THE OLMEC
&
THEIR NEIGHBORS

THE OLMEC
&
THEIR NEIGHBORS

Essays in Memory of Matthew W. Stirling

1981

Michael D. Coe and David Grove, Organizers
Elizabeth P. Benson, Editor

Dumbarton Oaks Research Library and Collections
TRUSTEES FOR HARVARD UNIVERSITY
Washington, D.C.

CONTENTS

Foreword

The first published catalogue of the Robert Woods Bliss Collection (*Indigenous Art of the Americas*) was issued by the National Gallery of Art in 1947 on the occasion of the installation of the collection as a loan exhibit in the National Gallery. Mr. Bliss, in his "Acknowledgments," first mentions Samuel K. Lothrop, who worked with him for many years in forming the collection. Next, he acknowledges another debt: "To Mr. Matthew W. Stirling, of the Smithsonian Institution, who collaborated with Mr. Lothrop in classifying certain of the objects, I express warm thanks for his interest and his clarifying discussion."

In 1961, in the Lothrop *Festschrift,* Matthew Stirling published three Olmec pieces from the Bliss Collection.

The second Pre-Columbian lecture presented at Dumbarton Oaks was given by Matthew Stirling, in 1965, to accompany the University of California film on excavations at La Venta.

The first Pre-Columbian conference held at Dumbarton Oaks, in 1966, was a conference on the Olmec. It seemed not only appropriate but inevitable that we ask Matthew Stirling to give the first paper. He began it with some remarks on what he called "The Impact of Olmec Art," saying that he had been "struck by the number of individuals who, after becoming involved with a single fine specimen of Olmec art, spent the rest of their careers as Olmec enthusiasts. . . . Mr. Bliss began his interest in Pre-Columbian art when he acquired in Paris an Olmec jade figure of a standing man. The ultimate result of that one acquisition is the magnificent collection in the adjacent room of this building."

The association between Matthew Stirling and Robert Woods Bliss was a long and fruitful one, and, although we tend to think of Matthew Stirling as "Mr. Olmec" and of the Bliss Collection as being particularly rich in Olmec objects and supportive of Olmec studies, interests were also shared in Panamá and other places yielding the high art with which Matthew Stirling worked and which Robert Bliss was dedicated to collecting. Matthew Stirling was always a part, not only of the Olmec activities at Dumbarton Oaks, but of all that went on in its Pre-Columbian world. He gave us advice; he participated in our conferences; and he and his wife, Marion, extended hospitality to our conferees—a very special kind of hospitality, which was not only lavish, but had a remarkable quality of warmth and good conversation, especially when the host would reminisce about his early days in the field. This generosity has extended to the present, with the very considerable backing given by Marion Stirling Pugh, June Stirling Sovey, and Matthew W. Stirling, Jr., to this publication.

Dumbarton Oaks owes a great debt to Matthew Stirling for many reasons, and it is with pride and pleasure that we issue this book in his memory.

Elizabeth P. Benson

Matthew Williams Stirling, 1896-1975

With the death on January 23, 1975, of Matthew W. Stirling, pioneer archaeologist, ethnologist, and the discoverer of the Olmec civilization, American archaeology has lost one of its grand men. He is survived by his wife, Marion, a son, Matthew, his daughter Ariana, and one grandchild.

Matt was born in Salinas, California, on August 28, 1896. His father was manager for the Southern Pacific Milling Co. and was in charge of establishing warehouses in the Salinas Valley, so he lived in various small towns while growing up. While a boy and young man, he also spent considerable time on the ranches of his grandfather Williams (for whom he was named) near Gonzalez and Salinas, in a milieu that has provided the setting for some of the novels of John Steinbeck, an old family friend who often discussed the pioneer days with Matt's maiden aunts, Did and Bee.

Chores such as milking cows and tending irrigation ditches, however, proved irksome to the young Matt, and he vowed never to follow that way of life. Instead, he was interested in reading and in collecting arrowheads. Matt gave credit for his initial interest in archaeology to his teacher in Gonzalez High School. In 1914 he entered the University of California, and graduated in 1920, having taken two years out for service as an ensign in the U.S. Navy during World War I. Although he had intended to be a geologist, he switched to anthropology because he enjoyed the courses, especially those given by T. T. Waterman. Other teachers were A. L. Kroeber and E. W. Gifford. Matt was subsequently made a teaching fellow, and William Duncan Strong, who remained a lifelong friend, was one of his students.

Matt's interest in sports and the outdoors developed while in college, and at California he was on the track team as a pole vaulter and hop-step-and-jumper (now called triple jump); after graduating he was a member of the Olympic Club team that competed in many meets in California and the West Coast in general. He remained a devoted sportsman and fisherman all his life.

In 1920 he made his first trip to Europe with his parents, and it was during this trip that Matt saw a "crying baby" masquette in the Berlin Museum that fired his interest in discovering more about the civilization that produced it, one that we know of as Olmec.

While visiting San Francisco with a friend who was taking the Civil Service examination for the post of Assistant Curator of Ethnology in the U.S. National Museum, Matt also took the exam to kill time. Characteristically, he then went off fishing. On his return, he learned that he got the appointment, which he took because he had wanted to live in the East for a year, although he actually remained in the post until 1924. While at the museum, he arranged the Ward Collection for exhibition, and rechecked acquisitions and identifications, giving him a superb knowledge of material culture which came in handy in later years. In 1921-22, he took night classes in anthropology at George Washington, under Truman Michelson, and received an M.A. in 1922.

In the early winter of 1923, J. Walter Fewkes, Chief of the Bureau of American Archaeology, sent Matt to conduct an intensive excavation at Weeden Island in Florida; a second season was spent the next winter. During the intervening summer, with an appropriation of $200, Matt was off to dig a historic site in Mowbridge, South Dakota. The 78 graves at

Mowbridge, with 128 skeletons and associated artifacts, were subsequently published by Aleš Hrdlička and Waldo Wedel (BAE Bull. 157, Anthrop. Pap. No. 25).*

Matt, however, still had considerable wanderlust left. With his friend Perry J. Patton, he had explored by bicycle the Paleolithic region of southern France and northern Spain in September 1922. In the spring of 1924, he resigned from the Smithsonian and left the United States in July with Perry Patton, bound by boat for Lima. They moved directly inland, and proceeded to explore the Montaña and upper Amazon by foot and dugout, crossing the territory of the Campa Indians. During much of this trip, Patton was ill with malaria and Matt was burdened down with Peruvian textiles which he had found discarded by *huaqueros* on the coast.

Dutch New Guinea was Matt's next destination. To help raise money for what was to be the largest expedition ever to explore that island, he returned to Weeden Island, in the winter of 1924-25, this time to sell real estate. From the end of 1925 to 1927, he was in the field as head of the joint Smithsonian Institution–Dutch Colonial Government expedition, one that totalled more than 800 people, including a military escort of 75 Ambonese soldiers, 130 Dyak canoemen and carriers recruited from central Borneo, and 250 Malay carriers. It was the first time that a plane had ever flown in Dutch New Guinea, and probably marked the first time serious use had been made of a plane in scientific exploration on this scale. Extensive work was done in ethnology, physical anthropology, botany, zoology, and medical research. Twenty thousand feet of motion picture film was made of a Stone Age people who had never before seen outsiders; unfortunately, most or all of this footage has been ruined in storage. The ethnological materials that Matt made for the U.S. National Museum make what is probably the largest documented collection ever gathered from a single tribe.

The Bureau of American Ethnology had been directed by a succession of four men, beginning with its founder John Wesley Powell, and con-

tinuing with William Henry Holmes, Frederick Webb Hodge, and Jesse Walter Fewkes. In 1928, a special committee selected Matt from a list of eligible applicants, to become the new Chief, a post that he held until succeeded by Frank H. H. Roberts, Jr., in 1958. Matt was a born leader of men, and knew how to pick the best; in addition to the staff that he had inherited, Matt brought in as the opportunity presented itself such outstanding anthropologists as W. D. Strong, Henry B. Collins, Jr., Julian H. Steward, William N. Fenton, Gordon R. Willey, Philip Drucker, George M. Foster, Jr., William C. Sturtevant, Winslow Walker, Alfred Metraux, and Homer G. Barnett. He always considered this roster of talent as his principal contribution to the Bureau's work.

In 1933, Matt married Marion Illig, who remained his beloved companion and collaborator for the rest of his life. Marion had been Matt's secretary at the Bureau, and had many personal connections with the staff of the National Geographic Society; through them, Matt eventually established the contacts that were to see his work supported through some of his most productive and important years of research.

During the early part of the thirties, Matt undertook a variety of investigations, both archaeological and ethnological, that reflected the many interests of the Bureau but that did not quite focus his own career. Among these were several seasons of excavation on the Gulf Coast of Florida, and a field trip to the Jívaro of the Ecuadorian Montaña. The growing WPA program in archaeology also claimed his attention. Probably more significant was a visit to Copan in Honduras and Quiriguá in Guatemala, drawing his attention to Mesoamerica for the first time.

It will be remembered that Matt had been intrigued with the jade masquette, now called Olmec, that he had seen many years before in Berlin. He had also been much interested in the article by Albert Weyerstall which appeared in the *Middle American Research Institute Papers* in 1932, describing abundant mounds, sculptures, and pottery artifacts in the Papaloapan Basin of southern Veracruz, the general area from which certain "Olmec-style"

*Ed. note: Wedel 1955.

carvings were said to have come. In 1938, Matt and Marion travelled to Mexico with Marion's parents, and he visited Tres Zapotes, Veracruz, where the first known Colossal Head had been found in the previous century. On their return, Matt showed a picture of the head to one of the editors of *National Geographic,* who suggested that Matt request a grant from the NGS Research Committee for an expedition to the site. Through the interest of Alexander Wetmore of the Smithsonian, a member of the Research Committee, the grant was approved.

Thus began Matt's long-term field project among Olmec sites of southern Mexico, beginning in 1939 and continuing through 1946, supported by the Smithsonian and the National Geographic Society. While sporadic Olmec finds had been made over a number of years, it is quite clear that it was Matt's vision, enthusiasm, and drive that resulted in the discovery of this ancient culture. As Gordon Willey has pointed out, Matthew Stirling was the John Lloyd Stephens of the Olmec civilization. This quest, usually with Drucker as assistant archaeologist, took Matt to Tres Zapotes in 1939 and 1940, to Cerro de las Mesas in 1941, to La Venta in 1942 and 1943, and to San Lorenzo (which he discovered) in 1945 and 1946, and has been recounted several times (see Michael D. Coe, *America's First Civilization,* 1968). Matt was one of the truly lucky archaeologists; among the highlights of his stupendous discoveries were the finding of Stela C at Tres Zapotes with its Cycle 7 date, the Cerro de las Mesas jade cache including Olmec heirloom pieces, the tombs and hidden offerings of La Venta, and the largest of all Colossal Heads, Monument 1 of San Lorenzo. To him must also go the credit for calling the attention of the archaeological world to the great site of Izapa in Chiapas, a key center for the transmission of Olmec culture to the earliest Maya.

The Stirlings had met the late Miguel Covarrubias and his wife Rose on their return from Tres Zapotes in 1939, and a warm friendship grew up. They shared a deep interest in the Olmec and a conviction that this was the *cultura madre* in Mesoamerica, far earlier than the much-vaunted Maya civilization. It should be said that this vision was shared by Alfonso Caso. The extent of the opposition to this point of view can hardly be imagined today, when the priority of Olmec is accepted by all. The Mayanists led the attack, which was hardly a credit to those who claimed to represent the intellectual achievements of the New World's most advanced civilization. Perhaps no group of scholars has ever been led in such a degree to the wrong conclusions for the "right" reasons. Even the Grand Panjandrum of Maya studies, Eric Thompson, badly erred in his attack on Matt's Stela C paper, by trotting out in awe-inspiring detail all the supposed evidence necessary to downgrade the Olmec, in an article innocuously entitled "Dating of Certain Inscriptions of Non-Maya Origin" (1941). It took another twenty to thirty years of dirt archaeology and the advent of radiocarbon dating to prove Thompson and his colleagues hopelessly wrong, and the Stirlings/Covarrubias/Caso absolutely right. To all those who like to think that archaeological knowledge proceeds by popular consensus, this ought to be a lesson. The discovery of the top part of Stela C in the last few years has fully confirmed Matt's contention that this was a true Cycle 7 monument, far more ancient than the oldest known Maya dated object.

After eight years of Olmec exploration by the Stirlings, the National Geographic began to be tired of Colossal Heads and were-jaguar jades, and the Stirlings were encouraged to look for other fields. Matt had a long-standing interest in Ecuador, and they decided to look for possible connections between Mesoamerica and South America. From 1948 to 1952 they spent four seasons digging in Panama (with Gordon Willey as assistant in the first year), one in Manabí Province of Ecuador in 1957, and a final season in 1964 in the Línea Vieja and Bagaces regions of Costa Rica.

In "retirement," Matt and Marion traveled extensively around the world, and Matt continued to do work for archaeology and ethnology as an important member of the Committee for Research Exploration of the National Geographic Society. Many an archaeological project, particularly those undertaken by younger members of our profession, owes its support to the direct interest of Matt on this committee.

Speaking personally, Matt was a prince among men. His incredible kindness to neophytes like myself was legendary. It is not easy for a scholar to grow old, but Matt achieved the status of elder statesman with grace and intellect; his interest in his younger colleagues, especially those who would "carry the ball for the Olmec," as he characteristically called it, was infinite. Matt was one of the greatest of all raconteurs, and it is a pity that his tales of early life in California, of the greats among early twentieth century American anthropologists, and above all of back-country Veracruz have not been recorded. In January 1973, Matt was operated on for cancer, which proved eventually to be terminal. He had several miraculous remissions from his fatal disease, during which time some of us had the great joy of seeing him once more with cigar in one hand and whiskey glass in the other, again recounting in his inimitable style his wonderful, humorous stories of early days in many lands, pursuing the variety of goals that had led his life since those arrow-collecting hunts of his boyhood in California.

One of the greatest joys of my life was when Matt and Marion came to visit us in San Lorenzo during the 1967 season. I knew of the high estimation in which the Stirlings were held in that remote part of the world since their 1945-46 expedition. In fact, I had flagrantly lied to the local people by claiming to be a godson of "Don Mateo" (or "Don Estirling"), for the latest archaeologist who had tried to work there had been nearly lynched by the populace. Upon their arrival, the word that these beloved friends had returned after a quarter of a century was spread to all the neighboring villages up and down the Coatzacoalcos River drainage. Most of their old workmen, a people incredibly proud and often violent in the southern Veracruz tradition, came in from the remote jungles and river settlements. The guitars were tuned up in the warm evening and the *huapango* began. In *trobas* composed and sung on the spur of the moment, these fierce men expressed their love and respect for "Don Mateo" and "Doña Mariana," after all these years had passed. I could well understand how the remote ancestors of these Veracruzanos, the mysterious Olmec, had conferred on Matt the glory of discovering their lost civilization.

Michael D. Coe

Reproduced by permission of the Society for American Archaeology from American Antiquity, *1976, vol. 41, no. 1, pp. 67-70. The Stirling bibliography, which was appended to this obituary, has not been reprinted here.*

An Intimate View of Archaeological Exploration
Marion Stirling Pugh

In the summer of 1931, I was out sailing on Long Island Sound and returned about midnight to find a telegram offering me a job as secretary to the Chief of the Bureau of American Ethnology of the Smithsonian Institution. I went to the dictionary to find out what "ethnology" meant and, since it sounded challenging and intriguing, I accepted.

I reported for work and my boss, Matthew W. Stirling, left the same day for South America, leaving me listening to his epigrapher visitor, Dr. Gates, who gave me an emotional discourse on Maya codices.

The Bureau received many inquiries regarding the American Indians, their origins, the variety of cultures among them, what they had contributed to civilization, etc. Also, there was considerable correspondence concerning the meanings of words and requesting the Indian names for concepts sometimes foreign to Indian thought, such as "love nest." Drs. J. P. Harrington, J. N. B. Hewitt, Truman Michelson, and John R. Swanton tried to accommodate, but sometimes the letters got buried on their desks. Being young and full of enthusiasm, I decided it would be a good idea to set up an efficiency system recording the receipt of letters, from whom, subject, to whom referred, and when answered. This follow-up was not popular with the scientists and was dropped when the Chief, my future husband, returned from South America.

In order to understand my work, I studied anthropology at George Washington University under Dr. Truman Michelson.

In December, 1933, Matt and I were married. Our archaeological honeymoon consisted of traveling around Florida, Georgia, and Tennessee, as he was in charge of the Southeastern archaeological projects for the Public Works Administration. At that time money was plentiful for archaeological excavations, as most of the money could be spent on labor, only picks and shovels being required for the workers. The problem was locating capably trained archaeologists to act as supervisors. Sites were worked on the west coast of Florida near Bradenton, on Lake Okeechobee, and on the east coast near Daytona Beach and Miami Beach.

In Tallahassee, Matt and I purchased a 1928 Ford sedan, green with orange trim, which we nicknamed Dixie. We toured around in her from one site to another. Since she was lightweight and had a high center, we could leave the highway, ford streams, straddle scrub palmetto, and if we got stuck in the sand, Matt and our guide could easily push the car out.

It was a marvelous introduction to archaeology for me. Many of the young archaeological supervisors working for us, such as Gordon Willey, James Ford, Jesse Jennings, and Marshall Newman, later became famous and respected in their fields. I was privileged to learn as they discussed their work with Matt.

Resulting artifacts ranged from shell hoes, gorgets, and pottery to a case of Gilbey's gin, found on Miami Beach, which we thought rum runners must have cached during Prohibition times and not recovered. Matt's brother, Gene, who was supervising this dig, kidded us about arriving shortly after its discovery. Coconut palms had been planted in rows along prospective streets when the big Florida real-estate boom of the twenties was in full swing, and the juice of the green coconut in its natural thermos shell made a delightful cool mix with the gin. Needless to say, none of this discovery was catalogued. Later, in Latin America, we became very fond of this refreshing, hygienic coconut juice. In Panamá, the green coconut is called a *pipa,* which I translated as "pipe" the first time it was offered to me. I refused, saying I didn't smoke, until further explanation made clear what was being offered.

Florida archaeology was not as glamorous as that we later encountered in Mexico, but it gave me an appreciation for the work and a background that was to prove useful.

In 1935, we spent Christmas with Matt's family in Berkeley, California, and cruised to Guatemala on the S.S. Santa Rosa. Matt had the bright idea of taking a cast of the Tuxtla statuette as a gift for the National Museum in Guatemala City. The Smithsonian made a cast that looked so realistic that we were delayed by Guatemalan customs authorities in San José when entering the country. It was forbidden to export archaeological specimens, and it was incomprehensible to them that anybody would want to bring in a Pre-Columbian object. Our Spanish was not fluent at that time, but we finally persuaded them of our good intentions, and the Tuxtla statuette was ceremoniously presented a few days later.

Our friends Oliver and Edith Ricketson were living in Guatemala City, and they urged us to visit Gustav Strómsvik who had just started working at Copán, Honduras, for the Carnegie Institution. I had not expected to "rough it" on this trip so had no suitable clothes. Edith Ricketson lent me her riding breeches and boots, and off we went by train and car to Esquipulas, the town famous for the Church of the Black Christ to which natives make pilgrimages from all over Latin America.

From here it took us about seven hours on horseback to reach the Honduran border, where we spent the night in a humble native house but were greeted with genuine, heartwarming hospitality. The owner hustled around and dispatched his sons to borrow for us a four-poster bed with crisscrossed leather thongs as mattress. We had a welcome supper of scrambled eggs, beans, and tortillas. The next morning, when Matt asked how much we owed, including feed for the horses, a great discussion ensued. Our guide told us to pay three cents American (U.S. currency being interchangeable in Guatemala.) The smallest coin Matt had was a dime. Our host told us he could not make change, so Matt magnanimously told him to keep it.

We reached Copán after another five- or six-hour ride, and Gustav Strómsvik put us up in his freshly cleaned quarters, which we proceeded to infect with fleas as, apparently, each crisscrossed leather thong had harbored a nest of them.

The next morning, we rode out to the ruins and were climbing the Hieroglyphic Stairway to see the remaining standing temple. Halfway up, an earthquake struck. Enormous trees swayed back and forth, making swishing noises. We hung on as several blocks of stone came loose and rolled down past us. When we thought it safe, we proceeded to the top of the stairway and found that the temple had collapsed; so, by three or four minutes, we missed immortality.

The bell tower of the church also collapsed, and the town suffered severe damage, but Gustav's quarters were spared.

About thirty years later, Matt and I returned by Jeep Wagoneer. We noticed many changes, there now being a hotel and a museum in Copán. A fiesta was taking place, and a gunfight developed between the soldiers and the city police, who used the hotel proprietor's car as a shield. The radiator and windshield were riddled, and two men were killed just outside the hotel entrance. If we had not moved our car into the patio about fifteen minutes earlier, it would have been wrecked. For us, life was never dull in Copán.

As a former track star, Matt always enjoyed attending the Olympic Games, so in 1936 we went to Berlin. We observed the crowd's instantaneous reaction to Hitler when he arrived at the Games. Each spectator leapt up, extended his right arm, and shouted "Heil Hitler!" We were told at the Tomb of the Unknown Soldier in Munich that he would rise again, symbolically meaning the country. When we returned home and told of Germany's strength and determination, nobody wanted to listen.

In 1938, Matt and I made our first trip to Mexico with my parents, driving down via Laredo and the Tamazunchale highway. Matt's objective was to visit Huayapan and see the colossal head there, discovered by Melgar in 1862. He thought that such an unusual carving must be located in an archaeological site, and that it should be worth investigating. As those of you who have read Matt's article "Early History of the Olmec Problem" in the 1967 Dumbarton Oaks Conference (1968) know, he had been fascinated by the "different" art style called Olmec for several years. He was intrigued by the artifacts of this type that were appearing in private collections without provenience.

Matt hired horses and a guide in Tlacotalpan, Veracruz, where they swam the Papaloapan River, rode eight hours to Huayapan, and spent the night. The next day he saw the colossal head at Tres Zapotes and was delighted both to find that it was located in the center of a large complex of earth mounds, and to observe a large stone tenon in the arroyo nearby, as well as a quantity of decorated sherds protruding from the banks. He returned to Mexico City scratching from *pinolillo* (tiny tick) bites, which we later learned to respect.

It was one of the few times I did not accompany him, as I was pregnant, so I visited Mitla and Monte Albán with my parents instead.

We showed pictures of the partially excavated head to some of the National Geographic Society editors and to Dr. Alexander Wetmore, then Director of the U.S. National Museum, who was a member of the National Geographic Committee for Research and Exploration. He encouraged Matt to apply for a grant to investigate the site, which was approved.

Thus began a series of eight National Geographic Society–Smithsonian Institution archaeological investigations in Mexico from 1939 through 1946. It is difficult to pick out highlights of those years because each site had its own. In some ways Tres Zapotes was the most exciting. Everything was new to us: not only the archaeology, but the manner of living in palm-thatched houses which the natives built for us, as well as making friends with the villagers and learning their customs.

In 1939, Tres Zapotes was quite isolated and we reached it by train, launch, small boat, and horseback (Figs. 1 and 2). We purchased supplies for the camp setup in the city of Vera Cruz. When the order arrived, there were six chamber pots and no wash basins. Consequently three of the pots were used as wash basins until they could be replaced. We grew accustomed to this, but when Karl Ruppert visited and wished to wash his hands before eating, I realized from the expression on his face that he was shocked. Here was a case of the function of a vessel being judged by its shape.

Tres Zapotes was a village of about two hundred people, half of whom lived on our side of the arroyo and were known as those from the *arroyo abajo* (lower) and the other half of whom lived on the *arroyo arriba* (upper). There was great rivalry between the two factions. *All* the men in the village wanted to work, as it was an unusual opportunity to earn cash wages. We were paying 2.50 pesos a day, the peso then being five to one American dollar. We were paying above the normal wages, as 1.50 or 2.00 pesos a day were considered good pay in Veracruz at that time, but we found that it was a wise policy.

In order to satisfy, or try to satisfy, everybody we agreed to work the men in shifts of twenty-five for three days each, thus employing seventy-five men. This definitely was not a satisfactory arrangement for us, as it meant that there was little continuity in the excavations. However, in general, the men were all good workers, as they were agriculturists and could spot changes in the soil, and they soon learned to be careful.

Because of the rivalry of the two factions in the village, one day the workers brought guns and stacked them in the trenches close at hand. They assured us that we would not be hurt, but we were happy that there was no shooting.

There were constant personal feuds, and the Saturday night *huapango* was often broken up

Fig. 1 On the trail near Tres Zapotes, Veracruz, Mexico, 1940. Photograph courtesy of the National Geographic Society.

Fig. 2 Fording the Arroyo Huayapan, near Tres Zapotes, Veracruz, Mexico, 1940. Photograph courtesy of the National Geographic Society.

by shots onto the dance floor, which occurred the only night we ventured two miles into town for the festivities and which discouraged us from attending again. Sometimes the dead bodies would be carried in a hammock along the trail in front of our camp.

The *aguardiente* the villagers drank was strong in alcoholic content, and we used it as a rub to sterilize the *pinolillo* bites, their removal being a nightly ritual before they could imbed themselves and the bite become infected. In fact, as a result of such neglected infections, Phil Drucker had to be carried to the launch for Tlacotalpan in a hammock.

A hoped-for but quite unexpected find was that of Stela C. Matt rushed back to camp with the exciting news. Carved on the stela in bars and dots were the numerals 15-6-16-18 with a terminal glyph 6 in front of a day sign. The cycle numeral and introductory glyph were missing. Fortunately, we had brought with us Sylvanus Morley's "An Introduction to the Study of the Maya Hieroglyphs," *Bulletin 57 of the Bureau of American Ethnology* (1915). Using the numbers 15-6-16-18, I computed the date and correlated it, arriving at the cycle number "9" with a date of 6 Eznab 16 Yaxkin, August 24, A.D. 478 (almost Matt's birthday—August 28).

Matt continued to study the stela every now and then, and the next day was sure he could see a dot above the three top bars, which would make the katun 16 instead of 15. I figured the date on this basis with a resulting cycle 7, 6 Eznab 1 Uo, or 31 B.C., according to the Thompson correlation. This date seemed plausible for the site but, lacking carbon-14 at the time, it could not be proved. When Matt published the stela date as 7-16-6-16-18, 31 B.C., the result was as expected. He was widely criticized, especially by the Mayanists, who claimed that the date was too early and not contemporary; but, when carbon-14 provided dates for Olmec sites, 31 B.C. was too late.

However, there was always some controversy as to whether or not the dot was present. Fortunately, about 1972, a farmer discovered the upper portion of Stela C and, thank heaven, there was the introductory glyph and the bar and two dots, indicating 7 for the cycle read-

ing. Matt said he never expected to live to know it and was delighted to be vindicated.

By our second year at Tres Zapotes the villagers had had eight months to conjure up demands. There were all sorts of annoyances, such as their wanting to be paid every day at the camp instead of receiving chits every three days to be honored at Ricardo Gutiérrez' store. Also they suggested that the sherd-washing girls should be rotated, along with a few other requests.

We sent off a letter to Dr. Caso in Mexico City stating that we were having problems. He dispatched a lieutenant and six soldiers, and the lieutenant persuaded the Presidente Municipal and his council to cooperate with us.

A few weeks later, two labor organizers from Vera Cruz came to see Matt, requesting 2000 pesos *not* to organize our workers and pointing out all the disadvantages if they were organized—such as paying for holidays, rainy days when they didn't work, vacations, etc. Matt told the *sindicato* organizers that we were foreigners and must obey the laws of the country, but that we had only so much money and, if we had to pay more, we would work less time. He also so informed the members of the town council whose response was: "Well, *Jefe*, what do you want us to do, kill them"? Matt replied that he didn't suggest they go that far. We don't know what they did, but we never heard any more from the *sindicato*.

Visitors and our workmen would watch Matt discarding plain sherds from test pits and beg him, or me, to explain which contained the gold. They never believed that we were spending so much money looking only for broken pieces of pottery. One villager wrote a poem lamenting the fact that the gold turned to clay when we dug it up.

Our workers were not religious and decided to work Easter week of 1940. We were working in the big trench in the mound behind Stela C. Rains had started and a huge section of the wall fell during the night. Matt had been concerned about slides, and for that reason had a very wide trench. The men decided this was a bad omen, so we took a trip to Lake Catemaco, where there was a big Easter fiesta. It was there I had my pocket picked for the first and only time, and, since I was dressed in male attire (riding boots and pants), I was asked to take off my hat in church.

There were a variety of gambling games going on in the plaza. For ten centavos, Matt took a chance on throwing rings over a table full of gadgets and proceeded to win a horn, glass vase, and pottery donkey, all of which he gave to bystanders. The next day he won a live cow, and stopped competing in order not to break the distraught proprietor of the stand. Apparently his baseball training was helpful and he was more adept than the average *campesino*.

In the light of present knowledge, Matt often recommended to modern archaeologists that further excavations should be carried out in the arroyo near the bar-and-dot number 6 carved in the living rock. It must be worked at the end of a very dry season.

In 1941, we traveled by station wagon to Cerro de las Mesas in Veracruz, a luxury compared to Tres Zapotes which was isolated and had to be reached by boat and horseback.

Here we made the astonishing discovery of 782 pieces of jade in a cache in the top of one of the large mounds. It was found at the end of the season when Miguel Baltazar, a Mexican foreman from Tres Zapotes days, took out a wheelbarrow ramp in order to make things tidy before filling the trench. Because this cache contained many heirloom pieces that were Olmec in style, many people erroneously assumed that we considered Cerro de las Mesas to be an Olmec site. There was great variety in the artifacts recovered there, from the fifty-two pottery vessels each containing a decapitated human skull, to the stone yoke encircling the little pottery figure seated cross-legged and holding a small pottery figurine on her lap, to the "Old Fire God" brazier, the abdomen of which contained the bones of an infant.

Miguel Covarrubias, the artist-anthropologist, was enthusiastic and voluble about our work, and visited us with his wife Rosa. When they left, she forgot her woolen jacket, and, the next morning, when I went to the house where they had stayed, it had been almost completely devoured by cockroaches.

It was here that the Presidente Municipal

threatened to confiscate our findings before we could transport them to the Museo Nacional. Fortunately, some friends from El Potrero visited us, so we took the opportunity to send our jade specimens with them. Dick Stewart, who was the photographer, and I would stop on the way back to Mexico City and pick them up. We would also bring Miguel Baltazar with us as a reward for finding the jade cache.

Matt and the pottery would travel with a truck carrying chili peppers. The truck driver stopped in Córdoba to call on a girl friend and got drunk, so Matt had to drive the truck over the mountains into Mexico City. This was no simple task, as he had not driven since our Florida days when he would be looking for Indian mounds and absent-mindedly drive off the road, leading me to take over as chauffeur indefinitely.

Each year, we would make a survey trip looking for new sites and following leads. From here we took time out to visit Izapa and take photographs of some of the monuments, including the "tree of life" that later inspired an extensive archaeological investigation by the New World Archaeological Foundation.

A couple of years later, near Izapa, we were given the "bum's rush" by the Mexican manager of a coffee *finca* that had been taken over from the Germans, this being during World War II.

For us to visit La Venta was natural, because of the colossal head published by Frans Blom and Oliver La Farge in "Tribes and Temples" (1926-7). When we visited the site in 1940, we had to hike in from the Blasillo River, and there was one family living in a palm-thatched house built on one of the smaller mounds. They let us use their chicken house for shelter. Jaguar roamed in the tropical forest and the bird life was prolific. It was a beautiful natural park. Later, unfortunately, oil was discovered, all the jungle was cut down, a small town grew up on the site, a landing strip was built in the main plaza, Petróleos Méxicanos moved all the monuments to Villahermosa, and that was "progress"—the end of La Venta as a park and archaeological site.

Highlights at La Venta were spectacular and almost unbelievable. With Philip Drucker, the sandstone sarcophagus with carved jaguar front and lid was found. No bones remained, but the jade earspools and necklace of beads were in place as if being worn. In front of the sarcophagus was a columnar basalt tomb, containing several burials in cinnabar with many jade offerings. Among them was the little seated jade figurine with the tiny hematite mirror on the chest that Alfonso Caso described as one of the masterpieces of Mexican art.

With Dr. Waldo Wedel, Matt found the mosaic stylized mask of the jaguar god fifteen-and-a-half feet square, composed of 485 neatly-cut squares of green serpentine set in yellow and orange sands and buried twenty-three feet deep. Other finds are too numerous to mention and are well known to most of the readers of this volume, as are the publications on later excavations by Robert F. Heizer and others.

The dig at Piedra Parada in Chiapas was a puzzling architectural problem. We saw some magnificent scenery as we took horseback rides to caves in the vicinity and to the gorge of the La Venta River. We had heard of some stone buildings on the rim of the gorge, which we decided to visit. We inquired if there was water available and our guide assured us that there was, as well as a house where we could stay. After riding seven hours on horseback, we reached the stone buildings all right, but found that the only water was in a small pond in which cattle wallowed. After boiling for twenty minutes and being flavored with tea, it was still muddy and odoriferous. The only other water was a couple of hundred feet below in the gorge. The "house" was a shelter for the cattle, and we slept in the loft above. This was another of those "poorly informed experiences" which many archaeologists encounter and which amuse us in later years but which are no laughing matter at the time.

I remember Chiapas especially for the beautiful flower shields, made with petals and used for the decoration of saints' altars, for marriage proposals, and for other special occasions.

We visited many Indian villages in Chiapas and Dick Stewart took photographs of fiestas. I bought some textiles—but not enough.

At a stop on our way to visit Tapijulapa in Tabasco, we had a hair-raising airplane accident due to faulty brakes. During the forties there were many Spanish refugee pilots who bush-hopped around Tabasco and Chiapas in small planes and were willing to take us any place where there was a field large enough to land. In a cave across the river from Tapijulapa we collected some blind fish that proved so interesting that the American Museum of Natural History in New York sent an expedition to study them and found them to be a new species. We usually carried a jar of *aguardiente* in which we could preserve any small specimens that Matt thought might prove of interest to scientists back home. When we got home, the Smithsonian scientists would sort them out and send them to appropriate specialists.

Our good friend Margarita Bravo in Coatzacoalcos wrote us about the possibility of there being monuments of interest at San Lorenzo. While hunting, Juan del Alto had seen a stone protruding from the soil which he thought looked like the top of one of the colossal heads we had excavated at La Venta.

Of course we had to see it, so when we closed camp at Piedra Parada we went to San Lorenzo. In 1946, we excavated there with Philip Drucker, finding five colossal heads (Figs. 3 and 4), stone altars, etc. Dr. Michael Coe later conducted an intensive investigation of the San Lorenzo area.

We became devoted to Mexico and its people. The many fine Mexicans who cooperated with us and helped us are too numerous to list here, but I want to mention a few of the anthropologists: Dr. Ignacio Bernal, Dr. Daniel Rubín de la Borbolla, Dr. Alfonso Caso, Miguel Covarrubias, Arq. Ignacio Marquina, and Dr. Wigberto Jiménez Moreno. Each year Miguel Covarrubias waited expectantly for our return to Mexico City to discuss our new finds. His enthusiasm was contagious and he persuaded Dr. Caso, as well as many other doubters, of the antiquity of the Olmec.

After Mexico, there were not as many highlights and unusual experiences. Perhaps we had become blasé. Generally speaking, our headquarters were now in *casas de material,* and not palm-thatched. We traveled over most of Panama, from the Costa Rican border almost to the Colombian, and from the Pacific Ocean to the Atlantic. Several Panamanian friends said we knew their country better than they did. The Gorgas Laboratory staff were great friends, and General Hale of the U.S. Air Force made a weapons carrier and jeep available to us, as well as the use of a helicopter for short hops to places where there were no roads.

During our four seasons of work in Panama, we found late material, such as graves containing gold, and quite early material, such as a pre-pottery site (later worked by Dr. Gordon Willey), but nothing that could be considered a link between Ecuador and Mexico. Alejandro Méndez, the Director of the Museo Nacional, was most courteous and helpful.

We wanted to visit the Choco Indians living on the Sambú River, and the supervisor of the Malaria Control Board in the Canal Zone arranged for us to accompany three soldiers from Fort Clayton who were going to trap mosquitoes at Garachiné on the Pacific Coast. On the Atlantic Coast of Panama there is very little tide, but on the Pacific side the tides range from sixteen to twenty feet. The waters along the coast of the Gulf of San Miguel are shoal, so that at low tide the waters recede a mile from the beach. Our U.S. Army Cargo Carrier anchored almost three miles from the beach, so three trips to shore were required to transfer the malarial equipment and us. By the time Dick Stewart and the sergeant made the third load, darkness had fallen and the tide was out. They groped their way, guided by our flashlights on shore, and had to land a half mile out on the mud flat. When he had finally unloaded, everybody was smeared with black mud from head to foot. Two of the natives from Garachiné helped rig a heavy stone as anchor for the skiff which had to be left stranded on the flat. It was a harrowing and dangerous experience for Dick and the sergeant.

Matt and I had come in on the first load, and had made arrangements with the *corregidor* to put us up in the school house. I was trying frantically to light the Coleman lantern to help out, as there were no lights in town.

From Garachiné we took a banana boat to Sábalo on the Sambú River. Thence, by dugout canoe with outboard motor, we photographed and interviewed the Choco Indians upriver.

We attended a Guaymí *balsería* in Veraguas and drank *chicha masticada* with them. I always tried to put the gourd to my lips without actually drinking any, as the thought of the corn being chewed by the women and spit into a jar to ferment was not appealing to me. Matt had developed a taste for it while with the head-hunting Jívaro in Ecuador. He said he got a pickup reaction from it similar to that from light beer.

In Parita, we celebrated Carnival by playing host to the various *tunas,* groups of serenaders who visit from one house to another, drumming, singing, clapping hands, and dancing.

One year we ascended the Coclé del Norte River off the Atlantic coast as far as possible. We were returning to the mouth when our canoe hit a submerged log and tipped over. We had the men dive for Dick's cameras, but all the pottery was lost. We arrived at the mouth of the river subdued and sad.

The next morning, to our surprise, a U.S. Air Force helicopter landed to pick up a skull that possibly belonged to a young aviator lost in the vicinity some years before. His parents had posted a reward for information regarding his death. (Later we were amused to read the newspaper account regarding this skull, describing the area where it had been found—and where we had just been working—as an "impenetrable jungle.") Dick Stewart rushed out and made arrangements to be carried back to the Canal Zone in the helicopter as cargo.

Dr. Robert Rands, Matt, and I would return with the next banana boat. Our workmen had told us that taking two canoe-loads of bananas to the boat was as exhausting as a full day's work in the field. The trip with us was their third and we almost swamped. Fortunately, the dynamic storekeeper was with us and shouted encouragement to the exhausted men. Matt and I bailed with discarded steel helmets. When we righted and were on course again, the storekeeper appropriately remarked: "Now we are relatives. We have been born again." We felt the same way, and tumbled gratefully onto the little banana boat as if it were a luxurious liner.

Over the years we made numerous trips on small boats with no toilet facilities and, along

Fig. 3 M. W. Stirling with Colossal Head 4, San Lorenzo, Veracruz, Mexico, 1946. Photograph courtesy of the National Geographic Society.

Fig. 4 Marion Stirling with "El Rey" (Colossal Head 1), San Lorenzo, Veracruz, Mexico, 1946. Photograph courtesy of the National Geographic Society.

with my typewriter, I threatened to carry a chamber pot in a case disguised as a "hat box."

We next worked a site about three hours from Panama City. After about a month, when Dick Stewart and I drove into town to leave a load of pottery and to pick up supplies, we found an urgent message for Dr. Matthew W. Stirling. He was wanted to identify the very same skull we knew about, but had never seen. Canal Zone officials had contacted Smithsonian physical anthropologists, who had advised that Matt was in Panama and could do so. When he returned to the Zone, Matt was ceremoniously conducted to the morgue. He was able to settle all doubts. The skull could not be that of a young male pilot. It was small, dolichocephalic, with the sutures closed, and Matt calculated it was the skull of an Indian woman at least forty years old.

In 1958, we made a survey trip to Ecuador and dug a site on the Pacific coast near Manta that produced solid and hollow figurines appearing together through fifteen feet of stratigraphic deposit. We were later kidded by archaeological friends because, by no more than 100 yards, we missed a jackpot cache of about one hundred, thirty-to-sixty-centimeter-tall, elaborate, pottery figurines that washed out a few years later. Our excuse was that, at the time we were there, a house was atop the mound.

Also, we photographed the Colorado Indians living near Santo Domingo. Their name derives from their custom of plastering their hair with red paint extracted from *achiote* seeds (*Bixa orellana*). This gives them such a bizarre appearance that the picture editor of the *National Geographic Magazine* thought they were phony.

We made a small dig at the famous archaeological site of La Tolita in Esmeraldas Province, where the site was operated as a mine for several years by the owners for the sole purpose of extracting gold with no consideration for the pieces as art objects. From here on the Cayapa River, above Borbón, we visited the "ghost town" of Punta Venado, a complete village occupied by the Cayapa Indians only twice a year—on December 25 and during Easter week.

In 1962, we worked on the "Old Line," in Costa Rica, finding jade and gold, but not in the same graves, although *huaqueros* claim they do.

After the *National Geographic Magazine* published an article on Costa Rica showing an eight-foot, man-made, stone ball we had excavated in the Diquís Delta, Matt received one-hundred or more letters regarding such balls in various parts of the world. A phone call from Ernest Gordon told of some in Mexico near Guadalajara at the Piedra Bola silver mine where he had worked many years ago. He said they were five or six feet in diameter and perfectly round. We were intrigued but unbelieving as we had never heard of stone balls so far north, although we had excavated a few in our archaeological investigations in Mexico. Matt suggested that he send us photos if he got down there again.

About a year later, along came the photographs and they definitely showed balls that were large and symmetrical. We determined to go see for ourselves and wrote to Mexico for permission to excavate there if necessary.

Our old friend Arq. Ignacio Marquina was again Director of Monumentos Prehispánicos and warmed our hearts with his instant reply. "Of course, dear colleague Dr. Stirling, you are welcome in Mexico any time."

Dr. Doris Stone, who first published on the stone balls in Costa Rica, accompanied us in December, 1967. We met Ernie Gordon and hired men to dig around the balls. We charted their locations, but were puzzled to find no pottery in association. After three days, one of our workmen remarked: "Why do you spend so much time digging out these balls when there are many more already exposed on the other side of the mountain?" We sent another workman to check and report. When he returned, his expression still showed astonishment and he told me: "Yes, Señora, there are many, many balls of many sizes from a half meter to two or three meters. I counted up to fifty and then stopped."

The next day we went to see for ourselves, and were surprised and amazed to find there were several hundred balls, ranging in size from two feet to a maximum of eleven feet. It would have taken years to make so many by hand, so they had to be natural. When we returned to Washington, Matt contacted geologist Dr. Robert Smith, who studied them for the National Geographic and determined that they were formed by crystallization in volcanic ash.

This made us wonder about the Costa Rican balls, so we asked Dr. Smith to examine one the National Geographic has in storage. He said it was made of granitic rock and could not be formed naturally, so had to be man made.

So ended our active archaeological career with a false alarm! Over the years we followed many leads that were failures, such as a stone wall in Panama that turned out to be a natural outcropping. Others were productive, such as our discovery of San Lorenzo. The most frustrating experience was to be led confidently to a spot, encouraged to look around for a half hour or so, and then be told, *"ya se fué"* ("it has gone") when we knew a stone couldn't disappear into thin air.

Matt and I treasured our years in the field,

our contacts with the native people, how much we learned from them and with them, as well as with the scientists and other friends who were so helpful. We owe special thanks to National Geographic Society photographer, Richard H. Stewart, who accompanied us on all our expeditions except that to Ecuador. Without his cheerful disposition and willingness to help in all situations, in addition to his superb photography, we would not have been able to accomplish what we did.

Matt was proud of his connection with the National Geographic Society. Had it not been for that organization we never could have found and investigated the Olmec. As a member of the Committee for Research and Exploration he kept up his interest and knowledge of the field, visiting many archaeological sites. He was sent to see the work of L. S. B. Leakey before the Society started to finance him.

After Matt's retirement we were free to travel and did so, always including museums and archaeological sites in the itinerary.

It was a fabulous life and I enjoyed every precious second of it with him.

Gift of the River: Ecology of the San Lorenzo Olmec

Michael D. Coe

YALE UNIVERSITY

The rise of the New World's first complex society in the swampy Olmec heartland has long puzzled archaeologists and anthropologists, some to the point that they even ignore it. And yet the ecological situation, discovered by the Yale Río Chiquito Project, made such a rise virtually inevitable. We found that San Lorenzo Olmec civilization, which flourished (in radiocarbon years) from 1200 to 900 B.C., was literally "the gift of the river," and I would like in this paper to explore the implications of this situation and to describe the human adaptation to it by past and present peoples. Although common to much of southern Veracruz and coastal Tabasco, the riverine way of life on the Gulf Coast is not even mentioned by Palerm and Wolf in their 1957 paper on ecological potential and cultural development in Mesoamerica.

The data on which these observations are based were gathered as an adjunct to an archaeological project, and included the study of a seventy-five square kilometer area around San Lorenzo, using aerial photography, fine-scale mapping, and field teams of botanists, zoologists, and soil scientists, along with ethnological research carried on by ourselves (M. Coe 1974). We believe that no human ecological study of a New World, tropical, lowland region has ever been carried out in such detail. We now realize that this was the last chance to conduct this research, for my colleague Richard Diehl discovered on a visit to the region in 1977 that practically all of the high forest and secondary growth had been turned into pasture land, and the entire local economy converted from agriculture, fishing, and hunting to the raising of cattle, a fate that has overtaken much of southeastern Mexico's jungles. Even the fish and game had disappeared, the former because of pollution from downstream petrochemical complexes. Thus, the way of life described here is now dead and gone.

THE NATURAL SETTING

The San Lorenzo Tenochtitlán complex of sites lies near the center of the Isthmian Saline Basin, a low-lying basin of marine origin, consisting mainly of eroded Tertiary uplands and Pleistocene and recent fluvial deposits. The entire basin is underlain by salt formations, and it is highly likely that the San Lorenzo plateau, as well as the hills or ridges on which other Olmec sites were founded, overlies a salt dome. The basin is drained by the Coatzacoalcos and its tributaries; in terms of volume, this is the second largest river in Mexico. To the east of San Lorenzo, it splits to run around Tacamichapa Island, the western branch being the Río Chiquito, and the eastern branch the Río Grande. Aerial photographs show numerous oxbows and old scars in the alluvium caused by the meanderings of this river system.

This is an exceptionally wet region: the minimal annual precipitation recorded is 1210 millimeters. But this does not tell the whole story. In this hot, humid area there is no strongly marked dry season, and evaporation is very low due to high humidity, so agriculture can be carried on throughout the year. While the rest of Mesoamerica is undergoing a winter dry season, the lower Gulf Coast is subject to periodic northers, which sweep down from Texas at intervals of one to two weeks, bringing drizzle and, at times, driving rains. Local soils thus never dry out, and moisture is always available for crops.

There is, however, an interval of much heavier rains which lasts from June through October, and this alternation between wetter and drier seasons controls the all-important rise and fall of the rivers and streams. At the height of the rains, the rivers have risen an average of 6.4 meters and overflow their banks, flooding not only their natural levees but also the low-lying *potreros* ("wet savannahs"); it is not until November that waters leave the *potreros*, and the levee lands are once again exposed with their layer of recent alluvium. It is this regimen to which all life in the zone, including human populations both past and present, must adapt.

Soil scientists working with our project have come up with a four-fold classification that coincides exactly with the local, "folk" soil classification: (1) Coatzacoalcos series soils, known as *tierra de primera*, on the natural river levees; (2) Tenochtitlán series soils, or *tierra de barreal*, above the contour of flooding; (3) San Lorenzo series soils, or *tierra de grava*, which are nothing more than artificial deposits on the top of the San Lorenzo plateau; and (4) Tatagapa series soils, or *tierra de potrero*, full of clay, covered by grass, and thus impossible to cultivate.

Given such conditions, the natural vegetation away from the savannahs should be high, perennial forest dominated by such giants as mahogany, but, in fact, by the time we were there, land clearing for agriculture had left only a patchwork of secondary growth or *acahual*. This is probably what it looked like in Olmec times.

Before we can interpret the ecological conditions of San Lorenzo Olmec civilization from modern data, we must establish the fact that there has been no major change in the environment over a period of three millennia. We believe that there has not been a major change, and that this is substantiated by the faunal remains from San Lorenzo Phase deposits examined for the project by Elizabeth S. Wing, and by the wood charcoal identified by B.

Francis Kukakcha; all plant and animal species can still be found in the area, with the exception of some highland pine, probably imported, which found its way into a San Lorenzo hearth. The only real change that we can detect is in the rivers and streams: examination of aerial photographs shows that these have certainly moved their beds, and it is highly likely that the Coatzacoalcos itself once flowed very near the San Lorenzo plateau, right next to the outlier site of Potrero Nuevo.

AGRICULTURAL PRACTICES

Abundant remains of *manos* and *metates* make it certain that the San Lorenzo Olmec were corn farmers, although like the modern villagers they probably planted a good deal of manioc as well as beans, squashes, and a host of other cultigens. Given the natural conditions that we have outlined above, they would have had to adapt to the river regimen in much the same way as have the modern farmers of the survey area.

Present-day farming in the San Lorenzo Tenochtitlán survey area is far more complex than the terms "slash-and-burn" and "swidden" farming usually imply, for the Tenochtitlán series soils can be cultivated the year round, but the prime Coatzacoalcos series only in the "dry" season when the river levees have become exposed. There are four maize crops a year, two primary and two secondary. The *tapachol* is the primary dry-season crop and is planted on both Coatzacoalcos and Tenochtitlán series soils. In the uplands, this is often carried out in young *acahual*, with the slashed brush and weeds left on the ground to rot as a mulch since they are too wet to burn. Along the river levees, the natural grass cover is cut with machetes, and the maize planted right down among the grass roots; the sprouting corn grows faster than its wild competitors. The primary wet-season crop is the *temporal*, necessarily grown only on the upland Tatagapa series soils, and usually in higher secondary growth or forest. Here a patch of forest is cut down, left to dry out, and burned, the seed being planted in holes poked down through the ashes. The two secondary crops, *chamil* and *tonamil*, entail a fair degree of risk due to various causes; the former is planted in March on low-lying soils, and the latter in late August or early September on Tenochtitlán series soils.

Present-day people plant a number of maize varieties, including hybrid maize, and, of course, production figures will vary according to the race sown. We have gathered fairly accurate data on production, but here I will only point out that the yield, using non-hybrid maize, on the Coatzacoalcos series soils is fifty-five percent above that on Tenochtitlán series soils. Furthermore, on the former no fallow at all is required, while on the latter the norm is five years fallow following two-and-one-half years use. Thus, in spite of the fact that the river levee lands can only be farmed for part of the year, the return on labor investment is so high that it is these areas that are the most desirable in this part of the Coatzacoalcos drainage. We believe that San Lorenzo is located where it is for two reasons. First, the farther up river one goes, the narrower the river levees become, until they virtually disappear. Second, the farther down river, the later the flood waters drop with the onset of the "dry" season, and therefore the shorter the growing season as a result of postponed *tapachol* planting. San Lorenzo is at a "nick point" along the river, where length of growing season and width of levees are at optimum coincidence.

Land tenure and land values are directly affected by productivity, and it is small wonder that in our day the river levee lands were almost all in private hands, while the uplands were communally owned by the local *ejido*. I will return later to the implications of this situation for understanding the rise of the San Lorenzo Olmec.

THE ANIMAL WORLD

The Olmec of the San Lorenzo Phase were clearly not interested in the hunting of game mammals, and in this they were similar to the super-sedentary Formative villagers of the Pacific Coast of Guatemala. In her analysis of faunal material from the San Lorenzo Phase, Wing (this volume) has shown that the Olmec mainly relied for their animal protein on fish, turtles, and dogs, although she may have underplayed the role of cannibalism; in fact, human beings as a source of animal protein were second only to snook among the warlike San Lorenzo Olmec.

The primary role played by the river regimen in Olmec ecology can be seen in contemporary fishing and turtle-hunting strategies in the survey area. As the rivers rise during the summer, the savannahs are transformed into one large lake, interrupted by islands and higher land. Local fishermen go out in dugout canoes, equipped with nets, fish spears, and harpoons to take the gar and tarpon on the flooded *potreros,* but the gar (which has a pronounced muddy taste) at any rate does not seem to have entered the Olmec diet. As the rains taper off, the water is drained into the river, leaving behind oxbow ponds and lakes; these gradually shrink as the "dry" season progresses, and vast numbers of cichlids and gar are concentrated and then can be taken in seine nets. This is, therefore, a constantly replenishing source of protein. The most highly prized dish among both the San Lorenzo Olmec and the modern villagers is snook, which is taken on the *potreros* in June and July; river fishing for this species reaches its height from September to the end of December. Various kinds of catfish, also important in the local diet, follow somewhat the same regimen.

Turtle hunting was and is an important activity, usually pursued while fishing. Because of the turtle's breeding habits, which are geared to the rains and to the rise and fall of the streams and river, collecting of these creatures is also highly seasonal.

Altogether, the annual river cycle not only provides superior habitats for the various fish and turtle species, it also ensures that there will be a natural restocking each year of these important resources. Thus, the abundant animal protein available to the ancient Olmec was as much a gift of the river as were the prized river levee soils.

THE *CACIQUES*

When we were working in the San Lorenzo Tenochtitlán area, most of the political power in the village was in the hands of a group of brothers, who filled the important political posts, ran the most prosperous local store, gave credit, controlled the *ejido,* and set the prices that would be asked on produce for sale. They were known as *caciques* (a derogatory term meaning "chiefs"), and were the subject for much resentment and envy by the villagers. Unlike everybody else, they did not drink, and they worked harder than was usual. Although they were members of the local *ejido* and thus had access to the communally owned Tenochtitlán series soils, their strategy was to get into their hands as much of the river levee lands as possible. In this they had been successful, and not only farmed these rich soils themselves, but hired labor to help them. They invested their agricultural profits in their store and in river boats so that they could act as middlemen in the sale of crops down river. Although they dressed and looked like everybody else, they had much larger and better-built houses and were obviously affluent. One sign of their prosperity was that they were able to maintain polygynous families, something that only the wealthy could afford.

We began to think about these men: how different were they from the Olmec rulers whose colossal portraits carved in basalt we had been excavating up on the San Lorenzo plateau? Diehl and I came to realize that we were seeing in action the transition from an egalitarian society (the way Tenochtitlán was in 1946, when the Stirlings were there) to a more complex one with social inequality. The immediate cause of the process was the concentration into the hands of a few ambitious men of the greatest natural resource of the area: the Coatzacoalcos series soils along the river. The result was the taking on of political and economic power by the newly risen *caciques.* We are firmly convinced that just this kind of process was taking place in the Chicharras Phase (1300–1200 B.C.), which directly presages the San Lorenzo Phase and in which one finds the first indication of the fashioning of large-scale sculpture, perhaps even a colossal head.

Of course the ancient Olmec *caciques,* in addition to their political and economic strength, would have also had religious power, for otherwise one cannot imagine that they would have

been able to command labor on such a stupendous scale and over such a wide area. There is little religion and less ceremony in modern Tenochtitlán, so here the analogy ends. But the most important factor in the transition from what was probably an egalitarian to a complex society, around 1200 B.C., would have been the ownership (probably by a single lineage) of the river levee lands.

WARFARE AND THE RISE OF OLMEC CIVILIZATION

We should not assume that the process was peaceful, however. In a very important theoretical paper, Carneiro (1970) has pointed out the weaknesses of most theories of the rise of the state, especially those that postulate (like Rousseau's *Social Contract*) the voluntary giving-up of autonomy by local groups in favor of an overriding, territorial organization. Wittfogel's "hydraulic theory" (1956) argues that civilization and the state arise in somewhat arid lands where irrigation is a necessity; the need for some form of control to defend, maintain, and distribute canal waters is supposed to lead to the state. Numerous authors have pointed out that this does not work in Mesopotamia and Mesoamerica, and, having taught a course on Peru, I can say that it does not work there either. In all cases, complex societies (like Chavín in Peru) *precede,* not follow, the establishment of irrigation. And I doubt that even the Pima and Papago would claim that the extensive irrigation carried out by their Hohokam ancestors ever produced a state.

I need hardly point out that the Wittfogel theory is totally inapplicable to the Olmec situation: we never discovered any signs of either irrigation or land drainage in the survey area. The spectacular San Lorenzo system of basalt drains seems to have had a purely ceremonial function.

Carneiro (1970) looks to coercion, *i.e.,* victory in war, as the only workable theory of state origin. This is the way, for instance, that many African kingdoms have arisen in the documented past. He views the decisive factor as an ecological one: in all those parts of the world where civilizations have arisen for the first time, the area is circumscribed—for example, the valleys of coastal Peru and the Nile, both areas bound in by desert hills. In areas of uncircumscribed lands, such as much of the Amazon Basin, dissident or defeated parties can leave to pioneer new lands. In a place like the Virú Valley in Peru, there is nowhere to go, and the defeated parties must submit to the victors, leading to social stratification and the concentration of scarce resources into the hands of an elite.

Most interestingly, Carneiro (1970:736–7) points to an apparent exception to his theory, namely, that early travelers along the middle Amazon River saw densely populated villages placed close together, some degree of social stratification, and even some paramount chiefs. The point that he makes is that this area *was actually* circumscribed. The margins of the Amazon and the islands within it comprise a type of land called *várzea* which is annually flooded and covered with silt; Carneiro comments that this land is of first quality, and was highly prized and coveted. Furthermore, the river itself was full of aquatic foods such as fish, turtles, and caymans "in inexhaustible amounts" *(ibid.: 736).* Concentration of resources along the Amazon therefore resulted in a kind of circumscription; overcrowding on these lands due to natural increase and immigration led to warfare over access to them; and there were losers who had to submit to the victors.

This scenario could have been written for the San Lorenzo Olmec, and is, I believe, what actually happened. Today's *caciques* would not have been able to carry out their designs by force, because of the presence of the Mexican state with its army and police. But at 1200 B.C. there was probably serious warfare;

in fact, we discovered abundant remains of cannibalized humans in both Chicharras and San Lorenzo deposits. We have no exact figures, of course, on ancient populations in the area, but archaeological remains show that there was a great increase during the transition from Bajío to Chicharras times, and an even greater one at the start of the San Lorenzo Phase. Using modern data, Richard A. Diehl (personal communication) calculates that the Olmec population was far below the actual carrying capacity of the land. However, the key factor is that the river levee lands make up only twenty-one percent of the total survey area today, and a similar figure probably prevailed in Olmec times. Thus, conflict over these scarce lands could have led, and almost certainly did lead, to social stratification and the complex way of life known as civilization.

In this, the rise of Olmec civilization was probably remarkably similar to that of ancient Egypt. Both were the "gift of the river" in two respects. First, the annual cycle of the river enabled large populations to live in the area; and, second, the most highly productive land (in the case of Egypt, *all* of the arable land) was highly concentrated or circumscribed. The best of all the land along the Coatzacoalcos was that in the immediate area of San Lorenzo itself. As the "prime mover" in the development of the New World's first civilization, the Coatzacoalcos deserves as much praise as the Nile.

ACKNOWLEDGMENTS I would like to acknowledge my debt to Richard A. Diehl and Elizabeth S. Wing for the general orientation of this paper; in particular, it was Diehl who called my attention to the significance of the recent rise of the *caciques* in San Lorenzo Tenochtitlán.

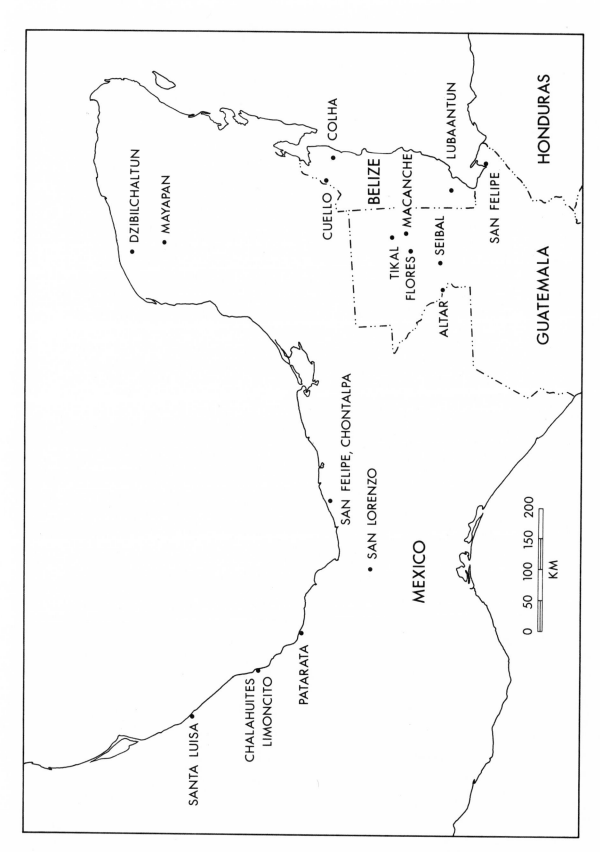

Fig. 1 Map of Mesoamerica showing sites of faunal assemblages. Map by Nancy Halliday.

20

A Comparison of Olmec and Maya Foodways

Elizabeth S. Wing

FLORIDA STATE MUSEUM, UNIVERSITY OF FLORIDA

The particular combination of plants and animals used for food is a distinctive culture trait. The concept of what organisms are edible is an overriding influence on the choice of resources used for food. These choices are clearly effected by the availability of resources within the catchment area of the home site. Therefore, the choice of habitation site becomes a crucial factor. People may be partially freed from these environmental constraints by the possession of domestic plants and animals. Where wild game and plants are important in the diet, the repertoire of collection, hunting, and fishing techniques acts as a selective filter resulting in a relative abundance of various organisms used for food that is quite different from the abundance in which they occur naturally.

If this proposition is as true for the past as it appears to be at present, one would expect to detect differences in animal use as part of the subsistence pattern associated with different cultural units. Thus, Olmec subsistence may be expected to be different from that of the Maya. A distinction should also be discernible between subsistence in the Formative Period and in the Classic Period.

The data I will use to shed light on this problem are identifications of faunal samples from twenty-three prehistoric occupations in Mesoamerica (Fig. 1). The faunal assemblages were all studied at the Florida State Museum except those from Mayapán (Pollock and Ray 1957) and the Petén sites, Tikal, Altar de Sacrificios, Macanché, Seibal, and Flores (Pohl n.d.). The sites range geographically from the Santa Luisa site (in Gutiérrez Zamora, Veracruz, Mexico) in the north, along the coastal lowlands to the San Felipe site (on Lake Izabal in Guatemala), which is the southernmost site under consideration. Nine are located in what is thought of as the Olmec heartland along the southwestern Gulf Coast, and ten are in the Lowland Maya area in the lowlands of the northwestern Caribbean Coast.

Chronologically, the faunal samples are divided approximately equally between Formative and Classic Period sites. The full time-range of these occupations is from 2000 B.C. (at the Cuello site, Belize) to A.D 1520 (at Mayapán, Yucatán). In the Gulf Coast area, five of the sites studied were occupied during Formative times and four during Classic times, whereas, in the Caribbean area, three sites date from the Formative Period and eleven from the Classic.

The cultural contexts of the faunal samples are as similar as possible. Animal remains associated with human burials or ceremonial contexts are excluded from this analysis. Differences are also expected to occur in the use of animals by people of different social strata. These differences of faunal association are more difficult to isolate. Two types might be expected. The proportions of foods from plant and animal sources might differ. Such differences have been demonstrated by a trace-mineral analysis which suggests, as one might expect, a proportionally greater intake of animal-derived protein among people of upper social classes (Brown n.d.). Secondly, the types of animals used by different social strata could differ. Certain food animals are known to have been reserved for particular feasts or for the exclusive use of particular people. At the time of the Spanish conquest, for example, turkey was reserved for elite consumption and was used as tribute payment (Schorger 1966:10). Existence of such differences can only be deduced from the cultural context of the faunal samples, and that is not precisely known for all of the samples examined. They do include food remains from the full range of social strata, however.

The region covered by this study, the southern segment of the Gulf coastal plain of Mexico and the adjoining coastal plain of Nuclear Middle America, is not uniform in respect to its flora and fauna. This tropical lowland region is divided into three biotic provinces: the Veracruz, which roughly coincides with the political boundaries of the state of Veracruz; the Yucatán, which coincides with the state of Yucatán and the coastal portions of Campeche; and the Petén, which covers the Yucatán Peninsula with the exception of the northwestern portion (L. C. Stuart 1964: 349). Of these three, the Yucatán province is probably the most distinctive, influenced by its greater aridity. Although the fauna varies throughout this lowland region, most of the animals that were used are found in their appropriate habitats throughout. In those cases in which one species or genus is not found throughout the region, for purposes of analysis I have combined it with an ecotype so that together they range throughout. For example, the two species of peccary are combined; together they occur throughout the region, whereas singly they do not. This was done in an attempt to eliminate the effect of animal distribution on patterns of animal use.

The method of analysis included the use of a cluster analysis (Bonham-Carter 1967) to group sites according to similarities of their faunal assemblages and characterization of the fauna of each cluster. The basis of analysis is the calculated minimum number of individuals (MNI). The sample sizes average 111 MNI (range 28-586) and include an average of twenty species (range 10-43). Incorporated

in this study are faunal samples presented by Pohl (n.d.). She indicates that the minimum numbers of individuals and number of specimens for her data are equivalent, and therefore I have used her data as she presents it on her figures 4-3 and 4-4. The cluster analysis presented in Table 1 is semiquantitative with parameters as follows: absent, rare (1-4 percent), present (5-14 percent), and abundant (over 15 percent). The species used as variables in the cluster analysis are presented in Table 2. These species occur in more than three faunal samples or are abundant in a site. All species that are represented in three or fewer sites are combined in a category such as "other mammals."

GROUPINGS OF SIMILAR FAUNAL ASSEMBLAGES

Three groups of sites emerge from the cluster analysis of these faunal data (Table 1). Samples from different occupations of the same archaeological site are most similar, as, for example, the different occupations at Santa Luisa, Patarata, Dzibilchaltún, and San Felipe. The sites that comprise the largest cluster are, with one exception, located in Veracruz. The second cluster includes sites from Yucatán and the Petén. The third, and smallest, cluster is composed of two sites located in southern Belize and coastal Guatemala. One site, Colhá, appears to be more closely associated with the sites of the Gulf region than with those of the Caribbean region where it is located.

Each of the two major groups has subdivisions. The Gulf Coast cluster is subdivided into northern and southern sites. The Caribbean cluster is divided into those in the northern lowlands of the Yucatán Peninsula, plus two sites from the eastern part of the southern lowlands, and sites strictly from the southern lowlands.

CHARACTERIZATION OF THE GULF
AND CARIBBEAN FAUNAS

The faunal assemblages in each of the cluster groups have distinctive characters. Table 3 shows the species that characterize these groups, represented in a majority of sites, and abundant where they are presently.

The Gulf Coast group of nine sites is typified

TABLE 1. CLUSTER ANALYSIS OF FAUNAL MATERIAL

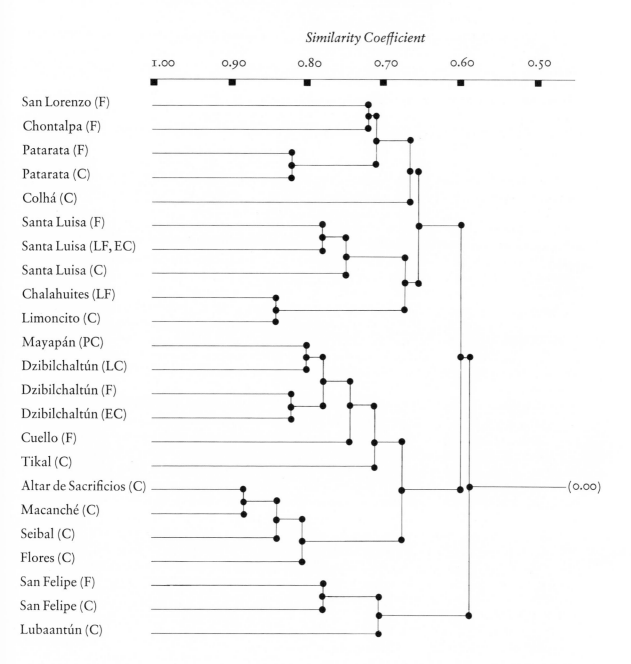

Similarity Coefficient

| 1.00 | 0.90 | 0.80 | 0.70 | 0.60 | 0.50 |

San Lorenzo (F)
Chontalpa (F)
Patarata (F)
Patarata (C)
Colhá (C)
Santa Luisa (F)
Santa Luisa (LF, EC)
Santa Luisa (C)
Chalahuites (LF)
Limoncito (C)
Mayapán (PC)
Dzibilchaltún (LC)
Dzibilchaltún (F)
Dzibilchaltún (EC)
Cuello (F)
Tikal (C)
Altar de Sacrificios (C)
Macanché (C)
Seibal (C)
Flores (C)
San Felipe (F)
San Felipe (C)
Lubaantún (C)

(0.00)

C—Classic
F—Formative
E—Early
L—Late

TABLE 2. SPECIES UPON WHICH THE CLUSTER ANALYSIS IS BASED

Didelphis virginiana	opossum
Sylvilagus floridanus	rabbit
Orthogeomys hispidus	pocket gopher
Dasyprocta spp./*Aguti paca*	agouti/paca
Canis familiaris	dog
Odocoileus virginianus/*Mazama* spp.	deer/brocket
Tayassu spp.	peccary
other mammals	
Meleagris spp.	turkey
other birds	
Dermatemys mawii	concha blanca
Kinosternon spp./*Claudius angustatus*	musk turtle
Staurotypus triporcatus	galápago
Iguana sp./*Ctenosaurus* sp.	iguana
other reptiles	
Arius felis/*Bagre marinus*	catfish
Centropomus spp.	snook
Epinephelus spp.	grouper
Cynoscion spp./*Sciaenops ocellata*	corvina/drum
Caranx spp.	jack
other fish	

by abundant remains of dog (*Canis familiaris*), musk turtles (*Kinosternon* spp. and *Claudius angustatus*), and snook (*Centropomus* spp.). Dog remains are absent from only one site; otherwise these three forms are uniformly present and also relatively abundant. On the average they each constitute between 12 and 16 percent of the faunal assemblages.

Remains of dogs are also a consistent feature of the eleven sites that make up the Caribbean group. Dog remains are only abundant in the two Formative Period samples, where they constitute between 10 and 23 percent of those faunas.

The Caribbean group of sites is typified by abundant remains of deer and brocket (*Odo-

TABLE 3. IMPORTANT FAUNAL ELEMENTS THAT CHARACTERIZE THE THREE GROUPS OF SITES

FORMATIVE

	Gulf of Mexico (5 sites)			Caribbean (2 sites)			Gulf of Honduras (1 site)		
	#	M	R	#	M	R	#	M	R
Pocket Gopher	3	3	0-11	0			0		
Agouti/Paca	0			1	2	0-3.9	0		
Dog	4	15	0-29	2	16.5	10.3-22.6	0		
Deer/Brocket	4	4	0-9	2	43	31.1-54.8	1	6.5	6.5
Peccary	3	1	0-4	2	3.2	2.6-3.8	0		
Turkey	2	2	0-6	1	1.0	0-1.9	0		
Musk Turtle	5	17	1-31	1	5.8	0-11.5	1	2.2	2.2
Snook	5	13	4-22	0			1	2.2	2.2
Jack	2	1	0-3	0			1	26.1	26.1

CLASSIC

	Gulf of Mexico (4 sites)			Caribbean (9 sites)			Gulf of Honduras (2 sites)		
	#	M	R	#	M	R	#	M	R
Pocket Gopher	3	5	0-12	2	0.2	0-1.5	0		
Agouti/Paca	0			4	1.8	0-9.9	1	2.7	0-5.4
Dog	4	18	10-24	9	3.2	0.5-9.7	1	1.8	0-3.5
Deer/Brocket	4	7	1-16	9	24.2	5.5-50.7	2	16.1	2.3-29.8
Peccary	2	1	0-2	9	7.3	2.2-31.4	2	5.0	4.7-5.3
Turkey	4	3	1-4	8	11.5	0-70.1	0		
Musk Turtle	4	8	2-21	5	2.5	0-8.1	0		
Snook	4	10	4-18	0			2	2.1	1.8-2.3
Jack	3	4	0-9	2	0.3	0-1.8	2	24.8	19.3-30.2

TOTAL

	Gulf of Mexico (9 sites)			Caribbean (11 sites)			Gulf of Honduras (3 sites)		
	#	M	R	#	M	R	#	M	R
Pocket Gopher	6	3.9	0-12	2	0.2	0-1.5	0		
Agouti/Paca	0			5	1.8	0-9.9	1	1.8	0-5.4
Dog	8	16.3	0-28.6	11	5.6	0.5-22.6	1	1.2	0-3.5
Deer/Brocket	8	5.2	0-16	11	27.6	5.5-54.8	3	12.9	2.3-29.8
Peccary	5	0.9	0-3.6	11	6.4	2.2-31.4	2	3.3	0-5.3
Turkey	6	2.2	0-6	9	9.6	0-70.1	0		
Musk Turtle	9	12.7	1.3-31.0	6	3.1	0-11.5	1	0.7	0-2.2
Snook	9	11.8	3.6-21.8	0			3	2.1	1.8-2.3
Jack	5	1.9	0-9.4	2	0.3	0-1.8	3	25.2	19.3-30.2

\# Number of Sites; M Mean percent of MNI; R Range in percent of MNI

coileus virginiana and *Mazama* spp.), peccary (*Tayassu* spp.), and turkey (*Meleagris* spp.). Landa and others who visited this area in the early sixteenth century report that the natives called this region the land of turkey and deer (Schorger 1966:7). Clearly, dependence on these two animals has great antiquity. Although turkey remains are absent from two of the Caribbean sites, their average abundance is 10 percent in faunas from the area as a whole. Peccary is represented in each of the Caribbean samples, ranging in abundance from 2 to 31 percent. Deer and brocket are, however, the most abundant, averaging 28 percent and ranging from 6 to 55 percent of the faunas.

Deer and brocket are also abundant in the Gulf of Honduras sites where they average 13 percent in the three samples comprising this group. The most important animal, in terms of abundance, is jack (*Caranx* spp.), which averages 25 percent in these faunas. Data are available for only three faunal samples from this area; however, preliminary data from the Selín Farm site immediately to the east of these sites on the coast of Honduras seem to bear out this characterization of relatively abundant deer and jack.

The data indicate a significant change in animal use through time only in the Caribbean group of sites. Evidence of this change, as indicated above, is a relative abundance of dog remains in sites occupied during Formative times as compared to a relative decrease in their remains in sites of the Classic Period.

DISCUSSION

The extent to which these data indicate environmental or cultural influences in the choice of food animals is not clear-cut. The faunal groupings derived from the cluster analysis discussed have a geographic characteristic which does not conform to the biotic provinces outlined above. The variables used in determining these groupings do not, however, have limited geographic distribution but are dispersed throughout the region under study. Animals, of course, are not uniformly distributed over a region, and for this reason the location of a home-site in respect to concentrations of certain species in various habitats within the

catchment area of the site may determine what resources were most intensively used. The location of the Caribbean group of sites, for example, away from large rivers, estuaries, and the sea shore, must have been an important factor in determining the more terrestrial character of the faunas of this group of sites. Access to choice resources is a factor in determining site location, although considerations other than meat resources go into such decisions.

The faunal element one would expect to be least affected by the environment is the domestic dog. Dogs were an important dietary constituent in the Gulf group of sites and in Formative Period sites of the Caribbean groups (Wing 1978). Evidently the role of dog changed in the Classic Period in the Caribbean group, and in the Gulf of Honduras group where dogs were used but were of relatively small importance in the diet. The consumption of dogs continued in the Gulf area at least throughout Classic times, and in parts of the highlands of Mexico through the sixteenth century. Dog meat was, in fact, greatly esteemed and preferred above other types of meat of domesticated animals (see Durán 1967, II:218-19).

The other meat that is known to have been particularly esteemed is turkey. The context of one of the faunal samples is the residential palace at Mayapán, which may account for the very high percentage of turkey (70 percent). Nevertheless, the Mayapán faunal sample fits in well with the other sites of this area. It has particularly close affinities with the faunal sample from the Dzibilchaltún site. Presumably, at least in this case, the dietary differences between different social strata are minor compared with differences between cultural units.

The effects of environmental potentials are most clearly seen in the use of aquatic resources. Faunal assemblages from sites located farthest from the sea or a large river generally include a small percentage of aquatic organisms. The Caribbean group of sites, for example, has far fewer aquatic vertebrates than do the Gulf of Mexico or Gulf of Honduras groups.

A more subtle difference in fishing is evidenced by the proportion of snook and jack in the two more coastal groups. Snook and jack are today almost equally abundant along the coasts of the southwestern Gulf of Mexico and the Gulf of Honduras. Generally, snook will ascend farther up rivers into fresh water than jack, but both are common estuarine genera. The proportions of the remains of these two fishes are not the same in the sites of these two areas. Snook are abundant (average 12 percent) and jack are rare (average 2 percent) in the Gulf of Mexico sites, whereas snook are rare (average 2 percent) and jack are abundant (average 25 percent) in the Gulf of Honduras sites. Such differences might be explained most easily as a result of prehistoric use of different fishing technology, perhaps dictated by dietary preferences.

The faunal remains from the Colhá site cluster with the Gulf groups rather than with the Caribbean group as one might expect from Colhá's location. The terrestrial fauna includes abundant deer and turkey but few peccary and dog. In these respects the faunal assemblage is most similar to other sites in the Caribbean group. The faunal sample differs from other samples in the Caribbean group in having abundant aquatic remains, particularly of crocodilians, sliders (*Chrysemys* sp.), and "galápago" (*Staurotypus* sp.). These are riverine resources available at Colhá and not as readily available in the other sites that make up the Caribbean group; they set the faunal sample from the Colhá site apart. This site may represent a riverine procurement pattern of the Caribbean group.

CONCLUSIONS

To return to the initial proposition that use of animals for food is influenced directly or indirectly by cultural attributes, these data provide insight into the complexity of the problem. Clearly the environmental potentials will have an effect on the procurement pattern. In order to predict the characteristics of a procurement pattern, both the environmental potentials and the cultural tradition must be known.

In any tradition or pattern, one may expect a site that appears to be an aberration, whose faunal assemblage does not fit in with the regional pattern and may be considered indica-

tive of a specialized hunting or fishing station. The Cancún site, located on the northern coast of Yucatán, may be such a site (Wing 1975). The primary resource used at that site was sea turtle, reflecting a distinctive economy based on a locally available resource. One might anticipate finding similar sites with specialized economies which may have supplied such non-subsistence commodities as marine shells, sharks' teeth, and stingray spines to people living inland. Such specialized sites reflect the range in resources used and probably not a modification in the basic procurement pattern.

Distinctive regional patterns in animal use are demonstrated. These patterns are evident in spite of the faunal samples coming from a variety of localities, each with its own combination of habitats and resource potential. For example, a similar subsistence tradition is seen in the arid northern lowlands and the more humid southern lowlands of the Caribbean coastal groups. The Caribbean group coincides with sites in the Maya area, and the Gulf Coast group coincides with sites in the Olmec heartland. The procurement pattern exemplified by the sites of the Gulf Coast group may be considered an Olmec subsistence tradition with intensive use of dogs, musk turtles, and snook for food. In Formative times this tradition, in respect to the intensive use of dogs, was similar to the Maya tradition emerging in Caribbean coastal areas. Subsequently, a distinctive Maya tradition based on the predominant use of deer, peccary, and turkey emerged. The Gulf of Honduras sites show dependence on the same terrestrial species, the deer, as the Caribbean group with the Maya subsistence tradition. By contrast, the Gulf of Honduras shows virtually no use of the key terrestrial species, the dog, of the Gulf group with the Olmec tradition, nor are fishing practices the same in these two groups. For these reasons the Gulf of Honduras group may best be viewed as having the estuarine-coastal pattern of the interior lowland Maya tradition. Faunal assemblages from this Gulf of Honduras region that are now being studied will add to our understanding of the relationship between these inland and coastal phases of the Maya subsistence tradition.

Elizabeth S. Wing

Subsistence patterns appear to change very slowly. Measurable changes seem to be slower than those for other cultural attributes. The data in this study indicate a faunal change only in the Maya tradition. The intensive use of dogs in the Formative sites of Maya tradition suggests similarities with the Olmec tradition. Otherwise changes in animal use are minor.

ACKNOWLEDGMENTS I am most grateful to my many friends and colleagues who have entrusted their archaeological faunal samples to me for study. Data for this presentation could not have been gathered without the generous support of the National Geographic Society and the National Science Foundation (NSF G 17948 and GS 1018).

On The Nature of Olmec Polity

Philip Drucker
UNIVERSITY OF KENTUCKY

The goal of this paper is to reconsider data from the region generally considered as the core area of Olmec culture in the southern and western portions, respectively, of the modern states of Veracruz and Tabasco,[1] to see what evidence there may be that can be adduced in support of one or another of the hypotheses that have been proposed concerning Olmec political structure and organization. I do not have any new data from recent excavations to offer, since to the best of my knowledge no new research has been carried out in the region since the termination of Robert Heizer's work at La Venta and Michael Coe's at San Lorenzo several years ago. However, increasing interest among archaeologists in types of archaeological evidence useful in casting light on ancient forms of political organization, such as those discussed by Bruce Trigger (1974) and admirably demonstrated by Joyce Marcus (1976), has suggested possible new lines of approach to utilization of data previously collected. The effort is worth making in view of the importance of Olmec culture to our understanding of Mesoamerican culture growth, and the widely diverse hypotheses that have been offered on the nature of Olmec polity.

Interpretations of Olmec political organization range from that of an empire (Caso 1965; Bernal 1969a; M. Coe 1968b), to a state (Heizer 1960), to a chiefdom (Sanders and Price 1968). (Thirty years ago I pointed out [Drucker 1947] that in view of the magnitude of the construction and quantity of heavy imported stone at La Venta, and the limited carrying-capacity of the swamp-ringed island on which the site had been built, the labor force had to have been brought in, implying a complex sociopolitical organization. I did not attempt to define this organization, however.) Recently, Timothy Earle (1976) has proposed an interesting evaluation of an aspect of Olmec political structure derived principally from use of the "nearest neighbor statistic."[2] What is involved in the

---

[1] The region of primary concern in this paper is that referred to by Bernal and others as the "Metropolitan Olmec" region, or the "Olmec Heartland." Many, but not all, of those who have written on Olmec culture consider this the scene of origin and development of the culture. The late Miguel Covarrubias proposed an undefined region in archaeologically scantily known Guerrero as the source, a view still held by some. The present paper will not approach this problem directly, but will concentrate on data from the southern Veracruz–western Tabasco region.

[2] It would be interesting to compare Earle's conclusions to those of the present paper, especially since they agree on certain findings, but it would not be useful because of major flaws in his baseline data and his use of them. In part, Earle was not at fault, because he did not have access to sufficient data, and in places he did not use what he had. Earle's inclusion (1976: 217) of San Lorenzo among the sites occupied 1000–600 B.C. creates difficulties, since M. Coe (1970) is clear that after 900 B.C., when San Lorenzo B ends, San Lorenzo ceased to be a major center. This left Tres Zapotes, Laguna de los Cerros, and La Venta. Earle's conclusions as to "competition" being the key factor in allocation of space does not take into account the possibility that Laguna de los Cerros may have been a distribution point for Cerro Cintepec andesite used in monuments at both San Lorenzo and La Venta (C. W. Clewlow, Jr., and Eduardo Contreras, personal communication), a key possibility he could not have known about.

determination of category of organization is far more than nit-picking over labels. It concerns our understanding of Olmec culture as a major or a minor manifestation on its time horizon, as the focus of a horizon style. It concerns, as well, our eventual understanding of factors involved in the growth of complex culture, including procedures for testing the Sanders-Price-Meggers hypothesis—or better, assertion—that high culture, that is, one so complexly structured as to fit the designation of "civilization," cannot be developed in the humid tropics.

To begin with the matter of chiefdoms, the magnitude of the works accomplished by the Olmec—construction of massive features of clay and other materials, and transportation of large quantities of stone for monumental sculpture, architectural ornament, and other purposes—points not only to a large labor force and hence large population, but also to a high degree of centralization of authority that makes possible control of such a large population. Such numerical estimates as can be made in terms of man/days of labor (Heizer 1960) corroborate this interpretation. Further, studies of modern peasant (i.e., unimproved) maize cultivation in the region (Drucker and Heizer 1960; Drucker 1961), make clear that the land area west of the Tonalá River across the river from the site could readily have supported a large enough population to carry out the massive public works at La Venta if properly organized. M. Coe (this volume) has emphasized the bounty of the flood-plain cultivation, which produces a major dry season harvest instead of a minor one in the San Lorenzo vicinity, again to demonstrate that that locality could support a population adequate to handle even the enormous "San Lorenzo artifact," as Coe has dubbed the artificial plateau forming the main part of the site.

Chiefdoms, it is generally accepted, do not attain the size needed to provide work parties to carry out Olmec-size projects. Nor are they characterized by strong enough centralized control to carry out long-term projects, such as the four-century progressive construction of the A, B, and C complexes at La Venta, adhering the while to the centerline orientation. Ad-

mittedly this is an opinion, but it is based on my ethnographically derived familiarity with chiefdoms on the Northwest Coast of America and in Micronesia. Chiefdoms could provide personnel and discipline for the building of large Northwest Coast plank houses, and the procuring, carving, and setting up of memorial poles. Similarly, chiefdom organizations could cope with construction of a Palauan *abai*, and the procurement, transport, and shaping of the Yapese calcite disks. These feats of planning, organization, and direction were maximal efforts to the chiefdoms concerned. All in all, it is apparent that a political order of more complexity than that of a "chiefdom"—more complexity in terms of a larger population base, subject to a central authority empowered to enforce a more rigid discipline—must have been essential to Olmec construction and sculpture. Political organization of the type of the primitive state is far more commensurate with these requirements.

By "primitive state" I mean an autonomous political unit significantly larger and more complexly structured than any chiefdom, with various but not all of the institutions of the fully developed state. In other words, it is a developmental aspect of the complete state. No one, to my knowledge, has claimed in writing that to merit the designation of Mesoamerican "state" the entity concerned has to be as large in population and territory and have as enormous a capital as Teotihuacan at its apogee. Nonetheless, that is clearly the measuring stick that Sanders and Price (1968) use in their cavalier dismissal of the propriety of use of the term "state" for Olmec and other lowland Mesoamerican political units. Their theme is essentially: if it can't match Xolalpan Teotihuacan point for point it can't be considered a state. Yet Xolalpan Teotihuacan did not suddenly appear full-blown, like a product of some mysterious spontaneous combustion. It developed over a long period from smaller, simpler beginnings. In its very beginnings, while containing the potential to develop into the superstate it became, it must have gone through the phase of primitive state being described here.

I define a primitive state as an entity in which

there is a highly centralized control over a population of about 5,000 to 20,000 souls, with a single major center and various dependent villages and hamlets. Control of the population would be direct from the center, that is, there would not be secondary and tertiary centers in the chain of command. There might be large villages with certain ceremonial responsibilities, but they would not otherwise control a network of satellite communities. The extent of primary territory of the primitive state would be limited, first, by the carrying capacity of the land in terms of the resource-exploitation technology of the group, which would define the minimum, and, second, by communications facilities, that is, trail or waterway distance to perimeters, modified by the nature of the terrain (level or rugged), which set the maximum area that could be controlled. The point here is that direct control of a populace must be maintained by reasonably easy direct contact. Distant subjects are less likely to be obedient subjects. As a rough measure I would suggest somewhere in the neighborhood of twenty-five to thirty kilometers over reasonably even ground (as in the Olmec heartland outside the Tuxtla Mountains) as representing the outbound distance of one leg of a hard day's round trip from a central point. This should set the limits of effective control by the primitive state. This would mean by rough estimate an area of about 2,500 to 3,000 square kilometers. I estimate that most domains would be smaller. Given a productive swidden-farming economy like that normal for Olmec country—two maize crops per year: main crop (*milpa del año*) yield about 1200 kilograms shelled maize per hectare, catch crop (*tonamil* or *tapachol*) about 800 kilograms shelled maize per hectare; as M. Coe (1974) has shown, the extensive river flood plains in the San Lorenzo vicinity produce catch crops as bountiful as the usual main crop—the lower limit of primary land controlled by the primitive state might be as small as 800 to 1,000 square kilometers.

The control structure would center on one individual, scion of a royal lineage, whose immediate subordinates would be a hierarchy of hereditary nobles. The breakdown of kinship ties and kinship-guided behavior would occur between the elite (royal, noble) sector and the mass of commoners. This is of course a major difference from the chiefdom where such a break does not occur. Some occupational specialization would be expectable in the lower class. The primitive state would have the ability to defend itself against aggression, external or internal, and to commit aggression, but by mobilizing a citizen militia, not by maintaining a standing army or professional officers' cadre.

Principal overt functions of this early state would be religious-ceremonial, including the planning and direction of both construction of sacred precincts and production of religious art, and the planning and direction of ceremonials for public benefit. Some economic functions of the state would be essential although viewed as incidental to the religious activities. They would include collecting and redistributing surpluses from the food producers to support the elite and to provision large crews laboring on public works. Incidentally, the public works would be entirely religious, not secular. Elegant permanent palaces, state storehouses, armories, etc., would be lacking at this stage. There would be external trade to acquire exotic materials in exchange for local products exotic to the trading partners. Craft specialties would consist of religious objects and status symbols for the elite. These objects would be viewed more as sacred objects than as wealth objects.

I submit that this model has utility as a measure of an early stage in the development of the complete state. The population, much larger than that of a chiefdom, would provide adequate manpower for large-scale labor-intensive construction. The patterns of social interaction of a population of such size have to be very different from those of frequent face-to-face interactions of chiefdoms. There would be too many people for total interaction. As numbers increased and the gulf between elite and commoners widened, impersonality would be the mode. Justice and injustice, too, would be impersonally administered.

All components are there for the final phases of evolution into the complete superstate. Let population increase and the social structure becomes more rigid, especially in the area of class distinction. Ceremonialism becomes more complex and spectacular, drawing vast crowds of offering-laden pilgrims from afar. Economic factors become more important. Not only are more sacred—now luxury—goods needed, but also necessities: salt, tools, and foodstuffs become involved in the trade system. People who do not want to trade have to be subjugated; trade becomes one-way tribute. For this, the army must be permanent and professionalized. The elite specialize; some become full-time religious personnel, others full-time military; some manage the redistribution systems. So, the chains of command multiply as well as lengthen. Lower-class specialization increases too, so that crafts become hereditary and guild-like, formalizing the pattern of sons learning their fathers' crafts. The whole lower class becomes complexly structured, and is increasingly regimented by the elite. All of a sudden it seems that we are sitting atop another Moon Pyramid observing the ceremonial processions along an Avenue of the Dead. Our hypothetical primitive state has become the superstate.

Of course, few primitive states really became superstates. Many, perhaps, marched on bravely for a time and then fizzled out. Others got into some sort of homeostatic dead-center condition, became at some point petty states, and then collapsed, too. All these political phenomena early on had to pass through the primitive-state phase.

There is general agreement among theorists that there is another characteristic of the sort of political organization postulated here: the appearance of numerous specialists in non-food-producing activities. Personnel so engaged are supported by redistributive systems, operated or regulated by the state, which bulks surpluses of the farming sector. Classes of specialists expectable on the Olmec scene would include: planners/administrators for both secular and religious affairs, graded in ranked series; craftsmen, including sculptors of monumental works and of miniature works of jade and other valued stones; craftsmen in other esteemed materials, such as feathers; maintenance personnel for the clay-surfaced structures; possibly far-ranging traders trafficking in exotic materials (jade, cinnabar, and the

like); and perhaps others. Evidence for such specialization is inferential, not direct. We shall review the listed categories to see what the weight of the inferences seems to be.

The argument for existence of a group of planners/administrators derives on the one hand from evidence of long-continued rebuilding of La Venta Complex A, retaining all the while adherence to the centerline orientation and symmetrical arrangement of features relative to it, and, on the other hand, from the magnitude, in terms of man/days of labor, of the projects accomplished (cubic yardage of clay structures, tonnages of stone transported long distances, etc.). The inference derived from the second set of facts is essentially a corollary of that concerning population size: if large work crews were necessary to carry out the various works, then a hierarchy of administrators must have been required to organize the crews and direct their efforts. M. Coe (1968b: 59) has estimated, for example, that it may have taken more than 1,000 men to move San Lorenzo Monument 20 overland by dragging it. Velson and Clark (1975), in a detailed study which draws on some interesting observations of actual recent moving of heavy objects by manpower alone, calculate 700 to 1200 men (median 950), or 750 to 1250 with a fifty-man relief crew, to move the thirty-eight-ton stone from which La Venta Altar 1 was carved. This work force, the writers propose, could move the stone, mounted on a sledge running over sleepers, with friction reduced by lubricants, at a rate of 71.8 meters per hour over reasonably smooth terrain. The estimated work force would include personnel to move up the sleepers, apply whatever lubricants were used, and repair worn ropes, and "a dozen or so supervisory personnel" (*ibid.*: 14). Whichever estimate one prefers, Coe's or that of Velson and Clark, it is obvious that a large labor force had to be involved. It would be quite impossible, in my opinion, for a task force of this size to operate effectively over a prolonged period of time (134.6 days at Velson and Clark's 431 meters per six-hour day[3])

[3] Velson and Clark's pocket calculator misplaced the

without coordination and supervision by persons with recognized authority. Rotation of the crews for shorter periods probably would require additional administrators. The "dozen or so supervisory personnel" posited seems too few, unless we assume that the count is of the upper-echelon category only. Lower-echelon persons, roughly equivalent to our foremen and straw-bosses, would increase the number substantially. Construction of massive features of clay and earth must have been accomplished under similar close direction.

That Olmec society was not egalitarian, but ranked, is clear from an analysis of behavior and dress and ornament depicted on Olmec sculptures (Drucker n.d.). There are strong suggestions (particularly in the presence and absence of head-deformation) that upper level status was ascribed, not achieved. There probably was gradation of rank within the upper class. These facts are supportive of the interpretation of specialization of upper-class activities. Planning and administration of secular and religious matters, as proposed here, seems the most probable domain for upper-class specialization. If, as has been proposed,[4] the Olmec

were pioneers in astronomy and calendrics, a number of priest/administrators—priests because of the religious associations of celestial phenomena—must have been dedicated to observing celestial bodies and recording their observations.

It is appropriate at this point to note that differences of opinion exist concerning the basis of legitimation of the state power. Heizer (1960), emphasizing the religious symbolism of structures and monuments, considers invocation of supernatural powers a major theme in Olmec political organization, and has suggested that the term "theocracy" best characterizes that organization. M. Coe (1968b: 65), on the other hand, sees militarism as a key component of Olmec polity and policy. Actually, theocratic and militaristic patterns are not necessarily mutually exclusive. Overt references both to religious activities and to use of force are frequent in Olmec sculpture (Drucker n.d.). Describing the much later Aztec, Alfonso Caso (1958: 90) characterized Mexica political organization as a "military theocracy," indicating a compatible integration of militaristic and religious themes. The same label seems appropriate for the Olmec. Their planning/administrative specialists most likely planned and directed military operations as well as construction works, rather than including a specialized military group among their ranks, to judge by absence of armed and armored personages in the art.

The proposition that sculptors formed a class of specialists, or most probably two distinct classes, is based on evaluation of skills required and probable length of time required for the pecking, hammer-dressing, sawing,

---

decimal point, giving them 13.5 days for their postulated force to drag the stone on the sledge at a rate of 431 meters per six-hour day over the assumed 58 kilometers from Cerro Cintepec to a point of embarkation on the Coatzacoalcos River. Actually, at 431 meters per day, it would require 134.57 days to travel the distance.

[4] Marion Popenoe Hatch (1971) has proposed an intriguing theory to account for the N 8° W orientation of La Venta Complexes A–C, in which she also considers Olmec astronomy, calendar, and writing. At about 2000 B.C. (when she believes systematic observations must have begun), the "Center Point" of Ursa Major, determined by diagonals of the trapezoid formed by Ursa Major α, β, γ, δ, transitted the horizon (set) at an azimuth of N 8° W at midnight (inferior meridian transit of the sun) on June 20 or 21, the summer solstice. This is astronomical fact, with no quibbles. From this she argues persuasively that various motifs on sculptures and incised on jade celts and other objects refer to constellations and celestial events. In fact she proposes that certain celts with numerous design elements incised on them are essentially ephemerides. Complexes A–C were built to point to the azimuth of the setting that signaled the summer solstice. The Great Mound, she avers, was built to provide an observation point for the phenomenon. Apart from some picky objections, which can be coped with (the Center-Point concept,

whether the sea horizon was actually visible from the Great Mound, etc.), her interesting argument has one fatal defect: she does not show any way in which the hypothetical Olmec astronomer, atop the Great Mound with his crossed-stick sighting device, could correlate sidereal and solar events. In other words, how could he determine *which* of the Center Points of Ursa Major's transits of the horizon, night after night in June, was the one which occurred precisely as the sun crossed the inferior meridian of La Venta, thus marking the summer solstice? If Hatch can solve this problem, she will have made a major contribution to our understanding of Olmec astronomy, calendrics, and iconography as well.

drilling, and polishing (in the cases of jade and iron ores such as hematite, etc.) of very hard materials with simple tools lacking any sort of mechanical advantage. In the case of jade objects and those of the iron ores, some special devices must have been used to retain small pieces, for some, like the "spangles" (Drucker 1952: 170–1, Pl. 58), are very small for sawing, drilling, and polishing. It is the differences in handling qualities that lead me to suggest that the artisans who worked the jade pieces, mirrors, and the like may have been a craft group distinct from those who made the monumental pieces. Even working full-time, shaping, drilling, and polishing a jade bead must have been a slow process; fabrication of a jade figurine from start to finish must have taken months, or even years. The monumental sculptures posed other problems, but at least several persons—Heizer (1960) has suggested, reasonably, a master sculptor and several apprentices—could work simultaneously on them. Even then, where large areas of stone had to be removed, for example, in the cases of La Venta Altars 4 and 5, completion of a monument must have been a very lengthy process. Manifestly, slow laborious technology does not demonstrate specialization. However, when it is coupled with the mastering of skills involving training and practice, as well as an understanding of the tenets of an art style, there is a strong possibility that full-time specialization was involved.

There may have been craftsmen, as specialized as the sculptors, who worked in other media, of whom we have no data because of the perishable nature of their products. Kent Flannery (1968) notes Gulf shell in his Formative Oaxacan materials. Presumably the Olmec were the source of such materials. Did they have specialists who worked glossy colorful shells into elaborate ornaments? Were the originals of all the necklaces and pectorals depicted on the monuments only of jade and serpentine and crystalline ores of iron? We cannot tell. A few jade specimens suggesting one valve of a pelecypod hint that some shells may have been esteemed. The acid clays of the structures have robbed us of more information.

We do have a few clues pointing to the possibility of another craft that might have offered a field for specialization: featherworking. There occur in the region a variety of birds, large and small, with strikingly colorful plumage (the quetzal, so esteemed in later Mesoamerica, of course, was not found in the low-lying region or even in the Tuxtla Mountains). Monuments, however, show almost no ornaments or other articles obviously made of feathers. La Venta Colossal Head 4 (Clewlow *et. al.* 1967: Pl. 4b) displays a headdress apparently of large feathers. Our best lead, however, comes from a jade figurine from Arroyo Pesquero, described in meticulous detail by Elizabeth Benson (1971). The figurine is shown wearing a bulky (fluffy?) short cloak of feathers, or covered with feathers. Cloaks of two kinds, short (like that of the figurine) or long (hanging almost to the wearer's ankles) appear on a number of monuments (La Venta Stelae 2 and 3, Altar 5 [sides]; Laguna de los Cerros Monolito 19, etc.). Since the bas-relief figures wearing these garments are shown in front view, or a sort of three-quarters simulation of a profile, only the inner surfaces are shown. Now the Gulf Coast Olmec region is not a place where one needs much cold-weather gear. There are a few raw blustery days in winter when the *nortes* blow when some sort of garment, preferably a waterproof one, feels comfortable. The rest of the year a cloak would be the last thing one would want. Thus, a reasonable inference is that the cloaks were status symbols. Some may have been of hide, perhaps jaguar with pelage. Some may have been of cotton cloth, with woven or painted symbolic designs. The Arroyo Pesquero figurine demonstrates, however, that some were of feathers, feathers on netting (?), feather-covered cloth (?), or feather-covered hide (some cloaks on the monuments have a stiff appearance, as though they were of dried, only partly dressed animal hide). If the feather cloaks, or feathered cloaks, were status symbols, it seems likely that they were made by specialists, rather than being household products. The argument for a class of specialists in featherworking is clearly based on inference piled on inference, but nevertheless I see it as a possibility.

Articles of dress depicted on stone monuments—breechclouts, sometimes with wide belts and a short back apron for men, and knee-length (wrap-around?) skirts for elite women—suggest cloth, presumably of cotton, although tapa (misnamed "barkcloth") might be represented. In either case the dress goods may have been household products. The representations give no indications of especially complex technologies used. Ceramics, too, would seem to have been a household craft, in view of the absence of highly specialized ceremonial forms.

The evidence for a caretaker force was cited frequently in the report on the 1955 excavations (Drucker *et al.* 1959). It consists of the lack of signs of heavy erosion on the floors of colored clays of the Ceremonial Court and similarly surfaced tops and sides of features, and of occasional traces of patching of floor surfaces. In addition, there was no accumulation of the drift sands blown in from the coastal and sand dunes during northers. The best specific case, of course, is the contrast between the heavily eroded surfaces of Construction Phase IV fill and the neat clean surfaces of the earlier phases. The complex was abandoned some time after the completion of the Phase IV construction. That surface was exposed to the frequent torrential summer thundershowers, more scattered rainstorms through the fall, and the heavy downpours that accompany the northers from November through January, a precipitation pattern that drenches the region with about 3000 millimeters annually. The bare surfaces of the final Construction Phase IV were sluiced away; the heavy clay fill was cut into a maze of small gullies, until finally the drift sand, accumulating first in low spots and areas downwind of elevations, gradually spread over the battered clay, ending the erosion. Something very different must have occurred during the four centuries or so of use of Complex A. A systematic procedure of cleaning drains, continual repairing of damaged surfaces, and cleaning away drift-sand accumulation, seems the most likely way the artificial surfaces could have been maintained. This would have required a permanent, or nearly permanent, maintenance force under the direction, of course, of some administrative personnel. The size of such a maintenance force cannot be estimated, except to speculate that it need not have been

large. Persons carrying out these tasks could have been specialists, full-time and life-long. There is also the possibility that these tasks may have been rotated among men of the lower class for periods of a year or so at a time. The skills needed do not appear to have been complex enough to require long apprenticeships.

The presence of a considerable variety of imported minerals, in addition to the basalts and andesites from the Tuxtla Mountains (and possibly from the Volcán La Unión locality) and the metamorphic stones whose nearest source is believed to have been near the crest of the Isthmus of Tehuantepec, has been interpreted as evidence of trade with distant groups. These exotic materials include, in addition to the andesites and basalts, principally jade, obsidian, cinnabar, and certain ores of iron. Numerous pieces—or quantities in the case of cinnabar—of these materials have been excavated. (In addition, from one to a few specimens of other exotic materials have been found: quartz crystal, amber, and amethyst.) Of the major imports, trace element analyses of some of the obsidian specimens point to sources in the Guatemalan highlands and to others in the Central Mexican highlands. The iron ores probably come from the Valley of Oaxaca (Flannery 1968:89). The only source of cinnabar of which I can find record is that referred to by Millon (1973:61–2), in the modern state of Querétaro, although there may be others. Jade sources are not identified as yet, but there may be several: there are known sources in highland Guatemala and, so it is speculated, there may be sources in the states of Oaxaca and Guerrero. While, as indicated, sources of some of these items are not precisely known, one thing is clear about them all: none occurs in or even very near Gulf Coast Olmec territory. The presence of these exotic minerals at La Venta and San Lorenzo indicates that there must have been communication between the Olmec and inhabitants of distant regions.

The nature of this communication is more difficult to determine. Most writers on the topic have interpreted the occurrence of materials from distant regions as indicative of "trade," involving exchange of goods from the

Philip Drucker

Olmec homeland for the exotics. The Olmec had a variety of goods that would have been prized by inlanders and uplanders, or better, goods that inlanders/uplanders could have learned to esteem. The list includes: marine shells (such as those Flannery reports from San José sites [1968:85] and/or ornaments made of them; cacao;[5] plumage and peltries of lowland birds and animals; possibly cotton or cotton goods (cotton does well in the region, having been a major commercial crop in the late eighteenth century in the Tuxtla district); possibly tobacco (on the same grounds as cotton: that the plant prospers and was widely cultivated in the recent past in southern Veracruz and Tabasco, and still is a major crop in the Tuxtlas); and, it has been suggested, finished jade products such as figurines.

That the trade was probably direct, rather than through a lengthy chain of village-to-village exchanges, is indicated by the fact that the minerals are not found at sites between the sources and the final destination, as would be expectable in the case of indirect transmission. While most writers on the topic have assumed that it was the Olmec who traveled the lengthy trails to procure the ceremonial materials they valued so, there is no supportive proof. In fact, the few depictions of outlanders in Olmec country suggest that at least at times persons from distant regions may have come to visit. On such occasions they may have brought their local raw materials as trade-goods, or as offerings if the trips were pilgrimage-like. We may suppose that the Olmec sought out the distant

sources of the materials and initiated the exchanges. Those uplanders who became sufficiently indoctrinated into Olmec values would have been the ones to make the journeys in the opposite direction.

While the term "trade" may have various usages, in the present connnection it is most useful to conceptualize it as referring to exchange of goods that has a certain continuity and frequency. As regards continuity, offerings containing jade and cinnabar have been found at La Venta in Construction Phases I, II, III, and IV, that is to say, over a time period of roughly 400 years. This time span is sufficiently long to take care of the matter of continuity. (The fact that only one offering including both substances is dated to Construction Phase I most likely can be accounted for by the possibility that, if any Phase I offerings occurred along the centerline, they may have been removed in Construction Phases III and IV in the excavation of the pits for Massive Offerings 3 and 2.) The frequency with which lots of the materials were imported by the Olmec and by uplanders cannot be discerned. Another aspect of this fact is that there seems to be no objective way to determine the frequency of contact between the Olmec and the various upland groups with whom they traded. Counting the tiniest beads, and even a few broken ones, more than 3,000 pieces of jade were recovered during the several seasons at La Venta (as reported in Drucker 1952; Drucker *et al.* 1959): from Structural Complex A, 3,022 pieces; from Altar 4 (1940), 99 pieces; 1942 stratitrenches, 5 pieces. This seems a substantial amount, but a reasonably robust man could carry it all in a single load. Moreover, we do not know how much more of the material remains in Complex A, let alone the other structures at the site. We do not know the number of specimens traded to uplanders—those that M. Coe (1968a:94) has suggested mark the "Jade Route" to a source or sources perhaps in Guerrero. Not knowing the exact sources, we do not know the abundance or scarcity of the material—how easy or difficult it was to find, in other words. Thus, we cannot know whether the Olmec would be content to make a long trek for a few nodules of raw

[5] Dillon (1975) has emphasized the fact, overlooked by some recent writers, that the southern Gulf Coast was a major cacao-producing region in early historic and certainly pre-Hispanic times. I am of the opinion that cacao cultivation in the region has a very long history; while firm evidence is not easy to find, it is at least supportive of the argument that the local environment is eminently suitable for this plant whose limits of tolerance to variations in temperature, moisture, and soils are very narrow. In proof, I have seen, albeit infrequently, wild *criollo* cacao in virgin forests there. A point too infrequently noted in discussions about cacao is the reason for the popularity of the bitter seeds and their great demand in Mesoamerica: the high oil content, appreciated by people on the high-starch diet of the maize cultivators.

36

jade, or whether they were satisfied only with several man-loads at a time. Not only the matter of trade procedures, but the question of Olmec influence on contemporary highland cultures is intimately tied to the solution of these problems.

We do have some information that suggests that throughout the utilization and rebuildings of Complex A at La Venta, during the apparent heyday of craftsmanship in jade, that mineral was scarce. The frequent placing of "serpentine"[6] celts and "serpentine" figurines instead of jade ones in offerings in La Venta Complex A suggests that the Olmec did not have as much jade to meet their requirements for offerings as they would have liked. This deduction is, of course, based on the assumption that objects of "serpentine"— or better, various kinds of metamorphic stone—although also imports, were imitations, or counterfeits, of jade specimens. While Garniss Curtis (1959: 287) notes that metamorphic stones are more fibrous and less brittle than the harder igneous rocks and jade, I believe they would be less suitable for real cutting tools—axes, adzes, and chisels. If serpentine and similar rocks were just simulations of jade it would appear to support the view that only relatively small lots of jade were imported at a time, that is, by any single expedition. Hence, it is probable that jade procurement expeditions were more frequent, and cross-(sub-)cultural contacts more numerous than has been previously thought.

The problems associated with the importation of cinnabar—lack of information on total amount, on probable amounts imported per trip (whether by La Ventans or by outlanders), or ease or difficulty of mining at the source— are like those relating to jade at La Venta. Thus it is difficult to derive conclusions as to the organization of the procurement system and as to the intensity of contacts with inhabitants of the region(s) where the substance was mined. It may well be that, as with jade, only relatively small amounts were brought in at a time.

In casting about for a model to account for the operation of this remarkable traffic in ceremonial materials, it has been suggested that Olmec traders may have been an organized group of specialists like the Aztec *pochteca*. Somehow, this model does not quite seem to fit. The general cultural milieu in which the Olmec operated was very different from that of the *pochteca*. The clientele of the *pochteca* were, by and large, on about the same cultural level as the traders. The Olmec, on the other hand, the most advanced Mesoamericans of their day, were dealing with simple village agriculturists, except perhaps in Oaxaca, where contemporary Guadalupe Phase villagers were far more advanced than other highlanders (Flannery 1968:89 ff.). Allowing for some differences of technology and motivation, the independent fur traders of our Far West provide a more appropriate model, for these too were representatives of an advanced culture dealing with less complexly organized peoples. Flannery (1968:102 ff.) has proposed similar models—one of the Tlingit, sophisticated by dealings with white traders, trading with interior Athabascans on the basis of personal alliances, and acculturating them in the process; another of the Shan's dealings with the tribal Kachin—to account for Olmec–early highlander relationships. The large forces, the paramilitary organization of the *pochteca*, their reported intelligence-gathering and plotting functions, would have been superfluous in the Olmec setting. This does not mean, of course, that Olmec travelers from the Gulf Coast would not have had to have the capability of defending themselves and their trade goods on occasion. Their foe at such times, however, would consist of a war party recruited from a village, not an army such as contemporaries of the Aztec could field. Taking and bringing back only small amounts of goods, and with a lesser security problem, the Olmec could operate with small expeditionary units. The

---

[6] In measuring, classifying, etc., the specimens from the La Venta offerings, in my mineralogical ignorance I designated everything that did not seem to be jadeite as "serpentine." Actually such specimens are made of a variety of metamorphic stones, as indicated by Curtis (1959: 288), who reports that of nine pieces labeled by me as "serpentine" only one was of that material, the others being other kinds of metamorphic rock. Other pieces, including a fair number of subglobular beads which I referred to as of "poorer quality jade," are probably of metamorphic rock also.

case for the trader-specialist in Olmec society seems weaker than that for other types of specialists. Nonetheless, it would have been efficient to have had a few individuals in each generation who knew the trails and had some ties to the villagers. Such persons, however, would not constitute a class, nor would they have any need to be organized as one.

To recapitulate our review of the possibility of classes of specialists characteristic of the primitive state, it is clear that cultural conditions were appropriate for the existence of several such occupational groups. The magnitude of the earthen structures, the transport of large amounts of heavy materials (stone), point to large work forces efficaciously directed. Elaboration of Complex A over a four-century time span, while adhering consistently to the centerline orientation and emphasis, and similar complicated layouts and construction (for example, the procurement and transport of many tons of columnar basalt to achieve certain architectural effects), indicates that continuous planning was involved. The most likely way to provide such planning and direction would have been through a distinct class, presumably an elite one, of planners/administrators. The probability that such status was ascribed is indicated by the occurrence of jade (and serpentine, etc.) figurines with and without head deformation. Personages with deformed heads were apparently those of higher status. Again, the skills required and the slow laborious technologies involved in the sculptor's art suggest the likelihood of full-time specialization, actually with two classes: one, the makers of monumental sculpture, the other, makers of miniatures and ornaments. There may have been specialists in featherworking. That there were persons performing more-or-less continuous maintenance and repair of the clay and clay-and-sand surfaces of the structures is apparent from the condition of such surfaces in the archaeological record, despite the formidable regional precipitation pattern. However, it cannot be determined whether this specialty was carried out as a career activity or was of a temporary nature, somewhat like the lower-ranked "cargoes" of recent and modern Indian communities in modern Latin America.

The case for an organized class of specialists in long range trade, comparable to the much later Aztec *pochteca,* is the weakest of all considered. Circumstances prevailing at the time—Olmec vis-à-vis their village agriculturist contemporaries, and the probably small amounts of raw materials (jade, cinnabar) procured at a time—would have made so complicated an institution as that of the *pochteca* unnecessary. While a few individuals, probably elite, may have guided and directed the expeditions and conducted the trade with natives of remote places, they were probably too few at any one time to constitute a class of specialists.

Thus far, we have seen that Gulf Coast Olmec remains, as we know them so far, can best be understood as the products of a primitive state, one with centralized authority over a sizeable population and with classes of specialists. In this situation there would, of course, have been another class, that of low status, the producers of maize and other foodstuffs, who performed as well the unskilled and semi-skilled labor in construction and in transport of heavy stones, and who must have borne the arms in police/military operations. It seems likely that they may have comprised the audiences at major ceremonials, and may even have participated in certain minor roles. Logic suggests that while lower class, they were not "peasants." They must have been too actively involved, albeit in a lowly way, in the Great Tradition of their time.

We have been discussing the probabilities of the existence of "an Olmec state" in broad terms. To turn to specifics, we must answer the question: was there one Olmec state on the southwestern Gulf Coast, or were there two, or more, at any one time? The answer to these questions should cast more light on the nature of political order among the Olmec. Fortunately, there are data that speak to the question.

In light of present knowledge, there are four major sites in the southwestern Gulf Coast region. Criteria for designation as "major sites" are based on areal extent, numbers of large structures (pyramids, platform mounds, etc.; in one case the site itself is an enormous structure supporting various features), and large numbers of stone monuments carved in Olmec style. In other words, these were centers of administrative control of sizeable populations from which enough labor could be drawn to accomplish all the construction. While it is most hazardous to predict what will be found in unexplored Olmec sites, it will be assumed that the following four are the only major ones: San Lorenzo, La Venta, Tres Zapotes, and Laguna de los Cerros. The first two have been well sampled and have good sequences of internally consistent carbon-14 dates. Tres Zapotes was tested before development of carbon-14 dating. Its occupations extended over a very long time-span, with, however, substantial unconformities between components (some of which eventually may be filled in by the sampling of untested areas of the very extensive site). Laguna de los Cerros is only slightly known, principally from surface survey.

The dates from San Lorenzo (1300–900 B.C.) and La Venta (1000–600 B.C.) demonstrate that the histories of those two sites were largely independent, but with a century of overlap, 1000–900 B.C. (There are some twelfth-century-B.C. dates from La Venta, but whether the site had achieved major importance so early is not known.) The next best data on site-contemporaneity can be derived from cross-site similarities of monuments, construction features, and the like. One characteristic of Olmec monumental sculpture is that most specimens are unique, unlike any other known. There are, however, a few instances in which identical themes portrayed in essentially the same manner have been found at two or more sites. Such specific thematic similarities of stone monuments at different sites are considered the best indicators of contemporaneity. The grounds for this assumption are as follows: (1) Olmec monumental sculpture was not just for art's sake, but was made for ceremonial purposes; (2) each monument was a symbol of certain specific religious and ceremonial concepts; (3) the monuments were not only symbols, but were foci of, and parts of, complex ceremonial behavior; (4) while the great variety of themes depicted indicates a wide variety of ceremonial concepts and resulting behavior in the individual Olmec sites,

duplication or near-duplication of theme can mean only that there was communication between the sites, through which not only the theme of the sculpture but also the procedures of the ceremonial acts were transferred by persons of one site to those of the other(s). A review of specific thematic similarities follows.

Themes common to all four sites
None[7]

Comment: It is not unlikely that careful exploration of Laguna de los Cerros and further work at Tres Zapotes may provide some cases fitting this distributional category.

Themes common to San Lorenzo, La Venta, and Tres Zapotes
Colossal heads

Comment: A point that has not been brought out in connection with these monuments, and one that strongly supports the interpretation of them as products of a thematic-technologic concept rapidly diffused among Olmec centers during a relatively short time period (1000–900 B.C.), is that they represent not only a thematic, but also a technological, innovation in Olmec sculpture: the use of stones of the approximate overall size and shape of the completed sculptures. The slopes of Cerro Cintepec, from which the stone used in many Olmec monuments came (Williams and Heizer

---

[7] There are a number of anthropomorphic statues shown seated with legs crossed tailor-fashion, leaning forward slightly with hands resting on or near the knees, from the four principal sites and from other localities in the region as well. These might be considered a unit group except for the fact that the heads of many have been destroyed so that there is no way to tell what distinctive features may have been carved on the faces and/or the headdresses. Also, the pose may or may not have been significant as thematic identification. It may have been instead a functional device to center the heavy upper body over its base to reduce the likelihood of the statues toppling over backward (see Drucker *et al.* 1959: 204). In addition, ornaments, belts, etc., depicted on these figures differ considerably, and may have been significant differentiators.

Philip Drucker

1965), in the vicinity of Guazuntlan Falls, Soteapan, and probably elsewhere, are peppered with large smooth boulders of roughly similar shape with elliptoidal, longitudinal cross-section with one flattish side, ranging in size from relatively small (guessed at less than 100 pounds) to about the size of the colossal heads. In the area I traversed, I do not recall seeing any of these stones much larger than the largest heads, indicating that materials for the largest heads were selected from the largest naturally occurring pieces. This means that the sculptures were accomplished through removal of minimal amounts of debitage (unlike freestanding statues, "altars," etc.), and that some areas of the sculptures, such as headdresses, backs of heads, and the like, were minimally modified, much of the original surface being retained in the design. Thus certain aspects of the completed sculptures, such as length/breadth proportions, etc., were determined by geologic processes, not cultural (aesthetic) ones (except insofar as the latter affected the choice of a specific stone). This technique was continued in the post-San Lorenzo stelae, such as La Venta Stelae 2 and 3, Monument 19, etc., in which the bas-relief design was applied to the unmodified stone surface. I do not know if boulders on the Cerro La Vigía used for the Tres Zapotes–Nestepe heads are less regular in shape, or if the representational differences are to be explained by a slightly lower level of contact and communication between Tres Zapotes and the other centers during the period 1000–900 B.C. than between San Lorenzo and La Venta.

"Tenon figures"
(San Lorenzo Monument 6, La Venta Monument 56, Tres Zapotes Monuments F and G)

Comment: Properly speaking, it is the overall form of these monuments, with the head or head and shoulders of a figure shown as though emerging from a massive shaft of stone extending behind it, that defines this class. As Stirling (1943b: 22) remarked ". . . it seems more likely that they were used as seats or altars" rather than as architectural ornament. Had the pieces been set into the ground to stand up vertically, most of the sculptural effect would have been lost; they were almost surely placed horizontally for, as Stirling suggested, some specialized ceremonial use. It is this probable special ceremonial function that justifies classing these monuments together as a unit.

Themes common to San Lorenzo and La Venta

Figure seated in niche holding infant, carved from large block of stone.
(San Lorenzo Monument 20, La Venta Altar 5, La Venta Altar 2)

Comment: This theme has been variously interpreted. Bernal (1969a: 58) has suggested a dynastic meaning: the presentation of the future heir. Others see it as a reference to a ceremony involving infant sacrifice. What is probably another version of this theme is that of an isolated full-round figure, not attached to a massive block, or "altar," holding an infant in the same posture as in San Lorenzo Monument 12 and the smaller figure from Las Limas, near the Coatzacoalcos River some distance upstream from San Lorenzo. The features of the figure La Venta Altar 5:2, the infant held by the principal figure (5:1), were weathered past distinguishing; those of the infant held by the Las Limas male figure, and of the three preserved infants depicted in low re-

40

lief on the sides of the La Venta example, are highly conventionalized, possibly to indicate monsters with stylized (feline) faces and bodies of human infants. Damage to, and weathering of, the matching specimen at San Lorenzo (Monument 20) make it impossible to determine if its sides bore comparable scenes.

Figure seated in niche of large block of stone, holding heavy rope to which smaller relief figure(s) on side of stone are attached
(San Lorenzo Monument 14, La Venta Altar 4)

Comment: The near-identity of the "captive" altars is highly probable, though not demonstrable, for damage and weathering have eliminated all traces of the rope that I believe was carved on the bottom edge of the stone to the arm of the figure on the side of San Lorenzo Monument 14. The emphasized Feline Monster design on the upper border of La Venta Altar 4 (not distinguishable on San Lorenzo Monument 14), suggests association with a supernatural feline being or beings. The San Lorenzo monument had an elaborate figure, now defaced past possibility of recognition, on the end opposite that of the captive, not found on the La Venta specimen.

Themes common to San Lorenzo and the Tres Zapotes vicinity
Naturalistic running feline
(San Lorenzo Monument 21,[8] Tres Zapotes vicinity)

Comment: This parallel is not quite as neat as the others proposed, but, if valid, it may be highly significant. One problem arises from the fact that the "Tres Zapotes vicinity" speci-

men was reported by Stirling (1943b: Pl. 16d) as being from "near Lirios" (a modern village eight to ten miles from Tres Zapotes). Another consists in the two figures facing in opposite directions (San Lorenzo Monument 21 toward viewer's left). Both specimens are alike in the naturalistic rendering, in the rather crude technological rendering, and in the pose: a feline in full motion, running or leaping. Naturalistic portrayal of violent motion is unusual in Olmec large works.

Since there is nothing thematically and technologically anywhere near similar at La Venta, it is possible that these specimens are pre-La Venta in date. They might, in fact, belong to a very early phase of Olmec art.

Themes common to San Lorenzo and Laguna de los Cerros
Figure on pedestal, principal figure kneeling on prostrate form expressing vanquishing/domination
(Río Chiquito Monument 1, Laguna de los Cerros Monolito 20)

Comment: The Río Chiquito monument, from a satellite site of San Lorenzo, belongs with the corpus of San Lorenzo sculptures. These figures are those interpreted as representing a jaguar copulating with a human female. A less picturesque but more factual interpretation will be presented in a later section of this paper. What matters here is that the two monuments are very similar not only in theme and use of pedestal, but in their somewhat cursory (and crude) treatment of the principal figure and of the very sketchy treatment of the inferior one. These monuments are probably pre-La Venta, and might belong to an early phase of Olmec sculpture. Potrero Nuevo Monu-

---

[8] M. Coe (1968b: 49) suggests that San Lorenzo Monument 21 may represent "a dog or coyote," but the squarish muzzle profile and the posterior attachment of the scrotum indicate that a feline was intended.

ment 3, whose remnants indicate that it was more vigorously and more proficiently executed, could reasonably be proposed as a later much elaborated expression of the same theme.

The foregoing list includes the most striking sculptural similarities shared by two or more Olmec sites.[9] As, and if, more work is carried out, more of them may well appear. In passing, a significant non-sculptural parallel between San Lorenzo and La Venta should be noted; construction of systems of stone drains, apparently to regulate the water levels of artificial ponds or catchment basins (M. Coe 1968b: 57; Heizer, Graham and Napton 1968: 144 ff.). The likelihood that the presumably ceremonial function of these systems was similar makes this parallel significant also.

It is worthwhile at this point to diverge briefly from the main theme to consider the chronological placing of certain monuments, an insight emerging as a spin-off from our search for information on Olmec political structure. A number of facts are pertinent. First, assignment of certain sets of monuments, and the drain systems, to the century or so of coexistence of San Lorenzo and La Venta is probably accurate because of two facts: the thematic and/or functional similarities within each set are precise, and the numerous internally consistent sequences of dates from San Lorenzo and La Venta make the chronological placing of the sites, including the overlap, quite reliable. The possible pre-La Venta (pre-1000 B.C.) placings suggested for other sets are less certain because of the limited number of examples, and, in the case of the feline figures, less precise formal similarities. However, there is an interesting hint, although no more than that, in this material. If other pieces are found to be referable to this same time segment, and if they tend to resemble those proposed here as

early in technologic simplicity and inferior execution, doubt would be cast on the present view that Olmec art burst forth full-blown, or had its origins and early development in some still-unknown site. We might be encouraged to look further into the early San Lorenzo levels, and levels contemporary with them in the other sites, for evidence of the developmental stages of Olmec sculpture.

For present purposes, the fact that these comparisons give us the first rational dating of several small sets of monuments is less important than what this means in terms of site interrelationships. During the tenth century B.C., there was considerable communication between San Lorenzo and La Venta, during which the complex involving the carving of the colossal heads and all the theological concepts and patterns of ritual associated with them, as well as the complexes or cults represented by the huge rectangular blocks of stone with figures carved on them to form semi-narrative scenes, were transmitted between the two sites. Similar but less intensive communication ties of one or both of these sites to Tres Zapotes permitted or caused the colossal-head cult to reach that center on the far side of the Tuxtla Mountains. Differing intensity of relationships would account as well for the differences in treatment of the monuments: the Tres Zapotes/Nestepe heads differ more in treatment from the San Lorenzo and La Venta sets than these latter do from each other. In which site the colossal-head complex originated cannot be determined. It might be possible to argue that San Lorenzo was the locus of origin. San Lorenzo is closer to Cerro Cintepec, from which the huge rounded bolders used for most of the heads at the two sites came. A long-established site, it may have had more skilled specialists in monumental sculpture. On the other hand, it might be argued that planners/administrators and sculptors at the then relatively new site of La Venta may have been more innovative. All such speculations fall far short of proof. The important fact is that all the shared complexes of monuments indicate strong ties and intercommunication between the sites. This is the significant fact to be derived from all the sets of parallels.

---

[9] One striking instance of very close duplication of two monuments, La Venta Monument 44 and that from San Martín Pajapán (Clewlow 1970), is not useful to us in the present connection because of the ambiguous context (apparent reuse in post-Olmec times) of the monument on the mountain.

That the cults represented by like monuments were not imposed by force, or threat of force, by the rulers of a dominant site on another entity, or on several subordinate entities, is indicated by the fact that there are so few of these duplicate or near-duplicate themes. Rather, during the history of each center, sculpting of individualistic unique monuments was the prevailing mode. This strongly implies considerable autonomy in ceremonial matters, and, since it is clear that ceremonial matters were of major importance in Olmec culture, it follows that the centers were autonomous in all respects during their individual histories.

Another set of data, that of the differing obsidian-procurement systems of San Lorenzo and La Venta, points to the same conclusion (Jack and Heizer 1968; Cobean *et al.* 1971). Had one center dominated the other, we should expect to find it distributing the monopolized material so that obsidian from the same sources would be common in both centers. Of course, there is an assumption involved here: that, in the vagaries of sampling, reasonable amounts of obsidian from both sites dated from the tenth century B.C.

In all probability, then, there was no single imperial realm in the Gulf Coast Olmec region, but rather a varying number of independent centers, with a fair amount of communication between them during periods of coexistence. In other words, there were several Olmec states functioning concurrently over much of the existence of the culture. They may have competed in some activities (Earle 1976), but they also cooperated in others.

This brings us to the question of the "Olmec Empire" as proposed by Caso, Bernal, M. Coe, and others. This concept involves the control of outlying areas, principally in the Valley of Mexico, Puebla, Morelos, and Guerrero—that is, the route or routes leading to suggested sources of jade in Guerrero, or what Coe has designated the "Jade Route." Caso (1965), considering the possibility of several autonomous Olmec states in the Gulf Coast region (he included non-Olmec Cerro de las Mesas among them), saw no difficulty in suggesting an alliance among them for purposes of maintaining the imperial control similar to that of the Triple Alliance of Tenochtitlan, Texcoco, and Tlacopan as it was structured centuries later. All proponents of the "Olmec Empire" attribute its origin and maintenance to military dominance by the Gulf Coast Olmec, and establishment of Olmec outposts or colonies in the distant lands. Bernal (1969a) adds another captive region, the "Soconusco" of the Aztec, which opened the way to the southeast. Lowe (1977) has stressed the evidences for an Olmec presence in this region, although not necessarily as a subordinate part of a Gulf Coast-based empire, on the evidence of his own investigations and those of Thompson, Navarrete, and others. Recent work by Heizer and Graham at Abaj Takalik has substantiated the occurrence of an early Olmec component of the long, complex set of culture sequences in this region (Robert F. Heizer, personal communication). The original site associations of the reused Olmec monuments could not be determined, and the battered carvings reveal no clear specific links to Gulf Coast sites. More data are needed before the Soconusco situation can be evaluated. Returning our attention to the Gulf Coast, the problem of empire is a difficult one. Occurrences of exotic materials presumably imported from distant places to Olmec sites, and occurrences of non-portable examples of relief carvings, stylistically Olmec, in remote places, are strong evidences of Olmec contacts with and Olmec influences on the inhabitants of such places; and yet, they neither prove nor disprove Olmec control and domination of people or places. It behooves us to begin by searching for answers to the intermediate question: What sort of evidence could we find, or should we look for, that would conclusively demonstrate Olmec control of the local inhabitants of Tlatilco, Chalcatzingo, Tlapacoya, and other places proposed as Olmec colonies?

In the best of all possible worlds, David Grove, Paul Tolstoy, José Luis Lorenzo, or some of the others who have been working so diligently at "Colonial Olmec" sites in the highlands would find the tomb of the Olmec Lord High Commissioner for Trade and Native Affairs. The remains of this worthy would be identifiable as Olmec, despite the lack of burials with measurable skeletons in the heartland, because of the massive bone with areas of attachment indicating heavy musculature (the body-type consistently pictured in the sculptures), and by the odd (constricted cylindrical) type of head deformation displayed by many La Venta jade figurines. The tomb (whose entryway would replicate the "Olmec niche" of the monuments, and whose walls would be adorned with bas-reliefs of Feline Monsters and of Catemacan volcanic cinder cones) would be cluttered with traded materials (unworked nodules of jade and ilmenite, man-loads of cinnabar, plus finished Olmec jade objects used in exchange) as well as many slim-boned skeletons of slight wiry highland servitors sacrificed with decorated jade celts (left embedded in the skulls) at the great man's funeral.

Since, despite the substantial amount of excavation done, nothing vaguely like this has been found, our pleasant fantasy remains and is likely to remain just that: fantasy. We must turn to more prosaic domains for evidence of empire. Let us look at the scenes depicted on the monuments, particularly those in which complex situations are displayed. To be convincing, the scene must overtly—"overtly" so that we can understand it—express interaction of symbols identifiable as Olmec and non-Olmec (highlanders), with designators of lower status or subjugation associated with the latter.

Careful review of sculptural themes shows that outlanders, personages or supernatural beings, in either case readable as symbols of non-Olmec groups, appear on certain monuments. Subordination/subjugation is also clearly depicted in some sculptures. Are the two concepts combined in a single monument?

La Venta Stela 3 indicates a face-to-face encounter of Olmec with non-Olmec. Figure 3:1,[10] he of the Uncle Sam chin-whiskers, stands before an Olmec niche. Therefore, he is the Olmec. In corroboration, among his supernatural back-up cohorts is a very Olmec being: 3:8, a figure with human body and feline face (mask?) nearly identical to the six subsidiary

10 See Drucker 1952: 173 for the system of designation of figures on multifigure monuments.

figures on La Venta Stela 2. If I see the less-clear, damaged figures 3:7 and 3:9 correctly (Drucker *et al.* 1959: Pl. 55 and Fig. 67), they may refer specifically to Olmec also; I read 3:7 as a being carrying a monstrous saurian with a guitar-shaped appendage on his tail, and 3:9 as a being carrying a huge bird on his back (is it too far-fetched to derive a meaning of alligator hides and bird feathers as trade goods?). Figure 3:2 is the outlander. The symbols on his towering headdress might designate his home, could we but read them, but the sure evidence of alien origin is his slightly upturned pointed-toe footgear. There is no question that some sort of footwear was intended and was carefully depicted, and that it was intended to contrast with the barefoot style of 3:1. To stress the contrast, a large toenail was emphasized on each foot of 3:1 (these can be seen most clearly in Bernal's illustration of the monument [1969a: Pl. 4]). This and two other depictions of footgear on the La Venta monuments were clearly emphasized to indicate non-local origin of personages so equipped. There is no reason to doubt that the principal figures on this monument represent a meeting of Olmec and non-Olmec personages. There is, however, no indication that either was superior to, or dominant over, the other. The figures are approximately the same size, and both stand firmly on the horizontal ground line. Apparently each had the same number of supernatural sponsors or supporters: remnants of three figures appear behind and above 3:2, and, if reconstructed over the damaged area of the monument, as Contreras did in his freewheeling reconstruction (Drucker *et al.* 1959: Fig. 68), would pretty well fill the pictorial space. In fact they would crowd it if any of them had been depicted as carrying bulky objects as were two of the figures associated with 3:1. In short, the two principal figures are meeting as equals.

Two other La Venta monuments show outsiders (non-Olmec individuals) arriving at the site: Monuments 13 and 19. The figure on Monument 13 is characterized by distinctive items of dress: a lumpy, turbanlike headdress, a breechclout without the front apron usually shown on Olmec sculptures, and a pair of ornate *huaraches* with heel guards. The foot-print carved behind him, probably to be read as "He has made [many] tracks [to get here]," seems almost superfluous in light of his alien garb. Monument 19's anthropomorphic figure, proffering a pouch of valued materials as he arrives in the protective coil of his formidable familiar, again is distinctively garbed. His feline-theme headgear, through whose open mouth he stares, is unique in the art style. It becomes common in artistic depiction in later centuries. His breechclout has not only a front apron, but ribbonlike strips dangling down the sides. He wears the same sort of peculiar footgear as figure Stela 3:2. Thus, he too represents a non-Olmec visitor. Neither of these representations is of use in our inquiry as to relative status, however, since no Olmec figure is shown with either of them.

La Venta Altar 3 has on one side two figures, 3:2 and 3:3, shown seated and engaged in conversation. Unequal status is shown by the fact that 3:2 sits on a bench, while 3:3, inferior in status, sits on the floor. No diagnostic details indicative of differing regional origins can be made out, however.

The "altars" portraying the captive theme, La Venta Altar 4 and San Lorenzo Monument 14, show a principal figure holding a line to which a lesser figure—lesser in size and boldness of relief, and hence in status—is attached. At least that is the scene on La Venta Altar 4. The San Lorenzo specimen is so eroded and battered that the rope is no longer visible, nor does the captive's lower arm, with the wrist caught between the strands of rope, remain. Nevertheless, there can be little doubt that these features were originally present. Domination of one figure by another was thus strikingly represented. The problem in this case is that the captive figures bear no indicators showing alien origin. The avian foot on the headgear of the San Lorenzo figure may have had some locative meaning, but we cannot translate it. Our only recourse is to assume that the captives represented unimportant persons.

There is another set of monuments that symbolize subjugation: Río Chiquito Monument 1, Laguna de los Cerros Monolito 20, and Potrero Nuevo Monument 3. The first and last of the set are those interpreted by Stirling (1955:19-20) as representing a jaguar *in copula* with a human female. The Río Chiquito and Laguna de los Cerros monuments are very similar in concept and crudity of execution. Both show an anthropomorphic figure with no feline features, from which the head has been battered and broken, kneeling with the left leg tightly flexed and thigh extended horizontally, the right leg flexed with knee upward. The posture is similar to that of the splendid (and much better executed) San Lorenzo Monument 34, except that the right/left positions of the legs are reversed, and in Monument 34 the leg with the knee upward is less tightly flexed—in fact, more realistically posed. The kneeling figures of the Río Chiquito and Laguna de los Cerros specimens are supported by massive rectanguloid blocks of the stone from which the pieces are carved. On the upper portion of each block is indicated in sketchy fashion what seems to be a prone human figure. The superior figure in both examples is placed with its right foot planted firmly on the lady's (if she *was* a lady) abdomen, its extended knee on her(?) chest. Obviously, the pose cannot have been intended to represent sexual intercourse. Medellín Zenil's interpretation (1960b: 95) that the carvings represent "domination and humiliation of the vanquished by the conqueror," is undoubtedly correct. Potrero Nuevo Monument 3, with the realistic clawed hind paws of the superior figure and with the inferior figure—although heavily damaged—clearly a human female, surely was meant to express the same concept. Had copulation been the theme, by all the realistic canons of the art style the feline copulatory posture would have been shown. Another version of the theme appears at Chalcatzingo in Relief 4, upper set (Grove 1968a: Fig. 5), where two feline monsters are shown vanquishing two anthropomorphs. However, none of the forms representing the victims carry any symbols to indicate place of origin. If there were such designators they were obliterated in the process of defacing the monuments. These three specimens (Río Chiquito Monument 1, Laguna de los Cerros Monolito 20, and Potrero Nuevo Monument 3) nevertheless come the closest of any of the compositions reviewed to the overt expression of conquest. Unfortunately, they do not tell us who was conquered.

It may appear that our survey of monumental scenes has ended on a somewhat uncertain note. I do not believe that this is quite so, for we have found a good deal of information in the monumental compositions, and there are some additional inferences to be made. I would summarize the total results as follows:

1. Figures represented as outlanders arriving at La Venta were of major importance:

   (a) because of their elaborate garb (even the La Venta Monument 13 figure, skimpily dressed though he appears at first glance, does not lack elegance: his elaborate turban, his necklace and nose ornament of large beads—jade?, ilmenite?—and the fancy tassels on his *huaraches*); and

   (b) one (La Venta Monument 19) obviously was bringing gifts.

   These, therefore, are symbols standing for the distant groups from whom the valued goods were obtained. This also means that the Olmec did not do all the traveling.

2. These foreign visitors were not conquered vassals:

   (a) they met the Olmec as equals (La Venta Stela 3); and

   (b) they came under the protection of mighty supernatural sponsors (La Venta Monument 19).

3. These foreign visitors may well have been honored by being shown the splendors of La Venta—the ceremonials and the monuments:

   (a) some visitors may have been impressed enough to want to emulate their hosts, and were lent (or given?) Olmec sculptors to do some carving for them; or

   (b) they arranged for some of their personnel to be trained by Olmec sculptors.

   Such procedures, which would add sculptural skills to the Olmec stock of "trade goods," would account for the wide, if scattered, distribution of sculptures in Olmec style better than speculation on Olmec proselytizing among folk of distant places by wandering about carving cliffs and boulders. Be it noted that it fits neatly Flannery's ethnographic model (1968:103 ff.) of the Shan-Kachin relationships. It would also serve to explain the scene of La Venta 1955 Offering 4 (Drucker *et al.* 1959:152 ff.), in which Figurine 7, highly distinctive in color and material from the others and hence an outlander, can be interpreted as a visitor observing the ceremonial procession from a place of honor.

4. Scenes symbolizing Olmec domination of other groups (La Venta Altar 4, San Lorenzo Monument 20, Río Chiquito Monument 1, Laguna de los Cerros Monolito 20, Potrero Nuevo Monument 3) refer to subjugation of obstreperous village/tribal groups, probably from nearby. Once subjugated they ceased to have major importance:

   (a) except as a possible source of sacrificial victims (La Venta Altar 4, San Lorenzo Monument 20);

   (b) they were not dignified by association with symbols of origins (as centuries later, tertiary and quaternary Classic Maya sites were not dignified with emblem glyphs [Marcus 1976]); and

   (c) the forms representing them were executed in a crude, sketchy manner (Río Chiquito Monument 1, Laguna de los Cerros Monolito 20).

The total effect of these interpretations is to negate the hypothesis of an Olmec empire exercising military control of distant sources of valued materials and, as well, the routes to and from them. There was no need to exile Olmec people to the arid plains of Morelos to colonize or to man garrisons, as long as the highland affines dutifully brought precious substances to La Venta. It should be noted that if the Olmec utilized, as suggested, primitive concepts of reciprocal gift-giving and kinship ties to exploit their highland neighbors, they did not compromise their own status as bearers of an advanced culture just as the Shan did not become tribalized by their dealings with the Kachin. Both groups were simply introducing an innovation (procurement of valuable materials) among their less advanced neighbors by setting it in a behavioral context the target population would find intelligible. Any modern applied anthropologist would approve of this technique. If the Olmec portrayed the village headmen and chiefs of petty tribes as an elegant nobility equal to their own for certain purposes, they differed but little from much later European explorers and traders who flattered their own egos by describing similar personages as native kings and princes, and their women as princesses.

To recapitulate, the archaeologic evidence we have from Olmec sites on such matters as extent of massive construction and tonnage of stone moved long distances indicates that only large populations under highly centralized control could have accomplished them. Evidence from sculptural works indicates existence of a hereditary elite. Consideration of technologies utilized suggests specialization of sculptors in two categories, those of monumental works and those of miniatures. Other categories of specialists such as featherworkers may have existed, although the case for a class of trade specialists similar to the Aztec *pochteca* is quite weak. Probably no such class existed in Olmec times. Overall, these conditions were clearly more congruent with the existence of a primitive state than with any other political order. Review of relationships between the four known major sites suggests that each was probably the center of an autonomous state, so that there would have been anywhere from two to four Olmec states at any given time during the existence of the culture. Presumably each state had its own set of relationships with highland villagers from whom unworked jade and like materials considered valuable were obtained. Rather than militarily based imperial control of highland trails and distant sources of jade, ilmenite, cinnabar, and the like, Olmec "trade" was probably based on reciprocal gift-exchange and real or fictive kinship linkages with the folk at the sources of the valuable raw materials.

Fig. 1 San Lorenzo Monument 20, an example of the extreme mutilation suffered by some Olmec altars. Photograph courtesy of Michael D. Coe.

Olmec Monuments: Mutilation as a Clue to Meaning

David C. Grove

UNIVERSITY OF ILLINOIS, URBANA

Almost all of the great stone altars and monuments have been broken and mutilated at the cost of considerable effort. This could not have happened by accident.... (Stirling 1940a: 334)

INTRODUCTION

Matthew Stirling's observation, following the 1940 discovery of the first large quantity of Olmec monuments at La Venta, marks the recognition of a prehistoric action which is still poorly understood. The Olmec not only created magnificent monuments, but many of these were later mutilated or destroyed. When and by whom remain matters of conjecture. The destruction was not limited to monuments at only one site. Almost four decades of explorations at La Venta, San Lorenzo, Laguna de los Cerros, and lesser-known Gulf Coast sites have produced numerous examples of battered and defaced carvings. Published speculation regarding this destruction tends to view it as a terminal event, marking the end of an Olmec site or of Olmec culture itself. But mutilation of Olmec monuments is not limited to Gulf Coast sites. My recent three-year project at Chalcatzingo (Grove *et al.* 1976), a central Mexican site, also recovered various mutilated Olmec-style monuments. The Chalcatzingo data do not fit well within a terminal-event explanation, and alternatives are explored in this article. Following their consideration, Gulf Coast and Chalcatzingo data are used as a basis for speculations regarding Olmec monument-building and Olmec chieftainship.

TYPES OF MUTILATION

The destruction and defacement of monuments assumed a variety of forms, primarily breaking, pitting and grooving, and the effacement of carved features. No publication to my knowledge has categorized this mutilation or correlated it with the various types of monuments. However, such a step seems necessary to understanding the mutilation of Olmec monumental art. The majority of Olmec monuments from San Lorenzo, La Venta, and Laguna de los Cerros are therefore categorized in Table 1, and the presence, or absence, and type of mutilation are recorded. The two main published sources for these data are Beatriz de la Fuente (1973) and Clewlow and Corson (1968). Plain or unidentifiable pieces are omitted from the list.

Many Olmec monuments suffered some form of purposeful breaking. Some were literally battered and broken into fragments. Others had merely one specific section broken off. Surprisingly, the monuments most damaged by breaking are also the largest: the monolithic table-top altars. These are often missing huge corner chunks, or, as in the case of San Lorenzo Monument 20 (Fig. 1), are broken until almost unrecognizable. Mutilation by breaking was no easy accomplishment in view of the size of most altars. It obviously required forethought and considerable effort (see Drucker *et al.* 1959: 228; Stirling 1940a: 334). While colossal stone heads were of a size nearly equal to that of altars, they were not subjected to serious battering and breaking (see discussion in M. Coe 1968b: 77), although they were slightly defaced by other means. The headdress and chin of La Venta Head 1 is fractured, the chin of La Venta Head 4 is fractured, and San Lorenzo Head 3 is missing its lower lip, but most of this damage may be natural (Clewlow *et al.* 1967: 20, 27, 37, Pls. 1, 9, 22). Even if the damage were purposeful, it is very minor in comparison to that of other monuments. Among other monuments, anthropomorphic statues are almost always found decapitated, and the heads are missing (Table 1). Some zoomorphic statues are left complete and others are decapitated, with no clear pattern to the breakage. Stelae are frequently broken, and unbroken stelae often show other types of defacement.

A less violent defacement is seen in the carving of shallow circular pits, elongated grooves, and small rectangular niches into monuments (Fig. 2). These occasionally obliterate some of a monument's carved features, but this does not appear to have been their primary purpose. Although instances of mutilation by grooves are found on all types of monuments, grooves are consistently found carved on colossal stone heads, generally atop the headdress and never on the face. Grooves are less common on San Lorenzo colossal heads and carvings, perhaps reflecting some temporal difference from La Venta carvings. Circular pits or "cup marks," some with a "nipple mark" (*e.g.*, Pohorilenko 1975) were first mentioned on Olmec monuments by Stirling (1955: 12). These too occur primarily on colossal heads and often *on* the face area. Rectangular carved niches are far more rare, occurring only on San Lorenzo Monuments 2 (colossal head) and 14 (altar).

In some instances when a monument is not broken, some of its carved areas are erased by

Fig. 2 San Lorenzo Monument 14, the effaced left side, showing also the small rectangular carved niches. Photograph by the author.

TABLE 1. GULF COAST MONUMENTS

		Unmutilated	Decapitated	Broken	Effaced	Grooves	Pits	Rectangles	Portrait/Stylized
Colossal Heads									
La Venta	1					●			P
	2					●	●		P
	3					●	●		P
	4					●	●		P
San Lorenzo	1					●	●		P
	2					?	●	●	P
	3						●		P
	4					●	●		P
	5						●		P
(Mon. 17)	6						●		P
(Mon. 19)	7						●		P
(Mon. 53)	8						●		P
(Mon. 61)	9	●							P
Tres Zapotes	A						●		P
	Q	●							
Altars									
La Venta	1			●					S
	2			●					P
	3			●					P
	4				?		?	●	P
	5			●					?
	6			?					?
	7					●			?
San Lorenzo Monument	14			●	●			●	P
	18			●					S?
	20			●					P
	33			●					?
	36			●					?
	38			●					?
	51			?					?
	60			●					?
Potrero Nuevo	2	●							S
Laguna de los Cerros									
Monument	5			●					P
	28			●					P

TABLE I. GULF COAST MONUMENTS (*cont'd*)

	Unmutilated	Decapitated	Broken	Effaced	Grooves	Pits	Rectangles	Portrait/Stylized
Anthropomorphic Statues								
La Venta Monument 5	•							S
8	•							S
9	•							S
10	•							S
11	?							S
21		•			•			P
23		•						P
30		•						P
31		•						P
39			•					?
40		•						P
57		•			•		•	P
70	?							S
72	?							S
73		•						P
75			•					S
San Lorenzo Monument 10	•							S
11		•						P
12		•						?
15			•					P
24			•					P
25		•						P
26		•						P
34		•						P
47		•						P
52	•							S
54		•						?
Laguna de los Cerros Monument 3		•						P
6		•						P
8	•							S
9			•					P
11		•						P
19		•						P
20			•					P/S

TABLE 1. GULF COAST MONUMENTS (*cont'd*)

	Unmutilated	Decapitated	Broken	Effaced	Grooves	Pits	Rectangles	Portrait/Stylized
Anthropomorphic Heads								
La Venta Monument 29		•						P
44		?			•			?
64		•						S
65					•			S
San Lorenzo Monument 6		•						P
Animal/Human Statues								
SL—Tenochtitlan 1		•	•					P/S
SL—Potrero Nuevo 3		•	•					P/S
Zoomorphic Statues								
La Venta Monument 12	•							Monkey
20	•							Whale
56	•							Monkey
74		•						Feline
San Lorenzo Monument 7		•						Feline
9		?	•					Duck vessel
37		•	•					Feline
43	•							Arthropod
SL—Tenochtitlan 2	?							Feline
SL—Potrero Nuevo 4	?		?					Serpent
Laguna de los Cerros Monument 13			•					Duck or paw-wing motif
Zoomorphic Heads								
La Venta Monument 28		•						Feline
Other Carvings in the Round								
La Venta Monument 59			•		•			S
Laguna de los Cerros Monument 1	•							S
2			•					S

TABLE 1. GULF COAST MONUMENTS (cont'd)

	Unmutilated	Decapitated	Broken	Effaced	Grooves	Pits	Rectangles	Portrait/Stylized
Reliefs (including Stelae)								
La Venta Stela 1	•							P
2	?							P
3				•				P
4			•		•			?
Monument 6	•							S
13	•							P?
15			•					S
19	•							S
25			•					S
26			•					S
27			?					S
42			•					S?
58			•					S
61			•					P
63	?							P/S?
66			•					S?
71	•							S?
San Lorenzo Monument 21					•	•		Dog
30			•					S
41			•					S
42			•					S?
56				•				P
58	•							S
Laguna de los Cerros Monument 27				?				S

grinding or battering in a purposeful attempt to obliterate them. I have termed this third major type of mutilation "effacement." Effacement is usually confined to bas-relief carvings occurring on stelae and altars. The most striking example of effacement is found on San Lorenzo Monument 14 (Fig. 2), a large stone altar. Almost the entire left side of the altar has been ground or pecked away to nearly an additional inch of depth (Stirling 1955: 16), wiping out all but the forehead and headdress of a human figure carved in bas-relief. In addition, ten rectangular niches have been cut into this effaced area.

PREVIOUS AND CURRENT EXPLANATIONS

The literature on Olmec carvings contains various explanations of their mutilation. Stirling (1940a: 334), based upon his initial La Venta finds, attributed the destruction to outsiders:

This could not have happened by accident; neither is it reasonable that it would have been done by the original makers. It seems plausible to suppose that some conquering group descended upon them and this mutilation represents their efforts to destroy the pagan gods which they found established here.

A slightly different interpretation for La Venta monument mutilation was given by Drucker, Heizer and Squier (1959: 230) in the report of their 1955 excavations. "The mutilation of the monuments in the Ceremonial Court area, and inferentially of those throughout the entire site, was most probably the work of post-Phase IV inhabitants of the island."

Michael Coe's San Lorenzo excavations, which began in 1966, produced further data on the act of mutilation, and partially laid to rest the concept that mutilation was carried out by outsiders. Coe (1967c: 25) states:

> Towards the end of the San Lorenzo phase [1150–900 B.C.] *all* of the great basalt monuments of San Lorenzo had been mutilated and then laid out in long lines on ridges around the peripheries of the site. . . . I take this to have been a revolutionary act, for we have no evidence that it was any other than San Lorenzo people themselves who carried out that great act of destruction.

This statement shows that not only did the San Lorenzo Olmec create their monuments, they destroyed them as well. In a slightly later article Coe (1968b: 63) takes a more regional viewpoint and concludes:

> Certainly the same cataclysm that resulted in the mutilation and burial of San Lorenzo sculptures also took place at La Venta. . . . this would suggest to me that an entire Olmec state fell into disarray about 900 B.C. San Lorenzo is subsequently abandoned, but La Venta goes on to even greater brilliance. . . .

The idea of revolution is further amplified in the comments that followed Coe's above-quoted paper at the Dumbarton Oaks Conference on the Olmec (M. Coe 1968b: 73–7).

A somewhat complementary explanation has been suggested by Heizer (1960: 220). "One could interpret such evidence as due . . . to the reaction against the old religion by a disillusioned people imbued with iconoclastic fervor." A similar explanation has been discussed by Drennan (1976b: 362–3).

MONUMENT DESTRUCTION AT CHALCATZINGO

As a site, Chalcatzingo is best known for its Olmec-style bas-reliefs (Cook de Leonard 1967; Gay 1966, 1971; Grove 1968a; Guzmán 1934; Piña Chan 1955: 24–5). Although the exact dating of these carvings is unimportant for this analysis, they share many design attributes with La Venta's monuments and can be considered to be contemporaneous in general terms with the La Venta Olmec period. While most of the reliefs known prior to our project's beginnings in 1972 (Reliefs I–VIII, X–XI) show no mutilation, monument mutilation did occur. Monument 1, found lying in a drainage stream near the center of the site by Eulalia Guzmán (1934: Figs. 12 and 13), is now on exhibit in the Museo Nacional de Antropología in Mexico City. The anthropomorphic statue is similar to La Venta Monuments 23 and 30. It depicts a seated personage, and, like so many Gulf Coast statues, it is decapitated (Fig. 3).

Fig. 3 Chalcatzingo Monument 1. Height, 53 cms. Photograph by the author.

TABLE 2. CHALCATZINGO MONUMENTS AND RELIEFS

	Unmutilated	Decapitated	Broken	Effaced	Grooves	Pits	Rectangles	Portrait/Stylized	
Reliefs									
I	•							S	
II	•							P?	
III	•							S	
IV	•							S	
V	•							S	
VI	•							S	
VII	•							S	
VIII	•							S	
(Mon. 6) IX			•					S	
X	•							P	
XI	•							S	
(Mon. 8) XII	•							S	
(Mon. 7) XIII			•					S	
XIV	•							S	
XV	•							S	
Monuments									
Monument 1		•						P	statue
5		•						P	statue-head
9	•							S	round drum altar
10			•					?	stela base
11			•					P	statuelike carving
12								S	table-top altar
13			•					P	stela
14	•		?					P	stela, female
15						•		P	stela
16			•					?	stela base
17	•							S	boulder with relief
18			•					S	stela

Our excavations from 1972 to 1974 uncovered other carvings, including free-standing bas-reliefs and stelae, some carvings in the round, and a Gulf Coast-like table-top altar. Reliefs XIV and XV are high on the hillside and form part of the agricultural fertility group centered around Relief I; they are unmutilated.

Also unmutilated is a free-standing relief, XII/ Monument 8 (see Table 2; a few monuments carry two identification numbers while the numbering system undergoes change). This carving, nicknamed the "Flying Olmec" (Grove 1974:122; Grove *et al.* 1976:1208), depicts a supernatural theme. The majority of other newly discovered carvings do exhibit mutilation and are commented upon below.

Relief XIII/Monument 7 (Fig. 4) is a free-standing carving quite similar to Relief IX/Monument 6 (Grove 1968a: 489–90, Fig. 7). This latter was illegally excavated and removed from Chalcatzingo and is now in a private gallery in Utica, New York. Both carvings represent frontal views of highly stylized earth-monster faces. Their large cruciform mouths are depicted in a manner identical to that of the earth-monster cave mouth so prominent (in profile) in Relief I, and all include sprouting-plant motifs. The inner mouth area of Relief IX/Monument 6 has a carved opening which passes through the stone, while the inner area of Relief XIII/Monument 7 is solid and carved in bas-relief. A cleft-headed baby-face figure is depicted sitting within the mouth (Fig. 4). Both monuments have been mutilated by breaking. Relief IX/Monument 6 was apparently in fragments when looted. Relief XIII/Monument 7 was found on the surface, hidden by vegetation. Only one half of the monument was discovered and subsequent investigations failed to locate the other half.

Chalcatzingo's table-top altar, Monument 12, is not monolithic, but constructed of large stone slabs (Fig. 5). The front face of the altar is carved with the large eyes of an earth-monster, but lacks the typical niche and seated figure of Gulf Coast altars. The altar's defacement was not achieved by breaking, for it is not monolithic. Stone slabs were simply removed from the top and ledge, and placed to cover the carved front face. The entire monument may have escaped heavy damage because its earth interior served as a tomb for two high-status individuals. Its function as a tomb may have been more important than its destruction.

Among smaller monuments recovered during excavations is Monument 11 (Fig. 6), a small carved and reworked boulder. The low-relief carving depicts bent arms with hands holding a "knuckle-duster" (see M. Coe 1965b: Fig. 50) and a torch. The boulder has been broken above the arms, indicating the decapitation of a carved human head.

The discovery of most value to understanding Olmec monument mutilation is Monument

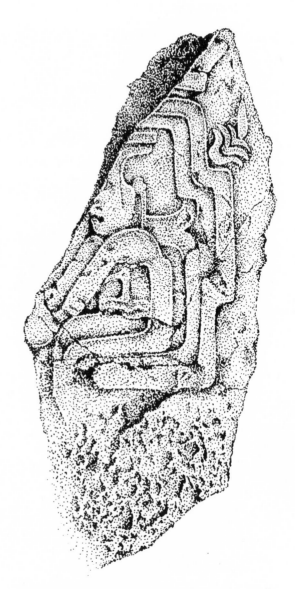

Fig. 4 Chalcatzingo Monument 7, a fragmentary earth-monster face. A seated cleft-headed figure sits within the mouth. Height, about 2.5 meters. Drawing by Barbara Wascher.

5 (Fig. 7). At the 1967 Dumbarton Oaks Conference, in response to questions regarding mutilation, Robert Heizer replied, "You will know the answer . . . when you find the heads" (M. Coe 1968b: 75). Monument 5 represents such a find. It was uncovered early in our 1972 field season, during the excavation of what we have since identified as an elite residential structure dating to *ca.* 600 B.C. A number of human burials were found in the sub-floor area of this structure, including high-status burials within

Fig. 5 Chalcatzingo Monument 12, a table-top altar. Approximate length, 4.5 meters; height, 1 meter. Photograph by Alex Apostolides.

stone-lined crypts. These latter burials were often accompanied by jadeite ornaments or, in one instance only, a La Venta-like greenstone were-jaguar figurine. The very first of the crypt burials excavated, Burial 3 (Merry n.d.: 74–80), was accompanied by Monument 5, a stone head obviously decapitated from a statue. This is the only instance to date in which a decapitated statue-head has been found in good archaeological association. The head is not the missing head from either Monument 1 or 11 and is obviously part of an undiscovered statue. The Burial 3–Monument 5 association will be discussed again later in this article.

Monuments 10, 13, 14, 15, 16, and 18 are stelae uncovered by our project. Two of these, 10 and 16, are broken stela bases, and their upper sections are missing. Monument 13 (Fig. 8) is important, for it still stands *in situ* in front of a long stone-faced Middle Formative platform mound. Only the stela base and one large upper fragment remain, and there is no doubt that this stela was purposefully broken. The

Fig. 6 Chalcatzingo Monument 11, a decapitated boulder statue. Carving in center of stone depicts arms with hands holding ceremonial objects, including a "knuckleduster" at the right. Photograph by the author.

Fig. 7 Chalcatzingo Monument 5, a decapitated statue-head found associated with a high status burial. Height, about 20 cms. Photograph by the author.

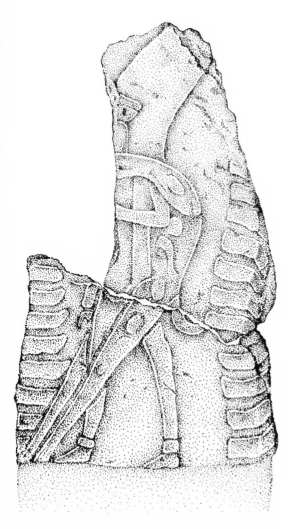

Fig. 8 Chalcatzingo Monument 13, a stela located *in situ* in front of a stone-faced platform mound. The stela shows a personage wearing an animal (deer?) skin. Height, about 1.8 meters. Drawing by Barbara Wascher.

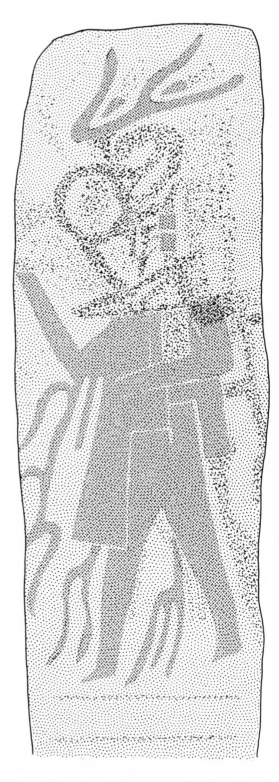

Fig. 9 Chalcatzingo Monument 15, a highly eroded stela depicting a plumed personage. The face area is effaced. Height, about 4 meters. Drawing by the author.

remaining sections show most of a walking personage, wearing what appears to be a deer skin. The missing section of the stela contains the face, headdress, and body front of the personage. Our excavations did not uncover the missing section, and it appears to have been purposely removed from the area, probably at the time of mutilation.

Monument 15 (Fig. 9) was found nearby, buried face down. The carving was heavily eroded, but appears to represent a standing human, resplendent in plumes. The person's face has been effaced.

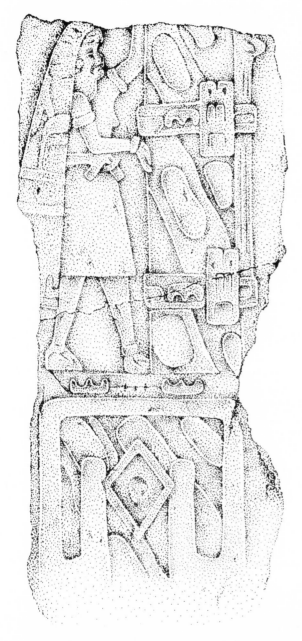

Fig. 10 Chalcatzingo Monument 14, a stela depicting a female standing above a stylized earth-monster face. Height, about 2.2 meters. Drawing by Barbara Wascher.

in La Venta Stela 1 and Relief I at Chalcatzingo have occasionally been identified in the literature as female, apparently because they wear skirt-like garments. I view these latter interpretations with suspicion, for, by the same reasoning, they could be Scotsmen.

Monument 18 (Fig. 11), the final stela, is too spalled and eroded for us to discern completely its motifs. It is apparently a stylized earth-monster face surmounted by two circular design elements. The top section of this monument has been broken. Other large stela-like worked stone fragments lie scattered on the surface of the site. All reliefs and monuments discussed here will be illustrated and discussed further in the Chalcatzingo book now in preparation.

Although Gulf Coast monuments are defaced by shallow circular pits, grooves, or

Fig. 11 Chalcatzingo Monument 18. Height, about 90 cms. Photograph by the author.

Monument 14 (Fig. 10), although broken in half (perhaps naturally) is otherwise undamaged. It is the earliest Mesoamerican monument (of which I am aware) specifically depicting a female, for the person depicted is shown with breasts. The personages depicted

carved rectangular niches, no Chalcatzingo monuments contain such defacement. Mortarlike depressions can be found on many flat boulders at Chalcatzingo, but these boulders are not actual monuments and the mortarlike holes are far deeper than the shallow depressions found on some Gulf Coast monuments (see Grove 1973b: 1139).

SOME INITIAL PATTERNS

Before proceeding, it seems of value to define two further categories of mutilation: specific and non-specific. Mutilation carried out with no intent to deface a specific carved feature or to destroy the monument is "non-specific." In other words, non-specific mutilation is also non-destructive. This is what Anatole Pohorilenko (1975) has referred to as "ceremonial markings"; it consists of the grooves, shallow circular pits, and rectangular niches carved on some monuments. These, I believe, are symbolically different from "specific" mutilation, which is breaking and effacement. I propose to omit "ceremonial," non-specific mutilation from further discussion and to concentrate upon specific mutilation and what was defaced, for with the latter we may gain some insight into why destruction took place at all.

In analyzing monument mutilation I am working under one further assumption, that Olmec monumental art can be divided into two general categories: natural representations and stylized-religious representations. I realize that ultimately both categories may be religious. I classify the great majority of naturalistic humans depicted in carvings as portrait art. Colossal heads provide an excellent example. Once thought of as depicting warriors or distinguished ball-game players (Piña Chan and Covarrubias 1964: facing p. 36) or generalized chieftains (Bernal 1969a: 56), colossal heads are seen by most Olmec specialists today as being portrait representations of Olmec chiefs—a view first expressed by Stirling (1955: 20, 1965: 733; M. Coe 1977: 186; Heizer 1971: 59). Colossal heads are not the only form of Olmec portrait carving, however. The human figures shown seated within the niches of Olmec altars also appear to be portraits of Olmec chiefs (Grove 1973a: 134–5). The iconography

of the altars symbolizes the chiefs' emergence from the underworld cave mouth and their divine origins, confirming their right to rule. Some altars have bas-relief carvings on their sides, depicting persons bound to the chief within the niche by a rope or cord which appears to represent kinship (*ibid.*: 130, 134). Where kinship ties are indicated, as on La Venta Altar 4 and San Lorenzo Monument 14, the persons shown in bas-relief are also portraits. Finally, personages represented on stelae and most naturalistic anthropomorphic statues are also, in most cases, portraits of chiefs. It seems likely in fact, that the same chief might appear in portrait on several monument forms.

Stylized-religious art is, on occasion, present on the same monument with portrait art. Altars provide a good example of this combination. In these instances the stylized-religious art is supplementary to the portrait art and places the chief portrayed in a particular symbolic setting, such as the entrance to the underworld. Stylized-religious art can be separated from portraiture because it involves the use of symbols of Olmec supernaturals. A statue may have an anthropomorphic body, but its face may exhibit attributes that are obviously non-human, for instance, fangs or the sharply downturned, L-shaped eyes of a saurian supernatural. In Table 1 I have attempted also to categorize monuments as either stylized-religious (S) or portrait (P). In cases such as decapitated statues, classification is more difficult and I have relied upon a relatively subjective judgment based on criteria such as body position or ornamentation. Some carvings are ambiguous; dwarfs and Chalcatzingo's "Flying Olmec" are classified as stylized because of their overall themes.

Although at first glance Table 1 seems to indicate random mutilation of both portrait and stylized monuments, this is not the actual case. Stylized-religious monuments remain relatively unmutilated. Likewise, with the exception of colossal heads, almost all portrait monuments are broken, decapitated, or effaced. There also seems to be a pattern to the type of mutilation a monument received. Among portrait carvings one particular feature was the target of destruction: the head. The main means of mutilation was by decapitation. Statues were decapitated and the heads removed elsewhere. Stelae showing portraits of personages were also decapitated; it can be seen that in almost all instances the attempt was made to break them at the neck area. The missing stelae sections include the head area, and, like statue-heads, were apparently removed elsewhere. When a monument was too large or thick to decapitate easily, the head area was effaced. This is true of stelae and some altar niched figures. I speak of a general pattern, and, of course, there are some exceptions. However, the pattern provides a clear step toward understanding mutilation.

At least one major aspect of Olmec monument mutilation is directed at portrait representations of Olmec chiefs. Most explanations of mutilation view it as a short-term and uncommon event. But if it was directed chiefly at portraits, such explanations seem unsatisfactory, unless all monuments were of one individual and an iconoclastic movement was directed at the person's monuments.

In considering alternative explanations, I find myself with a viewpoint diametric to those already proposed. First, revolution and iconoclasm are negative actions, but in thinking of acts of destruction available in the ethnographic record, many do not seem to represent negative acts. Secondly, in view of the sheer quantity of monuments destroyed, mutilation appears not to have been a singular or uncommon event. It might have been a recurring or repeated action by the society, and possibly an important symbolic act. These possibilities lead me to an alternative explanation which is proposed below. But first, one more point needs to be considered.

DATING ACTS OF MUTILATION

In order to be understood, the act or acts of mutilation require some time framework. Did mutilation occur only once or twice, as revolution or iconoclasm would suggest? Unfortunately, most mutilated monuments at La Venta and San Lorenzo do not occur in good stratigraphic context. The exceptions are those monuments which M. Coe (1967c, 1968b) found buried in a linear arrangement. Also, it

seems probable that at least some La Venta monuments had been moved and/or re-erected in pre-Hispanic times (Drucker *et al.* 1959: 229–30). It is, therefore, difficult to develop a stylistic sequence of monuments based upon stratigraphy, and we thus have only a general idea of their temporal placements. It does not seem that all the monuments are contemporaneous, as a revolt explanation would imply, but rather that they cover a long time-span. It is true that certain monuments, such as altars and colossal heads, seem to share a limited time range, but since carved monuments occur quite early in the San Lorenzo sequence and as late as Phase IV at La Venta, the total corpus of carvings spans at least 600 years. Since most monuments within this 600-year time span are mutilated, the defacement and breaking would have had to occur numerous times during that period.

The earliest evidence for monumental carving on the Gulf Coast is the carved stone fragment recovered by M. Coe (1970: 25–6) in a Chicharras Phase (1250–1150 B.C.) deposit at San Lorenzo. This carved but broken stone indicates monument-building in the Chicharras Phase, and it demonstrates monument destruction at that time as well. At the other end of the time span, it is impossible to place a terminal date for monument mutilation, for in actuality it did not end with the decline of La Venta. Stirling (1943b: 11) pointed out that many of the Tres Zapotes monuments (most of which are Late Formative and post-Olmec) suffered mutilation. Some Classic Period Maya monuments too are found effaced or mutilated. Mutilation appears to have been an on-going act which continued even after the decline of Olmec culture.

AN ALTERNATIVE EXPLANATION

Large-scale revolt or iconoclasm does not appear to me to have been the major cause of monument destruction. Indeed, the revolt explanation raises questions. Why would revolutionaries, or invading outsiders, or religious iconoclasts for that matter, take the time to decapitate carefully statues and stelae, rather than breaking them randomly? Why would the same pattern of mutilation occur at Chalcatzingo, several hundred miles away? Why did those destroying the monuments leave the colossal heads untouched? And why would revolutionaries, invaders, or iconoclasts take the time to bury the monuments in straight lines at San Lorenzo, or in clusters, as may be the case at La Venta (Clewlow 1974: 17), particularly if they were abandoning the sites? The actual data suggest to me an underlying symbolism to the act of mutilation which is not satisfactorily explained by previous hypotheses.

There are three basic alternative explanations which I find attractive.

(a) Mutilation was periodic or calendric, with monuments destroyed to begin or end a particular ritual cycle. An ethnohistoric analogy would be the New Fire Ceremony of late Postclassic central Mexico.

(b) Mutilation took place with a change of rulers or ruling dynasties at a site. Monuments destroyed were placed in clusters.

(c) Mutilation occurred with the death of a chief. Monuments depicting the chief or symbolically associated with the chief (certain stylized-religious monuments) were destroyed and then buried in clusters, etc.

The discovery at Chalcatzingo of Monument 5, a decapitated statue-head, in association with one of the rare elite crypt burials, lends support to the latter explanation. The burial probably represents one of Chalcatzingo's ruling elite, and Monument 5 is, in all probability, his stone portrait head. For the stone head to have been placed with the burial, the statue would have had to be decapitated soon after the person's death. Revolt or iconoclasm cannot account for the Monument 5–Burial 3 association. The model relating mutilation to the death of a site's chief is pursued in further detail below.

AN ETHNOGRAPHIC ANALOGY

Monument mutilation at a chief's death is an incomplete explanation. It fails to explain the underlying symbolism of the mutilation, and why colossal heads were untouched while other monuments were damaged, particularly if one varied group all represented the same individual. The current archaeological data do not provide answers to these questions either, but there are ethnographic analogies that do provide an explanatory model. Those discussed are derived from belief systems and symbolism of South American tropical-forest cultures. While such analogies must be used cautiously, South America's tropical-forest culture groups provide a logical data source. It is becoming increasingly clear that Olmec was basically a tropical-forest culture, with tropical-forest ancestral roots and a tropical-forest belief system. Parallels between the reconstructed Olmec belief system and those of South American culture groups have been noted by scholars (P. Furst 1968; Grove 1972: 55, 1973a: 133–5; Lathrap 1974: 145–52).

The analogies from which I have developed the following explanation of the symbolism underlying monument destruction I owe in large part to the research of two colleagues, social anthropologist Norman Whitten, Jr., and archaeologist Donald Lathrap. Both scholars work in tropical-forest South America. Whitten's work (*e.g.*, Whitten 1976) deals primarily with the Canelos Quichua of lowland Ecuador and their belief system and symbolism. Lathrap's archaeological research in Peru and Ecuador has demonstrated the great antiquity of some of the tropical-forest traits discussed. The following data derive primarily from Whitten (personal communication, 1976) and serve as the basic analogue for explaining monument mutilation.

Supernatural power—attaining supernatural power and controlling supernatural power—is a great concern to all members of Canelos Quichua society, as it is to most South American tropical-forest groups (for brevity I am restricting this discussion to the Canelos Quichua). Supernatural power is derived primarily from the underworld and resides in a variety of objects and places. Some of the most important objects containing such power are the wooden stools owned by each male in the society. These stools are quite literally *seats of supernatural power*. Although frequently referred to in the literature of South American

David C. Grove

Indians as "shamans' stools," they are not restricted to shamans, for all males have them and thus each male possesses a *seat of power*. This is true for the Canelos Quichua and for many other tropical-forest Indian groups as well. Symbolically, each stool or *seat of power* receives its supernatural power through connections with the underworld, a major source of supernatural power. Power can also reside within earthly places. The house, with its cave-like interior, can be seen symbolically as a cave and the underworld. Power can reside at the junction of cardinal directions within a house, and a person seated upon his stool at this junction is considered particularly powerful.

The most powerful individuals in Canelos Quichua society are the shamans, for they have access to the supernatural power of the underworld. Much of a shaman's power resides within his wooden stool and within his stone power objects. During his life, the shaman is in control of this supernatural power, but upon his death the power residing within the wooden stool and other power objects becomes uncontrolled. Uncontrolled supernatural power is both frightening and dangerous to the members of the society. The objects within which it resides must be destroyed or buried to neutralize or eliminate it. The shaman's house, the microcosm of his universe and power, is torn down. The stool, the repository of enormous supernatural power, is thrown into the forest. Stone power objects are buried. These are not negative acts against the shaman, but are carried out to guard society against the supernatural power left uncontrolled by his death.

The Canelos Quichua belief system relating to supernatural power is not unique, but, as mentioned, is widely shared by indigenous groups in tropical-forest South America. The basic symbolism of many Olmec monuments suggests that the Olmec, too, shared a similar belief structure. Through these analogies Olmec monuments can be viewed, in one of their aspects, as repositories of supernatural power. This power would have been controlled by the site's chief, the subject of the portraiture on many monuments. The chief, while apparently at least semidivine, also probably embodied many aspects of the tropical-forest

shaman as well. An Olmec chief's link to the underworld and its supernatural powers is consistently symbolized on stelae and altars, where the chief is shown sitting or standing in the stylized cave mouth of the underworld (see Grove 1973a). In fact, the Canelos Quichua view a person in the act of emerging from a symbolic underworld entrance (the doorway of a long-house or the mouth of a cave) to be at his most powerful. The Olmec chiefs seated or standing in the underworld cave-niche personify supernatural power.

Olmec monolithic stone altars, with their complex iconography, epitomize supernatural power. In fact they can be viewed as rather complex stone analogues to the shamans' stools. I have previously presented data (Grove 1973a) suggesting that Olmec chiefs actually sat upon the so-called altars. Here, as with the wooden stools, the altar literally served as a *seat of power*. Like the wooden stool, altars are connected with the underworld. Their niche symbolizes the entrance to this supernatural domain and links the person within the niche to the power of the underworld. The similarities between altars and shamans' stools suggest that the Olmec had the same general conceptualization of *seats of power* as do many South American Indians today. The three thousand years separating the Olmec concept from that of recent groups is well within the time range advocated by Lathrap (Zerries *et al.* n.d.) for the antiquity of shamans' stools.

The Canelos Quichua analogy can be used to view Olmec monument mutilation. If the Canelos Quichua see danger in uncontrolled supernatural power at the death of a shaman, consider the situation at an Olmec center at the death of the semidivine chief, when his vast supernatural power became uncontrolled. The altar of the deceased chief, as well as all his other power objects including portrait and supernatural carvings, had to be "neutralized." Neutralization was accomplished through mutilation. It is not surprising, in light of this belief system, that the greatest amount of attention and labor was directed toward the destruction of altars. The altar was the main symbol (and repository) of the chief's supernatural power. This is particularly evident in its complex iconography and its niche entrance to the underworld.

If monuments were primarily destroyed to neutralize supernatural power, then perhaps the destruction received by specific types of monuments can be taken as a *general* measure of their importance as repositories of power. By this measure, after altars, earth-monster-face monuments, such as La Venta Monuments 15, 25, and 26 and Chalcatzingo's Relief IX/ Monument 6 and Relief XIII/Monument 7, were very important. Their earth-monster/ underworld symbolism made them so, and they suffered extensive mutilation. On the other hand, the power within the portrait statuary and stelae of a chief could apparently be neutralized by decapitation or effacement of a portrait head. The removal of a decapitated head may also suggest a concept of the head as a seat of the soul. The colossal stone heads, however, received no significant damage and remain enigmatic. Were they unimportant as power objects, and if so why?

An important part of the ritual activity connected with monument mutilation (and presumably also with a chief's death) involved the burial of monuments (including some that were unmutilated). This action parallels the burial of a deceased shaman's stone power objects, and indicates that the monuments were still of symbolic value to the society. Colossal heads, although unmutilated except for "ceremonial markings," were included within this burial activity. Since buried monuments appear to occur in groups or clusters, it is highly possible that each group represents the monuments of a particular chief. Analysis of these groupings may yield data on individual chiefs. The large linear grouping of monuments found by M. Coe (1967c; 1968b: 48–52) at San Lorenzo may be one such chiefly group.

There have been two main points discussed in the sections above. One is the hypothesis that monument mutilation took place at the death of a site's chief. The second uses ethnographic analogies to explain monument destruction and the variability of mutilation, and discusses the monuments as possible repositories of supernatural power. These should be viewed as general hypotheses, for there are occasional examples of monuments which do not fit within the overall pattern. For instance, La Venta Altar 4, one of the iconographically most complex altars, is virtually unmutilated.

CLUES TO THE NATURE OF SOME OLMEC LEADERS

In analyzing monument mutilation, some other features of Olmec monuments came under close examination, and, because they are related to the overall theme of this article, they are presented here. In recent years, Mayanists have made important strides in identifying site glyphs and rulers' names, and in tracing kinship and dynastic succession (Haviland 1977; Jones 1977; Kelley 1962; Marcus 1973, 1976; Proskouriakoff 1960, 1963, 1964). During my analysis of Chalcatzingo's monuments, I arrived at a hypothesis which I subsequently tested with Gulf Coast monuments. The results were similar: some Olmec chiefs depicted in portrait monuments bear personal identification symbols or "names." Monument decapitation removes not only the portrait face, but in most instances the headdress as well. It is the headdress that serves as the identification or "naming" symbol. M. Coe (1977: 186) has independently reached a similar conclusion regarding the headgear of colossal heads, describing them as "idiosyncratic" and "badges." Although colossal heads provide the best examples, they are not unique in this regard. Personages shown on altars and stelae likewise often carry headdress identification symbols. The same is probably true of many statues, but in their decapitated state they are of little value in this regard (until, possibly, still-buried monument groups are studied as units). Other clues aid in identifying individual chiefs. The portrait quality of a carving is often important, for a particular physical trait may be depicted. Six of the fifteen known colossal heads show front teeth, and several can be said to be bucktoothed (Clewlow *et al.* 1967: Table 12; de la Fuente 1973: 232, 239). The form and decoration of pectorals, earspools, belts, and other ornamentation may prove in time to be of some value in identification.

In speaking earlier of monument destruction, I stated that a chief might have several

Fig. 12 La Venta Colossal Head 4, with eagle-foot head-gear motif. (After Stirling 1943b: Pl. 44a).

Fig. 13 San Lorenzo Monument 14, a bas-relief carving on the right side, with eagle-foot motif headdress. Photograph courtesy of Michael D. Coe.

portrait monuments of different types. If head-dresses serve as "naming" devices, repetition of headdress motifs should be expected to occur within the monument sample. The actual sample of monuments with undefaced headdresses is quite small (due to decapitation, etc.), but one pair of identical headdress identifiers can be isolated at this time. This pairing is interesting in that two different monument types and two different sites are involved.

The identification motif of La Venta Colossal Head 4 (Fig. 12) is a single eagle's foot. The motif has been also called a "jaguar paw" but is more probably avian and eagle. The eagle-foot identifier is also executed in bas-relief as the headdress of a personage shown on the side of a San Lorenzo stone altar, Monument 14 (Fig. 13). That the identifier repeats on different types of monuments and at different sites does not negate the identification. In fact, it increases the importance of the identification. The individual depicted on the two monuments has portrait qualities which aid in the identification. Teeth are rarely depicted in persons shown in bas-relief carvings, yet the

Eagle-Foot chief shown on Monument 14 has prominent teeth; so too does the Eagle-Foot chief of La Venta Colossal Head 4.

The Eagle-Foot colossal head in all probability represents a La Venta chieftain, for it is a major portrait monument at that site. At San Lorenzo the same chief is depicted in a secondary position on the side of the altar, bound to the main personage in the altar's niche by a rope of kinship (the rope has been destroyed by mutilation). The figure in the niche, mutilated beyond recognition, obviously represents a San Lorenzo chief. Therefore, a kinship tie between the San Lorenzo and La Venta chiefs is symbolized on this monument, an important fact for future reconstructions of the sociopolitical structure of the San Lorenzo Phase (to which these monuments apparently date).

The opposite side of the San Lorenzo altar is more enigmatic. By analogy to the other side, the personage once shown probably was a chief at an Olmec center and was symbolized in a kinship tie with the San Lorenzo chief, but the bas-relief portrait has been almost entirely effaced. Only a small portion of the face and headdress remain (Fig. 2). At some time, while this altar was still functioning as a monument, it apparently became important to remove the portrait of the third chief. The effaced chief may have died, or a conflict may have arisen between the two centers such that the kinship linking their chiefs was better left unsymbolized.

One clue provides us with the possible identity of the San Lorenzo chief of Monument 14, even though the portrait carving within the niche is highly damaged. Small ceremonial markings composed of carved rectangular depressions occur at San Lorenzo only on Monument 14 and on Colossal Head 2 (Table 1; Fig. 2; Clewlow *et al.* 1967: Pl. 20). Since these "ceremonial marks" are so unusual, they might have been carved at the same time, possibly on the death of this chief. If so, the chief of Monument 14 was probably identified by the Three-Parrot-Head motif of Colossal Head 2.

Another pair of headdress-motif similarities occurs between two La Venta monuments, but the situation is different. The headdress of La Venta Head 1 (Clewlow *et al.* 1967: Pl. 1) is a U-shaped element with three pendant "claws." This motif is repeated, within a larger set of symbols, in the headdress of the main personage on La Venta Stela 2 (Drucker 1952: Fig. 49). In this instance the same individual is apparently not portrayed, and I suspect Head 1 is one or two centuries older than the stela. The location of these monuments in the site of La Venta is important: they occur adjacent to each other (Heizer, Graham, and Napton 1968: Map 1). This suggests that the older colossal head was moved and re-erected near the stela so that together they would demonstrate a genealogical lineage linking Stela 2's

chief to an important deceased Olmec chief. The Stela 2 chief symbolized his descent by bearing his ancestor's identification symbol within his own headdress.

These monuments may not be the only ones erected to show genealogical links. Three La Venta colossal heads (2, 3, and 4) occur in a line, and apparently were purposely re-erected in that position. This may have been done to illustrate genealogical or dynastic succession.

Finally, I have a comment concerning colossal heads as portrait representations. It is easy to fall within a rigid pattern of thinking: headdresses identify individual chiefs, and since there is no repetition of headdress motifs among known colossal heads, each head represents an individual chief. In actuality, this may not be true. While not all heads have identification motifs, some share portrait characteristics. It is possible that a chief may have had several portrait heads carved over the period of a lifetime. Six colossal heads show prominent teeth. These could be six separate individuals, or they could be repeats of only a few chiefs. Both San Lorenzo and La Venta colossal heads exhibit tooth prominence. This may suggest that the kinship expressed between a La Venta and a San Lorenzo chief on San Lorenzo Monument 14 may actually reflect genetic kinship rather than fictive kinship, and that close kin may have ruled these two centers at *ca.* 900 B.C.

SUMMARY

Olmec monument mutilation shows patterns of destruction that suggest alternate explanations to the iconoclasm and revolt theories. The one alternative discussed is that monuments erected during an Olmec chief's lifetime were usually destroyed following his death. Using analogies drawn from the belief systems of present-day Indian groups of tropical-forest South America, it is suggested that monuments were destroyed because they were viewed as repositories of the supernatural powers controlled by a chief. Mutilation eliminated the danger to the society of uncontrolled supernatural power. Defaced monuments, their power neutralized, were then apparently ritually buried. This post-destruction act of burial is one of the data suggesting a peaceful rather than a violent cause of monument mutilation.

Many Olmec monuments can be classified as portraits of a site's chief, and headdresses sometimes contain motifs that serve to identify the chiefs individually. Not all headdresses served this purpose, however, and not all chiefs were "named." Through his headdress identifier (an eagle foot), a La Venta chief is seen to be depicted on a San Lorenzo altar, linked in kinship to the San Lorenzo chief (whose identification symbol may have been three parrot heads). This suggests that, at least during one period in their history, San Lorenzo and La Venta were governed by chiefs who believed it important to recognize symbolically kinship ties between themselves.

ACKNOWLEDGMENTS The Chalcatzingo archaeological research was funded by National Science Foundation Grant GS-31017, and supplemented in 1972 and 1973 by a grant from the National Geographic Society. Several illustrations for this article were graciously provided by Dr. Michael Coe (San Lorenzo) and Barbara Wascher Fash (Chalcatzingo). I am particularly indebted to Ann Cyphers de Guillen and Norman Whitten for discussions which provided a great deal of stimulus for this article.

Olmec Architecture: A Comparison of San Lorenzo and La Venta

Richard A. Diehl

UNIVERSITY OF MISSOURI

INTRODUCTION

The study of architecture was an important part of every project Matthew Stirling conducted in the Olmec area. His contributions to our knowledge of this topic were not as great as they might have been because of the limitations of time, manpower, and other resources he faced. Nevertheless, he and his associates trenched mounds and plaza areas at Tres Zapotes, La Venta, Cerro de las Mesas, San Lorenzo, Potrero Nuevo, and Río Chiquito (Tenochtitlan), providing the basis for later investigations at many of these sites.

In this paper I will describe and compare the Early and Middle Formative architecture from San Lorenzo and La Venta, and will attempt to highlight some of the cultural heterogeneity that has previously been neglected in Olmec studies. I have chosen these two sites because of the abundance and quality of the data available on them. My data come from the Yale University Río Chiquito Project, directed by Michael D. Coe, and the various La Venta projects conducted by Stirling, Philip Drucker, Waldo Wedel, Robert Heizer, and others.

Archaeologists who attempt to study Olmec architecture encounter numerous problems. Space limitations prohibit a detailed discussion of all, but a few must be mentioned. The typical Olmec structure consisted of a pole-and-thatch building with or without an earth substructure. Stone was used rarely, and then only as architectural embellishment. The earth surfaces of mounds have been subjected to erosion and other disturbances since their abandonment, thus they are often difficult to trace and in most cases we know more about the interior fill of mounds than we do about their original exterior appearances. The same is true of plaza and courtyard floors; most hardpacked earth surfaces have been completely destroyed by erosion and root action. We know nothing about the superstructures or actual buildings on top of the mounds. We were not able to define any Formative post-molds or packed earth floors at San Lorenzo and the same has been true at La Venta. These buildings were undoubtedly pole-and-thatch structures much like the traditional houses used in the area today, except that daub is used on walls today but we have no evidence for it in the past. Thus we can say nothing about the size and layout of houses, organization and use of space, or many other things so dear to the heart of the "contemporary archaeologist." Also, we know nothing about the presumably numerous houses and other structures that were built directly on the ground rather than on mounds. Their remains have been impossible to identify archaeologically, although they probably constituted the majority of the structures in every Olmec community.

Another major problem involves the exact chronological placement of excavated structures. Since the original surfaces are gone, and since chronologically sensitive dedicatory caches are rare, there are no *in situ* artifacts that date the actual use of the structures. Instead, we must depend upon the ceramic refuse found in the fill. Fortunately, the San Lorenzo inhabitants were not as fastidious as those of

La Venta; they frequently used midden soil as architectural fill, and very few fill layers lack debris. The reasoning I have used in assigning dates to fill layers goes as follows. The latest pottery in a fill layer indicates the layer's earliest possible disposition. Thus, if hypothetical stratum C contains Bajío, Chicharras, and San Lorenzo A Phase pottery, it could not have been deposited prior to the beginning of San Lorenzo A times but may have been deposited later. If stratum B on top of C contains San Lorenzo B pottery and C does not, I assume that C was deposited prior to the beginning of San Lorenzo B times. This approach to dating structures is not as good as one would like, but it is the best that can be done. Fortunately, we found several undisturbed, *in situ* midden deposits associated with charcoal-bearing hearths which provided unmixed ceramic samples for phase definition and absolute dating.

Another chronological problem that must be considered involves the comparability of the San Lorenzo and La Venta sequences. The La Venta chronology is based upon four architectural phases defined in Complex A and a substantial series of carbon-14 dates; that of San Lorenzo is based upon ceramic typology and a large number of radiocarbon dates. The lack of a La Venta ceramic sequence makes detailed intra-site comparisons difficult. Future research should produce a ceramic chronology for La Venta, but the work done there so far shows that it will not be easy to acquire the necessary ceramic samples.

The presently accepted time range of the La Venta occupation is 1000 to 500 B.C. There are indications of earlier occupation, but these have not been proven to date. According to the currently accepted chronology, La Venta Phase I is contemporaneous with San Lorenzo B and Nacaste Phases, Phases II and III occur during the Nacaste–Palangana hiatus, and Phase IV at least partially overlaps the Palangana Phase.

SAN LORENZO

Eighteen major excavations were conducted at the San Lorenzo site between 1966 and 1968; seven of these uncovered significant structural remains. In the following paragraphs, I will briefly describe what we know about each

structure. The excavations will be described in detail in a forthcoming monograph (M. Coe and Diehl 1980).

The Central Court

The Central Court is a rectangular mound group surrounding an interior plaza located at the center of the San Lorenzo plateau. The size of its mounds and its central location make it the dominant feature visible on the plateau today. It is bounded by the South Court, the North Court, and the Palangana (Fig. 1). These four mound complexes account for thirteen of the twenty mounds on the plateau that are over two meters high, and it is obvious that this section of the site was the focal point of the ancient community. However, the mounds represent discontinuous construction activities spanning two millennia, and all were not used simultaneously.

The Central Court is composed of Mounds C3-1, C3-2, C3-3, and C3-4. C3-1 is the tallest; it measures over six meters high and twenty-five meters along its east-west axis. Drucker excavated one trench into its north face and another into the plaza directly north of it in 1946; Paula Krotser excavated a trench into the south side in 1968. C3-2 and C3-3 are long mounds oriented north-south; C3-2 measures over three meters high and sixty-five meters long, C3-3 measures over two meters high and fifty-three meters long. C3-2 has never been excavated; the west side of C3-3 was trenched by me in 1967. C3-4 is an L-shaped mound about two meters high; the horizontal bar of the L closes off the north end of the Central Court. Drucker excavated a trench through this portion of the mound in 1946; Ramón Arellanos and I re-excavated this trench in 1967 and made profile drawings of the strata, but did not collect artifact samples. I partially excavated the plaza floor with a fifteen-meterlong trench in 1967.

The Plaza and Mound C3-3

The oldest remains in the Central Court were found in the plaza floor, where four construction stages have been defined. Stage I included sand, gravel, and clay fills capped by floors of red, white, and orange sand, and yellow gravel. This stage was deposited in San

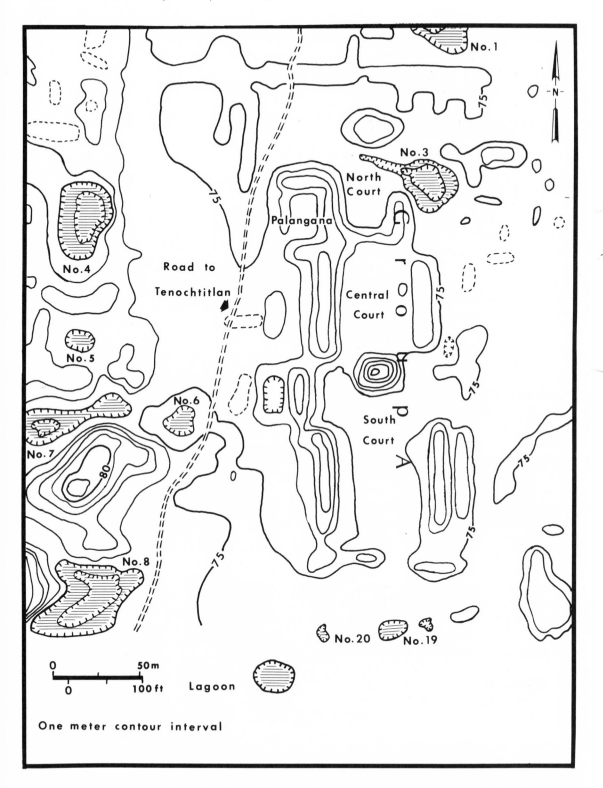

Fig. 1 Plan of the central section of San Lorenzo. Map by T. Majewski (modified from M. Coe 1967a: map in pocket).

Lorenzo A Phase times. Stage II featured red and brown sand and red clay fill covered by a yellow gravel and olive-yellow clay floor. It was constructed in San Lorenzo B Phase times. Stage III was initiated by digging several pits into the older strata, perhaps to recover buried caches; then yellow-brown clay fill and a tan-brown sandy floor were deposited. Stages III and IV were both Palangana Phase constructions. Stage IV was also initiated by digging several pits; then a brown clay fill was deposited. The Stage IV floor was undoubtedly the upper surface of this brown clay, although we could not define its surface in the excavations. Mound C3-3 was constructed in its entirety during this Stage IV operation, and it consisted of the same soil as the plaza. No surface features of the mound, such as steps, terraces, or floors, were identified in our trench profiles, and I assume they did not exist. The question that naturally arises is: what kinds of structures, if any, were associated with plaza Stages I through III? Two possibilities may be suggested: (1) the pole-and-thatch buildings were not placed on mounds and their remains either have not survived or are located somewhere outside the limited area we excavated, or (2) whatever mounds existed were dismantled and the fill removed for use elsewhere. There is no stratigraphic evidence in the Central Court to support the latter suggestion, and I offer it only because some of the fill around the monuments on the Group D ridge appears to be a mixture of soils that could have been derived from such a context. If this were the case, the San Lorenzo Phase mounds would have been dismantled during the Nacaste Phase. However, as things stand at the moment, there is no evidence for mound construction in the Central Court prior to the Palangana Phase.

Mound C3-1

M. Coe was able to study the ceramics in the United States National Museum from Drucker's excavations before Krotser began her excavations in C3-1. This study showed that at least the outer portions of the mound had been erected in Late Classic–Early Postclassic Villa Alta Phase times. We expected to find Formative structures buried under the

Villa Alta overburden, but such was not the case; in fact, the entire mound is a Villa Alta Phase construction. Three building phases have been defined; the fill materials include red, yellow, and blue clay and brown midden loam. The Stage II construction shows evidence of at least four and perhaps five terraces and a round shape. The stairway apparently faced north; we did not find any evidence of it on the south side, and Drucker uncovered several caches which conceivably were located under the stairway. We found enough Villa Alta pottery in the upper levels of the plaza and C3-3 to show that these areas were reused during the phase, suggesting that the entire Central Court was utilized at that time. The absence of a Formative mound at the north end of the Central Court should serve as a warning to archaeologists who automatically assume that mounds that form what appear to be functional groups are not necessarily contemporaneous. In the case of the Central Court, C3-3 existed in Palangana times; the C3-4 profile drawings suggest that it also was erected then. One might assume that C3-2 is also a Palangana Phase building, although there is no evidence to support this assumption other than the facts that it lies parallel to C3-3 and that the C3-1 area was moundless in Palangana times.

The Palangana

The Palangana is a mound complex northwest of the Central Court. M. Coe (1970:29) has assumed it functioned as a ball court, although there is no evidence to support this other than A. L. Smith's (1961) possibly mistaken assumption that similarly shaped mound complexes functioned as ball courts in highland Guatemala. The mounds that make up the Palangana include C3-5, C3-6, C3-7, and C3-8. C3-7, the mound that closes off the southern edge of the complex, is the largest; it measures thirty-eight meters long and over three meters high. The other three measure over two meters high. Frederick Bakunin excavated three pits in the plaza and a trench into C3-8 in 1967.

The Palangana plaza consists of a series of fill levels and earth floors. The earlier fill levels came from older Ojochi Phase occupation sites and were deposited during the San Lorenzo and Nacaste Phases. Palangana and Villa Alta Phase debris was found in the upper levels, but there were no definite plaza floors assignable to these phases. Four building stages were defined in the plaza. Stage I was erected in San Lorenzo B times and included red and brown sand and orange, red, yellow, and olive clay. Stage II also dates to San Lorenzo B times; the soils include olive clay fill and pink, orange, and red sand floors. A light green serpentine axe found in Stage II deposits presumably was placed as a dedicatory cache. Stage III had a single soil component, a Nacaste Phase brown sand floor. Stage IV was a brown sandy loam fill whose upper surface probably functioned as a floor although it is no longer detectable; this stage was deposited during the Palangana Phase.

Mound C3-8 consists of three superimposed earth structures; the earlier two (C3-8-1st and C3-8-2nd) were erected during the Palangana Phase; the latest (C3-8-3rd) is a Villa Alta addition. C3-8-1st was constructed of black loam midden soil fill, and it appears to have been conical rather than rectangular. C3-8-2nd was built by dumping a thick deposit of orange clay over its predecessor. Its outer surface had remnants of several steplike terraces, and the evidence suggests that it was rectangular. After lying abandoned for almost 1500 years, the mound was enlarged in Villa Alta times by dumping brown sandy loam over it, resulting in C3-8-3rd.

As in the case of the Central Court, there is no evidence of mound construction prior to the Palangana Phase, although there are earlier plaza floors. Unless the mounds were dismantled, as has been suggested previously, the entire central zone of the San Lorenzo plateau may have contained only plaza floors and pole-and-thatch buildings without substructures during the San Lorenzo Phase climax of monument carving.

Mound B2-1

By now the reader may wonder if the San Lorenzo Phase Olmecs really did build any artificial mounds; I assure him they did. Mound B2-1, the largest in a small group of four mounds located on the Northwest Ridge, is a definite San Lorenzo Phase structure. It mea-

sured over two meters high and fifteen meters long when Paula Krotser excavated a trench into it in 1967. The excavation revealed three construction stages. Stage I consisted of bright red clay deposited in San Lorenzo A times. Stage II was red and buff clay, and was placed in San Lorenzo B times; a hearth on the Stage II surface provided carbon-14 sample Y-1934 (1030 ± 100). Stage III was a light-brown sandy soil which may represent a naturally developed soil horizon or a Villa Alta Phase addition; in either case, the mound was reoccupied in Villa Alta times. The Stage III artifacts suggest a residential function but the San Lorenzo Phase function is not clear; the structure may have been a residence or a small temple. It would be interesting to know something about the other mounds in the complex but we lacked time to excavate them.

The Drains and Lagoons

The complex of artificial lagoons or water tanks on the plateau top and the drain systems associated with them form one of the most unusual aspects of San Lorenzo architecture. The circumstances of the initial discovery and excavation have been outlined elsewhere (M. Coe 1968a: 86–7; Krotser 1973; M. Coe and Diehl 1980) and will not be repeated here. Suffice it to say that an intact line of basalt troughs and covers was partially excavated by G. R. Krotser and the author in 1967, and that Krotser did an intensive study of the system in 1968. This system has been designated 4B-7 and is one of several on the site. It extended 170 meters almost due east-west from Laguna 8 to the eastern edge of the plateau. The system was constructed of U-shaped troughs with slightly convex covers; the total weight of the stone in it exceeds thirty metric tons. Entrance joints for three feeders or subsidiary lines were made in the main line but were never finished. The entire system was laid in a one-meter-deep trench which was left open while the system functioned. Massive quantities of fill were dumped over the system after it ceased to function. The fact that the fill above the drain contained San Lorenzo B pottery means that it was covered up during or after that phase: we assume this happened at the beginning of the Nacaste

Phase but cannot be certain. San Lorenzo A sherds below the drain demonstrate that it was constructed during this phase.

We did not do nearly as much excavation in and around the lagoons as we would have liked to have done. These features are depressions on the plateau surface; some may be natural, others may be borrow pits for architectural fill, but at least some were carefully excavated into geometric shapes. A small excavation in Laguna 10 uncovered chunks of bentonite, a very compact clay which modern people in the area use for lining wells. Although the lagoons are silted-in today, they still hold rain water well into the dry season and were undoubtedly used for water storage by the Olmec. The drains would have served to remove excess water and prevent overflowing during the rainy season.

The function of these reservoir systems is difficult to interpret. Several permanent springs at the foot of the plateau would have provided drinking and household water for the inhabitants, so this was probably not their function. The association of Monuments 9 and 52 (both of which depict water-related symbolism) with the drain system, the geometric shapes of some of the lagoons, and the fact that scarce and expensive (in terms of acquisition cost) basalt was used for the drain instead of wood, all suggest that the system had more than a strictly utilitarian meaning to the Olmec. M. Coe (1968b: 64) suggested that at least some were sacred or elite baths analogous to Netzahualcoyotl's baths at Tetzcotzingo. This idea is as good as any I can think of.

The Ridges

The artificial ridges that extend out from the plateau edges are a most unusual aspect of San Lorenzo architecture. Some may question their inclusion under the category architecture, but I think it is justified for two reasons. First, they seem to be analogous to substructure platforms or plazas; while we do not have any evidence of buildings on their surfaces, it seems unlikely that they did not support structures of some sort. Secondly, they represent a labor resource investment which surpassed anything previously attempted in Mesoamerica.

Six ridges extend out from the San Lorenzo plateau; they have been designated the Northwest, Group D, Group C, Southwest, South Central, and Southeast Ridges (see Fig. 1). Excavations on the Northwest Ridge showed that only the upper meter or so was artificial fill. Excavations on the Group D Ridge demonstrated that the top 6.5 meters were artificial fill, and we suspect that the same is true of the Group C Ridge. The three ridges on the south have not been tested, and so we have no evidence concerning them.

M. Coe began excavations on the Group D Ridge in 1967 to recover data on several monuments. At that time the dense vegetation permitted only a vague appreciation of the local topography, and we assumed that the area was a natural part of the plateau. Shortly thereafter, G. R. Krotser had his clearing crews cut and burn the vegetation so that he could map the area, and then we realized that the Group C and D Ridges were essentially mirror images of each other, keeping in mind that erosion has modified the ridge edges somewhat during the past 3,000 years. We excavated three areas on the Group D Ridge: the Monument 30 operation in the central part of the ridge, the Monument 23 operation at its eastern edge, and the Mound B3-5 operation, which was soon abandoned in order to utilize the workers elsewhere (it was terminated at 1.5 meters below ground level without hitting natural subsoil). The Monument 23 operation was concerned primarily with horizontal excavations designed to uncover buried monuments in the upper deposits, but one pit was excavated to a depth of 3.5 meters without encountering pre-occupation soils.

The Monument 30 operation likewise emphasized horizontal clearing of monuments, but here we were determined to reach the pre-occupation subsoil, so we did one of Kent Flannery's (1976) "telephone booth" excavations until we reached our goal at a depth of 6.5 meters. All the soils down to this level contained potsherds and other cultural debris. Near the bottom we penetrated a small terraced platform constructed of clean orange sand with a thin dark-gray sand facing. We did not have time to remove all the overburden and clear the entire structure, so we do not know its lateral dimensions but we do know that it measured 1.8 meters high. The pristine condition of the sand surface suggests that it was never exposed to rain and may have been covered over with fill shortly after it was built. The pottery in the soils above and below the mound belong to the Bajío Phase, and a carbon-14 sample from the area below it produced a date of 1310 ± 120 B.C. (Y-1933). The Bajío Phase deposits above the mound were covered by several strata and floors which contained only Chicharras ceramics. The uppermost Chicharras floor had an *in situ* hearth, which provided carbon-14 sample Y-1911 (1140 ± 80 B.C.), and another carbon-14 sample from within the floor strata was dated at 1120 ± 80 B.C. (Y-1912). The correct chronological placement of these strata is a matter of some importance. Although it is theoretically possible that all the soils were midden debris from older habitation areas which were deposited in their present position during the San Lorenzo Phase, this seems unlikely, given the total absence of San Lorenzo Phase ceramics. I see no reasonable alternative to the proposition that the lower levels were deposited in Bajío times and the upper levels during the Chicharras Phase. The Chicharras Phase floors were used for a long time because the monuments were placed on them as the first step in their burial at the end of San Lorenzo B Phase. In fact, it seems quite possible that the monuments were originally set up somewhere on the ridge, although probably not where we found them.

I assume that the entire Group D Ridge is an artificial construction down to a depth of six or seven meters, based on the evidence from our pits. The Bajío Phase deposits were 3.4 meters thick, and those of the Chicharras Phase were 1.6 meters thick. If the entire ridge was covered with deposits of similar thickness, approximately 46,000 cubic meters of fill were laid down in Bajío times and 21,000 cubic meters in Chicharras times, a total of 67,000 cubic meters, based on a total area of 13,400 square meters at a point five meters below the present ridge surface (six meters total fill minus 1.5 meters of post-Chicharras deposits). This is less than the 106,680 cubic meters calculated by Heizer and Drucker (1968) for the content of the Complex-C pyramid at La Venta, but the date and construction history of this pyramid is not known. The amounts of fill on the other ridges represent a major time and labor investment of the San Lorenzo area inhabitants, and they suggest a social and political organization that was more complex than those of any other Mesoamerican group at the time.

The purposes for the ridges and the reasons for building them are not known. I have already alluded to the possibility that they served as a base for at least some of the stone monuments. Our only evidence for the carving of monuments prior to San Lorenzo A times is a monument fragment, possibly from a colossal head in Chicharras deposits on the Group D Ridge. This, of course, does not necessarily mean that the monument was located in the immediate area, but it does at least suggest it. M. Coe (1967a) has suggested that the ridges were built to alter the basic shape of the plateau into that of an animal but that the project was never finished. Try though I have, I cannot make out any recognizable form in the plateau outline.

Before leaving the discussion of San Lorenzo architecture, I will mention some potentially confusing aspects of the community pattern and population of the plateau. M. Coe and I, independently, arrived at a hypothetical population of 800 to 1000 people based on the house-mound count. This figure assumes that every small mound supported a house, that all houses were situated on mounds, and that all house mounds were occupied simultaneously. The room for error in all three assumptions is apparent. Some house mounds may have supported auxiliary structures such as kitchens or storage facilities rather than domiciles, but our limited excavations did not shed light on this problem. This factor would mean that our calculations are too high. With regard to the second factor, it is undoubtedly true that at least some residences were placed directly on the ground; thus our figures would be too low. However, the third assumption bothers me the most. Until recently I assumed that the Villa Alta occupation at San Lorenzo was minimal

75

and had been concentrated in the Central Court–Palangana area. Examination of the data from all the excavations shows that this was not true. Every excavation had at least some Villa Alta pottery in the upper levels, and much of the civic architecture belongs to this phase. This indicates a respectable Villa Alta population size, and means that we can no longer assume that all the house mounds belong to the Formative occupations. We do not know how many are exclusively Formative, how many are exclusively Villa Alta, or how many Formative mounds were reoccupied in Villa Alta times. I suspect that excavation would show that the majority belong to the last category, but this is just a guess. Unfortunately, surface survey cannot resolve the problem because surface pottery is nonexistent. Nor can we automatically assume that the three or four mounds in a complex are contemporaneous; the excavation data from the Central Court show that this is not necessarily true. Before we can say anything reliable about San Lorenzo community patterns, we will need extensive excavations in a number of house-mound complexes for complete household pattern data, a large number of test pits on others for chronological information, and extensive testing of moundless areas. This should be coupled with excavations in villages and hamlets, such as Potrero Nuevo, and with a survey of the presumably numerous small communities where the bulk of the population lived.

LA VENTA

This section draws primarily on the following publications: the Drucker, Heizer, and Squier (1959) monograph and clarifications of it (Heizer 1964; Drucker and Heizer 1965) published in response to W. Coe and Stuckenrath (1964); and recent articles by Heizer (1968), Berger, Graham, and Heizer (1967), Heizer, Drucker, and Graham (1968), Heizer, Graham, and Napton (1968), and Morrison, Clewlow, and Heizer (1970). Two points should be made clear at the outset. First, all the La Venta data pertain to civic-ceremonial architecture; house mounds have not been located at the site. Second, there is no complete and detailed map of La Venta; the best map

presently available was published by Heizer, Graham, and Napton (1968: map at back of volume). While it is true that the site has been substantially disturbed by the Pemex refinery and associated structures, a map could and should be prepared in the near future.

Three architectural complexes (labeled A, B, and C) have been defined at La Venta (Fig. 2). Complex A is a series of low mounds and courtyards north of the large pyramid; it is the most extensively excavated part of the site. Complex B is located south of the pyramid; its content and areal extent is not clear, but I will use the term in its broadest sense to include the Stirling Group and Acropolis, the Great Platform, and all the associated structures. Complex C is the large mound or pyramid and its apron.

The thirty-meter-high Complex-C mound is one of the most distinctive structures in Mesoamerica. Its shape has been described as a fluted cone or conoidal frustum (Morrison *et al.* 1970: 1). This unusual shape is the result of a round ground plan and a series of ridges and troughs which ascend the sides. The surveyors assumed that the present configuration reflects the original rather closely and that the mound was modeled on similarly shaped hills in the Tuxtla Mountains, but some Mesoamericanists have suggested that the surface configuration is the result of erosion. There are no surface remains of a stairway, and the summit has been too badly disturbed to preserve any evidence of a structure. The mound has not been excavated, but a magnetometer survey suggests a subsurface concentration of basalt or other stone, perhaps a tomb, near the summit (Morrison *et al.* 1970). A low, wide apron surrounded most of the mound; it appears to have consisted of several arc-shaped extensions, although the area has been drastically modified in recent years and its original shape is almost impossible to determine. Several low circular earth mounds have been identified on top of the apron, and at least five monuments were found there.

Complex B

Complex B consists of at least nine square and rectangular mounds. Two of these, the

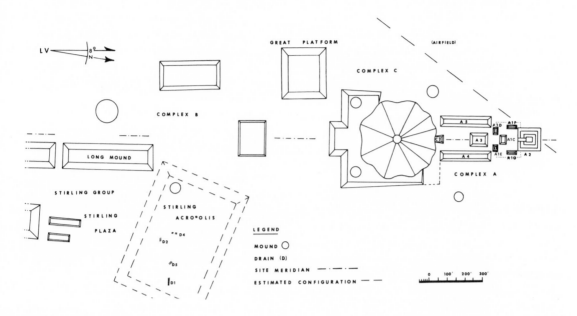

Fig. 2 Plan of La Venta. Map by T. Majewski (modified from Heizer, Graham, and Napton 1968: map at back of book).

Great Mound and the Stirling Acropolis, are large enough to be considered acropolises or platforms for at least several superstructures. A few stratigraphic test pits and monument excavations have been conducted in both of them, but none penetrated deep enough to provide much information on their interiors (Hallinan, Ambro, and O'Connell 1968). Both the Stirling Acropolis and an unnamed platform south of Complex C have numerous monuments on their surfaces, and the former has remains of a complex stone trough drain system. Carbon-14 dates from the Stirling Acropolis suggest that its occupation covered the entire Phases I-IV span as defined in Complex A.

Complex A

Complex A consists of two courtyards surrounded by earth mounds. Drucker, Heizer, and Squier (1959) divided its architecture into four construction phases and tentatively suggested that each lasted about one century (1000–600 B.C.) W. Coe and Stuckenrath (1964) have challenged the existence of this sequence and its chronology. I believe that the sequence and its beginning and terminal dates are sound, but

that the posited 100-year duration of each phase probably is not accurate.

The southern courtyard of Complex A is flanked by the Complex C mound on the south, two long low mounds (A-4 and A-5) on the east and west, and Mound A-3 on the north. The northern courtyard is bounded by two small rectangular mounds (A-1-D and A-1-E) on the south, rectangular mounds on the east and west (A-1-F and A-1-G), and a larger mound (A-2) at the north. A-2's shape is apparently open to question; the 1959 map (Drucker *et al.* 1959: Fig. 4) shows it as a featureless round structure, while the 1968 map (Heizer, Graham, and Napton 1968: map at back of volume) shows it as a rectangular stepped pyramid with a stairway. The excavation data suggest that the 1968 version is due to an overly imaginative draftsman. The area from the south end of A-2 to the A-1-D and A-1-E mounds was enclosed by a basalt column "picket fence" during Phase IV.

All the north courtyard structures have been excavated, and every one contained evidence of all four building phases. In the southern courtyard, A-3 has been extensively excavated

Richard A. Diehl

and shows definite occupations in Phases I and IV, a possible Phase II occupation, and no evidence of Phase III activity. Mound A-5 has been excavated but is difficult to place chronologically; the excavators suggest that it belongs to Phase IV on some rather tenuous evidence. Its twin, A-4, has not been excavated. The reader is referred to the original publications for more detailed information on the structures.

The bilateral symmetry of both surface structures and the underground caches and offerings is one of the most notable aspects of Complex A. This symmetry is expressed in the equidistant placement of mounds and caches from a north-south centerline and in a consistent equal sizing of features on both sides of the line. The assertion by Drucker, Heizer, and Squier (1959) that the bilateral symmetry was present from Phase I on, has been challenged by W. Coe and Stuckenrath (1964), but I prefer to accept the opinion of the original excavators. It should be noted that the latest, but still incomplete, version of the La Venta map makes it evident that only Complex A was bilaterally symmetrical, not the entire settlement.

All the known La Venta architecture consists of soil fills and surfaces with an occasional use of basalt, limestone, adobe blocks, and crushed serpentine for special purposes. The soils are primarily a wide color spectrum of clays and sands: the clays include red, yellow, white, blue, olive, brown, pink, purple, and tan shades; the sands are brown, white, old rose, gray, pink, yellow, orange, cinnamon, and red. Clay was used primarily for fill and mound surfaces, while sand was used for fill and plaza floors. A visit to La Venta in its heyday must have been a truly psychedelic experience. Although most of the fills consisted of dumped earth, sun-dried adobes were used on occasion. They formed the hearting of Mound A-1-E and were found at the northeast entryway into the northern courtyard and the outer border of the same court. The blocks were hand-formed out of red and yellow clay, and set in a clay mortar. In all cases their use dates to Phase II.

The use of basalt columns was one of the unusual aspects of Complex A architecture. They were used to form a "picket fence" around the northern courtyard, enclosures on top of Mounds A-1-D and A-1-E, steps leading from one courtyard to another, and the enclosures of Tombs A and E in Mound A-2. All the known basalt-column structures date from Phase IV. Other stones were occasionally used as architectural elements; a few dressed basalt blocks served as mound facing stones in Phase II, and limestone slabs were used for flooring or flagstones in Phase IV.

The deposition of underground caches and offerings was a recurring activity among the La Venta Olmec; more than fifty such caches have been discovered just in Complex A. Drucker, Heizer, and Squier (1959) divided these features into two categories: Massive Offerings and Small Dedicatory Caches. The Massive Offerings are huge deposits of serpentine blocks placed in deep pits, then covered up. Five of them have been found in Complex A; most were under mounds, although Massive Offering 3, the largest, lay between Mounds A-2 and A-1-C. Drucker, Heizer, and Squier (1959) suggested that at least one Massive Offering was placed at the beginning of each building phase.

The Small Dedicatory Offerings consisted of varying quantities of green stone celts, figurines, beads, etc.; pottery vessels; and other small objects. They occur during the full timespan of Phases I through IV, although most seem to date from the later phases.

Five features interpreted as tombs have been found in Complex A. Some lack bones, and the skeletal remains in the others are badly deteriorated; nevertheless, I assume that they were burials and not simply caches as suggested by W. Coe and Stuckenrath (1964). Four of the burials were located in stone enclosures or monuments: two (Tombs A and E) were in basalt column enclosures, one (Tomb B, Monument 6) was in a sandstone coffer, and one (Tomb C) was in a cist constructed of stone slabs. Tomb D was located directly in the ground. All the tombs were located on the north-south centerline which bisects Complex A, and all were deposited during Phase IV.

78

COMPARISON OF SAN LORENZO AND LA VENTA

The San Lorenzo and La Venta architectural complexes show some similarities and numerous differences. I will first describe these similarities and differences, and then attempt to explain their significance.

Similarities

Earth was the preferred material for mounds and plazas in both communities. In both cases the soil was probably acquired quite close to the construction site—at least there is no evidence of long distance transport of it. Both communities utilized the basic pattern of rectangular or square courts surrounded by mounds; although our evidence for them in San Lorenzo Phase times at San Lorenzo is not very convincing, it was certainly the pattern during the Palangana Phase. Both communities constructed drain systems of basalt troughs, although I find the 500-year gap between the San Lorenzo and La Venta systems difficult to accept, and think instead that the La Venta system may be older than has been assumed.

Traits Unique to San Lorenzo

Several architectural features known for San Lorenzo have not been reported at La Venta. These include artificial ridges, lagoons, numerous house mounds, and our suggestion of the demolition of mounds in order to obtain fill. Some of these absences at La Venta may be more apparent than real, and a complete, detailed map of La Venta may some day show ridges, lagoons, and house mounds. The sketch map of La Venta published by Drucker (1952: Fig. 1) shows features on the southwest side of the site which look tantalizingly like artificial ridges but which may be natural features. If the La Venta drain system functioned analogously to that of San Lorenzo, I would expect to find lagoons as the water source. The failure to discover house mounds at La Venta is not surprising in view of the fact that the site has never been completely cleared of vegetation and mapped in detail. We did not know about the San Lorenzo examples until this was done. Also, virtually all the La Venta research, with the exception of Drucker's test pits, has been concentrated in the areas of public buildings, and little attention has been paid to noncere-

monial areas. Nevertheless, two lines of evidence suggest that La Venta may have had a much smaller resident population than San Lorenzo. The lack of domestic refuse in mound fill, and the fact that Drucker's (1952) forty test pits yielded very few significant refuse concentrations, both indicate that refuse is scarce, in sharp contrast to San Lorenzo where every excavation recovered sherds and other debris. The demolition of mounds for fill at San Lorenzo is certainly not a proven fact, but rather a suggestion. If it did in fact occur, it was the product of a historical incident unique to San Lorenzo, *i.e.*, the probable conquest of San Lorenzo and the deliberate mutilation and burial of its monuments. There is no evidence of a similar event at La Venta.

Traits Unique to La Venta

La Venta's unusual architectural inventory makes it one of the most distinctive archaeological sites in the Americas. This uniqueness receives additional emphasis when the site is compared with San Lorenzo. The unique aspects of La Venta architecture can be discussed under two general categories: construction materials, and special forms and features.

Construction Materials. Although builders in both communities used earth as a basic material, the La Venta people placed great emphasis on collecting clean soil that lacked midden debris. Furthermore, while different-colored soils were used in both cases, the La Venta people seem to have sought out and used a wider variety of colors. Other materials used at La Venta but not San Lorenzo include basalt columns, cut blocks, limestone slabs, and shaped adobe blocks. It is true that Drucker found two basalt columns at the Remolino site on the Río Chiquito bank (Stirling 1955), but this is several kilometers from the San Lorenzo site, and their chronological position could not be verified by us. If the San Lorenzo builders used basalt columns, we have no evidence of it. This is not surprising, because basalt columns were used at La Venta in Phase IV when the contemporaneous Palangana Phase people at San Lorenzo imported no monumental stone at all. The absence of adobe blocks at San Lorenzo may be accounted for by the chronological differences between the two sites; they were used at La Venta only in Phase II, when San Lorenzo was unoccupied.

Architectural Features. The La Venta architectural features that are not duplicated at San Lorenzo or any other known Olmec site include the fluted-cone shape of the large mound, the acropolis-like rectangular platforms, numerous small caches with large quantities of jadeite objects, the Massive Offerings, the placement of elite burials in civic architectural contexts, and the bilateral symmetry of Complex A. None of the San Lorenzo mounds remotely approach the fluted-cone or acropolis configurations. We found very few caches and offerings at San Lorenzo, the most elaborate consisting of seven serpentine celts, several broken pots, and a few turtle-shell fragments under Monument 21. Others might have been found if we had excavated entire plazas and mounds, but I doubt that they would have approached those of La Venta in total number or wealth of contents. There is some evidence for Palangana Phase looting in the form of pits, but we do not know if the excavators found anything or not. Our excavations in the Central Court and the Palangana did not uncover Massive Offerings or any evidence that they had ever existed. We did not find any burials at all, although a few human bones were found in a midden context. Finally, the San Lorenzo map does not show any bilateral symmetry.

Discussion

San Lorenzo and La Venta are both considered Olmec centers because: (1) they were partially contemporaneous neighbors, and (2) they shared numerous culture traits, most notably an art style expressed in similar media and, presumably, a belief system which the art style expressed. I believe that up to now Mesoamericanists have been too concerned with the commonalities shared by the two communities and have underemphasized the differences. In this paper I have attempted to point out some of these differences as expressed in public architecture. The same could be done with the sculptural corpora, trade goods, community patterns, and areal settlement patterns of the

two sites; and I believe that such investigations would shed interesting and significant light on the dynamics of Mesoamerica's earliest complex society. I think the architectural differences are just one indication that we are dealing with two different social, economic, and political entities, both of which were leaders in the Olmec *Oikoumene,* probably in competition with each other throughout much of their existence. The sudden and violent changes that marked the end of the San Lorenzo B Phase suggest to me that San Lorenzo was physically conquered; that the stone monuments that symbolized its elite were destroyed and buried out of sight; and that the resident population (the elite of the San Lorenzo "state") was removed and replaced by migrants (who used, significantly, the Nacaste ceramic tradition). These events probably did not involve substantial population relocations in the hinterland, although there is no archaeological evidence on this topic. There is no evidence to suggest that La Venta was necessarily the conquerer; it may well have been Laguna de los Cerros or some unknown Olmec center. It is interesting that the Palangana Phase migrants to the San Lorenzo plateau built their civic architecture in a simplified version of the La Venta pattern of rectangular and square mounds enclosing courtyards, but the significance of this fact is not clear.

SUMMARY

The quantity of archaeological research in the Olmec area appears considerable to the nonspecialist, but it is pitifully small when viewed in light of the problems that remain unresolved. Much remains to be learned about Olmec architecture and other aspects of this ancient culture. There is a desperate need for a detailed site map of La Venta and for investigations in the Complex C mound, the Stirling Group, and other structures at the site. This research must be done before the Pemex refinery expands its facilities and causes further destruction. There is an equally pressing need for a survey to locate other major Olmec centers, particularly villages and hamlets. This is the only way we will ever have a fully integrated picture of the settlement patterns and their social, economic, and political correlates. Matthew Stirling did the right thing when he oriented his research program toward the big sites, but Olmec studies have remained oriented this way for too long. While the difficulties of areal survey are not to be dismissed lightly, they are not insurmountable. All one needs is Stirling's perseverance and ability to get along with people, a bottle of white lightning, a horse, a boat, and a set of aerial photographs. In addition, new techniques of remote sensing may soon provide a major breakthrough in the location of sites in tropical areas (see Bruder *et al.* 1975). I have a suspicion that, were Matthew Stirling beginning his career today, he would be out in the middle of nowhere mapping and testing Olmec hamlets and having a ball.

ACKNOWLEDGMENTS The information on San Lorenzo was collected under National Science Foundation Grant GS-715, awarded to Michael D. Coe and Yale University. My special thanks go to him for allowing me to participate in the project and for encouraging me to get involved in the write-up of the data. I also wish to thank the people who collaborated in the field work: Ramón Arellanos M., Frederick Bakunin, Francisco Beverido P., George R. Krotser, and Paula Krotser. Thanks are also extended to Dr. Ignacio Bernal, Professor José Luis Lorenzo, Professor Alfonso Medellín Zenil, Professor José García Payón, and Lic. Jorge Gurría Lacroix for their aid. Very special thanks go to the people of Tenochtitlan, without whom nothing would have been accomplished.

Toward a Conception of Monumental Olmec Art

Beatriz de la Fuente

INSTITUTO DE INVESTIGACIONES ESTÉTICAS,
UNIVERSIDAD NACIONAL AUTÓNOMA DE MÉXICO

For more than three decades we have used unquestioningly a definition of monumental Olmec art that is general, imprecise, and certainly incomplete. It now seems important to think about this traditionally accepted definition, and to examine it in the light of recent archaeological discoveries and within different theoretical frameworks.

The concept of "the Olmec" began when similar, and, in some cases, identical, features were observed on pieces that had not been placed within the cultures of ancient Mexico that were known at the time. Beginning with Beyer (1927) and Saville (1929a, 1929b), studies of these pieces centered their observations on features of an external nature, emphasizing particularly those that pointed to the presence of the jaguar. Elements common to the "diagnostic" vocabulary of Olmec sculptures are: slanting eyes, wide flat noses, flaring upper lips that give the appearance of a snarling mouth, cleft heads, and secondary features such as claws, baby faces, thick necks, and the presence or absence of fangs. In short, the list of visible elements that are assumed to show the image of the jaguar, jaguar-monster, or humanized jaguar has become very long.

It seems that all those who have attempted to understand this art and define its qualities—such as Stirling, Covarrubias, Westheim, Kubler, T. Smith, M. Coe, Bernal, Joralemon, and Clewlow—have put their main interest in defining the style in terms of those external features that resemble the jaguar or are derived from it.

Covarrubias (1942: 46) states that this is "el motivo básico del arte 'olmeca'." Kubler (1975: 68) says that "The style centres upon anthropomorphic representations of jaguars." T. Smith (1963: 140) limits herself to pointing out that "the presence of this feature [the jaguar's muzzle] in an art object has always been sufficient to identify it immediately as Olmec." M. Coe (1965b: 751) declares that "The Olmec style cannot be separated from its content, or iconography, for its weird jaguar-baby symbolism is the hallmark of the style." Bernal (1968: 252) sees the style as religious, and asserts that "Es alrededor del culto del jaguar y del ceremonialismo como se exporta más que nada el estilo olmeca." Joralemon, in his study of the iconography (1971), bases the identification of his Olmec deities principally on features attributed to the jaguar. And, lastly, Clewlow (1974: 95) accepts Coe's definition, which postulates that "The dominant theme of Olmec iconography is centered around the concept of the were-jaguar."

Within the group of authors who base their definitions of Olmec style on external features are those who have noticed the abundance of human representations. Along these lines, Stirling (1965: 721) emphasizes that "The bulk of Olmec representative art consists of human and anthropomorphic beings;" Drucker (1952: 201) concludes that "Representations are chiefly of adult human beings (both males and females, and only occasionally infants);" and Covarrubias (1946a: 159), even though he always grants first place to the humanized jaguar, at one point says "Los artistas 'olmecas' representaban casi exclusivamente al hombre,

83

es decir, a sí mismos . . ." It should be made clear that, although the authors cited above have noted the importance of the human figure in Olmec sculpture, they have never determined its full significance. More recent studies, particularly those dealing with the colossal heads, emphasize that the purpose of these heads is not exclusively that of reproducing human features, but also of giving to them the qualities of true portraits (see Clewlow *et al.* 1967:61; M. Coe 1972; de la Fuente 1975: 61).

To summarize, most of the definitions of Olmec sculptural style have had as their point of departure the description of external features, most of which are identified as characteristics of the jaguar. In the secondary position—in many instances not considered an element essential to the definition of the style—are human representations, among which are included the colossal heads. Other elements of an external nature, such as the presence of features of other animals (monkeys, birds of prey, fish, etc.), of physical deformities (dwarfs), and of symbolic designs (crossed bands, flame eyebrows, square eyes, etc.), have been added to the list of external traits that are supposed to hold the means of deciding whether a sculpture is Olmec or not. The interest shown in defining the style based on the external features mentioned above permits us to view the artistic objects from only one point of view: that of their resemblance to or disparity from nature.

Some authors have been concerned with another aspect of Olmec sculpture; I refer to those who consider it primitive and who believe it to be an art that has not reached its maturity, that has not been fully realized as an art style. M. Coe (1965b: 749) speaks of "primitive" and "certain archaic" features, and Westheim (1957: 200) places Olmec art in a place of transition between the "arcaico," which represented reality as it is perceived visually, and the "clasicismo" of the high cultures, which converted religious concepts into sculptural symbols. Actually, although it is not explicit, the idea of primitivism underlies much of the writing on Olmec sculpture, since such writings frequently start from the idea of a work of art as the approximation of nature. Heizer (1967: 37) makes it clearly understood

that in Olmec sculpture, with the exception of the altars and the colossal heads, "one senses that the art form had not arrived at a fixed, stable, formally patterned 'dogmatic' stage." It was only Fernández (1968: 6) who suspected that the Olmec sculptors "compusieron todas las cabezas según un patrón o canon que les daba ciertos puntos fijos, seguros para realizar la escultura."

On the other hand, there are also those writers who have concentrated on specific aesthetic qualities to complete the definition of style; they also rely on the degree of resemblance to visual data, and judge the works of art as objects resulting from a certain conception of the world and of reality. The opposite poles of this conception, which are inherent in a definite desire to create distinctive forms in art, are, on the one hand, naturalism—the strong attachment to visual data—and, on the other, abstraction—the radical withdrawal from nature.

Stirling (1940a: 325) recognizes the natural and even realistic postures of the figures; Drucker (1952: 191) speaks of "the skillful realism of the sculptures"; and, of course, all the authors who consider the colossal heads to be portraits share this same view, expressed with great clarity and conciseness in a paper by Willey (1962: 2): "the portrayals are carried out with a 'realistic' intent. It is thoroughly nongeometric and nonabstract. . . ." Within this tendency to prove naturalism in Olmec sculpture are the opinions of those who hold that the figures represented are full of movement. Stirling (1965: 721) refers to their "intensely dynamic" qualities; Drucker (1952: 201) says that "A trait especially prominent in the representation of human beings . . . is the dynamic movement of the figures;" and Kubler (1975: 68) declares that "The representation of vigorous motions of the body is common."

Other authors exhibit an intermediate point of view and speak, with ambiguity, of "un arte realista a la vez que abstracto" (Westheim 1957: 207). Concepts of naturalism in figurative elements and abstraction in geometric signs are also to be found in M. Coe's writings (see 1965b).

The concept of "powerful simplicity" noted

by Stirling (1965: 720), and held also by Covarrubias (1961: 59), preceded that of the abstraction of forms (Wicke 1971: 75; Kubler 1975: 68). Nevertheless, in the most recent studies, the idea of describing works as naturalistic or realistic when human beings are represented is accepted (Wicke 1971: 68). One speaks also, in relation to this group of sculptures, of the tradition of veristic sculpture (Kubler 1975: 68) and of the fact that these works tend toward abstraction as much as do the forms that represent stylized jaguars (Wicke 1971: 69) and those whose designs simulate glyphs, called by Kubler "ideographic forms" (1975: 68–71). In some cases, such as the colossal heads, an idealistic character is attributed to the art (Kubler 1961: 73); this concept is repeated by Wicke (1971: 106) when he says that "Olmec monolithic works fall under Sorokin's rubric of Idealistic art."

Therefore, within the traditional definition of Olmec sculpture, three methods of determination stand out. The most common and widespread is that of reducing its characteristics to the mere description of external features. Secondly, the supposed primitivism of this art is used by some as an expressive element for its definition; this is opposed by the majority because it is a nonexplicit category. Lastly, in a search for a more complete characterization, some have resorted to artistic categories such as naturalism, figural dynamism, abstraction, and idealism; but, even though these categories are handled in a perhaps correct manner in many instances, they lack a theoretical framework that would systematize them.

Certain concepts, observations, or ideals already presented in the traditional definition, I have used as a basis and theme for reflection in my study of Olmec monumental sculpture. It is evident that the external features that are traditionally accepted correspond in good measure to those that one sees in the sculptures: I refer, in particular, to the components of the jaguar, jaguar-monster, and humanized jaguar. I do not agree, however, that such features are the dominant ones or that they reproduce in an imitative way those of the real animal. In the monumental sculptures, I find that only the downward-slanted oval eyes

with internal sutures, the fangs, and the claws are features that can be seen in the true jaguar. Other elements that have been attributed to the feline—but which, in many cases, are the result of previously conceived interpretations, which rarely result from actual observation and which bear little resemblance to the feline— are: flaring upper lips, which on occasion give the impression of a snarling mouth and of which there are variations in representation; heads cleft in the center and down the forehead; and simple or bifurcated tails.

Certainly these features, as faithfully attached to visual reality as those that, despite their departure from the observation of that reality, have been extremely distorted, have been grouped into fixed types of images that can incorporate, in addition, other features that are not present in nature, such as eyes in the form of squares or half-moons, serrated or "flame" eyebrows, etc.

With regard to other external features, I group together with those that have been noted as the most frequently represented in Olmec imagery, those that show the human figure. Man is the principal theme of the monumental sculpture. Of the 206 pieces in my catalogues, 110 represent human figures. It is important to note that most of these sculptures were found decapitated; but, despite the possibility that some of the missing heads had features that would place them in the category of jaguar beings and their variations, all have obviously human bodies. Thus, it is only a minority of sixty-four sculptures that possess features traditionally considered feline or jaguar.

For those who are concerned with the degree of "naturalism" (attachment to visible reality) or "abstraction" (movement away from the same), I find that in Olmec art both those ways of seeing coexist and can be achieved through sculptural form. These were never carried to extremes; in no case was a slavish copy of the natural model made that would justify speaking of realism, but neither were forms created so distant from nature that they shared nothing with it, or that they could be called sculptural abstractions. Both ways of conceiving and creating appear to have been simultaneous, and were applied in accordance with what was being represented: greater realism for human forms; greater simplification, synthesis, or invention for forms that gave body to an idea or concept distant from the natural form.

I do not pretend to say totally new things here, in view of the already-extensive literature on this subject, but will confine myself only to supporting some of the already-established concepts and, departing from them, to proposing other aspects which, perhaps, when taken into consideration, will approach a more complete definition of the Olmec sculptural style.

My starting point is situated within a group of artistic works defined in space and time—the monuments of San Lorenzo, dated approximately between 1200 and 900 B.C.—and is limited to an analysis of the stone sculptures of monumental size. The reasons for making this choice are the following: (1) only those observations that derive from direct, diligent, and complete analysis of each and every one of the works in question can be elevated to objective and appraisable qualities; (2) the works considered here as the significant primary sample must come from a site that has not been altered by external events in its cultural circumstances; and (3) the formal features, like the aspects of content, must be appraised within the same artistic category.

The ambiguity of the contemporary definition of Olmec art derives unavoidably from an impressionistic appraisal of features common to works of different categories, coming from different places, and with very different temporal positions. Only by defining and limiting the discipline, place, and time through a legitimate geographic and temporal comparison can the characteristics of these features be extended to sculptures of other locations. In this way, the monumental sculptures of San Lorenzo, created during a definite period of time, permit us to establish the essentials of the features of the Olmec style, which, as such, is defined by its moments of full cultural integration; for, as style is not static, these already-defined features can be applied to the sculptures of La Venta, Laguna de los Cerros, Tres Zapotes, and other minor sites in order to determine whether or not they are Olmec

works. In this way, the forms and subjects that are separated out from those here considered to be essentially Olmec will no longer be considered as such, and thus the definition of Olmec sculptural style will remain necessarily confined to the sites on the Gulf Coast that produced monuments during a period that extended, perhaps, from 1200 to 400 B.C.

Qualities relating to regional styles, to changes and the devitalization of forms, and to processes of disjunction implicit in the development of style, as well as to the relationship to foreign contacts and influences, are problems that would draw me away from that which I consider essential.

I am of the opinion that, in order to reach an understanding of what the Olmec style is in its purest expressive form (which can only exist in an epoch of maximum cultural integration), we must take into account the visually recognizable external features, the organization and structure of the forms that give artistic life to these features, and the subjects or figurative themes which, as is known by all, must be read without the help of tradition and written documentation.

In Olmec scupture, in accordance with what one recognizes visually, there are three main categories: human figures, composite figures, and animal figures. The first group is, as I have already said, the most abundant; contrary to what has been asserted for years—that the jaguar dominates Olmec imagery—the statistical reality demonstrates that man is the main object of representation in the monumental sculptures. We are dealing, then, with a fundamentally homocentric art (Fig. 1); almost all of the depictions have the human figure as the basic subject matter. The forms with which this figure is constructed, although they are not removed from the natural data, are on occasion reduced to their essential features.

When I speak of composite figures (Fig. 2), I refer to those made up of a combination of human features with those of distinct animal species, of features of animals different from each other, and of features of this type mixed with imaginary and fantastic ones that lack a model in nature. Abundant among these are human bodies, some heads that resemble animals (particularly the jaguar), claws in place of hands and feet, and bifurcated tails. They are, in short, representations of strange beings that do not exist in perceptual sensory reality. I consider them as a group because they stand out visually as a mixture of features of a distinct kind.

The representations of the group of animal figures conform to their natural models only in a few examples. Usually their constituent elements are exaggerated or distorted, and, in addition, symbolic designs are usually superimposed on them.

In formal terms, the following fundamental characteristics are emphasized in the Olmec sculptural style: a marked preference for volume, that is, for the three-dimensional image; mass that is seen as solidly rooted because of its heaviness; structures of geometric forms that reveal order in their concept of the world; internal rhythm in the closed form; the predominance of rounded surfaces that disguise the harsh sternness of the geometry; and, above all, harmonic proportion. These characteristics are definitely applicable to that which can be called the purest "classic" Olmec sculpture and which best expresses the creativity of the culture that produced it. The Olmec sculptor did not like planes, angles, absolute symmetry, obvious dynamism, or rhythmic repetition; he preferred quiet and measured forms that kept sculptural movement within the confines of their volumes and that was adapted in a surprising manner to the canon, to the principle of harmonic proportion, that underlay the formal unity of his works.

I have already established that the central subject of representation in monumental sculpture is the human figure. It is primarily from within this group of images that we should proceed to look for the model or scheme from which its proportions are derived.

The assertion of equilibrium, unity, and proportion in the human figure, that is, the expression of form in geometric patterns, has shown itself differently in different civilizations (Panofsky 1955); the artistic expression of the great cultures and of significant eras has been revealed, by means of this expression, in a suitable and incontrovertible form. To have

been able to establish an art subject to a canon that governs and determines it reveals that, in the case of the Olmec, we are in no way dealing with primitive, immature, or transitional manifestations. We are, on the contrary, faced with manners of expression that have been fully realized, with forms conceived and structured within an organized world-view. I do not see in Olmec sculpture hesitations or stages of uncertain seeking; I find, on the contrary, that the monumental sculpture appears suddenly in the fullness of its maturity and with a core of structural composition that maintains its stylistic unity through many centuries. It is precisely when this directing principle of harmonic composition becomes weak and later disappears that the style fails, disintegrates, and is finally lost.

The great cultures have supported their artistic manifestations with systems of proportion that arose from solidly founded cultural bases; the art of the Olmec, as well as, for example, that of Classic Greek antiquity or of the Renaissance, utilized an exact system of proportion. This system—which explains the equilibrium, the harmony of the parts among themselves and as a whole, and the precise beauty of their formal rhythms—is what has variously been called "the divine proportion," "the golden section," and "the golden mean."

The golden mean was applied by Olmec sculptors. This can be easily demonstrated, for example, in the proportions of the colossal heads of San Lorenzo (Fig. 3), which are exactly defined by it, and in those of a series of complete full-figure sculptures (Figs. 4 and 5).

The Olmec method of using harmonic proportion reveals, it seems to me, a primordial aspect: the symbolization of the cosmos. Olmec man had a perfectly ordered vision of the world of nature and, perhaps, of the supernatural, and wanted to show it in a concrete way in his stone monuments. The ideal measure that he used in his monumental works of art is the same as that which forms our bodies and our universe, which is why there are stirred up within us echoes of identity, a sense of equilibrium, and the rightness of harmonic accord.

To the degree that the works lose the structure of this harmonic canon, they cease being

Fig. 1 San Lorenzo Colossal Head 4, showing man as the principal subject matter. Photograph by the author.

the "símbolo de fuerzas sobrenaturales . . . un dios y un antecesor . . ." (Covarrubias 1961:56); that the jaguar is the totemic antecedent of the people because it is believed that in some sculptures the sexual union between a jaguar and a woman is represented (Stirling 1955:19); that the jaguar-baby is associated with lightning and rain (Grove 1973a); and that the iconographic variations of jaguars represent different gods (Joralemon 1971, 1976) and include four whose identity has been sought in that of their assumed corresponding gods of the Aztec pantheon (M. Coe 1972: 3, Fig. 3). Alluding to ethnographic analogy, it has been said that the humanized jaguars are shamans (P. Furst 1968).

I do not intend to continue with speculations about the precise identity of the images or of the Olmec gods, since the points of depart-

Fig. 2 San Lorenzo Monument 10, a composite figure which combines human, animal, and fantastic traits. Photograph by Francisco Beverido.

Olmec; the loss of vigor of the arranged composition reveals that its significance has been weakened (Fig. 6). This phenomenon does not occur simultaneously at all the sites where there is sculpture. It is a fact, nevertheless, that the canon ceases to operate in works that were executed, I believe, between 600 and 400 B.C.

I said before that, in order to obtain a greater understanding of Olmec art and style, it is necessary to concern oneself with the themes, subjects, and contents that the monumental sculptures involve. I also pointed out the difficulties that exist in this part of the process.

There are some people, perhaps seeking explanations of Olmec ideology and religion based on accepting the notion that the primary image of Olmec sculpture is that of the jaguar being, who have assumed: that the jaguar is

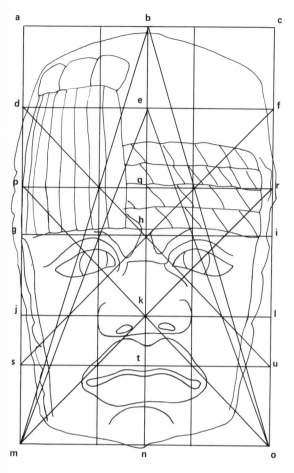

Fig. 3 San Lorenzo Colossal Head 4, the proportions of which allow it to be perfectly drawn within the rectangle of the golden mean.

ure used do not appear to me to be, strictly speaking, applicable. They are based on a comparison of the Aztec with the Olmec, the cultures having between them a span of some 2000 to 2500 years. They seek explanations for ancient forms in activities or beliefs of present-day peoples, whose societies have, furthermore, suffered the inevitable effects that result from the clash of native and western cultures.

I am interested in investigating the particular form in which the anxieties common to the soul of man are expressed in this monumental art. I intend, then, to approach an understanding of the intrinsic significance of the images represented, establishing that the Olmec could not have eluded the circumstances and foundations that give to all cultures—present-day and far-removed—a lowest common denominator,

which is none other than the fundamental syntax of the human condition.

I have already asserted that Olmec art is one whose center is man; one state of idealized man, of sacred man, is the primary theme of representation in these sculptures. From a strictly iconographic point of view, these can be gathered into three thematic groups in which man seldom does not appear: mythical images, effigies of supernatural beings, and simple human figures.

The mythical images that are shown in Olmec sculpture, while referring to events that occurred at the time of origin or while explaining the creation, do not resort to sculptural narrative processes but express in a succinct manner these primordial concepts. There are three subgroups that form the group I have called mythical images. The first is made up of only three sculptures: Tenochtitlan Monument 1, Laguna

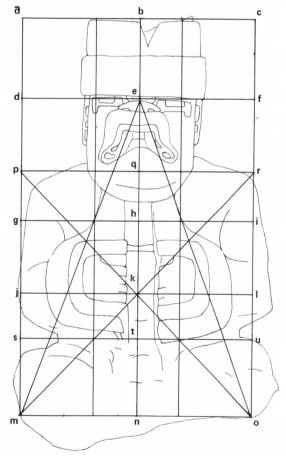

Fig. 4 San Lorenzo Monument 10, showing the application of the golden mean.

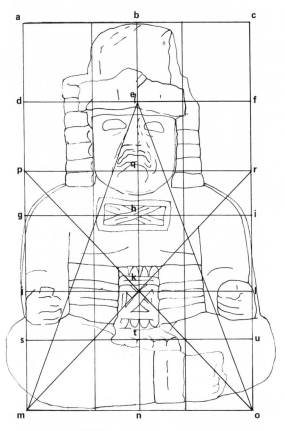

Fig. 5 La Venta Monument 77, showing the application of the golden mean.

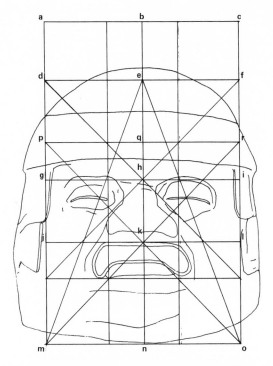

Fig. 6 Cobata Colossal Head, showing how the application of the golden mean has lost its vigor.

de los Cerros Monument 20, and Potrero Nuevo Monument 3. It has been said that they represent the sexual union of a jaguar and a woman, and that from this union there resulted the jaguar-monster so frequent in Olmec imagery. A careful analysis reveals that in the first two sculptures only human beings are represented, and, furthermore, in the sculpture from Potrero Nuevo the feet of a jaguar stand at the sides of the reclining body of a female monkey. In none' of these monuments is the reproduction of a real act intended, only the symbolization of an event of profound significance. These monuments are the petrified incarnation of a creation myth: the possession of the earth, the fertilization of the earth, the supernatural union that is established as a paradigm of all unions, the sacred origin of man. The second subgroup is formed of figures that emerge from a recess that reminds one of

a cave and of those that are found on the so-called altars (Fig. 7). Generally in these pieces a principal personage, whose bulky figure contrasts visually with the almost-flat reliefs of a symbolic character that are arranged round it, comes out of the cave, the threshold of the underworld; from it man emerges to establish and occupy his place on earth. These images reproduce an origin myth; the terrestrial cave, the great ancestral womb, is the generatrix of man. The sculptural symbol of origin, as part of the mystery of creation, resolved an existential tension; hence, its constant repetition. With minor alterations, one finds it at San Lorenzo (Monuments 14 and 20), La Venta (Altars 2, 3, 4, 5, 6, 7, and Stela 1), and Laguna de los Cerros (Monuments 5 and 28). Comprising the third and last subgroup are human figures that hold in their arms children with fantastic heads. These are of two kinds: those who hold

Fig. 7 La Venta Altar 4, an image which represents an origin myth. Photograph by Mariano Monterrosa.

children with flaccid bodies (San Lorenzo Monument 20, La Venta Altars 2 and 5, and Las Limas Monument 1), in which case it appears that the child is being treated as an offering (Fig. 8), the sacrificed child recalling that the original meaning of the word "to sacrifice" is "to make sacred"; and those who hold children with dynamic postures (La Venta Altar 5 and San Lorenzo Monument 12), whose lives presumably are destined for sacrifice. In combination with this concept, the myth of origin is then also a myth of fertility.

I proceed to the second thematic group: those images, always single figures, that incorporate into their essentially human aspect animal features together with others that are purely imagined. In this group of supernatural beings belong also stylized animals; there is a total of seventy-nine sculptures with representations that correspond to those that are traditionally called jaguars, jaguar-monsters, and humanized jaguars. The fantastic-animal fea-

tures are concentrated above all on the head and face; in a small number of cases they occur on the hands and feet, in which case claws are represented.

Among those images that are furthest from the human, I find two subgroups. The first is distinguished by parallel lines forming squares in place of eyes, and a thick upper lip turned upward, allowing one to see two large fangs that are bifurcated at their tips; San Lorenzo Monument 10, La Venta Monuments 6, 9, 11, and 64, and Estero Rabón Monument 5 (Fig. 9) belong to this group. The other group is well represented by San Lorenzo Monument 52 (Fig. 10), La Venta Monument 75, and the images of children that, in the arms of certain personages, are of the infantile type, recognizable by the slanting almond-shaped eyes with internal commissures pointing downwards, and the large, thick upper lip that turns up to reveal toothless gums. There are, on the other hand, features that are shared by both groups. This

91

Fig. 8 (above) Las Limas Monument 1, an image that represents a fertility myth. Photograph by Francisco Beverido.

Fig. 9 (below) Estero Rabón Monument 5, a supernatural being. Photograph by the author.

group of images represents creatures that do not exist in reality, and their hybrid character can be considered a pairing of symbols. I think that these figures, with an ambivalent cosmic–vital symbolic burden, are not gods but personifications of forces, concepts that are conceived as free from the ordinary laws of reality.

I have left for last the consideration of the most important group: images that have exclusively human features. In contrast to the preceding ones, they are natural representations; but I must warn that they do not deal with men in a world of historic dimension, but rather with the sculptural translation of the concept, with the idea of man who, anchored in myth, is the bridge between the supernatural world and the natural one of the terrestrial world. This group, in its turn, includes three subgroups. The first is made up of images that have been called lords under supernatural protection, because in them one or more human figures are beneath a composite or super-

Fig. 10 San Lorenzo Monument 52, a supernatural being. Photograph by the author.

natural figure, as for example, in La Venta Monument 44, San Martín Pajapan Monument 1 (Fig. 11), and the much later La Venta Stelae 2 and 3. The second subgroup of figures is formed by single figures that have been called mediators (Fig. 12); they are figures that lack individual features or expressions, although the totality of their characteristics is human. A number of these sculptures are decapitated; I am thinking particularly of San Lorenzo Monuments 12 and 47, La Venta Monuments 23, 31, and 40, and Laguna de los Cerros Monuments 3, 6, and 11. Among those that are preserved intact, apart from La Venta Monument 77, are some worthy of being included among the masterpieces of Olmec art: Cruz del Milagro Monument 1 and Cuauhtotolapan Monument 1 (Fig. 12). The mediators are, perhaps,

Fig. 11 San Martín Pajapan Monument 1, a human figure under supernatural protection. Photograph by the author.

Fig. 12 Cuauhtotolapan Monument 1, a human figure. Photograph by the author.

statues of those who mediate between chaos and cosmos; they express the fact that the human condition can be altered as a result of spiritual insight.

The colossal heads, the last of the subgroups of human figures that must be mentioned, are unique in the history of world art. Fifteen complete heads are known, and in them are shown the enduring changes in Olmec style. Eight—the most perfect ones—come from San Lorenzo, four from La Venta, and three from Tres Zapotes and its environs. I believe that the colossal heads are allegorical portraits in which the image of the represented person is associated with the image of a concept that ascribes, in its turn, to the subject of the portrait (Fig. 13) qualities that are inherent in it. I believe, then, that they are much more than simple portraits. The colossal heads carry within themselves

Fig. 13 San Lorenzo Colossal Head 5, a portrait. Photograph by the author.

an intrinsic significance more profound and universal than their mere exterior appearance. Their structure, with the exception of that of Cobata and of the so-called Monument A of Tres Zapotes, is determined by the perfection of harmonic proportion; their form, therefore, symbolizes the cosmos.

In this way, Olmec art, fundamentally humanistic, complete in its development, perfect in the use of its methods, and moderate in its essence, oscillates between naturalism and abstraction in its representations. It embraces the former when its elements of expression are purely human forms; it embraces the latter when it seeks to express itself with purely symbolic forms. Both the naturalistic forms and the abstract ones are constructed within a canon of proportions that is none other than the golden mean. This is another factor that serves to demonstrate that this art can in no way be considered primitive. The complexity of the subjects represented coincides with the external fullness of the representation. The human figure, the gravitational center of almost all of the forms of Olmec art, appears in this art with different metaphysical definitions which, at their extreme, seem to repeat, with their arrangement in perfect harmonic order, the entire order of the universe.

Some Olmec Objects in the Robert Woods Bliss Collection at Dumbarton Oaks

Elizabeth P. Benson

STANDING FIGURE (FIGS. 1 AND 2)

Matthew Stirling (1961: Fig. 7) published three Olmec pieces from the Robert Woods Bliss Collection. Among them was the object illustrated in the color frontispiece of the catalogue of the Robert Woods Bliss Collection published by the National Gallery of Art in 1947: a standing figure of highly polished, dark-green diopside-jadeite, the first Pre-Columbian object that Robert Woods Bliss acquired (Lothrop *et al.* 1957: 7). It was purchased from Joseph Brummer in Paris in 1914, when and where it was called "Aztec," since Stirling, Hermann Beyer (1927), and Marshall H. Saville (1929a, 1929b) had not yet made the world aware of the Olmec. After the "Aztec" description in the Bliss files, there is a penciled note: "Olmec (Professor Tozzer, Nov. 1939)." This was, of course, the year after Stirling began work at Tres Zapotes. The object was shown in 1940 at the Museum of Modern Art in New York in an exhibition entitled "Twenty Centuries of Mexican Art," and it was also seen in "An Exhibition of Pre-Columbian Art" at the Fogg Art Museum. These were two of the earliest exhibitions showing Pre-Columbian objects as "art," demonstrating a change in point of view toward these objects that was brought about, in part, by Mr. Bliss, who was probably the first Pre-Columbian collector with an aesthetic point of view. In later years, the figure was shown in Santa Barbara, San Francisco, Portland (Oregon), Cincinnati, Paris, and Stockholm, but its regular residence during a sixteen-year period was the National Gallery of

Art. It came to Dumbarton Oaks, with the rest of the Bliss Collection, in 1963.

The figure has a deformed skull, with a curving horizontal indentation at the back and sides, and the intimation of a cleft element above and perpendicular to this indentation; there is also a slight flattening along the vertical centerline of the skull below the indentation. There are small holes in the ear lobes, and a drilled indication of the ear opening (with an odd upper drilling on the proper left ear). The nostril is drilled through the septum. Eyes are formed by drilling at the ends and removing the stone between the drillings; it is possible that the eyes were inlaid. The mouth reveals a subtly carved gum ridge or, possibly, teeth; there is a small, shallow hole drilled at each side of the lower lip. The beard is formed by a polished, squarish, projecting block; it is not incised to indicate hair. A penis covering is the only clothing: it is simply rendered; there is no indication that this is a loincloth, and it shows no belt or means of attachment. The stance shows legs that are placed firmly apart and knees that are slightly bent.

There are old, mended breaks in both arms, both feet, and the left leg; the original parts have been reattached. Spinden (1947: 2), in publishing a jadeite figurine in the collection of Mr. and Mrs. Alastair Bradley Martin, quoted Covarrubias as saying that that figurine had been "ceremoniously 'killed' by breaking off the left leg, a type of mutilation noted in clay figurines of the Olmec."

Although the figure is generally like the fig-

95

Fig. 1 Jadeite standing figure of a man. Access. No. B-14.OJ.

Fig. 2 Front view of Figure 1.

urines found in greatest quantity at La Venta (Drucker 1952: Pls. 47–50; Drucker *et al.* 1959: Pls. 26, 33–6), it is about four centimeters taller than the largest La Venta figure (the Dumbarton Oaks figure measures 23.9 centimeters in height), and it is carved in a very different style. There are, of course, stylistic variations within the La Venta group, but the Dumbarton Oaks figure is generally more muscular, modeled, and monumental than his La Venta cousins; he is more broad-shouldered and has a firmer stance; a rather athletic figure, he makes the La Venta figures look mannered and effete. The conventions for forming shoulders, arms, chest muscles, buttocks, legs, and penis covering are quite different, as are the conventions for carving the cheeks and mouth, and the head deformation. Despite the size difference, it is closer in proportions and muscularity to the "Wrestler" in the Museo Nacional de Antropología (Corona 1962), and, like that figure, it has a beard—which does not exist on the La Venta figurines—and a face more human than those of La Venta.

The arms of the Dumbarton Oaks figure, more modeled and articulated than those of the La Venta figures, project farther to the side and forward, and the hands are drilled to hold something. The monuments suggest that it might have been something like a ceremonial bar or perhaps a "baby" that was held (de la Fuente 1973: Nos. 2, 5, 116, 136, 191), as in the jadeite figure in the Martin Collection, although it is hard to imagine the holding mechanisms that would have existed (Spinden 1947) to secure these objects in the holes of the Dumbarton Oaks figure. The position of the drillings immediately suggests the insertion of some sort of stick or pole, although I know of no precedent for such objects held in this way. Another—and perhaps the strongest—possibility is that there might have been a replica of a "torch" and/or "knuckle-duster," items that are represented with some frequency on small objects (Cervantes 1969; Benson 1971: 18–20) and monuments (Boggs 1950; Medellín Zenil 1971: Pl. 41; de la Fuente 1973: Nos. 117, 135, 151), and that are, in La Venta Offering No. 4, depicted on the celts associated with figures of this general type (Cervantes 1969).

The piece does not appear to have been made in La Venta; it would seem more likely that it was a lusty provincial imitation of a La Venta-type figure. The La Venta figures were, of course, highly portable (if they did not get buried before they got carried), and they may have been exported to, and copied with greater or lesser accuracy in, a number of places. Association of figures with specific places is not necessarily useful. There is, for example, a stone figurine from Tlatilco (Bernal 1969a: Pl. 55) that is very like the La Venta figures—much more so than is the Dumbarton Oaks figure. However, the resemblances of

the Dumbarton Oaks piece to the "Wrestler," which comes from Antonio Plaza (Santa María Uxpanapa), roughly halfway between La Venta and San Lorenzo, suggest a possible origin somewhere in the Olmec heartland; on the other hand, figures of more comparable size found in remote regions also share certain traits. A kneeling jade figure from the Ulúa Valley, Honduras (Bernal 1969a: Pl. 102), now in the Middle American Research Institute, Tulane University, shares the beard, the drilled hands, and the stocky muscularity, but has very different facial features and head shape. The jade figure, of unknown provenience, in the Martin Collection (Spinden 1947) has general similarities in the treatment of arms, fingers, neck area, brow, eye, and ear, and is perhaps the most nearly comparable figure. But I know of no figure that is closely similar to the Dumbarton Oaks one in style.

The difference between this figure and the La Venta prototypes may be chronological rather than geographical. It is possible that the beard suggests lateness in time, at least within the heartland. A number of late monuments—La Venta Stela 3 (Stirling 1943b: Pl. 35; Heizer 1967: Pl. 1 and Fig. 1), Tres Zapotes Stela D (Stirling 1943b: Pl. 14, left), and the Alvarado Stela (Covarrubias 1957: Fig. 29)—show a dominant, bearded figure at the right, facing a kneeling figure that usually has an "Olmecoid" face; outside the heartland, the Juxtlahuaca figure painting (Gay 1967: 29) may repeat the same scene. Such scenes suggest that truly or falsely bearded conquerors may have come into the Olmec area quite late. The major figure on La Venta Stela 2 (Stirling 1943b: Pl. 34; Heizer 1967: Pl. 2 and Fig. 2) is also bearded, and this is also a late monument; La Venta Monument 63 (Williams and Heizer 1965: Fig. 5 and Pl. 2d) is also probably bearded and probably late. If the figurines can be dated by the monuments, it would indicate that beards are a late phenomenon. (One of the seated figures—the dominant one—on the side of Altar 3 also has a beard—probably a false one. Altar 3 itself seems to be early in the La Venta seriation [Clewlow 1974: 172; Milbrath 1979: 32], but there is the possibility that the relief carving on the sides may be later. If the figure is bearded and the relief is early, then this throws out the likelihood of beards appearing only at a later time. On the other hand, beardedness may someday be used as an argument for the lateness of the sculpture—or, at least, of the relief carving on its side.)

I know of no small bearded carvings that were found archaeologically in the heartland.

A number of these unadorned standing figures, with considerable variation of style and subtlety, have been found over a wide area and possibly originated in a wide time span. Were such figures made simply to be placed in caches and scenes (see Drucker *et al.* 1959: 152, 161, Pls. 30, 33), or was that a secondary purpose? A still more basic question is: what sort of creature did they represent? To know the motivation for their manufacture and use would mean the possession of real insight into the Olmec mind. I have suggested elsewhere (Benson 1976: 70) that these figurines may have been made to be buried as gifts to the earth, and that they perhaps "represented progenitors, the race that had originally come from the earth and was tokenly returned there." But, even if this surmise is somewhat right, it does not tell us enough about the variations, subtleties, and specificities with which these pieces were made.

RECLINING FIGURE (FIG. 3)

Stirling (1961: Fig. 4) also published a small, flat figure with spindly arms and short legs, ankles together, one hand across the waist and the other by the ear, as if he were listening to a telephone or a seashell. It measures 11.2 centimeters long, and is carved from light gray-green serpentine. The hands are the only part of the body, other than the head, that is rendered with any care. A triangular penis sheath or loincloth is indicated, and buttocks are incised on the rear. The piece was at some time broken across the shoulders; the two sections were discovered several years apart.

This kind of figure is reminiscent of the standing La Venta figurines in the treatment of the head and general simplification of the body, although the facial features seem more exaggerated on the reclining figures than those on most of the La Venta examples. No reclin-

ing types are known from La Venta. Of the several published examples of figures of this type (Bernal 1969a: Pl. 74), that which is most similar to the Dumbarton Oaks figure is in the American Museum of Natural History (Covarrubias 1946b: Pl. 8; Bernal 1969a: Pl. 74b). The body proportions of both figures are particularly lean, and the ankles are together so that the legs outline essentially the same void in both figures, although the left hand of the American Museum figure is on the knee rather than on the torso. The American Museum figure is reported to have come from San Jerónimo, Guerrero, while the Dumbarton Oaks figure is said to be from San Cristóbal Tepatlaxco, Puebla. A figure in the Museo Nacional de Antropología, said to have come from Tzintzuntzan, Michoacán (Bernal 1969a: Pl. 74d), is incomplete, but one hand rests on the belly and the other on the head. Although it is closely comparable, it has an incised hairdress that does not appear on the other figures. All three of these pieces have a distinctive upside-down-V were-jaguar mouth, puffy eyelids, and an exaggerated glabella. Another figure in the Museo Nacional de Antropología is unlike the other examples, in that it has a profile face, L-shaped eye, and pronounced superciliary ridge, and it is shown in a crouching, rather than a stretched-out, position; it has no hand on the head, belly, or chest, but one hand clasps a knee. Miguel Covarrubias (1946b: 98), who describes it as a "dwarf," published it as "from Olinalá, Guerrero"; Bernal publishes it as "Provenencia dudosa" (1967: Fig. 183) or "Guerrero(?)" (1969a: Pl. 74a).

These objects are highly portable, of course, and could all have been made in the same area, or even in the same workshop, although I would find it difficult to believe that they were made by the same carver. Certainly the last one mentioned above is of a very different style and posture, and, if it belongs to the same iconographic group, would not likely have been made in the same place. Another figure of this type has been reported in a private collection in Mexico, and a jade pendant that is clearly imitative of the iconography, but carved in a quite different style, was found at Cerro Manicular in Panamá (Lothrop 1950:

Fig. 3 Serpentine reclining figure. Access. No. B-7.OS.

Fig. 142)—this last represents a female figure.

The same motif exists in clay examples (M. Coe 1965a: Fig. 199; Easby and Scott 1970: Nos. 8–10). Three of these published clay figures are from Central Mexico; a fourth (Easby and Scott 1970: No. 8) is published as from Playa de los Muertos, Ulúa Valley, Honduras, and clearly represents a pregnant woman. Here the hand on the belly suggests the easing of labor pains; it seems unlikely, however, that this is the original motivation for the other figures, but, rather, a local interpretation of the pose. Only the figures found far from the heartland are clearly female.

The clay figures shed some light on the understanding of the stone ones. The stone figures have most frequently been published as "dancing" (Lothrop *et al.* 1957: 242; M. Coe 1965b: Fig. 11; Bernal 1969a: Pl. 74), and there has been some discussion as to whether they should be exhibited vertically or horizontally. Stirling (1961: 50) published the Dumbarton Oaks figure in horizontal position, but appears to have grouped it with dancing figures. The answer to this question is not clear in the stone versions, although the weight and equilibrium of the objects seem more comfortable when they are presented horizontally. (The only drilling of the Dumbarton Oaks figure is through the ears.) I think that there is no question, however, that the clay versions are to be interpreted as reclining. The pose seems to grade into seated, rather than dancing, postures, for another clay figurine (M. Coe 1965a: No. 197), from Las Bocas, is seated with one hand on the

face and one on the belly, and with legs akimbo —that is, the limbs are placed similarly to those of the reclining figures—and a seated clay figurine from Gualupita (Vaillant and Vaillant 1934: Fig. 14-3) has one hand on the head and the other on the knee. What relationship these clay and small stone figures may have to the Monte Albán "Danzantes" will probably remain an open question.

The poses and gestures of these figures cannot have been completely random. Their iconography might well be worthy of particular study.

BUST (FIG. 4)

The third Bliss piece published by Stirling (1961: 48 and Fig. 5), a head of fine blue jade broken from a figurine, was acquired by Mr. Bliss from V. G. Simkhovitch. The head measures only 6.6 centimeters in height, but it has a monumental quality; a projected slide of it can be read as strongly as a colossal head. The face is slightly asymmetrical, a feature not uncommon in Olmec art, and one that gives a particularly alive quality to it. The remains of an arm thrust forward may indicate that the figurine had a pose similar to that of Laguna de los Cerros Monument 11 (Medellín Zenil 1960b: Lám. 23); this arm and the position of the head suggest that it was probably seated. Stirling commented on its "admirable realism." The style of this head denies the often-true dictum of Peter David Joralemon (1976: 33) that "The primary concern of Olmec religious art is the representation of creatures that are

Elizabeth P. Benson

biologically impossible." This face is not only biologically possible, but is undoubtedly a portrait. Its extraordinary naturalism makes one all the more curious about the nature of at least some of the heads that are missing from Olmec monuments or eroded beyond precise reading. The basic question raised here, of course, is that of what distinctions were or were not made between religious and secular art, between concepts of supernaturalism and naturalism, perhaps one of the most important questions that should be resolved in the study of any Pre-Columbian art.

George Kubler (1962: 70, Pl. 34B) published the piece as the head of a woman, and Michael D. Coe and I (Dumbarton Oaks 1963: No. 30) followed his lead; Samuel K. Lothrop (Lothrop *et al.* 1957: 242) and Stirling (1961: Fig. 5) called it a man; other authors have simply called it a head or bust, and not committed themselves to an opinion on its sex. Remarkably little has been determined about the well-kept secret of sex in Olmec art. The seated jade Figurine 1 from the La Venta Mound A-2 tomb (Drucker 1952: Pl. 46) is one of the few other sculptures to have been published as a woman. It is wearing a skirt and has some indication of breasts. The Dumbarton Oaks head is much more masculine— less pretty, more powerful—than the head of the La Venta figure, and its bare chest looks flat. Although both figures show unadorned, striated, incised hair, the hair styles are different. The hairdress of the Dumbarton Oaks figure has a general resemblance to that of the Las Limas figure (Medellín Zenil 1965), which M. Coe (1973a: 3) assumes to be "a young man or boy," as is indicated by the wearing of the loincloth. (The chief difference here, aside from technical distinctions, is that the hair covers the ears of the Dumbarton Oaks figure, whereas the ears of the Las Limas figure are exposed.)

The face on the Dumbarton Oaks object is not unlike that on the twelve-centimeter-high figurine from Arroyo Pesquero (Medellín Zenil 1971: Pl. 57), now in the Museo de la Universidad de Veracruz. The Dumbarton Oaks figure would have been somewhat larger in scale. The Arroyo Pesquero figure is helmeted and

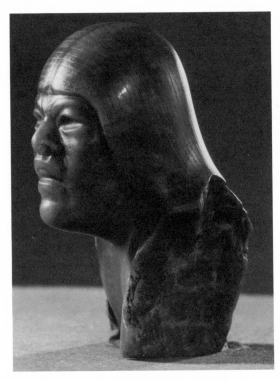

Fig. 4 Blue jadeite bust, broken from a figurine. Access. No. B-19.OJ.

the expression is not so intense, but brow, nose, and thick-lipped mouth are made in much the same way. The helmeted head of the Arroyo Pesquero figure seems to be related to the colossal heads. This piece, like the Dumbarton Oaks bust, begs the question of the relationship between the monuments and these small objects of precious material. (I am, for example, increasingly convinced that there is at least a family resemblance between the Dumbarton Oaks Arroyo Pesquero figure [Benson 1971] and the seated sculpture from Cruz del Milagro [Bernal 1969a: Pl. 19].)

BLOCKY STANDING FIGURE (FIG. 5)

A piece that had gone from Brummer to Walter Baker to Simkhovitch to Bliss is a small (8.5 centimeters high), blocky figure of pale, mottled, green jadeite, whose were-jaguar head is larger than its square, minimally indicated body. There is a horizontal rectangle incised on the "chest"; the hands are presented in low relief horizontally across the front of the body;

100

Fig 5 Small jadeite figure with were-jaguar face. Access. No. B-15.OJ.

the fingers are incised, and there is a vertical gap between the hands; the feet are formed by a projecting shelf of stone, with incisions to indicate toes. On the back, the stone is cut in relief to indicate a neck or shoulder line that goes straight across the body, and a parallel line intersects a perpendicular one to form the legs. Two incised lines on the back of the head form the rear of the handband; there is a horizontal line just above the center of the "torso," and there are two horizontal lines on each leg. The face has a were-jaguar mouth with broad upper "lip," gum ridge, *tau* tooth, and down-curving lower lip; it has a broad, flattened nose, and more-or-less even eyes that are curved on the outer corners and come to a point on the inner corners. The profile is carved in quite low relief.

The piece illustrates well the Olmec notion of the iconographic importance of the head over any other part of the body (Benson 1976: 69). As with various other Olmec monuments and figures, the head here is large and worked

in modeled detail, and the body, hands, and feet are sketchily represented with a few lines or simple planes. M. Coe (1973a: 11) has discussed the question of the oversized heads as a means of emphasizing the infantile qualities of the subject; I think that one must also take into account, however, the considerably greater care and detail with which the head is rendered in most instances.

Although it is small and has no blade-shape, the Dumbarton Oaks figure is more reminiscent of the large Olmec axes (Saville 1929a, 1929b), both in proportions and stockiness, than of any other Olmec form, with the exception of La Venta Monument 75 (de la Fuente 1973: No. 84) and a small jade carving that belonged to Alfred Maudsley (Bushnell 1964). The horizontally placed hands are a trait that Saville (1929b: 337) notes as characteristic of the axe type.

Joralemon (1971: 71) designates this figure as God IV, "an anthropomorphic dwarf or infant with Type C eyes and toothless mouth. A forehead band and wavy ear coverings are almost always worn by the deity." Joralemon further states (*ibid*.: 90) that "God IV is the rain god once thought to be the chief divinity of the Olmec culture. He is always depicted as an infant or dwarf." The Dumbarton Oaks figure has an incised forehead band with both horizontal and vertical elements, but lacks the wavy-lined ear ornaments.

The piece stands in perhaps the same relationship to the La Venta-type standing figurines as the baby on the Martin piece (Spinden 1947) does to the figure that holds it. It also shares similarities with the "baby" held by the Las Limas figure. Both of these held figures are designated by Joralemon as representations of God IV. Both have cleft heads, however, whereas the Dumbarton Oaks figure does not.

Saville (1929a: 295–7) suggested the association of the axe figures with thunderbolts, which would tie in with Joralemon's rain-god attribution, and Covarrubias (1944) made the association between rain gods and infants. The link that is still lacking is that which shows the connection between the infant-thunderbolt-rain gods and the La Venta-type figurines.

MASK (FIG. 6)

A large jadeite mask, measuring 20.8 centimeters in height, was acquired by Mr. Bliss with a statement from the dealer that it had been found in Italy and that:

> there is some evidence that it has been there since the 16th century. It was published some time ago by a Hungarian professor as a "Tang" mask; was sold by one collector to another as a Chinese piece and later returned because it was American and not Chinese.

I have been unable to document this information, but, in his obituary of Mr. Bliss, Lothrop (1963: 93) wrote that:

> there are only two objects [in the Collection] known to have reached Europe in the 16th century. One is . . . a life-size Olmec mask of jade which was taken to Italy in the 1530's.

One original piece of the brow is missing and has been replaced, and it was noted by the dealer that "the missing piece was present about 25–30 years ago and was subsequently lost and not recovered." The proper upper right quarter of the mask was also broken off, presumably at the same time that the missing fragment was broken. The right-hand piece was put back, leaving a crack from the ear to the middle of the mouth; another crack is visible from the mouth down into the proper right cheek. The mask has been cut down in the back from the top, at least on the inside, and there are indications that the mask once extended perhaps an inch behind the ears.

The mask could actually be worn for brief periods: there are holes for the nostrils and cross-eyed pupils. There are slight furrows in the brow, and an incised indication of an upper lid; the ears have S-curve incising above horizontal lines. The nose is turned up and flattened, and the mouth has an oblong upper projection with squared corners, outlined with incision, over a double-curved upper lip or gum ridge that is very deeply carved; a lower lip consists of a straight plane in the center drooping to a U shape on either side; there are two parallel lines incised on this lip. The mouth has no fangs, but there is a shallow-relief tongue in the mouth that presses against the

Fig. 6 Jadeite mask. Access. No. B-20.OJ.

middle of the lower lip. The droop of the lower lip, the curvaciousness of the gum ridge, and the decoration of the upper lip are perhaps more exaggerated in this piece than in any other such face.

This type of face is most commonly found on celts or *hachas* (Joralemon 1971: 56–7, 74–6), where the mouth and nose may also be accompanied by, among other variations, the crossed eyes of this piece and flame eyebrows, which this piece lacks. Joralemon (1971: 19, 24) lists this mask in his category of "Objects Unidentifiable as Specific Gods but Important for the Motifs They Bear." Elsewhere, he (Joralemon 1976: 29, 31, 33, 35) uses the mask as an example of the hybridization of human and feline elements in Olmec art, and does not give it a specific deity attribution, although it is the kind of face, most frequently found on celts, that he does classify as God I or God IV. It has the flattened nose and toothless mouth with the gum ridges of his God I-E,

Fig. 7 Seated figure of albite and jadeite. Access. No. B-18.OJ.

is no body to give it appropriate scale, this leaves something of a dilemma.

The corpus of Arroyo Pesquero masks includes only two with similar supernatural faces (David Joralemon, personal communication). Eyes, nose, mouth, and ears of all three masks are generally similar, but the two Arroyo Pesquero masks are closer to each other in style and more restrained than the Dumbarton Oaks mask. It would be interesting to ascertain the relationship between these and the masks of similar size and skillful rendering that are, in many cases at least, clearly portraits. It would be equally interesting to know the purpose served by these masks.

SEATED FIGURE (FIG. 7)

An albite-and-jadeite seated figure, ten centimeters high, is said to have come from Tabasco. The figure has a normal human face with narrow eyes, a large, blunt nose, and a beard. He wears a helmet, which has a three-pronged flame-eyebrow motif placed on either side of the lower border, so that the motif is above the eyes and normal brows of the figure. This is the only instance I know of the flame eyebrow on a helmet. The helmet also has a three-pronged element at the top, comparable to the projection on the headdress extension of the Dumbarton Oaks Arroyo Pesquero figure (Benson 1971). Between the two segments of the flame-eyebrow motif, there is a circular element, with a leaflike projection above; this is comparable to the similarly placed headdress element on the Arroyo Pesquero figure. There is a band around the back of the head.

The rib cage is fairly carefully denoted, front and back, giving the body an emaciated appearance. A tubular drill was used to make a blank hole in the middle of the front of the body. In unpublished notes Lothrop made, *ca.* 1960, he states that this is "an unusually early example of the use of this tool." Lothrop also notes that "the angles of the bent elbows at the back have been cut free by string sawing," a technique most frequently found in jade carving from the Guapiles, or Línea Vieja, region of Costa Rica.

The drilling of holes in the body of objects seems to have been a relatively late occupation,

although it lacks a cleft head or flame eyebrows.

I think that, given the mouth of this creature, it should probably be identified as a specific god under Joralemon's system, for this is the mouth of a supernatural. I believe that clues to what the Olmec were about are given us by the Martin figure. The large figure has the mouth and facial characteristics of a great many Olmec figures, notably the La Venta figurines; the mouth is only a little jaguar-haunted. Whether these people were to be identified as special human beings or characters with some supernatural quality is problematic; but the baby that the figure holds is clearly supernatural. I suspect that any figure with that kind of mouth is supernatural. Because it lacks the diagnostic flame eyebrows of Joralemon's God I, one is forced, according to Joralemon's categories, to put this mask in the category of God IV, the infantile rain god. Since it is not particularly infantile, and there

although many Central Mexican figurines have prominent navels (a phenomenon that may relate to the drilling of this stone figure) and the "figure" incised on a celt in La Venta Offering No. 2 (Drucker *et al.* 1959: Fig. 35b) has a small circle drawn on this part of the body. The kneeling figure from the Ulúa Valley (Bernal 1969a: Pl. 102; Easby and Scott 1970: No. 65) has a hole, smaller than that in the Dumbarton Oaks figure, drilled into the middle of the body. Post-manufacture holes were made in an Olmec stone pectoral in the Dumbarton Oaks Collection (M. Coe 1966a). A hole smaller than, but similar to, that in the Dumbarton Oaks seated figure is drilled in a stone figurine from Teotihuacan, now in the Museum für Völkerkunde in Vienna (Becker-Donner 1965: Taf. 12). It might be worthwhile exploring ethnographic material for an interpretation of this hole-drilling activity.

The pose of the Dumbarton Oaks piece is uncommon: the figure sits with legs drawn up at each side, so that the knees rest against the shoulders; the hands clasp the shins. The legs and the very flat arms are schematically rendered, and the knees are flat on top. The only similar pose that I know of is that of a male monkey, Monument 1 from Santa Rita Loma Larga, Hueyapan de Ocampo (Medellín Zenil 1971: Pl. 51). This figure appears to be obese, in contrast to the emaciation of the Dumbarton Oaks figure.

I would judge that the head of this figure is a portrait, and that the helmet denotes someone of importance—a king, a god-king, or perhaps a priest—yet the pose and the emaciated rib cage seem to indicate poverty or humiliation. It is conceivable that this is a conquered king, but I like better the possibility that the sculpture may commemorate ritual humiliation or mortification. It is the only example I know of a generally Olmec-style figure with a skeletal rib cage, with the exception of the monolith from Misantla (Bernal 1969a: Pl. 20), which is also probably a late piece. This suggests the possibility that the Dumbarton Oaks piece was made at a time when influences from elsewhere—perhaps the Izapan area—were coming into the heartland, if the piece was, indeed, made in Tabasco.

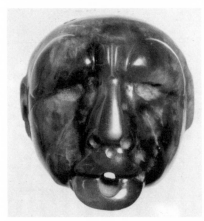

Fig. 8 (above) Miniature jadeite mask. Access. No. B-551.OJ.

Fig. 9 (below) Profile view of Figure 8.

MINIATURE PENDANT MASK (FIGS. 8 AND 9)

An unusual were-jaguar face is found on a finely carved small jadeite pendant mask which measures 5.4 centimeters in height. The blue-green jade is particularly fine and very highly polished, and there are traces of red pigment in the depressions; the stone is very thin at the rear edges. Two holes have been drilled at the top for suspension, and there are shallow drillings in the nostrils, ears, and the base of the nose, and two at each side of the mouth (one at the edge of the center of the mouth, and one between this and the nostril).

This face is perhaps more purely jaguar in many of its elements than most were-jaguar faces. There is a pronounced, and very feline, muscular area over the eyes. The glabella is marked with a vertical line leading to a slight depression, suggestive of the fontanelle. The eyes, which show no signs of inlay, slope down at the outer corners, where there is a forked crease at each side. The long, flattish nose is more feline than the squatter nose of the usual were-jaguar face, and raised planes at either side of the nose and mouth are, again, particularly feline. The ears, however, are placed in a human position. It is possible that this piece belongs in the category of transformation figures discussed in the next section.

The most exceptional feature is the mouth, which has no jaguar resemblances. Its center is formed by an open hole, drilled as if to hold a drinking straw. On the upper side, the hole breaks into an almost-triangular form, which runs into the bottom of the nose, and, on the lower side, the hole is drilled through a shape that reads, from the front view, as a thick lower lip, and, from the side view, as a possible beard. Although it is a most unusual form, a beard may be intended here. It is also possible that some sort of mouth mask is represented, for the triangular portion does seem to be attached to the septum. Mouth masks are uncommon on Olmec sculpture carved in the round, but they do appear on profile heads incised on celts and on slightly later relief-carved monuments. These generally appear to be quite different from the form on the Dumbarton Oaks pendant, but the mouth area of this piece is not essentially different from the mouth mask depicted on the profile figure on Cerro de las Mesas Stela 5 (Stirling 1943b: Pl. 21b; Medellín Zenil 1971: Pl. 25). Small Central Mexican clay masks may have unusual mouths with round holes in them (M. Coe 1965a: Nos. 162 and 164), and it is possible that there is some correlation of this mouth form with the mask form.

The only piece I have found that resembles the Dumbarton Oaks piece at all is a fuchsite pendant in the "Before Cortés" exhibition (Easby and Scott 1970: No. 67), which is described as a "Long-nosed head pendant" (I would describe it as long-lipped, rather than long-nosed). The piece is smaller than the Dumbarton Oaks pendant, and the mouth is quite different. A long upper lip curves downward, perhaps into a tongue; it is again possible that this represents a mouth mask. The nose is quite similar to that on the Dumbarton Oaks face, and both pieces have prominent musculature at the superciliary ridges. The "Before Cortés" pendant is said to have come from highland Guatemala, and is dated to the "Late Preclassic, 450–1 B.C." This may suggest a provenience for the Dumbarton Oaks piece, which must certainly come late in the Olmec period.

It is interesting to speculate on the possible use of such an object. Although the piece is small, the stone is fine, and it may have been worn as the central element in a necklace, or as a headdress element. It is also possible that it may have been used to ornament a basalt or other stone sculpture, for I think that it is not impossible that the Olmec clothed their sculpture (Benson 1971: 35).

KNEELING FIGURE (FIGS. 10 AND 11)

The most recent acquisition at Dumbarton Oaks is an Olmec kneeling figure acquired from the collection of Mr. and Mrs. John H. Hauberg, Seattle, and formerly in the collection of Ferdinand Ries, Eschborn, Frankfurt, Germany. It was exhibited in the "Before Cortés" exhibition at the Metropolitan Museum of Art (Easby and Scott 1970: No. 43). The piece is said to have come from Petalcingo, Puebla, in 1928. With it in the Ries Collection, and believed to have come from the same place, were the head of a larger figure and a standing figure of a man, not unlike the first standing figure discussed above, smaller than the Hauberg figure, and damaged.

The Hauberg–Dumbarton Oaks figure is of serpentine, with traces of red pigment, and measures nineteen centimeters high. The round, drilled eyes were, apparently, once inlaid. The figure is kneeling, with legs apart and thighs collapsed on calves; the arms go almost straight down and rest on the knees. The figure has a monumental quality—but most monumental figures with arms going straight down are seated cross-legged. The closest comparisons are with Arroyo Sonso Monument 1 (Nomland 1932) and La Venta Monument 74 (de la Fuente 1973: No. 83).

The figure has a nude human body, with no indication of sex; there is some indication

Fig. 10 Kneeling figure with were-jaguar head. Access. No. B-603.OS.

Fig. 11 Side view of Figure 10.

of pectoral muscles. The head is of the general type described as a "transformation figure" by Peter Furst (1968), who defines the type as having *"the human skin carved or peeled away to reveal the jaguar beneath" (ibid.:* 151). Hair is incised in two zones at the back and sides of the figure; the zones are marked off by thicker lines. In this plane, at each side, is a human ear. The top of the head is on a slightly lower plane; it is smooth except for a slight cleft, and it has feline ears at the top; these are placed rather high on the head, suggesting the possibility of a feline other than a jaguar

(Leopold 1972: 464–87). A raised pattern over each eye also suggests the musculature over the superciliary ridge that is more prominent on felines other than jaguars (*ibid.*). There is a hollow under the eyes, and the malar bone is exaggerated. The mouth is an unusual variant of the Olmec mouth, and the figure is bearded. There is a triangular form at the shoulder line at each side, which, together with a shape at the front of the neck, suggests that the head is bursting through the skin of the human body.

There are a number of these transformation

106

figures, and they have a considerable range of depiction. The Princeton Art Museum has a figure in almost-identical pose, with similar muscle modeling, hair incision, ear design, and carving of the hollows at the shoulder line. This piece and that at Dumbarton Oaks may well have been made by the same sculptor. The Princeton piece has been described as a man turning into a frog, for, instead of jaguar characteristics added to a human figure, it has a frog incised on the top of the head. It has the planar differentiation that suggests the peeled-away face, but here, instead of jaguar characteristics below, there is a strongly modeled human face that is clearly a portrait. A broken area on the chin suggests that it, too, once had a small beard. Perhaps there is the indication here that these figures show more than simple shaman transformation; felines and Olmec rulers were interchangeable (see M. Coe 1972). There is a great deal of cinnabar on the Princeton figure, except in the area around the lower torso and genitals, which suggests that it once wore some sort of kilt or short trousers, giving evidence for the theory that nude Olmec figures may have been dressed on certain occasions (Benson 1971: 35).

A small serpentine were-jaguar figure in the Constance McCormick Fearing Collection (P. Furst 1968: Fig. 3) has its proper right leg in a pose similar to that of the Princeton and Hauberg–Dumbarton Oaks figures, but the left leg is shown in a squatting position. The up-tilted head has a jaguar face with flame eyebrows beneath the line of a raised area along the upper part of the head. This figure looks as if it might have been made by the same sculptor who carved a head broken from a figurine, said to have come from Tabasco, that is now in the Museo Nacional de Antropología (*ibid*.: Fig. 2). The mouth, nose, and deep-set eyes are similar, although the head has a kind of vein-tracing instead of the flame eyebrows of the Fearing figure.

Peter Furst (1968: Fig. 1) published a standing serpentine figure at Dumbarton Oaks as one of the prototypical transformation figures. Another piece, carved of less fine stone, in a private collection in Los Angeles, is a standing figure of feline proportions, with the proper left arm down at the side and the proper right arm bent and raised to the height of the chest, where there is a deeply incised four-pointed "star." Rather than a peeled-back layer of skin, there is a thick band at the back of the head. There is also a line along the chin that looks as if it might indicate a mask; however, no other edge indicates a mask. The flame eyebrows again have a veinlike look.

A small standing figure in the Guennol Collection is a curious variation on these figures in that, in addition to a were-jaguar face, it has a caplike headdress with jaguar ears on it. It is, in some respects, closer to a small jaguar figure at Dumbarton Oaks (P. Furst 1968: Fig. 1) that stands like a human being.

The Hauberg–Dumbarton Oaks figure is also comparable to other figures that are *not* transformation figures. A figure from Puebla, which is similar in pose, is in the collection of Jay C. Leff (Easby 1966: No. 3). This is considerably larger ($11\frac{1}{2}$ in. high) than the Hauberg–Dumbarton Oaks figure, but has a body in the same position—although the Leff figure is slightly more erect—and with about the same degree of musculature. The technique of hair incision is comparable, and the figure is also bearded. This is a most extraordinary beard, for it seems to be attached below the chin and to go around the side of the jaw. A figure in similar pose, in the Museo Nacional (Bernal 1967: Fig. 188), is beardless and has a particularly long head with incised hair, falling, as does the Leff piece, in curving arcs. The Leff and Museo Nacional figures share the same dolichocephalic head that is rather small at the top and broader through the cheeks. They look almost as if they might have been a pair.

The bearded figure from the Ulúa Valley, Honduras (Bernal 1969a: Pl. 102; Easby and Scott 1970: No. 65), is in the same kneeling pose, but has arms that are rather more bent than those of most of the figures described above. It is not a transformation figure.

The Hauberg–Dumbarton Oaks figure thus seems to stand on a borderline between two types of figures—transformation figures and a nameless category of those that are in the same pose that it holds, are sometimes bearded, and are *not* transformation figures. One of the things that we most need to know is what these overlappings mean and how the iconographic material is interchanged. A further quest would be the understanding of the relationship between transformation figures and were-jaguar figures.

CONCLUSION

The history of the Robert Woods Bliss Collection, as indicated in the files and publications, essentially parallels the history of Olmec studies, reflecting changing opinions and descriptions. In addition to catalogue publications of the National Gallery of Art (1947), Lothrop *et al.* (1957), and Dumbarton Oaks (1963, 1969), other Olmec objects at Dumbarton Oaks have been published in some detail by Peterson and Horcasitas (1957), M. Coe (1966a, 1967b), P. Furst (1968), and Benson (1971); and the Olmec collection in general has been more sketchily illustrated by, among others, Covarrubias (1944, 1946b, 1957), Kubler (1962), M. Coe (1965a, 1965b), Bernal (1969a), Joralemon (1971), and Benson (1976).

Delgado's (1965) paper does not reproduce the Bliss object that belongs in the category he deals with (Access. No. B-11.05), but his observations are relevant to that object, and may be considered a publication of it.

Descriptions of the collection provide clues to information on seriation and geographical distribution, as well as raising a number of iconographic questions, some of which I have indicated here. Who has beards and when? What categories of creatures are being described in the various forms of sculpture? What degrees of supernaturalness can be defined in the representations? What is the significance of the poses in which figures are represented? What relationship do the small figures of jade and serpentine have to the basalt monuments? What do these figures tell us of myth and ceremony? What are the regional and temporal differences, and what are the influences that come from what places at what times? Matthew Stirling found and defined the material for us. But there is still a great deal of work left to be done to understand its significance.

Concave Mirrors from the Site of La Venta, Tabasco:
Their Occurrence, Mineralogy, Optical Description, and Function

Robert F. Heizer and Jonas E. Gullberg

UNIVERSITY OF CALIFORNIA, BERKELEY

The great Olmec ceremonial site of La Venta in the state of Tabasco lies on a small island formed by the sloughs and branches of the Tonalá River as it flows over the swampy coastal plain to empty into the Bay of Campeche. Findings resulting from the excavations of 1942 and 1943 by Philip Drucker, Matthew Stirling, and Waldo Wedel on joint Smithsonian Institution–National Geographic Society expeditions have been published by Drucker (1947, 1952), the Stirlings (1942), and Matthew Stirling (1943a). In 1955 an expedition under the auspices of the National Geographic Society, the Smithsonian Institution, and the University of California, under the direction of Philip Drucker and Robert F. Heizer, excavated at La Venta for nearly five months. In this period it was possible to make an accurate map of the site, and to carry out extensive and controlled stratigraphic excavations. Numerous buried offerings or dedicatory caches, usually consisting of carved and polished jade objects, such as celts, figurines, and beads, were found. These ritual offerings were buried by the builders of the La Venta site mainly along the centerline of the site, which runs seven degrees west of north, or in the low clay platform mounds inside the rectangular Ceremonial Court, which forms the central feature of the site. On the basis of nine radiocarbon dates for the La Venta site (Drucker *et al.* 1957) and the stratigraphy represented in the various layers of clay fills and floor-surfacings, four periods of construction have been identi-

fied in the site. These are designated Phases I to IV. The site was built at the beginning of Phase I, which is dated by radiocarbon at about 800 B.C. Phases II, III, and IV mark successive construction and restoration periods when the floor levels in the Ceremonial Court and mound structures were raised and resurfaced with brightly colored clays. The end of the last phase (IV) comes at about 400 B.C. Table I gives the information on La Venta radiocarbon dates. (See Postscript for a revised and corrected list of these dates.)

In the 1955 season, two complete concave mirrors were found. As the mirrors are closely similar in size, and therefore make a pair, so was their occurrence similar. One was found in each of the dedicatory offerings that were numbered 9 and 11 (Drucker *et al.* 1959). The two offerings lay at the same depth from the surface, and the center of each was precisely four and one half feet (1.47 m.) distant from the centerline of the site. A line connecting their midpoints crosses the centerline at right angles. Each offering contained, in addition to the mirror, nine jade or serpentine celts laid out in three rows, and many small globular jade beads (907 in one offering, 1274 in the other). The layout of the two offerings is shown in the accompanying illustrations (Fig. 1).

In addition to the two mirrors found in 1955 (Figs. 2 and 3)—which are the largest and most complete specimens known—five other examples, some of them fragments, were found in 1942 and 1943 at La Venta (Fig. 4). Table 2

TABLE 1. RADIOCARBON DATES OF CHARCOAL
SAMPLES COLLECTED AT LA VENTA IN 1955

Sample No.	Age in Years	Date (B.C.)	Phase
M-535	3110 ± 300	1154 ± 300	I
M-529	2860 ± 300	904 ± 300	I
M-530	2760 ± 300	804 ± 300	II
M-534	2670 ± 300	714 ± 300	I
M-532	2650 ± 300	694 ± 300	I
M-531	2560 ± 300	604 ± 300	I
M-536	2530 ± 300	574 ± 300	II?
M-528	2400 ± 250	444 ± 250	Post-IV
M-533	2130 ± 300	174 ± 300	Post-IV

Fig. 1 La Venta Offerings, 1955 excavations. *a.* Offering 11. *b.* Offering 9. Photographs courtesy of the National Geographic Society.

summarizes the measurements and characteristics of the several mirrors.

The materials from which the mirrors are made indicate a source in the metamorphic and granitic province to the south of La Venta. The mirrors are fashioned from fairly large pieces of material, 8 to 15 centimeters in diameter. The unpolished back surfaces have the appearance of stream-rounded boulders, and it is probable that the material was obtained from stream-bottoms in the form of float boulders which had eroded from their primary source.[1]

[1] Since an exact description of the materials may ultimately serve to identify the exact location of the source deposit, we give here the data on the mineralogy of the specimens. The large mirror from Offering No. 9 is a coarse-grained aggregate of three minerals—magnetite, hematite, and ilmenite—of which magnetite is the most abundant and hematite the least abundant component. The hematite occurs in streaks which envelop grains of magnetite, suggesting that the specimen is of hydrothermal, or vein, origin. The Knoop hardness number (Robertson and Van Meter 1951) of the ilmenite is 740-920; of the magnetite 525-555; and of the hematite 330-465. The material of the complete mirror from Offering No. 11 is composed of a fine-grained aggregate of optically anisotropic crystals which are weakly magnetic and identifiable as ilmenite. Under high magnification, exsolution intergrowths of hematite comprising about ten percent of the specimen may be observed. The Knoop hardness number of the ilmenite is 740-780, and of the hematite 480. Specimen No. 1942-A (Museo Nacional No. 13-267) is highly magnetic and is composed almost entirely of coarse grains of magnetite whose Knoop hardness is 525. The specimen from the Mound A-2 fill, found in 1942 (Museo Nacional No. 13-266), is very similar to the specimen last described, although the lower Knoop hardness number of the magnetite (485) suggests that the two

pieces were not cut from the same block of material. Specimen No. 1943-E (Museo Nacional No. 13-433) is distinctive in that lamellar blades of hematite constitute the entire specimen. The Knoop hardness number of the hematite is 600. Specimen 1943-F (Museo Nacional No. 13-435) is composed of a fine-grained aggregate of optically anisotropic crystals which are weakly magnetic and have a Knoop hardness number of 680 (ilmenite). Under high magnification, exsolution intergrowths of hematite comprising about ten percent of the specimen may be observed. This piece is very similar in properties to the specimen from Offering No. 11, although grain size of the hematite is smaller. Specimen 1943-N (Museo Nacional No. 13-438) is very similar to the material of the mirror from Offering No. 11, although the grain size is coarser. The Knoop hardness number of the ilmenite is 870-920. We are indebted to Dr. Garniss H. Curtis, Professor of Geology, University of California, for providing these data.

Fig. 2 Concave mirror from La Venta Offering 11. *a.* Obverse. *b.* Reverse. Photographs courtesy of the National Geographic Society.

Fig. 3 Concave mirror from La Venta Offering 9. *a.* Obverse. *b.* Reverse. Photographs courtesy of the National Geographic Society.

The technical and artistic quality of the La Venta mirrors is such that the present authors believe that, for their age, there are no specimens of lapidary art known from the aboriginal New World that exceed them. Such a judgment might be argued, but the Olmec mirrors are surely more than expert stone-fashioning, since they have specific optical properties that were deliberately aimed at and that were, no doubt, tradition-directed. There is an essential similarity in all of the specimens, even though their dimensions and focal lengths differ. The degree of polish of the concave surfaces is remarkably good, and seems to represent the limit of perfection which the material will allow. No clear trace of abrasion marks on the polished surfaces can be detected. One's first impression is that the mirrors are spheri-

cal, but careful study of the curvatures proves them to have a changing radius of curvature from the center to the outer edge, the radius of curvature becoming progressively greater as the edge is approached (Figs. 5 and 6). The effect is almost identical to the modern practice of parabolizing optical reflectors. The outer local flattening improves the performance of a reflector in focusing radiant energy. Such parabolizing is done along both the major and minor axes of the mirrors, and a description of the surfaces must take into account changing curvatures in at least two directions. This subtle and technically remarkable molding of the surface may be a result of either a high degree of manipulative sophistication or of something that inadvertently followed from the type of stroke and pressure employed in the hand-

111

Fig. 4 Mirrors from the 1942 and 1943 excavations at La Venta. Photograph courtesy of the National Geographic Society.

grinding-and-polishing technique. The theory that a characteristic handstroke explains the lesser curvature in the outer zones seems contradicted by the sharp clarity of the beginning of the flattened borders of each of the mirrors. The reversed border curvature on the specimens would seem to demand the use of a special bench tool for grinding and polishing the relatively narrow borders. In a culture that lacked metals, the selection of these minerals for making the mirrors leaves little room for doubt that the choice was deliberate and was determined by the favorable semi-metallic characteristics. Obsidian might conceivably have served for making such mirrors, but the obsidian used at La Venta is scarcely opaque enough for this purpose. Massive pyrite would have served also, but was perhaps not available.

Since theses mirrors seem to be optical devices, we may inquire as to their possible purpose and function. Attempts by us to kindle a fire with these reflectors met with no success, and we cannot now claim that this was one use to which they were put. Every one of the mirrors bears along one edge conical or biconical drilled holes (see Table 2). These were presumably for the purpose of attaching a cord. There is evidence that the mirrors were worn on the chest and attached to a cord which was looped around the neck. The heroic-sized seated human figure (Monument 23) excavated in 1955 from Mound A-5 at La Venta, and now in the Museo Nacional, wears on the chest a flat oval ornament which, by reason of its shape, size, and concave surface, is identifiable as a concave mirror. What may also be intended to represent such mirrors are plaques depicted on other La Venta sculptures, for example: Stela 2 (Drucker 1952: Fig. 49); the individuals numbered "1" and "6" on Altar 5 (*ibid.*: Fig. 52); and the seated jade figurine (*ibid.*: Pl. 46, Fig. 1) who wears an actual flat miniature mirror. This last specimen is paral-

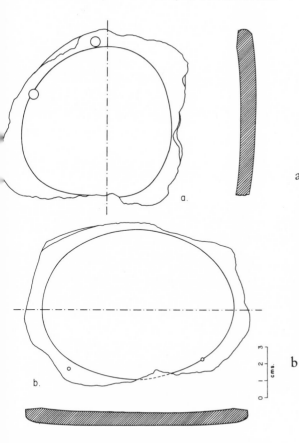

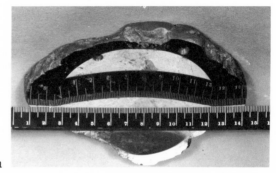

a

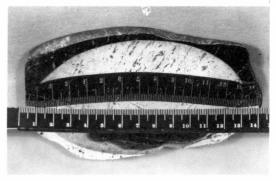

b

Fig. 6 Radius of curvature of mirrors in Figures 3 and 2. *a*. From Offering 9. *b*. From Offering 11. Photographs courtesy of the National Geographic Society.

Fig. 5 Radius of curvature of mirrors in Figures 3 and 2. *a*. From Offering 9. *b*. From Offering 11.

leled, incidentally, in some of the Tlatilco clay figures which have attached, presumably by some adhesive, miniature flat hematite reflectors on the upper chest (Porter 153: Pl. 4B). It thus appears probable that the concave mirrors were worn at La Venta on a cord about the neck. Its depiction on the statue and the small seated figurine, both of which were associated with the ceremonial center at La Venta, strongly suggests that the mirrors here served some ceremonial or ritual use, and that their use was reserved for the priests. Furthermore, mirrors are among the items that occur in the dedicatory caches or ritual offerings at La Venta, and their occurrence in this context emphasizes their nonsecular function in Olmec culture.

The reflected image of the sun is projected with some intensity for a short distance by these mirrors, and it is possible that the mirrors, when worn by priests who stood facing the sun, flashed the sun's light in the eyes of the audience. Such speculation should not be taken as anything but an effort to guess at the original function of the mirrors. The unique tableau represented by the sixteen jade and serpentine figurines found grouped together at La Venta in the 1955 excavations provides some suggestion of a small body of priests performing a ritual within a sufficiently restricted compass for the concave reflectors to have been really effective. It must be noted, however, that no mirror was found with the figurine group, and that none of the figurines wore either a miniature or carved representation of a mirror.

It has been suggested to us by Carmen Cook de Leonard and Willem Roos that the drilled holes near the edges of the mirrors may not have been made by the same persons who ground the specimens, since these holes (see

TABLE 2. LA VENTA CONCAVE MIRRORS: MEASUREMENTS AND CHARACTERISTICS

Phase	From Offering No.	Museo Nacional Catalog No.	Predominant Mineral Type	Mirror Diameter, Major Axis (mm)*	Mirror Diameter, Minor Axis (mm)*	Principal Focus, Major Axis (cm)*	Principal Focus, Minor Axis (cm)*	Weight (grams)	Mirror Thickness at Center (mm)*	Number and Type of Perforations	Illustration
IV	9	–	magnetite	96	90	24.5	21	391.2	7.9	2 biconical	Fig. 1a, b
IV	11	–	ilmenite	117	89	30	16	348.2	7.4	2 conical	Fig. 2a, b
IV	1942-A	13-267	magnetite	58	46	57	35.5	45.4	4.3	3 conical	Fig. 4c
IV?	Mound A-2 fill (1942)	13-266	magnetite	(9)	(9)	(14)	(14)	33.5	(3.8)	notches only	Fig. 4b
II	1943-E	13-433	hematite	75	(62)	8	6.5	88.9	3.6	2 conical	Fig. 4e
IV	1943-F	13-435	ilmenite	(91)	(74)	10	8	258.0	8.1	2 biconical	Fig. 4d
IV	1943-N	13-438	ilmenite	43	41	11.5	10.5	116.6	6.6	4 biconical 1 conical	Fig. 4a

*Reconstructed measurements are indicated by parentheses.

especially Fig. 4d) appear in many cases to be carelessly placed and at times are in the polished reflecting area rather than in the border or rim. With such virtuosity represented by the grinding and finishing, it is hard to believe that such lack of care in placing the holes would have been practiced by the same person who fashioned the pieces. It may be suggested, therefore, that the La Venta mirrors could be pieces secured by trade from some distant people who manufactured them. If this is the correct explanation of their presence at La Venta, future excavation in Mesoamerica at some archaeological site may be expected to produce additional undrilled examples. The alternative to an outland source of the mirrors is that the pieces date from an earlier period of Olmec culture development, and exist at the La Venta site as treasured heirlooms or antiques. An association with ancient times and the lost art of mirror grinding may have served to make the mirrors as precious as, for example, jadeite celts and figurines, and therefore deserving of burial in the ritual offerings so abundant at La Venta. In favor of this theory is the fact that fragments and broken mirrors (Fig. 4) were deemed sufficiently valuable to warrant being placed in important offerings.

Aboriginal mirrors in the New World have been discussed by several authors, among whom may be mentioned Merwin and Vaillant (1932: 87); Lothrop (1937: 102–5); Mason (1927); Kidder, Jennings, and Shook (1946: 126–33); and Nordenskiöld (1926). Nordenskiöld discusses concave mirrors and cites certain historical documents and specimens that would appear to indicate that these do exist. However, one of the present authors (J.E.G.), while in Europe in 1957, examined the obsidian and pyrite mirrors in the British Museum and the Musée de l'Homme, and discovered that the obsidian mirrors described by Nordenskiöld are massive rectangular blocks with *plane* or *convex* surfaces. The pyrite examples are generally small, and are also convex, and (as pointed out by some of the authors cited earlier) are probably not to be considered mirrors as such.

POSTSCRIPT

The above article about the metallic mirrors from the Olmec site of La Venta was written by Dr. Gullberg (now deceased) about 1959 for the Mexican journal *YAN* (now defunct). Much, but not all, of the data offered here were published in the main site report (Drucker *et al.* 1959: Appendix 3). Additional, though rather limited, scientific excavations at La Venta since 1955 (reported in *Contributions of the Archaeological Research Facility;* see Heizer, Drucker, and Graham 1968; Heizer, Graham, and Napton 1968; Morrison *et al.* 1970) did not turn up additional mirror specimens. But from other areas of Mexico, ilmenite artifacts have been discovered. One such is the broken and longitudinally grooved hematite bar recovered by Michael Coe from San Lorenzo, and illustrated and reported on by John B. Carlson (1975) who believes that it served as a lodestone compass. Why, and whether, the Olmec of San Lorenzo needed such a compass is puzzling, and I personally doubt that magnetic north meant anything to them.

More recently Gordon Ekholm (personal communication) informs me that the American Museum of Natural History owns two concave mirrors (of hematite-ilmenite presumably) which are "somewhat larger and somewhat better preserved than those from La Venta." Their provenience is unknown, but Ekholm says they are "typical Olmec objects." His opinion I accept. In June or July of 1972, at Pleasantville, New York, he succeeded in generating fire from one of these mirrors. The attempt to start fire with the second was unsuccessful. One of these mirrors has a concavity twelve inches in diameter, the surface being "a practically perfect circle," and a focal length of thirty-three centimeters. The second mirror has an oval concavity measuring 11 by 10.4 inches, and a longer (but unspecified) focal length. Dr. Ekholm tells me that the description of these two mirrors and his experiments in using them to generate fire is contained in Volume I of the 40th Congresso Internazionale degli Americanisti, Rome (Ekholm 1973). I have not been able to consult this paper.

So, *some* Olmec mirrors could have been used to start fires, and, if this was done in a ritual context, it could be one more bit of evidence of the existence at this early period of one element of the distinctive Mesoamerican culture pattern. Most such known mirrors could not have served this purpose, however, and their primary function (beyond serving as ornaments, which may be secondary) still remains a mystery.

The dating of the Gulf Coast Olmec sites has been difficult to determine. It was assumed before 1940 that the sites dated from the Classic Period—a reasonable guess in view of the size of sites such as San Lorenzo and La Venta, and the large stone sculptures. Radiocarbon dating of the charcoal samples collected in 1955 gave ages which placed the site (as Covarrubias had long, long insisted) in the Middle Preclassic Period (Drucker *et al.* 1957; Drucker *et al.* 1959: 264–7). The accuracy of these carbon-14 dates was questioned by W. Coe and Stuckenrath (1964), and, in an effort to resolve the question, we returned to La Venta in 1967 to reopen the site and to make careful charcoal collections from the deposits (Berger, Graham, and Heizer 1967). The results were surprising in that the age of the site in radiocarbon years was now pushed back about 200 years, our conclusion being that the main site was initially constructed about 1100 to 1000 B.C. and abandoned about 600 B.C. Some of the original charcoal samples dated at the University of Michigan in 1957 (Drucker *et al.* 1957) were redated at the UCLA radiocarbon laboratory, and new check samples were also analyzed. The results are given in the adjacent table and may be compared to those given earlier in this paper.

J. W. Pires-Ferreira (n.d.) has analyzed a number of small, flat, iron-ore mirrors from Oaxacan sites and San Lorenzo, all of Early Formative date. Her analytical technique employed Mössbauer spectroscopy. Iron-ore (hematite, ilmenite, magnetite) source samples were secured from fifty-four localities in the Valley of Oaxaca, the Isthmus of Tehuántepec, highland Chiapas, and Morelos.

Two of the hematite La Venta mirrors are

TABLE 3. RADIOCARBON DATES OF CHARCOAL SAMPLES COLLECTED AT LA VENTA IN 1955 AND 1967

Sample No.*	Date (B.C.) ($t^{1/2}$ 5568±30)	Date (B.C.) ($t^{1/2}$ 5730±30)
M-528	2400 ± 250	2475 ± 250
UCLA-1283	2380 ± 60	2450 ± 60
M-530	2760 ± 300	2845 ± 300
UCLA-1284B	2550 ± 60	2625 ± 60
UCLA-1284A	2530 ± 60	2605 ± 60
M-531	2560 ± 300	2540 ± 300
UCLA-902	2940 ± 80	3030 ± 80
M-532	2650 ± 300	2730 ± 300
UCLA-1285	2820 ± 60	2905 ± 60
M-533	2130 ± 300	2195 ± 300
UCLA-1287	2415 ± 60	2490 ± 60
UCLA-903	2460 ± 60	2530 ± 60
M-534	2670 ± 300	2750 ± 300
UCLA-1286	3000 ± 60	3090 ± 60

*Samples M-535 and M-529 were not redated because of insufficient sample size. M-536 was not redated because it could not be correlated with the La Venta building phases.

tentatively identified as coming from a geologic source of Cerro Prieto at Niltepec on the Tehuántepec Isthmus—a possible source earlier suggested by Williams and Heizer (1965: 12). The other La Venta mirrors did not match closely any known geologic sources. While these are limited results, they are important in showing how the source of the mirror material can be located.

No exact count of these concave metallic mirrors of Middle Formative Olmec age has been made, but Pires-Ferreira (*op. cit.*) mentions one from Arroyo Pesquero in Las Choapas, Veracruz, and Dr. Carlson (personal communication) tells me that he knows of one at Princeton and two others in the hands of private collectors.

A really thorough study of these concave mirrors of Olmec manufacture should be made because they are, for their age, the most remarkable technological artifacts known in the New World.

Olmec Concave Iron-Ore Mirrors:
The Aesthetics of a Lithic Technology and the Lord of the Mirror

(With an Illustrated Catalogue of Mirrors)[1]

John B. Carlson

THE UNIVERSITY OF MARYLAND

We believe that it is possible to make a burning-instrument of glass [a burning mirror] such that it has a special property, namely that one can make lamps from it which produce fire in temples and at sacrifices and immolations, so that the fire is clearly seen to burn the sacrificial victims; . . . especially on the days of great celebration: this causes the people of those cities to marvel. That is something which we too shall do. (From *Diocles: On Burning Mirrors,* Greek, *ca.* early second century B.C. [Toomer 1976: 44])

In its reflection one can read one's heart, And also see the image of one's face. (From an inscription on a Six Dynasties Chinese bronze mirror [Swallow 1937: Fig. 56 caption])

INTRODUCTION

The Formative Olmec civilization in Mesoamerica created unique, superbly crafted concave mirrors from iron-ore minerals. Words and photographs cannot convey a real feel for the technical quality and artistic power of these mirrors—they possess a remarkable appeal for both the eye and the mind. Of several dozen known examples, unfortunately only a few have been found in archaeological context. Nonetheless, it seems quite clear that they were produced only during the period of Olmec florescence—conservatively, within the Early and Middle Formative Periods (1500-300 B.C.).

This study will present a three-part analysis of this most ancient concave-mirror tradition, including: (1) an illustrated catalogue of all examples known to the author, with a technical analysis of those available for study; (2) the results of a successful series of experiments to duplicate and shed light on the Olmec-mirror lapidary technology; and (3) a four-part series of speculative interrelated hypotheses on the use and purpose of the mirrors in the Olmec and general Mesoamerican cultural contexts.

BACKGROUND: MIRRORS IN ANCIENT AMERICA

Nordenskiöld (1926) offered one of the earliest general accounts of New World mirrors; however, no Olmec concave mirrors appear in the European collections that he examined. He quotes (*ibid.:* 103) the well-known statement by the Inca Garcilaso de la Vega attributing ritual fire-making by a burning-mirror method to the Inca. According to Garcilaso (1966, I: 362), new fire was generated at the time of the great sacrifice of the Inca feast of the sun by the chief priest who employed a "highly burnished concave bowl," which was

---

[1] This article is an augmented revision of a paper entitled "Olmec Concave Iron Ore Mirrors: Technology and Purpose" originally presented at the XLII Congrès International des Américanistes in Paris, France, September 2-9, 1976.

part of the armlet of his costume. If sufficient sunlight was not available, a fire-drill was used. Both Nordenskiöld and, later, Cooper (1949) expressed serious doubts about Garcilaso's claim, but the method is clearly not implausible, as the discovery of this technique requires no theoretical knowledge of the laws of reflection and may have been the result of a much older native American concave-mirror tradition, as we shall see.

Mason (1927) discussed obsidian and pyrite or marcasite mirrors, most of which have been found in Mesoamerica. The iron pyrite (iron sulfide) minerals were most often used as inlays to make flat mosaic mirrors with elaborately carved slate backs. Perhaps the finest known example of this technique from the Formative Period is the large mosaic mirror from the Olmec site of Las Bocas in western Puebla (dated *ca.* 1000 B.C.) which was described by P. Furst (n.d.) and analyzed by Marshack (1975). The pyrite mosaic-mirror tradition in Mesoamerica has recently been carefully summarized and thoroughly documented by Strauss (n.d.) with an annotated catalogue of carved-slate mirror backs.

To the best of my knowledge, the first examples of Olmec concave iron-oxide-ore mirrors were discovered in the early 1940's at La Venta, Tabasco, during the archaeological excavations directed by Matthew W. Stirling. The results of the three seasons of work have been described in a series of popular articles in the *National Geographic Magazine* by Stirling (1940a, 1943a) and the Stirlings (1942), and in *Smithsonian Institution Bureau of American Ethnology Bulletins 138* (Stirling 1943b), *153* (Drucker 1952), and *170* (Drucker *et. al.* 1959). Although one small atypical magnetite mirror and a magnetite-mirror fragment were discovered in the 1942 season (Catalogue Nos. 3 and 4, respectively), the first complete mirror recognized as such was found during the 1943 season on the north arm of a cruciform cache of jade and serpentine celts (Drucker 1952). This find was designated Offering 1943-E and the mirror is Number 5 in the present catalogue (Fig. 5). Later finds from the 1955 season, including the spectacular mirrors found in Offerings 9 and 11 (Catalogue Nos. 1 and 2, Figs.

1 and 2), are described in detail by Drucker, Heizer, and Squier (1959).

In the only previous real analysis (the four-page Appendix 3 of the latter publication), Gullberg (1959) presented optical and mineralogical analyses of the seven La Venta mirrors and fragments with a few speculations as to the technique of manufacture and purpose. Curtis (1959) showed that the mirrors are made of all three major iron-oxide ores: magnetite, hematite, and ilmenite[2]. These are perhaps the ideal mineral substances to use for nontarnishing metallic-finish mirrors. Iron pyrites were apparently never used by the Olmec for concave mirrors. Pyrites are not fully oxidized minerals and tend to undergo almost total decomposition in an oxidizing environment. Most mirror backs now have little but a yellowish residue that was once a highly reflective metallic-finish pyrite surface.

The Olmec concave iron-oxide-ore mirrors, by contrast, still maintain the original high-quality polished reflective finish on the front faces, which have a concave center and convex beveled surround. The sides and backs were only crudely ground or sawed off as a general rule, but one example (Catalogue No. 18, Fig. 18) has a ground and polished convex back of spherical figure and mirror-quality finish. The concavity was found to be "paraboloidal"[3] in every artifact from La Venta that was examined by Gullberg, with either a circular or elliptical border, often with two separate focal lengths associated with the major and minor axes. The mirrors were apparently worn as pectoral pendants, usually possessing one or two drilled holes for suspension.

A CATALOGUE OF OLMEC CONCAVE IRON-ORE MIRRORS[4]

Table 1 is a catalogue of twenty-four concave mirrors and fragments, including those

---

[2] Pure varieties of magnetite have the composition Fe_3O_4; hematite is Fe_2O_3. Ilmenite is titanium iron-oxide-ore mineral with composition $FeTiO_3$.

[3] By "paraboloidal" I mean that the radius of curvature increases as we move away from the optical axis, *i.e.,* it is deeper in the center but not necessarily a true paraboloid.

[4] The catalogue contains all examples known to the

from La Venta, with a data list and derived parameters. Photographs of many of these artifacts are reproduced with the present study—for convenience, the figure numbers correspond to the catalogue numbers of those illustrated. Ten of the catalogued mirrors, not including the La Venta seven, were inspected and measured by the author. The mirrors are clearly divisible into two classes: Type 1 (see Figs. 19 and 20) is smaller and possesses only one hole for suspension; Type 2 (see, for example, Figs. 13–18) is larger, with two (or more) holes. Within those classes there is considerable variation in mirror boundary, composition, focal length, and most other parameters. The concave and convex portions of the mirror surfaces were examined with a microscope; the Foucault optical test for sphericity was performed (when practical); and a dial-gauge "spherometer" was used to determine the radii of curvature (this dial-gauge device was designed to measure the sagitta of curvature against a known chord length; see Figs. 15b and 17b). In addition, focal spots were observed in sunlight, and in some cases objects of the night sky were observed in reflection. Simple mineralogical tests were also performed.

From these analyses several generalizations emerge:

(1) Most mirrors were paraboloidal.

(2) All complete mirrors had drilled holes, presumably for the purpose of suspension.

(3) The shape of each mirror stone is unique, with the concavity usually, but not always, conforming to the peculiar shape of the stone. This aesthetic is striking—the mirror gains power from the shape of the stone. In a majority of cases, the stone is clearly sawed from a larger block and the edges are worked into a cartouche shape, but in several cases the shape of the original stone is apparent. No example has perfect symmetry—this almost seems to be purposely avoided.

(4) The major axes of the concavities with elliptical boundaries usually do not exactly align with the axis of the mirror stone itself (see Figs. 11 and 18).

(5) The drilled holes are often unsymmetrically placed relative to the boundary of the concavity, being either inside or outside of the concavity. They are conical or biconical—the conical examples are usually drilled from the back to the front.

Space does not permit a detailed commentary on each individual mirror, but some peculiarities are worthy of note. Though most were paraboloidal, two large mirrors (Catalogue Nos. 13 and 15, Figs. 13 and 15) allegedly found at Arroyo Pesquero[5] were determined to be quite spherical in optical figure. The border of Number 13 was circular, but that of Number 15 was ovoid and incomplete. Both were of the same mineral composition. Interestingly, Number 13 is the only example that has so far been successfully used to start a fire (Ekholm 1973—see Fig. 13b), but Number 15 is guaranteed to be equally Promethean. In general, most individual Olmec mirrors are not good burning mirrors in spite of their typical paraboloidal figure—they are too small and have relatively low surface reflectivity. However, their possible use for the production of smoke provides an intriguing speculation.

author. Peter Furst (n.d.: 189) refers to three other possibilities, but they may not be Olmec iron-oxide-ore mirrors of the type discussed in the present study. So far as Western Mexico is concerned, some metallic, parabolically concave "mirrors" of magnetite and ilmenite almost indistinguishable from those of La Venta have been found in Guerrero, and reportedly also in Michoacan and Nayarit. A small concave "mirror" of superb workmanship, said to have been part of a cache of carved stone objects found in the Mezcala River area in Guerrero, is now in a private collection in Mexico City. Another fine example is in the Michoacan State Museum in Morelia, along with a La Venta-style Olmec jade figurine. According to one of our workers, a small concave mirror cut from a pyrite nodule was found in a shaft tomb near Tequilita, but this could not be confirmed.
There are undoubtedly other mirrors in museums and collections around the world, and future Olmec archaeology cannot fail to unearth many more examples.

[5] Arroyo Pesquero is the generally accepted name of an important Olmec site located near the town of Las Choapas, Veracruz, on the border of the state of Tabasco. Four large mirrors are alleged to have been recovered from this site (Figs. 13-16).

John B. Carlson

TABLE 1. CATALOGUE OF OLMEC CONCAVE IRON-ORE MIRRORS

Catalogue Number	Whole or Fragment	Type	Identification	Provenience	Composition†	Hol
1	W	2	Offering 9	La Venta	Mag. II-A	2 bicon
2	W	2	Offering 11	La Venta	Il.	2 conic
3	W	2	Offering 1942-A	La Venta	Mag.	3 conic
4	F	?	Mound A-2 fill (1942)	La Venta	Mag. I-C	notches
5	~W	2	Offering 1943-E	La Venta	Hem.	2 conic
6	F	2	Offering 1943-F	La Venta	Il. III-A	2 bicon
7	W$_{br}$	2	Offering 1943-N	La Venta	Il.	4 bicon 1 conic
8	W	2	SPB 358	?	Mag.	2 bicon
9	F	?	SL-NW-MI-2zc	San Lorenzo	Il. III-A	?
10	F	?	RPC 02232	Río Chiquito	Il.	None
11	W	2	Small elliptical concave	Chalcatzingo	Mag.	2
12	2F	?	Sample 92 (2 fragments)	Las Choapas	Il. III-A	?
13	W$_{br}$	2	Large dark concave	Arroyo Pesquero	Hem. ?	2 conic
14	W	2	Large dark concave	Arroyo Pesquero	Hem. ?	2 conic
15	~W$_{br}$	2	Large dark concave	Arroyo Pesquero	Hem. ?	2 conic
16	W	2	Large dark concave	Arroyo Pesquero	Hem. ?	2 ?
17	W	2	"Saddle-shaped flat"	Xochipala	Mag.	2 bicon
18	W	2	"Small elliptical-convex back"	Guerrero	Mag. ?	2 bicon
19	W	1	Small spherical	Guerrero	Mag.	1 bicon
20	W	1	Small spherical	Guerrero	Mag.	1 conic
21	F	?	Small fragment	Guerrero	Mag.	?
22	F	?	MD	Guerrero	Mag.	None
23	F	1	ME	Guerrero	Hem. ?	1 conic
24	F	2	Large elliptical concave	?	?	?
f1	F	–	Small convex fragment	Guerrero	Mag.	None

*One half of the measured radius of curvature at center.
†Magnetite (Mag.), Ilmenite (Il.), Hematite (Hem.). Roman numeral designations are from Pires-Ferreira 197

120

Major Diameter (mm)	Minor Diameter (mm)	Focal Length, Major Diameter (cm)	Focal Length, Minor Diameter (cm)	Central Thickness (mm)	Reference
96	90	25.4	21	7.9	Gullberg 1959
117	89	30	16	7.4	Gullberg 1959
58	46	57	35.5	4.3	Gullberg 1959
(9)	(9)	(14)	(14)	3.8	Gullberg 1959
75	(62)	8	6.5	3.6	Gullberg 1959
(91)	(74)	10	8	8.1	Gullberg 1959
43	41	11.5	10.5	6.6	Gullberg 1959
39	38	17.5	17.5	3	Sotheby Parke Bernet 1975
—	—	—	—	—	Pires-Ferreira 1975
—	—	—	—	—	Coe, personal communication, 1974
21	16	—	—	~4	Grove *et al.* 1976
—	—	—	—	—	Pires-Ferreira 1975
119	119	~18*	~18*	9	Ekholm, personal communication, 1976
113	103	~20*	~14*	9.5	American Museum of Natural History, New York #30.3-1299
137	>110	~15*	~15*	6.4	Private Collection
—	—	—	—	—	Private Collection
73	67	>80*	>80*	11	Gay 1972
37	30	>18*	>12*	6	Private Collection
18	18	~ 5*	~ 5*	10	Private Collection
26	25	~ 8*	~ 8*	4	Private Collection
—	—	—	—	—	Private Collection
25	~17	~18	?	3	Private Collection
~27	17	~45	?	3	Private Collection
—	—	—	—	—	Museo Nacional de Antropología, Mexico
~35	—	~20*	—	9	Private Collection

Mirror Number 17, which comes from the state of Guerrero (Gay 1972: Fig. 38), has an almost flat surface inside an elliptical border and convex beveled surround. Under close examination, it was seen to be hyperboloidal or "saddle-shaped"—concave when viewed along the minor axis, and convex along the major (Fig. 17). This magnetite mirror is clearly of Type 2, but could never have been designed as a burning mirror.

EXPERIMENTAL ARCHAEOLOGY:
THE OLMEC MIRROR LAPIDARY TECHNIQUE

Gullberg (1959) was impressed by the manifest sophistication of the Olmec mirror lapidary technique, both in grinding and polishing the iron-ore minerals. He suggested that special grinding and polishing tools, perhaps of wood charged first with abrasive and then with polishing agents, were necessary to achieve the surface molding, parabolization, convex bevel, and sharply defined border region. He suspected that more than a "characteristic hand-stroke" was necessary to achieve the finished product. Having tried my hand at duplicating the Olmec mirror lapidary technology, I would disagree totally with these earlier speculations. With relatively little time and effort, I found that I could produce both spherical and paraboloidal "Olmec" mirrors of circular or elliptical border. The use of the correct technique is the key.

The method is fundamentally the same as that used in grinding modern concave telescope mirrors. Two "blanks" are used—a tool piece on the bottom and the work piece on top. With suitable grades of wet abrasive compound in between, the work piece is rubbed back and forth over the tool. The tool unavoidably becomes convex as the work piece becomes concave. Any good book on amateur telescope-making will give the details (e.g., A. J. Thompson 1973). A long back-and-forth stroke applied while occasionally rotating the work and tool blanks in opposite directions will almost assure a resultant spherical concave mirror with a circular border. This is true regardless of the original shape of the tool or work piece (see Figs. 3, 4, 7, and 9). The desired symmetry is imposed by rotating the pieces—

the longest axis of the tool seems to dictate the maximum diameter of the concavity. Furthermore, the use of very long circular grinding strokes tends to take more material out of the center and thus parabolizes the mirror in a natural fashion. The skilled lapidary has considerable choice in parabolizing the mirror or not.

The mirrors with elliptical borders are manufactured by using a smaller tool piece with a preselected major and minor axis. It need not be particularly symmetrical (see Fig. 7). The grinding stroke used is ovoid, and the pieces are *not* rotated relative to each other. A characteristic hand motion, without any great display of skill, yields a very symmetrical elliptical concavity indistinguishable from an Olmec original. The border is very sharp, and the surround region does not become scuffed by the interior grinding.

I would submit that these methods and results are so straightforward that they constitute the very origin of the Olmec concave-mirror tradition and aesthetic. In setting out to produce flat surfaces by rubbing two stones together, one inadvertently—and virtually inevitably—produces a concavity in the top piece and a convexity on the bottom. Grinding optically flat surfaces is a difficult task and involves the permutated grinding of at least three blanks.

A major enigma for me had been the nature of the Olmec aesthetic or utility of a concave mirror within a convex beveled mirror surround. The answer now seems clear. In the spirit of economy, the Olmec lapidary used his previous convex tool piece as the new work piece—a central concavity was ground in the old convex tool. In less than half an hour, I ground an elliptical concavity in the center of the spherical convex tool from my previous mirror (Fig. 9). The results were gratifying—it appears that the Olmec mirror aesthetic results from the economy of materials and the grinding technique itself!

In this context, I believe I have found a "missing link" in this process. There is a notable lack of convex-mirror examples among collections of Olmec artifacts. If the above hypothesis is correct, this fact is readily accounted for if the convex tools were virtually all used later to produce new concave mirrors having the unique Olmec aesthetic. Catalogue item f_1 is the only known *convex* spherical mirror fragment of high polish (Fig. 6). It had been broken, and has no holes drilled in it. I would speculate that it was a former tool piece that had been polished in preparation for the grinding of a central concavity. It broke and was discarded. Note that this fragment is very similar in size and appearance to the tool piece (Fig. 7) that was used to grind a concavity in a previous tool piece (Fig. 4) and produce a new mirror with a central elliptical concavity (Fig. 9). The back of mirror Number 18 (Fig. 18) is unique in that it was ground convex and polished. Perhaps this back was a former tool piece that did not seem to be of sufficient quality to proceed with the next phase of grinding a concavity. Measured radii of curvature of fragment f_1, of the back of mirror Number 18, and of the convex surrounds of several of the other mirrors are evidence in support of this hypothesis, as all possess radii of curvature characteristic of the concavities.

The iron-oxide-ore minerals used by the Olmec are not particularly hard. Magnetite, for example, is approximately six on the Mohs hardness scale, slightly harder than glass. Quartz sand (SiO_2) and natural emery (Al_2O_3) would serve well as readily available grinding compounds. The process of elutriation (mixing in water, decanting the water laden with fine suspended particles, and then evaporating) can produce a selection of coarse and fine grades of abrasive.

The exact polishing procedures are more problematical, but it is most straightforward to assume that the readily available red or brown ochre was used. This is essentially hematite jewelers' rouge or crocus, and it produces an excellent polish on glass and the iron-ore minerals in question. Using a fine polishing material like red hematite to polish a piece made of the same substance yields the highest possible degree of optical surface quality. Flannery (1968) found a section of the Early Formative San José Phase site of San José Mogote in the Valley of Oaxaca that was apparently an artisan-workshop area for crafting exotic trade items of shell, obsidian, and iron ores. Over 500

iron-ore mirror fragments, as well as quartz and iron-ore polishers, were found only in this one barrio. Ochres were found in conjunction with, and adhering to, mirror fragments. It would be most rewarding to inspect this collection of fragments for tool pieces and other items needed at various stages of the manufacturing process outlined above.

Fine ochre rouges for polishing the mirrors could have been prepared by either of two methods: (1) the elutriation process as described previously, or (2) the roasting of pure crystals of iron pyrite to produce colcothar, a brownish-red peroxide of iron that was used in Roman times to polish glass. For the present experiments, I used hematite jewelers' rouge in conjunction with both a "pitch lap" and pieces of leather impregnated with hematite rouge. Both wet and dry polishing were successful. The Olmec could conceivably have prepared a pitch lap from pine pitches and beeswax. Polishing to achieve high optical quality takes considerable time, and I will presume that the Olmec craftsmen had a sufficient amount of that natural commodity.

In summary, the Olmec lapidary created concave iron-oxide-ore mirrors of high optical quality and unique aesthetic design. The metallic-finish, nontarnishing, iron-oxide minerals are perhaps the ideal materials to use for making such stone mirrors. The singular Olmec aesthetic can be readily understood as a direct result of the technique of mirror-grinding itself in conjunction with the full utilization of the raw materials at hand. One must then wonder why this aesthetic and process were cultivated at the expense of what might seem from our perspective to be a simple utilitarian flat mirror.

OLMEC MIRRORS AS PECTORAL PENDANTS

Gullberg (1959) suggested several possible purposes or uses for the mirror: a burning mirror, a camera obscura, and a magnification device for self-contemplation. Schagunn (1975) has suggested astronomical uses. Ekholm (1973) has demonstrated that at least one large mirror (Catalogue No. 13) could be used as a burning mirror and suspects that perhaps several smaller mirrors might have been used in conjunction to produce sufficient heat. A possible eye association is speculated by Grove (1970) with the suggestion that a mirror might have been infixed in the prominent avian eye on Mural I from the Oxtotitlan cave in Guerrero. Various authors have suggested possible divinatory purposes.

It seems quite clear that the concave mirrors were high-status objects and were traded extensively in Formative times along with other elite goods (Pires-Ferreira 1975, n.d.). The mirrors were worn as pectoral pendants, as can be ascertained from numerous examples. A beautiful jade figurine from a La Venta tomb (Bernal 1969b: Pl. 60) is seen with an iron-ore pectoral mirror infixed (Fig. 25). Non-Olmec ceramic examples from the Formative Period from Tlatilco (Pires-Ferreira 1975) wear crystalline hematite mirrors, as seen in Figures 26 and 27. Joralemon (1971: 12) lists "Mirror Worn around the Neck" as Motif Number 63 in his Olmec iconographic motif index. Examples of Olmec monumental sculpture or relief carving with the mirror motif are: Stela 2, Monument 23 (Fig. 29), and Altar 5 front and sides (Fig. 28) from La Venta; the Las Victorias, El Salvador, bas-relief carvings (Boggs 1950); and Monument 34 from San Lorenzo (Fig. 30). A splendid jade *hacha* from La Venta Offering 1943-f (Fig. 32) representing Olmec God I (Joralemon 1971) may be wearing a concave mirror pectoral infix. God I is identified by Joralemon and by M. Coe (1973a) as the Mesoamerican Fire God and/or Fire Serpent, suggesting an intriguing association with concave burning mirrors.

One of the most notable and significant Olmec monuments to show the pectoral-mirror motif was discovered by Stirling (1955) lying in the village of Tenochtitlan, Veracruz, near the Olmec sites of San Lorenzo and Potrero Nuevo. This powerful sculpture, known as Río Chiquito Monument 1, and the similar Potrero Nuevo Monument 3 depict an anthropomorphic jaguar apparently in the act of copulation with a supine human female (see Fig. 31). The jaguar figure is seen to wear a prominent pectoral pendant of the same variety that is depicted in the other monumental representations. For the purposes of arguments to be developed later, it is worth noting the jaguar–mirror association, for both are probable symbols of power.

Chalcatzingo, in the state of Morelos, is the location of a movingly beautiful Olmec site. Grove *et al.* (1976: 1207) reported finding the only example of an Olmec concave mirror pendant in an archaeological context *in situ* near the pectoral position in a human burial. The magnetite mirror, with elliptical concavity and two holes for suspension, is shown in Figure 11. Chalcatzingo 1974 Central Plaza Burial 1 was a high-status, Phase C (Late Middle Formative, 750–550 B.C.) interment located in the Central Plaza area (see Fig. 12). The skeletal remains show that the male figure was interred lying stretched out on his left side. The mirror pendant was found lying on the mandible area of the fragmentary skull adjacent to a large spherical jade head. In addition, many iron-ore fragments (mainly hematite)—mirror fragments, and others showing grinding marks indicating probable use in making pigments—have been found at this site. The discovery of this unmolested high-status Olmec burial confirms the use of pectoral concave mirror pendants by the Olmec elite and brightens the hope for the possibility of future discoveries.

Several of the La Venta mirrors were found in carefully aligned ceremonial burial caches with beads, cinnabar, and celts of jade and serpentine. Offerings 9 and 11 (see Figs. 1 and 2) were buried aligned symmetrically on each side of, and parallel to, the central axis of Complex A—oriented 8° west of true north (Drucker *et al.* 1959). The other fascinating example is concave mirror 1943-E (Catalogue No. 5, Fig. 5), which was found ceremonially buried on the north-pointing arm of a cruciform cache of celts located beneath the brickwork of the East Platform of Ceremonial Court A-1 and lying above the famous Jaguar Mask Pavement Number 1 (Drucker 1952). M. Coe (1972) has presented a case for associating a "Tezcatlipoca" or "Smoking Mirror" figure with a pan-Mesoamerican deity of royal lineage and rulership. The Aztec Tezcatlipoca was really a quadripartite god associated with the four cardinal color directions and world-trees. The Black Tezcatlipoca of the North was specifically the Aztec bestower of rulership. M. Coe (1972: 9) suggests that the cruciform Offering 1943-E at La Venta may represent an Olmec version of Smoking Mirror associated with a "symbol of the quadripartite god who raised the World-Trees." From this and other evidence, I would submit a four-sided speculative argument to suggest that the Olmec concave mirrors were at the root of a general Meso-american mirror tradition associated with a Smoking Mirror deity and a system of deified royal lineage and rulership. To this end, if you will permit me, I must rely in part on ethnographic analogy and cross-cultural comparison.

A PAN-MESOAMERICAN MIRROR TRADITION OF DEIFIED ROYAL POWER AND CONTINUITY?

The Olmec concave mirror pendants appear to have been created primarily for their symbolic rather than utilitarian value. The wide variety of their forms and properties precludes any consistent use as burning mirror or camera obscura. The lapidary technology itself seems to have created the Olmec mirror aesthetic and perhaps the symbolic value as well—the meaning behind the pectoral display of such a mirror. The symbol of the Lord of the Sun, the Smoking Mirror as Lord of the Four Quarters and Creations, the mirror of divination, and the ruler as the mirror in which the people should see themselves reflected—these four interrelated aspects of the argument will only become a whole after all have been presented for reflection.

Mirrors are visual devices. The *first* and most obvious symbolic content of these concave mirrors is as a *representation of the sun*. A fine modern Mesoamerican example is given by a Huichol yarn drawing of the sun with mirror infix, illustrated in Figure 21. An individual wearing an Olmec mirror on his chest or forehead, standing before the people, would become an embodiment or representative of the sun itself. There is independent evidence that the Classic Maya rulers may have been deified or descended from deified ancestors (J.E.S. Thompson 1973) and that their power may have been closely associated with the sun (Schele 1976; Greene Robertson 1974). The

latter authors present complex arguments from Palenque inscriptions and iconography to associate the Quadripartite Badge Monster and a Scepter God, God K, with the Sun (see Figs. 37, 38, and 39). The daily and yearly movements of the sun are seen as bound up with the orderly transfer of, and accession to, royal power.

In addition, in the Olmec context, if the mirrors were used as burning mirrors to take fire from the sun, this would reinforce a mirror–sun relationship. If not fire, the creation of smoke from such a smoking mirror might inspire an equally potent ritual allocation of power.

The complex Aztec *Tezcatlipoca, Smoking-Mirror-God tradition* is the *second* part of the mosaic. Tezcatlipoca had many faces. He was the black martial god of the North in eternal opposition to Quetzalcóatl, the Tezcatlipoca of the East. He was a God of Sorcery and Divination because, with his smoking mirror, he could look into the hearts of men and foresee future events. Both Tezcatlipoca and his father Xiuhtecuhtli, the Old Fire God, bestowed rulership and were associated with the royal lineage and succession. Thus in the Aztec scheme we have a fire and mirror god associated with rulership.

Tezcatlipoca also had a transformational manifestation as the Jaguar God Tepeyollotl, the Heart of the Mountain. M. Coe (1972) demonstrates a strong long-standing Meso-american association of the jaguar with rulership, royal lineage, and power. The jaguar had an additional intimate relationship with the sun in the underworld Jaguar Sun God. These associations may bring to mind the powerful Olmec jaguar-mirror imagery of Río Chiquito Monument 1 (Fig. 31).

For the Maya, there seems to have been a parallel between Tezcatlipoca and God K or Ah Bolon Dzacab, the Lord of Nine or Infinite Generations. God K (Figs. 38 and 39) is usually seen with what appears to be a mirror infix in his forehead and a cigar or smoking tube with foliations of smoke passing through it. God K has been tentatively identified as the Maya version of Tezcatlipoca by M. Coe (1973b: 16), "for both give off smoke from bone tubes sunk into their heads, as well as being snake-footed. As a general attribute of deities, the sign

[Thompson affix 122, probably representing smoke foliations] may represent or symbolize the power of the divinity." At Palenque and for the Maya in general, God K and related deities are shown to be associated with royal lineage and power (Schele 1974, 1976). Indeed, Lord Pacal of Palenque is clearly depicted with the attributes of God K in the relief carving of his sarcophagus lid (Figs. 37 and 38). Those associations will be explored further in the final section.

Tezcatlipoca is also a cosmological deity— a force in space and time. He is four gods— the four Tezcatlipocas of the cardinal world-directions. They are also associated with the series of four previous world creations and destructions. There are mythological parallels between this quadripartite Tezcatlipoca and the four Bacabs or Sky Bearers of Maya cosmology. M. Coe (1972: 9) suggests that these traditions of quadripartite cosmological gods, bestowers of rulership, linked the ruler in space and time with the supreme generative forces.

> By means of a long series of structural oppositions, the divine nature of the royal line and its total separation from (and superiority to) the common people are stated in vivid terms. The kings are descendants of the Fire God and of Tezcatlipoca and are their living representatives on earth. By means of this, all of creation becomes the realm of the royal house, the well-being of the king and well-being of the external world having become identical.

In the Olmec context, this does recall the cruciform cache of celts at La Venta with the concave mirror to the north. Celts have a lightning-bolt connotation in Mesoamerican mythology, as does Tezcatlipoca. Olmec God I is identified by Joralemon (1971) and M. Coe (1972, 1973a) with the Fire God. Here again we have a Fire God–Four Tezcatlipocas association in the *hacha* with the mirror pendant infix from La Venta Offering 1943-f (Fig. 32).

The *third* side of the speculation involves the worldwide tradition of the use of the mirror in *divination*—scrying and catoptromancy (Besterman 1965). Tezcatlipoca could look into the hearts of men with his smoking divinatory mirror. The play of reflections in a mirror has often been equated with the observance of one's soul or inner self. This is in harmony with the dualistic pan-Mesoamerican tradition of a second or animal soul (Foster 1944). The mirror is also intimately associated with shamanism and curing practices. The magical and medicinal properties of the mirror in the Orient are described by P. Furst (n.d.: 190–1) quoting from Laufer (1915):

> The Chinese, writes Laufer, used concave mirrors of metal, metallic stone and other minerals during the Chou Dynasty (1027 to 223 B.C.), as well as later, both to ignite sacred or ceremonial fires and for magical and medicinal purposes. The noted Chinese alchemist and philosopher Liu An, Prince of Huai-nan, who died in 122 B.C., described plaques of bright metal which, when held toward the sun, "will ignite and produce fire" (Laufer, *ibid.*, pp. 187–88). So far as magico-medicinal use is concerned, Laufer (p. 209) describes an interesting early Chinese method of cauterizing by means of "burning mirrors." In this treatment young leaves of the *Artemisia vulgaris,* one of the Asian wormwoods, are ground up with water in a stone mortar; the coarse particles are eliminated and the remainder, rolled into pea-sized pellets, are placed on the ulcer or spot to be cauterized. The preferred method of igniting was in ancient times a burning mirror and more recently an optical glass. The same cautery treatment was adopted by the Japanese and is still in use there; in the West it became known as *moxa,* from the Japanese *magusa.* It is interesting to speculate whether the Olmec magician-priests, who are frequently depicted wearing concave mirrors, also utilized these remarkable instruments in a similar medicinal way. If they did, the treatment must have seemed utterly miraculous to the uninitiated, involving as it does the power to capture the sun's own sacred fire to alleviate man's afflictions. Be that as it may, the use of the optical mirror to produce fire for one or another ceremonial purpose seems beyond doubt in Mesoamerica.

From various lines of reasoning, including the ethnographic analogy of mirror use in Mesoamerican shamanistic healing practices, speculations on an original Olmec use of the concave mirror for divination, introspection, and the practice of medicine are well within reason. Furthermore, Ekholm (1973) recalls two accounts of Mexican rulers from the time before the Spanish conquest using magical obsidian mirrors to foretell the future. Moctezuma saw his fate in a mirror infixed in the forehead of a magical crane. The Lord of Tacuba, in consulting a clouded mirror, saw that Mexico would be lost to the Spanish invaders. Mesoamerican rulership was certainly bound up with priestly and divinatory function.

The *fourth* and final argument for a Mesoamerican association of mirror and rulership comes from the Maya. This is bound up with the Jeffrey Miller (n.d.) *"nen"/mirror hypothesis*. Miller noted that a Maya hieroglyph that appears in the Palenque inscriptions in the context of an event glyph looks like a hand holding an ovoid [concave or convex] mirror, the T617 grapheme.[6] This glyphic element is an ovoid cartouche in form with a second oval infixed, usually with three curved diagonal lines moving from the lower left to the upper right. Miller also noted the associated T116 affix which has been given one tentative phonetic reading as an *n* sound. This suffix is seen to function as a phonetic classifier in other contexts such as in the *kin* sign in a distance number, and in the Maya month glyphs *maun* and *yaxkin*. He then looked for a Maya word for mirror ending in an *n* sound in the Spanish–Maya *Bocabulario de Mayathan* (1972). The Yucatec word for mirror is *nen*. The same root is also found, for example, in the Tzotzil, Tzeltal, Lacandón, Chol, and Jacaltec languages.

The colonial period Yucatec Motul Dictionary (Martínez Hernández 1929: 669-70) has the following entry:

nen: espejo; *in nen, a nen,* ettc.

U nen cab, u nen cah, el sacerdote, cacique, gobernador de la tierra o pueblo, que es espejo en que todos se miran. [The priest, chief, or governor of the land or village who is the mirror in which all the people see themselves.]

U is the third person possessive; *cah* is the root for village or the people; *cab* is the root for earth: therefore the reading is "the people's or earth's mirror."

This remarkable entry very poetically relates the *nen*/mirror with the very person of leadership in whom the people should see themselves reflected.[7] In the Tzotzil language, *nen* is used in "Ritual speech, referring to scribes who are credited with special visual powers" (Laughlin 1975: 251). In the Quiché tongue, *nem* means to "succeed in office" (Edmonson 1965).

In most highland Maya languages, the root for mirror is *lem*. This provides an interesting connection with lowland Maya languages where *lem* has meanings related to "brilliance" and "lightning." The total *nen/lem* linguistic context relates the mirror root to rulership, succession in office, brilliance, lightning, contemplation, meditation, and imagination.

In the hieroglyphic inscriptions at Palenque, the *nen* T617 phrase has been shown in two

---

[6] T617 is a "Thompson number"—Glyph 617a, b from J. E. S. Thompson (1962: 238–9), *A Catalog of Maya Hieroglyphs*. This catalog lists the many occurrences of the T617 glyph in the Maya inscriptions and refers to its use on some Maya pottery. Glyph T712 is also seen to possess a similar "mirror" infix.

[7] Another such example may be found in Diego Durán's account of the selection of Moteczoma the Second as ruler of the Aztec empire. In chapter 52 of a recent English translation of Durán (1964), we find the following pasage (*ibid.:* 220) where Nezahualpilli of Texcoco, the principal elector, speaks:

O valorous monarch of Tacuba and great lords of Mexico! O rulers of the provinces of Chalco, Xochimilco and the low lands! With your vote and consent we are to choose the luminary that is to give us light like one of the sun's rays. We are to choose a mirror in which we will be reflected, a mother who will hold us to her breast, a father who will carry us on his shoulders and a prince who will rule over the Aztec nation.

After Moteczoma has been enthroned, Nezahualpilli continues his oration (*ibid.:* 221):

O you most powerful of all the kings of earth! The clouds have been dispelled and the darkness in which we lived has fled. The Sun has appeared and the light of dawn shines upon us after the darkness which had been caused by the death of the king. The torch which is to illuminate Mexico has been lighted and today we have been given a mirror to look into.

examples to be associated with an event in the life of a future ruler when he was between the ages of six and seven years old, and in one further case with the accession of an older ruler. This evidence is presented in detail by J. Miller (n.d.) and by Schele and Miller (n.d.). This event phrase also appears in a "succession in office" context at the Maya site of Quiriguá in Guatemala. Evidence from both Maya inscriptions and iconography are offered to show that there was probably a "mirror ceremony" involved with the transfer of royal lineal power, heir designation, or accession to rulership.

In addition, the same T617 grapheme is manifest as an iconographic element at Palenque. It is infixed in the foreheads of the Cross Deity of the Temple of the Foliated Cross, the lower border of the Temple of the Sun Tablet, and the Temple of the Inscriptions sarcophagus lid (Figs. 33–39). Indeed, the Maya "god markings" may be identified with the same iconographic element (see Fig. 35).

As previously noted, God K has been identified with the Smoking Mirror, and the T617 grapheme in his forehead clearly shows a protruding cigar or smoking tube complete with foliations of smoke (Figs. 38 and 39). Kelley (1965) has suggested the identification of God K (Ah Bolon Dzacab or He of the Nine, Infinite, Generations) as God II of the Palenque Triad of deities and would see him as a god of royal lineage. God K is also sometimes shown as a serpent-footed deity, and several rulers at Palenque show this embodiment in representations—perhaps due to actual physical deformity (Greene Robertson *et al.* 1976). They suggest that Lord Pacal and his son, Lord Chan-Bahlum, both important rulers of Palenque, may have had deformities of the foot. In summary, God K is the Manikin Scepter God, the ancestral deity whose birth is recorded on the Temple of the Foliated Cross Tablet, the deity of the Classic Maya 819-day count, and God II of the Palenque Triad. All of these forms possess some association with dynastic lineage and continuity.

The Jester God (see Fig. 35) is almost identical to God K—they form a duo—but the Jester God's forehead "mirror" infix does not have the smoking tube. This pair of deities is often depicted in dualistic opposition, as can be seen on the Palenque sarcophagus lid (Fig. 37). God K with "smoking mirror" is seen emerging from the gaping, westward-facing mouth (on the left) of the bicephalic serpent that is entwined around the central cross. The head of the Jester God with "clear mirror" emerges from the open jaws of the eastward-facing head of this serpent. This East-facing/West-facing; Sunrise (emergence from underworld)/Sunset (descent into underworld); Bright Mirror/Obscured Mirror set of oppositions strengthens the hypothetical "mirror" nature of the iconographic and functional associations of these brother deities. The "mirror" T617 glyph is the diagnostic iconographic element for both, and the general consensus is that they function as a pair as probable gods of rulership or lineal succession to office. The mirror is then a graphic symbol of their function.

It is most interesting that the T617 grapheme also appears on the foreheads of the Maya Sun God and God C variants (see Figs. 33–7). The Quadripartite Badge Sun Monster (Fig. 37) has a cartouche containing a *kin* sun symbol affixed to his forehead or headgear. This deity forms the head on one end of a Maya double-headed sky-serpent monster. Note that the cross motif depicted on the sarcophagus lid from the Palenque Temple of the Inscriptions (Fig. 37) is really two crossed double-headed serpent bars. The horizontal bicephalic bar has a jeweled serpent head at each end, each with a jeweled "mirror" infix at the throat. The vertical member of the cross has the Quadripartite Badge Monster at the bottom with another jeweled serpent head with jeweled "mirror" gorget. Possible "mirror" infixes appear on both bars of the celestial serpent-cross and a further fleshed dual-headed serpent bar is seen draped over the resultant cross.

The four-directional celestial framework depicted in this magnificent iconographic statement probably shows the Quadripartite Badge Monster as the setting sun graphically symbolizing the death of Lord Pacal who is seen falling with the sun into the underworld, only to be reborn at the beginning of the next cycle. This idea is reinforced by noting that the Monster has a fleshed face and eyeballs but a skeletal lower jaw—he is caught at the juncture of the upperworld and the underworld. Further support for these and related iconographic interpretations is given by Schele (1977).

The speculative association of mirrors and possibly concave sun mirrors with this four-directional cosmological framework certainly evokes the image of Tezcatlipoca and his probable Maya counterpart, God K. The depiction of the dying Lord Pacal as the incarnation of God K would make him the ruler over the death and rebirth of space and time itself—the Smoking Mirror God of the Four Directions, Destructions, and Creations and a symbol of the vitality of his dynastic lineage.

Among the Tzotzil Maya who reside in the municipio of Zinacantán in the highlands of Chiapas, the four Bacabs—the deities of the four quarters who support the corners of the night sky and direct the rains and storms from the four world-directions—are known as the Vashakmen or Vashaknen (Vogt 1969: 304). Klein (1976) associates the four Vashaknen with the four Aztec Tlaloques—the assistants of the goggle-eyed rain god Tlaloc. She suggests that the two ring-eyes of Tlaloc might have been mirrors, and hence the four Tlaloques of each world quarter would have eight mirror eyes. The word *vashaknen* in the Tzotzil language means "eight windows" or "eight mirrors." Vogt (1969: 304) observes from this translation that "All of this raises the interesting question of whether there is some belief about these gods either having mirrors or looking through windows at people." If these above arguments have credence, they demonstrate a series of Maya structural associations of sun, mirror, rulership, dynastic lineage, and cosmology.

Finally, the T617 grapheme appears as an element in the Primary Standard Text from Maya pottery (M. Coe 1973b), in the Dresden Codex Venus pages, and in a belt motif from Classic Maya costume representations. This latter head-mirror combination has been given a very tentative reading of *Ahau Nen* or "Lord of the Mirror." The details of the above argument are well presented by Schele and Miller (n.d.). Both the Yucatec *Book of Chilam Balam of Chumayel* and Landa's *Relación de Las*

Cosas de Yucatan contain ethnohistorical references to Maya mirror use. In the *Book of Chilam Balam* (Roys 1967: 110) one of the "angels" is described as follows: "Hebones was the only son of God. [Like] a mirror he was borne astride the shoulder of his father, on the stone of his father." Landa (Tozzer 1941: 89) recorded the use of mirrors as an element of the Yucatec male costume: "All the men used mirrors while the women had none; and to call each other cuckolds, they said that the wife had put the mirror in the hair at the back of their heads." Herrera reiterates (Tozzer 1941: 217): "They had mirrors in which they looked at themselves and the women did not use them." Floyd Lounsbury (personal communication, 1977), has pointed out that the mirror was placed at the back of the head as a humiliation for the cuckolded husband. This implies that the normal position for the mirror to be worn was on the forehead, as seen in the portrayals of the Classic Maya deities discussed above.

God K's smoking mirror has never been found with certainty in a Maya archaeological context. I would view his mirror infix as being a representation of a concave mirror, but there is as yet no evidence that the Maya manufactured concave mirrors. As a speculation, perhaps the Classic Maya used heirloom Olmec concave mirrors for their "mirror ceremonies." I would anticipate that such a mirror might be found in the context of a royal burial or dynastic monument.

I accept, in the broad context, that the Jeffrey Miller *nen*/mirror hypothesis is probably correct—the detailed support is an entire study in itself (Schele and Miller n.d.). The Classic Maya rulers were probably viewed as living gods, embodiments or representatives of perhaps God K or the Sun God. They had spiritual and secular power (J. E. S. Thompson 1973). The mirror ceremony might have conferred the all-encompassing office of wiseman, seer, and priest as well as of secular leader of the people—the "mirror in which all the people see themselves reflected."

We might note here that the ancient Siberian and Chinese bronze mirrors derived from a shamanistic divinatory tradition (Loubo-Les-

John B. Carlson

nitchenko 1973) and became associated with the dual function of "physical reflection and metaphysical contemplation" (Plumer 1944: 94). These mirrors were a "geometric ideograph for the sun" (*ibid.:* 97) on the front, and a square within a circle on the back—a cosmic diagram of the earth divided into four world-quarters and surrounded by the circular horizon boundary of heaven. A central knob on the back was the World Mountain at the center of the earth, the *axis mundi* or *omphalos*. As with the Tezcatlipocas, the four cardinal world-directions are associated with four world animals and colors. These too are usually depicted on the backs of the mirrors. Mirrors are seen to reflect the bearer's face and his inner soul, and the Chinese mirrors are perfect symbols of interior and exterior power and harmony both for the individual human microcosm and for the cosmos *in toto* (Hirth 1906; Rupert and Todd 1935). From the full spectrum of argument presented, it is most likely that the Olmec and the ancient Chinese alike used mirrors in a spiritually, if not physically, related context.

SUMMARY AND CONCLUSION

I would, therefore, suggest an Olmec or Early Formative origin for a pan-Mesoamerican mirror-cult tradition of royal lineage and power. The two main types of concave mirror may have had different functions, but of this we have no clue. I would agree with M. Coe (1972: 11) that probably "Olmec religion was therefore a royal cult, in general outline. . . ." The technology of concave-mirror grinding itself apparently yielded the Olmec concave iron-ore mirror aesthetic and perhaps gave birth to Sun-God-Mirror, Smoking-Mirror, and shamanistic divinatory-mirror traditions of Mesoamerican culture. A deified ruler may have possessed and maintained his power in part as a resultant benefit of this multifaceted symbolic structure.

One final speculative thought is that the Olmec may have discovered the principle of the lodestone geomagnetic compass as a result of their unique lapidary skills in fashioning the concave mirrors from naturally magnetic iron-ore minerals (Carlson 1975). If this were true for the Olmec (see Fig. 10) and later the Maya

(Fuson 1969; Carlson 1977), we have a further association of the Smoking Mirror with four-directional cosmology. The author (Carlson 1975) has suggested that the Olmec would have used a geomagnetic compass for geomantic purposes, as did the Chinese, to align cities, dwellings, and tombs so as to place them in proper balance and harmony with the perceived cosmic forces of the universe. Indeed, the cruciform La Venta Offering 1943-E with mirror Number 5 on the "north" arm was not oriented towards the cardinal directions, but 8° west of north, the prime axis of Complex A at La Venta. It might have been thus that the god Tezcatlipoca, the Lord of the Smoking Mirror, acquired his four-directional and succession-of-world-creations cosmological aspect that, as bestower of royal and priestly power, continuity, and wisdom, would make a ruler truly Lord of the Universe.

ADDENDUM

While attending the Tercera Mesa Redonda de Palenque in June, 1978, I had the opportunity to examine firsthand several artifacts in the Palenque Museum Collection. One item of interest was an irregular hexagonal piece of pyrite (less than two centimeters across and about two millimeters thick) that almost undoubtedly had once been part of a mosaic mirror. A drawing of this fragment appears as the sixth item of line six of Figure 15 of "Exploraciones arqueológicas en Palenque: 1956" by Ruz Lhullier (1958: 287). It is shown with six other artifacts described as fragments of a pyrite mosaic or mirror which were found in Tomb 2 of Temple 18A. Such pyrite mosaic mirrors are not often found in the Maya realm and this is the only example I know of from Palenque. However, Barbara MacLeod, working with Dennis Puleston on the exploration and excavation of Maya caves in Belize, announced that they had found the remains of three pyrite, slate-back mosaic mirrors in three separate caves during a recent season in the field.

The second item examined from the Palenque Museum Collection proved to be a unique and exciting find. The photograph in Figure 40 shows it to be a *convex,* highly polished

130

mirror fragment, roughly cartouche shaped, with the approximate dimensions of 25 by 38 millimeters. Though listed as the seventh pyrite mosaic fragment by Ruz Lhuillier (1958: 287, Fig. 15, line 6), the artifact is clearly not iron pyrite and is almost certainly composed of hematite. A check with a pocket magnet and a compass needle showed that it was not magnetite. This brittle iron-oxide mineral still possesses virtually all of its original high polish. The back had been ground flat showing the characteristic color and texture of hematite. This grinding has made the mirror so thin (about one millimeter at the center and perhaps less than 0.2 millimeters at some edges) that it had been subject to noticeable chipping at the edges. No drilled holes or attempts at perforation were apparent.

Though it was not possible to study the detailed optical figure of the convex surface, an approximate radius of curvature could be measured on the assumption that the mirror was of spherical figure. The radius of curvature measured was approximately nine centimeters, which is equivalent to a focal length of 4.5 centimeters for a spherical concave mirror (see Table 1). The implication is that whoever made this short-focal-length convex mirror would of necessity have created an equivalent concave mirror in the process.

There are extensive possibilities here for both speculation and further investigation. This mirror is completely unique in the Maya context, and resembles most closely the Olmec or Formative Period iron-oxide-ore concave mirrors in composition, quality and technique of manufacture. It is convex rather than concave, but nonetheless, would not now produce great surprise if found in an Olmec excavation.

One must now ask how this mirror came to be in Tomb 2 of Temple 18A at Palenque—a late Murciélagos (Early Tepeu II) Phase burial. The raw materials for the manufacture of either iron-oxide or pyrite mirrors do not exist in the Palenque vicinity, but the materials and technology could have been imported. It certainly would have been easier, however, to import these finished mirrors along with other high-status goods. Furthermore, these mirrors seem to be a unique find at Palenque, and nothing like a workshop for iron-ore minerals has yet been found there (Robert Rands, personal communication). The import of pyrite mosaic mirrors is quite logical, but the convex hematite mirror remains unique in the general Mesoamerican context. Either such convex and concave mirrors were being produced somewhere in Classic times where the raw materials existed, such as in the Valley of Oaxaca, or the piece is a Formative Period heirloom or looted from a Formative grave or ruin. A partial answer to the question of provenience may be available in the future through such techniques as those developed by Pires-Ferreira (1975, n.d.) in collaboration with B. J. Evans. It is certainly possible that techniques and traditions that developed in Early Formative times might have survived through the Classic.

In the context of the present study, one might speculate that the small cartouche-shaped convex mirror is what is being depicted in the T617 grapheme or iconographic element. Indeed, straight edges may appear to become curved lines when viewed from the correct perspective in either a convex or a concave mirror. The Palenque convex mirror might have been affixed to a figurine, a stucco relief, an item of costume, or perhaps even to the forehead or headgear of a young lord in the act of impersonating God K, the Jester God, or a Solar Deity as part of some ceremony of investiture or heir designation. This is speculation, but it adds yet another bit of evidence to help penetrate the enigma of Maya mirror use.

The convex mirror and the pyrite mosaic fragments were found in one high-status burial. One might hypothesize that these items were associated directly with the person or funerary costume of the deceased. This recalls the God K impersonation of Lord Pacal depicted on his sarcophagus lid. The lack of holes for suspension might contribute support for an argument that the mirror was not and never had been used as a pectoral pendant device, but of course there are other methods for the attachment of objects to cords worn around the neck. This recalls the figure depicted on a carved deer bone from the Island of Jaina on the west coast of Yucatán (Barthel 1967: Figs.

John B. Carlson

1 and 2). An aged, toothless male with elaborate headgear and ornamentation is seen sitting on a woven mat throne—a symbolic indication of his authority and rulership. He wears a breastplate device with no apparent perforations, which is indistinguishable from the T617 "mirror" element. This pectoral is suspended by a beaded or link-chain cord worn around his neck. The bone was found in a funerary context, and, furthermore, such scenes with aged lords are often shown on Maya polychrome funerary pottery.

The only statement one can make at this juncture is that the Palenque mirrors were placed in a high-status burial and could have served in any of these many possible capacities —as a pectoral device, as a forehead element, as a light to help the underworld traveler find his way (an analogue to the Chinese practice of placing a bronze mirror with the dead), etc. We can only hope that these recent discoveries and speculations will contribute to our appreciation of the fascinating question of the value and function of mirrors in the Pre-Columbian world.

ACKNOWLEDGMENTS A very long list is in order of persons who helped me with their advice, expertise, and generosity: Michael Coe, Philip Drucker, Mary Ann Durgin, Gordon Ekholm, Billy Joe Evans, Ben Goldberg, Gillett Griffin, David Grove, Robert Heizer, David Joralemon, Floyd Lounsbury, Jeffrey Miller, Linda Schele, Jerry Schnall, Joyce Strauss, Waldo Wedel, and Ann Gilbert Wylie. With their help, I looked into my magic mirror to see if there was truth in what I had conceived, but, alas, its depths remained murky. Obviously, all errors, misrepresentations, and ill-conceived notions are mine alone. Thanks are also due to the National Science Foundation, the American Anthropological Association, and the Astronomy Program at the University of Maryland for the financial support to attend the XLII Congrès International des Américanistes, where this work was first presented. The Astronomy Program and the Institute for Physical Science and Technology of the University of Maryland and The Tinker Foundation provided financial support for the completion of the present manuscript.

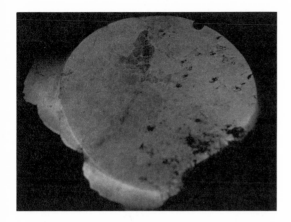

Fig. 1 Concave mirror, Catalogue No. 1. Magnetite mirror found as part of Offering 9 at La Venta along with nine jade and serpentine celts, jade beads, and cinnabar. Museo Nacional de Antropología, Mexico. Photograph by the author.

Fig. 2 Concave mirror, Catalogue No. 2. Ilmenite mirror found as part of Offering 11 at La Venta along with nine jade and serpentine celts, jade beads, and cinnabar. Museo Nacional de Antropología, Mexico. Photograph by the author.

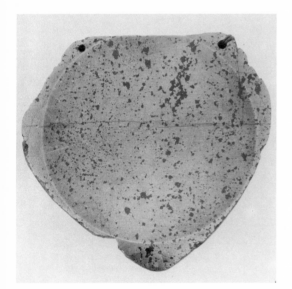

Fig. 3 The first Olmec-style concave mirror ground and polished by the author from a section of coarse-grained magnetite. *a*. Obverse. *b*. Three-quarters view. Photographs by the author.

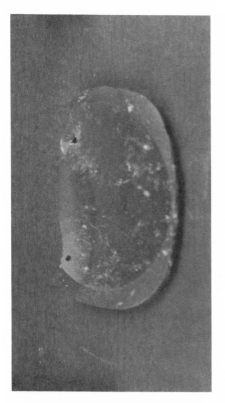

Fig. 5 Concave mirror, Catalogue No. 5. Hematite mirror found on the north side of the arm of a cruciform cache of jade and serpentine celts, La Venta Offering 1943-E. Museo Nacional de Antropología, Mexico. Photograph by the author.

Fig. 7 Small (approximately 35 mm.) convex tool piece used by the author to grind the second Olmec-style concave mirror (Fig. 9). Note the similarity to the convex-mirror fragment in Figure 6. Photograph by the author.

Fig. 4 The first convex tool piece as it looked after grinding the first Olmec-style concave mirror (Fig. 3). It was an irregularly shaped section of coarse-grained magnetite with the approximate dimensions of 4.5 x 7.0 centimeters. Photograph by the author.

Fig. 6 Fragment of a convex mirror, Catalogue No. f₁. The only example of a convex-mirror fragment known to the author. Note the similarity to the small convex tool piece (Fig. 7) used by the author to grind the second Olmec-style concave mirror (Fig. 9). Private collection, U.S.A. Photograph by the author.

Fig. 9 The second Olmec-style concave mirror ground and polished by the author. It has an elliptical border and convex surround. The small irregular tool piece shown in Figure 7 was used to grind the central concavity in this convex tool piece that was originally used to grind the first Olmec-style concave mirror (Fig. 3). *a.* Obverse. *b.* Three-quarters view. Photographs by the author.

Fig. 8 Concave mirror, Catalogue No. 8. *a.* Obverse. *b.* Near edge-on view. Note the extreme thinness (approximately 3 mm.) at the center. Private collection, U.S.A. Photographs by the author.

Fig. 12 Chalcatzingo 1974 Central Plaza Burial 1, located at coordinates 23-24S/3-5W. Catalogue No. 11 (Fig. 11) was found *in situ* lying on the mandible area of the fragmentary skull, adjacent to a large spherical jade bead. Photograph by Terry Majewski.

Fig. 10 Magnetized hematite bar, 34 millimeters long, from San Lorenzo, Veracruz. This may once have been part of an Olmec geomagnetic compass device (see Carlson 1975). Instituto Nacional de Antropología, Mexico. Photographs by the author.

Fig. 11 Concave mirror, Catalogue No. 11. This magnetite mirror pendant with an elliptical concavity is the only example of an Olmec mirror found in archaeological context *in situ* in a human burial. The mirror was found lying on the mandible area of the fragmentary skull (Grove *et al.* 1976) in Central Plaza Burial 1, Chalcatzingo, Morelos, in 1974 (see Fig. 12; David Grove, personal communication, 1977). Instituto Nacional de Antropología e Historia, Morelos. Photograph by David Grove.

Fig. 13 (left) Concave mirror, Catalogue No. 13. A large (119 mm.) concave mirror, of spherical figure, alleged to have been found at Arroyo Pesquero, Veracruz. *a.* Obverse. *b.* Shown here in a successful experiment by G. F. Ekholm to test the artifact's qualities as a burning mirror. A dried piece of wood was placed at focal point approximately 18 centimeters from the mirror surface. Private collection; on loan to the American Museum of Natural History, New York. Photographs by G. F. Ekholm.

Fig. 14 (above) Concave mirror, Catalogue No. 14, AMNH Catalogue No. 30.3-1299. A large concave mirror alleged to have been found at Arroyo Pesquero, Veracruz. American Museum of Natural History, New York. Photograph by G. F. Ekholm.

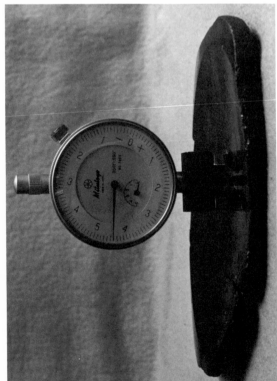

Fig. 15 (left) Concave mirror, Catalogue No. 15. This spectacular large mirror looks very much like the pectoral pendants seen on many Olmec monuments. Though broken into seven pieces (one is missing), this elliptical convex mirror has a spherical figure and possesses a collecting area and focal length that make it an excellent solar burning mirror. *a.* Obverse. *b.* A dial-gauge "spherometer" is shown measuring the radii of curvature. Private collection, U.S.A. Photographs by the author.

Fig. 16 (above) Concave mirror, Catalogue No. 16. A large concave mirror alleged to have been found at Arroyo Pesquero, Veracruz. Private collection, Mexico. Photograph courtesy of the owner.

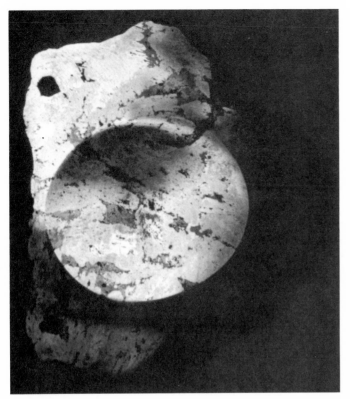

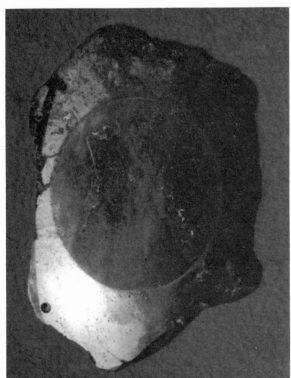

Fig. 17 (left) Concave mirror, Catalogue No. 17. This unusual magnetite mirror was found near Xochipala, Guerrero. The surround is convex, whereas the central mirror surface with elliptical border is almost flat but slightly "saddle-shaped." *a*. Obverse. *b*. A dial-gauge "spherometer" is shown measuring the radii of curvature. Private collection, U.S.A. Photographs by the author.

Fig. 18 (above) Concave mirror, Catalogue No. 18. This magnificent Type 2 pendant mirror is unique in that it has a polished convex back of spherical figure and mirror-quality finish. Private collection, U.S.A. Photograph by the author.

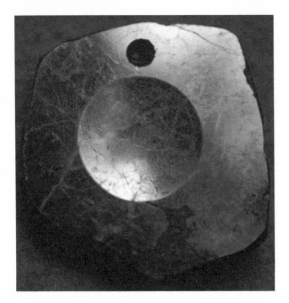

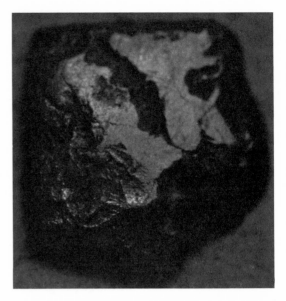

Fig. 19 Concave mirror, Catalogue No. 19. This is a small, thick, Type 1 pendant mirror. *a.* Obverse, showing clearly the conical drill-hole and sharp border between the concave center and the convex surround. *b.* Reverse, showing the essential contours of the original stone. Note the typical unfinished look of the crude grinding or sawing technique used to flatten the back of the pendant. Private collection, U.S.A. Photographs by the author.

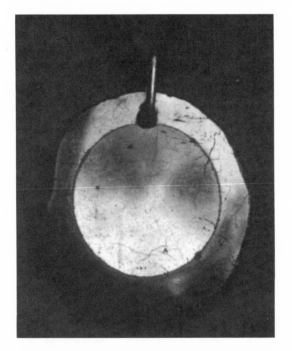

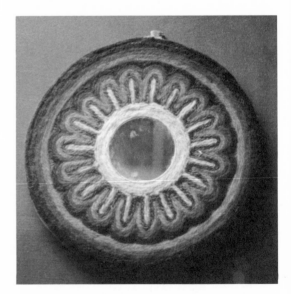

Fig. 21 Modern Huichol yarn drawing with a central mirror, symbolizing the sun. Museo Nacional de Antropología, Mexico. Photograph by the author.

Fig. 20 Concave mirror, Catalogue No. 20. Small Type 1 mirror found in the state of Guerrero. This mirror showed the greatest degree of symmetry and modification of the original stone of any of those examined. Private collection, U.S.A. Photograph by the author.

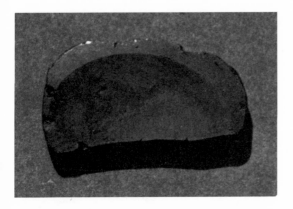

Fig. 22 Concave mirror, Catalogue No. 22. Small Type I magnetite mirror fragment found in the state of Guerrero. Private collection, U.S.A. Photograph by the author.

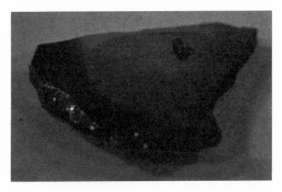

Fig. 23 Concave mirror, Catalogue No. 23. Small Type I mirror found in the state of Guerrero. This example had been broken, with a hole for suspension presumably drilled later from the back and through the face of the mirror. Private collection, U.S.A. Photograph by the author.

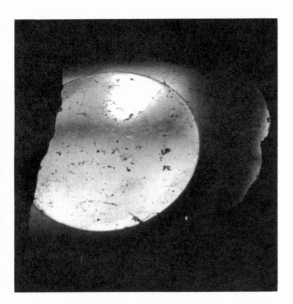

Fig. 24 Concave mirror, Catalogue No. 24. A large fragment of a mirror exhibited in the Museo Nacional along with Olmec mirrors from La Venta. The provenience is not known to the author. Museo Nacional de Antropología, Mexico. Photograph by the author.

Fig. 25 Jade figurine No. 1 from a tomb in Mound A-2 at La Venta (see Drucker 1952: Pl. 46). The 8-centimeter-high figurine was dusted with red hematite pigment, and carries an iron-ore mirror affixed in the pectoral position. Museo Nacional de Antropología, Mexico. Photograph by the author.

141

Fig. 26 (above, left) Ceramic figurine, wearing a crystalline hematite pectoral mirror, found at the Formative site of Tlatilco. Museo Nacional de Antropología, Mexico. Photograph by the author.

Fig. 27 (above) Ceramic figurine, wearing a crystalline hematite pectoral mirror, found at the Formative site of Tlatilco. Museo Nacional de Antropología, Mexico. Photograph by the author.

Fig. 28 (left) Olmec relief carving from the side of La Venta Altar 5. The personage on the left wears a probable pectoral concave-mirror pendant and holds an infant or were-jaguar dwarf in its arms. Photograph by the author.

Fig. 29 La Venta Monument 23. Note the probable concave-mirror pectoral pendant. Museo Nacional de Antropología, Mexico. Photograph by the author.

Fig. 30 San Lorenzo Monument 34. This probable ball-player-figure possesses unique ratcheted-disk shoulder sockets and wears a pectoral concave-mirror pendant. Museo Nacional de Antropología, Mexico. Photograph by the author.

Fig. 31 Río Chiquito Monument 1, found in the village of Tenochtitlan, Veracruz. It is similar to Potrero Nuevo Monument 3. These sculptures seem to depict an anthropomorphic jaguar presumably in the act of copulation with a human female. *a.* Side view. *b.* Three-quarters view. Note the probable pectoral concave-mirror pendant worn by the jaguar figure. (After Stirling 1955: Pl. 2.)

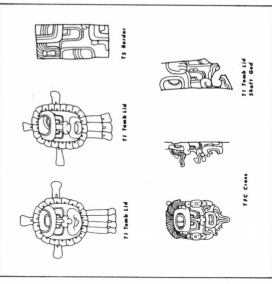

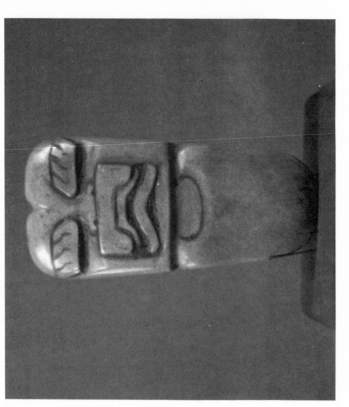

Fig. 32 (above) Jade *hacha* from La Venta Offering 1943-F. Joralemon (1971) identifies it as Olmec God I with flame eyebrows and a probable pectoral-mirror infix (Motif No. 63). Museo Nacional de Antropología, Mexico. Photograph by the author.

Fig. 33 (above, right) Carved-jade Maya head of the Sun God. Note the probable "mirror" infix in the forehead. Museo Nacional de Antropología, Mexico. Photograph by the author.

Fig. 34 (right) Comparison of Sun God motifs from Palenque (TI = Temple of the Inscriptions; TS = Temple of the Sun; TFC = Temple of the Foliated Cross). Drawings by Linda Schele.

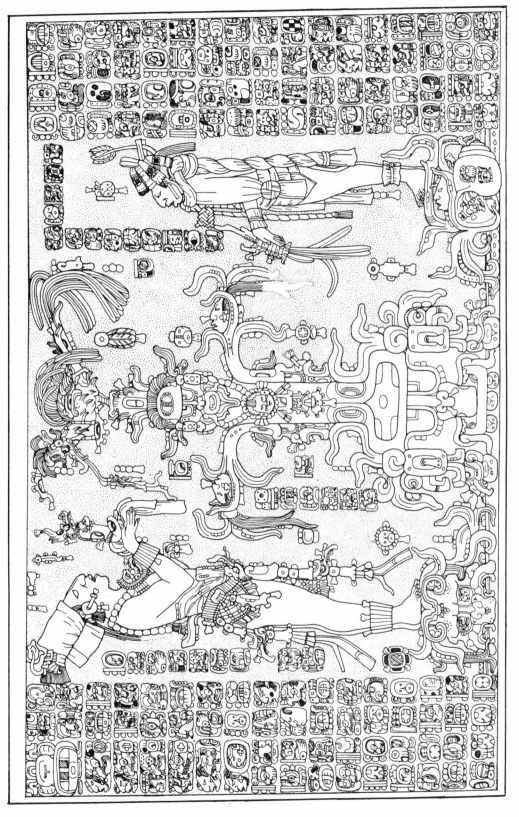

Fig. 35 Tablet of the Foliated Cross in the Temple of the Foliated Cross, Palenque, Chiapas. The face of a Maya Sun God with T617 "mirror" infix on the forehead appears on the top of the Foliated Cross and in profile on both sides of the main shaft of the cross (see Fig. 34). The tall standing figure on the left holds the diminutive Jester God in his hands. Note the use of the T617 element as an infix in the forehead and as "god markings" on his back and thigh. Drawing by Linda Schele.

Fig. 36 Face of the variant Maya Sun God at the top of the Tablet of the Foliated Cross, Temple of the Foliated Cross, Palenque. Note the T617 "mirror" infix used as an iconographic element (see Figs. 34 and 35). Photograph by the author.

Fig. 37 Sarcophagus lid from the Temple of the Inscriptions, Palenque. Note the probable depiction of Lord Pacal seated upon the head of the Quadripartite Badge Sun Monster. Pacal is wearing headgear virtually identical to that worn by God K, whose head is seen to emerge from the open serpent mouth on the left (see Fig. 38). Two Sun God motifs are displayed on each side of the relief above the open jaws of the dual-headed serpent. Note the T617 "mirror" infixes on their foreheads. A profile of this same solar deity may be seen on the main shaft of the cross directly adjacent to and above Lord Pacal's hands (see Fig. 34). Drawing by Agustín Villagra (after Ruz 1970: Fig. 75).

146

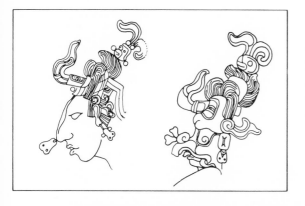

Fig. 38 Lord Pacal of Palenque (left) is seen depicted, probably after his death, as God K (right). Note the hypothetical "mirror" infix on the foreheads with the smoking cigar-tube thrust through it. Both depictions are from Lord Pacal's sarcophagus lid in the Temple of the Inscriptions at Palenque. God K is the "flare god" who is seen to emerge from the open jaws of the left west-facing serpent that is draped over the central cross. (From Greene Robertson *et al.* 1976: 80.)

Fig. 39 (above) Stucco panel of God K from the north side of the Palace substructure, Tier 1, Palenque. Note the probable T617 "mirror" infix in the forehead with a cigar or smoking-tube thrust through it. Photograph by the author.

Fig. 40 (right) Highly polished convex mirror found in Tomb 2 of Temple 18A, Palenque. It is probably composed of hematite, and has the approximate dimensions of 38 x 25 x 1 millimeters. Palenque Museum, Palenque. Photograph by the author.

147

Jaguar Baby or Toad Mother: A New Look at an Old Problem In Olmec Iconography

Peter T. Furst

STATE UNIVERSITY OF NEW YORK, ALBANY

INTRODUCTION

Virtually every discussion of Olmec iconography singles out the V-shaped cleft in the top of the head—along with the toothless "were-jaguar baby-face" mouth with which it is often associated—among the hallmarks of the Olmec style (Fig. 1). Thus far, however, no convincing explanation has been offered for the meaning of the cleft. This applies as well to the toothless gums and the curious split-ended narrow bands in the corners of some of these toothless mouths that are commonly—but, I am now convinced, erroneously—identified as "bifurcated fangs." Yet these traits are clearly diagnostic for Olmec iconography. It follows that if we had a better grasp of their real meaning we would gain a better understanding of Olmec cosmological structure. To that purpose, however, we will have to examine Olmec symbolism far more critically in the context of Mesoamerican symbolism and mythology in general, and to turn not only to analogies elsewhere in pre-Hispanic iconography but, equally important, to natural history.

As we shall see, the problem of identification is at once more complex and also more straightforward than one might have suspected. However it may vary in some details from example to example, the cleft-headed, toothless "were-jaguar baby-face" reveals itself to be unique only in style. In content and meaning it fits completely into the framework of Mesoamerican cosmological structure, and, in a sense, represents its very core. Neither "rain god," "maize god," nor "dragon," symbolic analysis and natural history in combination show it to be nothing other than the earliest recognizable ancestor of Tlaltecuhtli, the fundamental Mesoamerican Earth Mother Goddess (the Aztec "Heart of the Earth") in her animal manifestation as jaguar-toad. Whether

Fig. 1 Jadeite celt with pronounced V-shaped cleft, from the Mixteca, Oaxaca. Museo Nacional de Antropología, Mexico. Drawing by Jill Leslie Furst (after Covarrubias 1957: Pl. XVI).

149

the resemblance of the toothless mouth to that of a newborn baby is fortuitous or—and this is more likely—held some special meaning for the Olmec, it is a distinguishing characteristic of the toad, an animal that, although carnivorous, lacks teeth. What has for so long appeared to us as a "were-jaguar baby-face," is, I suggest, an anthropomorphically conceived toad with jaguar characteristics (Fig. 2). It is, in short, a classic example of transformation and mediation between contrasting but complementary beings, environments, and, by extension, cosmic realms.

No doubt the toad's life history—successive metamorphosis from egg to gill-breathing, fish-like aquatic vegetarian to four-footed, nocturnal carnivore[1]—as well as its almost legendary fertility, help account for its place in the symbolic universe. It is also likely that the psycho-pharmacological properties of the venom in its skin glands reinforced that role (see P. Furst 1972). However, as we shall see, there is in the toad's life history yet another extraordinary characteristic that fits it uniquely for its symbolic role as avatar and metaphor for the earth, not just in Mesoamerica but as far south as present-day Amazonia (*ibid.*). Toads grow by shedding their skin, but they do so in a most dramatic manner, one that also reveals the real meaning of the so-called "bifurcated fangs," and gives them a symbolic depth far beyond anything suggested by their present identification (Figs. 3–5). It also relates the toad to the Xipe complex in its several manifestations. In short, the natural behavior of few, if any, other creatures can rival the toad in degree of correspondence to some of the most fundamental

aspects of Mesoamerican cosmology and symbolism, the more so in complementary association with the jaguar.

THE V-SHAPED CLEFT

Miguel Covarrubias (1946b: 97–8), one of the earliest students of Olmec iconography and its influence on later art styles, at one point considered the possibility that the pronounced V-shaped cleft on the top of the head in Olmec art might refer to some form of sacrifice, perhaps by a blow of an axe—a suggestion for which there is no support in anything known of Mesoamerican ritual. Indeed, Covarrubias himself preferred the open fontanelle of the newborn baby as the more likely analogy, perhaps as a symbol of a connection between man and divinity through the occiput. Considering the strong emphasis on the fontanelle as a center of communication with the supernatural in Huichol symbolism, a Hopi tradition that the fontanelles of the first people in the world never closed so that they might remain in intimate contact with the gods (Waters 1963), the widespread concept of the life force residing in the head, and the numerous Pre-Columbian figurines with occipital openings, this suggestion from Covarrubias does not seem too far-fetched. At the very least he recognized that the cleft represented some sort of opening.

Ignacio Bernal (1969a: 72–3) also remarked on the V-shaped cleft as "one of the most characteristic traits" of the Olmec style and suggested that it might have been inspired by a real feature of the living jaguar—the deep furrow that often marks the head of the male.

No doubt the cleft could have held multiple associations for the Olmec, including those proposed by Covarrubias, and Bernal, but an examination of the motif elsewhere in Mesoamerican art suggests its primary function as a *sipapu*-like place of emergence from and reentry into the divine, female earth. Interestingly enough, it is precisely in the V or funnel form that Nahuat speakers in the Sierra de Puebla even now conceive of places from which supernatural beings emerge from Talocan, the divine earth generically called "Our Mother, Our Father," but supplicated as "Our Mother" in matters concerning the fertile milpa or

---

[1] In the wild, toads rely exclusively on live, moving food, including slugs, caterpillars, cutworms, grasshoppers, and other insects. They will, in fact, eat anything small within reach. According to Mary C. Dickerson (1913: 81-6), an estimated 88 percent of a toad's food consists of insects and other small creatures injurious to garden and field crops. As toads require a full stomach four times daily, but are inactive in daytime, they must hunt almost incessantly at night to fill their needs. Lacking teeth with which to grasp prey, the toad has a sticky tongue admirably adapted to catching food, being fastened in the front of the mouth instead of at the back and capable of extending two or more inches in exceedingly rapid movements.

Fig. 2 Mature female toad of the species *Bufo marinus.* Skeletal remains of this species were found by M. Coe at the Olmec ceremonial site of San Lorenzo. The characteristic V- or U-shaped cleft on the head is not as pronounced as that of *B. valliceps,* another impressive Mexican species with which *B. marinus* co-exists in the tropical lowlands, but it is nonetheless an unmistakable characteristic, as is the large, triangular protoid gland. Also to be noted is the typical skin pattern on the chest, which closely resembles the well-known "earth pattern" in pre-Hispanic Mesoamerican iconography and early post-conquest pictorial documents. Length, approximately 15 centimeters. Photograph by the author.

diseases associated with subterranean and terrestrial water (Tim Knab, personal communication).

In short, the triangular cleft, along with the ubiquitous U element, is a gender-specific female symbol in Mesoamerica (as it is virtually everywhere). As a kind of cosmic vaginal passage through which plants or ancestors emerge from the underworld, it can be found in many places (*e.g.,* on the side of Pacal's sarcophagus at Palenque); here I will limit myself to the Mixtec codices, particularly Codex Vindobonensis Mexicanus I, or Codex Vienna, for

whose fifty-two pages we have the recently published detailed *Commentary* by Jill Leslie Furst (1978).

In this Codex, the opening through which deities, people, and plants pass from one cosmic plane to another is represented as a V-shaped cleft, whereas the painter of Vienna's "sister" manuscript, Codex Zouche-Nuttall, employed the V form interchangeably with the U. If conceptual differences governed these choices, they are not now apparent. In any event, whether V- or U-shaped, the cosmic passage is usually depicted with a scalloped

Fig. 3 (above, left) The curving bands extending "fang-like" from the corners of the mouth of some Olmec "were-jaguar baby face" representations very likely found their inspiration in the behavior of the toad as an animal manifestation of the divine earth. Toads do not discard their skin while moulting but swallow it; here, the skin of the front of the body and the forearms dangles like black bands from the corners of the wide jaws of a female *Bufo marinus*, while that of the hind legs strikingly resembles the characteristic Olmec cleft element as it disappears into the mouth. Photograph by the author.

Fig. 4 (above) With the process of symbolic rebirth through the shedding of the dead skin almost completed, the giant toad. *Bufo marinus*—prototype for the Mesoamerican "earth-monster"—pulls the last of the old epidermis (that covering the forearms) into the corners of the wide, toothless jaws. As it disappears, it will assume the cleft appearance so characteristic of Olmec art. Photograph by the author.

Fig. 5 (right) The well-known V-shaped cleft and the ubiquitous U element in Olmec art may well have found their inspiration in the pronounced ridges on top of the head of *Bufo marinus*, the giant toad that from Preclassic to Aztec times served as animal avatar for the divine earth and prototype of the "earth-monster." If so, the Olmec U may be a shorthand hieroglyph for the earth or the Earth Goddess. Photograph by the author.

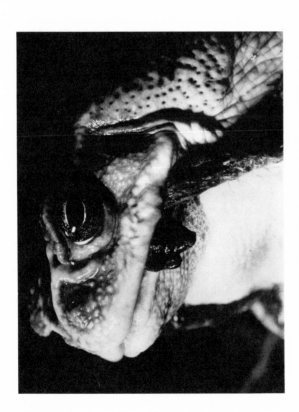

skin-like lining identified by J. Furst (personal communication), by analogy with scenes of birth and the conventional depiction of umbilical cords, as "birth skin." Although there are occasional exceptions, the "birth skin" is conventionally employed to denote V-shaped clefts that function, unlike other kinds of fissures in the earth, as cosmic passages, and presumably it symbolizes their identification with the female birth organs. The following consideration of some of the *sipapu*-like V-shaped clefts is adapted from J. Furst (1978).

The first two triangular openings occur side by side on the very first page of Codex Vienna, page 52² (Fig. 6), as emergence and re-entry holes of the curious small earth beings whom Alfonso Caso, in his many commentaries on the Mixtec genealogical codices, called "xolotls." Why the cleft at left, with the ascending xolotl, is unlined, while that at right, with the xolotl descending headfirst into the earth, has the "birth-skin" lining, is not clear, but their general correspondence to the Olmec cleft is unmistakable.

Codex Vienna's next V-shaped cosmic passage is found on page 49, on an elongated oval object—probably a place sign—identified by its diagonal multicolored stripes (the conventional Mixtec symbol for stone) as consisting of stone. It is, in fact, one of numerous stone forms magically generated by two deities, ♂ 8 Alligator and ♀ 4 Dog, a pair of creator deities who in Codex Vienna are responsible for the appearance not only of stone place signs but also the stone blade from which the Mixtec culture hero ♂ 9 Wind is born. ♂ 9 Wind is depicted on the same page, attached to the stone blade by an umbilical cord emerging from a skin-lined V-shaped cleft.

Another cleft occurs on the following page, 48, as a cosmic opening in the sky band through which ♂ 9 Wind descends from the heavens along a celestial rope. One of two

V-shaped clefts gives birth to a nude figure seated in a spout of water on page 27 (Fig. 7). Two more such clefts in the earth occur immediately above this scene, one with an emerging line of footprints, the other with a plant. The similarity of this latter motif to plants emerging from the V-shaped cleft in Olmec art (Figs. 8 and 9) is unmistakable.

The most striking representation of the V-shaped cleft as entrance and exit from the underworld is found on page 24 of Codex Vienna (Fig. 10), immediately below a scene that depicts the divine establishment of the ritual consumption of sacred mushrooms. Here, a male deity named 7 Wind is shown disappearing headfirst into the underworld through a V-shaped cleft in the surface of a river. In the following scene, below, the same god has emerged from his visit to the underworld, bearing a plant that has yet to be botanically identified. The river, conventionalized as a flattened double-outlined U filled with water and containing a hand grasping a bundle of feathers, is the customary toponym for Apoala, a town in the Mixteca Alta regarded by the ancient Mixtecs as the birthplace of their gods and noble lineages, who were believed to have sprung from a divine tree that stood beside the Apoala River. This miraculous birth from a sacred tree, whose personification J. Furst (1977) identified as the goddess ♀ 9 Reed, is depicted on Codex Vienna page 37 (Fig. 11). Here a nude male is shown emerging from a V-shaped cleft at the top of the tree, whose form suggests an upside down female, with her head (that of the goddess ♀ 9 Reed) at the base and the generative organ at the top. Above the emerging male is a nude female, and this pair is followed by a large number of other individuals who were also born from the divine tree.

To return to the scene on page 24 (Fig. 10), superimposed on the river is a circle divided into four quarters and containing footprints circling the intersection of the north-south and east-west axes. By linguistic analysis, M. Smith (1973) identified the four-quartered circle-with-footprints as the sign for market or plaza; J. Furst's analysis of its use in Codex Vienna suggests the additional meaning of sa-

---

² The fifty-two pages of Codex Vienna were erroneously numbered from left to right following its arrival in Europe shortly after the conquest of Mexico. In fact, like other Mesoamerican pictorial manuscripts, Codex Vienna reads from right to left, so that the page numbered 52 is actually page 1.

Fig. 6 Emergence and descent of xolotls through V-shaped clefts in the earth. Codex Vienna, page 52a. Drawing by Jill Leslie Furst.

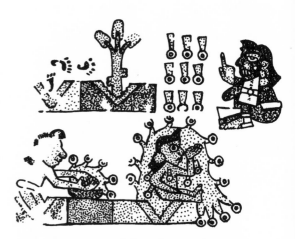

Fig. 7 Emergence of footprints, maize, water, and human figures from two pairs of V-shaped clefts in the earth. Codex Vienna, page 27b. Drawing by Jill Leslie Furst.

Fig. 8 Jadeite celt with tree or maize plant emerging from a V-shaped cleft. Said to be from Arroyo Pesquero, Veracruz. Height, 22.7 cm.; width, 5.8 cm. Private collection. Drawing by Jill Leslie Furst (after a photograph by Robert Sonin).

Fig. 9 Jadeite celt with an incised profile deity. Drawing by Jill Leslie Furst (after Covarrubias 1957: Fig. 33).

Fig. 10 Descent and re-emergence through the V-shaped cleft in the river at Apoala, in the Mixteca Alta. Codex Vienna, page 24b. Drawing by Jill Leslie Furst.

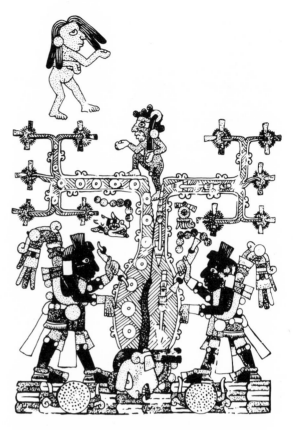

Fig. 11 The birth of Mixtec gods and nobles from the sacred tree at Apoala. The head at the base has been identified as that of the goddess 9 Reed (J. Furst 1977). Codex Vienna, page 37b. Drawing by the author.

cred center as a place of entry into the underworld.

The depiction of ♂ 7 Wind's descent and re-emergence through the cosmic passage in the river also suggests something of the extraordinary continuity that characterizes Mesoamerican cosmological structure and symbolism. The configuration of river, V-shaped cleft and circle divided into four quarters, painted not long before the Spanish conquest, replicates to a remarkable degree a similar configuration on an Olmec celt dating from the Early to Middle Formative Period, *i.e.*, nearly 2500 years earlier (Fig. 9). The top of the flattened head or headdress of the deity incised on the jade celt has a V-shaped cleft from which sprouts a plant resembling (but not necessarily

representing) maize. Immediately below the point of the V is a double-outlined flattened U with another V-shaped cleft in the line connecting the two sides. At the point of this second cleft is a circle in the center of two crossed bands that divide the field into four quarters. The total configuration could be read in much the same way as its Mixtec counterpart: as a symbol or even a toponym consisting of a uterine river with a triangular cleft as entry into and emergence hole from the center of the earth. A second U element, laid on its side, with the opening facing to the left and with four circles at the corners (possibly conjoining a cave as womb of the earth with the cardinal points), brackets the deity's open mouth. One may question the validity of an analogy be-

155

tween the Olmec and Mixtec configurations, however similar, on grounds of the enormous span of time dividing them.[3] But, as William Isbell (1978: 271) has noted in a stimulating contribution to the problem of continuity in New World cosmological structures, the "probability that a configuration of formal and relational criteria could be repeated by chance without communicating the same structural meaning is diminishingly small." It does seem to me that this configuration of separate symbols is sufficiently complex in this case to satisfy Nicholson's wise counsel that to make a compelling case for long-term ideological continuity, particularly from the Olmec to the late Post-Classic peoples, requires associated clusters of iconographic elements rather than a single trait (Nicholson 1976: 163).

As a final observation on the specifically *female* symbolism of the triangular cleft, we should not overlook the *quechquemitl*, the distinctive triangular female garment that, in pre-Hispanic times, was reserved for the fertility goddesses and certain human females of noble status who were in one way or another identified with these deities (see Heyden 1977). In Codex Vienna it is worn more often by ♀ 9 Grass, the Earth Goddess, than by any other deity, but the greatest number of different kinds of *quechquemitl* belongs to ♀ 9 Reed, the divine personification of the birth tree (Fig. 12), who is variously associated with a "Shell Quechquemitl," a "Flint Quechquemitl," and a "Jeweled Quechquemitl," all three of which are apparently also her personal names (J. Furst 1978). It is also an attribute of ♀ 1 Eagle, identified by J. Furst as the goddess of rivers, terrestrial water and steambaths, whose watery realm is symbolized by the U-shaped river sign with its evident uterine connotation. As Alfonso Caso (1964) was the first to demonstrate in his commentaries on the Mixtec historical codices Selden and Bodley, the *quechquemitl* was often incorporated into the personal names of human

Fig. 12 The Mixtec goddess of the divine birth tree, ♀ 9 Reed, wearing the V-shaped quechquemitl, with two additional quechquemitls as her personal names. Codex Vienna, page 28c. Drawing by Jill Leslie Furst.

females with direct affiliations with the goddesses, in particular ♀ 6 Monkey, the female ruler of a town called "Belching Mountain." Her calendrical and personal name at one point in her life was ♀ 6 Monkey "Serpent Quechquemitl," and at another ♀ 6 Monkey "Warband Quechquemitl." The latter name was conferred after a successful military campaign against her enemies, in which the goddess 9 Grass intervened on her behalf. As is evident from the pictoral documents, while males and females could share many other personal names, the honorific "Quechquemitl" was exclusively reserved for females.

Lest it be thought that the triangular shape of the *quechquemitl* bears no symbolic relationship to female sexuality but is entirely fortuitous, in the Sierra de Puebla to this day the garment serves as a metaphor for the female genitalia, as illustrated by this widely known male Nahuat joking riddle: "What does a woman wear when she wears nothing at all?" Answer: "Her *quechquemitl*" (Tim Knab, personal communication).

To repeat, like the "uterine U"—a common element in Olmec art that is prominent also on the monuments at Izapa (see Norman 1973, 1976)—the V-shaped cleft is a symbol of female

[3] The configuration of U-shaped river/crossed bands/ V-shaped cleft in Olmec art is not limited to the example illustrated here but occurs elsewhere, *e.g.,* as the eye of a cleft stone mask illustrated by Joralemon (1976:45, Fig. 13g).

Fig. 13 The Mixtec "earth-monster" with the year 5 Flint and the day 5 Flint. The head in the jaws is presumably that of the maize goddess ♀ 5 Flint (Nowotny 1948). Codex Vienna, page 47b. Drawing by Jill Leslie Furst.

sexuality and reproduction, directly associated with the life-bearing earth, a conclusion that has obvious implications for the conceptual gender of Olmec deities distinguished by this trait and that, of course, raises the question whether we are really dealing with discrete beings at all and not a single fundamental deity with multiple manifestations.

The foregoing is by no means intended to suggest Olmec monotheism, for that would be as much out of character for a Mesoamerican people as the thus-far exclusively male pantheon suggested for the Olmec by some of the recent literature (Joralemon 1971, 1976). Rather, it is intended to single out a Meso-american core concept—a master myth, if one will—within the pantheistic symbolic system of the Olmec who, if not the "mother culture" of a Mesoamerican co-tradition, are certainly its first complex manifestation.

THE "WERE-JAGUAR BABY-FACE" AS TLALTECUHTLI

If the V-shaped cleft on the top of the head is the feminine passage from and into the womb of the generative female earth, it follows that much of the literature about the cleft-headed "were-jaguar baby-face" has taken us in wrong directions: it is neither male nor ancestral to one or another masculine deity in later pantheons, nor, for that matter, really infantile. It is, in fact, not even a were-jaguar. Instead, as suggested, it appears to be nothing other than the

Olmec expression of a fundamental concept in pan-Mesoamerican cosmological structure— the sacred earth as paradoxical Great Mother, conceived heteromorphically as a feline toad, sometimes with added traits of birds and animals with related or complementary associations. The ideological link could be with any Mesoamerican species of toad, but for the Olmec it would have been either *Bufo marinus* or the Gulf Coast toad, *B. valliceps,* the latter distinguished by a deep valley or concavity between two prominent crests on top of the head that inevitably recalls the V-shaped cleft of Olmec art. The toad lacks teeth, but, divorced as we are from the natural world, we failed to perceive the real significance of those toothless gums, taking them for the mark of the newborn infant presumably because that is the sole analogy with which we have direct experience, and bolstering that tenuous model with speculations about infant sacrifice, infantile rain gods, and offspring of sexual unions between human females and male jaguars.[4]

The toad's jaguar attributes, in Olmec art confined mostly to the upturned lip and more rarely to a pair of realistic canines, eventually shifted to the fanged jaws and clawed extremities of the Mixtec "earth-monster" (Fig. 13) and her Aztec counterpart, Tlaltecuhtli, the Mother of the Gods and Heart of the Earth as a polymorphic creature in which, 2500 years

---

[4] The Olmec were certainly interested in infantilism, but it is unclear just where their focus lay. If the interpretation of the toothless mouth as that of the toad is correct, "infants" or dwarfs formerly taken to be "were-jaguars" may be infantile anthropomorphized toads or dwarfs with toad-feline characters. If so, what is their relationship to the naturalistic human figures with whom they are often associated in what appears like a parent-child relationship— *e.g.,* the standing jade figurine holding a dwarfish being with a wide, toothless mouth and cleft head in the Brooklyn Museum (see M. Coe 1965a:12), or, for that matter, the seated Las Limas figure with the "baby" across the lap? Another question is that of their gender. Are they, as has long been thought, males lacking genitals or, in fact, females? Considering that non-Olmec Early and Middle Formative figurines are overwhelmingly female, I suspect that this applies also to many, if not most, Olmec effigies (and also to the deity in Relief I at Chalcatzingo) and that much of our speculation about the absence of genitals has been due to an unconscious male bias in Olmec iconographic studies.

157

after the Olmec, the toad remains the fundamental and dominant component. This shift in emphasis on the devouring aspect of the earth is worth further exploration, for it may well reflect the same ecological concerns and fears for the continued ability of the gods—especially the Earth Goddess—to provide sustenance that on another level led to ever greater blood sacrifice as the price of cyclical renewal and human survival. The identification of the toad motif in Olmec art has the additional advantage of extending continuity in earth symbolism by half a millennium or more beyond the monumental toad "altars" at Izapa, of which several have feline traits. Parenthetically, it might be noted that the toad as Earth Goddess and originator of food plants is an important mythological motif not only in Mesoamerica but also over much of northern lowland South America, from the eastern slopes of the Bolivian Andes and upper Amazonia to the Guianas, a distribution that suggests a very ancient common ideological substratum (P. Furst 1972).

SYMBOLIC DEATH AND REGENERATION

If the true significance of the toothless mouth of the so-called "were-jaguar" has been missed, the misunderstanding has been compounded by the erroneous identification of the peculiar, cleft-ended bands in the corners of some of these mouths as "fangs" (Figs. 14–16). Naturalistic canines are represented in Olmec art; as mentioned above, some otherwise toothless effigies of the so-called "were-jaguar babyface" type have pairs of pointed canines projecting from the upper gums (see Dockstader 1964: Fig. 61; Joralemon 1971: 77–8). This alone should have suggested that the cleft-ended or split elements extending like curving bands over the upper and lower lips are of a very different order and even material from teeth, and so presumably convey a meaning or meanings unrelated to that of predatory feline, the more so since similar split-ended band elements that occur outside the specific context of the toothless mouth could hardly be understood as teeth. But even those that protrude from the mouth—especially where, as in Figure 14, the cleft, squared-off ends are bent almost at right angles—can be said to resemble fangs

only by suspending all reference to actual feline dentition.

But if not fangs of some special sort, what are those perplexing split-ended elements? The answer follows inevitably from the identification of the toad, for, if it is correct, they cease to be enigmas and even their symbolic function is suggested.

Toads are long-lived, with recorded lifespans of up to forty years. In Olmec times the oldest living toad would thus have outlived most of the human population. Such extraordinary longevity must have made the creature appear well-nigh immortal, especially if—as the priest-shamans of the Bolivian Tacana do to this day—toads were kept under direct observation in ritual captivity as avatars of the divine earth (see Hissink and Hahn 1961; P. Furst 1972). The discovery of numerous *Bufo* bones in Olmec middens on the artificial ceremonial plateau at San Lorenzo, Veracruz, raises the question of similar or related ritual practices by the Olmec, especially inasmuch as the possibility of intrusive burrowing toads is ruled out by the archaeological context and the non-articulated nature of the skeletal remains (Michael D. Coe, personal communication).

The growth of the toad proceeds, following metamorphosis from aquatic, gill-breathing tadpole into air-breathing four-footed carnivore, by the shedding of the outer horny epidermis. In the young, rapidly growing toad, this happens every few weeks, while adult toads shed their skin perhaps four times a year. So far this seems hardly unusual, since reptiles, other members of the Batrachia, and also spiders share this characteristic. What dramatically sets *Bufo* apart is that the dead skin is not only shed *in one piece* but is swallowed whole and digested by its owner. Indeed, it could be said that several times a year the toad swallows itself and is reborn. It is this extraordinary process of cyclical renewal that offers a reasonable explanation for the enigmatic split-ended curving bands in Olmec art, even as it tends to confirm the toad identification as essentially correct.

The shedding is described in detail for *Bufo americanus* by Mary C. Dickerson (1913: 73–5), from whose book on North American

Fig. 14 Basalt celt, provenience unknown. Height, 31 cm. The Metropolitan Museum of Art, New York. Drawing by Jill Leslie Furst (after Covarrubias 1957: Pl. XVI).

Fig. 16 The "Kuntz Axe," provenience Oaxaca(?). Height, 28 cm. American Museum of Natural History, New York. Drawing by Jill Leslie Furst (after Covarrubias 1957: Pl. XVI).

Fig. 15 Jadeite celt. Drawing by Jill Leslie Furst (after Covarrubias 1957: Fig. 34).

frogs and toads the following is abstracted. No peculiarities of behavior precede the cyclical moulting. When the toad is ready to shed its skin, it assumes a humped position, the head bent downward and the feet drawn up under it (the very position, it should be noted, of toad effigy "altars" at Izapa and elsewhere [Fig. 17]). The skin splits along certain definite lines, beginning along the midline of the head[5] and extending, in one direction, down the back, over the tail, and along the underside, and, in the other, across the breast from arm to arm to the base of the first finger. To understand the moulting process, it is necessary to know that the skin of the head is continuous over the lips with the skin of the mouth, and that the skin of the lips is shed together with the rest. After splitting, the skin begins to be drawn, or

---

[5] The cleft on the forehead in Figure 14 presumably represents the split in the moulting skin that begins at the midline of the head. Less easily explained is the bifurcated element projecting from the beaks of some so-called "Bird-Monster" (Joralemon's God III) representations. This, too, is usually called a "fang." Inasmuch as these birds are composite celestial-terrestrial beings, the bifid element might be read as a stylized forked serpent's tongue. More likely, if its meaning is similar to the bifurcated bands in the mouths of toothless feline toads, it may refer to celestial-terrestrial complementarity and cyclical renewal, especially inasmuch as birds, too, renew themselves by moulting. Might this be a case where the metaphor is extended from toad to bird, so that the split-ended element actually becomes a sign or glyph for "renewal" or a related concept? Perhaps the whole bird-serpent association so typical of pan-Mesoamerican iconography is not based just on complementary celestial-terrestrial opposition but also on perceived similarities in the cyclical moulting—*i.e.,* renewal or regeneration—of birds and reptiles. If so, the ancient Mesoamericans anticipated western science in recognizing essential relationships between the avian and reptilian fauna.

159

Peter T. Furst

sucked, into the corners of the wide mouth. It is, in fact, the mouth that does most of the work of removing the dead epidermis, repeatedly opening widely to suck in the bands of skin, while the humped body expands and contracts to loosen the old epidermis and help work it forward. In this way the skin is gradually pulled in bands into the angles of the mouth. When the hind end and back legs are freed, the old skin lies in two dark bands extending from the corners of the mouth around the upper parts of the arms, whose skin, along with that nearest the mouth, is the last part to be shed and swallowed. With a few final vigorous efforts, the epidermis, split on the underside to the fingers, is pulled off the hands and sucked as black bands, ending in the trailing split feet, into the angles of the mouth, to be transformed into nourishment in the toad's own belly.[6]

The so-called "bifurcated fangs" thus appear as nothing other than nature replicated to symbolize the drama of cyclical death and rebirth in the earth. By depicting in a composite image this extraordinary process in the toad as the earth's metaphor precisely at the point when the animal is altogether free of its dead epidermis, while the last of it is still being sucked into its own toothless mouth, the Olmec artist has admirably succeeded in synthesizing destruction and regeneration in a single image (Figs. 14–16), with the split feet reduced to their barest essentials. (For a strikingly similar conventionalization of the feet, see Figure 18, depicting the toad as earth-monster on a U-shaped *yugo* from Veracruz). If the analysis is even approximately valid, the cleft-headed toothless effigies and those with split bands in the angles of the toothless mouth, but generally lacking the cleft on top of the head, are not

Fig. 17 Basalt toad effigy "altar," Kaminaljuyú, Guatemala. Width, 57.2 cm.; length, 57.2 cm.; height, 6.4 cm. Museo Popol Vuh, Guatemala City. This extraordinary carving of a recumbent toad shares with later effigies of the male Maya solar deity the characteristic curling elements emerging from the corners of the mouth. From observation of the behavior of the living animal, it is now clear that these previously unexplained curls represent nothing less than the final stage of moulting —the moment of renewal or rebirth—when the last of the dead skin disappears into the toad's mouth (see Figs. 3-5). In the initial stages of the moulting process, which takes but a few minutes in nature, the old skin begins to split laterally along the back and underside of the animal. This characteristic presumably explains the thin engraved zigzag line extending from the top of the head to the tail on the back of this Late Formative effigy sculpture. Effigies of toads, especially in the form of small stone mortars, are quite common in the Late Formative in the Guatemalan highlands, particularly at Kaminaljuyú; likewise, the toad sometimes appears in direct association with effigies of mushrooms, presumably representing one or another species of the various psychoactive fungi used in Mesoamerican ritual to the present day. Although no inferences should be drawn for any direct pre-Hispanic contact between the two hemispheres, it is interesting to note that the toad-mushroom association also occurs in Eurasia, suggesting at the least the possibility of very ancient common origins. Photograph by the author.

---

[6] In this connection, it is significant that, at the conclusion of Aztec rites related to the Xipe, or flaying, complex, the skins of flayed sacrifices, after having been worn by the priests in personification of the gods, were customarily deposited in a cave (see Sahagún 1969, I:112, 148). Caves, of course, were (and still are) conceived as entrances to the underworld and the womb of the earth. It should also be noted that the costume of Xipe, as described by Sahagún (1950-69, Book I:40) in the Florentine Codex, included a headband with split or forked ends.

two different Olmec deities but the same being in different manifestations or symbolic contexts—the one the earth as genetrix, the other the earth in cyclical or seasonal renewal.

Some final observations are in order. If such iconographic peculiarities as the "bifurcated fangs" failed for so long to stimulate more than impressionistic consideration, this was a function of the bias of most investigators, myself

Fig. 18 Detail of *yugo* from Veracruz. Museo Nacional de Antropología, Mexico. Drawing by Jill Leslie Furst (after Bernal and Seuffert 1970: Fig. 7).

reconstruction succeeds only in further removing Olmec religion from the mainstream of Mesoamerican ideology; to accept it as valid would tend to mitigate against, rather than for, the very continuity in Mesoamerican cosmological structure for which Nicholson (1976) and, indeed, Joralemon himself have argued. By all means the Olmec must be granted many gods in many guises. But surely they were good Mesoamericans, and as such their pantheon must have included female as well as male supernaturals, with complementary as well as overlapping functions. Yet in all the attempts thus far at reconstructing Olmec gods one looks in vain for an acknowledgement of this fundamental characteristic of pan-Mesoamerican religion. It is time the balance was restored.

included, in favor of a "feline hypothesis": if the effigies are were-jaguars, what else would the double pairs of split-ended elements be but fangs, however much they diverge from the natural model or naturalistically depicted canines? Joralemon (1976) correctly deflated the jaguar as *the* predominant animal in Olmec iconography and drew attention to other creatures, including a cayman or alligator, in polymorphic Olmec symbolism. Unfortunately, his elaboration of his earlier God I into an iconographically more complex, but still exclusively male, "Olmec Dragon" as the principal, not to say functionally universal, god is no improvement.[7] In fact, in its own way such a

[7] "God I is a polymorphic dragon whose association [sic] include earth, maize, agricultural fertility, clouds, rain, water, fire, and kingship" (Joralemon 1976:58). Elsewhere (*ibid.*: 37), the same author writes "God I's primary associations are with earth, water, and agricultural fertility.... Representations that depict vegetation sprouting from the deity's body suggest that the Olmec identified God I with the earth itself and imagined *him* [italics mine] as the ultimate source of agricultural abundance." Considering the above, and Joralemon's conviction—with which I agree—that God I and other Olmec gods are ancestral to those of the Late Postclassic, it is difficult to understand his reluctance to draw the almost inevitable conclusion that, even if we accept his definition of this deity, God I would have had to be *female,* not *male.* The fundamental Aztec earth deity was Toci, Our Grandmother (also known by several other names), Tlaltecuhtli, the feline toad-monster, being her animal manifestation. The fundamental maize goddess was Chicomecóatl, also known as Xilonen; the terrestrial waters were the domain of Chalchiuh-

tlicue in the Aztec pantheon and ♀ 1 Eagle in the Mixtec (J. Furst 1978); agricultural fertility was primarily the realm of what Nicholson (1971) called the Teteoinnan (Mother of the Gods) Complex, and there are further examples which might be cited. If all this had its earlier manifestation in the Olmec pantheon, why refer to God I as "him?" Of course, fertility in Aztec ideology had its male patrons as well (indeed, fertility by definition is a function of male-female complementarity), but most of the attributes of God I in Joralemon's list are female in both Aztec and Mixtec cosmology. As for an analogy between God I as "the Olmec maize god" and the Aztec Centéotl (Joralemon 1971), Centéotl is a complex figure whose maize aspect may have been primarily the male, fertilizing maize—*i.e.,* the seed corn and the phallic *elote,* or new maize ear within its husk. The Huichols have much the same complementary categories for maize: maize as such is female (Our Mother 'Utuanáka), but there is a male aspect in the personification of the *elote* and the fertilizing seed corn. Centéotl as the new ear emerging from the husk is of a different (although obviously complementary) order from his mother, the maize plant born from the generative female earth. For that reason I would also caution against facile identifications of the apparently cleft-headed God E in Codex Madrid as "the maize god." The curving split in the head of this deity is quite different from the well-defined V-shaped clefts in Olmec and Mixtec art, and may refer to the opening husk rather than to the earth as genetrix. The same cautionary remarks apply to the depiction of this deity at Tancah, Quintana Roo, in a mural published by Arthur Miller (1977: Fig. 18). Here the curving of the split, which has a *kan* sign in the center, is very pronounced, longer toward the rear than to the front, suggesting even more strongly the falling away of the husk rather than the feminine V-shaped cleft in the earth as emergence hole of the sacred plant.

Clearly the iconographer, in addition to customary preconditions, needs to function at once as art historian, ethnographer and historian of religion, and naturalist, able, insofar as possible, to penetrate and assimilate native categories and symbolic associations. Above all, as in the study of such primary sources as the pre-Hispanic codices, he or she must assume that the ancient artist correctly transferred the oral traditions and perceptions of his time to his medium; in other words, the visual evidence must be believed and analyzed for what it says (see J. Furst 1978: 6–12). To lump together the naturalistic treatment of jaguar canines in Olmec art with very differently conceived cleft elements, to mention but one example, is not to listen to the primary data but to impose one's own categories and preconceptions on the material.

The complexities of Olmec iconography are considerable, and, as with other symbolic systems, the primary images of Olmec art were added to and subtracted from in accordance with their ritual and conceptual contexts. Much will defy our understanding, but the material need not all remain intractable. The task before us, it seems to me, is not to create gods or build models but to learn how Native American peoples divided and classified the world and how much of that aboriginal cosmological structure endured through time.

ACKNOWLEDGMENTS Jill Leslie Furst contributed considerably to the ideas expressed in this paper and her participation is gratefully acknowledged. It was, in fact, her analysis of Codex Vienna and her references to V-shaped clefts as emergence holes in the earth that initially stimulated a reconsideration of the Olmec cleft. This, in turn, led to a closer look at the meaning of the toothless mouth and, finally, to the split-ended bands in the corners of some of these.

The Old Woman and the Child:
Themes in the Iconography of Preclassic Mesoamerica

Peter David Joralemon
YALE UNIVERSITY

It is remarkable that the corpus of Olmec art includes so few identifiable female representations. La Venta Stela 1 (de la Fuente 1977: Lám. 66) portrays a woman, Relief 1 from Chalcatzingo (Gay 1971: Fig. 11) pictures an important female, and a seated jade figurine from La Venta (Bernal 1969a: Pl. 37a) is almost certainly a lady. There are few other examples. It is also very curious that Olmec sculpture seldom depicts old age. The kneeling transformation figure in the Princeton Art Museum is obviously a portrait of an old man, and there is another representation of a bearded old male at Dumbarton Oaks (Dumbarton Oaks 1963: Pl. 29). Other examples are rare.[1] The discovery of Olmec figures that portray old women is thus doubly important.

During the past ten years, I have had the opportunity to study eighteen Preclassic figurines that represent old hags. They generally have wrinkled faces, pendulous breasts, and exposed ribs. Several of the old women are pregnant, and two of them cradle Olmec infants in their laps. Although most of the figurines are Olmec in style, some of the sculptures were produced by Olmec-influenced Formative cultures of Mesoamerica. The following pages describe the figures in some detail and discuss what these ancient ladies might tell us about the early religious beliefs of Pre-Columbian America.

During the University of California's 1968 excavations at La Venta, a fragmentary Olmec figurine (Fig. 1) was discovered in Test Pit 1 in the Great Platform (Hallinan et al. 1968: 156–7, Pls. 8a and b). The coarse, orange clay sculpture depicts a seated old woman with pendulous breasts and outstretched leg. The eyes are formed by shallow troughs, the nose is short and arched, and the cheekbones are prominent. Her mouth is marked by a simple horizontal line; the lower jaw is thrust forward and the swollen lip protrudes. The old lady's cheeks are deeply sunken; vertical wrinkles frame her chin. The texture of the hair is indicated by rows of short incised lines. The ears are simple lugs. Although the body is badly damaged, it is clear that the figure leaned forward and turned to allow the arm to rest on the lower leg. The head tilts slightly to the right.

Two other fragmentary Olmec figurines, which are said to come from La Venta, are pictured in Cabecitas olmecas (González Calderón 1977: Fotos 157 and 162). Although the published photographs of the pieces are of poor quality, it is clear that both carvings represent old hags. The woman's wrinkled, hollow cheeks, toothless mouth, and long, flat breasts are evident in both cases.

A fourth representation of an Olmec grandmother (Fig. 2) is illustrated in *The Jaguar's Children* (M. Coe 1965a: Fig. 200). The figure is carved in buff clay and painted with red pig-

---

[1] Clay masks with caricatured old faces have been found at Las Bocas, Tlapacoya, and Tlatilco (M. Coe 1965a:Figs. 78, 161-4). Since these images only portray faces, the sex of the creatures represented is impossible to determine with certainty.

Fig. 1 Seated clay figurine from La Venta, Tabasco. Height, 9 cm. (After Hallinan *et al.* 1968: Pl. 8a.)

Three other figures of elderly females have been discovered in Preclassic sites in the Chalchuapa region of El Salvador. The two seated sculptures were reportedly found together, but the standing woman is said to have come from a different location. All show stylistic associations with Las Charcas figurines from Guatemala (Kidder 1965).

The seated hags are hunched and emaciated. The white-slipped clay figure sits with her long, thin legs crossed and her back sharply bent (Figs. 3 and 4). Her left arm rests on the thigh, and the right arm, which is now missing, touched her knee. The old woman's asymmetrical facial features give her a slightly pained expression. Her small, almond eyes are set in

ment. It is said to come from Las Bocas, Puebla. The woman sits cross-legged with her hands resting easily on her knees. The sculptor has given the hag a wonderfully wry, witty expression. The eyes are represented by simple slits between the swollen lids. Prominent cheekbones and brow ridges rim the large, sunken eye orbits. The old lady's mouth is held at a jaunty angle and, like that of her La Venta counterparts, her lower lip is swollen and protuberant. The hag's skin is deeply wrinkled and folded. The wrinkles are not confined to the face: the dangling dugs, swollen belly, and upper arms are also deeply furrowed. Diagonal rib markings appear on the old woman's back.

From the Chalchuapa Archaeological Project's excavations in El Salvador comes a white-slipped figurine fragment, a head with the features of an old woman (Sharer 1978, II: 160, Fig. 12e2). She has crescent eyes with slit pupils and well-formed eyeballs. Brow ridges, nose, and cheekbones are prominent. The cheeks are wrinkled and the toothless mouth hangs open to reveal her tongue. Hair is marked with three deep gashes. The figurine is associated with the Kulil ceramic complex at Chalchuapa.

Fig. 2 Seated pottery figure from Las Bocas, Puebla. Height, 9.2 cm. Private collection. Photograph by the author.

sunken hollows. The pupils are punched. The mouth has the limpness of extreme age and the forehead is covered with wrinkles. Curved, plaquelike motifs indicate the cheeks and jowls. Most of the head and upper torso is covered with red pigment, but a square patch on the back of the head was left unpainted. This may mark the place where a hair piece or head ornament was originally attached. The old woman's body is thin. She has small, limp breasts and a vaginal slit. Wrinkles appear on her chest and drooping belly. The figure's ribs, scapulae, spine, and vertebrae are all clearly shown.

A more fragmentary old-female figurine (Figs. 5 and 6) was found with the white-slipped lady. The style of the two pieces is so similar that they may have been fashioned by the same artist. The second grandmother is carved in coarse, buff clay and painted red. She sits in a stooped position, but her arms and legs are missing. The figure's twisted face has sunken, almond eyes, hollow cheeks, and a limp mouth with thin lips. Vertical folds of flesh extend from the nose to the jaw line. Deep wrinkles appear on the forehead, chest, and abdomen of the old lady. Her small, flat breasts hang down over the protuberant belly. The vulva is indicated. The woman's back is identical to the white-slipped lady's hindside: ribs, spine, and shoulder blades are all carefully marked. The figure is now in the Barbier-Müller Collection in Geneva.

A standing old lady from El Salvador is the only figurine in this group depicted in that position (Fig. 7). The buff-clay sculpture leans forward from the waist; its entire weight is supported by the heavy legs and arched feet. The woman's left hand rests on the upper pelvis, and the right arm presses against the small of the back. The hag's face is horrific. Her large, crescent eyes have deeply punched pupils. Prominent cheekbones and a bulbous nose accentuate the hollows of her cheeks. The mouth hangs ajar and the tongue lolls out of one corner. A curved line across the forehead marks the hair. The lug-shaped ears have large holes in the lobes. The hag's small, dangling breasts are asymmetrical; there are deep folds across her abdomen. The vaginal slit is incised.

Fig. 3 Seated ceramic figurine from the Chalchuapa region of El Salvador. Height, 7.2 cm. Private collection. Drawing by Elizabeth J. Kuether.

Fig. 4 Rear view of Figure 3. Drawing by Elizabeth J. Kuether.

165

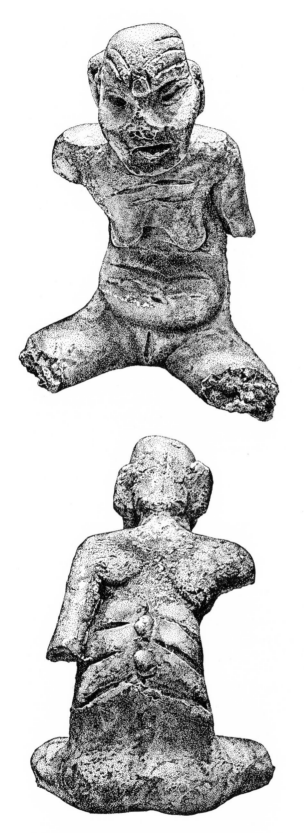

Fig. 5 (above, left) Fragment of a seated clay figure from the Chalchuapa region of El Salvador. Height, 7.8 cm. Collection Barbier-Müller, Genève. Drawing by Elizabeth J. Kuether.

Fig. 6 (left) Rear view of Figure 5. Drawing by Elizabeth J. Kuether.

Fig. 7 (above) Standing pottery figure from Chalchuapa, El Salvador. Height, 21 cm. Private collection. Photograph by the author.

Fig. 8 Fragment of a terracotta hollow figure from Veracruz. Height, 9.53 cm. Private collection. Photograph by Donald Hales and the author.

Fig. 9 Fragment of a ceramic hollow figure from San Lorenzo, Veracruz. Height, 7.8 cm. Instituto Nacional de Antropología e Historia, Mexico. Photograph by the author.

Although the back of the sculpture is relatively plain, small buttocks and knee joints are shown.

One of the most interesting Olmec ceramic objects yet discovered in Veracruz is the head from a large hollow figure (Fig. 8) with the same facial features we have seen on the old-female representations described above. The Veracruz lady has large, crescent eyes with punched pupils (like the eyes of the standing Salvadoran figure), high cheekbones, and sunken cheeks with prominent jowls. Her mouth hangs open and the tongue is partially extended. Deep wrinkles mark the forehead and cheeks. Punctations indicate the texture of the hag's hair, and a smooth area across the front of the hairdress suggests a headband. The ears have curved outlines and interior modeling. The head is carved in light-brown clay.

A second buff-clay Olmec hollow-figure fragment (Fig. 9) was unearthed at San Lorenzo Tenochtitlan, Veracruz, during the Yale University excavations at that site. Although the piece is in very damaged condition, it is almost certain that the sculpture originally represented an old hag. The curved eye has a punched pupil and the cheeks are deeply wrinkled. The lower facial features have shaled off, but the upper lip is undamaged. It is marked with tics which suggest the furrowed flesh left by the toothlessness of advanced age.

It is of great interest that both these objects from Veracruz are fragments of large, hollow, ceramic figures. This is added confirmation that the Olmec depicted a variety of creatures in large clay sculptures and not just the sexless infant forms for which they are so famous.[2]

Occasionally, the hag's face or body embellishes a Preclassic clay pot. A spouted blackware vessel from Tlatilco in the Valley of Mexico is decorated with an old lady's head (Fig. 10). Her face has a slightly pugnacious expression. The large eyes are almond-shaped.

[2] Several hollow clay-figure fragments from La Venta have vaginal slits and are clearly female (de la Fuente 1972:Color Pl. 27). There is also an Olmec hollow clay figure from Tenenexpan, in a private collection, which has a beard and moustache. It is obviously male, although the figure has no genitals.

167

Fig. 10 Spouted blackware vessel from Tlatilco, D. F. Height, 11.11 cm. Private collection. Drawing by Elizabeth J. Kuether.

The nose is short and wide, the lower jaw is thrust forward, and the lower lip is enlarged and protuberant. Wrinkles arch across the forehead and crow's-feet mark the corners of the eyes.

Another Tlatilco bowl has a kneeling grandmother (Fig. 11) attached to its walls (M. Coe 1965a: Fig. 149). Her asymmetrical face has trough eyes, prominent nose, toothless mouth, and protruding chin. A narrow groove runs across the forehead. The hag's face and upper torso are covered with wrinkles. Her arms and shoulder bones are thin and angular and her hands press against her pendulous breasts. The woman's obese body contrasts noticeably with her wasted limbs. The figure is modeled in buff clay and painted with red pigment.

One of the most powerful ceramic sculptures ever discovered in the New World is the skeletalized Olmec hag from Santa Cruz, Morelos (Fig. 12), which is pictured in *The Jaguar's Children* (M. Coe 1965a: Fig. 77). The whiteware figure is an effigy vessel: the old woman's open mouth serves as the vessel's spout. The hag is kneeling in the birth-giving position

traditionally used by Mexican Indian women. The face has a pained, even tortured, expression. Her bald head is turned upward and her mouth is wide open. The eyes have deep-cut pupils, the nose is large, and the cheeks are deeply wrinkled. The rounded ears are simply modeled. Long, pendulous breasts lie across her swollen, pregnant abdomen. The arms are emaciated and the large, awkward hands grasp her knees. The woman has skeletal rib cage, shoulder blades, and pelvis. The spine is exposed. Straining neck muscles and tendons are clearly delineated. The shoulders are stooped and rounded. The extraordinary contrast between the skeletalized body, emaciated limbs, and ancient dugs of the old woman and her grossly pregnant belly and parturition posture, strongly suggests that this female is not an ordinary human but rather a supernatural being.[3]

A second sculpture of an old personage with a swollen abdomen (Figs. 13 and 14) is part of the Olmec collection of the Museo de Antropología de la Universidad de Veracruz, Jalapa (Musée Rodin 1972: Fig. 24). Although the figure lacks breasts, it is sufficiently similar to the Santa Cruz hag to suggest that it also represents a pregnant female. This sculpture is an effigy vessel; the mouth of the *tecomate*-shaped bowl is on the side of the figure's abdomen. There are holes in the back of the sculpture which allow it to be suspended; additional holes are drilled in the belly. The piece is carved in serpentine. Its provenience is unknown. The grandmother looks upward with an amused expression on her face. The crescent eyes have drilled pupils and the nose is large and beaked. Her lips are pursed, her cheeks are hollow, and her chin is prominent and pointed. Wrinkles appear on forehead, cheeks, and chin. A vertically segmented band wraps around the head, but the top of the cranium is exposed. The very large ears are well modeled. The old woman is shown in a kneeling position with her extremely swollen belly resting on her thighs. She may be in parturition. Like the

[3] There is a remarkable similarity between the poses of the Santa Cruz hag and the Aztec birth goddess in the Pre-Columbian Collection at Dumbarton Oaks (Lothrop *et al.* 1957:Pl. XXXVII).

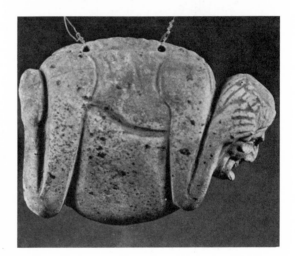

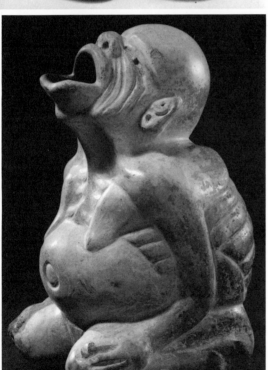

Fig. 11 (above, left) Pottery effigy *tecomate* from Tlatilco, D. F. Height, 8.57 cm. Private collection. Photograph by the author.

Fig. 12 (left) Whiteware effigy vessel from Santa Cruz, Morelos. Height, 20.64 cm. Private collection. Photograph by Rose and Mayer Photography, Inc.

Fig. 13 (top) Serpentine effigy *tecomate* of unknown provenience. Height, 11 cm. Museo de Antropología de la Universidad de Veracruz, Jalapa. (After Musée Rodin 1972: Fig. 24.)

Fig. 14 (above) Other side of Figure 13. (After Musée Rodin 1972: Fig. 24.)

Fig. 15 Serpentine effigy *tecomate* of unknown provenience. Height, 12 cm. Private collection. Photographer unknown.

Fig. 16 Other side of Figure 15. Photographer unknown.

Santa Cruz figure, the Jalapa hag has skeletal ribs and vertebrae, emaciated arms and legs, and oversized hands. Her left hand supports the lower abdomen and the right hand touches the side of her head.

Similar to the effigy *tecomate* in Jalapa is another Olmec stone figure of unknown provenience (Figs. 15 and 16). Again, the sculpture portrays a kneeling old person with a distended belly. The upturned head has a pointed top and a jutting chin. The eyes are deeply sunken and the brow ridges are prominent. The blunt nose has flaring nostrils. The sunken cheeks are incised with wrinkle lines. The lips are pursed and the lower lip is slightly protuberant. The large ears are naturalistically modeled. A carved ridge marks the hairline. Slender thighs support the swollen belly. The left arm is held across the chest and the right hand grasps the lower abdomen. The mouth of the *tecomate* is located on the right side of the belly. The figure's shoulders are rounded. The vertebrae are exposed, the ribs are skeletalized, and the

legs are long and thin. The swollen abdomen and the kneeling posture suggest that the figure is a pregnant female in parturition.

The last three sculptures we will discuss portray seated old women with infants in their laps. The first is a Preclassic figurine from Xochipala, Guerrero, and the other two are Olmec carvings from Las Bocas, Puebla.

The hag from Xochipala sits cross-legged and stares straight ahead (Fig. 17). The baby lies across her lap with his head resting in her right hand and his legs steadied with her left arm. The sculpture is modeled in reddish clay. The old woman's face is horrific. Her almond eyes are set in sunken orbits. The large nose has a low, curved bridge. The figure's lower lip is damaged, but the mouth was apparently slightly open. A network of crisscrossed lines cuts across the woman's cheeks; a pair of incised vertical lines indicates forehead wrinkles. The hair is parted down the middle and a queue extends down her back. Light incisions suggest strands of hair. The woman's body is smooth and unwrinkled, but her breasts are long and pendulous. Fingers and toes are clearly defined. A waistband with a round decoration at the back girdles the old lady's middle.

The baby has a large, round head with high cheekbones and a correctly proportioned body (Fig. 18). The elongated eyes have punched pupils and the nose bridge is arched. The mouth is naturalistically rendered; incisions suggest the channels of the ears. Around the neck is a segmented necklace with two strands. The child's torso is fleshy and fat. His nipples are marked with incised lines and his genitals are defined. The right arm is missing and the left arm is extended along the side of the body. The legs are bent and spread apart. Strangely enough, the skin around the kneecaps seems to have been flayed.

There is a considerable contrast between the hag, who sits bolt upright and stares straight ahead, and the lively little baby, who lies in her lap. The ancient artist avoids any suggestion of interaction between the woman and the child: the hag shows neither hostility nor affection toward the infant. It is this psychological void separating the two figures that gives the sculpture an enigmatic and troubling quality.

The first of the Las Bocas grandmothers has a tiny Olmec baby stretched out on a pallet in her lap (Fig. 19). The woman sits in a hunched position and gazes into the face of the child. Her legs are drawn up and her thighs rest on an oblong cushion. The old lady's asymmetrical face has large almond eyes (which may have been painted), a tiny crooked nose, and a small, straight mouth set at an angle. Brow ridges and cheekbones are clearly marked, and the cheeks are slightly sunken. The ears are unmodeled. The woman's shoulder-length coiffure is kept in place by a nar-

Fig. 17 Clay figure with infant in lap from Xochipala, Guerrero. Height, 10 cm. Private collection. Photograph by Laurin McCracken.

Fig. 18 Detail of infant in Figure 17. Photograph by Laurin McCracken.

Fig. 19 Seated clay female with child in lap from Las Bocas, Puebla. Height, 6.3 cm. Private collection. Photograph by the author.

Fig. 20 Face-on view of infant in Figure 19. Photograph by the author.

row band which extends across the forehead, continues down the sides of the head, and crosses the hair at the nape of the neck. The figure's hunched-over posture emphasizes the pronounced hump in the center of her back. The spinal column is indicated, and some of the vertebrae are even defined. The woman's saggy belly and dangling dugs suggest her advanced age. A short cape covers her shoulders and shorts girdle her middle. Although the fingers of the hands are well defined, the digits of the feet are undifferentiated. The left foot rests casually on the instep of the right foot.

The fat little baby stretched out in the hag's lap (Fig. 20) has a very round head with puffy cheeks, prominent brow ridges, a small nose, and a tiny Olmec mouth with flared upper lip and downturned corners. The ears are simple flanges. The infant wears a headband and loincloth. He lies flat on his back on the oval pallet with his legs and arms stretched out straight. The old woman cradles the baby's left hand in hers and supports its head on a tiny round pillow. The figures are modeled in white-slipped clay. Red pigment appears on the woman's face, hair, chest, feet, hands, and cape. The baby's face is unpainted, but the rest of its body is red. The old woman's shorts and the child's headband and loincloth are painted black.

Unlike the Xochipala sculpture described above, the Las Bocas figure depicts an intimate and affectionate relationship between the old woman and the child. The hag's hunched posture provides a protective envelope for the small, vulnerable baby. The old woman carefully cradles the infant in her lap and gently supports its head and limbs in her arms. She gazes into the face of the little one with tenderness. The intimate relationship between woman and child is masterfully captured in this small Olmec masterpiece.

The second grandmother from Las Bocas is also carved in pure Olmec style (Fig. 21). She sits with legs drawn under her body and cradles an infant in her lap. The old woman's face has a gentle and benign expression. The almond eyes are deeply set in the sunken eye orbits, and the lids are swollen and puffy. Her short nose has a gently curved bridge. The mouth is closed, the lower jaw is thrust forward, and the lower lip protrudes. The furrowed skin of the upper lip suggests advanced age. Grooved plaque forms mark the jowls and hollow, wrinkled cheeks. The hag's shoulder-length hair is neatly trimmed across the forehead. Incised lines indicate the hair strands. The ears are simple fillets of clay. The old woman's neck is short and fleshy, and her clavicles are clearly delineated. Her long breasts lie flat across her chest and belly. The hag's back is cut with diagonal rib markings. A pro-

nounced hump appears on the lower spine. Fingers and toes are shown with incised lines. She wears a pair of shorts around her middle.

The child (Fig. 22) has a large blocky head, elongated torso, and short, stumpy legs. He has plow eyes and a short, straight nose. His Olmec mouth has the usual trapezoidal form with full lips and downturned corners. The ears are simply modeled. A crest runs along the midline of the infant's head. The chest is subtly modeled and the belly is fat. The creature's sex is not indicated. The long, stiff arms are extended at the side of the baby's body, the stylized hands and feet are oversized, and incised lines mark the digits. The figure is modeled in grayish clay with a highly polished kaolin slip. Both old woman and child have red paint on various parts of their bodies. The hair, ears, mouth, hands, and feet of both figures and the woman's cheeks and garment retain especially large amounts of red pigment.

The psychological interaction between the old woman and the infant cradled in her lap is extraordinary. The woman leans forward protectively and surrounds the child with her arms, her right hand carefully supporting the

Fig. 21 (left) Seated ceramic figurine with baby in lap from Las Bocas, Puebla. Height, 12.8 cm. Private collection. Drawing by Eugenia Joyce.

Fig. 22 (below) Face-on view of infant in Figure 21. Drawing by Eugenia Joyce.

173

infant's head and her left arm gently resting across its body. The hag cocks her head so that she can look directly at the child, turning the baby's head so that she can gaze upon its face. The look that she gives the infant is full of maternal affection. Like the other Las Bocas grandmother, this sculpture is a masterpiece of Olmec art.

The sculptures described above come from the far corners of Preclassic Mesoamerica. Four of the old hags were found at great Olmec ceremonial centers in the Gulf Coast lowlands of Mexico; seven figures were discovered in the central Mexican highlands at Formative village sites with important Olmec components; and four carvings were excavated in Preclassic settlements in southern Mesoamerica that were influenced by the Olmec culture. Thus, images of the old woman have been found in most of the provinces of Middle America that were either under direct Olmec control or under strong Olmec influence during Preclassic times.

It is unfortunate that few of the old hags can be dated with any degree of certainty. Of the three pieces that were discovered under scientific conditions, only two were found in datable contexts. According to Michael D. Coe (personal communication), the hollow clay-figure fragment from San Lorenzo was recovered in San Lorenzo Phase deposits that date to 1200–900 B.C.[4] The figurine head from Chalchuapa is associated with Kulil-Complex ceramics; this complex, the earliest at Chalchuapa, dates to 1200–600 B.C. (Sharer 1978, II: 169–70). The old hags recovered during uncontrolled digging lack datable contexts. A comparison of the style, workmanship, and composition of all these figures with those of other Mesoamerican figurine traditions suggests that they were produced in Early and Middle Formative times (1500–500 B.C.) during the florescence of Olmec civilization. The scientifically excavated material fully supports this conclusion. More precise dating of the grandmothers must await further stratigraphic excavation, especially in

the central Mexican highlands and El Salvador, and more accurate seriation of Preclassic figurine types.

Having described the old-female figures, and reviewed their geographical distribution and probable placement in Mesoamerican chronology, we can turn our attention to the interpretation of the images.

Assigning meaning to Preclassic figures in general, and Olmec representations in particular, is a difficult enterprise at best. Olmec artists had a distinct preference for non-narrative, sculptural forms. Images are usually isolated, self-contained units. There are few scenes in Olmec art, and interaction between figures is rarely depicted. Thus, the iconographic clues that are provided by narrative compositions in other art styles are virtually absent in Olmec art. To make matters even more difficult, the vast majority of Olmec objects has been recovered under unscientific conditions. It is a rare Olmec piece that has a recorded archaeological context; many objects have no provenience whatsoever. Unfortunately, the interpretive approaches that depend on detailed analysis of the archaeological associations of an art work are useless in all but a few instances.

Despite the problems inherent in the study of Olmec sculpture, it is still possible to offer defensible hypotheses about the meaning of Olmec art forms. Close analysis of the images themselves provides the basic data. Comparison of the pieces under study with related Olmec sculptures supplies additional information. Finally, judicious use of appropriate archaeological and documentary sources from other Mesoamerican cultures allows the scholar to interpret Olmec objects in the broader framework of Pre-Columbian art and symbolism.

The figures described above tell us little about themselves. They clearly represent a female personage with a dual character. She is an ancient woman with a bony, emaciated body, and yet she is fertile and capable of bearing offspring. She is sometimes portrayed as a benign, affectionate grandmother, but at other times she is pictured as a malevolent, horrific hag. She seems to combine in herself

[4] M. Coe's dates for San Lorenzo are based on the 5730 year half-life for carbon-14. See Switsur (1973) for information on the recalibration of the radiocarbon calendar.

the opposing characteristics that mythology often attributes to females: a creative, fertile, nurturing aspect and a destructive, barren, life-devouring side.

Although it is possible to relate the old ladies to other Formative figurine traditions, such comparisons are not entirely apt. Vast numbers of small Preclassic figures have been discovered in archaeological sites throughout Mesomerica. Carved in a bewildering array of local styles, the sculptures usually portray young women with exaggerated hips and buttocks. They are sometimes pregnant, and they occasionally hold babies or dogs in their arms. Since old-female representations are exceedingly rare in the corpus of Formative figurines, it seems likely that the hags have a significance different from that of the young Preclassic ladies.

Most of the old-female sculptures mentioned in this paper bear no apparent relationship to known Olmec carvings. However, the hags with babies in their laps bear a formal resemblance to a number of important stone pieces from the Olmec heartland. Three large basalt thrones from San Lorenzo and La Venta show an Olmec lord seated in a niche with a supine infant cradled in his lap (de la Fuente 1973: Pl. 2; 1977: Pls. 9, 48–50). The monuments are eroded and mutilated and, while it is still clear that the seated adults are male, the details of the infants' bodies are too damaged to make out. In addition to a central-niche figure, Altar 5 from La Venta has relief carvings on its sides depicting pairs of active, dwarflike babies in the arms of adult Olmec males (Stirling 1943b: Pls. 40 and 41). Two other monuments from Veracruz portray similar themes, but these pieces are free-standing sculptures. The Las Limas figure depicts a young seated Olmec dignitary carrying a baby in his lap (de la Fuente 1977: Color Pl. 19 and Pls. 85-7; Joralemon 1976: Fig. 3). The lord's face and body are decorated with designs symbolizing important Olmec deities (Joralemon 1976). The infant is a were-jaguar creature with cleft head, almond eyes, wide nose, and toothless mouth with flaring upper lip and downturned corners. The baby wears the distinctive headband and ear coverings of God IV—the Olmec Rain God—

and a pectoral and loincloth emblazoned with St. Andrew's crosses. The infant's eyes are wide open, but the figure's body is stiff and inanimate. A battered, seated figure from San Lorenzo apparently portrayed a similar subject, although in this instance the baby is shown in an active posture and without the distinctive insignia worn by the Las Limas figure's child (de la Fuente 1977: Pl. 8).

Two portable Olmec stone objects of uncertain provenience depict the same theme shown in the monumental sculptures. A carving in the Metropolitan Museum of Art portrays an Olmec personage seated on a four-legged throne with a rigid were-jaguar baby in its lap (Metropolitan Museum of Art 1969: Fig. 551). The baby wears no symbolic regalia. An extraordinary standing jade figure in the Guennol Collection holds an infant God IV in his arms (M. Coe 1965a: Fig. 4). The baby has a were-jaguar face and a pudgy, sexless body with dwarflike proportions. He wears the headband and ear coverings of God IV. The deity is held in a vertical position against the standing figure's midsection. In both these stone sculptures the adult personages appear to be masculine.[5]

While there are definite formal similarities between the hags with infants in their laps and

---

[5] The relationship between the Olmec infant-bearers and the bearers of ceremonial bars and bundles is not yet clear. See for example, Relief 1 from Chalcatzingo (Gay 1971:Fig. 11); the incised jade celt from Arroyo Pesquero in the Museo de Antropología de la Universidad de Veracruz, Jalapa (Joralemon 1976: Fig. 8f); the incised jade celt from Arroyo Pesquero in a private collection (Joralemon 1976: Fig. 8e); the incised jade celt of unknown provenience now on exhibit in the Pre-Columbian Hall at the American Museum of Natural History in New York, but as yet unpublished; and the bearded-figure fragment of unknown provenience in the Guennol Collection (Rubin 1975:326, 328, 329). The bundles are held in the same position as the babies, and they usually appear in similar iconographic contexts. Only one bundle has facial features (Joralemon 1976:Fig. 8f), and its characteristics relate it to the scepter held by the main figure on La Venta Stela 2 rather than to the babies (*ibid.:* Fig. 11). As far as the gender of the bundle-bearers is concerned, the seated figure in Relief 1 from Chalcatzingo is almost certainly female, but the American Museum of Natural History's incised celt represents a male and the Guennol Collection statue is a bearded male. None of the bundle-bearers has aged physical features.

the stone carvings described above, there are very important differences that distinguish the two groups of sculptures. The adult figures carved in stone have neither aged features nor female sexual characteristics. Quite the contrary, the stone adults appear to be male figures in their prime. Second, several of the stone infants wear the diagnostic insignia of God IV (a deity who is never depicted in clay); the hags' babies display no such symbolism. Finally, most of the stone figures are large, public monuments from important Gulf Coast Olmec ceremonial centers; the grandmothers are small, clay objects which come from tombs in village sites in the central Mexican highlands. Thus, despite the formal similarities shared by all the infant-bearers, I see no reason to believe that the sculptures necessarily have the same meaning.

The infants held in the laps of the old women bear a close resemblance to large, hollow, clay figures found at Las Bocas, Tenenexpan, Tlapacoya, Tlatilco, Xochipala, and other Preclassic sites in Mexico (M. Coe 1965a: Figs. 184–6, 192). These sculptures show considerable stylistic variation, but most of them represent corpulent infants with large, uncleft heads and sexless, dwarflike bodies. The Olmec babies have slanted, almond eyes, flaring nostrils, and a trapezoidal mouth with bowed upper lip and downturned corners. They usually sit upright with legs splayed, and their hands and arms are held in a number of different positions. Occasionally, glyphlike motifs or deity insignia are carved on the figures. The Xochipala infants that most closely resemble the Xochipala hag's baby have subtly modeled faces with high cheekbones, and extended legs with flayed strips around the knees (Gay 1972: Fig. 25). Although these figures can stand upright, their posture suggests that they may have been placed in the laps of larger sculptures or cradled in the arms of human beings during ceremonial occasions. Both Olmec and Xochipala infants sometimes sport complex coiffures.

While the similarity between the hollow babies and the infants held by the old women is obvious, unfortunately the significance of the large clay figures has not yet been deter-

mined. They may portray pathological specimens—children afflicted with mongolism or Spina bifida (Covarrubias 1957: 58; M. Coe 1965b: 752). Such infants surely would have possessed supernatural powers in the eyes of the ancients. The babies may represent rain spirits or sacrifices to a rain god, for we know that infants and child sacrifices were associated with rain cults in later Mesoamerican cultures (Covarrubias 1957: 60, 62, 63, 65; M. Coe 1965a: 14). Another hypothesis suggests that the babies depict the supernatural offspring of the mating of a jaguar and a human being (Stirling 1955: 8, 19-20; M. Coe 1965a: 14, 105; 1965b: 751-2). These and other interpretations of the hollow figures are possible, but at this point all suggestions remain conjectures only. Whatever the significance of the hollow infants, their meaning is closely related to the symbolism of the hag's child.

Despite the apparent similarities between the old female sculptures and other Preclassic figures and Olmec carvings, not much interpretive data can be gained from these comparisons. Upon closer inspection formal resemblances turn out to be superficial similarities. The relationship between the hag's baby and hollow clay infant figures, however, is very close, and, when more information is discovered about the meaning of the hollow sculptures, we will learn more about the old women who carry these beings in their laps.

Representations of old females (with or without babies) are not common in the corpus of Pre-Columbian art, but such figures do appear throughout Mesoamerican culture history. There is not space in this brief article to discuss these later images in any detail, but a few of them should be mentioned. Stela 50 from Izapa (Fig. 23), a late Preclassic monument, depicts a hunched, seated, skeletal figure with a long umbilical cord extending from its midsection (Norman 1973: Pls. 49 and 50). A winged personage in the upper register of the carving grasps the cord in his hands. The association of the hunched, skeletal figure with the birth imagery of the umbilical cord suggests that the skeletal creature is female. The similarity between the Izapan bone-woman with umbilical cord and the Santa Cruz hag in the

Fig. 23 Stela 50 from Izapa, Chiapas. Height, 136 cm. Museo Nacional de Antropología, Mexico. (After Norman 1973: Pl. 50.)

birth-giving position is especially interesting.

From Late Classic burials on Jaina Island, off the coast of Campeche, and from the Petén, Guatemala, has come a number of Maya ceramic figurines that seem to be related to the Preclassic hags (Figs. 24 and 25). Often these Jaina figures represent wrinkled old women with drooping breasts (Piña Chan 1968: Figs. 56 and 61); sometimes the females take on a martial and horrific aspect (M. Miller 1975: Fig. 15); and occasionally the figurines represent old hags with infants in their arms.

A horrible old woman, clearly identifiable as Schellhas's Goddess O, appears on the last page of the Codex Dresden (Fig. 26), greatest of the Postclassic Maya manuscripts (J. E. S. Thompson 1972: Pl. 74). The goddess has a wrinkled face, a coiled-serpent headdress, and clawed feet. A knee-length black skirt decorated with crossed long bones circles her middle. The evil-looking creature holds an

upturned jar from which torrents of water cascade. The scene on this page illustrates the destruction of one of the world creations by flood.

Finally, images of Mexica old mother goddesses can be identified in the art of the late Postclassic Period. One aspect of this complex divinity is Coatlicue (Fig. 27), an old female deity with skeletal face, dangling dugs, and skirt of serpents (Ramírez Vázquez 1968: 92, 107, top right). Sometimes a necklace of human hands and hearts hangs across her chest. Coatlicue is a mother goddess, for the sun and all the stars were her children. However, because she represents the earth and because the earth is both womb and tomb in the Mexica world view, Coatlicue has both mortuary and fertility associations.

Having briefly examined images from later Mesoamerican cultures which may be related to the Preclassic hags, we can now turn to the problem of interpreting these ancient ladies. Since the evidence is not sufficient to allow us to reach any final conclusions on this matter at this time, it might be best to outline three possible interpretive approaches that might ultimately lead to the correct explanation of the figurines.

On the one hand, the old-female figures may represent real human beings. If this is the case, then the women depicted in the carvings were suffering from the ravages of advanced age. Some of them must have been afflicted with serious maladies which caused severe emaciation and wasting of the limbs, and swelling and bloating of the abdomen. Pathological conditions are portrayed in other Pre-Columbian art styles—notably the shaft-tomb sculpture from West Mexico—and it is possible that this is the case with the hags. If the figures do portray human beings, the grandmothers holding babies in their laps might celebrate the same miracle which so overjoyed Sarah in the Old Testament. Women certainly do not often conceive and deliver children late in life, but such occurrences are not unprecedented.

A second avenue of interpretation might suggest that the old women represent priestesses, sorceresses, or other religious practioners. Fasting, emaciation, and serious illness are asso-

Fig. 24 Seated pottery figure from Jaina Island, Campeche. Height, 15.3 cm. Museo Nacional de Antropología, Mexico. Photograph courtesy of the Instituto Nacional de Antropología e Historia, Mexico.

Fig. 25 Seated clay figure with baby from Jaina Island, Campeche. Height, 22 cm. Private collection. Photograph by the author.

ciated with shamanism and ecstatic religion in many parts of the world (Eliade 1964; Wilbert 1972). During shamanic initiations, it is necessary to produce a deathlike condition in the initiand before his or her rebirth into a changed existential state can be accomplished. In many traditions, shamans are given their new bodies or new organs by the spirits only after they have reduced themselves to the most elemental state possible—skin and bones—and purged themselves of all mortal corruption. In addition, fasting and illness can function as trance-inducers in shamanic religion. It is by trancing that the shaman breaks through the normal dimensions of time and space, and travels to the various levels of the cosmos to discover and combat the cause of illness in a sick per-

son or to determine the cause of some other medical or social difficulty. Some of the motifs often associated with shamanism appear on the Preclassic old women. The aged ladies may indeed be images of female shamans, and the hags with infants may represent some sort of child-curing ceremonies or rituals of childbirth.[6]

Finally, if the Preclassic old ladies are not

[6] It is interesting to note that the interior cavity of the old-hag effigy vessels is symbolically and actually the interior of the woman's body. Since several of these figures are obviously pregnant, the interior space represents the womb. If these objects were used as containers, they may have held a variety of liquid or solid substances, perhaps concoctions used in birth rites, shamanic ceremonies, or curing rituals.

human beings at all but deities or supernatural creatures instead, then they may represent the old mother goddess who in various guises and under a variety of different names appears in virtually all the cultures of ancient Mexico (Nicholson 1971; Sullivan n.d.; J. E. S. Thompson 1939). The goddess' most important role in Mesoamerican religion is as universal an-

cestress. She is the ancient mother of all the gods and of human beings. She and her consort are infinitely old, older than creation itself. The two of them live in the uppermost level of the stratified heavens in eternal union and send the spirits of children into their mothers' wombs. By determining the moment a creature is born, the moment it enters time and space, the old

Fig. 26 Dresden Codex, page 74. Height, 20.4 cm. Sächsische Landesbibliothek, Dresden. (After Codex Dresden 1882: 74.)

Fig. 27 Standing basalt figure of Coatlicue from Mexico Tenochtitlan. Height, 114.3 cm. Museo Nacional de Antropología, Mexico. Photograph courtesy of the Instituto Nacional de Antropología e Historia, Mexico.

179

goddess and her husband fix that creature's fate. Both gods and men took their birth date as their name, for it was that day upon which they entered the eternal round of fate. Not surprisingly, the old mother goddess is invoked in ceremonies that accompany and celebrate the birth of a child (Sahagún 1950–1969, Book 6: 175–7). Because the creator-couple determines the fate of all creatures and because the dual gods are, in a sense, beyond time and fate, they are the archetypical sorcerers and diviners. They are the ones who know all that has passed and all that is to come. Shamans who would use that kind of knowledge are under the patronage of the old deities. In another guise the aged goddess is a lunar divinity (J. E. S. Thompson 1939). As the waning moon, she is paired with the young moon goddess. Both of them are associated with various female arts, especially weaving and certain types of curing and midwifery. In still another manifestation the old goddess is an earth divinity and the provider of food and sustenance. It is her continuing fertility upon which all creatures ultimately depend. However, as we have seen above, because she is an earth goddess, she also has a sinister aspect. She is the devourer of the dead, the one whose clawlike hands strip the corpse of its flesh. Whether she is called Omecíhuatl or Alom, Cipactónal or Xmucane, Tlazoltéotl or Ix Chel, she is the same divinity, and all Mesoamerican cultures assigned her similar powers and associations.

All the iconographic features of the Preclassic hags described in this paper—the aged physical characteristics, the birth/death symbolism, the motif of ancient mother with newborn child—make sense together if we suppose that the old-female sculptures represent the old mother goddess. It is far beyond the scope of this article to provide a thorough account of all the characteristics and attributes of the old goddess. That is a major problem for students of Mesoamerican religion. However, an analysis of the rites and beliefs that are associated with the old mother goddess would surely help us to understand better the Preclassic grandmothers.

Although none of the approaches outlined above is entirely satisfactory, I think the third line of reasoning will be the most productive path to follow in interpreting the Preclassic figures. With further research into Preclassic art and archaeology, and additional investigation into Pre-Columbian iconography and religion, it should be possible to discuss the meaning of the old hags with greater confidence in future years. Until then, the little ladies present themselves for our consideration, sometimes with a wry smile, sometimes with a howling grimace, and sometimes with an affectionate gaze.

The Northern Olmec and Pre-Olmec Frontier on the Gulf Coast

S. Jeffrey K. Wilkerson
R. S. PEABODY FOUNDATION FOR ARCHAEOLOGY

Beginning with the pioneering explorations of Matthew Stirling in southern Veracruz and western Tabasco, Olmec civilization has been defined and increasingly examined anthropologically. North of the coastal-plain centers with concentrations of Olmec sculpture, however, relatively few Early or Middle Formative sites have been investigated. In the rain-shadow zone of south-central Veracruz interest has focused primarily on the Trapiche–Chalahuites–Limoncito Complex excavated by García Payón (1966), and later Ford, Medellín Zenil, and Wallrath (Fig. 1). Medellín Zenil (1960a) also explored Remojadas, of later date, and recovered a stela in an Olmec style at El Viejón. In the North Gulf area the excavations of Ekholm (1944) and MacNeish (1954) in the Panuco region established the first extended cultural sequence for any coastal site.

Until recently there has been no examination of early occupations in north-central Veracruz. Investigations in the area were directed largely to the Classic Period center of El Tajín in the Tecolutla drainage. In an effort to obtain evidence of earlier cultures, excavations were undertaken about forty kilometers downstream from El Tajín. This research has now produced a very long cultural sequence (Table 1) that allows us to consider the magnitude of Olmec influence in what appears to be one of the frontiers of early civilization.

The sequence is derived from excavations at the major riverbank site of Santa Luisa and the nearby hill site of La Conchita (Wilkerson 1972, 1973, n.d.a, n.d.b). From these explora-tions information can be brought to bear on the antecedents of the Olmec presence to help illuminate the nature of the pre-Olmec era. The Archaic Period occupations have been discussed elswhere (Wilkerson 1975a, 1975b) and will only be briefly described here.

La Conchita is located in the sandstone hills northwest of the Río Tecolutla. In deep erosional deposits at the site, just above a terminal Pleistocene stratum containing extinct faunal remains, the sparsely scattered artifacts of a sloping campsite were encountered. Near an amorphous hearth, which produced a sixth-millennium-B.C. date, were a limestone chopper and flakes of both sandstone and limestone. A few crude blades of obsidian were found nearby in contexts that cannot be positively associated with the same campsite. This limited material, tentatively labeled the Conchita Complex, fits within a generalized Early Archaic hunting-gathering tradition. It is quite possible that this seasonal campsite was associated with a base camp on the nearby Tecolutla River. Vestiges of later camps were also found, but these contained only a few obsidian chips and an empty hearth.

For the time period 4000 to 2400 B.C. there are abundant cultural remains (Palo Hueco Phase) from a large occupational area at Santa Luisa, stretching for at least a kilometer on what was then a deltaic island in the river mouth. No ceramics are associated. Artifacts are mostly crude obsidian blades made from nodules four to six centimeters in diameter. Most blades have prepared striking platforms,

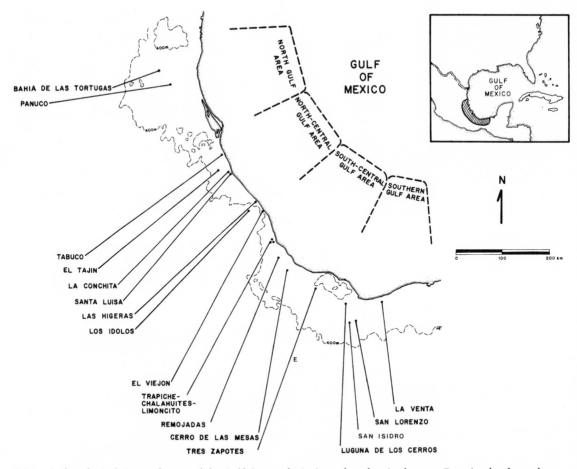

Fig. 1 Archaeological sites and areas of the Gulf Coast of Mexico referred to in the text. Drawing by the author.

although unprepared and pointed platforms also occur. Gravers, utilized flakes, drills, a few scrapers and choppers, net-sinkers, and a retouched flake are also present. Jasper, flint, sandstone, limestone, and chert were occasionally utilized in addition to obsidian. Cracked sandstone cobbles were employed extensively in cooking shellfish, especially oysters. Bone fragments (one of a howler monkey) and crab shells are also present in the midden deposits. The island occupation appears to have been a permanent village, and canoes were certainly in habitual use by this time. The entire Palo Hueco Phase occupational area is sealed throughout its extent by a culturally sterile sand cap which corresponds to a major inundation sometime shortly after 2400 B.C. Above

the sand stratum are abundant deposits of a densely settled Middle Formative Period (Esteros A and B Phases) village. There is, for the present, a hiatus between 2400 and 1700 B.C., during which pottery first appeared in the region.

Excavation of another alluvium-covered island revealed plentiful deposits for the 1700 to 1000 B.C. portion of the Early Formative Period. The material recovered to date characterizes four phases. The Raudal Phase, the earliest, is first recorded from a hearth yielding a date of (N-2434) 1660±105 B.C. Its termination about 1460 B.C is bracketed by two dates: (N-2432) 1450±95 B.C. and (N-2431) 1470±95 B.C. The phase as a whole has an aspect of transition about it, as attested by the

TABLE 1. THE CULTURAL CHRONOLOGY OF THE NORTH GULF AREAS COMPARED WITH SOME
RELATED SEQUENCES OF THE EARLY AND MIDDLE FORMATIVE PERIODS

NORTH GULF AREA					dates
	MODERN				
	POST-CLASSIC / CLASSICAL		LT.	OLARTE	1620
			EL.	TAPIA	1520
			LT.	CABEZAS	1300
		EPI.	EL.	EL CRISTO	1100
CLASSIC		LT.		ISLA B	900
		EL.		ISLA A	600
				CACAHUATAL	350
FORMATIVE	LATE			TECOLUTLA	AD BC
				ARROYO GRANDE	500
	MIDDLE			ESTEROS B	550
				ESTEROS A	1000
				OJITE	1150
	EARLY			MONTE GORDO	1350
				ALMERIA	1450
				RAUDAL	1700
				hiatus	2400
ARCHAIC	LATE			PALO HUECO	4000
	EARLY			LA CONCHITA COMPLEX	5600

SANTA LUISA	PANUCO	TEHUACAN	SAN LORENZO	PACIFIC CHIAPAS
ESTEROS B	AGUILAR	↑ ↑ LATE SANTA MARIA	PALANGANA	CONCHAS 2
ESTEROS A		EARLY SANTA MARIA	NACASTE	CONCHAS 1
				JOCOTAL
OJITE	PONCE	LATE AJALPAN	SAN LORENZO B / SAN LORENZO A	CUADROS
MONTE GORDO	PAVON	EARLY AJALPAN	CHICHARRAS / BAJIO	OCOS
ALMERIA			OJOCHI	BARRA
RAUDAL				
hiatus		PURRON		
PALO HUECO ↓ ↓		ABEJAS ↓ ↓		

(PRECERAMIC)

stone bowl fragments, simple ceramics, limited decoration, abundant shellfish debris, and restricted variation of lithic artifacts.

The ceramics of the early portion of the phase (Fig. 2) are mostly (46%) crude, simple *tecomates,* frequently with ridges suggesting a coiling technique. Shoulders and rims are covered with a red (non-hematite) wash applied with a brush, or more rarely, a red slip. Present also are flat-bottomed grater bowls with flaring sides and designs in the form of pinpoint-like punctate, opposed parallel lines, and swirls. There are a few red polished *tecomates* with short vertical rims; an incurved rim bowl; and a few Progreso Metallic *ollitas*. A few lumps of fired but untempered clay, probably for cooking, were found in a hearth from the lowest levels of the phase.

The latter part of the Raudal Phase (*ca.* 1550–1450 B.C.) has an increase in *ollitas*, both white and red surfaced; in convex- and insloping-wall bowls, now with triangular incised designs; and in pumpkin- and ellipsoidal-form *tecomates*. The first asphalt fragments and earliest decoration date to this time, as does a hollow animal head, probably a jaguar (Fig. 3e).

Fig. 2 Examples of ceramics from the Early Formative Period at Santa Luisa. Ojite Phase: *a.* black-white fired bowl; *d.* small, red incurved rim bowl with black mineral paint decoration. Monte Gordo Phase: *c.* jar fragment with suspension lug. Almería Phase: *e.* grooved wall fragment of a small jar; *f.* grater bottom with zoned punctate design. Raudal Phase: *b.* grater bottom; *g.* small bowl with geometric incision highlighted with white paint. Drawings by Lyn Cunningham Balck.

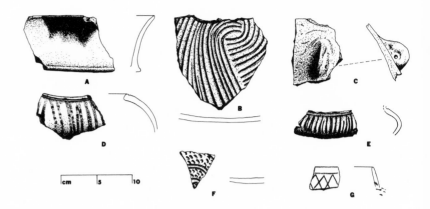

Lithic artifacts include a fragment of a flaring-sided stone bowl and a pumice abrader. Moderate quantities of small, sandstone cobble fragments may have been used for cooking and abrading.

Present throughout the phase are abundant obsidian chips which, like the Palo Hueco Phase examples, are derived from small nodules of poor quality (Fig. 4). A major distinction, however, is that the nodules appear to be crushed by a blow producing numerous chips with random cutting edges. There is nearly a total absence of crude blades, so common before 2400 B.C. Does this obsidian-chip occurrence imply the same manioc diet suggested by Lowe (1975: 10–4) for coastal Chiapas?

The answer for north-central Veracruz is a cautious maybe. The obsidian is still under study, but the chip sizes (averaging two to three centimeters in length) are much larger than known grater-chips from South America. A standard wear-pattern, such as one might expect on an object scraped against a grating board, is not apparent. The ceramic grater-bowl bottoms recovered from the same levels show effective use but are not necessarily diagnostic of manioc, especially as chile, or even bean, preparation cannot be ruled out at this time level.[1]

Assuming that the ubiquitous obsidian chips are related to a subsistence activity, which they must be, the basic shellfish-collecting/fishing/

hunting diet of the earlier Palo Hueco Phase was being modified. Oysters, marsh clams, and fish were still consumed in large quantities but new sources of nutrition appear. Dog is present for the first time and rapidly becomes a significant source of protein throughout the Early Formative Period (Wing, this volume). Plants such as beans, chile, and tomatoes may be associated with the new grater bowls. Important to note, however, is the absence of maize indicators, such as *metates*. The density of Raudal midden deposits, with packed earth floors and hearths, suggests that the subsistence pattern is very successful and can, for the moment, compete in cultural preference with early corn agriculture. At this time, manioc use cannot be conclusively proved or disproved. Nevertheless, it is a potential major staple which can be prepared with obsidian chips. The lithic and ceramic similarities between the Raudal Phase and the Barra Phase of Chiapas also suggest that the same early subsistence pattern existed on the Gulf Coast as on the Pacific.

The Barra Phase, with its present carbon dates of 1510 B.C. and 1449 B.C.[2] overlaps with Raudal but appears more sophisticated. It is similar in *tecomate* and bowl forms, the obsidian-chip complex, swirl designs, X-incising, and the absence of *metates* (Lowe 1975). Else-

---

[1] I thank Richard MacNeish for this suggestion and a provocative conversation concerning early bean and chile preparation.

[2] I have not added 200 years for atmospheric deviation to Barra dates, as Lowe (1975:29) has in his discussion of the phase, or to any of the Santa Luisa dates. All dates presented are based upon the 5,730 half-life calculation.

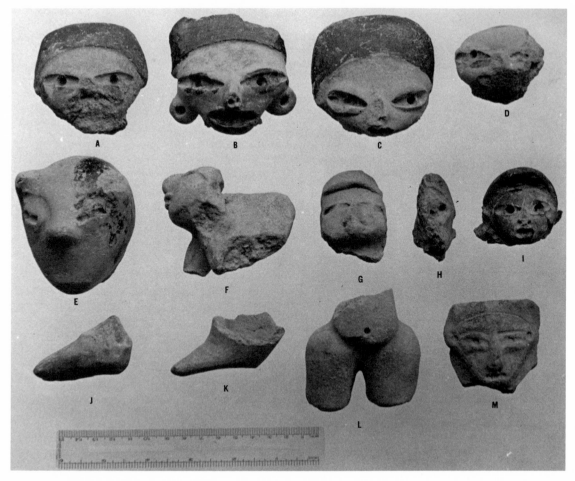

Fig. 3 Early figurines from Santa Luisa. Ojite Phase: *f, g, j–m.* Monte Gordo Phase: *a–d, h, i.* Raudal Phase: *e.* Photograph by the author.

where there are few affinities.[3] The Purron Phase (2400–1500 B.C.) of the Tehuacan Valley is quite different, implying that distinct highland and lowland traditions are functioning even this early in Mesoamerican culture history. The following Early Ajalpan Phase

(1500–1100 B.C.) at Tehuacan has sufficient similarities to imply lowland stimulation. Early Ajalpan ceramic types (especially Ajalpan Coarse Red), forms, and decoration are reasonably close to Raudal and may be derived from its yet-to-be-discovered counterpart in south-central Veracruz. In summation, the Raudal Phase can be said to represent a step beyond the late preceramic lifestyle and to form part of what may be a generalized and highly suc-

[3] At the time of this writing in the field I do not have sufficient data on the material excavated in Belize by Norman Hammond to analyze adequately its relationship with the Raudal Phase.

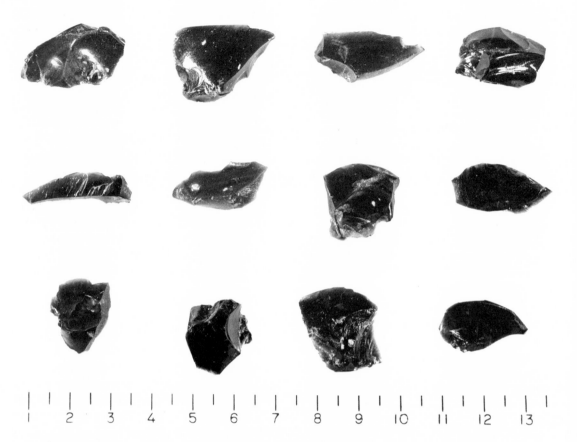

Fig. 4 Obsidian chips from midden deposits of the Raudal Phase from Santa Luisa (*ca.* 1700-1460 B.C.). Photograph by Curtis Craven.

cessful lowland subsistence pattern which does not yet include maize as a major staple.

The Almería Phase (1450 B.C. to *ca.* 1350 B.C.) develops from Raudal. The same ceramic forms continue but with an increase in flat-bottomed bowls with outflaring or outsloping sides, in pumpkin *tecomates,* and in *tecomates* with a small upturned rim. *Tecomates* now comprise 60 percent of the ceramic corpus, and surface undulation from coiling is more rare. Decoration, especially on *tecomates,* increasingly includes patterned polishing, stick polishing in latticework designs, and evenly applied red slips. Incised parallel lines in X's, triangular designs, or zoned diagonal lines continue on bowl exteriors. Asphalt paint decoration in parallel lines and slips is more common on Progreso Metallic and the newly present Progreso White. Small black convex-wall bowls,

which may be ancestral to Ponce Black appear in minor quantities. Grater-bottom designs, sensitive time markers at Santa Luisa, change to include zoned (reedlike) punctate and zoned chevron designs. A fragment of a hollow figurine or whistle was excavated. Turning to lithic artifacts, the corpus includes abundant quantities of the same obsidian chips as are found in the Raudal Phase, and a single *mano* fragment (long, subrectangular with a lenticular cross-section). The first burial underneath a packed-earth house floor occurs at the very beginning of the phase.

The late Almería Phase receives an influx of new traits, which certainly come from pervasive contacts with the Isthmian and Chiapas coastal regions. It appears that a complex of new ideas arrives from the south about 1400 B.C. to modify the local tradition. Apart from

186

the two-handed *mano,* and its implication for corn preparation, there are the first limited occurences of specular hematite slips and sherd-disk spindle-whorls, suggesting the arrival of cotton. Fluting and incised *tecomate* shoulders also occur for the first time. A few trade sherds may be Monte Incised and Cotan Grooved from Chiapas. Significant forms for the first time include vases, a few composite silhouette bowls, and convex-wall bowls. Gourd-shaped bottles continue from the latter part of the Raudal Phase.

While the grater-bowl designs and the white wares suggest similarities with the Pavón Phase of Pánuco, the majority of the external relationships point to the Early Ajalpan, Ojochi, and Barra Phases to the south. The common utility wares are fairly close, in surface treatment and form, to Ajalpan Coarse and Coatepec Plain at Tehuacan. However, the examples with a red surface finish do not have a hematite base, with the exception of a few sherds from vessels that may have been trade items. Hollow anthropomorphic figurines may appear in both areas at about the same time. Although there are no Ojochi trade sherds present, the fluting and, particularly, the vertical and latticework stick polishing are similar. As in the largely earlier Barra Phase, occasional recurved bottoms are found. The possible Chiapas trade sherds appear about midway through the Almería Phase. A fragment in the last level of the phase is a figurine headdress ornament reminiscent of those found in the Prognathic Elliptical-Eyed type at Pánuco in the much later Ponce Phase.

The Monte Gordo Phase begins about 1350 B.C. and ends approximately 1150 B.C. This dating is, for the moment, tentative but not inconsistent with the discernable external relationships. *Tecomates* continue to be the principal form, dropping in frequency to 51 percent of all forms, but there is a considerable increase in convex-wall bowls with incurved rims, and in flat-bottomed bowls with nearly vertical flaring sides. Grater-bottoms are somewhat less frequent, but are still common. Bottles became more frequent but are not numerous. Asphalt decoration on Progeso White, a minority type, continues. Red hematite slips on bowls with outflaring sides are slightly more popular. The obsidian-chip corpus continues to be abundant, suggesting a continuation of the Raudal-Almería pattern. Two stone *tecomate* bowl fragments and a single *mano* fragment were also found.

Figurines are numerous throughout the phase. The most common forms are variants of what MacNeish labeled "Prognathic Elliptical-Eyed" and "Realistic Projecting Eyeball" types, in the Ponce Phase at Pánuco (MacNeish 1954: 588–9), and the "Projecting-Eye Heads" in the middle of the Ajalpan Phase at Tehuacan (MacNeish, *et al.* 1970: 37). No figurines were encountered in the earlier Pavón Phase. The present evidence suggests that these figurine types began in north-central Veracruz and diffused north toward Pánuco and south toward the Tehuacan Valley.

The latter portion of the Monte Gordo Phase is marked by large, red, flat-bottomed bowls, often with grater interiors. Incurved-rim bowls, which are very similar to the later Aguilar Red examples, frequently have rough, undulating shoulders produced by the potter pulling the clay upward or downward with his hands while the vessel is still pliable. The first definite whistle fragments, covered in an asphalt slip, occur during this phase. Throughout the phase a gray-brown ware, which is very close to Ponce Black, occurs in significant, if minor, amounts, suggesting once more a more southerly origin for a number of the Ponce Phase attributes. Occasionally, and especially in late Monte Gordo, this ceramic is differentially fired to produce black-and-white surfaces. At no point in the present sample, however, does the process appear to be systematically or skillfully executed.

The external relationships of Monte Gordo suggest contemporaneity with the end of the Early Ajalpan Phase at Tehuacan and the Bajío Phase at San Lorenzo. Although no identical ceramic type is shared, decoration, forms, and lithic artifacts imply a rough temporal overlap. The Chicharras Phase of San Lorenzo is generally more complex and heralds the changes of the late Ojite Phase at Santa Luisa. Northward, the latter portion of the Pavón Phase should be coterminal, but there are few similarities.

Instead, the figurines, Aguilar Red, and Ponce Black of the later Ponce Phase appear to be foreshadowed in Monte Gordo.

The Ojite Phase begins about 1150 B.C. and ends around 1000 B.C. We have no carbon dates from Ojite times, but several dates from the beginning of the later Esteros A Phase cluster between 900 and 1000 B.C.[4]

This phase represents the introduction of numerous new artifacts and, in spite of the continuation of most previous domestic wares, the strong confirmation of a new lifestyle associated with the Olmec (Fig. 5). The phase, like its predecessors, can be conveniently divided into early and late segments. Early Ojite has true white-black pottery, both imported and locally made. Three distinct white ceramics are present: Progreso White and two imported types, one of which may be Xochiltepec White.

Tecomates now constitute only 39 percent of the ceramic forms, and are followed in frequency by flat-bottomed bowls with outflaring and outsloping sides, bowls with convex walls, and a few *ollas*. Some bowls have everted or bolstered rims. A few were decorated by gouging in broad parallel lines and highlighting the design with red hematite or ochre. This decorative technique, as well as the ceramic itself, is very similar to Calzadas Carved of the San Lorenzo A Phase in southern Veracruz, and to several Trapiche examples of "Cerámica raspada" (García Payón 1966: 76, 78, Nos. 4, 5, 8, 9) in south-central Veracruz. Figurine fragments denote large hollow seated figures (perhaps of the "Hollow Dwarf" type), a solid hunchbacked figure, and a "Trapiche-Bunned" head. Lithic remains indicate a decrease of obsidian chips in proportion to ceramics, and include: two types of footless *metates, manos,* and fragments of subrectangular stone bowls, one of which was finely finished.

Two additional features suggest the notable strength of the Olmec impact at this time. One is the first occurrence of a hearth that duplicates the form of flat-bottomed bowls with outflaring sides. The sides are evenly fired and

appear to have been formed with homogeneously mixed paste containing quartz temper. Later, in the Middle Formative Period, these hearths reach as much as a meter-and-a-half in diameter. This may represent the beginning of the "fired-clay tradition" for floors, structures, and hearths, which persists, and finally merges, with cement use in the Late Formative and Early Classic Periods.

The second feature, which will require definite confirmation in the future, is mound structures. On the basis of uniformly sloping fill observed in a test trench, surface survey, and the examination of river cuts, it appears that the first platform mounds may have been constructed early in Ojite times. Although the evidence is limited, heights were at least a meter, and there are no indications of revestment of any sort. Such data fits well with the first occurrence of mounds in the Bajío Phase at San Lorenzo, about a hundred and fifty years earlier (M. Coe 1970: 24).

The deposits of the latter portion of the Ojite Phase are in part disturbed, and they contain some intrusive material from later phases. Nevertheless, there is sufficient data to show that, while all the innovations of the beginning of the phase continue, there is a resurgence of local ceramic norms, especially incurved-rim bowls with parallel lines of black paint on the shoulders. Decorative designs, such as the double-line break on rims and the "hub-and-spoke" grater bottoms, appear in sparse numbers as harbingers of the Middle Formative Period which follows.

An important question for the Ojite Phase is the nature of the Olmec influence. Did Santa Luisa become an Olmec settlement at the end of the Early Formative Period? Given the reduced nature of the material at hand, it is not possible to come to a categorical decision. There is a definite shift in ceramic preferences, and an increase in technical complexity at the beginning of the Ojite Phase. Olmec norms, especially black-white fired bowls, are being imitated, and there is, relative to previous phases, considerable importation of white fired vessels from the south. All figurine fragments encountered to date are within known Olmec variation. Mound construction may begin at the

---

[4] Obsidian-hydration dating of all phases is pending. Dates should be available by early 1980.

Fig. 5 Ojite Phase ceramics, reflecting Olmec influence. Photograph by the author.

beginning of the phase, and *metates* appear in increasing numbers.

All of this represents considerable Olmec influence but not, in my mind, sufficient evidence for an Olmec settlement. At no time do the imported vessels or the local imitations of Olmec black-white vessels totally dominate the ceramic sample. Domestic wares continue and local ceramic types reassert themselves toward the end of the phase. Very significant is the continuation of the obsidian chips with their implication for the earlier non-maize subsistence pattern. While decreasing in number, they remain present throughout the Ojite Phase and imply a gradual rather than an abrupt change.

Farther south they disappear in the Cuadros Phase of Chiapas. The presently available evidence suggests a well-populated island village at Santa Luisa which not only was aware of Olmec culture and imitated it, but was also in direct trade contact with true Olmec centers to the south.

From the above data there are several conclusions we can draw about the north-central Veracruz area and its relationships to the Olmec and pre-Olmec cultures of southern Mesoamerica.

By the end of the Archaic Period *(ca.* 2400 B.C.), there were permanent population centers on the Gulf Coast, especially at convergent points of various ecological zones in the lower drainages. The basis of subsistence was primarily the extensive exploitation of the riverine and estuarine zones with supplementary savannah and forest hunting. It was a very successful lowland lifestyle which only changed significantly with the later introduction of corn agriculture during the ensuing Early Formative Period. It is very likely that the Palo Hueco Phase pattern was widely shared in the coastal regions of Mesoamerica.

By the 1700 B.C. time level of the Raudal Phase, modifications, but no massive alterations, in the lifestyle are perceivable. Ceramic technology had arrived earlier, perhaps with subsistence concepts involving grating with stone chips. The pottery of the Raudal Phase, although crudely executed relative to subsequent examples, is clearly not the beginning of the ceramic tradition. Its relationships, based on presently known material, are largely southward toward the Pacific coast of Chiapas. There the Barra Phase (Green and Lowe 1967; Lowe 1975) presents a similar ecological matrix and artifact corpus. Although the Barra ceramics tend to be more complex, they are certainly closely related. The same is also true for the lithic artifacts, principally obsidian chips which definitely suggest a new subsistence factor implying considerable reliance. Lowe's argument for manioc grating is very tempting but not yet conclusive. In the ceramic sphere, the numerous grater bowls are just as applicable to chile or even beans. I feel personally that manioc utilization, involving grating, is very probable, but that more exact methodologies for detecting its use are required. Nevertheless, as Lowe (1975) points out, the Barra affinities are southward toward South America, where manioc was widely used.

The Raudal–Barra horizon seemingly represents an early wave of South American influence in lowland Mesoamerican development. The Purron Phase of the Tehuacan Valley is at least in part contemporary with Raudal, but may represent a partially separate highland tradition. Its ceramics are distinct from the coastal examples and its lithic artifacts (MacNeish *et al.* 1967: 233) reflect a largely different subsistence orientation. Population densities at

this time in the lowlands were likely to be greater than in the highlands. What about the distribution of this Raudal pattern along the Gulf Coast?

The evidence from the later Pavón Phase at Pánuco, which may overlap with the end of the Almería Phase, suggests the remnants of a still-earlier pattern. Pavón lacks even the limited diversification of ceramic types, decorations, and forms—especially *tecomates*—common in Raudal and Almería. The presence in the lowest Raudal levels of a few sherds of a white ware, which may be the "prototype" of Progreso Metallic, hints at the possibility of a shared tradition at the beginning of the Early Formative Period (*ca.* 2400–1700 B.C.) for these two areas.[5] The origin of this earlier and undefined tradition is, pending further investigation, a moot point. Regardless of earlier manifestations, north-central Veracruz at about 1700 B.C. represents a type of cultural frontier in the northeast for an early south-to-north diffusion pattern.

Culture contact in the Early Formative Period was probably a continuum, but assuming that it can be segmented for descriptive purposes, there may be a second south-to-north pattern. It begins about 1450 B.C. in the Chiapas-Isthmian region and reaches the Santa Luisa area about 1400 B.C. during the Almería Phase. It is not Olmec, but it is a logical step in the direction of a cultural scenario that would be readily receptive to Olmec concepts. Besides new ceramic forms, figurines, and evidence of long-distance trade in items such as hematite for paint, one finds at this time level the first presence of sherd disks. The last, probably used as spindle whorls for cotton, may represent the arrival of this important domesticate, as well as weaving technology and backstrap looms, from South America (Richard S. MacNeish, personal communication). *Tecomates* receive an even greater emphasis at this time, and obsidian chips remain abundant. Again the Chiapas (Ocós Phase) and Isthmian

---

[5] Recently surveyed shell middens in the Lagua de Tortugas region north of Pánuco may be of Pavón or earlier date (Angel García Cook, personal communication, 1978).

(Ojochi and Bajío Phases) regions are more complex and dynamic. The conservative nature of the Pavón Phase in the North Gulf area suggests that once more the north-central Veracruz area is still the frontier for these north-bound cultural features. It also implies that the Pavón cultural pattern, although conservative, may also have been sufficiently vigorous to resist the southern influence.

This second Early Formative pattern may end in the south about 1250 B.C. with the Chicharras Phase at San Lorenzo and the arrival of the first verifiable Olmec people on the Gulf Coast. Olmec influence arrives at Santa Luisa during the third discernible north-to-south pattern. It is represented by the Ojite Phase, which roughly corresponds temporally with the San Lorenzo A Phase in the south.

It was certainly not by chance that many of the earliest Olmec centers, such as San Lorenzo and La Venta, were on lagoons, islands, or the banks of major rivers near the Gulf itself. This was simply where the majority of the pre-existing lowland populations were located, and probably had been since the end of the Preceramic Period. The underlying subsistence orientation of intensive gathering, hunting, and fishing had made it possible. Throughout the Early Formative Period this base, apart from tropical fruits, must have been expanded by an increasing number of domesticated plants such as beans, chile, squash, tomatoes, and, probably, manioc. The Olmec addition to the subsistence formula appears to have been a major insistence on maize agriculture.

Manos and *metates* at Santa Luisa are not common until the Ojite Phase. In fact, there is only a single *mano* fragment in both the Almería and Monte Gordo Phases and there are no *metate* fragments until Ojite times. Obsidian chips drop in proportion to other artifacts during the Ojite Phase and disappear as a major category by the beginning of the following Esteros A Phase. The inverse ratio implies that the subsistence activity associated with the chips, probably manioc grating, decreased as maize became the major plant staple. Although the existing evidence is sparse, it implies the spread of an intensive reliance on maize with Olmec influence in the north-cen-

tral Veracruz area. This relationship parallels Lowe's interpretation of the spread of corn agriculture in Chiapas (Greene and Lowe 1967: 59–60). It is also in accord with implications of possible sculptural maize motifs, as on the slightly later Stela 1 at not-too-distant El Viejón (Fig. 6) and the Xoc rock-sculpture in Chiapas (Ekholm-Miller 1973: 17). Although these sculptures correspond more closely to the later Olmec representational format common at La Venta, they do exhibit the Olmec religious concern for plants, most probably maize.

The Olmec impact at the end of the Early Formative Period was intensive, including not only a probable manioc-to-maize subsistence shift, but also the introduction of platform mounds, distinct figurine types, Olmec icon-

Fig. 6 Stela 1 from El Viejón, Veracruz. Museo de Antropología de la Universidad de Veracruz, Jalapa. Photograph by Milinda Berge.

191

ography, and new ceramics and ceramic technology. Relative to Trapiche, in the northern region of south-central Veracruz, Santa Luisa appears not to have been as severely affected. In comparison to the contemporaneous Ponce Phase at Pánuco, however, Ojite looks rather Olmec.

The cultural pattern in the North Gulf area was much more conservative than that at Santa Luisa throughout the Early Formative Period. Unless the lithic distribution noted by Mac-Neish in the Pavón levels in 1949 is somehow aberrant, it would appear that the "obsidian-chip complex" may not have reached Pánuco until Ponce times (*ca.* 1150 B.C.), peaking in the following Aguilar Phase. Even then, it is not as strong proportionately as in the much earlier Raudal Phase to the south.[6] Sherd-disk spindle whorls do not appear until the end of the Ponce Phase (post-1000 B.C.), suggesting that the arrival of cotton in the area, or at least its use in cloth fabrication, was quite late. In general, with its limited ceramic variation and the late arrival of many traits, the Pánuco region certainly appears to have been quite conservative for the time. It would not be a primary area for Olmec penetration. Seemingly, there would be little for the dynamic Olmec to obtain from this area in terms of unique items for trade or tribute. While Olmec artifacts and influence are bound to have penetrated the area, the nature of the Olmec presence is unlikely to have been as intense as at Santa Luisa.

The North-Central Gulf at the end of the Early Formative Period once more appears to be a cultural frontier region, reflecting strongly events and innovations to the south but not reaching the point of being a full participant in the modifications. It also constituted the buffer or screen through which many diffusing artifact concepts, and the cultural processes they imply, must have moved to the then

remote and conservative North Gulf area. This frontier status seems to be more formalized in the beginning of the subsequent Middle Formative Period.

While the nature of Olmec influence in the Ojite Phase was pervasive, it did not completely overcome local ceramic traditions, and settlement location did not change. During the early portion of the Middle Formative, the Esteros A Phase at Santa Luisa, the local traditions are again emphasized.[7] Obsidian chips disappear, indicating that, although slower than in the south, the subsistence change was pervasive in the long run. Olmec influence is seen at this time in modest numbers of imported ceramic vessels and figurines, portable art (Fig. 7), and some outright ceramic imitations.

The physical Olmec presence appears concentrated at a limited number of sites, such as El Viejón, a hundred kilometers to the south. At that point the coastal plain with a fringe of salt-producing lagoons, contracts almost to the water's edge on both sides of the small valley and stream where El Viejón is located. The site location fits very well the Olmec site/pass/trade-route correlation originally proposed by Grove (1968b) for the western highlands. I suspect that ample study of Los Idolos in the nearby Sierra de Chincoquiaco will show a similar correlation.

Both of these sites have sculpture of the major La Venta horizon (Figs. 6 and 8), illustrating a "provincial" or "colonial" styling. Both are also located in the topographically abrupt area separating the then more "Olmec-ized" south-central Veracruz from the more "frontierlike" north-central Veracruz. Trade in such items as obsidian, salt, basalt, ceramic vessels, hematite, pyrite, shells, and asphalt certainly passed through such strategic locations and could easily have been regulated.

In summing up the Late Archaic to early Middle Formative cultural levels at Santa

[6] The current evidence suggests that the cultural unity for the North-Central and North Gulf areas, hypothesized in an earlier analysis for the entire Early Formative Period (Wilkerson 1974: Fig. 3), ought to be set back to before the Raudal Phase. The North-Central Gulf area would be included in the same subcultural area with the South-Central and South Gulf areas for the 1700-1000 B.C. time period.

[7] The generalized nature in north-central Veracruz of the Middle Formative materials found at Santa Luisa has been confirmed by stratigraphic tests accompanying salvage projects at Tuxpan (Ortiz Ceballos n.d.b) and Las Higeras (Arellanos *et al.* 1975).

Luisa, it is possible to define: (1) a successful lowland lifestyle allowing population concentration at the end of the Archaic Period; (2) successive patterns of pre-Olmec cultural complexes moving south to north (*ca.* 1700-1450 B.C. and *ca.* 1450-1150 B.C.), which seemingly make north-central Veracruz a type of frontier with respect to the North Gulf area; (3) a strong Olmec intrusion (*ca.* 1150–1000 B.C.), which greatly modified the lifestyle, its artifacts, and its subsistence base; and (4) a reassertion of local traditions (*ca.* 1000–600 B.C.) and a probable formalization of the frontier status with the establishment of Olmec sites at the potential trade-control points to the south.

The Olmec "aftermath" on the Gulf Coast is a subject requiring its own careful examination, but it is interesting to note briefly how successive cultural florescence moves also from south to north as the Olmec cease to be the focus of early civilization. The Tres Zapotes and Cerro de las Mesas regions prosper as

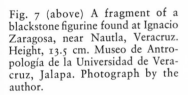

Fig. 7 (above) A fragment of a blackstone figurine found at Ignacio Zaragosa, near Nautla, Veracruz. Height, 13.5 cm. Museo de Antropología de la Universidad de Veracruz, Jalapa. Photograph by the author.

Fig. 8 (right) Large seated figure from Los Ídolos, Veracruz. Museo de Antropología de la Universidad de Veracruz, Jalapa. Photograph by Milinda Berge.

Fig. 9 Olmec sculpture of a seated man dressed in a loincloth and wearing a mirror-like ornament on his chest. He is holding a partially destroyed infant on his lap. This basalt sculpture, probably of San Lorenzo Phase date, is from the Ejido San Isidro. The site is located in close proximity to the hematite sources of Los Amagres and is on the high ground just across the Coatzacoalcos flood plain from San Lorenzo Tenochtitlan. Photograph by the author.

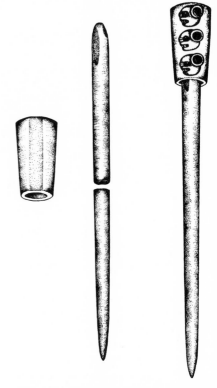

Fig. 10 A light-green jade "perforator" with a jaguar-decorated handle found near Rodríguez Clara, Veracruz. Present location unknown. Drawings by Elsbeth Gordon.

major social units during the Late Formative and Early Classic Periods. El Tajín in north-central Veracruz reaches its peak in the Late Classic and Epiclassic Period before losing impetus to the Huastec centers of the North Gulf area during the Early Postclassic Period. This pattern of cultural peaks is rough and only approximates historical reality. Nevertheless, each cultural subarea of the Gulf Coast reacted to the forceful Olmec presence and each had a turn at its legacy.[8]

ACKNOWLEDGMENTS Much of the data contained in this presentation is derived from research sponsored by grants (1973-78) from the National Geographic Society. The investigation was undertaken in collaboration with, and under the supervision of, the Instituto Nacional de Antropología e Historia in Mexico. I am indebted to the late Matthew Stirling for much encouragement and discussion of the research in the initial years of the project.

[8] Although they are not from the Santa Luisa region, I have included two Olmec items which should go on record (Figs. 9 and 10).

Guerrero and the Olmec

Louise Iseut Paradis

UNIVERSITÉ DE MONTRÉAL

INTRODUCTION

The Olmec have been approached from many directions: iconography, chronological position, culture, and economic structure. Common to all these approaches is the recognition of an Olmec art style distributed all over Mesoamerica, from Costa Rica to northwestern Guerrero. Art styles travel well and quickly; however, their meaning in terms of the cultural system and subsystem in which they are found is not so easily understood.

The overall perspective on the nature and importance of the Olmec phenomenon has changed considerably over the last twenty years. Present-day interpretations are a direct result of new theoretical and methodological orientations in archaeology. The kinds of data and the manner in which they are collected and analyzed determine the kinds of interpretation they generate, and vice versa. In very general terms, interest has switched from a more artifactual and typological approach to a more processual appreciation of archaeological evidence. The interpretations provided for Olmec-style artifacts found in Mesoamerica illustrate this trend. After a period of recognition and identification of Olmec-style artifacts, and a preoccupation with their placement in space and time, came a first attempt at interpretation. Diffusion—with or without migration—from a Veracruz–Tabasco heartland was to account for the widespread distribution of the art style. Religious, military, and/or economic processes were seen underlying this diffusion (Caso 1965; M. Coe 1968a; Grove

1968b). Unfortunately, no way of verifying this theory presented itself immediately, and the hypothesis itself remained vague. Yet there was nothing else to propose in its place in the absence of the kind of evidence needed to confirm or disprove it. Since the mid-sixties, however, a considerable amount of evidence has been uncovered and has made possible the testing of this type of hypothesis and the formulation of new ones. Chronological placement has been achieved for several regions, and the "heartland" of Olmec culture has been defined by work at La Venta and San Lorenzo Tenochtitlan. Parallel to the archaeological discoveries in Veracruz and Tabasco, the Mexican highlands were searched for contextual evidence related to the Olmec presence. New kinds of data are now considered and integrated into a more structural perspective. Archaeological sites are increasingly seen, not as mere collections of artifacts but as loci of prehistoric cultural behavior. Ecological, economic, and social correlates of the material evidence can be suggested and, in a growing number of cases, proved. Archaeological literature on the topic over the last decade illustrates well this new orientation (Benson 1968; Flannery 1976). The Olmec phenomenon can now be defined more precisely and understood in the context of an early Mesoamerican society. How does Guerrero fit into this perspective? In the ensuing section, I will attempt to clarify this question. After presenting the recent archaeological evidence for the Early and Middle Formative Periods in this region, I will re-

195

evaluate some hypotheses concerning the nature and importance of the Olmec presence in Guerrero in the light of the present state of knowledge of the Olmec phenomenon in the rest of Mesoamerica.

Guerrero is well known for the variety of its remains of the Olmec, Teotihuacan, and even Classic Maya traditions. Other cultural styles —Xochipala, Mezcala—are even more intriguing, and appear to be unique to this area. Almost all of these styles are known because of their high value on the collectors' market and the well-organized looting activities in Guerrero. These styles are frequently mentioned in publications, but their presence in Guerrero is not well understood due to a lack of archaeological context. The consequence of this situation is that Guerrero has yielded evidence of prehistoric art styles that have not been associated with identifiable societies. The few identified cultural remains found thus far cannot unequivocally be assigned to either Xochipala, Olmec, or Mezcala.

This state of affairs has led often to speculations concerning the prehistory of the region. One hypothesis, brilliantly formulated by Miguel Covarrubias (1946a), claimed Guerrero as the source of the Olmec art style. The quantity and quality of Olmec-style artifacts, often of jade, found in the region supported his idea. Unfortunately, this hypothesis remained unverified for lack of context and chronological placement. Recent work in the region, however, has produced a great deal of information. More specifically, the placement in time, the distribution in space, and the significance of acknowledged Olmec evidence have begun to be understood. Archaeological investigations on the coast (E. Brush n.d.; C. Brush n.d.) and in the northeastern (Henderson n.d.), northwestern (Paradis n.d.), and central (Stark 1977: 274) portions of Guerrero shed light on the Pre-Columbian occupation of the area. My survey of the evidence will be restricted to the Early and Middle Formative Periods, a time when the local populations seem to have participated in a vast Mesoamerican exchange network in which Olmec-style

artifacts played a still not totally explained function.

There are good grounds for claiming the existence of village life in the Early and Middle Formative Periods in various parts of Guerrero. Systematic archaeological investigations are still scarce, as compared to the extensive outflow of looted artifacts, but they do give a framework for discussing prehistoric activities in the area. I will first discuss one region, for which I have more detailed information: the Middle Balsas River Basin. I will then attempt a general survey of other archaeological finds.

THE MIDDLE BALSAS RIVER BASIN (MBRB)

The discovery of an Olmec-style stela in the village of Amuco de la Reforma in 1967 (Grove and Paradis 1971) triggered my choice of the MBRB for archaeological investigations: this find suggested that chronological and, above all, contextual placement of Olmec-related artifacts might be achieved in Guerrero. The results of this archaeological and ethnohistorical research were rewarding although often puzzling, as I will show.

The MBRB lies in the extreme northwestern corner of the modern state of Guerrero (Fig. 1). It borders the state of Michoacán to the northwest and the state of México to the north. It covers an area of 18,350 square kilometers between parallels 17°26' and 18°52' north latitude, and meridians 100°08' and 101°11' west longitude. The Middle Balsas River itself constitutes that portion of the main river that lies between Tetela del Río and the Infiernillo dam. In this region the Balsas River broadens and flows into a wide open valley with low hills; the mean elevation of the basin is 260 meters above sea level. From all points, however, the presence of the mountains limits one's view: on the north and northeast, the neovolcanic range, and on the south, the threatening Sierra Madre del Sur enclose the MBRB like the setting of a precious jewel. Paradoxically, the region is both supplied with, and deprived of, valuable water by these mountains. Tributaries from the northern neovolcanic range flow into the Balsas and provide most of the discharge into the basin. A few tributaries from the Sierra Madre del Sur also contribute their water to

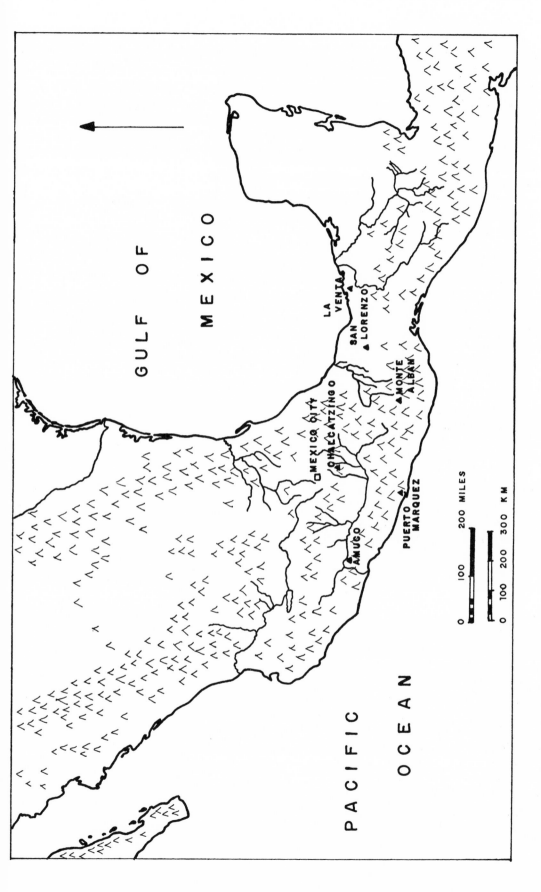

Fig. 1 Map of Mesoamerica showing the location of Amuco, Guerrero. Drawing by Suzan Klein.

197

the Balsas River. But at the same time, the mountains block the basin from moisture-bearing winds, and it is thus comparatively dry. Locally, the MBRB is called *Tierra Caliente* and it deserves its name. At times, it becomes unbearable even for the people who have spent their lives there. The climate as a whole can be described as semidry, with hot and dry autumn, winter, and spring seasons and no defined cold season. Eighty percent of the annual rains fall from June to October and are torrential. The average annual precipitation varies between 1000 and 2000 millimeters, but the year-round evaporation rate (2492 millimeters) seriously attenuates the effects of this precipitation.

I worked in the southern MBRB, and more particularly in the area between Ciudad Altamirano and the village of Tlapehuala. In dealing with the physical environment, I subdivided the southern MBRB into four microenvironments on the basis of topographic features and vegetation (Fig. 2): (1) the river network and riverbanks with their alluvial soils and semitropical vegetation; (2) the valley floor, which lies between the river network and the piedmont area, and which supports a dry shrub vegetation; (3) the piedmont area, south of the region studied, which anticipates the first escarpments of the Sierra Madre del Sur and has a shrub-and-tree-vegetation cover; and (4) the Sierra Madre del Sur, which closes the MBRB from the south and the Pacific coast, and has an escarpment which reaches to the Balsas River immediately south of Amuco de la Reforma.

The MBRB forms the only wide valley floor in the Balsas River system and, as such, an opening suitable for settlement. The Balsas River itself crosses the rugged state of Guerrero from northeast to southwest and offers a natural outlet from the highlands to the Pacific coast. The MBRB, surrounded by high mountains, is also relatively isolated from the rest of the country. This setting contributes to its being an isolated area economically as well as culturally.

The evidence for the chronological sequence established in the southern MBRB comes from archaeology and ethnohistory. The archaeological sequence spans the period from *ca.* 1600 B.C. until *ca.* A.D. 500; the ethnohistorical sequence, from A.D. 1250 until 1580. I will concentrate here on the early part of the archaeological sequence, as reconstructed from analysis of data excavated in two sites: Amuco Abelino and Los Terrones. Archaeological remains from four other excavated sites and from surface collections were used as comparative material. A summary of this sequence is shown in Table 1.

The site of Amuco Abelino lies at the southwestern end of the modern village of Amuco de la Reforma. It is situated about 800 meters west of the location where the Olmec-style stela is said to have been found. The Amuco River, a southern tributary of the Balsas River, flows northwest of the site, which is located on the valley floor. The excavation at Amuco Abelino indicates a long and diversified occupation of the site. This occupation was more-or-less continuous, with at least four distinct structural features reflecting human activity. Two foundation walls, associated with hearths and cooking debris, are separated by seventy centimeters of dirt, and underneath these, a white ash floor supporting three whole vessels and a contemporaneous stone-wall foundation seal off an even earlier occupation at the site. Ceramic analysis, in conjunction with the study of the natural and cultural stratigraphy, led me to recognize two main phases in the local sequence: Sesame Phase (subdivided into Sesame Subphases 1, 2, and 3) and Guacamole Phase.

The site of Los Terrones lies less than a kilometer from Amuco Abelino. It is located on the left bank of the Amuco River, in the hamlet of the same name. There is evidence for a single occupation at the site; ceramic analysis leads me to believe that the site was occupied during the Guacamole Phase. In fact, whereas Amuco Abelino appears to have been occupied only near the beginning of the Guacamole Phase, that phase was widespread in the region as a whole and well represented in Los Terrones. I thus subdivided Guacamole into two subphases: Guacamole 1, represented in Amuco Abelino, and Guacamole 2, at Los Terrones.

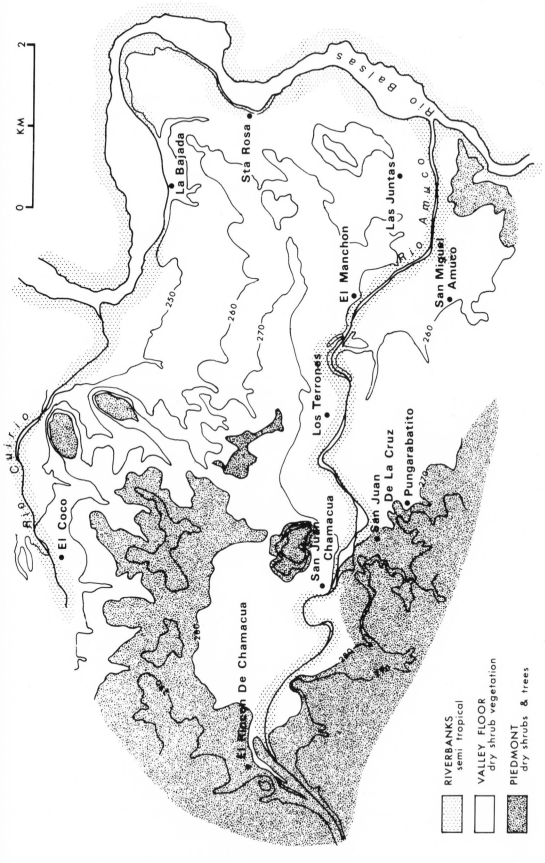

Fig. 2 Map of the vegetation patterns in the Amuco area. Drawing by Lucien Goupil.

RIVERBANKS
semi tropical

VALLEY FLOOR
dry shrub vegetation

PIEDMONT
dry shrubs & trees

199

In terms of chronological placement, the Sesame Phase starts *ca.* 1600 B.C and lasts until *ca.* 900 or 800 B.C. A temporal gap follows and the Guacamole Phase tentatively begins *ca.* 600 B.C to end in the first centuries of the Christian era. This tentative sequence is based on a combination of radiocarbon dating and ceramic comparisons in a stratigraphic context.

It is in the Sesame Phase that I found evidence of Olmec-style artifacts associated with local ceramics. The ceramics from the southern MBRB are generally representative of a local tradition. The overall impression when looking at the ceramics from Sesame Phase is one of homogeneity and of a relative lack of imagination from an artistic or comparative point of view. The sherds are of a general orange-to-red color, well fired, and of uniform size and thickness. The shapes most often represented are open, straight-walled vessels and *ollas*. There is comparatively little emphasis on surface treatment and plastic or painted decoration: punctations on the lip, zoned punctation on the exterior wall of vessels, star-shaped incision on the interior, semilunar incision on the interior rim of open vessels. The Guacamole Phase differs from the earlier Sesame Phase by the addition of new elements to the ceramic assemblages. There is greater contrast between coarse and finer ceramics and a greater overall variety in the ceramic inventory. Plastic decoration is different and geometric patterns are common. On the whole, however, the ceramic tradition shows great conservatism during the Formative Period. In the rather extensive amount of archaeological material recovered from excavation and surface collection, there is a relatively small number of artifacts of exotic appearance, that is, artifacts that are distinct from the rest of the archaeological remains and are of rare occurrence in the sample studied. The Olmec-related finds are among these.

OLMEC-RELATED FINDS IN THE MBRB

Surface survey, excavation, and private collections from the southern MBRB have produced a total of four recognizable Olmec-style objects (Fig. 3). Two of these, a stela (Fig. 4) and a jadeite mask (Fig. 5a), were found in private collections, although their provenience is known with some degree of reliability. In addition, a ceramic masquette and a figurine head were excavated at the Amuco Abelino site (Fig. 5b, c). The stela and ceramic figures are all from within a radius of 500 meters of Amuco de la Reforma. The jadeite mask comes from La Arboleda, some thirty-five kilometers to the southwest. Only the two ceramic artifacts were found in a cultural context and could be chronologically placed.

The ceramic masquette (Fig. 5b) was found in the lowest layer of the trench at Amuco Abelino, a gray-clay stratum lying at 3.5 meters below the surface, beneath a floor and cooking area. The mask is seven centimeters long, not including the top of the helmet, and approximately seven centimeters wide at ear level. It is incomplete; slightly less than half of the left side of the face is missing, as is the upper portion of the helmet. The latter circles the face down to the chin, which does not seem to be covered; the left ear protrudes from the helmet. The eyes bulge, and a diagonal slit punched in the center indicates the iris and pupil. The nose is broken. The upper portion of the lip is missing, but two fangs protrude from the upper portion of the mouth. The corners of the mouth are turned down and the lower lip is well marked; the chin is slightly pointed. The masquette represents a human head with feline features—the fangs.

The Olmec-style figurine head, also found in Amuco Abelino (Fig. 5c), comes from a layer of light-colored clay, at a level lower than that of the second-lowest floor and cooking area. The head has human features. The upper part of the forehead and the body are missing. The head is pear-shaped; it is 3.5 centimeters long, not including the missing top portion, two centimeters wide at the narrow upper part of the face, and 2.5 centimeters wide at the bottom. The back of the head is flat and deformed. The eyebrows are indicated by incised lines that extend to the nose area. The eyes are depicted as coils inside an almost-square outline, and a hole is punched for each pupil. The upper lip is raised and formed with its corner sloping down; the mouth is open, letting the tongue show, but is toothless. The lower lip is

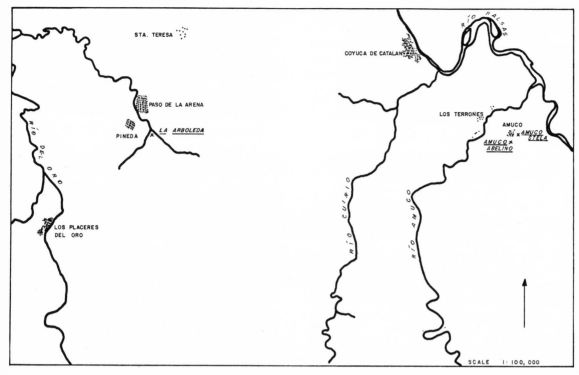

Fig. 3 Map showing the sites from the Amuco area where Olmec-style artifacts were found. Drawing by Suzan Klein.

not depicted and the receding chin is accompanied by two vertical-slit incisions extended from the mouth; these incisions might be intended to indicate fangs.

Two radiocarbon dates were obtained from the excavation at Amuco Abelino (the analyses were carried out at the Centre Radiogéologique in Nancy, France). The Olmec-style masquette and figurine head were not directly associated with the charcoal used for dating. The masquette was under the lowest floor, which was dated (Sample No. 8: 3480 ± 230 B.P.) 1530 B.C. ± 230. The figurine head was slightly beneath and outside the wall structure and cooking area for which another date was obtained (Sample No. 5: 3170 ± 110 B.P.), 1220 B.C. ± 110. The ceramic associations, however, indicate both figurines to be part of the dated assemblages. Ceramics directly associated with the masquette are characteristic of Sesame Subphase 1; those found with the figurine head are attributable to Sesame Subphase 2. The ceramics are locally made and show no direct influence or resemblance to Olmec-style ce-

ramics as represented in the heartland (M. Coe 1970), in Oaxaca (Flannery 1968), in the Basin of Mexico (Tolstoy and Paradis 1970; Niederberger 1976), or in Morelos (Grove 1970; Grove *et al.* 1976).

Two comments can be made at this point. First, Olmec-related artifacts have now been found in an archaeological context in Guerrero and dated. If we accept the radiocarbon dates for the site of Amuco Abelino, they provide a very early date for the occurrence of Olmec-style objects in Guerrero—in fact, one of the earliest in Mesoamerica. But, and equally important, these artifacts are found embedded in a local cultural tradition that has nothing to do with one commonly labeled Olmec. For this reason, it seems justifiable to consider these artifacts as alien to the local context.

EVIDENCE FROM OTHER PARTS OF GUERRERO

Excluding for the moment Olmec-style artifacts known from private collections, the only other well-documented archaeological sequence comes from the Pacific coast (C. Brush n.d.). Here, as in the case of the southern MBRB, I shall restrict my comments to the early part of the ceramic occupation, that which corresponds to the Early and Middle Formative Periods. A long ceramic sequence has been established for Puerto Marqués. The sequence begins with one of the earliest dates for ceramics in Mesoamerica: Pox Phase, with an average date of 2440 B.C. ± 140 (C. Brush 1965). As a whole, the sequence represents a local tradition. In fact, the closest similarities I could find for the ceramic assemblages from the MBRB were with the Pacific coast. Most similarities between the two areas are found in the early part of Brush's sequence: the Tom, Rin, Et, and Fal Phases of Puerto Marqués, which probably correspond to the Early, Middle, and Late Formative Periods. The Sesame Phase shows similarities with the Tom and Rin Phases. Although the ceramics from Puerto Marqués show no relation to Olmec-style ceramics, the presence of Olmec figurines was noticed there and more generally on the Pacific *Costa Grande* (E. Brush n.d.). The first identifiable type from the coast is the baby-face type from levels 17 and 18 at Puerto Marqués (end of Tom and beginning of Rin Phases) and from level 9 at Zanja II (equivalent to Tom Phase). There are earlier Olmec-style body fragments; in effect, it looks as though at Puerto Marqués the earliest figurines may have been Olmec-style. In that case they would date back to Uala Phase, probably of the Early Formative Period. There are no radiocarbon dates for these levels at Puerto Marqués, but they are considered Early and Middle Formative in relation to earlier and later radiocarbon dates from both sites (Puerto Marqués and Amuco Abelino) and to the nature of the ceramic assemblages. Thus, as seen from the Pacific coast as well as from the MBRB, Olmec archaeological evidence is both early and scarce, in the context of very strong local tradition.

A review of Olmec-related finds in other parts of Guerrero would add little here since it would consist of an enumeration of artifacts without any contextual correlates. Suffice it to say that there is a large corpus of Olmec-style evidence, of various materials and shapes, that has come out of Guerrero. The Amuco stela

Fig. 4 Stela from Amuco, Guerrero. Private collection, Arcelia, Guerrero. Photograph by the author.

and the Oxtotitlán and Juxtlahuaca paintings are among the few examples of monumental art in Guerrero and the Mexican highlands, aside from Chalcatzingo, Morelos. Jadeite objects are frequently reported from Guerrero, and, although no actual jade source has been discovered yet, it has been hypothesized that Guerrero could have been one of the sources for La Venta and Olmec jade (M. Coe 1968a). A considerable amount of Olmec jadeite appears in private collections as portable objects: bowls, masks, pendants, celts, spoons, earspools, etc. The most productive areas center around the Balsas River drainage, east and west of the road to Acapulco. Olmec jadeite

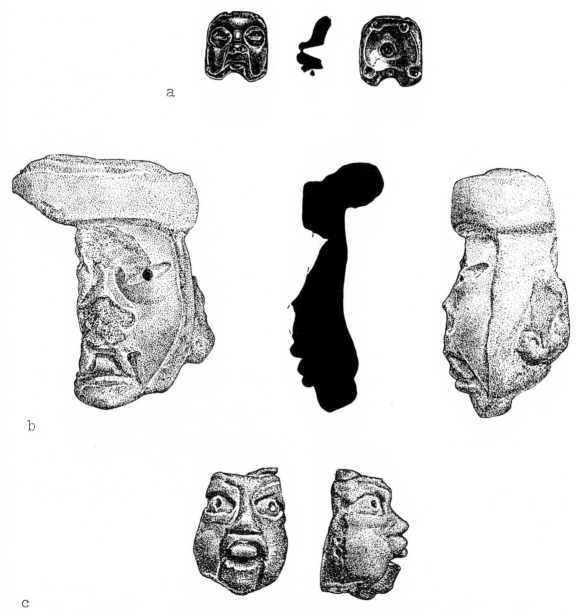

Fig. 5 Olmec-style figurines. *a*. Jadeite mask from La Arboleda. Private collection, Paso de Arena, Guerrero. *b*. Ceramic masquette from Amuco Abelino. Instituto Nacional de Antropología e Historia, Mexico. *c*. Ceramic figurine head from Amuco Abelino. Instituto Nacional de Antropología e Historia, Mexico. Drawings by Suzan Klein.

from Guerrero has a highly polished surface; blue-gray and dark green are the colors most often found. Engraved jadeite usually depicts human or feline features that have been interpreted as illustrations of Olmec gods (Joralemon 1971). Finally, ceramic figurines are also part of the Olmec-style inventory in Guerrero: they have been encountered in the same general area as the jadeite objects, *i.e.*, at Ahuelicán and Tetipa, and particularly on the Pacific coast.

To sum up, we are left with a picture of Guerrero as an area rich in Olmec-style objects, most of which are neither dated nor placed in context. The only evidence of chronological and contextual placement comes from the somewhat marginal region of the MBRB and from the Pacific coast. There, Olmec occurrences seem intrusive into an otherwise local cultural inventory. On chronometric grounds alone (more work will have to be done to check this), Guerrero could actually have been the source of Olmec art style. That could account for the early dates from Guerrero, as well as for the amount and variety of examples of the Olmec style that is not equaled in other parts of Mesoamerica. If such is the case, the birth and development of Olmec civilization cannot be understood on the basis of evidence from Veracruz and Tabasco alone. The possibility I have suggested, once discussed by Covarrubias, still remains to be investigated fully.

Leaving aside for the moment the early dates for the Olmec-related finds in Amuco Abelino, I would like to turn to other evidence, of an economic and social nature, that might explain the Olmec presence in Guerrero in the light of present knowledge of the Olmec in the rest of Mesoamerica.

UNDERLYING PROCESSES

The study of the socioeconomic patterns in the MBRB has led me to believe that the presence of a few exotic artifacts there is not an anomaly and can very well be explained. The evidence for the Formative Period is not precise enough to allow general inferences concerning socioeconomic patterns. However, the study of modern and ethnohistorical evidence indicates patterns that could well have existed throughout the occupation of the MBRB by a sedentary and agricultural society. Only a short summary of these patterns can be presented here.

Subsistence is based on agriculture. The environment offers excellent conditions for this activity. Rich soils and the climatic conditions favor a fast growing season and the possibility of cultivating a large variety of plants. The environment, however, does present limitations. Productive soils are limited to certain environmental niches. Climatic and hydrologic conditions limit the availability of water and the kinds of soils that can be successfully cultivated. Adapting to this environment, four patterns are observed.

(1) Riverbanks and the valley floor are intensively exploited for agricultural and settlement purposes, much more so than any other environmental zone in the MBRB.

(2) Under normal conditions, only one crop can be grown during the rainy season. A minor crop, grown on river levees at the end of the rainy season, is also possible. However, unless water-control techniques are used, no crops can be grown during more than half of the year. Three types of response to this limitation have been observed locally: (a) *temporal* (rainy season) and *bajial* (river levee) agriculture may be sufficient to support the population; otherwise, the inhabitants resort to (b) seasonal out-migration or (c) irrigation.

(3) Collecting, hunting, and fishing activities contribute to subsistence. These activities are proportionately minor today and were so in the sixteenth century. Moreover, they are not sufficient today to complement fully the agricultural production where no irrigation is practiced.

(4) Movements of goods and people in and out of the MBRB form a recurrent pattern during contemporary and ethnohistorical times. In modern times, products are exchanged with the Pacific coast and with the Mexican highlands. Agricultural products are exported to Mexico City. Local industrial products (palm hats, *mezcal*) are exported to Morelos, Michoacán, and other parts of Guerrero. In return, finished products—electrical appliances, textiles, and tools—are brought in by truckloads and sold in Ciudad Altamirano. The sixteenth-century system of specialized long-distance carriers (*arrieros*) is almost entirely replaced by modern means of communication. The traffic is intense both in and out of the region. Although I did not make a systematic study of this, I noticed a social network (kinship, alliances) superimposed on the economic-exchange network.

In the sixteenth century, an elaborate exchange network linked populations from the Pacific coast, the *Tierra Caliente*, northeastern Guerrero, and the central highlands. Long-distance trading and seasonal out-migration were

TABLE I. TENTATIVE ARCHAEOLOGICAL SEQUENCE FOR THE FORMATIVE PERIOD OF GUERRERO, MEXICO

	Amuco (Balsas)		Puerto Marqués (Pacific coast)	Northeastern Guerrero*
100	La Molienda Sample 2:	Guacamole 2	Fal	
BC/AD	A.D. 110±110			
100				
200				
300				
400		Guacamole 1	Et	
500				
600				
700		?	Rin	
800				Tecolotla
900				
1000		Sesame 3		Atopula
1100			Tom	
1200	Amuco Abelino Sample 5:			Cacahuananche
1300	1220 B.C. ±110	Sesame 2		
		Olmec figurine		
1400				
1500	Amuco Abelino Sample 8:	Sesame 1		
1600	1530 B.C. ±230		Uala	
		Olmec mask		
1800				
2000				
2200				
2400			Pox	

*Henderson 1979:28

then common patterns in the MBRB. Figure 6 gives a summary of this network, showing the products exchanged and the directions of exchange.

Thus, the geographical isolation of the *Tierra Caliente* of Guerrero is counterbalanced by a network of exchange with surrounding regions. The patterns observed in modern and ethnohistorical times are the basis for the following inferences and hypotheses concerning the preconquest occupation of the region.

(1) The settlement patterns give good evidence for a predominantly agricultural society in the MBRB. Riverbanks and the valley floor were the most favored locations for settlement.

(2) The evidence for the Formative Period is not sufficient to inform us of agricultural practices. The lack of evidence for irrigation in preconquest times leaves two possibilities. *Temporal* and *bajial* agriculture could have been sufficient in some cases to support the living population. Where and when this was not the case, seasonal out-migration could have been practiced.

(3) Hunting, collecting, and fishing were part of the subsistence activities in preconquest times and, most probably, proportionately more important than today.

(4) An exchange network could have existed in preconquest times. The archaeological evidence indicates contact with, or at least knowledge of, societies outside the MBRB. Olmec- and Teotihuacan-related objects are found in the region of Amuco. This could have occurred as a result of seasonal out-migration and/or interregional commercial exchange. Interregional exchange networks have now been established on firm grounds, thanks to technical analyses of source and distribution of material (Cobean *et al.* 1971; Pires-Ferreira 1976). Results from such study confirm the hitherto vague hypothesis of trade in Early and Middle Formative times. The mechanisms insuring the flow of goods and the commercial system have yet to be specified, but distinctive patterns have been identified. Obsidian, shell, and iron ore, in view of their nature and the manner of their utilization (both as utilitarian and as luxury goods) are good comparative materials.

The archaeological evidence alone allows one to think that Guerrero was part of the Early and Middle Formative exchange network. In addition to the obsidian and shell network already documented, I would hypothesize a third one: jade.

The Zinapécuaro obsidian source lies north of the MBRB and was linked to Oaxaca (Pires-Ferreira 1976: 304). The obsidian from Amuco has not yet been studied for sources, but could very well have been part of the Zinapécuaro–Oaxaca exchange network in Early Formative times. The Balsas River is a good travel route and passes through regions where a large number of Olmec objects have been privately collected.

A Pacific shell-exchange network has been established only between the Chiapas and western Guatemala coasts and highland Oaxaca. Testing of the Guerrero Pacific coast and other Guerrero sites might provide another link to this exchange network.

Jade has always been the motive cited for movements of Olmec traders from the lowlands up to the highlands and Guerrero. To date, however, no definite sources of jade have been found in Guerrero. The quantity of Olmec jade objects found in Guerrero can be interpreted as the result of the activities of local craftsmen. In the same way that San José Mogote had a specific portion of the village responsible for the manufacture of iron-ore mirrors and beads, some definite regions of Guerrero might have specialized in jade luxury goods. Lapidary work was and has remained one of the salient features of Guerrero's cultural tradition. Exchange of jade or serpentine objects could have been channeled through the same exchange network as obsidian or possibly shell. Jade is found at La Venta but not at San Lorenzo. If the jade products could be shown to have reached the lowlands only in Middle Formative times, three interpretations could be offered: (a) Olmec jade objects found in Guerrero date to the Middle Formative; (b) they were produced earlier but did not reach the lowlands at an early date; or (c) there is jade at San Lorenzo but it has not been found.

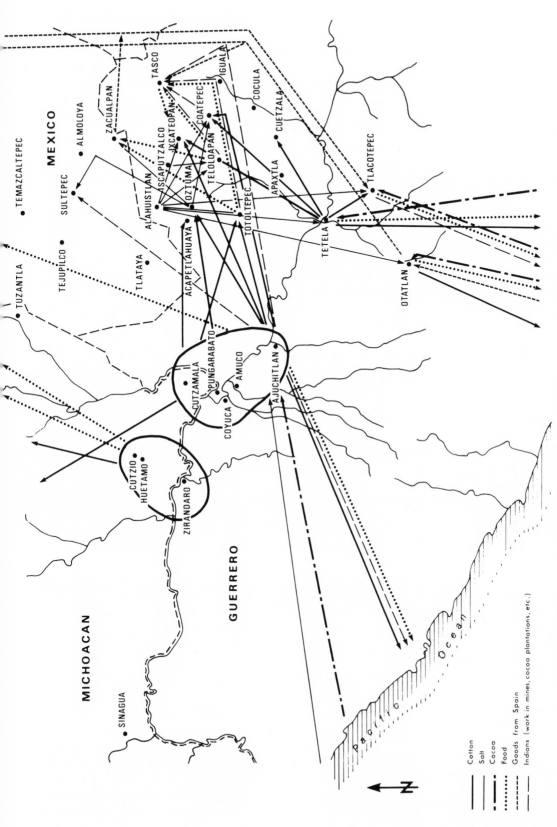

Fig. 6 Map showing the commercial networks of the Amuco area during the sixteenth century. Drawing by Lucien Goupil.

207

The chronological placement of Olmec lapidary work needs to be settled before any conclusions can be reached on the mechanisms of exchange and its overall relation to the Olmec. If the Zinapécuaro obsidian-exchange network actually went through the Balsas drainage, it could have served to make the lapidary craftsmen of Guerrero aware of Olmec art style; they could have subsequently applied their knowledge to the manufacture of Olmec-style jade and serpentine objects. If one agrees with the early date for Olmec-style ceramic figurines in the MBRB, the reverse could also be possible.

CONCLUDING REMARKS

We are still far from a solution to the Olmec enigma, but we are getting closer. From Guerrero, recent evidence can be summarized as follows: (1) the Olmec art style occurs early in an otherwise local cultural tradition characterized by sedentary agricultural villages; and (2) the region participated in an Early and Middle Formative exchange network in which obsidian, shells, and perhaps jade were circulated.

Two questions remain to be answered: What is the origin of the Olmec art style (a chronological problem) and what is the meaning of its spread along the commercial networks (a processual problem)? Are we dealing with luxury goods and/or status symbols? Flannery has answered this question adequately in the case of Oaxaca (Flannery 1968). Along the same line, I propose to investigate further the relations between Guerrero and the other regions of Mesoamerica in the Early and Middle Formative times.

Olmec Forms and Materials Found in Central Guerrero

Gillett G. Griffin

PRINCETON UNIVERSITY

The Dumbarton Oaks Conference on the Olmec, held in late October of 1967, was pervaded by the generous and gentle spirit of the "grandfather of Olmec studies," Matthew Stirling. It was my first conference on a Pre-Columbian theme and my first sight of the great man. He and his wife, Marion, invited the participants and those associated with Dumbarton Oaks to their home for dinner on Saturday night. It was there that I found myself sitting at the feet of all of the North American archaeologists who had been present at the actual excavation of the great Offering 4 at La Venta—the famous group of thirteen stone figures and six halved celts arranged as a ritual group. They described how it all had to be recorded, photographed, and removed in the same day for fear that it might be stolen that night. Robert Heizer told how the next day they were able to pinpoint exactly the balancing offering, which appeared to be wizardry to the laborers. But the most moving part of that conference was Matthew Stirling, the man who had excavated all the important Olmec sites and had unerringly called attention to most of what we still know about that mysterious civilization. His love affair with the Olmec sites began with a blue-jade masquette in the Berlin Museum which he had gone to see in 1920.

What attracted Matthew Stirling and all *olmecistas* from José Melgar through Miguel Covarrubias to the present generation, is the remarkable conception and mastery of form and technique in the working of materials—especially the working of hard stones such as jade and serpentine. It might be said that no other lithic culture in world history has been as precise in choice of stones and as accomplished in the working of them as the Olmec. I would like to discuss Olmec forms and materials from the highlands of Mexico—especially north-central Guerrero (Fig. 1).

There survives no Olmec architecture *per se*. Earthen mounds and clay pyramids abound; these must have supported buildings and temples of perishable materials. The site layouts of the Olmec heartland have been mapped; aerial photographs have been taken of unexplored sites; and a particular form of Olmec layout has emerged which is very intriguing in its overall concept, arrangement, and possible effigy connotations. But in central Guerrero, for years a source of Olmec lithic art, little serious archaeological reconnaissance has been attempted because of the wildness of the terrain and the often unpredictable disposition of the people. To my knowledge, no whole Olmec site has yet been mapped there. There have appeared in Guerrero, however, three possible depictions of temples: two flat blue-jade pectorals in what might be construed as temple forms (Fig. 2); and, deep in Juxtlahuaca Cave, a crude smudgy painting, partly defaced by a lime coating, which could be interpreted as a long temple with a high roof-comb (Fig. 3).

We are fortunate in having found Olmec cave paintings in Guerrero, and certainly others will be found. The arid climate and general dryness of southern highland Mexico is more conducive to preservation than the humid air and acid soil of the steamy lowlands. Dry caves have yielded, and will, we hope, continue to

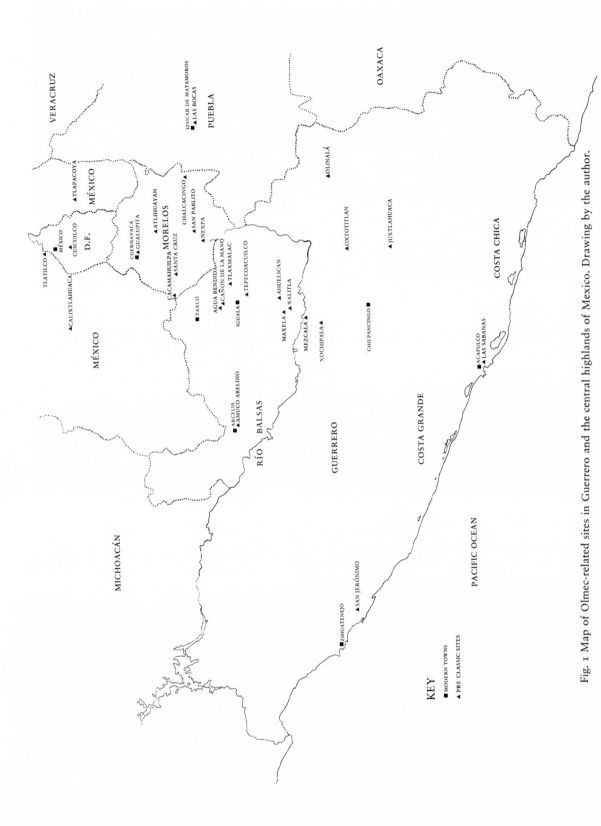

Fig. 1 Map of Olmec-related sites in Guerrero and the central highlands of Mexico. Drawing by the author.

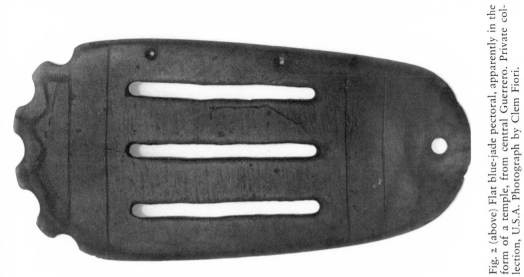

Fig. 2 (above) Flat blue-jade pectoral, apparently in the form of a temple, from central Guerrero. Private collection, U.S.A. Photograph by Clem Fiori.

Fig. 3 (right) Drawing on a stalagmite which appears to be a structure with a roof-comb, Juxtlahuaca Cave, Guerrero. Photograph by Carlo Gay.

yield, Olmec materials of a perishable nature, such as the great wooden mask (Fig. 4) found in a cave high up in the Cañon de la Mano, near Iguala. The mask tells us eloquently what we all must have intuited, that the Olmec were masters of wood-carving and that a body of their artistic output in wood and other perishable materials is probably lost forever. But it also holds out the hope that more Olmec wooden objects and possibly even cloth ones, remain to be found.

The Olmec also worked shell. Surviving examples, mostly from Xochipala, are few but handsomely executed. Shell was used for pectorals, beads, inlays, and probably earspools.

A number of stone bark-beaters survive, which is a strong indication that the Olmec probably had a *ficus* paper similar to contemporary Otomí sacred paper. Frederick V. Field (1974: xiii) offers a theory that the great number of seals, or *sellos,* with Olmec designs on them were the property of shamans who used them to print magical symbols on sacred paper to be used as charms to be burnt, to be planted with the corn, or to be strewed on the trail to insure success in some endeavor. Several *sellos* have survived with traces of red pigment on them (Fig. 5); a coating of specular hematite

on various examples indicates that this blood-red substance, when ground, may have been the pigment used for printing. Field further notes (*ibid.:* x, xi) that he knows of no *sellos* from the great central ceremonial sites—only examples from provincial areas. This may reflect their association with a provincial religion, or indicate that they may have served the same function as Buddhist or Christian printed charms intended to disseminate the religion into remote regions. If Field is right about their function of printing on paper, this might constitute the earliest evidence of printing on paper in the world (Mayor 1971: Fig. 2).

Another rich highland source of Olmec iconography is to be found on incised and excised pottery vessels and bowls. Negative painting on pottery vessels is found more rarely, the most famous coming from Tlapacoya. Heartland pottery has suffered from the ravages of the acid soil of the region, but the same forms and iconography appear in the highlands, often in excellent condition. The finest have come from the Las Bocas region in Puebla and from Olmec burials at Tlatilco. Not so well known are a number of excellent, pure Olmec examples from Xochipala. Certain clays, such as a reddish-brown ware, seem to be unique to Xochipala which also has yielded blackwares and kaolin-slipped wares. Since only fragments from the San Lorenzo horizon at San Lorenzo survive, as eroded sherds, it must be said that vessels from the highlands comprise the finest examples of Olmec ceramics that we know at present. David Joralemon (1976: 36–7), from an exhaustive study of numbers of ceramics from all these areas, has been able to trace their ideographic, almost calligraphic, symbols—in many cases, from highly abstract notations—back to an original naturalistic image, thereby recovering depictions of deities as the Olmec conceived them.

The earliest ceramic figurine fragments in Olmec style, to my knowledge, are two ceramic head fragments (Fig. 6) excavated by Louise Paradis at Amuco Abelino, in western Guerrero, under carefully controlled conditions. Their radiocarbon dates center at 1500 B.C. Their style is reminiscent of certain pieces from Xochipala, although cruder. The term Xochi-

Fig. 4 Wooden mask in Olmec style found in a cave in the Cañon de la Mano, near Iguala, Guerrero. Photograph courtesy of the American Museum of Natural History, New York.

pala has come to indicate a region which includes a rather large territory and a number of sites located between Zumpango del Río and Mezcala, its center being the modern village of Xochipala. Xochipala material ranges in time from very early mid-Preclassic to late Postclassic, including a pure Olmec stratum. The Olmec material at Xochipala appears to have strong ties with Las Bocas. Several pieces found at Xochipala seem to be of Las Bocas clay and workmanship (Gay 1972: 32, Figs. 17 and 18). Certain iconographic subjects, such as an old hag cradling a baby in her lap, appear thus far only in these two sites.

The most renowned objects from Xochipala are a group of solid clay figures which are tiny portraits having great energy and power. Only a dozen or so of these are known; none has been excavated scientifically. The first was purchased at Xochipala in 1897 by William Niven, and found its way into the Peabody Museum collections at Harvard. The major part of the remaining material passed in the 1970's from local farmers to local dealers. This small group constitutes some of the greatest miniature ceramic sculpture made in the Americas. The figures stand out in intensity and naturalism from all other works. I feel that they are very

Fig. 5 Two Olmec seals from Las Bocas, Puebla. The stamp seal above has an ancient thick coating of specular hematite pigment on the printing surface. Private collection, U.S.A. Photograph by Clem Fiori.

Fig. 6 Two ceramic heads found at Amuco Abelino, near Arcelia, western Guerrero, in a stratum dating to 1500 B.C. Instituto Nacional de Antropología e Historia, Mexico. Photographs by Peter David Joralemon.

early. They seem closely related, along with other cruder products from Xochipala, to a Preclassic style, as yet undefined, which is found with regional variations along the Pacific coast from El Salvador to Michoacán. The figures from both areas share a liveliness, a careful finish, and punctate eyes.

Sculptures of solid clay can be manufactured only up to a certain size and thickness before they are liable to explode upon firing. The answer to making large ceramic figures is to model thin-walled, hollow figures with several ventilation holes. The construction of such figures without the support of interior armatures, or without using molds (the Peruvian solution), is highly sophisticated technically. On the Olmec horizon, there are a number of anthropomorphic forms in hollow ceramic vessels, but the majority of human representations are the hollow so-called "babies." Some of these are indeed babies, while others are ambiguous in age and androgynous in sex. Curiously enough, fragments of a large "baby" carved in chalk were discovered at San Pablito, Morelos, in 1969 (Franz Feuchtwanger, personal communication). Does this indicate that these effigies were produced also in other media?

The Olmec hollow babies run the aesthetic gamut in their own special canon from sublime sculpture to mediocrity. The most impressive, alive, and powerful ones come from Las Bocas (not far from San Pablito), Xochipala, and Tlatilco (Fig. 7). The vast majority of surviving examples are second-rate products, but the very few prime examples must rank with the world's great art. These extraordinary pieces (most still unpublished) are as powerful, moving, and inventive as anything we know. Fragmentary examples from San Lorenzo survive in battered sherds, recognizable only by their shape. Other areas of the Gulf Coast, such as Tenenexpan, have produced a number of dismally repetitive and pedestrian examples, possibly slightly later and derivative from the highland examples. Their lowland versions tend to denigrate the image of Olmec art.

What are these babies, or adolescents, and what do they mean ceremonially? We may work towards a meaning someday, using the hag-with-baby figures from Xochipala and Las

Fig. 7 Olmec ceramic hollow baby figure found at Tlatilco, Mexico. Franz Feuchtwanger Collection, Cuernavaca. Photograph by the author.

Bocas (Figs. 8 and 9) in conjunction with Monuments 12 and 20 from San Lorenzo, Monument 3 from Cerro el Vigía, Altars 2 and 5 from La Venta, the Las Limas figure (Fig 10), and such pieces as a small bench figure in the Nelson Rockefeller Collection (Fig. 11). In these monumental sculptures (which I feel are a later evolution of the theme), the iconography has changed radically; but, if the two themes are related, as I believe they are, we may be led to a hypothesis of the meaning and its important relation to Olmec iconography. It is interesting to note that the two clay figurines from the highlands depict an aged female cradling a baby. The Xochipala hag is nearly toothless and blind, her cheeks scarified with crosshatching; the Las Bocas hag is not a portrait but represents the same sort of aged person. The Xochipala baby is very much alive and has male genitalia—a rarity in Preclassic art—while the Las Bocas baby is already removed from humanity through stylization, and

Fig. 8 Snaggle-toothed, blind hag with scarified cheeks holding a male baby in her lap, from Xochipala, Guerrero. Paul Tishman Collection, New York. Photograph by Laurin McCracken.

Fig. 9 Seated hag cradling a dwarf or were-baby in her lap, from Las Bocas, Puebla. Private collection, U.S.A. Photograph by Peter David Joralemon.

Fig. 10 Seated Olmec figure holding a baby corn god or manikin in his lap, from Las Limas, Veracruz. Museo de Arqueología de la Universidad de Veracruz, Jalapa. Photograph courtesy of the Instituto Latinoamericano de la Comunicación Educativa, Mexico.

Fig. 11 Seated bench figure holding a manikin on his lap. Nelson Rockefeller Collection, Metropolitan Museum of Art, New York. Photograph courtesy of the Metropolitan Museum of Art, New York.

215

Fig. 12 Adolescent ballplayer from Xochipala, Guerrero. Mr. and Mrs. Edward Strauss Collection, Denver. Photograph by Laurin McCracken.

Halfway down into the painted sanctuaries of the Juxtlahuaca Cave were several traces of child burials with the imprints of bowls. Were these sacrifices, buried nearly half of a kilometer into a sacred cave, and were the remains found in Tomb A at La Venta, royal children or token ritual sacrifice? Were children sacrificed because the earliest Xipe was a child god or a god to whom children were sacrificed? Altar 5 at La Venta (Fig. 13) seems to depict graphically the offering of deformed or monstrous children for sacrifice. This same (possibly sacred) deformation may be apparent in some, although not all, of the ceramic hollow babies.

The most important and permanent Olmec medium, which they manipulated incredibly well, is stone. As I implied before, the Olmec were possibly the greatest lithic technicians of the ancient world. The Olmec never mixed stones. There was a hierarchy of certain stones to be used for certain objects. Occasionally there were surrogate materials selected, because of their color, to stand for unavailable or too-precious stones, such as impacted clay or greenstone, which were sometimes substituted for jade or serpentine. There are a number of attractive stones that the Olmec seemed to avoid, such as turquoise, malachite, obsidian, onyx, opal, amethyst, and even rock crystal (although there is at least one example of an Olmec-shaped celt in rock crystal, from the Pacific coast of Guerrero). The most surprising avoidance of an obvious material is that of obsidian, easily obtainable in the volcanic Tuxtla area and later used so splendidly by Postclassic lapidaries for mirrors, paper-thin earspools, and even large anthropomorphic vessels. Let me review types of objects made of various stones that are found in the Olmec highlands.

A large group of finely shaped straight- and flare-walled stone bowls from the Xochipala area (Fig. 14), made of a very hard stone, appeared about 1967. Michael Coe (personal communication) stated at that time that fragments of vessels like these had been found at Ocós at a pre-Olmec level. A number of those from Xochipala had unusual anthropomorphic designs incised on the sides in a fine but scratchy line, heightened by traces of cinnabar.

is sexless. The babies of the heartland have become monsters (or in the case of the Las Limas figure, the rain god) and the cradling figures are male.

It is also interesting to note that among Xochipala figures are represented several ballplayers. One is a tiny "portrait" of an adolescent (Fig. 12)—a boy of about fourteen or fifteen. Another, less specific representation appears to depict a youth (possibly an adolescent).

Fig. 13 Altar 5, the "Quintuplets Altar," La Venta, Tabasco. Photograph courtesy of the Instituto Latinoamericano de la Communicación Educativa, Mexico.

To my knowledge, stone bowls of this sort have not been found in the heartland.

Celts of serpentine and jade have been found in great numbers in Guerrero. Most of these are functional tools rather than ceremonial objects. Incised celts, such as those found at Arroyo Pesquero, appear to be of later, or La Venta horizon, Olmec manufacture. Many of the 1500 or more celts reported recovered from Arroyo Pesquero are "token" celts—that is, celt-shaped pieces or split celts.

Concave mirrors of magnetite, hematite, and ilmenite have been found in numbers in Guerrero. These extraordinary examples of lithic genius are worked from nodules of those unusual iron ores, sliced and then ground. The inner area is ground to an oval or round concave surface (Fig. 15); the frame, or outer edge (often left in an irregular but balanced shape), is usually polished to be convex; the back is generally left unfinished. The polish itself is a remarkable achievement, and the concavity is worked with optical precision (see Carlson, this volume). The mirrors are not simply to reflect; they obviously possess magical properties. The reflected image enlarges the viewer and distorts his features when the mirror is held closely. But, as the mirror is moved away, the image flips upside down. It has been demonstrated by Gordon Ekholm (1973) that cer-

tain of the mirrors can be used to create fire through focusing the sun's rays. The mirrors made of magnetite are magnetic, and the smoky black surface creates its own sense of mystery in all of these mirrors. Four large mirrors were found at Arroyo Pesquero, including the largest Olmec mirror yet discovered. Most of these appear to be heirloom pieces, since areas of some have been sawed off for reuse. Four mirrors were uncovered in the caches at La Venta, and four were discovered at Cerro de las Mesas. No record has been kept of the number of mirrors found in Guerrero. Most of them

Fig. 14 Fine flare-walled stone bowl from Xochipala, Guerrero. Private collection, Mexico City. Photograph by the author.

Fig. 15 Oval concave magnetite mirror from central Guerrero. Private collection, U.S.A. Photograph by Clem Fiori.

came from the Tepecuacuilco–Xochipala area of north-central Guerrero. Some of these are oval and concave; at least one is round and concave. One magnetite mirror from Xochipala has a flat, oval surface; one is made of one unusually large nodule of pyrite, polished flat with a round back. The most remarkable Olmec mirror is a mosaic, made up of several hundred eccentrically faceted pieces, from Las Bocas. It is interesting to note that no subsequent cultures used these special iron ores for mirrors, nor were mirrors ground to be concave. Most later cultures used either pyrite mosaic mirrors, supported by slate or wood backs, or obsidian mirrors.

Another kind of object survives in numbers considerable enough to be important. Called *pulidores,* because they have been mistaken for polishing tools, it is certain from the lack of wear and from their very precise shapes that polishing was never their function. True *pulidores,* used for burnishing clay or stone objects, have been found. Some have rough attachment surfaces for wood handles (at least one of these has survived with the original wood bound to the stone with sinew and pitch [Fig. 16]), but the majority were conceived to be held in the hand directly. The other varieties of so-called *pulidores,* which I shall describe here, were most probably of a divinatory or magical na-

ture and, I am convinced, were the special property of shamans. An example of a grave containing *pulidores* is Burial 154 at Tlatilco, reconstructed in the Museo Nacional de Antropología in Mexico City. Here large, triangular, chalcedony *pulidores* are found, with other special objects, on the pelvis of the interred. These may have been contained in a sacred medicine pouch placed on his stomach. In this same burial was also found the famous kaolin-slipped acrobat pot, surely a magical vessel, which was placed by the right hand.

The *pulidores* discussed here, like the *sellos* mentioned above, are not, to my knowledge, found in the great ceremonial centers, but in the provincial sites of central Veracruz and central Guerrero, and at Las Bocas and Tlatilco. They were probably manufactured in pairs, as a number of matched pairs are known.

Fig. 16 Three ancient true *pulidores* (polishers), one with its original wood handle bound with sinew and pitch. Private collection, U.S.A. Photograph by Clem Fiori.

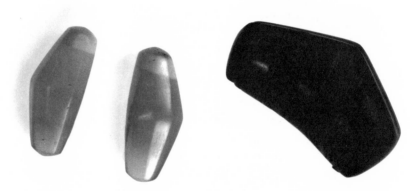

Fig. 17 Pair of banded chalcedony so-called *pulidores,*
right- and left-handed. Private collection, U.S.A. Photograph by Clem Fiori.

These pairs, in certain styles, were carefully fashioned to be right- and left-handed (Fig. 17). This can be seen in certain pairs made of banded chalcedony with matching milk-white tips and translucent bodies, the markings giving a visual balance to the pair. The forms of these *pulidores* are varied and hard to describe in their complexity. All come to a peak at the top and are usually narrower at the ends; some are triangular, some crescent-shaped; some have flat bottoms, some concave ones. The most sophisticated type is basically a football shape with a flat bottom, four precisely ground facets on one side, and a rounded opposite side. These faceted *pulidores* are ground to as near an optical polish as neolithic technology could produce. It is this type of *pulidor,* usually of an attractive stone of the agate family, which is often found in matched pairs. With such care and workmanship—rivaled only by the tech-

nology of concave-mirror-making or the execution and polish of jade figures—these objects are certainly of a most sacred nature. The selection of agate rather than jade may refer to a hierarchy of stones for degrees of ritual use, for no "jade" *pulidores* that I know of have been made of jade. One pair of faceted *pulidores* made of impacted clay, which is often a surrogate for jade, has come from Guerrero. Another crescent-shaped pair exists in contrasting colors—black and white—matching perfectly in size and shape.

Pulidores never had attachment holes for wearing, seldom show signs of use, but were probably designed for casting, somehow, for divination. On a flat surface they spin like a gyroscope. A very few have carved designs or inlays in them (Fig. 18); one odd *pulidor* was curiously fashioned as a human foot, complete with anklebone.

The Olmec "spoon" is another misnomer. Shaped like a razor-clam shell with a bulge, it probably had a ritual function in bloodletting or in the absorption of hallucinogens for ritual purposes. These are often of jade or a green stone. Many are incised with Olmec designs. Some have come from Guerrero (Fig. 19), as have long, needlelike bloodletters, which probably have their origins in the stingray spine. Many of the bloodletters have anthropomorphic handles in the form of humans, serpents, or birds (Fig. 20). The Tepecuacuilco Valley area of Guerrero has yielded a great number.

The Olmec jade generally associated with Guerrero is that remarkable blue-to-blue-green variety which was possibly traded in from Costa Rica, where a few Olmec pieces have

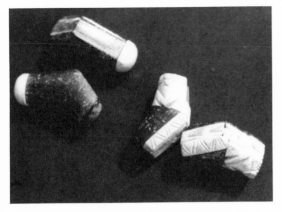

Fig. 18 Inlaid and incised so-called *pulidores* from Xochipala, Guerrero. Private collection, Mexico City. Photograph by the author.

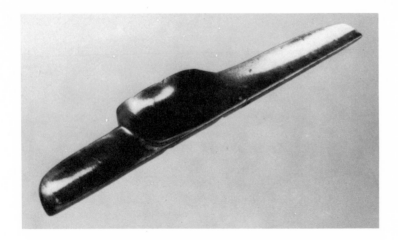

Fig. 19 Olmec jade "spoon" from central Guerrero. Private collection, U.S.A. Photograph by Clem Fiori.

been found. To me it is the most beautiful jade utilized in Preclassic Mexico, and I rather feel that the Olmec preferred it, before the source and supply ran out. A number of sets of matched blue-jade beads have come from the north-central Guerrero area. These beads are of extraordinary quality and polish; they are usually round or tubular in shape. The Olmec also used, as pendants or in necklaces, jade worked into the shape of a feline incisor (Fig. 21) or a talon of a bird of prey. One spectacular necklace, formerly in the collection of Miguel Covarrubias, was composed of tiny blue-jade human legs, like a chorus line (Fig. 22). Other pendant shapes include mirror forms, human teeth, small round bowl-shaped pieces, and a corn symbol (Fig. 22).

Also found in central Guerrero have been figures in jade of extraordinary beauty, such as the great figure of translucent jade holding the baby rain god, in the Guennol Collection, on view at the Brooklyn Museum, or the famous figure from Olinalá, collected by Miguel Covarrubias. The peculiarly high polish on the

Fig. 20 Stone bloodletters from central Guerrero. Private collection, U.S.A. Photograph by Clem Fiori.

finest pieces of blue jade is unique and instantly recognizable—very different, for instance, in form and finish from the contemporary jades of the Chou period in China. A number of sculpted "axes," also from Guerrero, are made from a variety of stones. The masks found in Guerrero, with the exception of the wooden one, tend to be smaller than those found in Veracruz. Until the approximately thirty-five masks turned up in the hoard at Arroyo Pesquero, comparatively few life-sized ones of jade or serpentine were known. The Arroyo Pesquero masks, some of which David Joralemon (personal communication) feels represent historical personages (his "Lord of the Double Scroll" appears in jade works from Guerrero [Fig. 23] as well as from the heartland), are probably of the La Venta horizon. Central Guerrero, especially the Tepecuacuilco Valley area, became the manufactory of lithic masks, figures, and vessels for many late Olmec and subsequent cultures. It finally became a center for fine obsidian-working in Postclassic times.

Until the discovery of the great hoard at Arroyo Pesquero, it could be said that the majority of Olmec jade had come from Guerrero. The Arroyo Pesquero cache and the cache found by the Stirlings at Cerro de las Mesas are heirloom assemblages representing more than

Fig. 21 Two Olmec pendants in the form of feline incisors, from central Guerrero. Private collection, U.S.A. Photograph by Clem Fiori.

Fig. 22 Olmec stone pendants in the form of a human leg (green stone), bifurcated serpent tongue (jade), and corn symbol (jade), from central Guerrero. Private collection, U.S.A. Photograph by Clem Fiori.

221

Fig. 23 Jade masquette, possibly the "Lord of the Double Scroll," from near Zumpango del Río, Guerrero. Private collection, U.S.A. Photograph by Peter David Joralemon.

one period. How did the Olmec sculptors master the refined knowledge of stones and lithic technology if they had always lived and developed in an area quite bereft of those very special stones that they ultimately selected for their own exacting purposes?

It seems simplistic to assume that the Olmec culture arrived full-blown at San Lorenzo with an established pantheon, iconography, symbolism, extraordinary knowledge of stones foreign to the heartland, an incredible lithic technology, organization, hierarchy—in short, a well-honed civilization—without a succession of centuries in which to congeal this information and to establish Olmec power and Olmec order. I talked at length with Matthew Stirling at a conference on Xochipala and the Olmec held at Princeton in February of 1972. He regretted that he had never worked in the central highlands or in Guerrero and expressed his enthusiasm for the discoveries at Juxtlahuaca and Xochipala. He mentioned Miguel Covarrubia's conviction that the Olmec had developed there. But before him was always the

haunting memory of seeing an ancient stratum with archaeological material underlying a deposit of volcanic ash in the Río Huayapan when it was unusually low, just as he was about to leave at the end of his last season at Tres Zapotes. He was convinced that the origins of the Olmec civilization lay there.

I know of no primal civilization in world history that did not take centuries to jell after the initial surge towards civilization. It took four centuries from the establishment of the First Dynasty for the Egyptians to reach the point when monumental and relief sculpture, glyphs, conventions, and technology had fused to become Egyptian art as we think of it today. This was also true for the Sumerian civilization and for the peoples of the Indus Valley and China. All of these had metals and writing systems, which cannot be said of the Olmec.

In the heartland, no Olmec material so far has been identified as any earlier than the San Lorenzo horizon, dated by radiocarbon to 1200 B.C. (M. Coe 1970: 21), unless the unexcavated stratum below the ash level at Tres Zapotes contains the Formative materials that Matthew Stirling was convinced were there. The three heartland sites which have been worked extensively were selected for the presence of monumental sculpture. Traditionally, monumental sculpture belongs to a later developmental period in a primal culture, and I see no reason why the Olmec culture should differ. The transportation and sculpting of multi-ton blocks of volcanic rock is a sophisticated concept, especially if the stone heads are portraits of rulers. The intention of such sculpture would be as much to impress the subjugated local people as to immortalize or deify those portrayed. In heartland sites not as yet disturbed by archaeology, we may find the complete development of the enigma we call the Olmec. Yet their advanced lithic technology strongly indicates a long highland development or sojourn—not merely a later transient contact. A vast stage of Olmec cultural development seems to be entirely lacking in our present knowledge. When archaeological discoveries shed light on this developmental stage, I expect that the highlands will play a more important role than they are credited with at this time.

The Dainzú Preclassic Figurines

Ignacio Bernal

COLEGIO NACIONAL, MÉXICO

How can I not light at least a little candle to the memory of the first of the Olmec? When such a wonderful person as Marion Stirling suggested I write a paper in Matthew Stirling's honor, I accepted at once. Some Olmec subject would have been more appropriate, but, having none, I remembered that, after all, the flowers on funeral wreaths are held together by humble greenery. Let an herb be my offering.

Preclassic figurines—as are most of the Dainzú ones—have been little studied in the Oaxaca Valley in an organized fashion. As Drennan (1976a: 233) writes, only interim types can now be recognized until the day when a study of all Preclassic figurines can be achieved. This paper is a step towards that end.

Although the ceramics of Dainzú are, in general terms, very similar to the already-published ones from Monte Albán (Caso *et al.* 1967), the figurines, apart from following the pattern of the Oaxaca Valley ceramics, present certain peculiarities. Thus, they are of interest, even if far too few in number for the definition of types; some elements, being frequent, may help to plot local varieties within the unified pattern of culture inside the three large sections that form the Oaxaca Valley area.

There is a general similarity between Preclassic figurines from the Oaxaca Valley that makes them differ, as a block, from contemporaneous figurines in other parts of Mesoamerica, even though all Preclassic figurines share common traits. This is another of the several characteristics of the Oaxaca Valley that indicate that it is a cultural unit with a common history. As has been pointed out, the figurine complex of the Preclassic Period appears only occasionally similar to that of the Olmec. Rather, there seems to be a highland style that is present from the central plateau of Mexico down to Guatemala, and another style that is typical of the lowlands. Of course they intermix, as happens in Olmec-influenced sites such as Gualupita or Tlatilco. Thus, the division cannot be considered too rigorous.

Figurines, at least at Dainzú, were obviously not meant as objects intended to accompany the dead, and, therefore, they are not usually found in burials. None appeared in any of the seven tombs and numerous burials excavated; only in one instance was there an animal effigy in an offering. Thus, very seldom do we find figurines in association with other objects that indicate to us a moment in time. Mostly they come from fills with no possible stratigraphy, and occasionally from dumps. The latter were not really piles of discarded refuse, but, rather, manmade holes where pottery and other objects were thrown, perhaps in obeisance to certain ceremonial rites celebrating dates. In most instances, our attribution of a figurine to one determinate period according to the Monte Albán sequence is typological and not stratigraphic.

Figurines obviously alike in shape appear in either gray or brown clay (G1 or K1 in the Monte Albán typology of Caso *et al.* 1967). None belongs to the cream or yellow wares. As their types indicate, they are unpolished but not of too rough a texture. This demonstrates that it was immaterial whether gray or brown clay was used. The only exceptions are one

223

figurine in polished gray (G3) in Figure 2e, another in polished brown (K3) in Figure 3b, and both figurines in Figure 7. These last are fashioned in a reddish ware, slightly polished. These last two are quite different from the usual types not only in color and polish but in all other traits as well. All figurines are solid and, of course, handmade. Molds, a product of Teotihuacan influence, appear only much later.

The bodies of the few figurines recovered at Dainzú were all naked. They wore only necklaces, headdresses, and earplugs (sometimes very complex ones). On one occasion (Fig. 3a), we see a red line above and a yellow line below painted over the fired piece, under the necklace. Another body (Fig. 5d) is painted red all over its front. Bodies are always fashioned with widely separated legs, frequently curved, as seems typical of the Oaxaca Preclassic. The figurines in Figure 7—unfortunately headless—are extremely thin, and of the gingerbread variety. One of them wears a necklace of beads. Their type did not appear at Monte Albán.

Headdresses are quite imaginative. Some are tall, night-cap affairs that usually do not rise straight upwards from the forehead but instead slant to the side (Figs. 2a and 4a). That in Figure 2f recalls an open bivalve shell, while the one in Figure 1e is split in two and has a different design on each side. It would look fine on a modern lady, if ladies still wore hats. In two instances (Figs. 2e and 8), the face of the figurine emerges from the open mouth of an animal in a fashion that would later become frequent in Mesoamerican art. Some, without a headdress, show only their hair, either tied in a knot (Figs. 1a and b) or falling in a braid from the back of the head down to the shoulders (Fig. 3h). Another very small head, not illustrated here since it was just published elsewhere (Bernal and Seuffert 1979), has its face covered by a sort of mask, like the ones worn by the ballplayers at Dainzú on the façade of Mound A.

Yet another Dainzú group consists of bodies —we do not have a single head to go with them —that have a curious and very marked circle or large hollow around the navel, brought about by adding strips of clay to the already-fashioned body (Fig. 6). There is a similar figurine from Fábrica San José (Drennan 1976a: Fig. 82.1), unfortunately also beheaded. None like them comes from Monte Albán, suggesting that this group may be quite early, perhaps dating before Monte Albán I times. The figurine in Figure 6d was possibly intended as a whistle, although I cannot see how it would have functioned. This possibility is somewhat enhanced by the two figurines shown in Figures 8 and 9, where the whistle corresponds to the sex organ, which is possibly masculine. This whistle is, therefore, placed in a similar position to the body as that in Figure 6d. Should this be correct, the whistle is in front of the figurine instead of in the back, as was the usual custom, particularly from the Classic Period onwards. In Figure 9 we see an animal represented. As far as I know, the two pieces in Figures 8 and 9 are unique. Since, as already mentioned, all the figurines are solid, it is difficult to accept them as intended whistles. Those in Figure 6 all appear to be feminine and, except for 6d and perhaps 6a, do not have a cavity for air. The two possibly masculine bodies (Figs. 8 and 9) might suggest the very remote possibility of the origin of the Mexican slang word *pito,* expressing both a whistle and the penis. In this sense, the word does not occur in Spain, and seems, therefore, to be an Indian association of ideas. On the other hand, the hole or circle around the navel may have been meant to hold an inlay of some sort, perhaps of another material. Stone or even metal inlays are found occasionally in later sculpture.

The difficulty at Monte Albán of distinguishing between figurines of Periods I and II, except in a few cases, is also encountered at Dainzú. This corroborates the fact that, as much as many ceramic shapes change greatly from one period to the other, certain traits remain unchanged. The implications of this conservatism are meaningful, although this is not the place to elaborate on that problem. Such a consideration would concern not only Dainzú and its small lot of figurines, but the cultural history of the entire Oaxaca Valley during the Preclassic Period.

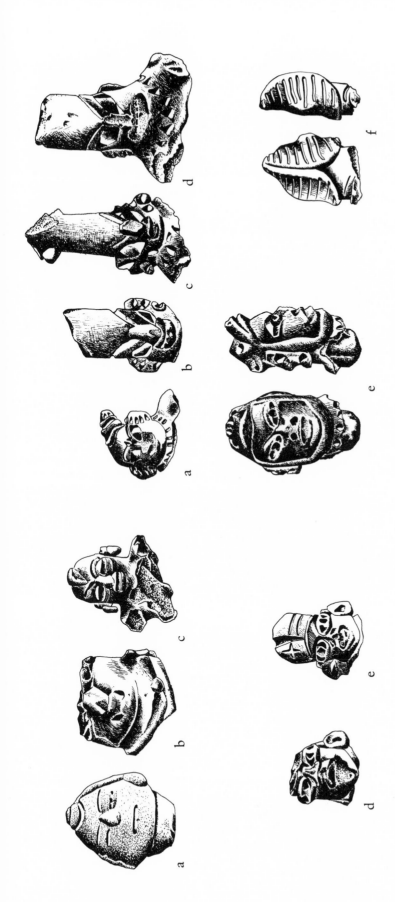

Fig. 1 Ceramic heads of type K1 from the 1967 excavations at Dainzú, Oaxaca. *a.* Object No. 7 from surface at the foot of West Wall. *b, d.* From surface of Mound F. *c.* From Bag 89. *e.* From Mound B, South Wall, southeast corner. These and other drawings by Andy Seuffert.

Fig. 2 Ceramic heads. *a.* Type G1 from surface, 1966 excavations. *b.* Type G1 from surface of Mound B, Section B, 1967 excavations. *c.* Type G1 from Bag 116, 1969 excavations. *d.* Type K1 from surface of Mound F, 1967 excavations. *e.* Type G3 from Bag 89, 1967 excavations. *f.* Type K1 from surface of Mound J South, West Wall, 1967 excavations.

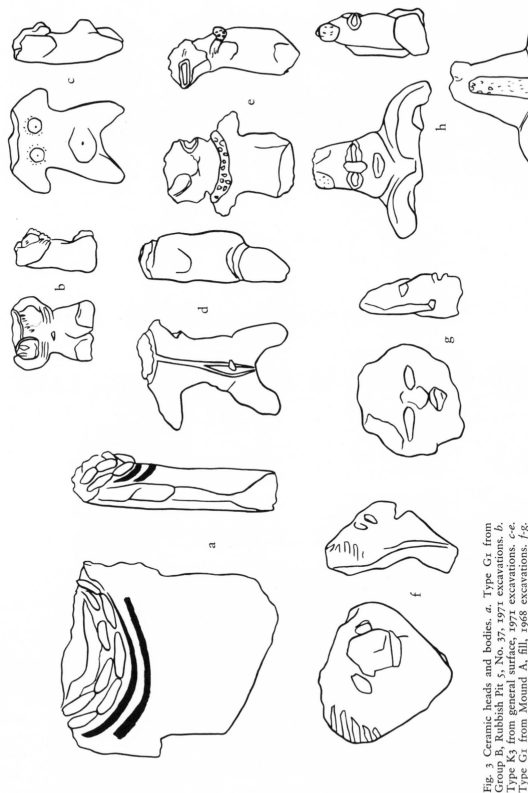

Fig. 3 Ceramic heads and bodies. *a.* Type G1 from Group B, Rubbish Pit 5, No. 37, 1971 excavations. *b.* Type K3 from general surface, 1971 excavations. *c-e.* Type G1 from Mound A, fill, 1968 excavations. *f-g.* Type K1 from above the floor, Mound B, Pit 1, 1971 excavations. *h.* Type K1 from Mound B, Section A-2, fill, 1968 excavations.

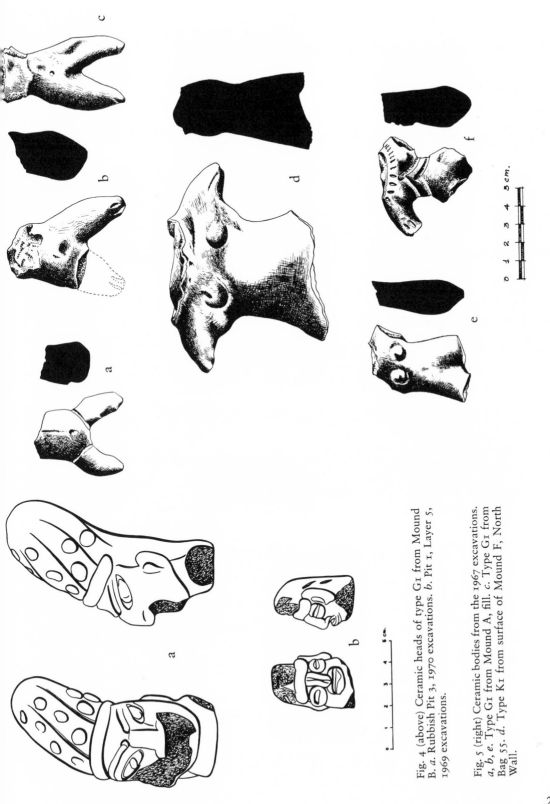

Fig. 4 (above) Ceramic heads of type G1 from Mound B. *a.* Rubbish Pit 3, 1970 excavations. *b.* Pit 1, Layer 5, 1969 excavations.

Fig. 5 (right) Ceramic bodies from the 1967 excavations. *a, b, e.* Type G1 from Mound A, fill. *c.* Type G1 from Bag 55. *d.* Type K1 from surface of Mound F, North Wall.

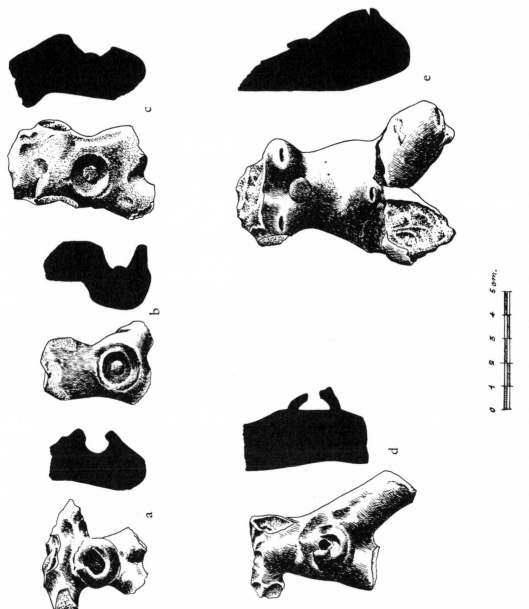

Fig. 6 Ceramic bodies. *a, c, e.* Type Kɪ from surface, 1966 excavations. *b.* Type Kɪ from Mound A, fill, 1967 excavations. *d.* Type Gɪ from Mound J South, Pit ɪ, Layer 4, 1967 excavations.

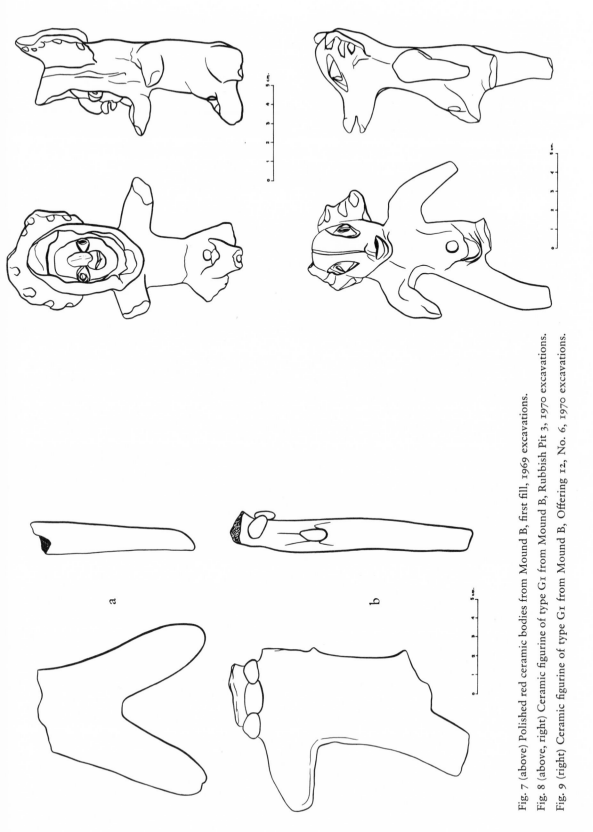

Fig. 7 (above) Polished red ceramic bodies from Mound B, first fill, 1969 excavations.

Fig. 8 (above, right) Ceramic figurine of type G1 from Mound B, Rubbish Pit 3, 1970 excavations.

Fig. 9 (right) Ceramic figurine of type G1 from Mound B, Offering 12, No. 6, 1970 excavations.

Olmec Horizons Defined in Mound 20, San Isidro, Chiapas

Gareth W. Lowe

NEW WORLD ARCHAEOLOGICAL FOUNDATION, BRIGHAM YOUNG UNIVERSITY

In the spring of 1944, Matthew W. Stirling led a National Geographic Society–Smithsonian Institution expedition up the tortuous Río de las Playas, principal headwater tributary of the Río Tonalá, into the mountain ridges separating southeastern Veracruz from Chiapas; he was in search of rumored major archaeological sites which he hoped would extend southward the known Olmec domain. Defeated in this purpose by the difficult terrain and the finding only of apparently late ruins at Pueblo Viejo and Ceiba Grande, the Stirling group was forced to return with its immediate goal un-achieved (Weber 1945; Stirling 1957: 219–24). Ironically, had this expedition continued south-ward or eastward another twenty or thirty miles, it would have dropped into the Middle Grijalva Basin (Fig. 1), a lush, wet region rich in early archaeological sites, many of them closely related to the famed Gulf Coast Olmec centers. It is, nevertheless, unlikely that the Stirling party would have recognized Olmec characteristics in these ruins, for two reasons. First, the Middle Grijalva settlements were confined to narrow riverine terraces closely surrounded by encroaching hills and densely covered by either near-virgin forest or the al-most equally dense shade trees sheltering the cacao groves then still tended on most of the more favored riverbank lands. Second, these provincial sites possessed none of the massive stone sculpture characterizing the few major Olmec "heartland" centers on the Gulf Coast. The early Middle Grijalva occupation and its Olmec relationships thus could only have been determined via the recognition of other, less-obvious traits, most of them likely to appear only in the course of intensive excavations. This fortune did not befall the region until the winter and spring of 1966, and then it was almost too late, for the waters of the Mal Paso Dam were soon to cover both the valleys of the Middle Grijalva River and its major tributary, the Río La Venta.

In June of 1966, the huge Netzahualcoyotl (Mal Paso) Dam at the confluence of the Grijalva and La Venta Rivers was closed. Within thirty days an area approximately sixty kilometers long and up to five kilometers wide was flooded. The archaeological survey of this westernmost Chiapas region had begun only in September of the previous year (Fig. 2). A gradually increasing rhythm of salvage excava-tions did not begin until January of 1966 (Navarrete 1966). Excavations at the largest site in the region, San Isidro, commenced fi-nally in mid-March of 1966, and were con-cluded by the encroaching waters of the rapidly forming lake in mid-June (Fig. 3). The remote-ness of the area, incessant winter rains, and the unexpectedly brief period available for rescue of archaeological data permitted little planning, so operations were confined to an expensive, time-consuming clearing of the for-est that covered most of the site, and to the digging of a series of test pits and some rather intensive mound explorations (Matos Mocte-zuma 1966, 1968; Lee 1974a, 1974b). Results of the brief but very important excavations in Mound 20 at San Isidro, directed by the author, are the subject of the present article.

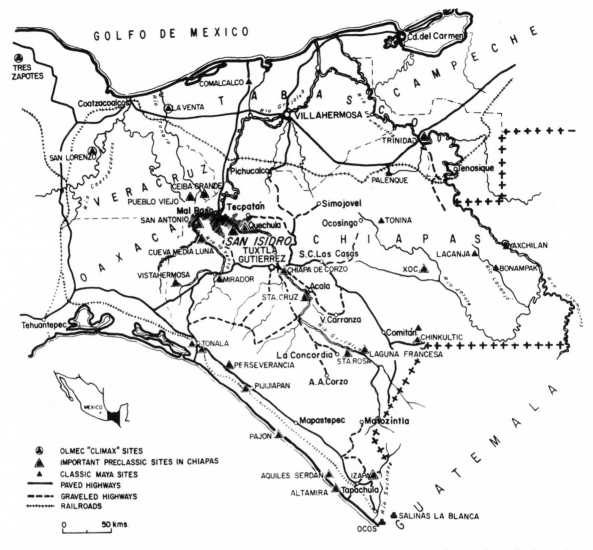

Fig. 1 Map of Chiapas and the Greater Isthmus Area of Mexico, showing the location of San Isidro and other major archaeological ruins as well as some minor but related Olmec horizon sites. Drawing by Eduardo Martínez E.

THE MIDDLE GRIJALVA REGION AND SAN ISIDRO

The Grijalva River in the vicinity of San Isidro and Quechula, the Spanish-conquest-period village (Díaz del Castillo 1964: 387), flowed through a district characterized by very high rainfall, broken high hills, and extreme isolation. Entry into this little-known zone, even in 1965 and 1966, was possible only by difficult rapids-plagued boat travel from downstream, or via the precipitous, usually muddy,

foot and horse trails crossing the mountains. The area is now conveniently referred to as the Mal Paso or Middle Grijalva region, with upstream limits at the lower end of the Sumidero Canyon above Quechula and lower limits at the Mal Paso *raudales*, or rapids, at the confluence of the Grijalva River and its Río La Venta tributary entering from the west. The Netzahualcoyotl or "Mal Paso" Dam was constructed just below these major rapids, and

Fig. 2 Map of the Mal Paso Basin Archaeological Survey, Chiapas, showing the sites located and those receiving some excavation prior to the closing of the dam. Las Palmas and López Mateos are described by Piña Chan and Navarrete (1967). Pueblo Viejo and Ceiba Grande are sites investigated in 1944 by Matthew W. Stirling (1957; see also Weber 1945). Drawing by Eduardo Martínez E.

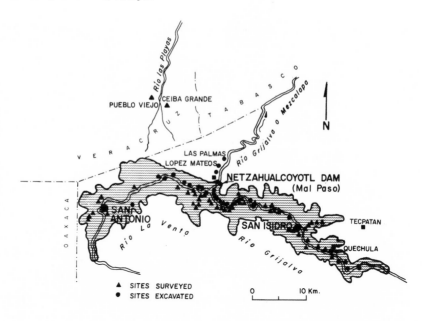

Fig. 3 View of the ruins of San Isidro being flooded by dam waters, June 30, 1966, after the beginning of the rainy season. Mound 20 may be seen at left center with whitish backdirt on the summit. Photograph by the author.

the resultant lake has effectively flooded the entire Middle Grijalva region since mid-1966. The Mal Paso Lake includes the lower Río La Venta arm of the Middle Grijalva (or Mezcalapa) River which is so topographically and otherwise similar to the latter that it may be considered an extension of the Middle Grijalva region; culturally and ecologically the two subregions appear indistinguishable in both known pre-Hispanic and more recent times (see Agrinier 1969 for a report on San Antonio, one of the most important Late Classic ruins in the Río La Venta Basin).

Daily rains and, often, cool mists typify the Middle Grijalva region during much of the year, due to its peculiar orographic "funnel" position midway in the Isthmian mountains. This extremely wet nature contrasts the region with the low, open Tabasco plain to the north, which has less rain and a marked dry season, and much more so with the Upper Grijalva region (or Central Depression of Chiapas), an interior basin over 1500 feet above sea level with a dry tropical climate (Lowe 1959). It is interesting to remember that Stirling, in a 1942 expedition, had already explored the dry upper, or southern, arm of the Río La Venta canyon-and-plateau country around Piedra Parada, Ocozocoautla, Chiapas (Stirling 1947; Ekholm-Miller n.d.), but found there little Olmec evidence.

The historical role of so wet and, at least today, sparsely inhabited an intermediate region as is that of the Middle Grijalva obviously is one of some perplexity. The area, nevertheless, seems always to have had importance as an alternative riverine transportation route across the Isthmus, and also for the production and distribution of cacao, the principal trade commodity of southern Mesoamerica. At the head of canoe navigation on the Grijalva River and in a principal cacao-producing zone, San Isidro was the obvious ceremonial center for the region during a long period of time (Lee 1974b).

The Middle Grijalva region pertains to the Zoque ethnic province once crossing the Isthmus from ocean to ocean (Thomas 1974); it formed a central part of the Mixe-Zoque territory, which extended from the Tuxtlas mountain-and-plain region of southeastern Veracruz

and Oaxaca into western Tabasco, western and Pacific-coast Chiapas, and parts of southern Guatemala (Foster 1969; Báez-Jorge 1973: 57–63; Campbell and Kaufman 1976; Lowe 1977).

The site map, chronological sequence, and Mound 4 report for San Isidro have been presented by Thomas Lee (1974a, 1974b). An English-language summary of the Mal Paso and San Isidro salvage operations may be found in Lowe 1967, and a preliminary description of the Late Classic double-ball-court complex at San Isidro has been published by Eduardo Matos Moctezuma (1966). The San Isidro ceremonial center was composed of thirty-one numbered pyramidal or platform-mound groups arranged across a relatively wide river terrace and adjacent hills. All of the mounds were badly eroded, with Mound 20 occupying a central position within the community. Mound 20 was pyramidal in form, roughly circular (originally square in plan), and twelve meters high (see plan and section, Figs. 4 and 5).

MOUND 20 EXCAVATIONS

The eroded Mound 20 pyramid at San Isidro was explored by the deep Pit 2 in its summit, by the shallow Pit 2a on its eastern mid-slope, and by the joined, deep Pits 5 and 17 dug at its eastern base; the even more eroded low platform at the eastern foot of the mound was tested by the wide Pits 20 and 27 (Figs. 6 and 7). The principal discoveries of these excavations were a series of burials and an axial line of offerings and stone-celt mosaics extending eastward from the base of the Mound (Figs. 5–7). This burial-and-offering pattern and the earlier cultural matrix into which it was often intruded can best be described chronologically in terms of three distinctive Olmec "cultural horizons" (see Lowe 1971, 1977). The "Early Olmec" horizon includes the "San Lorenzo" horizon of Michael Coe (1977: 184), and the "Later Olmec" and "Modified Olmec" horizons divide in two the "La Venta" horizon proposed by M. Coe (1977: 184–5).

THE EARLY OLMEC HORIZON
(CA. 1350–1000 B.C.)

The earliest identified ceramic collection from San Isidro, included in the Bombana ce-

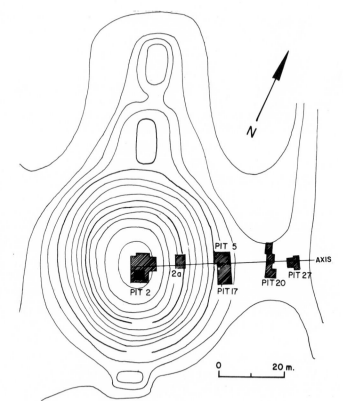

Fig. 4 (right) Plan of Mound 20, San Isidro, Chiapas, showing excavations. Contour interval, 1 meter. Drawing by Eduardo Martínez E.

Fig. 5 (below) West-to-east section drawing of Mound 20 showing excavations. Burials B-9 and B-10 and Caches C-10 through C-14 are intrusive. Drawing by Eduardo Martínez E.

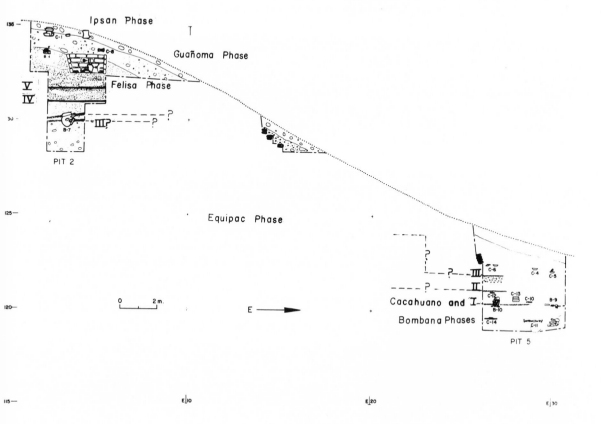

235

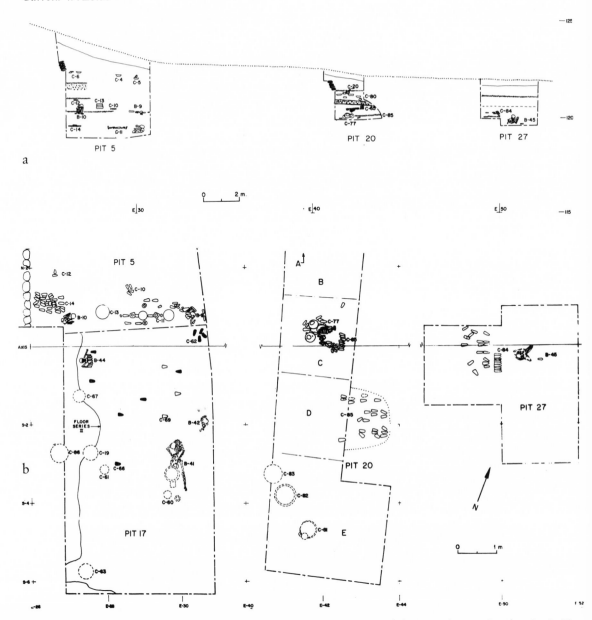

Fig. 6 Section and plan of Pits 5, 17, 20, and 27, Mound 20. *a*. Continuation of the Mound 20 section drawing in Figure 5, looking north. *b*. Plan showing the early Modified Olmec horizon (Equipac Phase) offerings (solid line) and the late Modified Olmec horizon (Felisa Phase) caches and burials (broken line). Drawings by Eduardo Martínez E.

ramic complex, came from the lowest level of Pit 17 (Figs. 7 and 8), 4 to 4.6 meters below the surface and beneath the level of Floor Series I. Outstanding type-sherds from this lot (Fig. 9b) represent deep flat-bottom bowls with specular hematite red interiors or rims, white wares, white-and-black wares, brushed and stick-punched *tecomates* (neckless jars), fluted red-and-white jar bodies, and a hollow figurine leg and foot. These sherds are in unusually good condition in spite of the very wet climate and the early period of time to which they belong; apparently they are from undisturbed portions of an occupation underlying the earli-

236

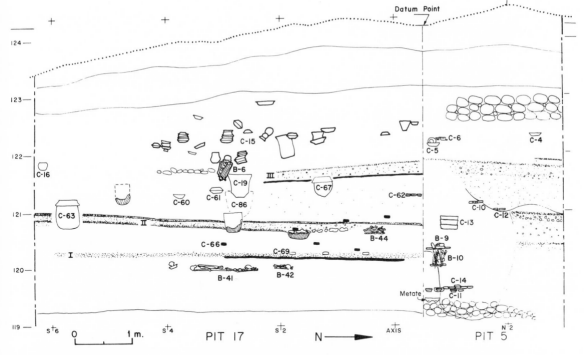

Fig. 7 (above) Profile of Pits 17 and 5, Mound 20, looking west. Floor Series I-III were cut anciently by intrusive caches. Compare with Figures 5, 6, and 8. Drawing by Eduardo Martínez E.

Fig. 8 (below) West wall of Pit 17, Mound 20, at the termination of the excavation. Floor Series I-III are clearly seen and labeled; compare with profile drawing in Figure 7. Note the reddish pigment deposit (A), the barely visible Cache 86 urn (B), and the vessels remaining in the wall from the Guañoma Phase Cache 15 (C). The two cords across the face are one meter apart. Photograph by the author.

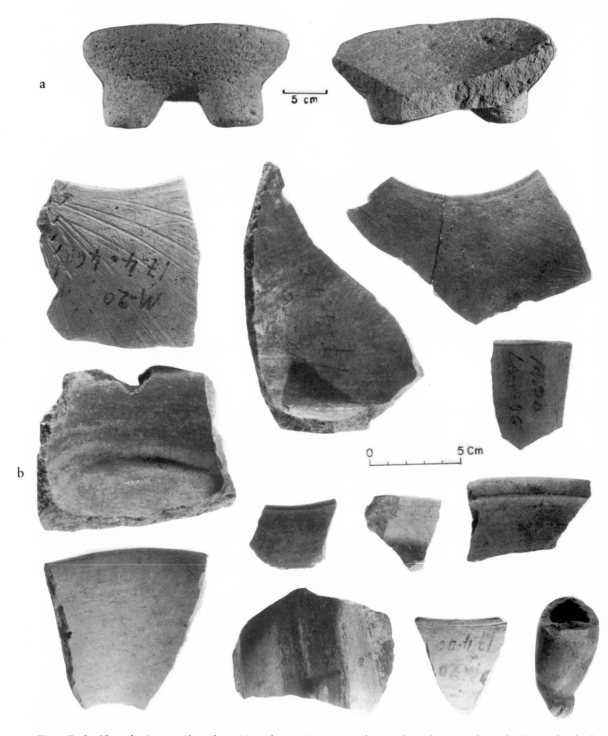

Fig. 9 Early Olmec horizon artifacts from Mound 20. *a.* Fragment of a two-legged *metate* from the lowest level of Pit 5, probably from the Cacahuano Phase (see Figs. 5-7). Exterior and interior views. *b.* Bombana ceramic complex sherds from the lowest level of Pit 17. Photographs by Mario Vega Román.

Fig. 10 Early Olmec horizon sherds of the Cacahuano ceramic complex from San Isidro. Incised and excised sherds from the lowest levels of Pit 20, Mound 20, and related plaza pits. Photograph by Mario Vega Román.

est Mound 20 platform. This initial San Isidro ceramic manifestation seems best aligned with the Chicharras Phase at San Lorenzo (M. Coe 1970), although Lee (1974b: 5) prefers an earlier, Bajío Phase, alignment; in either case, a "proto-Olmec" occupation is indicated (Lowe 1977: 212). All of the infrequent sherds from nonintruded zones below 3.40 meters in our Pit 5, and those few from undisturbed deposits below the level of the Series I floors in Pit 17, appear compatible with the Chicharras ceramic complex. Nevertheless, M. Coe (1970: 27) states that there are many continuations of Chicharras pottery types into the San Lorenzo Phase, and I will refrain here from a definite Chicharras alignment for the earliest San Isidro Mound 20 floors.

That San Isidro was occupied contemporaneously at least with the following fully Olmec San Lorenzo Phase at the San Lorenzo site, however, is evidenced by the widespread Cacahuano-ceramic-complex sherd distribution under several mounds and the occurrence of a peculiar San Lorenzo type of two-legged stone *metate* in Pit 5 (Fig. 9a). This artifact distribution is closely related to an architectural development, noted in Mound 20 particularly. To all appearances, there was a large flat terrace or platform, certainly measuring more than 10 by 30 meters in area, maintained during the Early Olmec horizon on the gentle slope where the Mound 20 pyramid was to rise very soon after. The platform, which we may assume most probably to have been ceremonial, was refloored at least once with a whitish sand or volcanic ash, and parts of it had been burned subsequently (see Floor 1 in Figs. 5, 7, and 8). Construction seems to have leveled off a natural, narrow rise cutting across the broad river-levee zone first occupied by the Bombana Phase "proto-Olmec" populace.

The incised-excised black pottery of the San Isidro Cacahuano complex (Fig. 10) is a key diagnostic trait of the Early Olmec horizon. At the San Lorenzo site in Veracruz, a broadly parallel ceramic type named Calzadas Carved is considered to be a major "ceramic marker" for the San Lorenzo Phase, although it typically has "familiar Olmec elements like crossed-bands, jaguar-paw–wing, flame brows, and

fire-serpent jaws" (M. Coe 1970: 26), motifs that are rare at San Isidro.

Additional pottery types from Cacahuano proveniences at San Isidro are shown in Figure 11. Sherds included are from red-on-white *tecomates;* plain thin *tecomates* (other, brushed examples are common but not illustrated); coarse-incised, red-slipped heavy *tecomates;* white wares; and white-rim black ware. There seems every reason to suppose, from this and related evidence, that San Isidro experienced a long and probably unbroken development extending from at least beginning Early Olmec-horizon times (*ca.* 1350 B.C.) through the entire period of the San Lorenzo Phase occupation at that Veracruz "climax Olmec" capital center.

The two lowest floor series in Pits 5 and 17 (I and II in Figs. 5, 7, and 8) are dated to the Early Olmec horizon on the basis of sherd lots for arbitrary levels maintained as the pits were dug. Despite the intrusion of a dozen Modified Olmec-horizon Equipac Phase offerings made through or onto these floors, no sherds later than the Cacahuano Phase were found in the surrounding fill. The stratigraphy of Pits 5 and 17 was complicated by the large number of intrusive pits, including cuts into the underlying sterile soil (see Figs. 5–8), but there is no question of the Early Preclassic (Early Olmec horizon) date of the lower floors and the broad platforms which they covered. Both Equipac and Felisa Phase offerings were intrusive through part or all of the Series III, II, and I floors seen in Figures 7 and 8; particularly devastating destruction was caused by the intrusion of the Felisa Phase Burials 41 and 42 through the Series II and I floors or floor levels to a position directly above sterile subsoil. All three floor series were entirely missing a short distance into the pit area (note ancient edges in Fig. 8).

THE LATER OLMEC HORIZON (CA. 1000–700 B.C.)

The Later Olmec horizon (Lowe 1977: 218–22, Fig. 9.3) is known at San Isidro only from occasional surface, mound-fill, and test-pit sherds (analysis in process), and apparently it is not represented in the Mound 20 architec-

Fig. 11 More Early Olmec horizon sherds from San Isidro. Red-on-white, incised-red, white, and white-rim sherds (top to bottom rows) from the Cacahuano ceramic complex in the lower levels of Pit 20, Mound 20, and related plaza pits. Photograph by Mario Vega Román.

ture. This is the early part only of the period labeled the "La Venta horizon" by M. Coe (1977: 184; see also the "Middle Preclassic I Subperiod" described by Lowe 1978: 358–61, Fig. 11.8, lower). Presumably the platform covered by the Early Olmec Series II floors in the Mound 20 locale remained unused for a time before it was enveloped by the later Modified Olmec-horizon platform and pyramid represented by the Series III floors, but there may be intermediate architectural details, including even Dombi Phase terraces, within the core of the Mound 20 pyramid (note, in Fig. 5, the horizontal and vertical space available). Unfortunately, it was impossible to probe deeper into the pyramid before it was flooded (less excusably, perhaps, no excavation at all was made at the opposite, or western, base of the mound to test for continuation of deposits or construction in that direction).

THE MODIFIED OLMEC HORIZON
(CA. 700–400 B.C.)

The Equipac and Felisa Phase offerings in Mound 20 represent early and late aspects of a widespread Modified-Olmec-horizon occupation contemporaneous with the closing centuries in the life of the La Venta Olmec capital center seventy-five miles away in Tabasco (Lowe 1977: 222–6, Figs. 9.3, 9.4; 1978: 365–73, Figs. 11.8, 11.9). The intermediate stratigraphic position of these offerings in Mound 20 and their important architectural situations can best be understood through a brief description of the excavations which discovered them, starting with Pit 2 in the summit of the pyramid and proceeding eastward. The offerings themselves will be described following this review.

Pit 2 was dug 3 by 3 meters square in the summit of Mound 20 to clear a group of Ipsan Phase ("Protoclassic" horizon) cache vessels exposed there (Cache 1). The excavation was subsequently enlarged to permit investigation of an adobe-brick tomb and its occupant (Burial 11), discovered one meter below the surface of the pyramid; Burial 11 pertained to the Late Preclassic Guañoma Phase of the "Epi-Olmec" or early Chicanel horizon. The tomb had been intruded into the summit of an earlier Felisa Phase pyramid, as evidenced by Burial 4 of that phase and stratigraphical position (see Fig. 5, upper left). Beneath Burial 11 appeared clay fill, two clay floors, and, at about five meters below the summit, the urn burial designated Burial 7, of the Equipac Phase. Pit 2 was continued down below this burial to the 6.5-meter depth and stopped in nondistinctive sandy clay fill.

Had it been possible to continue the Pit 2 mound center probe to greater depth and areal extent, it is certain that details of the central portions of the Early and possibly Later Olmec horizon platforms would have been encountered. As it is, the fill sherds from the lower 1.5 meters of Pit 2 (below the lowermost floor) are mainly pre-Equipac Phase and indicate an early Modified-Olmec-horizon date for an eight-meter-high pyramidal structure. The lower summit floors apparently correspond to the earlier of the Series III floors found in Pits 5 and 17 (Figs. 5 and 7), and we must envision a number of vertical or sloping terrace surfaces to have connected the two vestiges. The resulting earthen pyramid is one of the earliest known in Mesoamerica.

Pit 5 was excavated at the slightly elevated eastern base of Mound 20. The upper 1.5 meters of the pit were disturbed, and were in part talus from the eroding pyramid slope above; however, just below this point a river-boulder wall appeared, and at its base a number of apparently related and presumably subfloor offerings were found. These small groups of vessels (Caches 4, 5, and 6) dated to the Guañoma Phase and may be part of the huge Cache 15 found later just to the south in Pit 17, all contemporaneous with the Burial 11 adobe tomb intruded into the surface of the pyramid as described above for Pit 2. Below these offerings, Pit 5 went through Equipac Phase platform fill between broken floors, visible in the face of the west wall shown in Figure 8 and drawn in Figure 7. Below or within this construction level were Caches 10, 11, 12, 13, and 14, and Burials 9 and 10, all Equipac Phase interments, each of which (except for Cache 13) included from two to twenty-eight stone axes or celts. Most of these offerings had been intruded into holes cut into the earlier Cacahuano Phase platform and in some instances into the sterile sandy subsoil underlying this earliest structure known at San Isidro.

With the discovery of the impressive celt offerings along the southern edge of Pit 5, it was deemed important to uncover a larger section of the contiguous mound base. Accordingly, Pit 17 was laid out four meters wide and six meters long and extended south from Pit 5 (see Fig. 6b). The sequential pattern uncovered here was the same as that found in Pit 5, with the exception that several offerings, mainly urn burials, of the Felisa Phase (Caches 19, 43, 61, 63, 67, and 86) appeared below the level of the huge Guañoma Phase Cache 15. Level with, or, more usually, below these certainly intrusive offerings, appeared three groups of widely separated celts (Caches 62, 66, and 69) and the celt-equipped Burial 44. Through these were intruded the lower but later Felisa Phase Burials 41 and 42. Although we cannot be certain, it is most probable that all of these burials and offerings were intrusive through the same Series II floors disturbed by the similar celt offerings in Pit 5, inasmuch as no intact floor appeared above any of them. Except for the Burial 44 offering, nevertheless, no large compact group of stone celts appeared in Pit 17, and we are left to conclude that such groups of celts were centered closely along the approximately east-west-axis primary centerline for such offerings encountered by Pit 5 (Fig. 6).

Pit 20 was excavated about ten meters east of, and in line with, the southern edge of Pit 5 (Fig. 6) to test for continuation of the centerline of celt offerings. The pit did not disappoint us in this regard. After passing by a riverboulder wall and a Guañoma Phase offering (Cache 20) within the first meter below the surface, the central 'C' section of the long north-south trench encountered Cache 65, an offering of over forty-five tuff pseudocelts. Beneath this offering was found Cache 77, a group of three *tecomates* (neckless jars) and twenty-one celts. Apparently related to the latter offering, Cache 85 was then uncovered in Section 'D' of Pit 20 by knocking down the trench wall prior to abandoning the site to the rising lake waters (Fig. 14).

The Equipac Phase and earlier occupations in the southern sections ('D' and 'E') of Pit 20 were badly disturbed by the intrusion of three large Felisa Phase urn burials (see Caches 81, 82, and 83, drawn in broken lines in Fig. 6b), and no sherd stratigraphy was recovered there. In the northern sections ('A' and 'B'), on the other hand, the deposits were found to be undisturbed below the 1.40 meter level, and there again we recovered sherd lots of only the Cacahuano and/or Bombana Phases.

The axial alignment of celt offerings was reconfirmed in Pit 27, which was hurriedly excavated six meters east of Pit 20 as the dam waters began to enter the ruins. Here no sherds were saved, but the Cache 84 celt offering and Burial 45, encountered at approximately two meters below the surface indicate that at least the Modified-Olmec-horizon occupation still continued along the ridge or platform extending east from Mound 20.

Primary Centerline Caches and Burials (Equipac Phase)

The recovered objects from the Mound 20 Equipac Phase (early Modified Olmec horizon) offerings are summarily listed in the following paragraphs by cache and burial provenience, numerically arranged in order of discovery. All locations are shown in Figures 5 and 6. It will be noted in Figure 6 that the offerings cluster along an early, primary axis line running almost straight east from Cache 14 at left; the La Venta Olmec character of this lineal pattern is apparent (Drucker 1952: Pl. 13; see also Bernal 1969a: 39–40). The few Felisa Phase burials and caches of the late Modified Olmec horizon in a secondary and later alignment are summarized following the primary centerline axis description.

Cache 10. Four fine-grained tufaceous stone "pseudocelts" (for this term see Drucker *et al.* 1959: 135) at elevation 121.10 meters in the east-central section of Pit 5, found lying horizontally, two with bits to the southeast and two with bits to the northwest.

Cache 11. At the south edge of Pit 5, this was the lowest of the Mound 20 caches (elevation, 119.60 meters), and it appears to be the initial deposition and perhaps the central point in the primary axis line of offerings (Fig. 12b). Two pairs of jadeite earspool flares were set at right angles around a central pottery bowl of brown-black, poorly fired, and disintegrating ware (Fig. 13). Laid out in three unequal rows were eleven pseudocelts and one perfectly formed elliptical celt of hard gray stone with whitish banding. Two of the pseudocelts were placed vertically, with bits upward.

The axis-aligned pair of earspools from Cache 11 is one of the most remarkable sets of jade flares in all Mesoamerica. Each flare face is extremely wide, sharp-angled at the

a

b

Fig. 12 Modified Olmec horizon finds in Pit 5, Mound 20. *a.* Cache 14 at the west edge of the pit (see Figs. 6 and 7). *b.* Burial 10 and Caches 11 and 13. See Figure 13 for a close-up of Cache 11. Photographs by the author.

244

Fig. 13 Modified Olmec horizon Cache 11 in Pit 5, Mound 20. Photograph by the author.

throat, and squarish, with one side longer than the other and with corners rounded. Each flare is made from a different piece of dark green marblelike jade, with only very slightly differing measurements. These are among the largest earplug flares known, measuring over ten centimeters across the shorter dimension of the face; they seem, in fact, to be the largest squared examples reported. The flares are unperforated, highly polished, and very attractive. In spite of their extreme hardness, however, they were badly chipped and broken into numerous pieces. The missing fragments could not be found in the cache area, indicating that the flares had suffered damage prior to deposition.

The other pair of earspools consists of mottled white-and-green flares of crystalline jadeite, both cut from the same stone. Neck

and flare edges show old chipped and worn indentations, across which each flare had subsequently broken into unequal halves (Fig. 13). They measure 7.5 centimeters across the face, and are "Type A" flares (as identified by Kidder, Jennings, and Shook 1946: 106–8, and Shook and Kidder 1952: 113–4). These examples are unperforated, as is typical of Preclassic flares, but they compare very closely in form, color, and size with one of the perforated pair from the final Complex A burial in the Stone Coffer at La Venta (Drucker 1952: 161, Pl. 56 f).

Cache 12. Two pseudocelts lying horizontally near the west wall of Pit 5, at elevation 121.05 meters, with a third celt beneath.

Cache 13. Three rather crude nested black-brown bowls (32 by 11 centimeters) with flat bottoms, slightly outflaring walls, and thick-

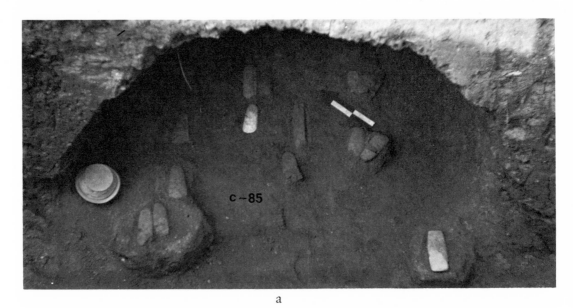

a

b

Fig. 14 Modified Olmec horizon caches in Pit 20, Mound 20, looking east. *a.* Cache 85, Pit 20-D. The bowls at left are intrusive from the Guañoma Phase. *b.* Caches 65 and 77, Pit 20-C, showing a figurine fragment (X) (see Fig. 15). Cache 65 is superimposed over Cache 77; note their relative positions in Figure 6. Photographs by the author.

Fig. 15 Modified Olmec horizon celts and figurine fragment from Caches 77 and 65 in Pit 20-C, Mound 20. Tufaceous pseudocelt (18) shows the fracturing pattern common to the type as found upon excavation. See text for a description of the top row of true celts and Figure 14 for the figurine location. Photograph by Mario Vega Román.

ened rounded lips, were found near the south wall of Pit 5 at elevation 120.65 meters. (Fig. 12b); each of the lower two bowls contained fourteen small roughly oval stream-bed pebbles, from five to fifteen centimeters in diameter. The vessels appear very similar in shape, construction, and finish to one recovered from La Venta Offering 18 in Phase II of Complex A (Drucker *et al.* 1959: 190, Fig. 42c).

Cache 14. Mosaic of twenty-seven rather large pseudocelts lying horizontally, all with bits to the east, at the western edge of Pit 5 (elevation 119.65 meters), with a huge celt of dense green stone with its bit to the west lying directly upon the smaller celts beneath it (Fig. 12a). Remains of a deteriorated river shell were stuck to the upper surface of the large axe. The entire offering was placed directly on sterile sandy subsoil and apparently had been arranged at the bottom of a pit (the profiles of the Cache 14 intrusion pit were lost as a result of consecutive ancient disturbances above, around, and even undercutting the sand on the offering's southwestern edge). Cache 14 formed the western limit of the primary offering axis line as discovered, but this line may, and probably does, continue farther west, under the Mound 20 pyramid. The enormous central stone celt of Cache 14 unfortunately was stolen from storage at the San Isidro field camp and cannot be described in detail. It was of a dense, highly polished, dark-green stone, 26 centimeters long and 12.5 centimeters wide at the bit, roughly elliptical in cross-section and slightly asymmetrical in outline.

In general characteristics, Cache 14 follows closely the frequent pattern of grouped axe offerings at La Venta (Drucker *et al.* 1959: 135–7).

Cache 62. Four roughly formed pseudocelts of tuff were found grouped together, apparently without order, at the northeast corner of Pit 17, just south of the offering axis line, at elevation 121.65 meters. There were no vestiges of floors directly above this offering, the highest of the early Modified Olmec horizon caches (originally probably related to the lower of the Series III floors).

Cache 65. A group of forty-five pseudocelts of very soft tuff was found on the west side of

Pit 20-C, 1.68 meters below the surface of the Mound 20 frontal platform (Fig. 14b). Cache 65 was located directly over the eastern edge of Cache 77, described below, but is probably a separate and somewhat later offering (see Fig. 6). The celts in the northwest segment of Cache 65 were badly disturbed and broken; this apparently disrupted condition, together with a vacant area in the center of the offering, suggests that some looting had taken place. This postulate is sustained by the absence of even a single igneous or other nontufaceous celt in this largest of the San Isidro axe offerings.

The two eastern rows of pseudocelts had their bits to the east, whereas the two rows on the west had their bits to the west. A clay anthropomorphic-figurine body fragment was found on the south edge of the cache, but may have had only an accidental relationship with it (Figs. 14b and 15, left center).

Cache 66. Six pseudocelts of soft tuff were found scattered across Pit 17 at levels ranging from elevations 120.30 to 120.65 meters (celts drawn in Figs. 6 and 7 with solid lines). These celts may have been individual and unrelated offerings; the four found farthest west had their bits to the west, but their differing levels do not indicate an association between them.

Cache 69. Three typically crude pseudocelts of weathered tuff were found at 4.04 meters below datum (elevation, 120.20 meters) in the northeast sector of Pit 17 arranged in an apparently purposeful manner (Figs. 6 and 7). The central celt was farther east than its companions.

Cache 77. A group of three *tecomates* and twenty-one celts was found just west of, and below, Cache 65 (Fig. 14b). The offering was about 2.40 meters below the surface of the Mound 20 frontal platform (Fig. 6). The celts seemed to have been placed indiscriminately about the jars, but the majority had their bit ends to the west or south, and only three, on the east side of the vessels, had their bits pointing northward. It is equally significant, no doubt, that those on the northern (Celt 6, pointing north), southern (Celt 7, pointing south), and western (Celt 5, pointing north) extremities of the offering—each quite separate from the offering center—were all of hard igneous rock or soapstone of varying shades of green (Fig. 15, top row); two other small celts of green igneous rock were west of the *tecomates*, Celt 2 pointing north and Celt 3 pointing east. As a group, these celts are somewhat smaller than the average for similar celts at La Venta, but otherwise they fit well the La Venta norms (Drucker *et al.* 1959: 137).

The three *tecomates* were of a coarse-paste, reddish-brown ware, each with a single groove around the mouth and a small hole, about two centimeters across, cut into its shoulder ("kill-holes" made to "let out the spirit" of the vessels and thus render up their utilitarian character). *Tecomates* of this rather uniform, simple type are a hallmark of the Middle Preclassic Period in the Greater Isthmus Area (Lowe 1978: Fig. 11.8). Most appropriately, such neckless jars have been reported as common at La Venta by Drucker (1952: 117, Fig. 39a), who makes the following significant comment: "These rims, which are among the more abundant rim sherds of all levels especially in the Coarse Paste wares, are more commonly decorated than any other form or jar rim. . . . one to three circumferential lines [are] incised about the exterior of the rim. . . ."

Cache 84. A large group of celts was found beginning eighty centimeters west of and eighty centimeters above the pelvis of Burial 45 in Pit 27, at elevation 120.0-120.30 meters (Fig. 6). Twenty-one pseudocelts were recovered, but an unknown number, probably twelve or more, were removed from the excavation clandestinely; these latter are drawn in on the plan.

Cache 85. Prior to abandoning San Isidro to the invading waters of the Mal Paso Lake, a short tunnel was dug into the east wall of Pit 20-D to follow an offering of pseudocelts which had become visible at about two meters below the surface and just south of Cache 77 (Fig. 6). The tunnel was continued to a depth of 1.40 meters before it collapsed, and this excavation uncovered a group of twenty-three pseudocelts at elevation 120.10 meters (Fig. 14a). Two of the discovered pseudocelts were too disintegrated for removal, and most of the balance remained buried by the sudden cave-in of the tunnel. The distribution pattern of these

ritual axes was indicative of deliberate ordering, with all but two bit-ends to the west, but without apparent meaning.

Burial 7. Quite probably at a time nearing the close of the Equipac Phase, Burial 7 was intruded through the two poor earthen Series III floors at the summit of the earliest Mound 20 pyramid known; these floors are suspected of corresponding to the upper or Series III platform floors in Pits 5 and 17 (Figs. 5–7). The position of the burial urn and its offering buried beneath the Series IV and V floors is clearly seen in the photograph of Pit 2 (Fig. 16). It is probable that Floors IV and V represent late or final Equipac Phase building platforms on top of the pyramidal substructure.

Burial 7 was of a young adult (bones fragmentary) placed in a large coarse-ware *olla* with low outflaring neck. Amid the bone fragments were found numerous small jade beads and a duck-billed amulet, all undoubtedly pertaining to a necklace (Fig. 17g). Placed around the urn (Fig. 16) were three flat-bottom flaring-wall bowls or plates (Fig. 17b, e, and f) and two composite silhouette bowls (Fig. 17c and d), all of a polished orange ware closely similar to the Nicapa Slipped Group of the Chiapa de Corzo Escalera Phase and the Naranjo Nebulosa pottery of Middle Preclassic Tres Zapotes (Ortiz Ceballos n.d.a: 35–6, 107–10, Figs. 38–48). A sixth vessel in the offering was a fine-paste white-and-black effigy bowl with restricted orifice (Fig. 17a); this is also a common Tres Zapotes Middle Preclassic ware (*ibid.*: 96–7, 113).

The absence of celts in this otherwise quite elaborate burial offering indicates that its function was distinct from that of the centerline-axis caches and burials at the foot of the pyramid.

Burial 9. In the southeastern corner of Pit 5, at elevation 120.35 meters, and just below the level of the whitish segment of the Series I floors (entirely absent in this section of the pit), was found Burial 9, directly on the primary offering axis centerline (Figs. 5–7). Apparently it was of a seated child, buried in a pit, with only a few remnants of long bones and the smashed skull recognizable; the deceased appears to have faced east. The burial was sur-

Fig. 16 Modified Olmec horizon Burial 7, an urn and offering in Pit 2, Mound 20. At upper right are the remains of the intrusive Burial 11, a Guañoma Phase adobe tomb. The floors below the worker delimit the Equipac-to-Felisa Phase construction transition (see Fig. 5). Photograph by the author.

Fig. 17 Modified Olmec horizon artifacts from Burial 7, Pit 2, Mound 20. *a*. Equipac Phase effigy vessel, white-and-black fine-paste ware. *b-f*. Polished orange vessels. *g*. Jadeite necklace from the floor of the urn (see Fig. 16 and the section in Fig. 5). It includes a duck-head effigy pendant. Photographs by Mario Vega Román.

rounded by three perfectly formed and polished grayish stone celts of typical La Venta elliptical shape; eighteen pseudocelts, some of them upright; and a plain, brownish, poorly fired, flatbottom, flaring-wall bowl, badly smashed.

Burial 10. On the south side of Pit 5, just to the south of the axis centerline of the offering, at elevation 120.10 meters, was a seated adult burial, facing east, right leg inside the left and arms over chest (Fig. 12b, lower right); a large, flattish, pinkish seashell with perforations was over the face and forehead. The deceased was sitting directly upon a row of three tufaceous pseudocelts laid parallel to each other. In line with the central celt of this group and under the flexed legs of the skeleton was a single pseudocelt, and in front of this was another row of three parallel ones. The bits of all seven pseudocelts apparently faced west. Twelve other pseudocelts were found scattered beneath this group of seven.

Burial 44. In the northwest corner of Pit 17, one meter south of the primary axis centerline (Figs. 6 and 7), at elevation 120.85 meters, was a seated adult burial facing east, with the skull collapsed at the feet and the bones badly disintegrated. The deceased rested upon a north-south row of ten celts, nine of which were parallel to each other and the tenth placed horizontal to these and beneath the chin (that is, at the buttocks position originally). Eight of the celts were of the rude pseudocelt type, but one was of a fine-grained light-green stone with both poll and bit ends battered or chipped, as if from use as a chisel.

Burial 45. This was a seated adult burial facing east, with the skull collapsed over the rib cage and pelvis, with other bones fragmentary; it was found in Pit 27, on the primary offering axis line and at its eastern extreme (as known; see Fig. 6), at elevation 119.70 meters, 2.25 meters below the ground surface. A single soft tuff pseudocelt was found in front of the feet at the pelvis position, and all the remains were above what appeared to be a burned floor over sterile subsoil. At approximately head level, and forty centimeters behind or west of the burial, was a large offering of pseudocelts, described above as Cache 84, which possibly was related to this burial.

Secondary Axis Caches and Burials (Felisa Phase)

A secondary east-west offering-alignment axis several meters south of the primary centerline seems to have guided the interment of caches and nonpyramid burials during the Felisa Phase (broken-line drawings in the plan, Fig. 6). A separate burial was made in the summit of an addition to the pyramid.

Caches 19, 60, 61, 63, 67, 81–83, and 86. These Felisa-Phase offering vessels will not be described in this paper except for the small bowls with Caches 81–83 (Fig. 18). Positions of all are indicated in Figure 6, and similar Felisa Complex burial urns and bowls from San Isidro Mound 4 have been described in detail by Lee (1974b: 37–46, Figs. 41–4). The Mound 20 caches appear to have been intruded through or into the various Equipac and Cacahuano platform superimpositions in front of the pyramid. The cache evidence indicates that by late Modified Olmec times (*ca.* 550–400 B.C.) the offering pattern had changed from celt groups and possible adult sacrifices to an emphasis upon child (or animal?) burials in an alignment probably related to a now-modified platform and center around the pyramid.

Burial 4. At about 1.50 meters below the surface of Mound 20 in Pit 2 (Fig. 5) was found a clustering of bone fragments, an offering of three pottery vessels (Fig. 19), and a group of stone abrading tools. The situation suggests that some erosion of the pyramid summit, as from disuse, had occurred after placement of Burial 4 and before the massive excavation was made to intrude the Guañoma Phase adobe-brick tomb for Burial 11 (note Fig. 16). Such a period of disuse would correlate with a similar disjunction in the constructional history of Mound 4 (Lee 1974b: 11; note absence of Stage G construction in his section drawing, Fig. 4). This evidence of disruption at San Isidro coincides remarkably with the full demise of La Venta and the near-abandonment of San Lorenzo, all of these events occurring between about 400 and 300 B.C. The Burial 4 pottery shows, as does that of Burial 41 described below, the expected correspondence to final Middle Preclassic San Lorenzo and La

Fig. 18 Late Modified Olmec horizon vessels from Caches 81-83, Pit 20, Mound 20, Felisa Phase (see Fig. 6, Pit 20-E). *a*. Coarse buff ware. *b, d*. Felisa Phase Polished red ware. *c, e*. Polished brown ware. Photograph by Mario Vega Román.

Fig. 19 Late Modified Olmec horizon vessels from Burial 4, Pit 2, Mound 20, Felisa Phase (see Fig. 5, upper left). *a*. Incised brown ware. *b, c*. Polished red-orange ware. Photographs by Mario Vega Román.

Fig. 20 Late Modified Olmec horizon vessels from Burial 41, Pit 17, Mound 20, Felisa Phase. *a*. Pedestal bowl, incised polished brown ware. *b*. Coarse buff ware. *c-g*. Polished orange-red double-slip ware. *h*. Incised polished black ware. Photograph by Mario Vega Román.

Venta ceramic complexes (see Lowe 1978: Fig. 11.8, top; also M. Coe 1968b: discussion at close of article, and M. Coe 1970: 29).

Burials 41 and 42. Excavations almost two meters deep were made by the Felisa folk to intrude Burials 41 and 42 into sterile sand beneath the earlier platforms at the base of the Mound 20 pyramid (Figs. 6 and 7). There was no significant offering with the jumbled and perhaps secondary Burial 42, but Burial 41 was accompanied by a handsome pottery offering of eight vessels (Fig. 20). These pots find closest correspondences in the final offering vessels in late Complex A Phase IV at La Venta (Lowe 1978: Fig. 11.8, upper right; see Drucker 1952: Figs. 29, 41d).

CONCLUSIONS

Though brief and incomplete, the excavations made in Mound 20 at San Isidro uncovered an instance of La Venta Olmec ceremonialism so striking in extent and position that it at once testifies to the more-than-local importance of that previously near-unique ritual pattern and also establishes its relative place in time and culture. The finding at San Isidro of an extensive "Early Olmec" occupation, better known at San Lorenzo, underlying that of the late La Venta or "Modified Olmec" horizon provides needed confirmation of a basic sequence for Olmec culture history that is of critical importance for Mesoamerican archaeology. In addition, a pyramidal construction over eight meters high was shown to be related to the La Venta-like centerline axis offerings at San Isidro.

The Mound 20 investigations have produced a truly companion-site occupation for Modified-Olmec-horizon La Venta. Other, and probably closer, La Venta-horizon-site occupations certainly must exist, but none revealing similarly extensive Olmec offering patterns have been excavated to date (a single mosaic celt offering was found at Seibal [Sabloff 1975: 57]). San Isidro, at this early time, was undoubtedly a lesser center, but its available data contribute to the definition of a clearer Olmec chronology and also suggest the actuality of a Greater Isthmus Area Olmec-influenced territory. Such a territory, to all appearances, shows more thorough cultural cohesion than any other so far postulated for the Olmec "homelands."

ACKNOWLEDGMENTS   The archaeological investigation of San Isidro was a joint project of the Departamento de Prehistoria of the Instituto Nacional de Antropología e Historia, Mexico, and the Brigham Young University—New World Archaeological Foundation. The then Departamento de Prehistoria director, José Luis Lorenzo, supervised the Mal Paso archaeological salvage project from Mexico City, and Carlos Navarrete served as overall field director. It is a pleasure to acknowledge the assistance and facilities provided by these officials both in the field and subsequently in Mexico City. Special appreciation is extended to Ingeniero Enrique Marrón V. and the Comisión Federal de Electricidad for supplying half of the sixty workmen eventually utilized at San Isidro, and for providing most of the food and transportation for the entire crew. Particular gratitude is expressed to Jorge Acuña for field assistance and to Eduardo Martínez Espinosa for topographic and excavation drawings.

Post-Olmec Stone Sculpture: The Olmec-Izapan Transition on the Southern Pacific Coast and Highlands

Lee A. Parsons

THE ST. LOUIS ART MUSEUM

The sheer quantity of monumental stone sculpture on the southern Pacific coast of Chiapas and Guatemala and adjacent highlands is no less than staggering. Some is published, more is unpublished, and even more is coming to light every year. The site of Kaminaljuyú alone, in the Valley of Guatemala, now has over one-hundred catalogued monumental sculptures assigned to it. (By "monumental" I mean relatively unportable stone carvings over two feet in height.) About the published sculptures in this southern Pacific region there has been conflicting opinion as to age and style, and the published illustrations are extremely scattered in the literature. I wish to concentrate on one class of this material, which may be considered post-Olmec in both style and time, a period that I will bracket between approximately 500 and 200 B.C. Some forty-four representative examples of the style have been selected in order to illustrate them together for comparative purposes. (About twenty of these have never before been published.) Following the precedent of Miles (1965),[1] I define

four stone-sculpture Divisions for the Preclassic Period: (I) Early Olmec, (II) Late Olmec, (III) Post-Olmec, and (IV) Izapan (Table 1). (Division V begins the Classic Maya period in southeastern Mesoamerica.)

Roughly two-thirds of the known stone monuments in the area under concern were carved in Preclassic to Early Classic times and the other third in Middle and Late Classic times, with a small residue of Postclassic monuments. I have already defined the Classic Period Cotzumalhuapa style (Parsons 1969),

[1] The first synthesis of sculptural styles in the southern Chiapas–Guatemala–El Salvador region was brilliantly achieved by the late Suzanna Miles in her contribution to the *Handbook of Middle American Indians* (1965). She recognized all the basic style divisions that we now work with, but at that time she seriated them in a somewhat different manner. My research effort has been directed toward updating and revising her seriation with the advantage of new archaeological information and a greater number of sculptures to support each stylistic subdivision. With the excavation of Monte Alto, Escuintla, Guatemala, and with Michael Coe's ex-

cavation of the early Olmec site of San Lorenzo (Coe 1968b), it is necessary to re-examine the subject matter. Formerly it was plausible to postulate that certain rude boulder sculptures and rock carvings in the Pacific coastal zone were early enough to be pre-Olmec, if not Olmec-contemporary (Parsons and Jenson 1965; Miles 1965). However, we now have good reason to believe that most of them are not; therefore, on reassessment, Miles's sculptural Divisions I and II are best grouped together in my Division III (Post-Olmec), though a few examples may eventually prove to belong to my Division II (Late Olmec). Miles's sculptural Divisions III and IV fit comfortably within my Division IV (Izapan). (To my eyes, Miles's tentative assignment of certain Izapan narrative stelae to her Division II was incorrect.)

A key to the entire Preclassic sequence lies in the wide range of sculpture found at the pivotal site of Kaminaljuyú. This author is preparing a comprehensive monograph on all this sculpture, and thereby will elaborate upon the Miraflores–Izapa period as well as the Post-Olmec period (Table 1). One may assume that any major Preclassic stone monuments obviously omitted from this article are to be classified within the general Izapan horizon. The reader should note that all monument numbers cited for Kaminaljuyú in this article follow, and continue from, those given by Miles (1965); however, there were certain errata in her printed article which are here corrected.

TABLE I. PRECLASSIC SCULPTURAL DIVISIONS

		STYLE DIVISIONS	SUB-DIVISIONS	Kaminaljuyu	La Venta	San Lorenzo
400	EARLY CLASSIC	V EARLY MAYA	MAYA	Aurora		
200	TERMINAL & PROTO-CLASSIC	IV IZAPAN	IZAPA / ARENAL	Verbena / Arenal		
AD/BC			MIRAFLORES ("Proto-Maya")			
200	LATE	III POST-OLMEC	MONTE ALTO / OLMECOID / DANZANTE	Providencia / Majadas		
500					IV	Palangana
	MIDDLE	II LATE OLMEC	COLONIAL OLMEC	Las Charcas	III	HIATUS
800					II	Nacaste
	EARLY	I EARLY OLMEC	OLMEC		I	San Lorenzo
1200						

which dominated the area between A.D. 400 and 900. Many sculptures discovered in the last decade may be appended to that category. That style owed its origin to non-Maya, Gulf Coast, and Mexican highland origins. Before A.D. 400, however, and before the Middle Classic Teotihuacanoid intrusions, the sculptural styles of this area may be considered "Proto-Maya," and they extend back to Olmec and Olmecoid influences. They also include the locally developed Izapa style. Among the Preclassic corpus of stone sculpture, about one-third may be placed in a broad Izapan horizon; another third is concentrated in a transitional Olmec–Izapan, or "Post-Olmec," style period; and the few remaining examples are doubtlessly Late Olmec.

It is time to devote serious attention to the Post-Olmec Division, which has not been sufficiently recognized as a discrete entity or art-style period.[2] In most discussions of Preclassic sculpture, authors jump directly from a general "Olmec" to a general "Izapan" classification (*e.g.*, M. Coe 1966b) or add a nebulous, floating, "Olmecoid" category which has been applied to both contemporary, provincial Olmec and to a later derived Olmec, if not including the Izapan manifestation (*e.g.*, Bernal 1969a). The rampant confusion and controversy over what stone sculpture in Mesoamerica may be classed as Olmec, as opposed to Olmecoid, or even Izapan, may be clarified by the consideration of a post-Olmec interim, especially as manifested on the Peripheral Coastal Lowlands (for definition of this area see Parsons 1978).

The stone sculpture of incipient civilizations, with or without sound archaeological context, must be analyzed. This writer is heartened by the trend for an increasing number of art history students to apply themselves to the field. However, it should be emphasized that much

more archaeological field work is necessary before any final judgments can be made. This is not to say that preliminary hypotheses as to art-style sequences cannot be proposed in order to examine critically the enormous reservoir of extant sculptural art. There are enough guidelines in existing field research to allow us to surmise broad stylistic classes and sequences. Individual stone sculptures inevitably are difficult to assign to specific phases. Some of the most impressive monuments were moved from place to place in Pre-Columbian times and reused in successive periods. Direct structural or ceramic associations rarely exist or, if they do, only provide a terminal date for the use or deposit of the sculpture. Proskouriakoff (1968) has raised the valid point of archaistic revivals of early sculptural styles in Late Classic times, but it seems that on close analysis, such situations can usually be recognized. There are too many documented instances of actual Preclassic monuments having been rediscovered, reused, and newly revered by Late Classic peoples (*e.g.*, the "potbelly" sculpture found on the surface of the Monument Plaza at Bilbao [Parsons 1969: 122]). Furthermore, it has been disconcerting that so many classical Olmec monuments on the Gulf Coast were discovered in association with Late Classic ceramic levels (Medellín Zenil 1960b).

My thesis, like M. Coe's (1968b: 63), is that there was a development in southeastern Mesoamerica of sculptural styles from Olmec to Maya, with certain probable offshoots, regional developments, and feedbacks from region to region (Parsons 1967b).[3] In outline (Table 1), we must begin with a sculptural Division I encompassing Early, or "classic," Olmec (1200–800 B.C.) which is typified by the famed colossal stone heads and full-round

---

[2] On the other hand, John F. Scott may be credited for having carefully perceived a Post-Olmec period (Easby and Scott 1970: Chap. 4; Scott 1978, I:7-9), but, for the purposes of the "Before Cortés" exhibition, he combined Post-Olmec and Izapan sculpture into one chapter. In another recent paper (1976), he outlined a Post-Olmec period. His insights into these problems parallel mine.

[3] Matt Stirling also directed his Mesoamerican field work toward the whole spectrum of Preclassic sculpture, which also led well into the Classic Period. In my opinion, it has always been an injustice to Stirling that the archaeological "gold" he so consistently struck was invariably considered "Olmec" by less informed scholars. Granted, Stirling followed Blom and La Farge's lead to La Venta and then his own exploration led him to the Río Chiquito and the discovery of San Lorenzo (Stirling 1955). These indeed were sensational Olmec discoveries. The fact that he

seated figures naturalistically and skillfully executed at San Lorenzo, Laguna de los Cerros, and early La Venta. There is as yet no known precedent for this class of monumental stone sculpture. In this Early Olmec period cultural interchanges were already being communicated between the Gulf Coast and the Mexican highlands, though this apparently was not expressed in monumental stone sculpture.

There is increasing justification for defining a Division II, Middle Preclassic, "Late Olmec" Phase (*ca.* 800–500 B.C.), which corresponds to the dissolution of San Lorenzo and the innovations seen in late La Venta sculpture. Although the Early Olmec had reciprocal contacts with Oaxaca and central Mexico, in Late Olmec times there is compelling evidence of pan-Mesoamerican influences, including monumental stone sculpture. This period was appropriately called "Colonial Olmec" by Bernal (1969a), and I shall briefly characterize it below.

My Division III, in evolving stone sculpture styles (*ca.* 500–200 B.C.), is best labeled Post-Olmec, and corresponds with the beginning of the Late Preclassic Phase in Mesoamerica. We shall concentrate on that phase. I divide the Post-Olmec into three stylistic subdivisions which may be called "Danzante," "Olmecoid," and "Monte Alto." I would like to insist that the overused term "Olmecoid" be limited to this class and time-period of sculpture; in other words, a very particular substyle derived from, and later than, Olmec.

Division IV, then, is Terminal Preclassic and, if you will, "Proto-Classic" (*ca.* 200 B.C.–A.D. 200). It subsumes what has been called the Iza-

pan horizon style in southeastern Mesoamerica, and represents the full florescence of the Preclassic development. (Space will not allow the treatment of that Division in this article.) The divergent styles of the Post-Olmec phase were perfected during Division IV as new regional art styles, the most notable of which was essentially "Proto-Maya." I see three subdivisions in that phase: Miraflores and Arenal (centering at Kaminaljuyú in the highlands), and the Izapan narrative style itself (centering at the type site of Izapa on the Pacific coast).

I consider the Danzante, Monte Alto, Arenal, and Izapan art styles (Table 1) to be specialized regional offshoots from a mainline tradition that extends from classical Olmec through Colonial Olmec and Olmecoid to Miraflores (in essence, Proto-Maya) to Early Classic Maya. Between about 200 B.C. and A.D. 200 (150 B.C. to A.D. 150 may prove to be tighter chronological boundaries), the innovative sculptural and iconographic modes of the Peripheral Coastal Lowlands were transferred through the highlands to the central Maya lowlands, where a full Classic sculptural style was destined to emerge (Parsons 1967b, 1973).[4] Southern Guatemala and the Pacific coast were destined at the same time to be dominated by Mexican influences during the Middle Classic Period, although some Preclassic concepts continued into the Cotzumalhuapa sculptural tradition. I wish to emphasize my belief that, before A.D. 400, our area was culturally and stylistically thoroughly Mayoid.

DIVISION II: LATE OLMEC
(800–500 B.C.)

In order to place a Post-Olmec sculptural division in its proper developmental context, art expressions of the prior Late Olmec, Middle Preclassic Period should be summarized. By this time the classic Olmec style was breaking up and changing in new directions. Notably, low relief on panels and stelalike slabs (with-

---

also was the first to excavate Tres Zapotes, Cerro de las Mesas, and even Izapa (Stirling 1943b) has perpetually confounded the issue of what is Olmec, owing to some writers who mistakenly took all the sculpture of these sites to be *a priori* classic Olmec. Stirling (1940b) did not claim that Stela C at Tres Zapotes represented anything other than an art style corresponding to the calendrical date inscribed on the monument—a period we now refer to as Izapan. Both Tres Zapotes and Cerro de las Mesas had long sequences, but Stirling intuitively recognized that not all Tres Zapotes sculpture could be considered classic Olmec, and that Cerro de las Mesas demonstrated both Olmec heirlooms and archaistic sculptural trends in its Classic Period.

[4] Recent archaeological discoveries at Abaj Takalik on the coast (Graham 1977), San Jerónimo, Baja Verapaz (de la Haba 1974: 689, which mentions the work of Sharer and Sedat), and La Lagunita, El Quiché (Ichon n.d.) promise to confirm and strengthen this hypothesis.

out associated altars), as well as rock carvings, received greater emphasis. The style itself became more dynamic, incorporated a great number of signs and symbols (if not true hieroglyphs), and saw the appearance of a new, linear, aquiline, bearded physical type. Low-relief carvings featured more complex interaction scenes of two or more figures, and included supplementary figures, as well as serpent and bird motifs. Also, the first profile "dragon" motifs appeared (Parsons 1967b: Fig. 8A, from a La Venta jade earplug, and Fig. 8B, from a Las Charcas bowl), which were to become so important in later Preclassic times. These elements diffused to the distant provinces of Mesoamerica where local traditions were already entrenched. They portended styles that were to become established in the Post-Olmec era.

Also widely distributed in this Colonial Olmec Period were full-round portable sculptures, jade (or other fine-grained stone) figures, celts, and votive axes. Incentives and mechanisms for this distribution undoubtedly involved trading networks for jade and cacao (Parsons and Price 1971). Colonial outposts may have been maintained as far south as Costa Rica. This was also the time of the pan-Mesoamerican popularity of the hollow ceramic "baby-face" figurine complex so well known in the central and west Mexican highlands as well as in the southern highlands and along the coast (Las Charcas and Bolinas figurine types). In Guerrero there are the Late Olmec painted caves, which have received much publicity, and in Morelos there is the group of rock carvings on the cliffs at Chalcatzingo (with the exception of Petroglyph 1, which I will argue is Post-Olmec).

The Gulf-Coast Olmec heartland produced a number of Late Olmec stone sculptures during Phase IV of La Venta. I specifically wish to point out the following, which relate to Post-Olmec developments (for a catalogue of these La Venta monuments see de la Fuente 1973): Stelae 1–3, Monument 13 (the low-relief bearded figure with a column of three glyphs), Monument 19 (the low-relief slab with a dynamic human figure surrounded by a serpent), Monument 40 (a seated figure on a bench),

Monument 21 (a torso on a table altar), Monument 5 (the full-round *abuelita* with crest and offering tray), and Altar 6 (with its rigid "hunched-shoulder" figure seated in a niche). The several aberrant colossal heads found in and around Tres Zapotes probably should be assigned to this Late Olmec phase, as well as the low-relief stela at the central Veracruz site of Viejón (Medellín Zenil 1960b: Pl. 9).

Colonial Olmec, Division II, sculptures also have been found evenly distributed along the southern Pacific coast and adjacent highlands, an area that was to blossom with monumental sculpture in the subsequent Post-Olmec phase. Curiously, however, none of the monumental sculptures at Kaminaljuyú can as yet be assigned confidently to the Late Olmec category, although its Las Charcas ceramic complex indicates substantial Middle Preclassic settlement. Three well-known petroglyphs carved on the flat faces of enormous boulders are probably Late Olmec: Pijijiapan, Chiapas (Navarrete 1974), Abaj Takalik, western Guatemala (J. E. S. Thompson 1943), and Chalchuapa, western El Salvador (Boggs 1950). All of these are located in the cacao-growing zone of the Pacific slopes. There also is the low-relief stela at Padre Piedra in highland Chiapas (Navarrete 1960: Fig. 11), and the newly discovered Late Olmec panel from the Pacific coast of Guatemala (Fig. 1; Shook and Heizer 1976). The style of the latter relief relates to both the Abaj Takalik petroglyph and Petroglyph 2 at Chalcatzingo (Covarrubias 1957: Fig. 24). Navarrete also reported (1974: Figs. 19-23) two full-round Colonial Olmec sculptures from coastal Chiapas. Other apparently Late Olmec Monuments, such as a niche figure on a boulder, are being unearthed at Abaj Takalik (Graham 1977: 197) and at San Jerónimo, Baja Verapaz, in highland Guatemala (de la Haba 1974: 689).

DIVISION III: POST-OLMEC
(500–200 B.C.)

At the beginning of the Late Preclassic, a diversified period of stone sculptural activity may be discerned, which in many respects was transitional between Olmec and Izapan. It was also a period of coalescing, specialized, re-

Lee A. Parsons

Fig. 1 Late Olmec low-relief panel, south coast of Guatemala. Andesite. Diameter, *ca.* 81 cm. Private Collection, Guatemala. Photograph by Nicholas Hellmuth, courtesy of the Foundation for Latin American Anthropological Research, Guatemala.

gional developments, such as the low-relief "Danzante" style centering at Monte Albán, Oaxaca, and the "Monte Alto" style of coastal Guatemala (comprising the boulder sculpture at the type site and a full-round, potbelly stylistic derivative). Both substyles indicate a vague rentention of prior Olmec concepts. In addition, there is a widespread "Olmecoid" style whose canons were more directly derived from the Olmec and prognosticated the innovations of the Terminal Preclassic Izapan Period. Olmecoid carving is expressed in three basic categories: low-relief, full-round "naturalistic," and full-round "engaged" relief. Olmecoid monumental sculpture was particularly prevalent at the highland Guatemalan site of Kaminaljuyú during its Majadas and Providencia/Sacatepequez phases. All three substyles were more-or-less contemporary, or occasionally mixed and overlapping. New concepts in sculptural art were also freely interchanged on the coastal lowlands (Gulf and Pacific) and included communication with highland Mexico. (For example, the Guerrero-based "Mezcala" style of

small stone carvings probably was inspired during this period.) The centers of these styles had shifted away from the Olmec heartland, and, in fact, certain outside regional styles evidently diffused back to that region.

Overall, there was a balanced emphasis on low-relief and full-round carvings in this Post-Olmec Division, although the technical quality of the latter diminished in the direction of simplification or an unfinished "crudity" (factors which previously led to the hypothesis that some of the sculptures may have been proto-Olmec). Classes of monumental sculpture included petroglyphs, stelae and wall panels, columnar basalts, boulder sculptures, and full-round sculptures. A very specialized subclass of sculptures proliferated in southern Guatemala at this time in the form of tall, vertical pedestal sculptures as well as portable "bench figures" and "mushroom stones." Other special classes of portable carvings widespread in the Post-Olmec period include Olmecoid stone masks, stone spheres with faces, and seated or kneeling figures. Although it is difficult to generalize as to stylistic qualities of Post-Olmec sculpture, I suggest that in low-relief carving there was a continued tendency toward more dynamic postures and linear proportions, while full-round carving included naturalistic full-rounded contours, as well as sculptures with "engaged" relief and fat-featured faces with puffy, closed eyes.

Subject matter emphasized anthropomorphic feline figures or grotesque feline-masked figures, seated human and feline figures, crude colossal heads, and human figures within open feline jaws. Other prevalent subjects were captive prisoners, serpents, birds, and profile "dragon monsters." Common motifs included broad, flat scrolls; double-voluted earplugs; rounded rectangles; scroll-ended benches; arm and leg ligatures; beards or false beards; and simplified indications of clothing and adornment (such as belts and breechcloths; stiff capes; collars; medallions; ear, waist, and ankle ornaments; and, occasionally, fancy headdresses). Footgear is absent. Glyphs and glyphlike symbols (such as the omnipresent U motif) are more commonly found, as is the first undisputed hieroglyphic writing in columns (*e.g*, the Alvarado columnar basalt monument [Cervantes 1976] and Monte Albán's well-known Danzante panels). Many of the above features carried over from the Middle Preclassic and many were continued and elaborated during the Terminal Preclassic Period.

Danzante Substyle (Low-Relief)

Monte Albán's Phase I in the southern Mexican highlands has been securely dated to 500–150 B.C., which establishes time limits for our Post-Olmec period (Scott 1978, I: 12). Some 300 carved wall panels featuring contorted, genitally mutilated, captives with associated hieroglyphic texts characterize this style at the type site. (Superficially similar stone panels at the nearby site of Dainzú should be assigned to the Izapan period). The so-called Danzantes have been labeled both Olmec and Olmecoid, but in view of the existence of related carvings in outside regions, and more-precise dating, they deserve a discrete stylistic category. For example, a recently published Danzante-style monument was found near Angel R. Cabada

(El Mesón), southern Veracruz (de la Fuente 1973: 268). I would include the tall Alvarado columnar basalt relief (Covarrubias 1957: Fig. 29) and the related El Mesón column (Stirling 1943b: Pl. 16a)[5] in the Post-Olmec Danzante style also. All three of the above may have come from the same site. The dynamic, linear quality of the central figure on the Alvarado column, with its upraised arm, is especially comparable to one Monte Albán Danzante (Covarrubias 1957: Fig. 61). It also bears an eroded glyph-column on one side. The headdress type relates to Petroglyph 1 at Chalcatzingo (*ibid.:* Pl. 13), which we place in the same period for other reasons. Precocious features of this Alvarado carving consist of the seated obeisant figure on one side and the geometric basal panel which presages Izapan conventions, but which is also present on Post-Olmec Stela D at Tres Zapotes (Stirling 1943b: Fig. 4 and Pl. 14a) and Monument 2 at Izapa (Fig. 9). (It is well to point out here that I would place the well-known "Matisse" and "Tepatlaxco" stelae [Covarrubias 1957: Pl. 17] in the subsequent Izapan period.)

Moving to the southern Guatemalan region, there are two examples of the Danzante style at the distant site of Kaminaljuyú. Stela 9, the low-relief figure on columnar basalt (Fig. 2) has been discussed by both Miles (1965: 252) and Proskouriakoff (1968: 123). The linear, phallic, standing figure with upraised arm again reminds us of the above-mentioned Monte Albán Danzante. The trefoil headdress-element is duplicated on another Monte Albán Danzante (Martí and Kurath 1964: Fig. 66b), as well as on archaistic Stela 9, Cerro de las Mesas (Stirling 1943b: Fig. 11a). The top and bottom scroll motifs also relate to other Post-Olmec low-relief conventions. Stela 9 was discovered by Shook (1951) in Mound C-III-6 at Kaminaljuyú associated with three other plain basalt columns, two broken shafts from vertical pedestal sculptures, a cache of Majadas Phase pottery, and almost 300 jade beads and pendants.

[5] Since this article was written John F. Scott (1977: Fig. 1) republished this columnar "Monument 1" from El Mesón, with the only existing drawing of its relief. His analysis fully confirms my placement of the sculpture in the Post-Olmec period.

Lee A. Parsons

One accompanying jade figure with drilled eyes, drooping mouth, and forward-turned headdress fits well into a Post-Olmec category of portable sculpture (Fig. 3). While the first radiocarbon determinations for this cache were *ca.* 1000 B.C., a Yale laboratory correction read as 372 ± 50 B.C., which now seems ideal for this assemblage of artifacts. Stela 17 (Fig. 4) is the second Danzante-type low-relief stela from Kaminaljuyú, which came to light in 1962. The contorted, old-man figure, with beard and staff and beaded necklace, imitates the qualities of Stela 9. (Beaded necklaces are also common on Monte Albán Danzantes.) The expanded belt is similar to that on archaistic Stela 9 at Cerro de las Mesas (Stirling 1943b), and the two-part skirt looks like that on the C-III-6 jade figure (Fig. 3), as well as one worn by a figure on Stela D at Tres Zapotes. Stela 17 precociously features a celestial band with a central symbol which reminds us both of the headdress-element on the local Stela 9 and, more particularly, the one featured on Stela 2 at La Venta (Heizer 1967: Pl. 2 and Fig 2).

Olmecoid Substyle (Low-Relief)

Another group of low-relief sculpture assigned to Post-Olmec Division III is only partially related to the special Danzante style and will be referred to as "Olmecoid" because of its obvious derivation from the earlier Olmec. (Two other variants of the Olmecoid substyle consisting of full-round sculpture will be treated separately). Stones included in the low-relief class are rock carvings, stelae and wall panels, and columnar basalts. The continued utilization of naturally occurring, volcanic, columnar basalt may be traced from Olmec La Venta to Post-Olmec Alvarado/El Mesón, Mound C-III-6 at Kaminaljuyú (Stela 9 and the three associated plain columns), and Naranjo on the northern outskirts of the same site where rows of such plain columns had been erected (Williamson 1887; Villacorta and Villacorta

Fig. 2 Stela 9, Kaminaljuyú, Mound C-III-6. Columnar basalt. Height, 145 cm.; width, 22 cm. No. 2359, Museo Nacional, Guatemala. Drawing by Ryntha J. Gibbs (after photographs courtesy of the Peabody Museum, Harvard University, Cambridge).

1927: 62), to Monument 2, Kaminaljuyú, which we are about to discuss. Stylistic qualities emphasize broad, flat relief and, for the first time, tightly rounded scroll motifs. Scenes lack framing borders, and profile "dragons" (Miles 1965: Fig. 2) become firmly entrenched in the iconographic repertoire.

Outside our southern area, I would like to suggest the following monuments as being representative of this substyle. First, Chalcatzingo's large Petroglyph 1 (Covarrubias 1957: Pl. 13), which is generally accepted as being Middle Preclassic and at the very least Late Olmec, has some special features (unlike the other petroglyphs at the site) that lead me to believe that it is Post-Olmec in style, although it may have been carved around 500 B.C. and may be one of the earliest examples in this new mode. The low-relief scene displaying a seated figure within a great, open, feline mouth illustrates a La Venta Olmec concept (*i.e.,* the niche figures on altars), but that concept also is perpetuated in Post-Olmec times, as we shall see in several examples to be cited. However, it is the mass of flat, tightly curved scrolls emanating from the open mouth that relates its carving style to others in this category.

Four low-relief stelae that may be considered Post-Olmec are found at San Miguel Amuco, Guerrero (Grove and Paradis 1971); Cerro de la Piedra, Alvarado, Veracruz (Medellín Zenil

Fig. 4 Stela 17, Kaminaljuyú. Height, 116 cm.; width, 62 cm.; depth, 36 cm. Museo Nacional, Guatemala. Photograph by the author, courtesy of the Milwaukee Public Museum, Milwaukee.

Fig. 3 Figurine from Kaminaljuyú, Mound C-III-6 cache. Jade. Height, 11.6 cm. Museo Nacional, Guatemala. Photograph by Edwin M. Shook, courtesy of the Peabody Museum, Harvard University, Cambridge.

1960b: Pl. 6); and Los Mangos, Catemaco, Veracruz (de la Fuente 1973: 160). Both the Guerrero and Catemaco stelae have geometric base-line motifs that relate their style period to the Alvarado stela and Stela D, Tres Zapotes (for the best photograph see Kubler 1975: Pl. 41). Stela D has several features that confirm a Post-Olmec assignment, most especially its conceptual relationship to the archaeologically dated Monument 2 at Izapa (Fig. 9), to be discussed below. The low-relief scene on Stela D is contained within a high-relief jaguar mouth. Carved on two sides are downward-directed dragon masks from whose snouts depend

265

Fig. 5 Stela 19, Kaminaljuyú. Height, 109 cm.; width, 105 cm. Joya Hairs Collection, Guatemala. Photograph courtesy of Joya Hairs.

broad, tightly curled volutes (Stirling 1943b: Pl. 14b and c).

In our southern coastal and highland region there are two rock carvings in Chiapas, one at Abaj Takalik, and five sculptures at Kaminaljuyú that may be accepted as Olmecoid low

reliefs. The first is a petroglyph at Xoc in northeastern Chiapas (Ekholm-Miller 1973). This is drafted in a provincial manner similar in many details to the San Miguel Amuco carving in Guerrero. The second is Petroglyph 1 at Tonalá on the Pacific coast of Chiapas (Ferdon 1953:

Pl. 23b), which may be classed as Olmecoid also. Its unusual features strongly resemble the full-round head from Medias Aguas, Sayula, Veracruz (Medellín Zenil 1960b: Pls. 4 and 5), a monument correctly called non-Olmec by de la Fuente (1973: 274).

Stela (wall panel?) 19 from Kaminaljuyú (Fig. 5; Easby and Scott 1970: No. 59) depicts a kneeling, dragon-masked figure grappling with a serpent that issues from the base of an upside-down, dragon-masked, trophy head. Its style and motifs can be placed confidently in the Post-Olmec period when compared with other sculptures. It has the flat relief, tightly rounded volutes, dynamic posture, and dragon masks replicated elsewhere. The tripart breast-medallion is duplicated on a Providencia Phase ceramic bowl in the Museo Nacional, Guatemala (personal observation). The peculiar knobbed elbow also is seen on a limb of the dragon on Monument 2, Kaminaljuyú (Miles 1965: Fig. 4a). The double scrolls on the cheek and earplug of the main figure are repeated on monster-masked Monument 3 at Monte Alto (Fig. 20), which in itself probably is a trophy head. An incomplete stone panel from Kaminaljuyú (Stela 4), which is a mate to Stela 19, was published by Miles (1965: 250 and Fig. 11c). Monument 2 from the *palangana,* or monument plaza, at the same site has a full-length dragon monster carved on two facets of a shaft of columnar basalt (Monument 2 is illustrated and described in Miles [1965: 247 and Fig. 10d; see also the drawing in Stone 1972: 47; and see Lothrop 1926: 155]). This suffices to confirm that the style and the dragon motifs of Monument 2 parallel details of Stelae 19 (Fig. 5), 4, and 5 at Kaminaljuyú. The important Stela 5 is also illustrated and discussed by Miles (1965: 251, Fig. 11b). Once again, its flat relief and complex dragon-mask details complement Monument 2. Its profile, puffy human face matches other Post-Olmec visages, especially in the Monte Alto subdivision. Stela 3, Kaminaljuyú (Miles 1965: 251 and Fig. 5a), bears a single, grooved-incised image of a ring-tailed fish; and I concur with Miles's argument for placing this in the same style division.

Finally, the grooved-incised boulder, Monument 6 from Abaj Takalik (Fig. 6; and Miles

Fig. 6 Monument 6, Abaj Takalik, Retalhuleu. Basalt boulder. Height, 110 cm.; length, 130 cm.; width, 90 cm. Museo Nacional, Guatemala. Photograph by the author, courtesy of the Milwaukee Public Museum, Milwaukee.

1965: 247 and Fig. 10b, which shows the opposite side), fits the Post-Olmec Division both on the basis of the unshaped basalt boulder and the simplicity of the broad, concentric grooves outlining the motifs. On two sides are depicted the profiles of a toad with avian characteristics, and on the top there is a grooved bird image with outstretched wings.

Olmecoid Substyle (Full-Round "Naturalistic")

Post-Olmec sculptures in full round seem to be unusually prolific in the Chiapas–Guatemala area. The remaining groups of sculpture to be analyzed fall into the full-round category (I will refer to comparative examples outside the area only where especially appropriate). Certain expressions, such as the Monte Alto colossal heads, seem to recall Olmec ideas, but tendencies toward regional idiosyncrasies, such as boulder sculptures and pedestal sculptures, seem to dominate.

The first substyle is a relatively naturalistic one and is included within the Olmecoid cluster because of its demonstrable Olmec heritage. In this, limbs and contours on seated or kneeling figures are modeled in the round; human faces may be fat, but take on a simplified

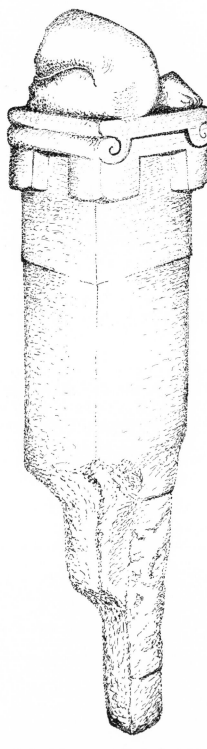

naturalism. Full-round animal representations are common, as well as pedestal bases to sculptures of several kinds. Before looking at the prime monumental examples of this class, we should examine briefly a group of related sculptures that are, in the main, portable.

The most remarkable special type consists of tall, vertical pedestal sculptures having square or round shafts, which may be two to three meters in height. (Recall that two such shafts were found in the Majadas Phase pit, along with Stela 9, at Kaminaljuyú.) These pedestals support naturalistically modeled human figures (often a scroll-ended bench is indicated under them) or full-round animal figures, such as monkeys, *pisotes,* and jaguars (*cf.* Miles 1965: 248 and Fig. 11d; Stone 1972: 68). Illustrate Pedestal Sculpture 6 from Kaminaljuyú (Fig. 7). Although broken, it exemplifies nicely the full-modeled, kneeling-human-figure type on a scroll-ended bench. Vertical pedestal sculptures seem to have their principal locus in the central Guatemalan highlands, from Patzún, Tecpan, and Chimaltenango, to Kaminaljuyú—a site that yielded at least seven. Other examples are reported from Chiapas to El Salvador.

Another type of sculpture which is more specifically "portable" than the above, has a short, stubby pedestal support; its distribution is similar to that of the tall pedestal monuments. The example from Tecpan shown by Doris Stone (1972: 69, right) is typical, with its leg and arm ligatures (emphasizing the heavy shoulders), the perforations between the limbs (recalling Diquís-region sculpture in Costa Rica), and its fat-featured face. The forward-turned-headdress type is identical to that on the Majadas jade figure from Kaminaljuyú (Fig. 3). A full-round seated-jaguar sculpture, about two feet in height, from Patzún (Linden Museum 1967: Pl. 86) relates to this group in general feeling, and in the way its arms are freed from the body.

A third specialized type of portable sculpture having the same distribution and the same probable time period is the so-called bench figure (which deserves a separate study in itself). I illustrate one, characteristically seated on a scroll-ended bench (Fig. 8; see also Miles

Fig. 7 Pedestal Sculpture 6, Kaminaljuyú, Mound C-III-4 complex. Height, 132 cm.; width, 25 cm. (pedestal base incomplete). Government zone, Kaminaljuyú. Drawing by Ryntha J. Gibbs (after photographs by Richard M. Rose).

1965: 250 and Fig. 10c; Easby and Scott 1970: No. 66). The prototype of such a figure originated on the Gulf Coast in La Venta IV times (*cf*. Monuments 21 and 40 at that site), but the small bench figures on the Pacific coast have Olmecoid faces and carving techniques. Like the above stubby pedestal sculptures, the arms are cut free from the body, and the heavy shoulders are always emphasized (*cf*. Altar 6, La Venta). Also, there is at least one variety of "mushroom stone" widespread in the southern highlands and coast which assuredly is Post-Olmec.[6] Their hemispherical caps are supported by full-round human or animal figures on square or round bases. They are stylistically identical to the effigies on pedestal sculptures (*cf*. Easby and Scott 1970: No. 63).

A unique type of stone carving that one normally associates with Olmec La Venta and San Lorenzo is the monolithic U-shaped drain trough. However, the fact that U-shaped stone drains also occur at Izapa (personal observation, 1970) and at Kaminaljuyú (Monuments 45 and 46) strongly suggests that their use may have continued into the Post-Olmec period in the south, or that there are other Late Olmec monuments yet to be discovered at those sites. Other unusual portable carvings associated with the Olmecoid classification are stone spheres with fat faces (for a possibly later example from Kaminaljuyú, see Easby and Scott 1970: No. 53), as well as various ball-game "knee yokes" (*yugitos*) and "handstones" (Covarrubias 1957: Pl. 9, lower right; Borhegyi 1961a: Fig. 8), and some of the widespread stone funerary masks (Covarrubias 1957: Pl. 10, lower left, which bears Olmecoid incised scrolls; see also Easby and Scott 1970: No. 70). Finally, I wish to mention the green soapstone mask we found at Monte Alto (Stuart and Stuart 1969: 198). It will be argued elsewhere that this also is a Post-Olmec kind of expression.

To return to the more monumental exam-

Fig. 8 Bench figure, from near Villa Flores, highland Chiapas. Fine-grained black stone. Height, 17.5 cm. The Metropolitan Museum of Art, New York. Photograph by Charles Uht, courtesy of the Metropolitan Museum of Art, New York.

ples of Olmecoid full-round, "naturalistic" sculpture, we should begin with Monument 2 at Izapa (Fig. 9). This much-battered monument portrays a life-sized, Olmecoid seated figure within the open jaws of a jaguar. It is probably one of the earliest sculptures at Izapa, having been dated to at least 500 B.C. by ceramic associations in its original platform (Gareth Lowe, personal communication, 1965). Stela D at Tres Zapotes is entirely comparable,

---

[6] See Borhegyi (1961b) for one of the best general classifications and discussions of mushroom stones. A recent in-depth study (Rose n.d.) of these enigmatic objects relates their function to the ball-game complex rather than to their fortuitous mushroom shapes.

Fig. 9 Monument 2, Izapa, Group B, Mound 30. Andesite. Height, 235 cm.; width, 175 cm.; depth, 60 cm. *In situ,* Izapa, Chiapas. Photograph by the author, courtesy of the Milwaukee Public Museum, Milwaukee.

with its half-round jaguar mouth framing a low-relief scene, and with its basal motif. The geometric base line, with diagonal and Tau motifs, on Monument 2 is almost identical to that on the Alvarado stela, as mentioned. More important for chronology, the same base line is represented on a Francesa Phase (*ca.* 450–250 B.C.) incised shell from Chiapa de Corzo which also has Olmecoid-looking human figures (Lee 1969: Fig. 129). There is a similar Olmecoid monumental sculpture from Tiltepec on the Pacific coast of Chiapas now in the Tuxtla Gutiérrez regional museum (personal

observation), with jaguar mouth surrounding a high-relief squatting figure.[7]

Another naturalistically modeled sculpture long known from the vicinity of Izapa is sufficiently Olmec in feeling that Easby and Scott (1970: No. 35) included it in their Olmec chapter. This writer, on the other hand, has always considered that particular anthropomorphic rampant jaguar to be Post-Olmec because of its stylistic relationship to the Sin Cabezas sculptures (Figs. 10 and 11), its non-Olmec ankle ruffs, and details of the feline face which may be compared with certain pedestal sculpture figures. (The forward-turned headdress, once again, has been established as occurring in this phase by the figurine in Fig. 3).

In addition to the above, the epitome of this category of Olmecoid sculpture is represented by the four sculptures from Sin Cabezas, near Tiquisate, Escuintla (Shook 1950; Parsons and Jenson 1965). Two of them are illustrated here (Figs. 10 and 11). These are seated, cross-legged human figures with full-rounded modeling and a minimum of adornment. One of them (see Parsons and Jenson 1965: 143) seems to have held a baby in its lap, and another (Fig. 11) has a potbelly like those of a large category of Monte Alto-related sculptures (see Fig. 42). It also has leg ligatures, and the right hand is perforated. Interestingly, this group retains rough-rounded pedestal bases showing the original outlines of the boulders from which they were carved (a feature that aligns well with this Post-Olmec phase). Fortunately, there is for comparison, another similar small sculpture from a private collection in Antigua (Fig. 12), which has not lost its head. Although helmeted in a way reminiscent of Olmec figures, the character of its face would never be confused with classic Olmec. Also, there is a pair of small *sin cabezas* sculptures, shown kneeling on

---

[7] Stirling (1965:723) has logically suggested some kind of developmental sequence of this theme including Stela 1 at La Venta (the half-round standing figure in a rectangular niche with a jaguar mask above), Stela D at Tres Zapotes, and Monument 2 at Izapa, which leads to the conceptual layout of later Izapan narrative stelae with their celestial and terrestrial bands, derived from the framing-jaguar-mouth concept.

Fig. 10 Monument 1, Sin Cabezas, near Tiquisate, Escuintla. Total height, 105 cm.; figure height, 35 cm. Bartolomé de las Casas School, Tiquisate. Photograph by Edwin M. Shook, courtesy of the Peabody Museum, Harvard University, Cambridge.

heavy, rounded pedestal bases, recently found on the coast in the Department of Suchitepequez (Jorge Castillo Collection, Guatemala City, personal observation, 1977). These are without question the same type and style, and all of them resemble certain vertical pedestal figures (Fig. 7). In addition, a sculpture from the Preclassic site of El Balsamo, Escuintla, was misidentified by me (Parsons 1969: Pl. 54a). This actually is a Sin Cabezas-type rounded pedestal sculpture which has lost its head. In Classic Period times a Xipe-like face was pecked into its broken neck area.

Olmecoid Substyle (Full-Round "Engaged" Relief)

The last class of monumental sculpture that can be called in any sense Olmecoid comprises an even larger group of stones in the southern area. The subject matter mainly consists of seated or rampant anthropomorphic feline monsters and grotesque feline masks. Their eyes are consistently delineated as rounded rectangles. Included in the forms are rigid seated figures with hands on knees and flat bases and backs. (It may be significant to note here that the backs of Gulf Coast colossal stone heads invariably are artificially flattened.)

Fig. 11 Monument 3, Sin Cabezas, near Tiquisate, Escuintla. Total height, 78 cm.; figure height, 46 cm. Bartolomé de las Casas School, Tiquisate. Photograph by the author, courtesy of the Milwaukee Public Museum, Milwaukee.

271

Fig. 12 Seated rounded pedestal sculpture, provenience unknown. Height, *ca.* 50 cm. Private collection, Antigua, Guatemala. Photograph by Edwin M. Shook, courtesy of the Peabody Museum, Harvard University, Cambridge.

Glyphlike symbols, medallions, and disks on torsos are regular additive elements. Zoomorphs, boulder sculptures, and Monte Alto-related full-round forms also occur. On all of the above, limbs and features are carved in a half-round or flat "engaged" relief. In other words, in this substyle Olmecoid subject matter is predominant, but the handling of the stones employs both Olmecoid and Monte Alto techniques.

One of the new, unpublished, sculpture discoveries made by Pennsylvania State University during its extensive excavation project at and around Kaminaljuyú (beginning in 1968 under William Sanders) is a headless seated figure with hands on its folded legs (Monument 62, Fig. 13). Carved on the torso is an Olmecoid face with knotted headband. That face, the posture, and the relatively flat bottom and back of the monument introduce the first category of Olmecoid full-round "engaged" relief. Surprisingly, there is a comparable seated, headless sculpture with the known provenience of Chalcatzingo, Morelos (Fig. 14). Like Petroglyph 1 at that site, I feel that this full-round work may be Post-Olmec. It has the same compact character as Monument 62, and its torso is emblazoned with both a St. Andrew's cross and a double crenelated emblem which retains Olmec iconography. Another broken, newly discovered sculpture from Solano in the Valley of Guatemala (Fig. 15) represents a seated, cross-legged figure with hands on the knees. It has a beaded belt on the front, and the base and back are pecked flat, with a straight groove dividing the lower and upper body. Unfortunately, the above three sculptures being head-

Fig. 13 Monument 62, Kaminaljuyú, *palangana* (monument plaza). Height, 69 cm.; width, 74 cm. Government zone, Kaminaljuyú. Photograph courtesy of the Pennsylvania State University, University Park.

Fig. 14 Seated figure, Chalcatzingo, Morelos. Height, *ca.* 60 cm. Museo Nacional de Antropología, Mexico. Photograph by the author, courtesy of the Milwaukee Public Museum, Milwaukee.

Fig. 15 Seated figure, from Solano, Valley of Guatemala. Height, *ca.* 90 cm. Finca Solano(?), Valley of Guatemala. Photograph courtesy of the Pennsylvania State University, University Park.

Fig. 16 Monument 60, Kaminaljuyú. Height, 57 cm.; width, 45 cm.; depth, 30 cm. Private collection, Antigua, Guatemala. Drawing by Ryntha J. Gibbs (after photographs by Edwin M. Shook).

less, we cannot be certain if their faces were anthropomorphic-feline or human, though I suspect the latter. A small sculpture from Kaminaljuyú (Monument 60, Fig. 16) has the same flat base and back with dividing groove. This compact fat figure is seated in the hands-on-knees posture, though the presumed folded legs have been flaked away. (Also, the nose has been filed down and the sagittal crest is damaged.) The rectilinear sagging breasts remind one of the treatment on the peg-based pedestal sculpture illustrated by Stone (1972: 69). The hooded human face has a feline aspect to its mouth (note the fanged corners, exposed upper gum, and single tooth), and scrolls curl back from the sides of the head. The latter trait is also featured on the next sculpture (Fig. 17b) and on Monument 3 at Monte Alto (Fig. 20).

A remarkable, monumental, Olmecoid sculpture has long been known from Palo Gordo, Suchitepequez, on the Guatemalan Pacific coast (Fig. 17a), having been photographed by Robert Burkitt about 1929 (Fig. 17b). It was then published by the late Franz Termer (1942, 1973) who excavated at the site. To this day it is worshipped by migrant highland Indians as the local *piedra santa*. Although mentioned by Miles (1965: 246), its iconographic significance has not been fully appreciated. This is an enormous flat-backed and flat-based sculpture representing a seated, anthropomorphic feline monster with hands resting on the knees. The feet are turned to the centerline, and arm bands emphasize the heavy shoulders. The feline head has flat scrolls above the spooled ears on each side, and a huge, projecting "upper lip." Note, in front view, that the real nose and nostrils are perched above this "snout."[8] For comparison see Monument 42, Kaminaljuyú (Fig. 18), Altar 12 at the same site (Fig. 19), and Monu-

a

b

Fig. 17 *Piedra santa*, Palo Gordo, Suchitepequez. Granite. Height, 155 cm.; width, 123 cm.; depth, 70 cm. Approximately *in situ*, Palo Gordo. *a*. Front view. Inset at upper left is the 70-centimeter-square shield emblem on the back of the head. Drawings by the author (after photographs by Robert Burkitt and the actual monument). *b*. Side view. Photograph by Robert Burkitt, *ca.* 1929, courtesy of the University Museum, University of Pennsylvania, Philadelphia.

---

[8] This element was broken off even before Burkitt's time and reattached by a *finca* administrator. It was cemented in place when I saw the monument in 1961, but today it is missing again. The Burkitt photo (Fig. 17b), however, shows the snout in place. Termer had good reason to believe that the replaced snout was not the original one (personal communication, 1967), though comparative evidence of related sculptures convinces me that the snout in the Burkitt photo, or one very much like it, must have belonged to this sculpture.

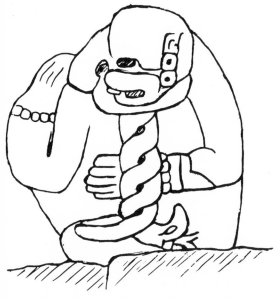

Fig. 18 Monument 42, Kaminaljuyú, between Mound C-III-2 and *palangana* (monument plaza). Height, 130 cm.; width, 124 cm.; depth, 50 cm. *In situ,* Kaminaljuyú. Drawing by the author (from photographs and the actual monument).

ment 3, Monte Alto (Fig. 20). The rounded-rectangle eyes are bracketed by scrolled supra- and suborbital elements. Below the drooping mouth, and under the pendent upper lip, emerge a pair of twisted serpents which trail off to each side. This feature has its prototype in the seated Olmec feline from Los Soldados, Veracruz (de la Fuente 1973: 162), where a

pair of twisted serpentlike elements drops from the mouth. (A braided serpent also hangs from the collar of the sculpture to be discussed next [Fig. 18]).

The Palo Gordo sculpture also bears several symbols that carry over from Olmec iconography. Carved on the flattened back of the head is a "feathered"-shield emblem (Fig. 17a, upper left) containing the ubiquitous Preclassic U motif; it is surrounded by imbricated U forms. On the front torso, below the collar, is a series of three stacked symbols, with the U motif featured in the belt area. Resting above this, in the navel area, is a crenelated motif already noted on the belt of the Chalcatzingo figure (Fig. 14), which also occurs on the Humboldt celt (see Joralemon 1971: motif 159, for this symbol in Olmec art). Falling from the collar is a Tau-shaped medallion with five water-drop elements. A pectoral on the left figure of La Venta Stela 3 (Heizer 1967: Fig. 1) is comparable to this, as is a Monte Albán Danzante glyph (Paddock 1966: Fig. 36, lower left). All three of these examples have five pendent water drops. Does this trinity of symbols connote sky (Tau-with-water), earth (crenelated "vegetation"), and underworld (U-shaped "earth bowl")? If so, we have a simple glyphic statement in Post-Olmec times on the southern coast. Further, the shield emblem on the back of the head possibly encompasses the same statement in one sign, showing the cosmos in "plan" view. The less glyphic iconography of

Fig. 19 Zoomorphic Altar 12, Kaminaljuyú, *palangana* (monument plaza). Length, 150 cm.; width, 106 cm.; depth, 50 cm. Museo Nacional, Guatemala. Photograph by Richard M. Rose.

Fig. 20 Monument 3, Monte Alto, Escuintla. Height, 153 cm.; width, 85 cm.; depth, 150 cm.; circumference, 430 cm. Plaza, La Democracia, Escuintla. Photograph by the author, courtesy of the Milwaukee Public Museum, Milwaukee.

Petroglyph 1 at Chalcatzingo may well represent the same series of concepts, but I do not have space to elaborate here.

Monument 42 (Fig. 18) was unearthed at Kaminaljuyú by Gustavo Espinoza (1960). It was located on a stone-lined platform in flat terrain just north of Mound C-III-2, and just south of the *palangana,* where the large sculpture remains *in situ* (for an excellent published photograph see Kusch 1962: Pl. 4). While this is an anthropomorphic boulder sculpture (the back is unworked and the carving follows the contours of the stone), the subject matter resembles the Olmecoid monument at Palo Gordo. Here, the feline-monster head is shown in left profile, with its prodigious "snout" projecting to the side. The eye is a rounded rectangle, as are the double-scrolled earplugs; a single upper tooth is shown under heavy lips. (Note also the eye-ear line, which may be

demonstrated on other Post-Olmec pedestal sculptures and mushroom stones.) The right arm is drawn up with the hand touching the shoulder, and the legs seem to be tucked in at the bottom. The figure wears beaded bracelets, and the left arm has a cuff. A braided serpent with forked tongue depends from the plain collar.

The Pennsylvania State University project discovered the enormous zoomorphic Altar 12 (Fig. 19) in its *palangana* excavations at Kaminaljuyú. This reptilian monster sports our same projecting upper lip with nose on top and rounded-rectangle eyes (not visible in Fig. 19). Not unexpectedly, in the Post-Olmec context, we also find well-defined bunched shoulders. Related zoomorphic stone altars become more prevalent in the subsequent Izapan period.

Monument 3 at Monte Alto (Fig. 20; Parsons and Jenson 1965: 138) is an aberrant boulder sculpture at that site, in that it is clearly in the Olmecoid tradition rather than the baby-faced Monte Alto style. It is a feline-monster-masked head which resembles the anthropomorphic felines I have been writing about (including the profile-masked figure on low-relief Stela 19 at Kaminaljuyú, Fig. 5). Further, this kind of mask becomes common in the Izapan horizon where a number may be cited, including Uaxactún's E-VII-sub stucco masks and the three large stone censers from Kaminaljuyú's Miraflores Phase (*cf.* Miles 1965: Fig. 16a). In fact, this boulder sculpture may be an early example of a much larger tradition leading into Classic Maya architectural masks. Be that as it may, we see here in relatively high relief the familiar fanged jaguar mouth, the blocky protruding upper lip with nostrils above, rounded rectangular eyes, volutes leading off the sides of the head, double-scrolled earplugs, and double-scrolls on the cheeks.

Two comparable, unpublished, feline-headed sculptures may be cited from the Guatemalan coast. One is a small, eroded, full-round head that we discovered at Finca Santa Clara, Santa Rosa, in 1969 (Fig. 21). It has a down-turned feline mouth with fangs, a tongue or bib, projecting upper lip and nose, and the Post-Olmec eye form. Another sculpture was found by Francis B. Richardson at Finca La

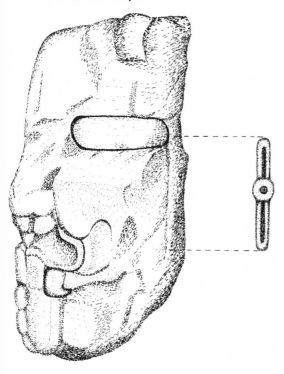

Fig. 21 Feline head, Monument 5, Santa Clara, Santa Rosa. Inset to the right shows the ear form which is extant only on the opposite side of the head. Height, 78 cm.; width, 45 cm.; depth, 42 cm. Finca Santa Clara, Santa Rosa. Drawings by Ryntha J. Gibbs (after photographs by the author).

Flora, Escuintla (Fig. 22). This unusual full-round sculpture has a smoothed cylindrical base surmounted by a very eroded feline head resembling the last object.

The remaining group of Olmecoid monuments relates to the Monte Alto style of full-round human potbelly sculptures, although the subject matter shows predominantly anthropomorphic felines. The relief is "engaged," and legs are shown wrapped around the bases of the figures. The first is another sculpture from La Flora (Fig. 23), discovered and published by Richardson (1940: Pl. 19c). This depicts a hooded, fang-face creature whose arms hold a scored "pad" at the midriff. The ovoid breast medallion has three pendent hooked elements reminiscent of the Palo Gordo medallion. The back of this sculpture, typically, is flattened.

Monument 5, Kaminaljuyú (Fig. 24), has a deeply indented feline mouth and ovoid eyes

(the top of the head is sheared off). The treatment of the mouth and nose area is remarkably similar to that on the curiously non-Olmec stone head from Medias Aguas, Veracruz (Medellín Zenil 1960b: Pls. 4 and 5), as well as on Petroglyph 1 at Tonalá, Chiapas (Ferdon 1953: Pl. 23b). The figure wears a plain collar, and its low-relief arms grasp a disk-shaped medallion on the front of the torso, which is attached to the collar by a band. Its legs are pulled around the base and the back of the sculpture is flattened. Monument 15, Kaminaljuyú (Fig. 25) has a turret-shaped head with ovoid eyes and mouth (the right corner has a drilled pit). Its right arm holds a forked wand and its legs are wrapped around the bottom. A kind of low-relief chasuble is draped over the shoulders with a disk-shaped medallion on the front and a shieldlike emblem, with knotted bow, on the back. (Headless Monument 11 from the same site is a mate to Monument 15, while Monument 9 [Lothrop 1926: Fig. 55b] is also comparable in its torso disk and eye-mouth treatment.) A concave disk broken from

Fig. 22 Feline-headed sculpture, La Flora, Escuintla. Dimensions unknown; probably comparable to Figure 23. Finca La Flora(?), Escuintla. Photograph by Francis B. Richardson, 1938, courtesy of the Peabody Museum, Harvard University, Cambridge.

Fig. 23 Full-round sculpture, La Flora, Escuintla. Height, 140 cm. Finca La Flora(?), Escuintla. Photograph by Francis B. Richardson, 1938, courtesy of the Peabody Museum, Harvard University, Cambridge.

such a sculpture was excavated in the fill of a Terminal Preclassic mound at Kaminaljuyú (Shook 1971: 75), suggesting an even earlier date for the original monument type.

In 1970 we discovered a full-round rampant-jaguar sculpture at Finca Hamburgo, Suchitepequez (Fig. 26), which may be placed in this general group of Post-Olmec monuments. Its paws are poised upward, while its legs crouch at the base. The head is perfectly feline and the eyes, characteristically, are rounded rectangles.

A half-dozen, unpublished, full-round sculp-

tures were found by Carlos Navarrete at the site of Tiltepec on the Chiapas coast near Tonalá. (These may be seen today in the regional museum at Tuxtla Gutiérrez; for a related sculpture, see Navarrete 1959: Fig. 8d). They feature puffy, closed-eyed faces and engaged low-relief arms and legs which encircle minimally shaped cylindrical boulders. The top of one of these monuments has a series of simplified faces in cartouche forms that are identical to the seemingly non-Olmec colossal-head fragment found at San Miguel, Tabasco (Stirling 1957: Pl. 50). Taking into account excavation information from Navarrete, John Scott

Fig. 24 Monument 5, Kaminaljuyú, *palangana* (monument plaza). Height, 100 cm.; width, 68 cm. Aurora Park Zoo, Guatemala. Photograph by the author, courtesy of the Milwaukee Public Museum, Milwaukee.

Fig. 25 Monument 15, Kaminaljuyú. Height, 90 cm., width, 80 cm. Museo Nacional, Guatemala. Photograph by the author, courtesy of the Milwaukee Public Museum, Milwaukee.

(1976: 384) places these Tiltepec sculptures in our Post-Olmec period. A final Olmecoid sculpture that should be mentioned from our area is Monument 5, Tonalá (Ferdon 1953: Pl. 20e). This is a relatively small stone head showing a trefoil form falling from its heavy upper lip. The head features a sagittal crest reminiscent of both Monument 5, La Venta (Stirling 1943b: Pl. 45a), and potbelly Monument 47, Bilbao (Fig. 41).

For comparative purposes, I shall list a few Post-Olmec, Olmecoid, full-round monuments outside of the southern Chiapas–Guatemala area. I would include duck-billed Monument 5 from Cerro de las Mesas (Stirling 1943b: Pl. 28) and, of course, the Olmecoid monument from Huamelulpan in northern Oaxaca (Paddock 1966: Fig. 2). Then, at a site near Ometepec on coastal Guerrero is a headless crouching-jaguar sculpture (Fig. 27) which, curiously,

is nearly identical in form to the Preclassic sculpture found by Dieseldorff and Maudslay in the fill under Stela 5 at far-away Copán, Honduras (Fig. 28).

Monte Alto Substyle (Colossal Heads)

I will finish this survey of Post-Olmec monuments with the Monte Alto style itself, and illustrate herewith all eleven of the boulder sculptures found at the type site (Olmecoid Monument 3, Fig. 20, has already been discussed). Three categories of Monte Alto sculptures may be distinguished: colossal stone heads, full-figure boulder sculptures (the only two types found at Finca Monte Alto, Escuintla), and full-round potbelly sculptures (widely dispersed in the southern Chiapas–Guatemala region, following the distribution of Olmecoid full-round sculpture). All Monte

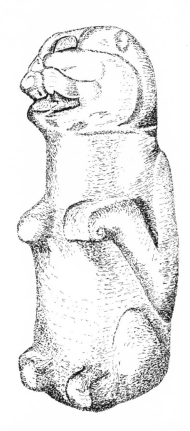

Fig. 26 Rampant jaguar, Hamburgo, Suchitepequez. Height, 125 cm.; width, 60 cm. Finca Hamburgo, Suchitepequez. Drawing by Ryntha J. Gibbs (after photographs by the author).

279

Fig. 27 Headless jaguar sculpture, from near Ometepec, Guerrero. Height, *ca.* 75 cm. Now at a site called Piedra Labrada, Guerrero. Photograph courtesy of Louisa Stark and Jane Rosenthal.

Fig. 28 Headless jaguar sculpture, from beneath Stela 5, Copán, Honduras. Height, *ca.* 90 cm. Archaeological zone, Copán. Photograph by the author, courtesy of the Milwaukee Public Museum, Milwaukee.

Alto-style sculptures have modified "baby-face" features, and usually have puffy, closed eyes. They are relatively devoid of adornment except for occasional earplugs, collars, medallions, and, rarely, loincloths. Relief is low and engaged to the stones. Boulder sculptures, including the colossal heads, are just that: carved features tend to follow the contours of volcanic basalt boulders like those still strewn on the alluvial plain, while the bottoms and backs of the stones are not worked at all. The smaller, full-round, potbelly sculptures, however, almost invariably have intentionally flattened backs. Limbs tend to encircle the stone forms, with the soles of the feet almost touching.

A few comments are in order for evidence on the absolute dating of Monte Alto sculpture, although this is not the place to summarize fully the Parsons and Shook excavation project at Monte Alto. Miles (1965) argued on stylistic grounds for a pre-Olmec dating and assigned the group to her sculpture Division I. Recent Guatemalan propaganda (see Girard 1969) also insists that the monuments now moved to the plaza at La Democracia, Escuintla, belong to the "cradle of Olmec civilization." Shook (1971: 75), on the other hand, cautiously equates their carving to the peak, Late Preclassic, occupation phase at Monte Alto, which he dates to 300 B.C.–A.D. 1. This researcher would accept the early part of this range as overlapping the style period but, on the basis of all the comparative evidence already presented, places them in a Post-Olmec 500–200 B.C. phase. The firmest evidence for this earlier dating comes from Santa Leticia, El Salvador, where Stanley Boggs excavated beneath three huge Monte Alto-style boulder sculptures (Fig. 39). These apparently had been *in situ* on a terraced platform, where radiocarbon analysis associated charcoal yielded the dates 561 ± 150 B.C. and 620 ± 150 B.C. (Ball 1975). Therefore, our date of 500 B.C. for the inception of the style could be slightly conservative.

As has been noted frequently, even sculptures weighing many tons were moved about in Pre-Columbian times and reused. (This tradition has not ceased; in 1970, the newly discovered Monument 10 (Fig. 33), was moved to New York City for the "Before Cortés" exhibition [Easby and Scott 1970: No. 52], and later returned to La Democracia.) The eleven monuments at Monte Alto were no exception, and, therefore, little evidence was obtained as to their primary dating. (Only Monument 11, Fig. 38, was found on some sort of original stone rubble platform, on the north-south centerline of the mound group. The latest associated pottery was Terminal Preclassic, so even this may not have been in its first location.) Six of the other monuments were found haphazardly lined up on the east margin of the site (four of these were illustrated in Richardson 1940: Pl. 18), and the remaining four turned up on the west side. None of these were *in situ* in terms of construction platforms or meaningful associations.

Another common class of sculptures at Monte Alto was plain, tabular stone stelae (fifteen) and plain altars (three). Considering the abundance of both plain and carved stelae and altars at Terminal Preclassic Izapa, farther west on the coast, I would conjecture that these represent the true sculptural effort contemporary with the major occupation phase at Monte Alto, with the boulder sculptures having been reset from the previous phase when the site was also occupied. In other words, by Izapan times, Monte Alto must have been surpassed in creative accomplishment by both Izapa and Miraflores Kaminaljuyú.

Five of the boulder sculptures at Monte Alto are colossal heads (plus the aberrant Monument 3, Fig. 20). These comprise Monuments 1, 2, 7, 8, and 10 (Figs. 29–33). Numbers 1 and 2 were on the east side of the site, and 7, 8, and 10 on the west side. All of them

have smooth-pecked bald heads, heavy-lidded closed eyes, and expressionless mouths. An inverted V-shaped groove separates the nose, mouth, and chin from the fat cheeks, and there usually is a bulge or indented furrow between the brows (see Monuments 8 and 10). Three of them have C- or hook-shaped ears with either round or rounded-square earspools. (Comparable ear types may be seen on the Monte Albán Danzantes.) Two (Monuments 8 and 10) have simple, tabular-shaped ears, like some of the Olmecoid stone funerary masks. As with the ancestral Olmec colossal stone heads, these seem to represent the severed trophies of departed dignitaries. At Monte Alto, unlike the Olmec area, the heads are clearly depicted as dead. New evidence for the trophy-head concept is provided by the intentionally headless potbelly sculpture from El Baul (Fig. 44). As yet, Monte Alto-style colossal heads have not been found at any but the type site.

Monte Alto Substyle (Full-Figure Boulders)

Five monuments at Monte Alto are human-effigy boulder sculptures: Monuments 4, 5, 6, 9, and 11 (Figs. 34–8). Three were found on the east margin of the site (Monuments 4–6), one on the west (Monument 9), and one in the center (Monument 11). All of them have neckless fat-faced heads comparable in style to the colossal heads. All but one (Monument 6, Fig. 36) have the same closed eyes and a similar variety of ear forms. The bulging bodies have low-relief limbs wrapped around their circumferences, and there is an attempt to join the soles of the feet at the midline. Monument 6 (Fig. 36) differs from the others not only in the fact that its eyes are open, but in that it has upper arm ligatures, a plain collar, and an attached scroll-bracketed breast medallion containing four horizontal bands. Monument 11 (Fig. 38) also differs in having a squared depression in its breast, which must have contained some kind of inlay.

The only other known site with comparable large boulder sculptures is Santa Leticia, near Apaneca, on the coast of El Salvador not far from the Guatemalan border. The three human-effigy boulder sculptures there were first reported by Habel (1878: 32), and recently re-

Fig. 29 Monument 1, Monte Alto, Escuintla. Height, 127 cm.; width, 143 cm.; depth, 140 cm.; circumference, 417 cm. Plaza, La Democracia, Escuintla. Photograph by Peter S. Jenson, courtesy of the Milwaukee Public Museum, Milwaukee.

Fig. 30 Monument 2, Monte Alto, Escuintla. Height, 147 cm.; width, 200 cm.; depth, 180 cm.; circumference, 605 cm. Plaza, La Democracia, Escuintla. Photograph by Peter S. Jenson, courtesy of the Milwaukee Public Museum, Milwaukee.

Fig. 31 Monument 7, Monte Alto, Escuintla. Height, 140 cm.; width, 102 cm.; depth, 185 cm.; circumference, 477 cm. Plaza, La Democracia, Escuintla. Photograph by Francis E. Ross.

Fig. 32 Monument 8, Monte Alto, Escuintla. Height, 91 cm.; width, 105 cm.; depth, 88 cm., circumference, 335 cm. Plaza, La Democracia, Escuintla. Photograph by Francis E. Ross.

Fig. 33 Monument 10, Monte Alto, Escuintla. Height, 145 cm.; width, 110 cm.; depth, 130 cm.; circumference, 376 cm. Plaza, La Democracia, Escuintla. Photograph by Edwin M. Shook.

investigated by Boggs. (The possible sixth-century-B.C. dating for these has already been mentioned.) These differ from the Monte Alto figures mainly in displaying large, ruptured navels (see Fig. 39 for Monument 3 at that site).

Monte Alto Substyle (Full-Round Potbelly Sculptures)

The last Post-Olmec variety of stone monument is apparently an offshoot of the effigy boulder sculptures at the central site of Monte Alto. However, we have no clue as to whether they are contemporary, or somewhat earlier or later, although a seriation could be proposed. I have selected five representative potbelly sculptures for illustration, but see Table 2 for a more complete tabulation and distribution. (There is a total of thirty-four, to my knowledge, in the southern Chiapas–Guatemala region, not including a dozen portable "potbellies.") The greatest single concentration of this type of sculpture is at Kaminaljuyú (other than the cluster in the Department of Escuintla). Several of them were found in the *palangana*, which I have always called a "monument plaza" for Preclassic sculpture (see

TABLE 2. DISTRIBUTION OF MONTE ALTO-STYLE FULL-ROUND POTBELLY SCULPTURES

Pacific Coast (Chiapas to El Salvador)

Tonalá–Tapanatepec, Chiapas	1
La Unidad, Chiapas (near Guatemalan border)	2
Abaj Takalik, Retalhuleu	2
Sololá (Tiquisate), Escuintla	3
Bilbao, Escuintla	3
El Baul, Escuintla	1
La Gomera, Escuintla	2
Concepción, Escuintla	3
Obero, Escuintla	2
La Nueva, Jutiapa (near El Salvador border)	2
	21

Guatemalan Highlands

Lake Atitlán	1
Utatlán	1
Antigua	1
Kaminaljuyú	10
	13
Total	34

Fig. 34 Monument 4, Monte Alto, Escuintla. Height, 157 cm.; width, 180 cm.; depth, 170 cm.; circumference, 570 cm. Plaza, La Democracia, Escuintla. Photograph by Peter S. Jenson, courtesy of the Milwaukee Public Museum, Milwaukee.

Fig. 35 Monument 5, Monte Alto, Escuintla. Height, 138 cm.; width, 203 cm.; depth, 202 cm.; circumference, 635 cm. Plaza, La Democracia, Escuintla. Photograph by Peter S. Jenson, courtesy of the Milwaukee Public Museum, Milwaukee.

Fig. 36 Monument 6, Monte Alto, Escuintla. Height, 122 cm.; width, 120 cm.; depth, 125 cm.; circumference, 417 cm. Plaza, La Democracia, Escuintla. Photograph by Joya Hairs, Guatemala.

Fig. 37 Monument 9, Monte Alto, Escuintla. Height, 185 cm.; width, 130 cm.; depth, 110 cm.; circumference, 336 cm. Plaza, La Democracia, Escuintla. Photograph by Francis E. Ross.

Fig. 38 Monument 11, Monte Alto, Escuintla. Height, 154 cm.; width, 150 cm.; depth, 180 cm.; circumference, 505 cm. Plaza, La Democracia, Escuintla. Photograph by Francis E. Ross.

Lothrop 1926: Fig. 57). Some of them have been found reused in Late Classic settings, but most have no known chronological context. Many of them were discovered with their heads mutilated or broken off.

Full-round potbelly sculptures are of smaller scale than the boulder sculptures at Monte Alto, but most of them have similar "baby faces" with heavy closed eyes; engaged, wrap-around limbs with hands holding protruding bellies; and characteristically flattened backs. There is a tendency for somewhat greater orna-mentation (like Monument 6 at the type site, Fig. 36), including plain or dentate collars, medallions, and occasional navels and loin-cloths. Ears and earspools are in the Monte Alto fashion.

My first example is an unpublished stone presently in the storeroom of the Museo Na-cional de Antropología in Mexico City, which came from the coast of Chiapas (Fig. 40). Its most special feature is a deer-head(?) medallion

attached to a plain collar. Its flat back shows tassels behind the collar. Monument 47 from Bilbao, Escuintla (Fig. 41), now in Berlin, is one of the few that has a rough-rounded back and that presents a more fetal aspect. Note the navel, dentate collar, and sagittal crest (remi-niscent, once again, of Monument 5 at La Venta [Stirling 1943b: Pl. 45a]). Monument 58 from Bilbao (Fig. 42) has as its peculiar features crossed legs, a true potbelly, and up-ward-tilted head. Another sculpture, which has been in the American Museum of Natural His-tory since 1863 (Fig. 43), has as its recorded provenience Utatlán in the Guatemalan high-lands. It is the most typical of the group illus-trated here, closely resembling the ten recorded for Kaminaljuyú. The fifth example (Fig. 44) was discovered in 1976 or 1977 at El Baul, Escuintla. Its unique feature is not that the head is presently missing, but that it was conceived as a decapitated figure. The round stump of the neck is finished carving, raised four centi-meters from the shoulders. This fact lends sup-port to the idea of a trophy-head cult on the

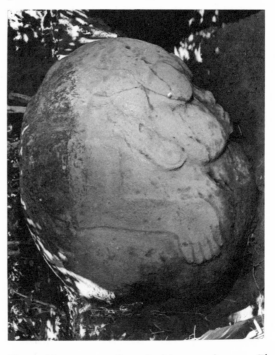

Fig. 39 Monument 3, Santa Leticia, near Apaneca, El Salvador. Height, 170 cm.; width, 140 cm.; depth, 150 cm. Finca Santa Leticia, El Salvador. Photograph cour-tesy of Stanley H. Boggs.

Fig. 40 (above, left) Potbelly sculpture, from between Tonalá and Tapanatepec, Chiapas. Height, 68 cm.; width, 58 cm. No. 24-1249/46719, Museo Nacional de Antropología, Mexico. Photograph by the author, courtesy of the Milwaukee Public Museum, Milwaukee.

Fig. 41 (above) Monument 47, Bilbao, Escuintla. Height, 110 cm.; width, 90 cm. No. IV Ca 7197, Museum für Völkerkunde, Berlin. Photograph courtesy of the Museum für Völkerkunde, Berlin.

Fig. 42 (left) Monument 58, Bilbao, Escuintla. Height, 132 cm.; width, 80 cm. Ricardo Muñoz Collection, Finca Las Ilusiones, Santa Lucia Cotzumalhuapa. Photograph by the author, courtesy of the Milwaukee Public Museum, Milwaukee.

Fig. 43 Potbelly sculpture, Utatlán, Guatemala. Height, 114 cm. No. 30/76, American Museum of Natural History, New York. Photograph courtesy of the American Museum of Natural History, New York.

coast in Post-Olmec times. Also, the unusual cross-armed posture (not unusual in Classic Period Cotzumalhuapa sculpture) may be another sign of a death pose. This potbelly figure has a navel, loincloth, and legs hunched close to the base.

In conclusion, I should mention some far-flung examples of potbelly-related sculptures, which, in this case, may indicate reverse diffusion of an established, regional, southern Pacific style to the Gulf Coast and other regions during the Post-Olmec period. In contrast, during Late Olmec times, movements of ideas had been primarily in the opposite direction, help-

ing to create new Olmecoid sculptural styles in remote regions. A headless potbelly sculpture found in the foundation of Stela 4 at Copán, Honduras has been cited by Richardson (1940: Fig. 37); it probably represents a Late Pre-classic intrusion from the Pacific region. Also in the Classic Maya area, William Coe reported (1965: Fig. 18) a miniature stone potbelly figure from Cauac fill (first century A.D.), but, of course, the sculpture itself could be earlier. Recently, Nicholas Hellmuth sent me a photograph of another eroded, but monumental (about 70 centimeters in height), potbelly sculpture, with a serrated medallion on its torso, that just turned up at Tikal.

The most obvious Monte Alto-style pot-

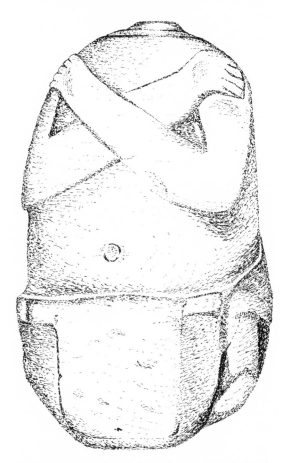

Fig. 44 Decapitated potbelly sculpture, El Baul, Escuintla. Height, 123 cm.; width, 65 cm.; depth, 70 cm. Finca El Baul, Escuintla. Drawing by Ryntha J. Gibbs (after photographs by the author).

belly on the Gulf Coast is the eighty-centimeter sculpture from Polvaredas, Veracruz (Medellín Zenil 1960a: Pl. 69). Monte Alto-related sculpture also occurs among the Tres Zapotes inventory: Monuments F, K, and L (Stirling 1943b: Pls. 8a; 9, lower left; and 10c). Blom and La Farge (1926–7, I: Figs. 21 and 40) also reported two small quasi-potbelly sculptures from Veracruz, from Catemaco and Piedra Labrada, respectively.

Miniature stone carvings also seem to imitate the Monte Alto style. Two from Tabasco are reported by Stirling (1957: Pls. 62c and 69b). Many other similar Preclassic stone figurines from West Mexico might also be cited. Furthermore, the ultimate inspiration for this fat-figure style perhaps may be traced to Middle Preclassic Olmec ceramic figurine types. Parallels are readily observed in some of the Tlatilco and Los Bocas figurines as well as in the Las Charcas and Bolinas types from Guatemala–El Salvador. David Joralemon informed me of five, solid-clay, fat figurines from the Guatemala–El Salvador border zone which are astonishingly Monte Alto-like, but unfortunately undated. However, a particular figurine from Chiapa de Corzo in highland Chiapas, and specifically dated to my Post-Olmec period, is directly parallel to Monte Alto (Lee 1967: Fig. 3d). While all of this is supportive for the proposed placement of the Monte Alto style, it must be remembered that fat-faced, fat-bodied figures and deities recurred in all regions and time periods in the Mesoamerican co-tradition.

Following the Post-Olmec, initial Late Preclassic (500–200 B.C.) innovative diversity in monumental sculpture presented in this article,

the Izapan horizon (200 B.C.–A.D. 200) witnessed a Terminal Preclassic florescence both on the coast in the vicinity of Izapa, and in the Guatemalan highlands in the vicinity of Kaminaljuyú in its Miraflores/Verbena and Arenal Phases. In that period, new ideas were once more disseminating outward from the southern Pacific coast and highlands. These ideas—especially those from the Kaminaljuyú source—profoundly influenced all of southeastern Mesoamerica. Elsewhere I will review this phenomenon in depth.

ACKNOWLEDGMENTS This article is the result of research beginning fifteen years ago when Matt and Marion Stirling visited me during one of my field seasons at Bilbao, Escuintla, Guatemala. I took them to see the nearby boulder sculptures at Monte Alto, six of which were then partially exposed. We decided that day that Monte Alto should be excavated, that I would make it my next field project, and that we would approach the National Geographic Society for possible funding. Through the encouragement and help of the Stirlings, National Geographic grants numbers 678, 814, and 916, 1968-1970, were received under the consecutive auspices of the Milwaukee Public Museum and the Peabody Museum, Harvard University; and the Monte Alto excavation project was carried out through the 1971 season.

Appropriately, this is the first substantial report to appear relating to that work (see also Parsons and Jenson 1965; Parsons 1976; and Shook 1971); the final Monte Alto monograph is presently under preparation by Edwin M. Shook and Marion P. Hatch. My early years of stone-sculpture research in Guatemala were personally guided and inspired by the presence of Suzanna Miles, Joya Hairs, and, ultimately, Ed Shook, who was at first chosen as my field director and finally as project director for Monte Alto. My debt to these pioneers is profound. Indirectly I also have been influenced by the prophetic insights of Miguel Covarrubias (1957) and Francis B. Richardson (1940). I would also like to acknowledge the capable assistance of Richard M. Rose in stone-sculpture reconnaissance.

Tricephalic Units in Olmec, Izapan-Style, and Maya Art

Jacinto Quirarte

THE UNIVERSITY OF TEXAS, SAN ANTONIO

This is a study of tricephalic units in Olmec, Izapan-style, and Maya art. The unit, similar to a serpent bar, has two duplicate heads usually facing away from or toward a single frontal or profile head presented in the center. It appears in a great variety of contexts. It is incised, carved, or painted on a number of Olmec objects—earplugs, pendants, sceptres, vessels, masks, and monumental sculpture. It is also seen on Izapan-style stelas, and on Maya relief panels and painted vases.

The unit occupies a unique position visually in a number of Olmec portable objects: it makes up the entire image. It is also relegated to framing functions in monumental sculpture, as in La Venta Altar 4 and the later Izapan-style top-line designs of most stelas. It appears, less often, as a basal panel. It becomes the major protagonist in the narrative scenes depicted on a number of Izapan styles. In Maya art it is one of many motifs in elaborate thematic units.

Morphological and iconographic questions will be posed in this paper. What is the significance of the tricephalic unit? Is it a formal problem of representation? What does the unit actually represent? What are the characteristics of the constituent heads? Which ones are duplicated? Which ones are presented in the central position? What is the relative position of the heads—front or rear—within the tricephalic unit? Is the unit associated with specific types of thematic contexts?

It will be demonstrated that the tricephalic unit is a two-dimensional representation of at least two bicephalic units arranged in bilateral or perpendicular fashion. It will be shown that the serpent bodies are arranged in the form of a Greek cross with a head occupying each arm and facing directions that are ninety degrees apart. An analysis of the constituent heads—their identifying characteristics, their position within bicephalic and tricephalic contexts—and of the themes in which the units are found, will help us to answer questions regarding significance and meaning. Ultimately, this study will help us establish a relationship between Olmec, Izapan-style, and Maya art.

MOTIFS AND ELEMENTS

The composite heads of bicephalic and tricephalic units will be designated as motifs. A cluster of motifs usually comprises a theme. Since the thematic contexts are not always clear, a reference will be made to such clusters as units, in this case bicephalic and/or tricephalic units. The constituents of a motif will be referred to as elements. Examples of elements are crossed bands, U shapes, and others. (For a discussion of these elements, see Quirarte 1977: 251-64.)

Compound serpent-saurian heads found in bicephalic and tricephalic contexts are variously referred to in the literature as dragons, monsters, Serpent X, composites, and even "beasties" (Schele 1976: 27). The heads will be referred to in this paper as composite or compound creatures exhibiting feline, serpent, and/or saurian traits. Their association with other similar or different heads joined by serpent bodies or quadrupeds will be noted by a reference to bicephalic, or two-headed, units and/or tricephalic units.

TRICEPHALIC UNITS IN OLMEC
AND OLMECOID ART

The presentation of compound creatures in multiheaded contexts in Olmec and Olmecoid art[1] is similar to later practices in Izapan-style and Maya art. Bicephalic creatures are found in the art of the three areas. While there may be some morphological parallels, the meaning expressed by the motifs may not be the same. In addition, the multiheaded units are not always presented in figurative terms, but sometimes through a combination of images and signs, such as U shapes, crossed bands, or other elements; the latter combinations signal, rather than show, the presence of the creatures. What holds true in all three areas is the persistence of the tricephalic unit as a motif appearing in numerous contexts.

La Venta Earplugs

One of the earliest representations of the tricephalic unit is found on two jade earplugs presently held in the collection of the Museo Nacional de Antropología in Mexico City (Fig. 1a). The pieces were found in 1943 by Matthew Stirling in a tomb at La Venta (Stirling 1943a: 325; Drucker 1952: 160, Fig. 46b and Pl. 52). The tricephalic unit here is unlike any of the others included in this study; it is in the shape of a U on its side. However, the number of constituent heads is the same—one unique and two duplicates—and their relative placement, respectively, in the center and at the sides of the unit is retained. It is as if the standard horizontal unit with three heads had been bent out of shape with its sides turned upward. Once formed, the U shape was then turned on its side.

The tricephalic unit of each earplug is comprised of a single profile head in the middle forming the base of the U, and duplicate heads on each side forming its parallel arms. The distinctive heads face in opposite directions. The single head with feline-serpent (?) traits has a U shape on its cheek. The two serpent-saurian heads, or dragons with serpent bodies, grow or extend from the forehead and chin of the single head. The latter has a line running from its forehead through the eye and continuing beyond the chin. It divides the serpent bodies and functions as a ledge for the eyes or U shapes, flared nostrils, and serrated eyebrows of the dragon heads.

The downward-turning snouts of the dragon heads point to an open area filled by a simple sign—a circle with a dot in the center and double scrolls on the outer side. This completes the design arranged within the circular band of each earplug.

Philip Drucker (1952: 160, 191, 195, Fig. 46b, and Pl. 52) discussed the earplugs, and reproduced a drawing by Miguel Covarrubias (1946b: 94) and a photograph of both alongside the other objects found in the tomb. He read the single head as a stylized human profile and the dragon heads as bird monsters, that is, comprised of avian and reptilian traits. Other students of Mesoamerican art have since reproduced versions of Covarrubias's drawing. Agrinier (1960: 13 and Fig. 7g) used it alongside other examples of Olmec-style felines to point out their similarity to the bearded feline (his Fig. B) of the Chiapa de Corzo Carved Femur 1. He did not refer to the dragon heads.

Lee Parsons (1967b: 187, Fig. 8) placed the earplug at the beginning of an evolutionary series (chronological development) of the dragon-monster motif in Mesoamerica, and suggested an Olmec through Maya con-

---

[1] A number of objects usually designated as Olmec are here considered Olmecoid, using Parson's discussion (1967b:178, 181-3) as a basis for the classification. These objects usually date from the Middle to Late Preclassic Periods (600-400 B.C.). Some of the Olmecoid-style objects bear a Protoclassic date (such as Tres Zapotes Stela C, 7.16.6.16.18 6 Eznab 1 Uo—31 B.C.). Although Parsons's basis for the classification—the use of scrolls—is too broad, it is useful for our purposes. He includes objects from the "Peripheral Coastal Lowlands" that are clearly Izapan in style. He also includes a number of sculptures from the Gulf Coast (El Mesón, Alvarado, Cerro de las Mesas, and Tres Zapotes) and central Mexico (Chalcatzingo). The small mask (Fig. 1d) in the Peabody Museum clearly falls under the Olmecoid category (Parsons 1967b:183). The El Mesón stela (Covarrubias 1957: Fig. 68), considered Olmecoid by Parsons (*op cit.*:182), has a tricephalic unit comprised of duplicate profile dragon heads flanking a central head. Although the single head in frontal view is unclear, a U shape occupies a prominent position in the center.

tinuity. He excluded from his drawing the circle with a dot in the center and double scrolls on the outer side (Fig. 1a). In addition, his interpretation of the design on the cheek of the large single head follows Piña Chan and L. Covarrubias (1964: Fig. 27), who leave no doubt as to its configuration as a U shape by completing its contours. Parsons identified the single feline as an Olmec were-jaguar and called the entire image, concentrating on the dragon heads, a "double headed conception" which later became an important symbol in classic Maya iconography (Parsons 1967b: 188).

David Joralemon (1971: 45, 90, and Fig. 131) suggested that the single head may represent his God VI, ". . . the god of spring, renewal, and resurrection, the gruesome Xipe Totec of Aztec times." He interpreted the dragons as God I. He considers God I—the jaguar-dragon—to be linked with fire, yet also identified with the earth and soil, water and rain. God I may also refer to royal lineage and dynastic succession. Although God I is reptilian, Joralemon prefers to call it a jaguar-dragon.

As already noted, the images of the earplugs have morphological links as well as iconographic relationships with the other tricephalic units to be discussed below.[2]

The two earplugs are to be considered as one basic image because of their visual arrangement. Since the otherwise identical images of the two earplugs are reversed, each mirrors the other. When worn, the distinctive head of each tricephalic unit faces in the same direction as its counterpart. Whether it faces the front or rear depends upon the wearer. If the wearer were to be visualized in frontal view and the earplugs were then turned outward so as to make them visible, one of two configurations would be created. Each would depend upon how the plugs were worn. If worn with the single head facing the front, or the observer, the resultant shape would be an elaborate X

with its outward serifs extended. It could also be described as an H-shaped unit on its side. If, instead, the dragon heads faced the observer, a flattened-out O would be created. It is likely that the single head with the U shape on its cheek faced the front. This is in keeping with its central position within other tricephalic units. The companion dragon-heads facing to the rear may correspond to the creatures normally located on both sides of the central head.

The top dragon of each earplug (Fig. 1a) bears minor distinguishing marks on its snout —two opposed diagonal lines—which demonstrate one aspect of that head's characteristics. Duplicate heads often have such references attesting to their distinction even when they appear to be identical. The trapezoid marking is an important distinguishing element in Maya representations of a bicephalic serpent. When one of the heads of such a bicephalic creature is presented in frontal view (in this case the single head with the U shape), the other head is normally hidden from view (see Quirarte 1974: 131).

On the La Venta earplugs, the double scrolls, attached to each of the circles with dots, probably refer to a serpent's bifurcated tongue. The circle may symbolize the continuous nature of the serpent body to which heads are attached at 90° intervals or within two or more quadrants.[3] Finally, the serpent head may be the other side of the bicephalic unit to which the single head with U shape is attached.

Thus, the tricephalic units of the two earplugs are to be considered as one single image (mirrored) comprised of two distinct but interrelated bicephalic creatures.

Quartzite Pendant

Another early piece, related morphologically

---

[2] Although the intent in the present study is not to establish a developmental sequence of the tricephalic unit, it is necessary to place the objects under discussion within a temporal framework (see Table 1). The following is based on Parsons (1967b:181-3) and Quirarte (1973c: Chronological Table).

[3] Several years ago, I proposed, in a paper entitled "Actual and Implied Visual Space in Maya Vase Painting: A Study of Double Images and Two-Headed Compound Creatures" (Quirarte 1978), that the cylindrical vessel may symbolize the (serpentine) body connecting bodiless heads depicted on opposite sides of the vessel. Further research on Maya polychrome vases demonstrates that the circle as a sign may stand for the serpentine bodies to which a number of heads may be attached.

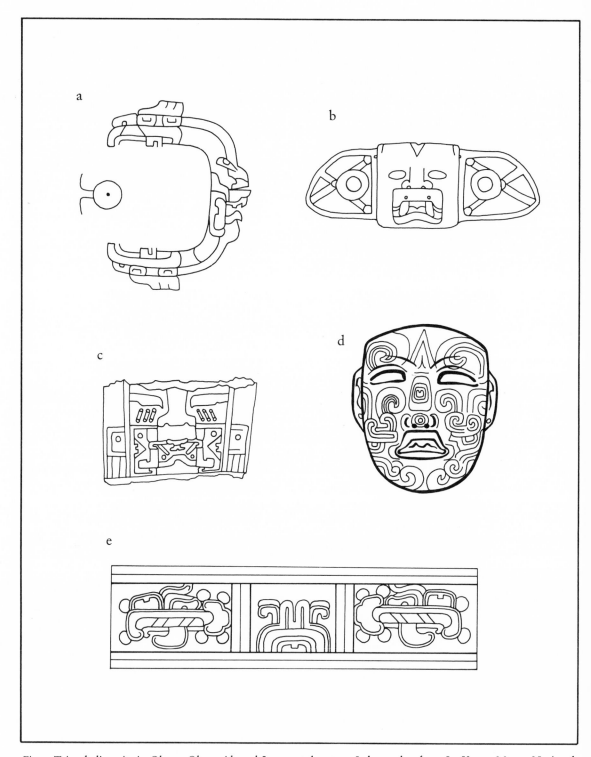

Fig. 1 Tricephalic units in Olmec, Olmecoid, and Izapan-style art. *a.* Jade earplug from La Venta. Museo Nacional de Antropología, Mexico. (After Joralemon 1971: Fig. 131.) *b.* Quartzite pendant from the Yucatán Peninsula. Dumbarton Oaks, Washington, D.C. (After Joralemon 1971: Fig. 230.) *c.* Tres Zapotes Stela C. (After Covarrubias 1961: Fig. 19.) *d.* Serpentine mask from the coast of Veracruz. (After Covarrubias 1961: Fig. 35.) *e.* Abaj Takalik Stela 3. (After Miles 1965: Fig. 8.) These and other drawings by David M. Barrera.

to the jade earplugs, is the quartzite pendant from the Yucatán Peninsula now in the Dumbarton Oaks Collection (Fig. 1b). The pendant has a composite head presented in frontal view and in the center of the piece. It has framed crossed bands on both sides, within winglike panels or flanges. It was discussed by Michael Coe (1966a: 8, Fig. 1), who placed it within the same temporal horizon as Stela C at Tres Zapotes. Joralemon (1971: 77, Fig. 230) read the central head as God V initially. Later he considered this a false category (Joralemon 1976: 33).

The snarling mouth with fangs is typical of Olmec representation of this head with a notched forehead. The central head is in relief with some incising (the lower-lip outline and the V-shaped notch). The winglike flanges are pierced by centrally located circular holes, made after the framed crossed bands had been incised (M. Coe 1966a: 6). Two smaller holes, obviously used to suspend the piece, were made on either side of the forehead composite. The larger holes are funneled on one side (obverse) and cylindrical toward the other (reverse).

A reading of the image (the frontal relief head), the sign or emblem (the crossed bands), and the drilled funnel-shaped holes, requires a number of assumptions. First of all, images such as the composite head represent, as well as express, ideas in space. Signs, such as the crossed bands, refer to, but do not show the attributes of, whatever it is they stand for. Perforations, such as the holes in the pendants, do not appear to me to function primarily either as images or signs; they could conceivably do so, but to interpret them as such seems highly speculative.

M. Coe's interpretation (1966a: 6) of the perforated holes as ear flares is based on a reading of them as images. Their configuration and their location bring such objects to mind. Although Coe's reading may not be far off, the reasons may be due to the possible symbolism involved rather than to a simple transcription of objects in space. The unbroken line of a cylindrical and/or flared hole, like the unbroken line of the previously mentioned earspool or cylindrical vessel, probably refers to and symbolizes the connecting serpentine body

of the composite creature. The scroll earplugs in Izapan-style art and the varied Maya examples are probably shorthand references to the concept of quality more dramatically expressed by the bicephalic creatures.

The centrally located composite head is given prime importance by its definition in space (as an image) and placement. The flanges on either side refer to its serpentine creature, duplicated as in the La Venta earplugs.

Stone Mask

Another version of a tricephalic unit is found in the incised design on a serpentine stone mask (Fig. 1d) from the coast of Veracruz (Piña Chan and L. Covarrubias 1964). The head exhibits the typical characteristics of this type of object in Olmecoid style. There is a single reference to the feline-serpent (?) with the inclusion of a U shape within a rounded-square frame on the nose of the head. The serpentine-saurian characteristics—the dragon heads—are incised on the cheeks of the mask and presented upside down. Furthermore, the heads face inward and are not actually attached to the U shape.

Covarrubias (1961: Fig. 35 and Lám. X) included a drawing and a photograph of the mask, along with three others, to illustrate such designs in Mesoamerican art. He did not specifically refer to the images in his text.

Joralemon (1971: Fig. 187) identified the mask as his God II ". . . with spiral flame eyebrows, . . . rounded nose, and snarling mouth." He also referred to the "pointed vegetation motif . . . between the eyes and spiral incising . . . [over] the cheeks." Joralemon (1971: 90) considered God II to be ancestral to such Aztec corn gods as Centéotl.

There is no question that the U shape refers to the same creature depicted on the La Venta earplugs. This is in keeping with some of the other examples in which this composite occupies the central position, with the duplicate serpent-saurian (dragon) heads presented one on each side. The circle below and/or the designs on the forehead may refer to the other side of the bicephalic unit with the U shape.

Other possible tricephalic representations may be found on a pottery vessel from Las

Bocas (Fig. 3b), on La Venta Altar 4, and on a small portable piece found in Guanacaste, Costa Rica (Joralemon 1971: Figs. 144 and 196). The highly abstracted design of the Las Bocas pottery vessel may be the same as that represented on the Dumbarton Oaks pendant (Fig. 1b). The design has a cleft head in the center, and crossed bands within smaller panels on both sides. La Venta Altar 4 has a central head flanked by diagonal bands and a notched element on one side. The latter is found in numerous representations of a terrestrial creature in Olmec and Izapan-style art (Fig. 1c; and Quirarte 1973c: Fig. 7a-d.) The reference to a tricephalic unit in the small winged figure from Costa Rica is very schematic; it is found around the belt area (Joralemon 1971: Fig. 196). A U shape is presented in the central position as a "buckle" with possible serpent-saurian references on both sides.

Tres Zapotes Stela C (Fig. 1c) demonstrates, through the use of signs and images, the same breakdown of dual traits expressed by the tricephalic composites exhibiting feline, serpent, and saurian traits. The mouth is primarily feline. The bifurcated tongue and large J-shaped elements on the sides of the mouth are serpent references. The J elements are the scrolls (fangs?) represented at the corners of the mouth of numerous serpentine and feline composites usually shown in profile. The notched elements within triangular units (cleft heads?) are references to a crocodile. The diagonal band is very likely a saurian reference. This is demonstrated by the diagonal band incised on the long-lipped head of Izapa Stela 2 which may specifically refer to an iguana (Quirarte 1976a: Fig. 12a). Thus Tres Zapotes Stela C represents, in abbreviated form, the feline serpent in frontal view and the serpent-saurian dragon duplicated and presented at its sides.

BICEPHALICS AND MASK PANELS IN OLMEC ART

The genesis of the tricephalic unit may be found by studying a number of Olmec bicephalic creatures and mask panels. These images demonstrate that mask panels and Izapan-style top-line designs are simply representations of two bicephalic creatures facing inward. When two identical profiles of the "front" serpent-saurian, or dragon, head are presented in bilateral fashion, the resultant image is a composite head seen in frontal view. The rear heads remain as duplicates on each side. The front, or central heads become the second bicephalic's head seen in frontal view.

Tabasco Sceptre

The best example of the "ancestral" bicephalic creature can be found in the black stone sceptre from Cardenas, Tabasco (Fig. 2a1). The small piece discussed by Navarrete (1974: 15) and Joralemon (1971: 64) has a serpent-saurian-dragon head on one side (front) and a cleft head on the other (rear). A unit with a double-contour band appears to grow from the cleft. The heads are attached to a bundle tied with three bands.

If the entire unit is duplicated and presented with the front dragon heads facing each other, a tricephalic unit is created (Fig. 2a). The single fang of the dragon becomes the double J shape of the later Izapan-style top-line designs (Quirarte 1976a: Fig. 2). The configuration of the dragon's mouth—a horizontal bar with a slight curvilinear upswing at the corner—is echoed by the Oxtotitlan mural mask panel discussed by Grove (1970).

The Oxtotitlan mask panel has crossed bands within the creature's eyes and a U shape in the center (Fig. 2b). The notched or cleft head of the Cardenas sceptre is relegated to the fang in the Oxtotitlan design. The double contour bands are now slanted and contained within the creature's mouth. These clearly are related to the double opposed diagonal bands of the Izapan-style top-line designs. This can also be seen in the mural found in Tikal Structure 5D-Sub 10-1st (Fig. 2c). The double contour vertical bands incised on the outermost unit of the Cardenas sceptre are included on both sides of the Tikal Izapan-style top-line design. Two U shapes occupy the central part of the design. The double scrolls directly below the vertical bands are the fangs of the creature. These could be ancestral to the scrolls attached to the corners of the mouths of numerous creatures in Maya art.

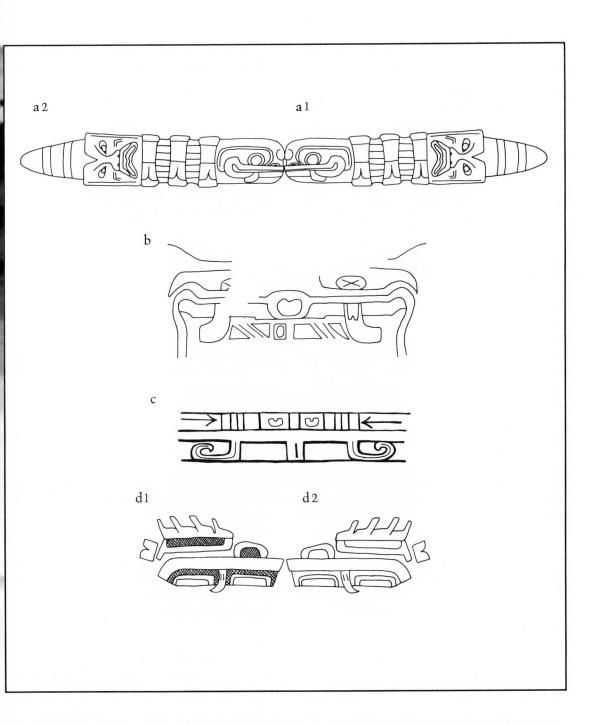

Fig. 2 Bicephalic units and mask panels in Olmec, Olmecoid, and Izapan-style art. *a1*. Sceptre from Cardenas, Tabasco. (After Joralemon 1971: Fig. 183 and Navarrete 1974: Fig. 16.) *a2*. Mirror image of sceptre. *b*. Oxtotitlan mural mask panel. (After Grove 1973a: 132.) *c*. Tikal Structure 5 D-Sub 10-1st mural. (After a photograph from the University Museum, University of Pennsylvania, Philadelphia.) *d1*. Design from Tlapacoya ceramic vessel. (After Joralemon 1976: Fig. 6c.) *d2*. Mirror image of design.

Tlapacoya Pottery Vessel

Another profile head that may be related to the mask panels, with crossed bands associated with them, is found on a pottery vessel from Tlapacoya (Fig. 3a), discussed by Joralemon (1976: 37 and Fig. 6c). A single left-profile head, with fang, crenellated (flame) eyebrow, and nostril, faces a similar head presented in frontal view. The latter has a cleft head, crenellated (flame) eyebrows, and crossed bands in its open mouth, but no fangs. The profile head has a small detached cleft unit on the left or behind the head. This is probably a reference to the rear cleft head of the Cardenas sceptre, but without the "vegetation" seen by Joralemon (1971: 64).

If the profile head of the Tlapacoya image is duplicated so as to appear on both sides of the single head presented in frontal view, the result is another mask panel (Fig. 2d; only the profile head is duplicated in the drawing).

Once the mask panels and other related units, such as the Izapan-style top-line designs, are seen as two bicephalics facing inward, then tricephalic units become "legible." Such is the case with the Tlapacoya image and the ledge design of La Venta Altar 4 (Joralemon 1971: Fig. 144). The crossed-bands element of both central units is comparable to the U shape used in similar contexts.

TRICEPHALIC UNITS IN IZAPAN-STYLE ART

Unlike Olmec and Olmecoid art, Izapan-style art exhibits an obsessive interest in compound creatures with serpent-saurian characteristics, which are represented within narrative scenes. Rarely are felines presented. Although the standard tricephalic units are not as clearly articulated in this art, the same concepts are expressed in these and in a number of related images.

Izapa Stela 11

The best example of the tricephalic unit is seen on Izapa Stela 11 (Fig. 4a). The full saurian figure is presented in frontal view at the bottom of the narrative frame in a squatting position. Its head, with open jaws, is shown in profile and looking upward. A figure with outstretched arms is shown, from its waist up, within the mouth. The saurian creature has crossed bands on its chest or abdomen area. Framing the squatting figure on either side are identical heads shown in profile and facing away from it. These are presented at 90° angles to the frontally positioned body of the compound creature (Quirarte 1974: 131).

A similar, toothless, open-jawed composite is seen on Izapa Stelas 3 and 6 (Fig. 5b, a). Each balances a U-shaped canoe (?) with a human figure inside. Unlike the squatting Stela-11 figure, these have bifurcated tongues and no crossed bands.

Abaj Takalik Stela 3

Examples of tricephalic units found at the site of Abaj Takalik demonstrate in more elaborate fashion the same concept expressed in the Olmec pieces and in Izapa Stela 11. On Abaj Takalik Stela 3, the composite creatures appear within a basal panel on which a human figure stands (Fig. 1e). The basal panel is divided into three smaller framed panels—one square and two rectangular—in which references are made to the two bicephalic creatures. The U shape placed in the lower center within a glyphlike cartouche is reminiscent of some Izapan-style top-line designs (Quirarte 1977: Fig. 10.2b). Flanking the central panel are two others in which serpent-saurian, or dragon, heads are shown in profile facing toward the center. The highly stylized representations of these bicephalic creatures, with U shapes within plates in lieu of eyes and with diagonal bands on the snouts, are discussed by Miles (1965: Figs. 8g and 16g), Parsons (1967b: 186 and Fig. 7b), and Quirarte (1973c: 22 and Fig. 12b; 1977: 256 and Fig. 10.2b).

The basal panel of Stela 3, comprised of inward-looking composites on each side of the centrally located U shape, may contain two bicephalics rather than single heads. That is, each duplicate head may represent a complete bicephalic creature.

Abaj Takalik Stela 4

On Abaj Takalik Stela 4, combined two-headed creatures are represented in their entirety (Fig. 4b). Identical serpent-saurian heads, facing inward, are shown as water-suppliers at

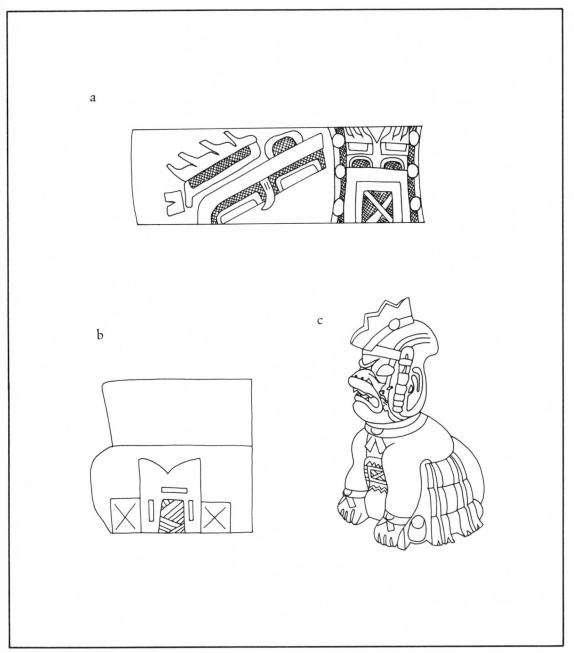

Fig. 3 The crossed-bands element in various contexts in Olmec art. *a.* Tlapacoya ceramic vessel. (After Joralemon 1976: Fig. 6c.) *b.* Las Bocas pottery vessel. (After Joralemon 1971: Fig. 123.) *c.* Jade figure from Necaxa, Puebla. American Museum of Natural History, New York. (After Joralemon 1971: Fig. 216.)

the base of the stela. A composite creature with distinctive heads is shown emerging from the water band as a bicephalic serpent undulating toward the uppermost part of the stela. The "tail" head of the serpent is actually a U shape within a glyphlike cartouche with scrolls on both sides. A human head looks upward from within the jaws of the saurian head at the top of the stela. Duplicate heads (dragons) are seen at each side of the body of the serpent.

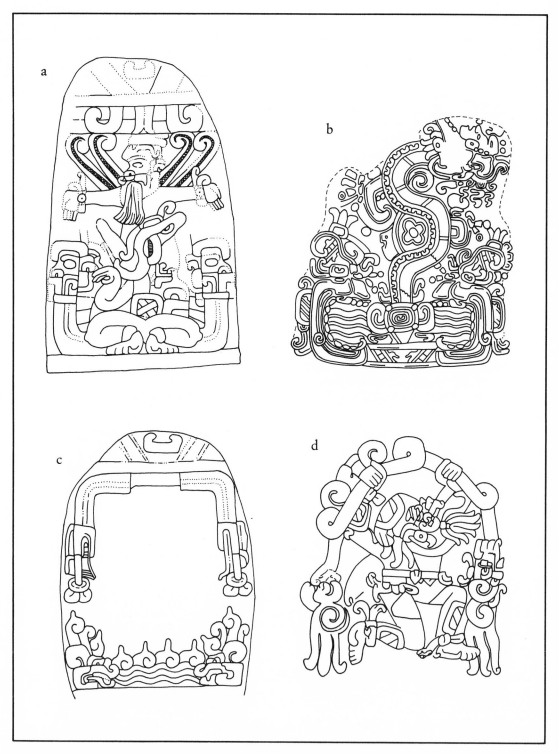

Fig. 4 Tricephalic units in Izapan-style art. *a*. Izapa Stela 11. (After Norman 1973: Pl. 22.) *b*. Abaj Takalik Stela 4. (After Parsons 1973: Fig. 1.) *c*. Izapa Stela 23. (After Norman 1973: Pl. 38.) *d*. Kaminaljuyú Stela 19. (After Proskouriakoff 1968: Fig. 4.)

Fig. 5 Bicephalic units in Izapan-style art. *a*. Izapa Stela 6. *b*. Izapa Stela 3. *c*. Izapa Stela 67. *d*. Izapa Stela 22. (After Norman 1973: Pls. 12, 6, 36, and 54.)

Parsons (1973) discussed the piece, dealing with its form and meaning. I have interpreted the U shape at the base of the bicephalic unit as a reference to the rear head (Quirarte 1977: 269).

As on Izapa Stelas 1, 22 (Fig. 5d), 23 (Fig. 4c), and 67 (Fig. 5c), the water-suppliers of Abaj Takalik Stela 4 are shown as bodiless heads facing inward. The heads of Izapa Stelas 1 and 23 (Fig. 4c) are definitely feline-serpent composites occupying a tail position in other contexts, as demonstrated by Kaminaljuyú Stela 19 (Fig. 4d) and El Baul Stela 1 (Quirarte 1973c: 20 and Figs. 10a, c-e, 11a, b).

The water-supplier heads of Izapa Stelas 22 and 67 (Fig. 5d, c) are more saurian in aspect and, therefore, are closer to the Abaj Takalik Stela 4 heads (Fig. 4b). Both Izapa stelas have long-snouted heads with distinctive earplugs. Both have crossed bands above the eye area within bunlike headgear. The Stela 22 head has a fleshless jaw. A plantlike unit grows from the headdress of the Stela 67 head. Both frame a similar scene in which figures with outstretched arms, holding axes (?) in Stela 67 and serpents in Stela 22, are shown in a canoe supported by serpent bodies.

Izapa Stela 23

The bicephalic creature with duplicate heads (two front and two rear) is used as a frame on Izapa Stela 23 (Fig. 4c). The double J forms of the typical top-line design represent the fangs (scrolls) at the corners of the mouth of the composite, but, on Stela 23, these are suppressed. In their place are two serpentine creatures extending downward. They effectively frame the narrative scene (see Quirarte 1974: 131). Both are attached to serpent bodies and have stylized bifurcated tongues. Only the one on the left appears to have teeth.

The suggested reading of the frame on Izapa Stela 23 is as follows: The U shape and diagonal bands at the top stand for frontal and profile views of two bicephalic creatures. Their serpentine traits (fangs), normally included in these top-line designs by the double J shapes (scrolls), are represented as images by the two descending serpents. These are the front heads of this aspect of the composite creature. The diagonal bands with double contours probably represent the rear of the bicephalic creature. An additional reference to tail heads is made at the bottom with duplicate heads facing inward and functioning as water-suppliers. This is a variation on the usual way in which the two-headed creatures are presented. Each distinctive head is duplicated, thus showing very clearly the multiple aspects of each side of the bicephalic creatures.

FRONT AND REAR HEADS IN TRICEPHALIC UNITS

Front heads are primarily saurian in character. Such heads, associated with quadrupeds, have crocodilian jaws and crenellated-element markings within triangular units. The saurian's obesity is pronounced in Izapa Stela 6 (Fig. 5a). Its serpent traits are demonstrated by the bifurcated tongue. When the saurian appears in the Chiapa de Corzo Femur 1 (Quirarte 1976b: Fig. 2a), it has squared-off teeth and downward-turning snout, but no bifurcated tongue. When its markings are used as a baseline on Izapa Stela 5, the double saurians framing the sides of the scene (*ibid.*: Fig. 5) have the same squared-off teeth of the Chiapa de Corzo femur front head. On Izapa Stela 12 (*ibid.*: Fig. 2e), the framing serpents(?) have vegetation growing from identical heads. Crenellated elements, diagonal bands, and slanted U shapes are on the serpent bodies. The inward-looking serpents appear to be toothless. These may be the same design as the tail head seen on Izapa Stela 6. Since serpent bodies are clearly intended in Izapa Stela 12, it may be that a relationship exists between Izapa Stelas 6 and 12. Both heads of the Izapa Stela 6 figure have bifurcated tongues (Fig 5a).

Vegetation is associated with the tail/rear positions of related creatures on Izapa Stelas 12 and 25 (Norman 1973: Pls. 24 and 42). On Izapa Stela 12, duplicate serpentine creatures form a tricephalic unit within the basal panel. An upturned crocodile is seen on Izapa Stela 25. The Tabasco sceptre (Fig. 2a1) has a toothless cleft head with a banded motif growing from it. It occupies the tail position of the bicephalic creature. Joralemon (1971: 64) classifies it as God II-E, with "maize symbols" growing from its cleft head. These three examples demonstrate that whenever vegetation is represented, it is associated with a head exhibiting serpentine traits and occupying the rear position of the bicephalic creature.

CROSSED BANDS AND U SHAPES[4]

Crossed bands are usually associated with saurian creatures and, like the U shapes, are also found within tricephalic contexts.

The squatting quadruped represented on Izapa Stela 11 (Fig. 4a) has crossed bands on its chest. It does not have the bifurcated tongue of the Stela 6 figure (Fig. 5a) nor the crenellated element on its cheeks. The duplicate serpent dragons on either side also do not have bifurcated tongues.

The similar squatting figure from Necaxa, Puebla, in the collection of the American Museum of Natural History, New York, has saurian and serpentine references (Fig. 3c). It has a crest similar to the one worn on its snout by the upturned crocodile tree of Izapa Stela 25 (Norman 1973: Pl. 42). The Necaxa figure also has the crossed bands on its chest and skirt, comprised of what may be parallel cleft bands of bifurcated tongues. This figure has the famed snarling expression discussed by Covarrubias (1946a) and others. However, given its saurian, and possibly serpentine, traits, it is unlikely that a feline head is intended. It is probably the same composite creature represented on Izapa Stela 11 (Fig. 4a).

The Dumbarton Oaks pendant (Fig. 1b) may

be related to the Necaxa and Izapa Stela 11 figures. Like the Necaxa figure, it has the fangs and toothless gums of the serpent. The two small circles directly above the fangs and within the upper lip may be serpentine references as well. The double crossed-band units, also with circles associated with each flange, are additional serpentine references.

All examples reviewed demonstrate that crossed bands are associated with heads occupying a front position.

The U shape may refer to a composite head which occupies the rear position when presented in a bicephalic or tricephalic context. The rear heads of the two Chiapa de Corzo carved femurs (Quirarte 1976b: Fig. 2a) and Abaj Takalik Stela 4 (Fig. 4b) have U shapes within the supra-orbital plates. Stylized vegetation units are attached to the headgear of each profile head.

There is no figurative reference to a feline in Abaj Takalik Stela 4. Yet the U shape is prominently displayed in the lower center of the image. The water-suppliers face toward it. The U shape placed within a glyphlike cartouche has scrolls on either side and is balanced on a triangular element. The serpent appears to grow from the U shape. In addition, the U shape is depicted repeatedly along the entire length of the serpent's underside.

CONTENT AND FUNCTION

The Izapan-style stelas demonstrate the thematic and functional contexts in which the bicephalic and/or tricephalic units are found. In some cases, it is possible to determine whether a scene takes place within the terrestrial sphere, even though the details or significance of the event remain obscure. Sometimes the tricephalic unit becomes the ground itself or the container (a cave?) in which events take place. In others, it is shown as a water-supplier or a more direct provider of sustenance.

The tricephalic unit as a top frame (mask panels and top-line designs) provides the location where events take place on most Izapan-style stelas. Part of the tricephalic unit functions as a side frame on Izapa Stela 23, and as narrative on Izapa Stelas 6 and 3 (Figs. 4c and 5a, b).

---

[4] Covarrubias (1946a:Pl. 31), Drucker (1952:199-200 and Fig. 60w, x, y), M. Coe (1965b:759 and Fig. 43), and Joralemon (1971:14 and Figs. 67-76) refer to the incidence of the crossed-bands element in Olmec art without attempting to interpret it. Similar references are made to the U-shaped element. Drucker assumed the crossed bands to be a "borrowing" from Maya art, since he assigned La Venta art to the Early Classic Period. I have proposed elsewhere (Quirarte 1973c:18) that the crossed-bands element in Izapan-style art may symbolize the serpent. It is likely that it refers to the same creature in Olmec and Maya art.

The meaning of the U shape is less clear. In all previous studies, I read the element as a reference to a predominantly feline creature. I still believe that, but now would propose that serpentine traits are also involved. The U shape associated with so-called were-jaguar heads (Fig. 1a) in Olmec art, and with long-lipped heads in Izapan-style and Early Classic Maya art, may refer to a composite bearing both serpentine and feline(?) traits.

On other stelas, references are specifically made to earth, vegetation, and water. The basal panel of Abaj Takalik Stela 3 (Fig. 1e) refers to the earth. Izapa Stela 12 has a tricephalic figure that clearly refers to the earth at base level and to vegetation along the sides and just under the top-line design. Bodies of water are provided by inward-facing feline-serpent heads on Izapa Stela 23 (Fig. 4c). The other water-suppliers have crossed bands (Izapa Stelas 22 and 67) and a diagonal band with blips (Abaj Takalik Stela 4) associated with them (Figs. 5d, c and 4b). The latter element refers to the terrestrial sphere (see Quirarte 1976b: 84). It is unknown whether the crossed-bands element refers to terrestrial or celestial spheres.

A review of the serpent bicephalic unit with its attendant duplicate dragons shown on Abaj Takalik Stela 4 (Fig. 4b) may clarify the thematic content in which some of the tricephalic figures are found. The front saurian head (top), like others on Izapa Stelas 11, 6, 3, and possibly 67 and 22 (Figs. 4a and 5a–d), supports or contains a human or deity figure. The tail U shape (bottom) occupies both levels of the narrative frame. It functions as the center of a base-line tricephalic unit. The water-suppliers, with terrestrial elements and vegetation growing from their heads, are either front- or rear-position heads functioning as the duplicates of those on the tricephalic unit. The undulating serpent, normally hidden from view, takes up the entire scene on the stela. The vertically placed bicephalic unit, in turn, has the usual duplicate dragons of the standard tricephalic complex, one at each side of its body. The duplicate dragon heads are probably related to the duplicate dragons with downward-turning snouts seen on the La Venta earplugs.

The several bicephalic units in concert may have been conceived as a source of all things (earth, water, and vegetation), as protector, and as a power- and/or status-conferring entity (Quirarte 1976a: 236 and 1976b: 83).

The various interconnecting bicephalics are very clearly shown on Abaj Takalik Stela 4 (Fig. 4b). How each unit interconnects can be demonstrated by a drawing of the image in simulated three dimensions and a diagram of the same image dissected and labeled (Fig. 7).

Each bicephalic unit is labeled with a Roman numeral. The identifying elements of the composite heads are also labeled (with Arabic numerals) for purposes of exposition. This will enable us to "read" the two-dimensional image as follows: the central bicephalic (Fig. 7b I) has another attached to it at right angles (Fig. 7b II). The third and fourth bicephalics (Fig. 7b III and IV) function as a complete band at baseline to create a tricephalic unit (Fig. 7a I). They also provide a focus for the central bicephalic by drawing our attention to the U shape, which performs a double function. It is the tail head of the serpent bicephalic and the source for the inner heads of the two bicephalics at baseline; it is the central unit to which all attention is drawn; it is part of each of the several bicephalic units represented on this stela.

Specifically, the front saurian head (top) of Abaj Takalik Stela 4, like others on Izapa Stelas 11, 6, 3, and possibly 67 and 22 (Figs. 4a and 5a–d), support or contain human or deity figures. The rear "head," a U shape within a cartouche at the bottom, occupies both levels of the narrative frame. It also functions as the center of a baseline tricephalic (Fig. 7a I). The tricephalic is comprised of two bicephalics with outer heads facing inward. The latter are water-suppliers with terrestrial elements and vegetation growing from their heads. Terrestrial heads "normally" occupy the front position. In this context the heads function as the duplicates of the tricephalic unit and may occupy the usual front position if the reading of the large scrolls flanking the U shape as rear heads is correct (Fig. 7b III and IV). The large scrolls are reminiscent of the scroll-eyed heads used as water-suppliers on Izapa Stela 23 (Fig. 4c). The flared nostril makes this reading plausible (Fig. 7b 4).

Finally, the undulating serpent, normally hidden from view, takes up the entire scene of the stela. The vertically placed bicephalic has the usual duplicate heads (dragons) of the standard tricephalic on both sides of its body (Fig. 7b I and II). The duplicate dragons are probably related to the duplicate dragons with downward-turning snouts seen on the La Venta earplugs (Fig. 1a).

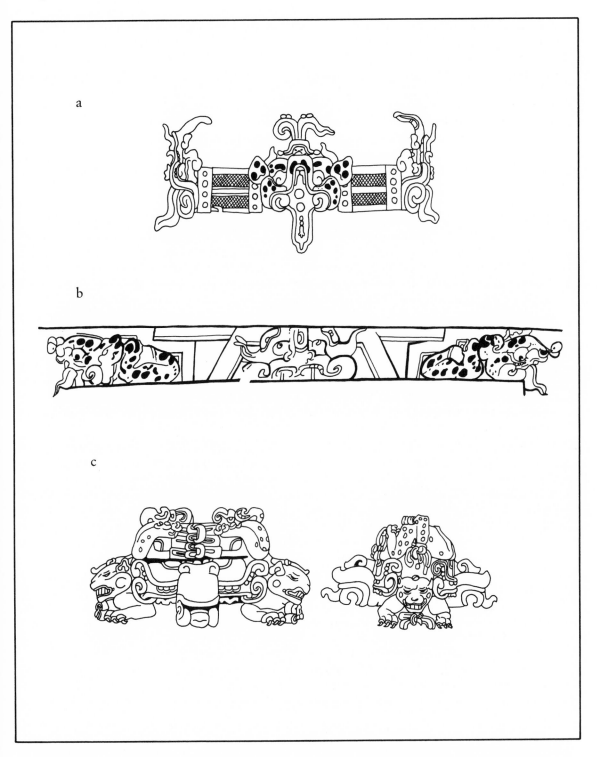

Fig. 6 Tricephalic units in Maya art. *a*. Sanctuary panel from the Temple of the Sun, Palenque. (After Schele 1976: Fig. 12.) *b*. Vase in "codex style," southern Campeche or northern Petén. (After M. Coe 1973b: 92, upper right.) *c*. Altar in front of Stela F, Copán. (After Spinden 1913: Fig. 99 and Maudslay 1889-1902, I: Pl. 114f, g, and h.)

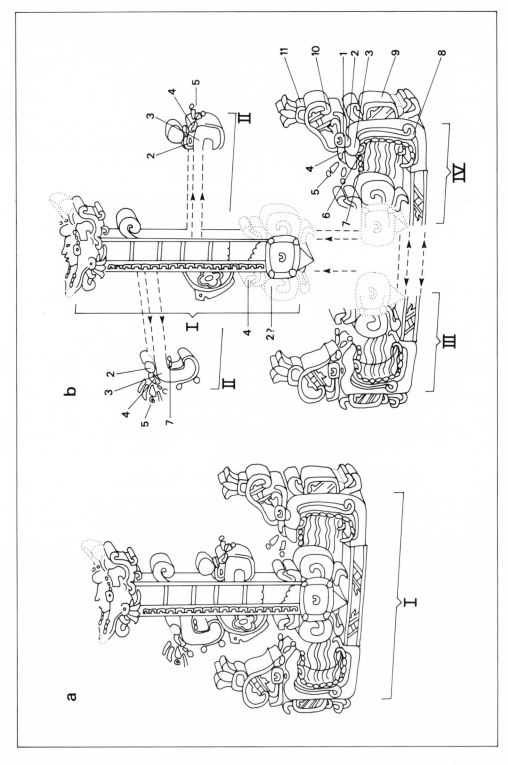

Fig. 7 Drawing (a) and diagram (b) of Abaj Takalik Stela 4, showing the various bicephalic units. Each bicephalic unit is designated by a Roman numeral. The constituent parts of the composite heads are numbered in Arabic numerals as follows: (1) supra-orbital plate, (2) eye, (3) snout, (4) flared nostril, (5) noseplugs, (6) fang, (7) teeth, (8) scroll, (9) ear unit, (10) headgear, and (11) stylized plant unit.

MAYA TRICEPHALIC UNITS

There are a number of Early Classic Maya examples of bicephalic creatures presented in the manner discussed above, but none corresponds so clearly as the Late Classic examples found at Palenque (the sanctuary panel in the Temple of the Sun) and Copán (the altar in front of Stela F) or on several Late Classic polychrome vases from the Petén (Fig. 6). The Maya tricephalic units are always presented clearly in visual terms. The constituent heads of the units are always presented as images. Elements or signs do not stand for the heads. Whenever a feline or saurian is intended, whether occupying a central or side position, it is presented clearly and naturalistically.

Sanctuary Panel, Temple of the Sun, Palenque

The bar held by two seated deity figures in the Temple of the Sun at Palenque is the clearest representation of the tricephalic unit in Maya art (Fig. 6a). Taylor (1941: 49) classified it as a ceremonial bar. Numerous studies on the panel and other sanctuary tablets found at Palenque have included references to this unit. One of the most recent is Cohodas's intriguing interpretation of the unit as a serpent bar symbolizing the earth while the feline with open mouth symbolizes the west where the sun is literally devoured as it starts its nightly journey through the underworld (Cohodas 1976).

The naturalistic representation of the jaguar with serpentine references is presented in the central position of the three-headed unit. The serpent traits are indicated by the scrolls at the corners of the mouth. The head has no lower jaw. The unit coming out of the creature's mouth is its tongue. This can be seen in the profile representation of the same feline-serpent heads on a painted vase (Fig. 6b). There is an *ahau* unit attached to the head which designates it as a lord of the underworld (see Quirarte 1976c: 21). The bar to which it is attached is represented at right angles, as is appropriate for this unit. A serpent-saurian head, without the usual lower jaw, is represented at each end. The single diagonal bar, placed within a cartouche on the snout of the serpent on the right, distinguishes it from its opposite on the left; otherwise they are identical. The bar itself is similar to numerous examples represented in underworld scenes on so-far unpublished Maya polychromes.

Pottery Vessel

That the Palenque tricephalic unit deals with the underworld is clearly demonstrated by representations of a similar unit in the upper part of a temple depicted on a vase discussed by M. Coe (1973b: 90–3). God L, surrounded by five women, is shown seated inside a temple, while to the extreme left of the scene there are two standing figures, one of whom is about to behead a victim. The architectural(?) frieze shows a scroll-eyed figure with upturned snout, scrolls at the corners of the mouth, and markings that clearly identify it as a saurian creature (Fig. 6b). It is contained within a frame with sloping sides. This may be related to the markings (trapezoidal) on the snout of the upper head incised on the La Venta earplugs (Fig. 1a). The horizontal unit above the trapezoid in the vase painting extends on either side and functions as a directional device by drawing our attention to the outward-facing jaguars presented in profile. Each is framed by a stepped unit on the inner side. If both jaguars were placed side by side facing inward, the resultant frame would be the typical notched unit or Tau shape, often associated with the jaguar. Drucker (1952: 193) interpreted this shape as a stylized representation of the jaguar's upper jaw. In the vase painting, the identical jaguars have scrolls flowing out of the corners of their mouths, with long lolling tongues. The scroll-eyed jaguars with serpentine references (*i.e.*, the scrolls) are found in a number of Maya reliefs. Linda Schele (1976: 27 and Figs. 17, 18) pointed these out in her discussion of the sanctuary tablet of the Temple of the Sun at Palenque. She clearly distinguished between these and other representations of the jaguar she discussed in an earlier paper (Schele 1974: 45). She specifically points to scrolls coming out of the corners of the mouth as a distinguishing feature. The same jaguar with serpent references appears in Lintel 3, Temple I at Tikal (W. Coe, Shook, and Satterthwaite 1961: Fig. 15).

Stela F Altar, Copán

That the two distinctive sets of bicephalic creatures, arranged at right angles, are represented by the tricephalic unit, is clearly demonstrated by a drawing published by Maudslay (1889–1902, I: Pl. 114f, g, h) and later by Spinden (1913: Fig. 99) of the altar in front of Stela F at Copán (Fig. 6c). On one side is shown the drawing of the saurian head, presented frontally with two jaguars scrambling off its sides at right angles. The markings directly above the eyes, within the supra-orbital plates, are identical to those markings on the temple frieze painted on the vase (Fig. 6b), but this time they are on the creature's snout. Spinden reproduces a drawing of the bicephalic creature represented in the Copán altar in which the jaguar is now seen in frontal view. The long-lipped head without lower jaw is seen in profile on both sides.

The foregoing three examples of the tricephalic unit in Maya art are enough to demonstrate that this arrangement of bicephalics was important iconographically. Its relationship to Olmec and Izapan-style art is clear.

SUMMARY (TABLE 1)

(1) The bicephalic creature in Olmec, Izapan-style, and Maya art is comprised of distinctive heads demonstrating basically opposite characteristics. On one side are the feline-serpent traits, while on the other are the serpent-saurian traits. These are most often joined by a serpent body, sometimes by a quadruped with saurian characteristics. The clearest serpent-body examples are seen on an Olmec sceptre from Tabasco (Fig. 2a1) and on Izapan-style Stela 19 at Kaminaljuyú (Fig. 4d). The two-headed quadruped is seen on Izapa Stela 6 (Fig. 5a). Maya examples of both creatures have been noted in the literature since the late nineteenth-century (Maudslay 1889-1902).

(2) The heads of the compound creatures on either one side or the other, or both, can be duplicated. In Olmec art the combination of two bicephalic creatures in bilateral fashion was presented visually as a tricephalic unit. One head of one of the bicephalic creatures was included in a central position and presented, either in frontal view (Fig. 2b) or in profile, flanked by the other bicephalic creature in duplicate fashion on either side (Fig. 1a). A tricephalic unit can be created by combining two bicephalic creatures facing inward. The result is similar to a mask panel (Fig. 2b). This was demonstrated by duplicating the Tabasco sceptre and presenting it, dragon-face to dragon-face (Fig. 2a).

When a frontal view of a head was included in the tricephalic unit, identifying elements such as crossed bands or U shapes occupied the singular central position. This was demonstrated with profile and frontal views of the Tlapacoya vessel design (Figs. 3a, 2d). The tricephalic units in Olmec and Izapan-style art can, therefore, represent two bicephalics facing toward a central head with crossed bands (Figs. 3a, 4a) or a U shape (Figs. 1a, d, 2b, c, 4b). These in turn can be crossed with other bicephalic units at right angles. Sometimes the crossed bands are duplicated and presented on either side of a composite head (Figs. 1b, 3b). In Maya art the feline and saurian traits of each head are always presented in figurative terms (Fig. 6).

(3) The mask panel and other similar tricephalic units are ancestral to the Izapan-style top- and baseline designs. The temple frame in Chenes architecture may be related to the same panels.

(4) In Izapan-style art, front and rear heads of bicephalic creatures were duplicated and presented, as on Izapan Stela 23, in bilateral rather than Greek-cross fashion (Fig. 4c). While presented as two separate entities, the duplicate heads are undoubtedly interrelated.

(5) Composite heads in tricephalic contexts retain the same relative position occupied in bicephalic contexts in all three areas.

(6) Saurian heads with crenellated markings occupy the front position in multiheaded units (Fig. 5a). The crossed bands associated with serpents and saurians may be relegated to the same position (Fig. 4a). U shapes associated with feline-serpent composites occupy the rear position of a bicephalic creature (Fig. 4b). The element is often placed within the central position of the tricephalic creature (Figs. 1a–c, 2b, c).

It may be that front and rear positions do not correspond to hierarchical systems of values.

TABLE I. SUMMARY OF OCCURENCES OF TRICEPHALIC UNITS

Date	Periods	Olmec	Olmecoid	Izapan	Maya
A.D. 800	Late Classic				Copán altar in front of Stela F (A.D. 721?)
					Vase
A.D. 600					Palenque panel (A.D. 692)
A.D. 200					
A.D. 400					
A.D. 200	Early Classic				
A.D. 100					
0	Protoclassic		Tres Zapotes Stela C (31 B.C.)	Abaj Takalik Stelas 3 and 4	
100 B.C.					
200 B.C.					
300 B.C.	Late Preclassic		Mask		
400 B.C.		Tlapacoya vessel(?)		Izapa Stelas 3, 6, 11, 23	
500 B.C.		Las Bocas vessel(?)		Kaminaljuyú Stela 19	
600 B.C.	Middle Preclassic	Necaxa figure(?)			
		Pendant			
700 B.C.		La Venta earplugs			

The vegetation often associated with saurians and other composites grows from heads occupying rear positions in bicephalic and tricephalic contexts (Figs. 2a, 4b, 5c).

The diagonal band may be a reference to a rear head which is also associated with vegetation (Fig. 2a).

CONCLUSIONS

The tricephalic unit in Olmec, Izapan-style, and Maya art is a special formal solution to a thematic problem of great complexity. The units signal, as well as show, the attributes of the heads comprising the joined bicephalic creatures. These are the prime carriers of meaning in the images.

The distinctive heads of the bicephalic units symbolize the dual nature of everything in the Pre-Columbian world. Under certain circumstances it was appropriate to point to this duality with only one head of a bicephalic creature while its opposing face was presented in two. Thus, the concept of a two-headed creature was multiplied so that the duality was not presented in back-to-back terms only but at right angles as well. This means that a composite creature with two feline, or feline-serpent, heads was crossed in perpendicular fashion to another composite creature with saurian-serpent heads to create a four-armed unit in the form of a Greek cross.

In effect, we are dealing with the duality referred to above, personified and symbolized by serpent-saurian heads on one side and feline-serpent heads on the other. Whenever the artist dealt with the representation of this creature with dual characteristics on a two-dimensional surface, whether in relief or painting, the solution was to select one for emphasis by presenting it in the center while the other was duplicated and presented on both sides.

The Olmec Style and Costa Rican Archaeology

Anatole Pohorilenko

TULANE UNIVERSITY

I speak with personal feeling on this subject... (Stirling 1968: 1)

What in 1918 was only a fascination became a fully blossomed love affair by 1920 when Matthew Stirling saw the "crying-baby" jade masquette at the Berlin Museum. When Matt joined the Smithsonian Institution in 1921, he was struck, he admitted, by the number of Olmec examples made of blue jade, a material apparently not otherwise found among the many jade specimens from Mexico, although present in Costa Rica (Stirling 1968: 4).

In 1964, accompanied by his lovely wife, Marion, and assistants, Matt led an expedition to Costa Rica. It was apparent then that his fascination with Costa Rican blue jade had never diminished for a moment; now, forty years later, among the problems to be investigated, one would be to locate the sources of Costa Rican blue jade. As in all great love stories, the lover is denied the pleasure for which he undergoes lifelong epic exploits: Matt never found those sources. Nonetheless, in his fruitful life, Matt made many discoveries and contributions, and two generations of archaeologists after him are still asking the questions that he posed forty years ago. In an attempt to honor the memory of this great man, Matthew Stirling, I submit a study of Olmec blue-jade artifacts from Costa Rica. They will be described, analyzed, compared, and discussed within the context of Costa Rican archaeology.

Since the fifties, more than anyone else, Carlos Balser (1959, 1961, 1969, and 1974) has been consistently writing on the Olmec presence in Costa Rica. Important contributions by Stirling (1961), M. Coe (1962b, 1965b), Stone (1966, 1972), and Easby (1968) have continually related the jade-working in Costa Rica to cultural developments in northern Mesoamerica. As a consequence, many specialized publications in the field of archaeology have included Costa Rica's Nicoya Peninsula as an integral part of Pre-Columbian Mesoamerica. But, surprisingly, up to this date, no one has systematically analyzed the few Olmec or Olmec-related artifacts from Costa Rica (Fig. 1). As a result of such an analysis, it is possible to propose that:

(1) The Olmec material from Costa Rica is stylistically very late. In the sequence of Mesoamerican temporal development it could be placed conservatively within the late Middle Preclassic to Late Preclassic Periods, *ca.* 400–200 B.C., if not later.

(2) Stylistically, this material relates to artifacts found in Guerrero, Chiapas, highland Guatemala, and El Salvador much more than it relates to those of La Venta.

(3) As a result of the above, and in addition to the contextual information that surrounds the recovery of this material in Costa Rica, it could not have been ancestral to, have influenced, or in any way have been responsible for, the development and cult of the Costa Rican axe gods.

(4) The presence of the Olmec-related material found in Costa Rica does not warrant the incorporation of the Nicoya

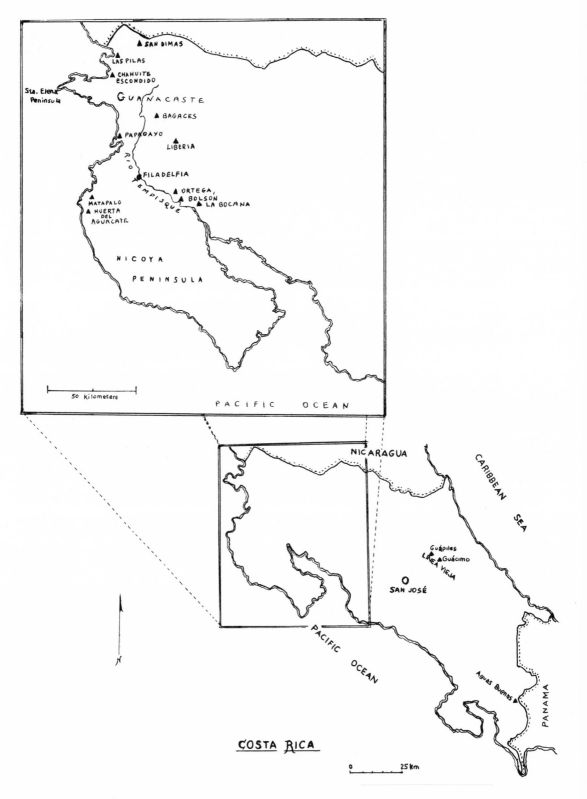

Fig. 1 Map of Costa Rica showing some of the sites that have yielded Zoned Bichrome pottery and/or Olmec and Maya artifacts. Drawing by the author.

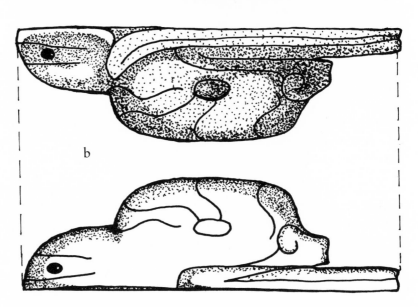

Fig. 2 *Atepocate,* from Bagaces, Guanacaste. Cat. No. 4428, Museo del Instituto Nacional de Seguros, San José. *a.* Photograph by Héctor Gamboa P., courtesy of the Museo del Instituto Nacional de Seguros. *b.* Dorsal and ventral views. Drawing by Robert J. Twardzik (after a drawing by the author).

Peninsula within the Mesoamerican cultural sphere.

OLMEC-STYLE ARTIFACTS FROM COSTA RICA

Atepocates ("*Spoons*")[1]

1. *Atepocate.* Catalogue Number 4428, Museo del Instituto Nacional de Seguros, San José (Fig. 2). This measures 9.2 centimeters in length by 2.9 centimeters at its maximum width, and weighs *ca.* 175 grams. It is reported to be from Bagaces, Guanacaste. The material used for its manufacture is greenish-blue jadeite, excep-

tionally translucent. Incised with carefully executed fine lines, a duck's head appears depicted on the dorsal side. These wavy incisions are carefully repeated, exactly over the dorsal ones, on the ventral side of the piece. Given the differences in surface this would not have been possible were it not for the extraordinary translucence of the material. The tail of the *atepocate,* which, in effect, constitutes the duck's bill, is broken in two different places, indicating that the bill was cut slightly open. The lower part of the bill is broken at one of the two angled perforations for horizontal suspension. If one hung the *atepocate* the way it normally hangs, the duck's head would hang upside down. It is quite possible that the incision of the duck was not made by the artist who originally carved the *atepocate,* but by a later artist who was impressed by the magnificent transparency of the jadeite. Another perforation pierces the piece approximately at the

[1] A detailed study of the so-called Olmec "spoons" (Pohorilenko 1972:36 and Fig. 57) revealed that these artifacts may be representations of tadpoles. They are rendered plain, and in composite or compounded representations. The Nahuatl name for tadpole is *atepocate.* This identification fits very well within the overall thematic aspects of Olmec representation, which is characterized by an extraordinary interest in the genetic process, as is the case with the Olmec "baby-face" representations.

level where the eye of the tadpole should be. This perforation must have been added in Costa Rica where, except for the winged pendants, jades of such size hang vertically. Among the Olmec, the *atepocates* were horizontal pectorals. It is quite possible that this beautiful artifact was first intended, by the Olmec, to be an *atepocate*. The form, finish, and type of drilling for horizontal suspension all seem to indicate an Olmec type of execution. Later perhaps, for reasons already mentioned, a compounded representation was created by reworking the piece into a duck's head by means of incision and modification of the *atepocate's* tail. A compounded representation is different from a composite representation. The latter combines different referential signs into an anthropomorphic or zoomorphic figure, as in a bird-monster *atepocate* (Pohorilenko 1977: 3). A compounded representation occurs, not when different referential signs are articulated to form a composite design, but when one or more designs, composite or not, are expressed by the same artifact, usually in a nonrelated fashion. Our *atepocate* expresses two unrelated concepts. Both of these representational forms are typical in Olmec representations. This piece has been illustrated by Balser (1974: Pl. VIII, Fig. 1).

2. *Atepocate*. Catalogue Number 4429, Museo del Instituto Nacional de Seguros, San José (Fig. 3). This artifact, reported to be from Bagaces, Guanacaste, measures 10.7 centimeters by 4.2 centimeters. The medium used is an opaque bluish-green jadeite. Its weight is approximately 212 grams. There are two angular, tubularly drilled holes for horizontal suspension on the top (straight) side of the piece. As in Figure 2, these holes are not visible from the ventral side of the artifact, a characteristically Olmec method of placing suspension holes. This highly polished artifact exhibits several major incised lines. One runs the length and along the upper edge of the head of the *atepocate,* which, in this case, faces right. Another, dividing the upper edge, follows the spinal length of this larva. Parallel to the spinal incision, another incised line begins at the base of the tail. It seems to follow the upper edge of the ventral depression. A short, arched, in-

cised line is placed between the head and spinal incisions. A fifth incision follows the base of the head and extends, for a short distance, along the edge of the ventral depression, emphasizing the lower outline of the artifact. These incisions are not as carefully executed as the ones in the above piece. In addition to the broken and repaired tail, the head of the *atepocate* also shows signs of wear and repair. It is possible that the wear or breakage of the end portion of the head was the result of an attempt to drill a frontal perforation for vertical suspension. This piece has been illustrated by Balser (1974: Pl. VIII, Fig. 2).

3. Incomplete or modified *atepocate*. Museo del Instituto Nacional de Seguros, San José. This artifact measures 13.4 centimeters by 2.6 centimeters, and is listed as being from Bagaces, Guanacaste. It is carved out of opaque grayish-blue jadeite. At the narrow end of the piece, one finds two biconically drilled perforations, one above the other, for vertical suspension. There are two incisions on the ventral side of the artifact, which may be interpreted as being either canines or claws. Technically they are not very well rendered, and their interpretation is open to speculation. This artifact has a peculiar aspect to it. It looks as if the artisan had made a mistake in executing the design. It is obvious that the intended design is that of an *atepocate*. This is possible to establish because the stages of the execution of the design are evident. First, the artist began by placing two parallel lines sufficiently wide to contain the upper loops of the three bodily sections that compose the *atepocate*. The first mistake was that he never removed the jade between the loops inside the parallel lines. Second, and more important, he overlooked the fact that compositionally the neck loop should have been brought farther down, and not remain as short as the other loops within the parallel lines. Furthermore, the arch that corresponds to the back of the neck in the figure is too close to the outer edge of the piece, suggesting that a strip of jade has been removed along the whole upper length of the *atepocate*. This is further indicated by the absence of the angularly drilled holes for horizontal suspension which would be found on the spinal portion of the piece.

Fig. 3 *Atepocate,* from Bagaces, Guanacaste. Cat. No. 4429, Museo del Instituto Nacional de Seguros, San José. Photograph by Héctor Gamboa P., courtesy of the Museo del Instituto Nacional de Seguros.

But, if the artist realized his mistake, he might have left the piece unfinished without bothering to place the suspension holes. The poorly made incisions and the double holes for vertical suspension may have been applied at a later time. This piece has been illustrated by Balser (1974: Pl. VIII, Fig. 4).

4. Composite *atepocate.* Private collection. This artifact of bluish-green jadeite with cloudy spots is reported as having been found in the vicinity of Guácimo, Línea Vieja. It measures 10.3 centimeters in length by 4.2 centimeters in width. This artifact shows a composite representation made up of a hooked, raptorial bird's beak, a flaming eyebrow, and a down-projecting curved fang. This combination is placed on the head portion of the larva. However, the overall morphology of the piece is that of the *atepocate,* with its appropriately hollowed-out belly and tail. String-sawing was apparently used for cutting the openings between the upper and lower beaks. A faint incised line outlines the opening between the beaks and the fang. Another faint incision runs the spinal length of the piece, beginning in the head portion before the eyebrow. A similar line is evident on the lower edge of the belly and tail. It appears that the tail has been shortened and smoothed. Two obvious frontal and conically drilled perforations appear below the flam-

ing brow. On the upper edge of the figure, not visible from the front, there are two angular, tubular-drilled perforations for horizontal suspension. They are placed on either side of the flaming brow. It is interesting to note that the later-applied biconical perforations also appear to be for the purpose of horizontal suspension. Stylistically similar artifacts are reported by Easby (1968: 90) to have come from El Salvador, Michoacán, and Guerrero, as an indication of Olmec–Costa Rican contact at the Late Preclassic level. This piece has been illustrated by Easby (1968: Fig. 64).

5. Composite *atepocate.* Private collection. The material used for the carving of this artifact is bluish-green jadeite, and it is reputed to have come from Línea Vieja. No dimensions were available, but it is slightly larger than the one above. This particular "bird monster," as this kind of composite *atepocate* is called in the specialized literature, has a much larger and more rounded beak than its above counterpart. In this figure, the raptorial aspects of the design are much more emphasized. The tail is explicitly depicted by means of parallel incised lines. Another fine incised line, as if defining the figure's morphology, runs along its spinal, ventral, and tail edges. This figure is carved to face the viewer's left side. As in the preceding piece, this one has a three-pointed flaming eye-

brow, with the last point subdivided. A large, frontal, biconical perforation, placed below the hump preceding the eyebrow, lends a huge nostril to this figure's head. Another frontal, biconical drilling in the upper right hand side of the tail indicates that at one time, despite its upper angular holes for horizontal suspension, this *atepocate* hung vertically by its tail opening.

6. Composite *atepocate*. Private collection (Fig. 4). Carved out of bluish-green jadeite, this piece constitutes one of the best examples of reworked Olmec material yet found in Costa Rica. Its dimensions are 10.4 centimeters in length by 5.0 centimeters in width, with Línea Vieja as its place of provenience. There is little distinction between this and the other composite *atepocates* of the bird-monster variety described previously. The hooked raptorial beak, the three-pointed flaming eyebrow, and the upward-curved rictus of the mouth are the characteristic elements that relate this particular composite *atepocate* to the bird-monster subclass or variety. A lower beak, possibly an egg-tooth, and a down-projecting curved fang may have been part of the composition; the piece shows break-marks in the places where these elements previously appeared. There is a small curved incision following the outline of the lump connecting the hooked beak to the beautifully rendered flaming eyebrow. The base of the eyebrow is incised in a semicircular petaloid motif, forming a three-looped pattern. The tip of these rounded petals rests on the inner edge of the raised surface that delimits the spinal length of the *atepocate*. Another fine incision follows the outline of the buccal rictus. The tail of this *atepocate* has been cut and extensively reworked. On the surface of the tail, two drilled depressions, a bit off line, suggest that these may have been intended as perforations for vertical suspension. Inspired by the birdlike design at the head of the piece, incisions suggesting feathers were placed on the tail end of the figure, obviously in post-Olmec times. Two angularly placed, minutely drilled, tubular perforations are located in areas before and after the flaming eyebrow. These perforations are for the purpose of horizontal suspension. Not satisfied with these, a post-Olmec

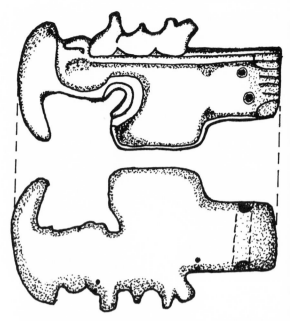

Fig. 4 Composite *atepocate*, dorsal and ventral views, from Línea Vieja. Private collection, San José. Drawing by Robert J. Twardzik (after a drawing by the author).

craftsman drilled a wide orifice the width of the tail. This kind of perforation for vertical suspension is also typically Costa Rican, as is shown by several animal pendants published by Easby (1968). In this piece, the Costa Rican artisan intended to drill the holes for vertical suspension frontally. Realizing, however, the thickness of the material, he decided to drill it through the width of the tail.

Head Pendants

7. The Butterfly Man pendant. Catalogue Number L65.7.1, Guennol Collection of Mr. and Mrs. Alastair Bradley Martin, Katonah, New York (Fig. 5). Exquisite imperial green jadeite was used for the manufacture of this splendid artifact. Found in the vicinity of Unión de Guápiles, Línea Vieja, this piece measures 4.9 centimeters in height by 3.8 centimeters in width. This small pendant depicts the upper torso of a winged and helmeted "baby-face." The helmeted head is depicted in relief, showing puffy eyes, a nose with a perforated septum, and a toothless mouth that is typically Olmec. A small quasi-conical pit is drilled into each

Fig. 5 The Butterfly Man pendant, from the vicinity of Unión de Guápiles, Línea Vieja. Cat. No. L65.7.1, Guennol Collection of Mr. and Mrs. Alastair Bradley Martin, Katonah, New York. Photograph courtesy of The Brooklyn Museum.

of the mouth corners. The eyes appear exceedingly swollen. The incised outline of the "bags under the eyes" not only emphasizes the swollen aspect of the eyes, but is carried down to meet the upper lip. On the outer side of each tumid palpebra there is a small drilled pit, a feature I consider unusual. Each ear is incised and adorned with a circle that may be regarded as an earspool, although the right one is barely visible. The face is surmounted by a helmet composed of a band and a crown. The band shows some semicircular incisions. Rising above the band, and located in the central front portion of the crown, a corncob-like incision appears flanked by two pit depressions. Each of these depressions is further outlined by a finely incised line. The curvaceous wings have their dynamic contour further emphasized by an equally fluid incised line. Arms and shoulders are depicted by means of incision. These incised lines are characterized by a superb mastery and control of this difficult technique of drawing on stone. The elegance and assurance with which they are rendered may be compared only to the brush-strokes in some Japanese paintings from the late seventeenth century. The central and upper tips of the wings show small biconical perforations. The back of the pendant has two large holes for suspension. This piece has been illustrated by Balser (1959: Fig. B; 1961: Fig. 1).

8. Stirrup-shaped pendant. Catalogue Number NW-CR-37-CC, private collection, on loan to the Denver Art Museum, Denver (Fig. 6). This fine dark bluish jadeite artifact comes from Hacienda "El Viejo," near Filadelfia, Nicoya Peninsula. It measures 6.0 centimeters in height and 4.1 centimeters in width, with a depth of 2.54 centimeters. Except for two cracks in the upper bow section of the piece, it is in excellent condition, exhibiting an even polish with little trace of wear. Apparently it was broken in modern times but has been well repaired. This artifact is carved in the round and depicts a helmeted head held by two hands whose arms create an arched loop above the head. The helmet or skull cap is shaped like a deep concave basin. In fact, it bears a close morphological resemblance to the shape of the caps of the highland Guatemala mushroom stones, which have been dated to the Late Preclassic Period. Under this helmet, two horizontally slit eyes appear imbedded in swollen tissue. The well-carved nose is short and wide, with a perforated septum which has been broken. The half-open mouth is typically Olmec. It is characterized by a thick projecting upper lip and a less-prominent lower one. The visible upper gums show no teeth, and two small drill pits are placed at the corners of the mouth. Two finely drilled biconical perforations at about earlobe level may possibly depict pierced earlobes. The chin is formed by two pits drilled on the sides. A beard, perhaps false, appears on the projection below the chin and is indicated by six incised straight lines. The stirrup effect is created by the two arms fused together at the level where they would normally join the shoulders. The hands holding the helmeted head meet under the chin and are indicated by four incised lines. A lapidary technique known as string-sawing was used in the manufacture of this carving. This technique is not common in the Olmec pieces from the heartland. It is interesting to note that this artifact has no drilled perforations for suspension. However, this fact in no way prevents

Anatole Pohorilenko

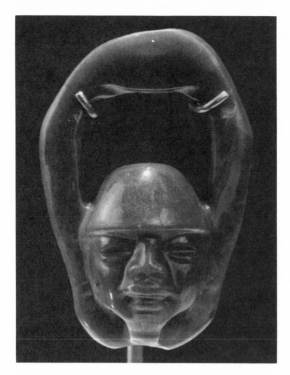

Fig. 6 Stirrup-shaped pendant, from Hacienda "El Viejo," near Filadelfia, Nicoya Peninsula. Cat. No. NW-CR-37-CC, private collection, on loan to the Denver Art Museum, Denver. Photograph courtesy of the Denver Art Museum.

the artifact from being a pendant, since the space provided by the welded arms is suitable for a hanging attachment. Although it is a miniature, the proportions and general aspect of this remarkable helmeted head remind one of the colossal heads from the Olmec heartland. This figure has been previously described and illustrated by Balser (1969: 244, Figs. 1, 2).

Figure Pendants

9. Standing winged figure. Catalogue Number L56.10.1, Guennol Collection of Mr. and Mrs. Alastair Bradley Martin, Katonah, New York (Fig. 7). Bluish-green jadeite was used in the manufacture of this piece. It measures 5.7 centimeters in height by 4.8 centimeters in width. Its general provenience is given as the Nicoya Peninsula. Of all the Olmec pieces from Costa Rica, this one is the best known. Stylistically, this figure has a classic Olmec head, whereas the rest of its body exhibits a different

pictorial tradition. Except for the three-dimensional aspect that characterizes the workmanship of its head, there is a predominant flatness characterizing the rest of the figure. This and the Butterfly Man are the only carved Olmec winged representations known. The elements that characterize this representation as Olmec are the rendering of the head and the cleft-rectangle emblem on its buckle. The head of this figure is a classic Olmec "baby-face" representation. The skull is very high and looks deformed as a result of possible binding practices. Almond-shaped and excised horizontally, the eyes are set into swollen tissue. The small, wide nose has a perforated septum. Toothless gums appear through an open, but small, trapezoidal mouth. Although not placed exactly where they should be, two drilled pits serve as hinges to a thick, trapezoidal upper lip and a thinner, arched, lower lip. A heavy, rounded chin separates two fleshy, low-hanging jowls. The long barlike ears, with drilled pits in the lobes, compress the head from both sides. The figure is virtually neckless. Starting somewhere under the jowls, a line in low relief defines the shoulders and bends at the elbows, giving this stocky torso a triangular upper half. The arms are held horizontally at chest level with the summarily incised hands pointing downward. Attached to the waist is a skirt. This skirt shows two parallel incised lines that serve as decorations. Both terminate at the buckle after circling the figure. The upper one exhibits a stepped design toward the sides of the figure. The stepped designs are not equidistant from the buckle; the one on the figure's right is closer. Below the lower horizontal line, one finds paired, short, vertical incisions, four on each side of the buckle. The legs are short, flat, and turned outward, not in typical Olmec execution. They are placed widely apart, but the cut separating them is curved and low. A pair of wings—the unusual and distinguishing feature of this piece—begins at the waist and extends upward to about the height of the forehead. The outer edge of each wing is serrated into three sections, a fact responsible for the interpretation of this artifact as a bat or butterfly. In addition to the two large biconical holes appearing on the upper-middle section of the

316

wings, there are two perforations for suspension placed where each wing joins the shoulder. These perforations are of the same type as those exhibited by the man-holding-a-jaguar piece, from Alta Verapaz, Guatemala (Easby and Scott 1970: Fig. 68). Part of the left leg and skirt are broken off. This piece has been illustrated by Balser (1959: Fig. A) and Bernal (1969a: Pl. 103).

10. Standing masked figure. Collection of Mr. and Mrs. Juan Dada, San José. This pendant, of whitened albitic jadeite, was found at Potrillos de Liberia, Guanacaste. It is 6.8 centimeters high, 2.9 centimeters wide. This is a curious piece, for its stylistic associations are not classically Olmec, and, consequently, it would not necessarily belong among the pieces that would qualify as such. But since it exhibits many post-Olmec Mesoamerican stylistic traits, and also some characteristics that relate it to Costa Rican pieces bearing Olmec traits, this, and the next, piece will be considered here. The strongest representational elements that characterize this piece are the various sections that form the face mask, particularly the motif found on the forehead, the mouth-plate, and the cheek plaques or scrolls. Over the forehead and exactly above the nose, there appears a three-tipped vegetal motif. A conical perforation, slightly off center, cuts through it. On each side of this motif, a quasi-rectangular plaque covers the brow region. The large rounded eyes peer from behind the brow plaques and the scrolls covering the cheeks. On the cheeks and nested inside the semicircle formed by the scrolls, two circularly drilled pits could appear to be dimples. Apparently this figure also wears a nose mask. A rectangular plate covering the mouth descends to, rises from, or in some form is attached to, a necklace or some other kind of neckgear. It is very likely that the facial scrolls may be attached to such a harness. The rectangular mouth-plaque strongly resembles the downturned mouth-masks depicted on some Izapan stelae. The plaques over the eyes may also be a version of the semi-elliptical eye-plaques found in some figures depicted on Izapan stelae. An example of a downturned mouth, or a mouth with an overextended upper lip, appears in a highland Guatemala piece

Fig. 7 Standing winged figure, from the Nicoya Peninsula. Cat. No. L65.10.1, Guennol Collection of Mr. and Mrs. Alastair Bradley Martin, Katonah, New York. Photograph courtesy of The Brooklyn Museum.

described by Easby and Scott (1970: Fig. 67). The neck is short but wide; around it is a necklace or collar. The shoulders are narrow. The pinched upper arms are fused to the body. The pinching of the upper arms appears to be an important stylistic element in Mesoamerican representation. It is the distinguishing trait in a type of figurine from Chiapas and highland Guatemala during the Late Preclassic Period (Navarrete 1972) and from Guerrero (Bernal 1969a: Pl. 62). Hands and arms are depicted as if holding an object. The same hand and arm position has been found depicted on a human-figure pendant from Guácimo, Línea Vieja (Easby 1968: Fig. 22). There is no stylistic relationship between this figure from Línea Vieja and those from Mesoamerica. This figure also wears a wide belt. It is not clear from the design whether the figure is holding a ceremonial bar or whether the horizontal incision at hand level is the upper part of the wide belt. Attached to the belt, a double-strand loincloth

317

hangs down over each thigh. Easby and Scott (1970: 110) note the resemblance between the double-strand loincloth worn by this figure and another one from Alta Verapaz, Guatemala (*ibid.:* Fig. 68). The short, squat, out-turned legs of this figure are very similar to those of our standing winged figure (Fig. 7). An illustration of this figure may be found in Easby and Scott (1970: Fig. 73).

11. Standing figure. Private collection, San José. The provenience of this saussurite or bowenite artifact is given as Bagaces, Guanacaste. The size of this pendant is 11.0 centimeters lengthwise by 4.6 centimeters widthwise. As in the preceding artifact, the aspect of this figure is very flat. The head is rather squarish. On the forehead one finds the same three-pointed motif that appears on the forehead of the previous figure. Below it is a strongly incised horizontal line delimiting, at the same time, both the upper portion of the rectangular eyes and the triangular nose. Rising from this line and flanking the three-pointed motif of the forehead is a pair of incised canine- or clawlike designs. Continuing the outer incised lines of the triangular nose, two incised lines descend as far as the mouth, strongly emphasizing and delimiting the cheeks. The trapezoidal mouth is the only feature lending this piece a certain Olmec character. Slightly projecting bars on the sides of the head suggest some form of stylized ears. The figure has no neck. The width of the head is carried downward, boxing in the shoulders and upper arms, and further emphasizing the size of the head. Two frontal perforations at the shoulders permit suspension. Lightly incised hands touch at the chest. As in the two previous pieces, the legs are short, squat, and placed widely apart, while exhibiting a low, carved separation. Only the front of the piece is polished. On the back, it is cut flat and shows a dorsal crest, evidence of a breakage technique typical of the axe gods of Costa Rica. The placement of the incised lines depicting its various features is quite angular and technically similar to that generally evident on Costa Rican lapidary work. The overall aspect of this artifact is strongly geometrical. It appears to be a Costa Rican copy of an Olmec-derived artifact. I was denied permission to photograph or draw this piece.

Masks

12. Split-mask pendant. Private collection, San José (Fig. 8). This pendant, carved of light bluish-green jadeite and reported to have been found at Bagaces, Guanacaste, measures 12.5 centimeters long by 3.7 centimeters in width. With large almond-shaped eyes and a widely open, Olmec-like mouth, this mask reminds one of the kind of Olmec mask that Navarrete (1971: Lám. 3) published as being from Chiapas, Mexico. The stylistic correspondence is further confirmed by the shape of the piece, the careless incising technique, and the general treatment of the mouth. Similar stylistic degeneration characterizes some of the Olmec Late Preclassic pieces of Chiapas and the Pacific coast of Guatemala. A similar piece was also reported from El Salvador by Boggs (1971: Figs. 1–4). In addition to the realistically executed eyes, nose, and mouth, the piece has a series of facial incisions. There are parallel incisions extending from the right side of the nose and over the cheek. Two connecting lines, vertically placed and carelessly incised, extend downward by the edge of the piece. It is not clear whether the artifact was cut in half in Costa Rica or in Mesoamerica. This practice, to a certain degree common in Mesoamerica during Preclassic times, is frequently observed in the material from Costa Rica. I am confident that someday we will be lucky enough to find the matching half. It is possible to suggest that its state as a pendant was acquired in Costa Rica. After the piece was cut in half, in order to transform it into a pendant, the far side of the face was further removed, cutting off part of the outer corner of the eye. It is likely that during the cutting process the upper-right-side tip of the mask cracked or broke off. This might have forced the artisan to cut and polish the broken edge. The placement of the biconical perforation for suspension takes into consideration the section that was removed, as it affects the vertical balance of the pendant. As a result, the piece hangs perfectly straight. Although it is very likely that, as an Olmec mask, this piece was fashioned elsewhere, I am con-

vinced that its condition as an *herencia* pendant was achieved in Costa Rica. The removal of the end portion of the right side of the face; the large, frontal, biconical drilling for vertical suspension; and its condition as a pendant, all seem to conform to the general format and function of the Costa Rican *colgantes*.

13. *Mask*. Catalogue Number NW-CR-37-J, private collection, on loan to the Denver Art Museum, Denver (Fig. 9). This squarish small mask is carved out of grayish-blue translucent jadeite and measures 7.28 centimeters in height and 6.98 centimeters in width. It is reported to be from Línea Vieja, on the Atlantic watershed. Despite its overall excellent condition, there are evidences of cutting on the upper right-hand side of the artifact. Also on the same side of the piece, the upper portion of the ear and a small section of the face are missing. On the left-hand corner, this carving has a tiny pair of suspension holes that exhibit a fracture which must have occurred in ancient times. On the upper portion of the mask, this figure sports two "horns," similar to those appearing on what Easby (1968: Fig. 21) and Stirling (1969: Fig. 2) regard as typical Costa

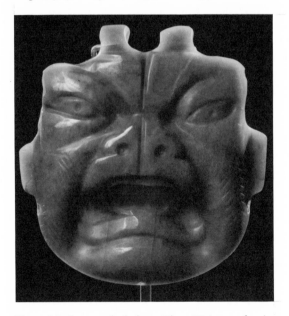

Fig. 9 Mask, reworked, from Línea Vieja, on the Atlantic watershed. Cat. No. NW-CR-37-J, private collection, on loan to the Denver Art Museum, Denver. Photograph courtesy of the Denver Art Museum.

Fig. 8 Split-mask pendant, from Bagaces, Guanacaste. Private collection, San José. Photograph by Héctor Gamboa P.

319

Rican bird celts from the same general area. These "horns" are laterally perforated, probably for suspension. The nose is wide and flat with frontally drilled nostrils. Over the upper lip, nose, and forehead a deep and wide incised vertical line seems to divide the mask into two sections. This line seems to indicate an attempt to saw the piece into two equal halves, possibly to create two *herencias*. As it is, this line only underscores the bilateral symmetry of the composition. The eyes are almond-shaped and placed on an inclined axis. Each eye shows drill pits in the center and outer edges, with the center ones suggesting pupils. As a result of the pressure created by the snarling mouth, the eyes appear to be set in tumid triangular planes. The large mouth is typically Olmec in outline. Its interior, however, is divided into three sections, as if scooped out by three jointly held fingers. Adding to the tension and ferociousness of this composition, parallel rows of short, chevron-like incisions slash the figure's cheeks. In addition to those in the "horns," there are five small holes on the edges of the mask: one under the chin, one below each of the short, barlike ears, and one at each corner on the top of the forehead. Based on the distribution of these openings, it is possible to suggest that this carved piece could have been worn either as a pendant or been sewn or attached to some unspecifiable surface. On the back of the piece, in the top left corner, there appears a single drill pit. It is very likely that this mask is an imported Olmec artifact that has been reworked by local artisans to conform with local usage. The wide incising technique, the presence of "horns," and the drilling through them, all suggest either reworking or adapting a foreign image to local representational concepts.

General Pendants

14. Incised bar pendant. Catalogue Number 4593, Museo del Instituto Nacional de Seguros, San José (Fig. 10). Of highly polished and translucent dark bluish-green jadeite, this piece is of exquisite simplicity and beauty. It is reported to be from Bagaces, Guanacaste. Rectangular in shape, it measures 11.1 centimeters by 1.7 centimeters. It is an *herencia*,

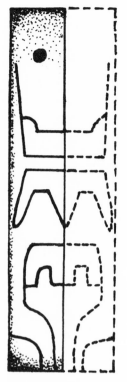

Fig. 10 Bar pendant, from Bagaces, Guanacaste. Cat. No. 4593, Museo del Instituto Nacional de Seguros, San José. Drawing by Robert J. Twardzik (after a drawing by Carlos Balser).

that is, the piece has been cut in half. This highly polished rectangular bar tapers off into almost a cutting edge on the end that has a frontal perforation for vertical suspension. It is delicately incised with some Olmec "glyphs." When the piece became an *herencia,* the cut seems to have divided the "glyphs" exactly in half. Since these "glyphs" are quite familiar to Olmec students, their reconstruction is not difficult and can be accurately done. Set vertically, below the suspension hole, there is an open-ended cartouche with a double-line base. Immediately below it there is a downturned E motif. This is followed by a possible torch motif, similar to the ones that are held by three of the Chalchuapa relief figures from El Salvador (Boggs 1950: Fig. 1). A curved incised line marks off the left lower corner of the piece.

15. Shell pendant. Catalogue Number 4430, Museo del Instituto Nacional de Seguros, San

Fig. 11 Shell-shaped pendant from the vicinity of Bagaces, Guanacaste. Cat. No. 4430, Museo del Instituto Nacional de Seguros, San José. Photograph by Héctor Gamboa P., courtesy of the Museo del Instituto Nacional de Seguros.

José (Fig. 11). Of highly polished blue-green jadeite, this pendant has the shape of a large clamshell. Reported to have been found in the vicinity of Bagaces, Guanacaste, it measures 12.1 centimeters in length by 4.5 centimeters in width and weighs 285 grams, approximately. This shell-like artifact has two small angular perforations on the hinge edge for horizontal suspension, probably as a pectoral. As in the case with many of the Olmec pieces found in Costa Rica, this piece has been reworked. One of its narrow ends has been cut and reworked into a point. At the opposite end, a large biconical hole has been drilled frontally, through the ventral side of the artifact. This perforation, which was very likely made in Costa Rica, although the manufacture of the piece itself took place elsewhere, indicates that the artifact was suspended vertically, with the point facing downward. This artifact has been illustrated by Balser (1974: Pl. VIII, Fig. 3), but it is not to be regarded as an *atepocate*, as Balser (*ibid.*: 21) claims.

DISCUSSION

Despite the small size of this sample, the fifteen Olmec or Olmec-related artifacts that comprise it were sufficient to allow me to detect and isolate, and then later to compare and explain, certain trends that characterize them. They do permit us to raise several important points of comparison related to Olmec materials in Costa Rica, and, further, to consider their possible archaeological implications.

Technique

In terms of the technical evidence exhibited in the manufacture of these pieces, a combination of local and Preclassic Mesoamerican traditions appears. Easby's (1968: 16–26) treatment of Costa Rican lapidary techniques is the best in the specialized literature and will serve as our comparative standard.

Most, if not all, jades in Mesoamerica and Costa Rica are, in fact, jadeite (Balser 1965: 34; Easby 1968: 15). Valued between six and seven on the Mohs scale of hardness, jadeite is harder than steel and has one of the highest resistances to scratching. Moreover, jadeite is among the toughest of minerals. It is tougher than all the precious gems that exceed it in hardness. As a result, it is more durable and, at the same time, more difficult to work than other minerals of equal hardness (Easby 1968: 19). Except for Number 11, all of the Olmec or Olmec-related pieces from Costa Rica use jadeite as the manufacturing medium. Pecking, incising, abrading, drilling, string-sawing, and polishing are techniques that appear both on Olmec and Costa Rican artifacts. However, different aspects of the same technique are emphasized in each area. For instance, jadeites from the Olmec heartland emphasize tubular drilling, whereas in the many Costa Rican jadeites that I examined, I found a significant predominance of conical and biconical drilling. In the case of conical drilling, as in Number 10, the narrower opening appears on the pictorial side of the artifact, that is, the piece is drilled conically from behind. In Mesoamerica, conical and biconical drilling is much less evident than in the Costa Rican material. There it begins to be noticeable in the material that stylistically belongs to the end of the Middle Preclassic Period, as in the stonework from Guerrero, Chiapas, and the Guatemala Pacific coast. String-sawing, a jadeite-working technique also found in Mesoamerica, has an uneven or localized distribution even in Costa Rica (Lothrop 1955; Stone and Balser 1965; Balser 1969), since it is predominantly found on objects from the Línea Vieja vicinity. While Lothrop (1955: 48) noted that the string-sawing technique had been used on the large and stylistically late Olmec figure in the Puebla Museum, Mexico, Stirling (1961) questioned whether this technique was even known by the early Olmec lapidaries.

The evidence that lapidaries in both Mesoamerica and Costa Rica used the same stone-working techniques is inconclusive. Given the hardness and toughness of jadeite, it is not surprising to find a certain similarity in the techniques used to work it, even if great distances separate the areas under consideration. What should be noted, perhaps, is whether there is a marked predominance in the use of certain techniques and their execution, with particular stress on the temporal and spatial information.

Execution

Greater differences become apparent when one considers the manner in which these techniques were used by both the Olmec and the Costa Rican lapidaries.

Olmec lapidaries avoided frontal perforation for purposes of suspension. Artifacts Numbers 1, 3, 4, 5, 7, 9, 10, 11, 12, 14, and 15 show frontal perforations, most of them biconical, except for Numbers 1 and 10, which have conical perforations. It must be pointed out that Numbers 1, 2, 4, 5, 6, 9, and 15 already had angularly drilled perforations for horizontal suspension. Two pieces, Numbers 6 and 13, have biconical perforations running the horizontal width of the piece, the latter through the "horns" and the former through the tail. Except for Number 8, which could hang as a pendant without perforations, all of the Olmec

artifacts have been reworked to hang vertically in the form of pendants. It must be pointed out that, among the Olmec, *atepocates* and shell-shaped pectorals hung horizontally.

Another problem of execution relates to the type and stylistic similarity of the legs in Numbers 9, 10, and 11. All three figures have short and widely separated legs, although the cut separating them is rather low. They also have turned-out feet. I have been unable to identify specifically this style of rendering lower limbs and feet in Mesoamerica. The closest that anything comes to it are some Mezcala, Guerrero, pieces in which the execution of legs and feet bears some similarity.

The application of drilled pits in mouth corners is a common practice among both the Olmec and Costa Rican lapidaries when rendering anthropomorphic representations.

Full-bodied figurines were, among the Olmec, three-dimensionally carved, and normally did not serve as pendants. In Late Preclassic Mesoamerica, however, in possibly post-Olmec times, there are full-bodied figurines which were used as pendants, as in a figure from Alta Verapaz, Guatemala, which shows double suspension holes on the back (Easby and Scott 1970: Fig. 68). Numbers 7 and 9 have similar suspension holes. Full-bodied figurines Numbers 9, 10, and 11 are drilled to serve as pendants. The only Olmec full-bodied figurines to serve as pendants are the plaque-axes. They are related pictorially but not morphologically, to the votive axes. They may be compared in M. Coe (1965b: Figs. 27 and 28). The only Costa Rican piece that tenuously resembles an Olmec plaque-axe is Number 11. Another Mesoamerican representational characteristic to have appeared recently in Costa Rica consists of a figure, or part of a figure, that is depicted inside a circle. This principle, which appears represented by our Number 8, may also be found in a stone sculpture from Guatemala (Shook and Heizer 1976: Figs. 1 and 2). The importation of such a piece into Costa Rica is understandable, for, structurally, it conforms to local representational principles (Easby 1968: Figs. 55–7). The back portions of Olmec artifacts, even of such "flat" objects as celts and plaque-axes, are appropriately carved and polished. In a great majority of cases, the back portions of Costa Rican celts are sawed flat with a visible attachment or "umbilicus." This dorsal ridge may be left rough or may be partly smoothed. Number 11 shows such a dorsal ridge. This lapidary practice is never found among Olmec stone artifacts.

Except for the bird celts, particularly those of the pointed-top variety, most Costa Rican celts are representationally two-dimensional. three-dimensional. Only three of the Olmec Except for the Olmec celts and plaque-axes most of the portable Olmec lapidary work is three-dimensional. Only three of the Olmec pieces from Costa Rica may be said to be three-dimensional. They are Numbers 7, 8, and 9. In each case, the three-dimensionality is expressed by the head of the figure, which, stylistically, is classically Olmec. It appears that the Olmec pieces that were of interest to the Costa Ricans were of the representationally "flat" type, such as the *atepocates,* shell pendants, and masks. Apparently, these pieces were preferred because their "flatness" resembled the Costa Rican types. Indeed, those that did not were often reworked in accordance with local tradition. Such is the case with Numbers 3, 6, 10, 11, 12, 14, and 15.

Although both lapidary traditions made use of incising as a technique to execute a design, there are some minute but important differences between them. The incising that appears on most of the La Venta lapidary material is extremely fine and sure in its application, and characterized by an absence of sharp angles and overlapping lines. Costa Rican artifacts show an incised line that is wider and characterized by a slashlike pattern where lines often cross one another. A stylistic angularity characterizes Costa Rican incisions and representation in general. This "geometricity" that characterizes Costa Rican lapidary production does not exist in classical Olmec stonework. In Mesoamerica, only Late Preclassic lapidary work from Guerrero, particularly that in the Mezcala style, reflects a comparable "geometricity."

Motifs

The buccal mask, facial scrolls, and the three-pointed motif that appears on Numbers 10 and 11 may be easily related to Monument 2 (Piña Chan and L. Covarrubias 1964: Pl. 1; Medellín Zenil 1971: Pl. 28) and Monument 5 (Stirling 1943b: Fig. 14b) from Cerro de las Mesas. In fact, the skirt of Monument 5 resembles that of our Number 9. The mouthplate on Number 10 resembles that on Monument 5.

The rendering of the lower limbs in Numbers 9, 10, and 11 is virtually identical. Among these figures, only Number 9 has a classic Olmec head. Number 10, on the other hand, has the pinched shoulders of the bench figurines from Chiapas and highland Guatemala (Shook 1971: 74; Navarrete 1972: Pls. 1–3) and may also be related to the Bolinas figurines from El Salvador reported by Stanley Boggs. Cursory analysis revealed that both the Bolinas and bench figurines may stem from a similar representational tradition.

Although not present in the Olmec or Olmec-related material from Costa Rica, I find that the tongue motif that characterizes some of the so-called "Olmecoid" pendants (Easby 1968: Fig. 8) may not be Olmec at all. It has been reported from South America, and Boggs (1976: Fig. 6) indicated its presence as far north as El Salvador.

As noted before, the double-strand loincloth also appears on figures from Alta Verapaz, Guatemala (Easby and Scott 1970: Fig. 68).

The "horn" motif shown on Number 13 seems to be strictly Costa Rican; there it is rendered in pairs and predominantly on bird celts. In Mesoamerica, the "horn" motif appears only on some of the bench figurines from Chiapas and highland Guatemala, always with a single "horn." Balser (1974: Pl. II, Fig. 3) publishes a single-"horn" steatite celt from Bagaces, Guanacaste. He implies that the piece might have been imported from Kaminaljuyú, Guatemala.

The unusual feature about Numbers 7 and 9 is that they have wings. Even though wings are indicated in some Olmec representations—the Tuxtla Statuette, for instance—they are generally rare. Even so, these two Olmec pieces from Costa Rica have a stronger representational connection with Mesoamerica than with

Costa Rica. In Preclassic Mesoamerica, there is a strong tradition of representing shamans wearing masks, or even whole outfits, of different animals. Both the Butterfly Man and the standing winged figure belong to this tradition. In the Costa Rican tradition of lapidary work, there are no representations of winged anthropomorphic figures. All of the winged figures are either birds or bats (Easby 1968: Figs. 46–8). Numbers 7 and 9 must have been originally carved in the Oaxaca–Chiapas area during the Middle to Late Preclassic Periods. There is evidence that in that area the cult of the bat was highly developed at that time.

Temporal Affiliation

In our descriptive analysis of the Olmec and Olmec-related materials found in Costa Rica, especially at the level of execution and motifs, there is no evidence of a direct connection between this material and the Olmec heartland in the Mexican southern Gulf Coast area. We have found, however, that stylistically the areas of Mesoamerican contact are Guerrero, Chiapas, highland Guatemala, El Salvador, and to a lesser degree Oaxaca and Honduras.

Given the late stylistic manifestation of the materials under consideration and the areas of affiliation in Mesoamerica, these contacts could not have occurred before the late Middle Preclassic or Late Preclassic Periods. I am not suggesting that this material entered Costa Rica during this time, although some of it may have. I am proposing, given the evidence, that the stylistic affiliation of the Costa Rican Olmec material, in its majority, corresponds temporally to Mesoamerican Late Preclassic material. This makes it almost coeval with the earliest dates given to the jadeite axe gods from the Nicoya Peninsula, which are temporally placed in the Zoned Bichrome Period, 300 B.C.–A.D 300 (Stone 1972: 95; Lange 1975: 95). A radiocarbon date of A.D. 144 was obtained by Stirling (1969: 240) for a fine string-sawn human figure of blue jadeite. It is unlikely that the Olmec pieces found in Costa Rica contributed in any way except quantitatively to the establishment of the cult of the Costa Rican axe gods. Balser (1959: 282; 1969: 243) reports that Numbers 7 and 8 were found buried

together with axe gods. Furthermore, some *huaqueros* told me, upon being shown photographs of Olmec material, that they recognized and had seen some of it, and that in most cases they found it together with Maya jadeite artifacts. This is corroborated by Balser (1969: 243) who notes that Number 8 was found in a cache that contained a green cut-jade celt with remnants of incised decorations "which are similar to those of the personage on the famous Leyden plaque."

This temporal information, together with the evidence regarding foreign jade materials in Costa Rica, begins to offer some concrete possibilities toward the solution of the problem regarding the Olmec presence in that country.

Balser (1974: 31–45, Pls. X–XX) shows a total of sixteen reworked jadeite plaques with Maya hieroglyphs, all of them from the province of Guanacaste. Stone (1972: 149) dates them A.D. 300–500. The reworking of these Maya jadeites is similar to that of the Olmec pieces: biconical drilling for vertical or, in a few cases, horizontal suspension; disregard for the possible original significance of the pieces; and splitting them into *herencias*. It is very likely that the Olmec jadeites entered Costa Rica together with, or as part of, the same distributional mechanism that brought in the Maya pieces. The stylistic "lateness" and their regional affiliation in Mesoamerica certainly support this position.

EARLY COSTA RICAN ARCHAEOLOGY

Apparently, the initial contact between the Greater Nicoya area (Norweb 1964) and Mesoamerica first took place during the Zoned Bichrome Period established by M. Coe and Baudez (1961). The corresponding period in Mesoamerica is the Late Preclassic. Lange (1975: 94) reports that at Las Pilas, on the Pacific coast near the Costa Rica–Nicaragua border, he found pottery fragments of the Paso Caballo Ceroso type that indicate to him indirect commercial contact with the Maya lowlands. These fragments occur temporally within the Catalina Phase, *ca.* 300 B.C.–A.D. 200. Lange adds that this initial contact is intensified in later periods. Aguilar (1976: 76) supports Lange's assertion by showing that, in the central highlands of Costa Rica, during his Curridabat Phase, there is an intensification in the presence of some Mesoamerican traits. Aguilar notes that Curridabat Phase materials relate to those of the Linear Decorated Period in the Nicoya Peninsula, which dates from A.D. 300 to 500. Aguilar (*ibid.*) adds that he found, in association with López Polychrome pottery, "uno de los más bellos ejemplares de jade del tipo olmeca." Alas, he does not illustrate it. Although I mention these contacts with Mesoamerica, they are in no way extensive. On the contrary, the cultural connections are much stronger with areas to the south. Ceramic evidence from different areas of Costa Rica indicates sufficient similarity and standardization by the time of the Zoned Bichrome Period to permit me to suggest a cultural cohesiveness of a developed nature characterized by a local syncretic tradition with strong affiliations to the south, rather than to the north. The Pavas Phase in the central highlands (Aguilar 1975: 25–6), the El Bosque Phase in the Atlantic watershed (Snarskis 1976: 106), and the Concepción and Aguas Buenas Phases in the southeast of Costa Rica (Haberland 1976: 116), all share significant attributes with Zoned Bichrome materials (Baudez 1967). They also relate to the ceramics from Santa María, at the site of Girón, Panamá (Aguilar 1975: 26), and to those from Momil, in Colombia (Aguilar 1975: 26; Snarskis 1976: 106). Sweeney (1976: 39) states categorically: "The inclusion of Nicoya in Mesoamerica is unwarranted."

It is clear that by Early Classic times two major jade-working centers existed in Costa Rica, one in the Guanacaste region and the other along the Atlantic watershed (Easby 1968: 96). Apparently, the lapidary work of the latter reflects more South American trading influences, and that of the former, those from the north. Contact between these centers is also evident (Balser 1974). Trading contact between Costa Rica and Mesoamerica is apparent from the distribution of Costa Rican manufactured artifacts, such as the axe god, in Guerrero and the Maya highlands where local lapidaries occasionally copied them (Easby 1968: 96). An axe god was also present in the Cerro de las Mesas jade cache (Stirling 1941). This is

further evidence that this trade took place during Late Preclassic or Early Classic times.

The connective route between the Greater Nicoya and Mesoamerica was probably overland, with northeast Honduras as the gateway. Referring to Baudez (1970), Healy (1975: 66) notes that the Costa Rican axe gods (200 B.C.–A.D. 800) are broadly similar to many serpentine pieces from northeast Honduras. These pieces are found during the Selin Period (A.D. 600–900), thus overlapping in time with the Costa Rican material. However, evidence suggests that this trade route was already in use during earlier times, when Usulatán pottery was traded as far south as Costa Rica. Andrews (1977: 119) believes that Usulatán pottery originates in western El Salvador or in Guatemala. Sharer (1974: 171) notes that Usulatán pottery greatly contributed to Chalchuapa's Late Preclassic prosperity. However, this pottery does not reach the shores of Lake Yojoa, Honduras, until the Eden I Phase (400–100 B.C.) at Los Naranjos (Andrews 1977: 119). It is about this time that Usulatán pottery reaches El Hacha, Guanacaste, where it was found with early Palmar ware and jadeite (Stone 1972: 54). Later, Usulatán pottery inspired some local styles of coastal Nicoya during the Linear Decorated Period (Sweeney 1976: 38). Despite this evidence, we should not discount the possible importance of coastal maritime routes between the Nicoya Peninsula and Pacific-coast Mesoamerica. It is possible to conclude from this evidence that the first contacts between Mesoamerica and the Nicoya Peninsula are in the form of trade and not a settlement by Mesoamerican peoples or shamans who came to teach the Costa Ricans Mesoamerican cultural traditions. These contacts were apparently established during the Zoned Bichrome Period, with Olmec materials coming into Costa Rica at that time or thereafter and possibly following the Greater Nicoya–northeast Honduras trade route overland.

Despite suggestions that the Olmec came to Costa Rica in search of blue-green jadeite, no sources of this material have yet been found in Costa Rica. I agree with Easby (1968: 89) that the most obvious—and perhaps the only—La Venta–Costa Rica similarity is the emphasis in both places, but to different degrees, on the ritual significance of celts. However, it is not possible to accept as an explanation, even if the jadeite sources were known, that the demand for Costa Rican jadeite at La Venta should necessarily account for the transmission to Costa Rica of Olmec concepts, particularly when the isolation of such concepts is based on such loose iconographic methods as those that suggest Olmec *chaneques* whenever one finds crouched anthropomorphic figures on Costa Rican celts. On the other hand, I do believe that the Costa Rican axe gods may embody some Mesoamerican concepts, but not necessarily Olmec ones. The concepts expressed by the Costa Rican axe gods relate to jade, celts, avian elements, and possibly agricultural practices (Pohorilenko, in preparation). Except perhaps for the use of jade, these individual elements must have been part of the Mesoamerican cultural inventory in pre-Olmec times, rather than being introduced by the Olmec. Olmec art seems to reflect their systematization and institutionalization into a body of beliefs that still maintained many shamanistic characteristics (Pohorilenko 1977: 14). Such Mesoamerican concepts, as generally reflected by the artifacts under consideration, existed before the appearance of the Olmec and surely thereafter. Still, when one superficially examines and compares such representational elements as pits drilled in the corners of mouths, composite representations, the splitting of artifacts into *herencias,* and so on —that is, when one compares lists of characteristics without any regard for their representational systemic context—it becomes easy to discover points of contact between the La Venta and Costa Rican styles of jade-working and, given the temporal precedence of the former over the latter, consequently to attribute to the latter the significance of the former. A more profound analysis will reveal that the representational elements usually considered in such comparisons may not have been exclusively Olmec, but generally appear in Guerrero, Chiapas, highland Guatemala, El Salvador, and Honduras during the Late Preclassic and Early Classic Periods. By the time the described Olmec pieces found their way to Costa

Rica, local stone carvers had already incorporated and systematized the above-mentioned traits into their lapidary tradition. One possibility is that such traits reached Costa Rica without the aid of the Olmec, but overland via the trade route that brought in the Usulatán pottery. Ferrero (1975: 63), using different evidence, has also expressed doubts about the Olmec influence in Costa Rica.

One often sees the term "Olmecoid"—a most unfortunate term—applied to the axe gods of Costa Rica. It must be pointed out that the term "Olmecoid," even when applied in a derivative sense—that is, a representation derived from or related to the Olmec style—should never carry any content or thematic connotations, but be strictly limited to those aspects that are stylistic or descriptive. Even stylistically, I do not find Costa Rican axe gods to be "Olmecoid."

As I have shown, the available Olmec pieces from Costa Rica should never be used as evidence for direct contact between La Venta and the Nicoya Peninsula. The most likely explanation for their presence in Costa Rica is that they were traded into that area by the Maya. Increasing archaeological evidence seems to support this position. The reason for their import may be the same as the one Easby (1968: 77) proposed for the import of Maya artifacts: "The reworked jades hint that the supply of raw material was running low."

Recently, new evidence of certain Mesoamerican ceremonial practices has appeared in Costa Rica. Carlos Balser had the kindness to send me a photograph of some "striations" and "pit marks" (Pohorilenko 1975). He claims that these Olmec ceremonial markings are found in the Guanacaste area and on the Atlantic coast. The reproduced boulder was from the Diquís region. As I noted in my paper, this practice of applying such ceremonial markings on Olmec sculptures and boulders was not limited to the Preclassic Period, but there is evidence that it continued in post-Olmec times as well.

To conclude, I present a summary of the evidence:

(1) Sources for the Costa Rican bluish-green

jadeite—a material much esteemed by local lapidaries—are unknown.

(2) Artifacts of bluish-green jadeite carved in Olmec or Olmec-related styles have been found in Costa Rica.

(3) Most, if not all, of the Olmec or Olmec-related pieces found in Costa Rica have strong stylistic relationships to the Late Preclassic–Early Classic lapidary work from Guerrero, Chiapas, highland Guatemala, and El Salvador.

(4) Many of the Olmec or Olmec-related pieces have been found in Costa Rica together with local axe gods and imported Maya artifacts.

(5) Early Costa Rican archaeology does not evidence a significant Mesoamerican cultural influence.

(6) There is, however, evidence for trading contacts between Costa Rica and Mesoamerica during the Late Preclassic Period and later.

(7) It appears that the Olmec or Olmec-related materials entered Costa Rica during Late Preclassic–Early Classic times. Their entrance into this region in even later times is not discarded as a possibility.

(8) The Olmec or Olmec-related materials found in Costa Rica did not influence local lapidary work.

(9) The majority of the Olmec-style pieces found in Costa Rica was reworked according to the local lapidary tradition. Apparently, the Olmec conceptual significance of these artifacts was unknown to the Costa Ricans.

As a result of this evidence, it is not possible to suggest that the Olmec were *in* Costa Rica or that they traded directly with local populations. If these pieces were traded-in by the Maya, which is very likely, we should not speak of an Olmec presence in Costa Rica. Since the inclusion of the Nicoya Peninsula in the Mesoamerican culture sphere is the result of the presence of the Olmec or Olmec-related materials found there, the evidence presented in this paper does not support such a practice.

ACKNOWLEDGMENTS The author wishes to thank the following persons for their kindness and assistance during his search for Olmec materials in Costa Rica. My special gratitude goes to Héctor Gamboa P., head of the Departamento de Antropología e Historia of the Museo Nacional de Costa Rica, and to Zulay Soto, Director of the Museo del Instituto Nacional de Seguros, San José. Most valuable help was provided by Carlos Balser, Luis Ferrero, Carlos Aguilar, Alfonso Jiménez-Alvarado, Randolph von Breymann, Mr. and Mrs. J. Dada Olijia, Frederick Lange, Michael Snarkis, Maximo Acosta, and Elizabeth K. Easby, with whom discussion was most illuminating. This research trip to Costa Rica was sponsored by a generous grant from the Shell International Studies Fellowships allotted to Tulane University for the purposes of doctoral research by the Shell Companies Foundation, Inc., and it is gratefully acknowledged.

Bibliography

AGRINIER, PIERRE

1960   The Carved Human Femurs from Tomb 1, Chiapa de Corzo, Chiapas, Mexico. *Publication No. 5: Papers of the New World Archaeological Foundation,* no. 6. Orinda.

1969   Excavations at San Antonio, Chiapas, Mexico. *Papers of the New World Archaeological Foundation,* no. 24. Brigham Young University, Provo.

AGUILAR P., CARLOS H.

1975   El Molino: Un Sitio de la Fase Pavas en Cartago. *Vínculos,* vol. 1, núm. 1, pp. 18-56. Museo Nacional de Costa Rica, San José.

1976   Relaciones de las Culturas Precolombinas en el Intermontano Central de Costa Rica. *Vínculos,* vol. 2, núm. 1, pp. 75-86. Museo Nacional de Costa Rica, San José.

ANDREWS, E. WYLLYS, V

1977   The Southeastern Periphery of Mesoamerica: A View from Eastern El Salvador. *In* Social Process in Maya Prehistory: Studies in honour of Sir Eric Thompson (Norman Hammond, ed.), pp. 113-134. Academic Press, London, New York, and San Francisco.

ARELLANOS, RAMÓN, LOURDES BEAUREGARD, PAULA HOMBERGER KROTSER, RAMÓN KROTSER, ALFONSO MEDELLÍN, JUAN SÁNCHEZ, and LUIS SÁNCHEZ

1975   El proyecto de investigación "Higueras." *In* Balance y perspectiva de la antropología de mesoamérica y del centro de México, Arqueología I, *XIII mesa redonda,* pp. 309-314. Sociedad Mexicana de Antropología, Mexico.

BÁEZ-JORGE, FÉLIX

1973   Los zoque-popolucas: estructura social. *Serie de Antropología Social,* no. 18. Instituto Nacional Indigenista, Secretaría de Educación Pública, Mexico.

BALL, HAL C.

1975   Radiocarbon Dating of "Pot Belly" Statuary in El Salvador. *Newsletter,* vol. 4, no. 10, p. 4. Institute of Maya Studies of the Miami Museum of Science, Miami.

BALSER, CARLOS

1959   Los "Baby-Faces" Olmecas de Costa Rica. *Actas del XXXIII Congreso Internacional de Americanistas, San José, 20-27 Julio 1958,* tomo II, pp. 280-285. Lehmann, San José.

1961   La Influencia Olmeca en algunos motivos de la arqueología de Costa Rica. *Informe Semestral,* enero a junio 1961, pp. 63-78. Instituto Geográfico de Costa Rica, Ministerio de Obras Públicas, San José.

1965   El jade precolombino de América. *Boletín Informativo,* no. 15, pp. 31-50. Museo Nacional de Costa Rica, San José.

1969   A New Style of Olmec Jade with String Sawing from Costa Rica. *Verhandlungen des XXXVIII. Internationalen Amerikanistenkongresses, Stuttgart-München, 12. bis 18. August 1968,* Band I, pp. 243-247. Kommissionsverlag Klaus Renner, München.

1974   El jade de Costa Rica: Un Album Arqueológico. San José.

BARTHEL, THOMAS S.

1967   Notes on the inscription on a carved bone from Yucatan. *Estudios de Cultura Maya,* vol. VI, pp. 223-241. Seminario de Cultura Maya, Universidad Nacional Autónoma de México, Mexico.

BAUDEZ, CLAUDE F.

1967   Recherches archéologiques dans la vallée du Tempisque, Guanacaste, Costa Rica. *Travaux & Mémoires de l'Institut des Hautes Etudes de l'Amérique Latine,* 18. Université de Paris, Paris.

1970   Central America. (Trans. by James Hogarth.) *Archaeologia Mundi.* Nagel Publishers, Geneva, Paris, and Munich.

BECKER-DONNER, ETTA

1965   Die Mexikanischen Sammlungen. Museum für Völkerkunde, Wien.

BENSON, ELIZABETH P.

1971   An Olmec Figure at Dumbarton Oaks. *Studies in Pre-Columbian Art and Archaeology,* no. 8. Dumbarton Oaks, Washington.

329

1976   Motifs in Olmec Sculpture. *Actas del XXIII Congreso Internacional de Historia del Arte: España entre el Mediterráneo y el Atlántico, Granada 1973,* vol. I, pp. 65-80. Universidad de Granada, Departamento de Historia del Arte, Granada.

BENSON, ELIZABETH P. (ed.)

1968   Dumbarton Oaks Conference on the Olmec, October 28th and 29th, 1967. Dumbarton Oaks Research Library and Collection, Washington.

BERGER, RAINER, JOHN A. GRAHAM, and ROBERT F. HEIZER

1967   A Reconsideration of the Age of the La Venta Site. *In* Studies in Olmec Archaeology, pp. 1-24. *Contributions of the University of California Archaeological Research Facility,* no. 3. Department of Anthropology, Berkeley.

BERNAL, IGNACIO

1967   Museo Nacional de Antropología de México: Arqueología. Aguilar, Mexico.

1968   El mundo olmeca. Editorial Porrúa, S.A., Mexico.

1969a   The Olmec World. (Trans. by Doris Heyden and Fernando Horcasitas.) University of California Press, Berkeley and Los Angeles.

1969b   100 Great Masterpieces of the Mexican National Museum of Anthropology. Harry N. Abrams, Inc., Publishers, New York.

BERNAL, IGNACIO, and ANDY SEUFFERT

1970   Yugos de la colección del Museo Nacional de Antropología. *Union Académique Internationale, Corpus Antiquitatum Americanensium, Mexico,* IV. Instituto Nacional de Antropología e Historia, Mexico.

1979   The Ballplayers of Dainzú. *Artes Americanae,* vol. 2. Akademische Druck- u. Verlagsanstalt, Graz.

BESTERMAN, THEODORE

1965   Crystal Gazing: A Study in the History, Distribution, Theory and Practice of Scrying. University Books, New Hyde Park, New York.

BEYER, HERMANN

1927   Review of *Tribes and Temples* by Frans Blom and Oliver La Farge. *El México Antiguo,* tomo II, nos. 11-12, pp. 305-313. Mexico.

BLOM, FRANS, and OLIVER LA FARGE

1926-   Tribes and Temples: A Record of the Ex-
1927   pedition to Middle America Conducted by The Tulane University of Louisiana in 1925. 2 vols. *Middle American Research Series, Tulane University of Louisiana, Publication* 1. New Orleans.

BOCABULARIO DE MAYATHAN

1972   Bocabulario de Mayathan: Das Wörterbuch der yukatekischen Mayasprache. Vollständige Faksimile-Ausgabe des Codex Vindobonensis

S.N. 3833 der Österreichischen Nationalbibliothek. Einleitung Ernst Mengin. *Bibliotheca Linguistica Americana,* vol. I. Akademische Druck- u. Verlagsanstalt, Graz.

BOGGS, STANLEY H.

1950   "Olmec" Pictographs in the Las Victorias Group, Chalchuapa Archaeological Zone, El Salvador. *Notes on Middle American Archaeology and Ethnology,* vol. IV, no. 99, pp. 85-92. Carnegie Institution of Washington, Department of Archaeology, Cambridge.

1971   An Olmec Mask-Pendant From Ahuachapan, El Salvador. *Archaeology,* vol. 24, no. 4, pp. 356-358. Archaeological Institute of America, New York.

1976   Las esculturas espigadas y otros datos sobre las ruinas de Cara Sucia, Departamento de Ahuachapán. *Anales del Museo Nacional "David J. Guzman,"* nos. 42-48, 1968-1975, pp. 37-55. Ministerio de Educación, San Salvador.

BONHAM-CARTER, G. F.

1967   Fortran IV Program for Q-Mode Cluster Analysis of Nonquantitative Data Using IBM 7090/7094 Computers. *Computer Contribution 17.* State Geological Survey, The University of Kansas, Lawrence.

BORHEGYI, STEPHAN F. DE

1961a   Ball-game Handstones and Ball-game Gloves. *In* Essays in Pre-Columbian Art and Archaeology (Samuel K. Lothrop and others), pp. 126-151. Harvard University Press, Cambridge.

1961b   Miniature Mushroom Stones from Guatemala. *American Antiquity,* vol. 26, no. 4, pp. 498-504. Society for American Archaeology, Salt Lake City.

BROWN, ANTOINETTE B.

n.d.   The Uses of Bone Strontium Assay in Dietary Reconstruction. Paper presented at the 41st Annual Meeting of the Society for American Archaeology, St. Louis, May, 1976.

BRUDER, J. SIMON, ELINOR G. LARGE, and BARBARA L. STARK

1975   A Test of Aerial Photography in an Estuarine Mangrove Swamp in Veracruz, Mexico. *American Antiquity,* vol. 40, no. 3, pp. 330-337. Society for American Archaeology, Washington.

BRUSH, CHARLES F.

1965   Pox Pottery: Earliest Identified Mexican Ceramic. *Science,* vol. 149, no. 3680, pp. 194-195. American Association for the Advancement of Science, Washington.

n.d.   A Contribution to the Archaeology of Coastal Guerrero, Mexico. Doctoral dissertation, Columbia University, New York, 1969.

BRUSH, ELLEN S.

n.d.   The Archaeological Significance of Ceramic

Figurines from Guerrero, Mexico. Doctoral dissertation, Columbia University, New York, 1968.

BUSHNELL, GEOFFREY H. S.

1964 An Olmec Jade Formerly Belonging to Alfred Maudslay. *XXXV Congreso Internacional de Americanistas, México, 1962, Actas y Memorias,* vol. 1, pp. 541-542. Instituto Nacional de Antropología, Mexico.

CAMPBELL, LYLE, and TERRENCE KAUFMAN

1976 A Linguistic Look at the Olmecs. *American Antiquity,* vol. 41, no. 1, pp. 80-89. Society for American Archaeology, Washington.

CARLSON, JOHN B.

1975 Lodestone Compass: Chinese or Olmec Primacy? *Science,* vol. 189, no. 4205, pp. 753-760. American Association for the Advancement of Science, Washington.

1977 The Case for Geomagnetic Alignments of Precolumbian Mesoamerican Sites — The Maya. *Katunob,* vol. X, no. 2, pp. 67-88. Museum of Anthropology, University of Northern Colorado, Greeley.

CARNEIRO, ROBERT L.

1970 A Theory of the Origin of the State. *Science,* vol. 169, no. 3947, pp. 733-738. American Association for the Advancement of Science, Washington.

CASO, ALFONSO

1958 The Aztecs: People of the Sun. (Trans. by Lowell Dunham.) University of Oklahoma Press, Norman.

1964 Interpretación del Códice Selden 3135 (A. 2)/ Interpretation of the Codex Selden 3135 (A. 2). (Trans. by Jacinto Quirarte and revised by John A. Paddock.) Sociedad Mexicana de Antropología, Mexico.

1965 ¿Existió un imperio olmeca? *Memoria de El Colegio Nacional,* tomo V, año de 1964, núm. 3, pp. 11-60. Editorial del Colegio Nacional, Mexico.

CASO, ALFONSO, IGNACIO BERNAL, and JORGE R. ACOSTA

1967 La cerámica de Monte Albán. *Memorias del Instituto Nacional de Antropología e Historia,* XIII. Secretaría de Educación Pública, Mexico.

CERVANTES, MARÍA ANTONIETA

1969 Dos elementos de uso ritual en el arte olmeca. *Anales del Instituto Nacional de Antropología e Historia,* época 7a., tomo I, 1967-1968, pp. 37-51. Secretaría de Educación Pública, Mexico.

1976 La estela de Alvarado. *Actas del XLI Congreso Internacional de Americanistas, México, 2 al 7 de septiembre de 1974,* vol. II, pp. 309-322. Instituto Nacional de Antropología e Historia, Mexico.

CLEWLOW, C. WILLIAM, JR.

1970 Comparison of Two Unusual Olmec Monuments. *In* Magnetometer Survey of the La Venta Pyramid and Other Papers on Mexican Archaeology, pp. 35-40. *Contributions of the University of California Archaeological Research Facility,* no. 8. Department of Anthropology, Berkeley.

1974 A Stylistic and Chronological Study of Olmec Monumental Sculpture. *Contributions of the University of California Archaeological Research Facility,* no. 19. Department of Anthropology, Berkeley.

CLEWLOW, C. WILLIAM, JR., and CHRISTOPHER R. CORSON

1968 New Stone Monuments from La Venta, 1968. Appendix II to The 1968 Investigations at La Venta (Robert F. Heizer, John A. Graham, and Lewis K. Napton). *In* Papers on Mesoamerican Archaeology, pp. 171-182. *Contributions of the University of California Archaeological Research Facility,* no. 5. Department of Anthropology, Berkeley.

CLEWLOW, C. WILLIAM, JR., RICHARD A. COWAN, JAMES F. O'CONNELL, and CARLOS BENEMANN

1967 Colossal Heads of the Olmec Culture. *Contributions of the University of California Archaeological Research Facility,* no. 4. Department of Anthropology, Berkeley.

COBEAN, ROBERT H., MICHAEL D. COE, EDWARD A. PERRY, JR., KARL K. TUREKIAN, and DINKAR P. KHARKAR

1971 Obsidian Trade at San Lorenzo Tenochtitlan, Mexico. *Science,* vol. 174, no. 4010, pp. 666-671. American Association for the Advancement of Science, Washington.

CODEX DRESDEN

1882 Die Mayahandscrift der Königlichten Öffentlichen Bibliothek zu Dresden. Herausgegeben von Prof. Dr. E. Förstemann. Verlag von A. Naumann & Schroeder, Leipzig.

CODEX ZOUCHE-NUTTALL

1975 The Codex Nuttall: A Picture Manuscript from Ancient Mexico. The Peabody Museum Facsimile edited by Zelia Nuttall; with new introductory text by Arthur G. Miller. Dover Publications, Inc., New York.

COE, MICHAEL D.

1962a An Olmec Design on an Early Peruvian Vessel. *American Antiquity,* vol. 27, no. 4, pp. 579-580. Society for American Archaeology, Salt Lake City.

1962b Preliminary Report on Archaeological Investigations in Coastal Guanacaste, Costa Rica. *Akten des 34. Internationalen Amerikanistenkongresses, Wien, 18.-25. Juli 1960,* pp. 358-365. Verlag Ferdinand Berger, Horn-Wien.

1965a The Jaguar's Children: Pre-Classic Central Mexico. The Museum of Primitive Art, New York.

1965b The Olmec Style and its Distributions. *In* Handbook of Middle American Indians (Robert Wauchope, ed.), vol. 3, pp. 739-775. University of Texas Press, Austin.

1966a An Early Stone Pectoral From Southeastern Mexico. *Studies in Pre-Columbian Art and Archaeology,* no. 1. Dumbarton Oaks, Washington.

1966b The Maya. *Ancient Peoples and Places,* vol. 52. Frederick A. Praeger, New York.

1967a Map of San Lorenzo: An Olmec Site in Veracruz, Mexico. Department of Anthropology, Yale University, New Haven.

1967b An Olmec Serpentine Figurine at Dumbarton Oaks. *American Antiquity,* vol. 32, no. 1, pp. 111-113. Society for American Archaeology, Salt Lake City.

1967c Solving a Monumental Mystery. *Discovery,* vol. 3, no. 1, pp. 21-26. Peabody Museum of Natural History, Yale University, New Haven.

1968a America's First Civilization. American Heritage Publishing Co., Inc., New York, in association with the Smithsonian Institution, Washington.

1968b San Lorenzo and the Olmec Civilization. *In* Dumbarton Oaks Conference on the Olmec, October 28th and 29th, 1967 (Elizabeth P. Benson, ed.), pp. 41-78. Dumbarton Oaks Research Library and Collection, Washington.

1970 The Archaeological Sequence at San Lorenzo Tenochtitlán, Veracruz, Mexico. *In* Magnetometer Survey of the La Venta Pyramid and Other Papers on Mexican Archaeology, pp. 21-34. *Contributions of the University of California Archaeological Research Facility,* no. 8. Department of Anthropology, Berkeley.

1972 Olmec Jaguars and Olmec Kings. *In* The Cult of the Feline: A Conference in Pre-Columbian Iconography, October 31st and November 1st, 1970 (Elizabeth P. Benson, ed.), pp. 1-18. Dumbarton Oaks Research Library and Collections, Washington.

1973a The Iconology of Olmec Art. *In* The Iconography of Middle American Sculpture, pp. 1-12. The Metropolitan Museum of Art, New York.

1973b The Maya Scribe and His World. The Grolier Club, New York.

1974 Photogrammetry and the Ecology of Olmec Civilization. *In* Aerial Photography in Anthropological Field Research (Evon Z. Vogt, ed.), pp. 1-13. Harvard University Press, Cambridge.

1977 Olmec and Maya: A Study in Relationships. *In* The Origins of Maya Civilization (Richard E. W. Adams, ed.), pp. 183-195. *School of American Research Advanced Seminar Series.* University of New Mexico Press, Albuquerque.

COE, MICHAEL D., and CLAUDE F. BAUDEZ

1961 The Zoned Bichrome Period in Northwestern Costa Rica. *American Antiquity,* vol. 26, no.

4, pp. 505-515. Society for American Archaeology, Salt Lake City.

COE, MICHAEL D., and RICHARD A. DIEHL

1980 In the Land of the Olmec. 2 vols. University of Texas Press, Austin.

COE, WILLIAM R.

1965 Tikal, Guatemala, and Emergent Maya Civilization. *Science,* vol. 147, no. 3664, pp. 1401-1419. American Association for the Advancement of Science, Washington.

COE, WILLIAM R., and ROBERT STUCKENRATH, JR.

1964 A Review of La Venta, Tabasco and Its Relevance to the Olmec Problem. *The Kroeber Anthropological Society Papers,* no. 31, pp. 1-43. Department of Anthropology, University of California, Berkeley.

COE, WILLIAM R., EDWIN M. SHOOK, and LINTON SATTERTHWAITE

1961 The Carved Wooden Lintels of Tikal. *Museum Monographs, Tikal Reports,* no. 6, pp. 15-111. The University Museum, University of Pennsylvania, Philadelphia.

COHODAS, MARVIN

1976 The Iconography of the Panels of the Sun, Cross, and Foliated Cross at Palenque: Part III. *In* The Art, Iconography & Dynastic History of Palenque, Part III: Proceedings of the Segunda Mesa Redonda de Palenque, December 14-21, 1974—Palenque (Merle Greene Robertson, ed.), pp. 155-176. The Robert Louis Stevenson School, Pebble Beach.

COOK DE LEONARD, CARMEN

1967 Sculptures and Rock Carvings at Chalcatzingo, Morelos. *In* Studies in Olmec Archaeology, pp. 57-84. *Contributions of the University of California Archaeological Research Facility,* no. 3. Department of Anthropology, Berkeley.

COOPER, JOHN M.

1949 Fire Making. *In* Handbook of South American Indians (Julian H. Steward, ed.), vol. 5, pp. 283-292. *Smithsonian Institution, Bureau of American Ethnology, Bulletin 143.* U.S. Government Printing Office, Washington.

CORONA, GUSTAVO

1962 El Luchador Olmeca. *Boletín del Instituto Nacional de Antropología e Historia,* no. 10, pp. 12-13. Secretaría de Educación Pública, Mexico.

COVARRUBIAS, MIGUEL

1942 Origen y Desarrollo del Estilo Artístico "Olmeca." *In* Mayas y Olmecas: Segunda Reunión de Mesa Redonda Sobre Problemas Antropológicos de México y Centro América, Tuxtla Gutiérrez, Chiapas, pp. 46-49. Sociedad Mexicana de Antropología, Mexico.

1944 La Venta: Colossal Heads and Jaguar Gods. *DYN,* no. 6, pp. 24-33. Coyoacan, Mexico.

1946a El arte "olmeca" o de La Venta. *Cuadernos Americanos,* vol. XXVIII, no. 4, pp. 153-179. Mexico.

1946b Mexico South: The Isthmus of Tehuantepec. Alfred A. Knopf, New York. (British edition 1947: Cassel & Co., London.)

1957 Indian Art of Mexico and Central America. Alfred A. Knopf, New York.

1961 Arte indígena de México y Centroamérica. (Trans. by Sol Arguedas.) Universidad Nacional Autónoma de México, Mexico.

CURTIS, GARNISS H.

1959 The petrology of artifacts and architectural stone at La Venta. *In* Excavations at La Venta, Tabasco, 1955 (Philip Drucker, Robert F. Heizer, and Robert J. Squier), pp. 284-289. *Smithsonian Institution, Bureau of American Ethnology, Bulletin 170.* U.S. Government Printing Office, Washington.

DELGADO, AGUSTÍN

1965 Infantile and Jaguar Traits in Olmec Sculpture. *Archaeology,* vol. 18, no. 1, pp. 55-62. Archaeological Institute of America, New York.

DÍAZ DEL CASTILLO, BERNAL

1964 Historia verdadera de la conquista de la Nueva España. (Introducción y notas de Joaquín Ramírez Cabañas.) Tercera edición. Editorial Porrúa, Mexico.

DICKERSON, MARY C.

1913 The Frog Book. Doubleday, Page & Company, Garden City, New York.

DILLON, BRIAN D.

1975 Notes on Trade in Ancient Mesoamerica. *In* Three Papers on Mesoamerican Archaeology, pp. 79-135. *Contributions of the University of California Archaeological Research Facility,* no. 24. Department of Anthropology, Berkeley.

DOCKSTADER, FREDERICK J.

1964 Indian Art in Middle America. New York Graphic Society Publishers, Ltd., Greenwich.

DRENNAN, ROBERT D.

1976a Fábrica San José and Middle Formative Society in the Valley of Oaxaca. *In* Prehistory and Human Ecology of the Valley of Oaxaca (Kent V. Flannery, ed.), vol. 4. *Memoirs of the Museum of Anthropology, University of Michigan,* no. 8. Ann Arbor.

1976b Religion and Social Evolution in Formative Mesoamerica. *In* The Early Mesoamerican Village (Kent V. Flannery, ed.), pp. 345-368. Academic Press, New York, San Francisco, and London.

DRUCKER, PHILIP

1947 Some Implications of the Ceramic Complex of La Venta. *Smithsonian Miscellaneous Collections,* vol. 107, no. 8. The Smithsonian Institution, Washington.

1952 La Venta, Tabasco: A Study of Olmec Ceramics and Art. *Smithsonian Institution, Bureau of American Ethnology, Bulletin 153.* U.S. Government Printing Office, Washington.

1961 The La Venta Support Area. *In* A. L. Kroeber: A Memorial, pp. 59-72. *The Kroeber Anthropological Society Papers,* no. 25. Department of Anthropology, University of California, Berkeley.

n.d. The Ethnography of Olmec Sculpture. MS. 1979.

DRUCKER, PHILIP, and ROBERT F. HEIZER

1960 A study of the Milpa System of La Venta Island and its Archaeological Implications. *Southwestern Journal of Anthropology,* vol. 16, no. 1, pp. 36-45. University of New Mexico, Albuquerque.

1965 Commentary on W. R. Coe and Robert Struckenrath's Review of *Excavations at La Venta, Tabasco, 1955. The Kroeber Anthropological Society Papers,* no. 33, pp. 37-70. Department of Anthropology, University of California, Berkeley.

DRUCKER, PHILIP, ROBERT F. HEIZER, and ROBERT J. SQUIER

1957 Radiocarbon Dates from La Venta, Tabasco. *Science,* vol. 126, no. 3263, pp. 72-73. American Association for the Advancement of Science, Washington.

1959 Excavations at La Venta, Tabasco, 1955. *Smithsonian Institution, Bureau of American Ethnology, Bulletin 170.* U.S. Government Printing Office, Washington.

DUMBARTON OAKS, WASHINGTON

1963 Handbook of the Robert Woods Bliss Collection of Pre-Columbian Art. Dumbarton Oaks, Washington.

1969 Supplement to the Handbook of the Robert Woods Bliss Collection of Pre-Columbian Art. Dumbarton Oaks, Washington.

DURÁN, DIEGO

1964 The Aztecs: The History of the Indies of New Spain. (Trans. by Doris Heyden and Fernando Horcasitas.) Orion Press, New York.

1967 Historia de las Indias de Nueva-España y islas de Tierra Firme. Notas é ilustraciones de José F. Ramírez. 2 vols. plus atlas. Editora Nacional, Mexico.

EARLE, TIMOTHY K.

1976 A Nearest-Neighbor Analysis of Two Formative Settlement Systems. *In* The Early Mesoamercian Village (Kent V. Flannery, ed.), pp. 196-223. Academic Press, New York, San Francisco, and London.

EASBY, ELIZABETH KENNEDY

1966 Ancient Art of Latin America From the Collection of Jay C. Leff. The Brooklyn Museum, Brooklyn.

1968   Pre-Columbian Jade from Costa Rica. André Emmerich Inc., New York.

EASBY, ELIZABETH KENNEDY, and JOHN F. SCOTT

1970   Before Cortés: Sculpture of Middle America. The Metropolitan Museum of Art, New York.

EDMONSON, MUNRO S.

1965   Quiche-English Dictionary. *Middle American Research Institute, Tulane University, Publication 30.* New Orleans.

EKHOLM, GORDON F.

1944   Excavations at Tampico and Panuco in the Huasteca, Mexico. *Anthropological Papers of the American Museum of Natural History,* vol. XXXVIII, part V. New York.

1973   The Archaeological Significance of Mirrors in the New World. *Atti del XL Congresso Internazionale degli Americanisti, Roma–Genova, 3-10 Settembre 1972,* vol. I, pp. 133-135. Casa Editrice Tilgher, Genova.

EKHOLM-MILLER, SUSANNA

1973   The Olmec Rock Carving at Xoc, Chiapas, Mexico. *Papers of the New World Archaeological Foundation,* no. 32. Brigham Young University, Provo.

n.d.   The Olmec Presence in Chiapas. *Papers of the New World Archaeological Foundation,* no. 43. Brigham Young University, Provo. (In press.)

ELIADE, MIRCEA

1964   Shamanism: Archaic Techniques of Ecstasy. (Trans. by Willard R. Trask.) *Bollingen Series LXXVI.* Pantheon Books, New York.

ESPINOZA, GUSTAVO

1960   Newspaper article. *El Imparcial,* no. 12797, November 24. Guatemala City.

FERDON, EDWIN N., JR.

1953   Tonalá, Mexico: An Archaeological Survey. *Monographs of the School of American Research,* no. 16. Santa Fe.

FERNÁNDEZ, JUSTINO

1968   Arte olmeca. *Los Olmecas,* 10. Museo Nacional de Antropología, I.N.A.H.-S.E.P., Mexico.

FERRERO, LUIS

1975   Costa Rica precolombina: arqueología, etnología, tecnología, arte. Editorial Costa Rica, San José. (2nd edition 1977.)

FIELD, FREDERICK V.

1974   Pre-Hispanic Mexican Stamp Designs. Dover Publications, Inc., New York.

FLANNERY, KENT V.

1968   The Olmec and the Valley of Oaxaca: A Model for Inter-Regional Interaction in Formative Times. *In* Dumbarton Oaks Conference on the Olmec, October 28th and 29th, 1967 (Elizabeth P. Benson, ed.), pp. 79-117. Dumbarton Oaks Research Library and Collection, Washington.

1976   Research Strategy and Formative Mesoamerica. *In* The Early Mesoamerican Village (Kent V. Flannery, ed.), pp. 1-11. Academic Press, New York, San Francisco, and London.

FOSTER, GEORGE M.

1944   Nagualism in Mexico and Guatemala. *Acta Americana,* vol. II, nos. 1 y 2, pp. 85-103. Sociedad Interamericana de Antropología y Geografía, Mexico and Los Angeles.

1969   The Mixe, Zoque, Popoluca. *In* Handbook of Middle American Indians (Robert Wauchope, ed.), vol. 7, pp. 448-477. University of Texas Press, Austin.

FUENTE, BEATRIZ DE LA

1975   Las cabezas colosales olmecas. *Colección Testimonios del Fondo,* 34. Fondo de Cultura Económica, Mexico.

1977   Los hombres de piedra: escultura olmeca. Instituto de Investigaciones Estéticas, Universidad Nacional Autónoma de México, Mexico.

FUENTE, BEATRIZ DE LA (ed.)

1972   El arte olmeca. *Artes de México,* no. 154, año XIX. Mexico.

FUENTE, BEATRIZ DE LA (with the collaboration of Nelly Gutiérrez Solana)

1973   Escultura monumental olmeca: catálogo. *Cuadernos de historia del arte,* 1. Instituto de Investigaciones Estéticas, Universidad Nacional Autónoma de México, Mexico.

FURST, JILL LESLIE

1977   The Tree Birth Tradition in the Mixteca, Mexico. *Journal of Latin American Lore,* vol. 3, no. 2, pp. 183-226. UCLA Latin American Center, Los Angeles.

1978   Codex Vindobonensis Mexicanus I: A Commentary. *Institute for Mesoamerican Studies, Publication No. 4.* State University of New York, Albany.

FURST, PETER T.

1968   The Olmec Were-Jaguar Motif in the Light of Ethnographic Reality. *In* Dumbarton Oaks Conference on the Olmec, October 28th and 29th, 1967 (Elizabeth P. Benson, ed.), pp. 143-178. Dumbarton Oaks Research Library and Collection, Washington.

1972   Symbolism and psychopharmacology: The toad as earth mother in Indian America. *In* Religión en Mesoamérica, XII Mesa Redonda, pp. 37-46. Sociedad Mexicana de Antropología, Mexico.

n.d.   Shaft Tombs, Shell Trumpets and Shamanism: A Culture-Historical Approach to Problems in West Mexican Archaeology. Doctoral dissertation, Department of Anthropology, University of California, Los Angeles, 1966.

FUSON, ROBERT H.

1969   The Orientation of Mayan Ceremonial Centers. *Annals of the Association of American Geographers,* vol. 59, no. 3, pp. 494-511. Lawrence, Kansas.

GARCÍA PAYÓN, JOSÉ

1966   Prehistoria de Mesoamérica: Excavaciones en Trapiche y Chalahuite, Veracruz, México, 1942, 1951 y 1959. *Cuadernos de la Facultad de Filosofía, Letras y Ciencias,* 31. Universidad Veracruzana, Xalapa.

GARCILASO DE LA VEGA, EL INCA

1966   Royal Commentaries of the Incas and General History of Peru. 2 vols. (Trans. with an Introduction by Harold V. Livermore.) University of Texas Press, Austin and London.

GAY, CARLO T. E.

1966   Rock Carvings at Chalcacingo. *Natural History,* vol. LXXV, no. 7, pp. 56-61. American Museum of Natural History, New York.

1967   Oldest Paintings of the New World. *Natural History,* vol. LXXVI, no. 4, pp. 28-35. American Museum of Natural History, New York.

1971   Chalcacingo. Drawings by Frances Pratt. Akademische Druck- u. Verlagsanstalt, Graz. (Reprint 1972: International Scholarly Book Service, Portland.)

1972   Xochipala: The Beginnings of Olmec Art, The Art Museum, Princeton University, Princeton.

GIRARD, RAFAEL

1969   La misteriosa cultura olmeca: últimos descubrimientos de esculturas pre-olmecas en Guatemala. 3a. edición. Guatemala.

GONZÁLEZ CALDERÓN, O. L.

1977   Cabecitas olmecas: orígenes de la primera civilización de América. Dr. Luis González Calderón, Mexico.

GRAHAM, JOHN A.

1977   Discoveries at Abaj Takalik, Guatemala. *Archaeology,* vol. 30, no. 3, pp. 196-197. Archaeological Institute of America, New York.

GREEN, DEE F., and GARETH W. LOWE

1967   Altamira and Padre Piedra, Early Preclassic Sites in Chiapas, Mexico. *Papers of the New World Archaeological Foundation,* no. 20. Brigham Young University, Provo.

GREENE ROBERTSON, MERLE

1974   The Quadripartite Badge—A Badge of Rulership. *In* Primera Mesa Redonda de Palenque, Part I: A Conference on the Art, Iconography, and Dynastic History of Palenque; Palenque, Chiapas, Mexico. December 14-22, 1973 (Merle Greene Robertson, ed.), pp. 77-93. The Robert Louis Stevenson School, Pebble Beach.

GREENE ROBERTSON, MERLE, MARJORIE S. ROSENBLUM SCANDIZZO, and JOHN R. SCANDIZZO

1976   Physical Deformities in the Ruling Lineage of Palenque, and the Dynastic Implications. *In* The Art, Iconography & Dynastic History of Palenque, Part III: Proceedings of the Segunda Mesa Redonda de Palenque, December 14-21, 1974—Palenque (Merle Greene Robertson, ed.), pp. 59-86. The Robert Louis Stevenson School, Pebble Beach.

GROVE, DAVID C.

1968a   Chalcatzingo, Morelos, Mexico: A Reappraisal of the Olmec Rock Carvings. *American Antiquity,* vol. 33, no. 4, pp. 486-491. Society for American Archaeology, Salt Lake City.

1968b   The Pre-Classic Olmec in Central Mexico: Site Distribution and Inferences. *In* Dumbarton Oaks Conference on the Olmec, October 28th and 29th, 1967 (Elizabeth P. Benson, ed.), pp. 179-185. Dumbarton Oaks Research Library and Collection, Washington.

1970   The Olmec Paintings of Oxtotitlan Cave, Guerrero, Mexico. *Studies in Pre-Columbian Art and Archaeology,* no. 6. Dumbarton Oaks, Washington.

1972   Preclassic religious beliefs in Mexico's Altiplano Central. *In* Religión en Mesoamérica, XII Mesa Redonda, pp. 55-59. Sociedad Mexicana de Antropología, Mexico.

1973a   Olmec Altars and Myths. *Archaeology,* vol. 26, no. 2, pp. 128-135. Archaeological Institute of America, New York.

1973b   Review of *Chalcacingo* and *Xochipala: The Beginnings of Olmec Art* by Carlo T. E. Gay. *American Anthropologist,* vol. 75, no. 4, pp. 1138-1140. American Anthropological Association, Washington.

1974   The Highland Olmec manifestation: a consideration of what it is and isn't. *In* Mesoamerican Archaeology: New Approaches (Norman Hammond, ed.), pp. 109-128. University of Texas Press, Austin.

1976   Olmec Origins and Transpacific Diffusion: Reply to Meggers. *American Anthropologist,* vol. 78, no. 3, pp. 634-637. American Anthropological Association, Washington.

GROVE, DAVID C., and LOUISE I. PARADIS

1971   An Olmec Stela from San Miguel Amuco, Guerrero. *American Antiquity,* vol. 36, no. 1, pp. 95-102. Society for American Archaeology, Washington.

GROVE, DAVID C., KENNETH G. HIRTH, DAVID E. BUGÉ, and ANN M. CYPHERS

1976   Settlement and Cultural Development at Chalcatzingo. *Science,* vol. 192, no. 4245, pp. 1203-1210. American Association for the Advancement of Science, Washington.

GULLBERG, JONAS E.

1959   Technical notes on concave mirrors. *In* Excavations at La Venta, Tabasco, 1955 (Philip Drucker, Robert F. Heizer, and Robert J.

Squier), pp. 280-283. *Smithsonian Institution, Bureau of American Ethnology, Bulletin 170.* U.S. Government Printing Office, Washington.

GUZMÁN, EULALIA

1934   Los Relieves de las Rocas del Cerro de la Cantera, Jonacatepec, Mor. *Anales del Museo Nacional de Arqueología, Historia y Etnografía,* época 5, tomo I, núm. 2, pp. 237-251. Secretaría de Educación Pública, Mexico.

HABA, LOUIS DE LA

1974   Guatemala, Maya and Modern. *National Geographic,* vol. 146, no. 5, pp. 660-689. National Geographic Society, Washington.

HABEL, S.

1878   The Sculptures of Santa Lucia Cosumalwhuapa in Guatemala, with an Account of Travels in Central America and on the Western Coast of South America. *Smithsonian Contributions to Knowledge,* 269. Smithsonian Institution, Washington.

HABERLAND, WOLFGANG

1976   Gran Chiriquí. *Vínculos,* vol. 2, núm. 1, pp. 115-121. Museo Nacional de Costa Rica, San José.

HALLINAN, P. S., R. D. AMBRO, and J. F. O'CONNELL

1968   La Venta Ceramics, 1968. Appendix I to The 1968 Investigations at La Venta (Robert F. Heizer, John A. Graham, and Lewis K. Napton). *In* Papers on Mesoamerican Archaeology, pp. 155-170. *Contributions of the University of California Archaeological Research Facility,* no. 5. Department of Anthropology, Berkeley.

HARVARD UNIVERSITY, CAMBRIDGE

1940   An Exhibition of Pre-Columbian Art, January 15 through February 10, Arranged by the Peabody Museum and the William Hayes Fogg Art Museum. William Hayes Fogg Art Museum, Harvard University, Cambridge.

HATCH, MARION POPENOE

1971   An Hypothesis on Olmec Astronomy, with Special Reference to the La Venta Site. *In* Papers on Olmec and Maya Archaeology, pp. 1-64. *Contributions of the University of California Archaeological Research Facility,* no. 13. Department of Anthropology, Berkeley.

HAVILAND, WILLIAM A.

1977   Dynastic Genealogies from Tikal, Guatemala: Implications for Descent and Political Organization. *American Antiquity,* vol. 42, no. 1, pp. 61-67. Society for American Archaeology, Washington.

HEALY, PAUL F.

1975   H-CN-4 (Williams Ranch Site): Preliminary Report on a Selin Period Site in the Department of Colón, Northeast Honduras. *Vínculos,* vol. 1, núm. 2, pp. 61-71. Museo Nacional de Costa Rica, San José.

HEIZER, ROBERT F.

1960   Agriculture and the Theocratic State in Lowland Southeastern Mexico. *American Antiquity,* vol. 26, no. 2, pp. 215-222. Society for American Archaeology, Salt Lake City.

1964   Some Interim Remarks on the Coe–Stuckenrath Review. *The Kroeber Anthropological Society Papers,* no. 31, pp. 45-50. Department of Anthropology, University of California, Berkeley.

1967   Analysis of Two Low Relief Sculptures from La Venta. *In* Studies in Olmec Archaeology, pp. 25-55. *Contributions of the University of California Archaeological Research Facility,* no. 3. Department of Anthropology, Berkeley.

1968   New Observations on La Venta. *In* Dumbarton Oaks Conference on the Olmec, October 28th and 29th, 1967 (Elizabeth P. Benson, ed.), pp. 9-40. Dumbarton Oaks Research Library and Collection, Washington.

1971   Commentary on: The Olmec Region—Oaxaca. *In* Observations on the Emergence of Civilization in Mesoamerica (Robert F. Heizer, John A. Graham, and C. L. Clewlow, Jr., eds.), pp. 51-69. *Contributions of the University of California Archaeological Research Facility,* no. 11. Department of Anthropology, Berkeley.

HEIZER, ROBERT F., and PHILIP DRUCKER

1968   The La Venta Fluted Pyramid. *Antiquity,* vol. XLII, pp. 52-56. W. Heffer & Sons Ltd., Cambridge.

HEIZER, ROBERT F., PHILIP DRUCKER, and JOHN A. GRAHAM

1968   Investigations at La Venta, 1967. *In* Papers on Mesoamerican Archaeology, pp. 1-33. *Contributions of the University of California Archaeological Research Facility,* no. 5. Department of Anthropology, Berkeley.

HEIZER, ROBERT F., JOHN A. GRAHAM, and LEWIS K. NAPTON

1968   The 1968 Investigations at La Venta. *In* Papers on Mesoamerican Archaeology, pp. 127-154. *Contributions of the University of California Archaeological Research Facility,* no. 5. Department of Anthropology, Berkeley.

HENDERSON, JOHN S.

1979   Atopula, Guerrero, and Olmec Horizons in Mesoamerica. *Yale University Publications in Anthropology,* no. 77. Department of Anthropology, Yale University Press, New Haven.

n.d.   Preclassic Archaeology in the State of Guerrero, Mexico. Doctoral dissertation, Department of Anthropology, Yale University, New Haven, 1974.

HEYDEN, DORIS

1977   The Quechquemitl as a Symbol of Power in the Mixtec Codices. *Vicus Cuadernos,* vol. 1, pp. 5-23. John Benjamins B.V., Publisher, Amsterdam.

HIRTH, FRIEDRICH
1906   Chinese Metallic Mirrors, with Notes on Some Ancient Specimens of the Musée Guimet. *In* Boas Anniversary Volume: Anthropological Papers, pp. 208-256. G. E. Stechert & Co., New York.

HISSINK, KARIN, and ALBERT HAHN
1961   Die Tacana: Ergebnisse der Frobenius-Expedition nach Bolivien 1952 bis 1954. Band I: Erzählungsgut. W. Kohlhammer Verlag, Stuttgart.

ICHON, ALAIN
n.d.   Esculturas de piedra del Preclásico Tardio en La Lagunita, El Quiché, Guatemala. Paper presented at the International Symposium on Maya Art, Architecture, Archaeology and Hieroglyphic Writing, Guatemala, 1977.

ISBELL, WILLIAM H.
1978   Cosmological order expressed in prehistoric ceremonial centers. *Actes du XLIIe Congrès International des Américanistes, Congrès du Centenaire, Paris, 2-9 Septembre 1976,* vol. IV, pp. 269-297. Société des Américanistes, Musée de l'Homme, Paris.

JACK, ROBERT N., and ROBERT F. HEIZER
1968   "Finger-Printing" of Some Mesoamerican Obsidian Artifacts. *In* Papers on Mesoamerican Archaeology, pp. 81-100. *Contributions of the University of California Archaeological Research Facility,* no. 5. Department of Anthropology, Berkeley.

JONES, CHRISTOPHER
1977   Inauguration Dates of Three Late Classic Rulers of Tikal, Guatemala. *American Antiquity,* vol. 42, no. 1, pp. 28-60. Society for American Archaeology, Washington.

JORALEMON, PETER DAVID
1971   A Study of Olmec Iconography. *Studies in Pre-Columbian Art and Archaeology,* no. 7. Dumbarton Oaks, Washington.

1976   The Olmec Dragon: A Study in Pre-Columbian Iconography. *In* Origins of Religious Art & Iconography in Preclassic Mesoamerica (H. B. Nicholson, ed.), pp. 27-71. UCLA Latin American Center Publications and Ethnic Arts Council of Los Angeles, Los Angeles.

KELLEY, DAVID H.
1962   Glyphic Evidence for a Dynastic Sequence at Quiriguá, Guatemala. *American Antiquity,* vol. 27, no. 3, pp. 323-335. Society for American Archaeology, Salt Lake City.

1965   The birth of the gods at Palenque. *Estudios de Cultura Maya,* vol. V, pp. 93-134. Seminario de Cultura Maya, Universidad Nacional Autónoma de México, Mexico.

KIDDER, ALFRED V.
1965   Preclassic Pottery Figurines of the Guatemalan Highlands. *In* Handbook of Middle American Indians (Robert Wauchope, ed.), vol. 2, pp. 146-155. University of Texas Press, Austin.

KIDDER, ALFRED V., JESSE D. JENNINGS, and EDWIN M. SHOOK
1946   Excavations at Kaminaljuyu, Guatemala. *Carnegie Institution of Washington, Publication 561.* Washington.

KLEIN, CECELIA F.
1976   The Face of the Earth: Frontality in Two-Dimensional Mesoamerican Art. Garland Publishing, Inc., New York and London.

KROTSER, G. RAMÓN
1973   El agua ceremonial de los olmecas. *Boletín del Instituto Nacional de Antropología e Historia,* época II, no. 6, pp. 43-48. Mexico.

KUBLER, GEORGE
1961   Rival Approaches to American Antiquity. *In* Three Regions of Primitive Art, pp. 61-75. *The Museum of Primitive Art, Lecture Series,* no. 2. New York.

1962   The Art and Architecture of Ancient America: The Mexican, Maya, and Andean Peoples. Penguin Books, Baltimore. (2nd edition 1975.)

KUSCH, EUGEN
1962   Guatemala im Bild: Land der Maya. Verlag Hans Carl, Nürnberg.

LANGE, FREDERICK W.
1975   Excavaciones de Salvamento en un Cementerio del Período Bicromo en Zonas, Guanacaste, Costa Rica. *Vínculos,* vol. 1, núm. 2, pp. 92-98. Museo Nacional de Costa Rica, San José.

LATHRAP, DONALD W.
1974   The Moist Tropics, the Arid Lands, and the Appearance of Great Art Styles in the New World. *In* Art and Environment in Native America (Mary Elizabeth King and Idris R. Traylor, Jr., eds.), pp. 115-158. *Special Publications, The Museum, Texas Tech University,* no. 7. Lubbock.

LAUFER, BERTHOLD
1915   Optical Lenses. *T'oung Pao,* vol. XVI, pp. 169-228. E. J. Brill, Leide, The Netherlands.

LAUGHLIN, ROBERT M.
1975   The Great Tzotzil Dictionary of San Lorenzo Zinacantán. *Smithsonian Contributions to Anthropology, no. 19.* Smithsonian Institution Press, Washington.

LEE, THOMAS A., JR.
1967   Figurillas antropomorfas de Chiapa de Corzo. *Estudios de Cultura Maya,* vol. VI, pp. 199-214. Seminario de Cultura Maya, Universidad Nacional Autónoma de México, Mexico.

1969   The Artifacts of Chiapa de Corzo, Chiapas, Mexico. *Papers of the New World Archaeological Foundation,* no. 26. Brigham Young University, Provo.

1974a The Middle Grijalva regional chronology and ceramic relations: a preliminary report. *In* Mesoamerican Archaeology: New Approaches (Norman Hammond, ed.), pp. 1-20. University of Texas Press, Austin.

1974b Mount 4 Excavations at San Isidro, Chiapas, Mexico. *Papers of the New World Archaeological Foundation,* no. 34. Brigham Young University, Provo.

LEÓN-PORTILLA, MIGUEL

1963 Aztec Thought and Culture: A Study of the Ancient Nahuatl Mind. (Trans. by Jack Emory Davis.) University of Oklahoma Press, Norman.

LEOPOLD, A. STARKER

1972 Wildlife of Mexico: The Game Birds and Mammals. University of California Press, Berkeley, Los Angeles, and London.

LINDEN MUSEUM, STUTTGART

1967 Kunst der Maya, aus Staats- und Privatbesitz der Republik Guatemala, der USA und Europas. Linden Museum für Völkerkunde, Stuttgart.

LOTHROP, S. K.

1926 Stone Sculptures from the Finca Arevalo, Guatemala. *Indian Notes,* vol. III, no. 3, pp. 147-171. Museum of the American Indian, Heye Foundation, New York.

1937 Coclé, An Archaeological Study of Central Panama: Part I. *Memoirs of the Peabody Museum of Archaeology and Ethnology, Harvard University,* vol. VII. Cambridge.

1950 Archaeology of Southern Veraguas, Panama. *Memoirs of the Peabody Museum of Archaeology, Harvard University,* vol. IX, no. 3. Cambridge.

1955 Jade and String Sawing in Northeastern Costa Rica. *American Antiquity,* vol. XXI, no. 1, pp. 43-51. Society for American Archaeology, Salt Lake City.

1963 Robert Woods Bliss, 1875-1962. *American Antiquity,* vol. 29, no. 1, pp. 92-93. Society for American Archaeology, Salt Lake City.

LOTHROP, S. K., W. F. FOSHAG, and JOY MAHLER

1957 Robert Woods Bliss Collection: Pre-Columbian Art. Phaidon Publishers Inc., New York.

LOUBO-LESNITCHENKO, E.

1973 Imported Mirrors in the Minusinsk Basin. *Artibus Asiae,* vol. XXXV, no. 1/2, pp. 25-61. Institute of Fine Arts, New York University, New York.

LOWE, GARETH W.

1959 Archeological Exploration of the Upper Grijalva River, Chiapas, Mexico. *Papers of the New World Archaeological Foundation,* no. 2. Orinda.

1967 Eastern Mesoamerica. *American Antiquity,* vol. 32, no. 1, pp. 135-141. Society for American Archaeology, Salt Lake City.

1971 The Civilizational Consequences of Varying Degrees of Agricultural and Ceramic Dependency within the Basic Ecosystems of Mesoamerica. *In* Observations on the Emergence of Civilization in Mesoamerica (Robert F. Heizer, John A. Graham, and C. W. Clewlow, Jr., eds.), pp. 212-248. *Contributions of the University of California Archaeological Research Facility,* no. 11. Department of Anthropology, Berkeley.

1975 The Early Preclassic Barra Phase of Altamira, Chiapas: A Review with New Data. *Papers of the New World Archaeological Foundation,* no. 38. Brigham Young University, Provo.

1977 The Mixe-Zoque as Competing Neighbors of the Early Lowland Maya. *In* The Origins of Maya Civilization (Richard E. W. Adams, ed.), pp. 197-248. *School of American Research Advanced Seminar Series.* University of New Mexico Press, Albuquerque.

1978 Eastern Mesoamerica. *In* Chronologies in New World Archaeology (R. E. Taylor and Clement W. Meighan, eds.), pp. 331-393. Academic Press, New York, San Francisco, and London.

MACNEISH, RICHARD S.

1954 An Early Archaeological Site Near Panuco, Vera Cruz. *Transactions of the American Philosophical Society,* n.s. vol. 44, part 5, pp. 537-641. Philadelphia.

MACNEISH, RICHARD S., ANTOINETTE NELKEN-TERNER, and IRMGARD W. JOHNSON

1967 The Prehistory of the Tehuacan Valley, Volume Two: Nonceramic Artifacts. University of Texas Press, Austin and London.

MACNEISH, RICHARD S., FREDERICK A. PETERSON, and KENT V. FLANNERY

1970 The Prehistory of the Tehuacan Valley, Volume Three: Ceramics. University of Texas Press, Austin and London.

MARCUS, JOYCE

1973 Territorial Organization of the Lowland Classic Maya. *Science,* vol. 180, no. 4089, pp. pp. 911-916. American Association for the Advancement of Science, Washington.

1976 Emblem and State in the Classic Maya Lowlands: An Epigraphic Approach to Territorial Organization. Dumbarton Oaks, Washington.

MARSHACK, ALEXANDER

1975 Olmec Mosaic Pendant. *In* Archaeoastronomy in Pre-Columbian America (Anthony F. Aveni, ed.), pp. 341-377. University of Texas Press, Austin and London.

MARTÍ, SAMUEL, and GERTRUDE PROKOSCH KURATH

1964 Dances of Anáhuac: The Choreography and Music of Precortesian Dances. *Viking Fund Publications in Anthropology,* no. 38. Aldine Publishing Company, Chicago.

MARTÍNEZ HERNÁNDEZ, JUAN (ed.)

1929 Diccionario de Motul: Maya Español, atribuido a Fray Antonio de Ciudad Real, y Arte de lengua maya, por Fray Juan Coronel. Compañía Tipográfica Yucateca, S.A., Mérida.

MASON, J. ALDEN

1927   Mirrors of Ancient America. *The Museum Journal,* vol. XVIII, no. 2, pp. 201-209. The Museum of the University of Pennsylvania, Philadelphia.

MATOS MOCTEZUMA, EDUARDO

1966   Un Juego de Pelota doble en San Isidro, Chiapas. *Boletín del Instituto Nacional de Antropología e Historia,* no. 25, pp. 36-37. Mexico.

1968   Arqueología de rescate en Malpaso. *CFE Sirviendo a México,* vol. 1, no. 2, pp. 32-37. Comisión Federal de Electricidad, Mexico.

MAUDSLAY, A. P.

1889-   Biologia Centrali-Americana: Archaeology.
1902   1 vol. text, 4 vols. plates. R. H. Porter and Dulau & Co., London.

MAYOR, A. HYATT

1971   Prints & People: A Social History of Printed Pictures. The Metropolitan Museum of Art, New York.

MEDELLÍN ZENIL, ALFONSO

1960a   Cerámicas del Totonacapan: exploraciones arqueológicas en el centro de Veracruz. Universidad Veracruzana, Instituto de Antropología, Xalapa.

1960b   Monolitos Inéditos Olmecas. *La Palabra y el Hombre,* no. 16, pp. 75-97. Universidad Veracruzana, Xalapa.

1965   La Escultura de las Limas. *Boletín del Instituto Nacional de Antropología e Historia,* no. 21, pp. 5-8. Mexico.

1971   Monolitos olmecas y otros en el Museo de la UnUiversidad de Veracruz. *Union Académique Internationale, Corpus Antiquitatum Americanensium, Mexico,* V. Instituto Nacional de Antropología e Historia, Mexico.

MERRY, MARCIA PAULETTE

n.d.   Investigation of a Middle Formative Area of Burials: Chalcatzingo, Morelos, Mexico. Master's thesis, University of the Americas, Cholula, 1975.

MERWIN, RAYMOND E., and GEORGE C. VAILLANT

1932   The Ruins of Holmul, Guatemala. *Memoirs of the Peabody Museum of American Archaeology and Ethnology, Harvard University,* vol. III, no. 2. Cambridge.

METROPOLITAN MUSEUM OF ART, NEW YORK

1969   Art of Oceania, Africa, and the Americas from the Museum of Primitive Art. An exhibition at The Metropolitan Museum of Art, May 10-August 17, 1969. The Metropolitan Museum of Art, New York.

MILBRATH, SUSAN

1979   A Study of Olmec Sculptural Chronology. *Studies in Pre-Columbian Art and Archaeology,* no. 23. Dumbarton Oaks, Washington.

MILES, S. W.

1965   Sculpture of the Guatemala–Chiapas Highlands and Pacific Slopes, and Associated Hieroglyphs. *In* Handbook of Middle American Indians (Robert Wauchope, ed.), vol. 2, pp. 237-275. University of Texas Press, Austin.

MILLER, ARTHUR G.

1977   The Maya and the Sea: Trade and Cult at Tancah and Tulum, Quintana Roo, Mexico. *In* The Sea in the Pre-Columbian World: A Conference at Dumbarton Oaks, October 26th and 27th, 1974 (Elizabeth P. Benson, ed.), pp. 96-140. Dumbarton Oaks Research Library and Collections, Washington.

MILLER, JEFFREY H.

n.d.   Untitled paper presented at the Segunda Mesa Redonda de Palenque, Palenque, December 14-21, 1974. Tape transcription.

MILLER, MARY ELLEN

1975   Jaina Figurines: A Study of Maya Iconography. The Art Museum, Princeton University, Princeton.

MILLON, RENÉ

1973   The Teotihuacán Map, Part One: Text. *In* Urbanization at Teotihuacán, Mexico (René Millon, ed.), vol. 1. University of Texas Press, Austin and London.

MORLEY, SYLVANUS GRISWOLD

1915   An Introduction to the Study of the Maya Hieroglyphs. *Smithsonian Institution, Bureau of American Ethnology, Bulletin 57.* Government Printing Office, Washington.

MORRISON, FRANK, C. W. CLEWLOW, JR., and ROBERT F. HEIZER

1970   Magnetometer Survey of the La Venta Pyramid, 1969. *In* Magnetometer Survey of the La Venta Pyramid and Other Papers on Mexican Archaeology, pp. 1-20. *Contributions of the University of California Archaeological Research Facility,* no. 8. Department of Anthropology, Berkeley.

MUSÉE RODIN, PARIS

1972   L'art olmèque: source des arts classiques du Mexique. Musée Rodin, Paris.

MUSEUM OF MODERN ART, NEW YORK

1940   Twenty Centuries of Mexican Art/Veinte Siglos de Arte Mexicano. The Museum of Modern Art, New York, in collaboration with the Mexican Government.

NATIONAL GALLERY OF ART, WASHINGTON

1947   Indigenous Art of the Americas: Collection of Robert Woods Bliss. National Gallery of Art, Smithsonian Institution, Washington.

NAVARRETE, CARLOS

1959   A Brief Reconnaissance in the Region of Tonalá, Chiapas, Mexico. *Papers of the New World Archaeological Foundation,* no. 4. Orinda.

1960   Archeological Explorations in the Region of Frailesca, Chiapas, Mexico. *Papers of the New World Archaeological Foundation,* no. 7. Orinda.

1966   Excavaciones en la presa Netzahualcoyotl, Mal Paso, Chis. *Boletín del Instituto Nacional de Antropología e Historia,* no. 24, pp. 36-40. Mexico.

1971   Algunas piezas olmecas de Chiapas y Guatemala. *Anales de Antropología,* vol. VIII, pp. 69-82. Instituto de Investigaciones Históricas, Universidad Nacional Autónoma de México, Mexico.

1972   Fechamiento para un tipo de esculturas del sur de Mesoamérica. *Anales de Antropología,* vol. IX, pp. 45-52. Instituto de Investigaciones Históricas, Universidad Nacional Autónoma de México, Mexico.

1974   The Olmec Rock Carvings at Pijijiapan, Chiapas, Mexico and Other Olmec Pieces from Chiapas and Guatemala. *Papers of the New World Archaeological Foundation,* no. 35. Brigham Young University, Provo.

NICHOLSON, H. B.

1971   Religion in Pre-Hispanic Central Mexico. *In* Handbook of Middle American Indians (Robert Wauchope, ed.), vol. 10, pp. 395-446. University of Texas Press, Austin.

1976   Preclassic Mesoamerican Iconography from the Perspective of the Postclassic: Problems in Interpretational Analysis. *In* Origins of Religious Art & Iconography in Preclassic Mesoamerica (H. B. Nicholson, ed.), pp. 157-175. UCLA Latin American Center Publications and Ethnic Arts Council of Los Angeles, Los Angeles.

NIEDERBERGER, CHRISTINE

1976   Zohapilco: cinco milenios de ocupación humana en un sitio lacustre de la cuenca de México. *Colección Científica,* 30. Instituto Nacional de Antropología e Historia, Mexico.

NOMLAND, GLADYS AYER

1932   Proboscis Statue from the Isthmus of Tehuantepec. *American Anthropologist,* vol. 34, no. 4, pp. 591-593. American Anthropological Association, Menasha.

NORDENSKIÖLD, ERLAND

1926   Miroirs convexes et concaves en Amérique. *Journal de la Société des Américanistes de Paris,* n.s. tome XVIII, pp. 103-110. Paris.

NORMAN, V. GARTH

1973   Izapa Sculpture, Part 1: Album. *Papers of the New World Archaeological Foundation,* no. 30. Brigham Young University, Provo.

1976   Izapa Sculpture, Part 2: Text. *Papers of the New World Archaeological Foundation,* no. 30. Brigham Young University, Provo.

NORWEB, ALBERT HOLDEN

1964   Ceramic Stratigraphy in Southwestern Nicaragua. *XXXV Congreso Internacional de Americanistas, México, 1962, Actas y Memorias,* vol. 1, pp. 551-561. Instituto Nacional de Antropología e Historia, Mexico.

NOWOTNY, KARL ANTON

1948   Erläuterungen zum Codex Vindobonensis (Vorderseite). *Archiv für Völkerkunde,* Band III, pp. 156-200. Museum für Völkerkunde, Wien.

ORTIZ CEBALLOS, PONCIANO

n.d.a   La cerámica de los Tuxtlas. Master's thesis, Universidad Veracruzana, Jalapa, 1975.

n.d.b   Informe preliminar de las excavaciones realizadas en Tabuco. Unpublished manuscript on the August 1977 excavations in the Museo de Antropología, Jalapa, 1977.

PADDOCK, JOHN

1966   Oaxaca in Ancient Mesoamerica. *In* Ancient Oaxaca: Discoveries in Mexican Archeology and History (John Paddock, ed.), pp. 87-242. Stanford University Press, Stanford.

PALERM, ANGEL, and ERIC R. WOLF

1957   Ecological Potential and Cultural Development in Mesoamerica. *In* Studies in Human Ecology: A Series of Lectures Given at the Anthropological Society of Washington, pp. 1-37. *Social Science Monographs,* III. Social Science Section, Department of Cultural Affairs, Pan American Union, Washington.

PANOFSKY, ERWIN

1955   Meaning in the Visual Arts: Papers in and on **Art History**. Doubleday & Company, Inc., **Garden City, New York**.

PARADIS, LOUISE ISEUT

n.d.   The Tierra Caliente of Guerrero, Mexico: An Archaeological and Ecological Study. Doctoral dissertation, Yale University, New Haven, 1974.

PARSONS, LEE A.

1967a   Bilbao, Guatemala: An Archaeological Study of the Pacific Coast Cotzumalhuapa Region, Vol. 1. *Publications in Anthropology,* 11. Milwaukee Public Museum, Milwaukee.

1967b   An Early Maya Stela on the Pacific Coast of Guatemala. *Estudios de Cultura Maya,* vol. VI, pp. 171-198. Seminario de Cultura Maya, Universidad Nacional Autónoma de México, Mexico.

1969   Bilbao, Guatemala: An Archaeological Study of the Pacific Coast Cotzumalhuapa Region, Vol. 2. *Publications in Anthropology,* 12. Milwaukee Public Museum, Milwaukee.

1973 Iconographic notes on a new Izapan stela from Abaj Takalik, Guatemala. *Atti del XL Congresso Internazionale degli Americanisti, Roma-Genova, 3-10 Settembre 1972,* vol. 1, pp. 203-212. Casa Editrice Tilgher, Genova.

1976 Excavation of Monte Alto, Escuintla, Guatemala. *National Geographic Society Research Reports, 1968 Projects,* pp. 325-332. Washington.

1978 The Peripheral Coastal Lowlands and the Middle Classic Period. *In* Middle Classic Mesoamerica: A.D. 400-700 (Esther Pasztory, ed.), pp. 25-34. Columbia University Press, New York.

PARSONS, LEE A., and PETER S. JENSON

1965 Boulder Sculpture on the Pacific Coast of Guatemala. *Archaeology,* vol. 18, no. 2, pp. 132-144. Archaeological Institute of America, New York.

PARSONS, LEE A., and BARBARA J. PRICE

1971 Mesoamerican Trade and Its Role in the Emergence of Civilization. *In* Observations on the Emergence of Civilization in Mesoamerica (Robert F. Heizer, John A. Graham, and C. W. Clewlow, Jr., eds.), pp. 169-195. *Contributions of the University of California Archaeological Research Facility,* no. 11. Department of Anthropology, Berkeley.

PETERSON, FREDERICK, and FERNANDO HORCASITAS

1957 Recent Finds at Tlatilco. *Tlalocan,* vol. III, no. 4, pp. 363-365. La Casa de Tlaloc, Mexico.

PIÑA CHAN, ROMÁN

1955 Chalcatzingo, Morelos. *Informes,* 4. Dirección de Monumentos Pre-hispánicos, Instituto Nacional de Antropología e Historia, Mexico.

1968 Jaina: la casa en el agua. Instituto Nacional de Antropología e Historia, Mexico.

PIÑA CHAN, ROMÁN, and LUIS COVARRUBIAS

1964 El pueblo del jaguar (Los olmecas arqueológicos). Consejo para la Planeación e Instalación del Museo Nacional de Antropología, Mexico.

PIÑA CHAN, ROMÁN, and CARLOS NAVARRETE

1967 Archeological Research in the Lower Grijalva River Region, Tabasco and Chiapas. *Papers of the New World Archaeological Foundation,* no. 22. Brigham Young University, Provo.

PIRES-FERREIRA, JANE W.

1975 Formative Mesoamerican Exchange Networks with Special Reference to the Valley of Oaxaca. *In* Prehistory and Human Ecology of the Valley of Oaxaca (Kent V. Flannery, ed.), vol. 3. *Memoirs of the Museum of Anthropology, University of Michigan,* no. 7. Ann Arbor.

1976 Obsidian Exchange in Formative Mesoamerica. *In* The Early Mesoamerican Village (Kent V. Flannery, ed.), pp. 292-306. Academic Press, New York, San Francisco, and London.

n.d. Formative Mesoamerican Exchange Networks. Doctoral dissertation, University of Michigan, Ann Arbor, 1973.

PLUMER, JAMES MARSHALL

1944 The Chinese Bronze Mirror: Two Instruments in One. *The Art Quarterly,* vol. VII, no. 2, pp. 90-108. Detroit Institute of Arts, Detroit.

POHL, MARY E. D.

n.d. Ethnozoology of the Maya: An Analysis of Fauna from Five Sites in the Peten, Guatemala. Doctoral dissertation, Harvard University, Cambridge, 1977.

POHORILENKO, ANATOLE

1972 La Pequeña Escultura: El Hombre y su experiencia Artístico-Religiosa. *In* El Arte Olmeca (Beatriz de la Fuente, ed.), pp. 35-62. *Artes de México,* no. 154, año XIX. Mexico.

1975 New Elements of Olmec Iconography: Ceremonial Markings. *In* Balance y perspectiva de la antropología de mesoamérica y del centro de México, Arqueología I, XIII mesa redonda, pp. 265-281. Sociedad Mexicana de Antropología, Mexico.

1977 On the Question of Olmec Deities. *Journal of New World Archaeology,* vol. II, no. 1, pp. 1-16. Institute of Archaeology, University of California, Los Angeles.

POLLOCK, H. E. D., and CLAYTON E. RAY

1957 Notes on Vertebrate Animal Remains from Mayapan. *Current Reports,* vol. II, no. 41, pp. 633-656. Department of Archaeology, Carnegie Institution of Washington, Cambridge.

PORTER, MURIEL NOÉ

1953 Tlatilco and the Pre-Classic Cultures of the New World. *Viking Fund Publications in Anthropology,* no. 19. New York.

PROSKOURIAKOFF, TATIANA

1960 Historical Implications of a Pattern of Dates at Piedras Negras, Guatemala. *American Antiquity,* vol. 25, no. 4, pp. 454-475. Society for American Archaeology, Salt Lake City.

1963 Historical data in the inscriptions of Yaxchilan, Part I. *Estudios de Cultura Maya,* vol. III, pp. 149-167. Seminario de Cultura Maya, Universidad Nacional Autónoma de México, Mexico.

1964 Historical data in the inscriptions of Yaxchilan, Part II. *Estudios de Cultura Maya,* vol. IV, pp. 177-201. Seminario de Cultura Maya, Universidad Nacional Autónoma de México, Mexico.

1968 Olmec and Maya Art: Problems of Their Stylistic Relation. *In* Dumbarton Oaks Conference on the Olmec, October 28th and 29th, 1967 (Elizabeth P. Benson, ed.), pp. 119-134.

Dumbarton Oaks Research Library and Collection, Washington.

QUIRARTE, JACINTO

1973a   El estilo artístico de Izapa. *Cuadernos de historia del arte,* 3. Instituto de Investigaciones Estéticas, Universidad Nacional Autónoma de México, Mexico.

1973b   Izapan and Mayan Traits in Teotihuacan III Pottery. *In* Studies in Ancient Mesoamerica (John Graham, ed.), pp. 11-29. *Contributions of the University of California Archaeological Research Facility,* no. 18. Department of Anthropology, Berkeley.

1973c   Izapan-Style Art: A Study of Its Form and Meaning. *Studies in Pre-Columbian Art and Archaeology,* no. 10. Dumbarton Oaks, Washington.

1974   Terrestrial/Celestial Polymorphs as Narrative Frames in the Art of Izapa and Palenque. *In* Primera Mesa Redonda de Palenque, Part I: A Conference on the Art, Iconography, and Dynastic History of Palenque; Palenque, Chiapas, Mexico. December 14-22, 1973 (Merle Greene Robertson, ed.), pp. 129-135. The Robert Louis Stevenson School, Pebble Beach.

1976a   Izapan style antecedents for the Maya Serpent in Celestial Dragon and Serpent Bar Contexts. *Actas del XXIII Congreso Internacional de Historia del Arte: España entre el Mediterráneo y el Atlántico, Granada 1973,* vol. I, pp. 227-237. Universidad de Granada, Departamento de Historia del Arte, Granada.

1976b   The Relationship of Izapan-Style Art to Olmec and Maya Art: A Review. *In* Origins of Religious Art & Iconography in Preclassic Mesoamerica (H. B. Nicholson, ed.), pp. 73-86. UCLA Latin American Center Publications and Ethnic Arts Council of Los Angeles, Los Angeles.

1976c   The Underworld Jaguar in Maya Vase Painting: An Iconographic Study. *New Mexico Studies in the Fine Arts,* vol. I (Pre-Columbian/Spanish Colonial Issue), pp. 20-25. The College of Fine Arts, The University of New Mexico, Albuquerque.

1977   Early Art Styles of Mesoamerica and Early Classic Maya Art. *In* The Origins of Maya Civilization (Richard E. W. Adams, ed.), pp. 249-283. *School of American Research Advanced Seminar Series.* University of New Mexico Press, Albuquerque.

1978   Actual and Implied Visual Space in Maya Vase Painting: A Study of Double Images and Two-Headed Compound Creatures. *In* Studies in Ancient Mesoamerica, III, pp. 27-38. *Contributions of the University of California Archaeological Research Facility,* no. 36. Department of Anthropology, Berkeley.

RAMÍREZ VÁZQUEZ, PEDRO (and others)

1968   The National Museum of Anthropology, Mexico. Harry N. Abrams, Inc., in association with Helvetica Press, Inc., New York.

RICHARDSON, FRANCIS B.

1940   Non-Maya Monumental Sculpture of Central America. *In* The Maya and Their Neighbors, pp. 395-416. D. Appleton-Century Company, Incorporated, New York and London. (2nd edition 1962: University of Utah Press, Salt Lake City.)

ROBERTSON, FORBES, and WILLIAM J. VAN METER

1951   The Kentron Microhardness Tester, A Quantitative Tool in Opaque Mineral Identification. *Economic Geology and the Bulletin of the Society of Economic Geologists,* vol. 46, no. 5, pp. 541-550. Lancaster, Pennsylvania.

ROSE, RICHARD

n.d.   Mushroom Stones of Mesoamerica. Doctoral dissertation, Harvard University, Cambridge, 1977.

ROYS, RALPH L.

1967   The Book of Chilam Balam of Chumayel. University of Oklahoma Press, Norman.

RUBIN, IDA ELY (ed.)

1975   The Guennol Collection, Volume I. The Metropolitan Museum of Art, New York.

RUPERT, MILAN, and O. J. TODD

1935   Chinese Bronze Mirrors. Peiping. (Reprint 1966: Paragon Book Reprint Corp., New York.)

RUZ LHUILLIER, ALBERTO

1958   Exploraciones arqueológicas en Palenque: 1956. *Anales del Instituto Nacional de Antropología e Historia,* tomo X, no. 39, pp. 241-299. Secretaría de Educación Pública, Mexico.

1970   The Civilization of the Ancient Maya. *Serie Historia,* XXIV. Instituto Nacional de Antropología e Historia, Mexico.

SABLOFF, JEREMY A.

1975   Excavations at Seibal, Department of Peten, Guatemala: Ceramics. *Memoirs of the Peabody Museum of Archaeology and Ethnology, Harvard University,* vol. 13, no. 2. Cambridge.

SAHAGÚN, FRAY BERNARDINO DE

1950-   Florentine Codex: General History of the
1969   Things of New Spain. (Trans. by Arhur J. O. Anderson and Charles E. Dibble.) 13 parts. *Monographs of The School of American Research,* no. 14. The School of American Research and the University of Utah, Santa Fe.

1969   Historia General de las Cosas de Nueva España. (Annotated by Angel María Garibay K.) Segunda edición. 4 vols. Editorial Porrúa, S.A., Mexico.

SANDERS, WILLIAM T., and BARBARA J. PRICE

1968   Mesoamerica: The Evolution of a Civilization. Random House, New York.

Bibliography

SAVILLE, MARSHALL H.

1929a   Votive Axes from Ancient Mexico. *Indian Notes,* vol. VI, no. 3, pp. 266-299. Museum of the American Indian, Heye Foundation, New York.

1929b   Votive Axes from Ancient Mexico, II. *Indian Notes,* vol. VI, no. 4, pp. 335-342. Museum of the American Indian, Heye Foundation, New York.

SCHAGUNN, JAMES O.

1975   La Venta Mirrors' Possible Use as Astronomical Instruments. *In* Balance y perspectiva de la antropología de mesoamérica y del centro de México, Arqueología I, XIII mesa redonda, pp. 293-298. Sociedad Mexicana de Antropología, Mexico.

SCHELE, LINDA

1974   Observations on the Cross Motif at Palenque. *In* Primera Mesa Redonda de Palenque, Part I: A Conference on the Art, Iconography, and Dynastic History of Palenque; Palenque, Chiapas, Mexico. December 14-22, 1973 (Merle Greene Robertson, ed.), pp. 41-61. The Robert Louis Stevenson School, Pebble Beach.

1976   Accession Iconography of Chan-Bahlum in the Group of the Cross at Palenque. *In* The Art, Iconography & Dynastic History of Palenque, Part III: Proceedings of the Segunda Mesa Redonda de Palenque, December 14-21, 1974—Palenque (Merle Greene Robertson, ed.), pp. 9-34. The Robert Louis Stevenson School, Pebble Beach.

1977   Palenque: The House of the Dying Sun. *In* Native American Astronomy (Anthony F. Aveni, ed.), pp. 42-56. University of Texas Press, Austin and London.

SCHELE, LINDA, and JEFFREY H. MILLER

n.d.   The Mirror, the Rabbit, and the Bundle: "Accession" Phrases of the Classic Maya. *Studies in Pre-Columbian Art and Archaeology,* no. 25. Dumbarton Oaks, Washington. (In press.)

SCHORGER, A. W.

1966   The Wild Turkey: Its History and Domestication. University of Oklahoma Press, Norman.

SCOTT, JOHN F.

1976   Post-olmec Mesoamérica as revealed in its art. *Actas del XLI Congreso Internacional de Americanistas, México, 2 al 7 de septiembre de 1974,* vol. II, pp. 380-386. Instituto Nacional de Antropología e Historia, Mexico.

1977   El Mesón, Veracruz, and its Monolithic Reliefs. *Baessler-Archiv: Beiträge zur Völkerkunde,* N.F. Band XXV, Heft 1, pp. 83-138. Museum für Völkerkunde and Verlag von Dietrich Reimer, Berlin.

1978   The Danzantes of Monte Albán. 2 vols. *Studies in Pre-Columbian Art and Archaeology,* no. 19. Dumbarton Oaks, Washington.

SHARER, ROBERT J.

1974   The Prehistory of the Southeastern Maya Periphery. *Current Anthropology,* vol. 15, no. 2, pp. 165-187. The University of Chicago Press, Chicago.

SHARER, ROBERT J. (ed.)

1978   The Prehistory of Chalchuapa, El Salvador. 3 vols. University of Pennsylvania Press, Philadelphia.

SHOOK, EDWIN M.

1950   Tiquisate UFers Scoop Archaeological World, Find Ruined City on Farm. *Unifruitco,* August, pp. 62-63. United Fruit Company, New York.

1951   Guatemala. *Year Book No. 50, July 1, 1950-June 30, 1951,* pp. 240-241. Carnegie Institute of Washington, Washington.

1971   Inventory of Some Pre-Classic Traits in the Highlands and Pacific Guatemala and Adjacent Areas. *In* Observations on the Emergence of Civilization in Mesoamerica (Robert F. Heizer, John A. Graham, and C. W. Clewlow, Jr., eds.), pp. 70-77. *Contributions of the University of California Archaeological Research Facility,* no. 11. Department of Anthropology, Berkeley.

SHOOK, EDWIN M., and ROBERT F. HEIZER

1976   An Olmec Sculpture from the South (Pacific) Coast of Guatemala. *Journal of New World Archaeology,* vol. I, no. 3, pp. 1-8. Institute of Archaeology, University of California, Los Angeles.

SHOOK, EDWIN M., and ALFRED V. KIDDER

1952   Mound E-III-3, Kaminaljuyu, Guatemala. *Carnegie Institution of Washington, Publication 596, Contributions to American Anthropology and History,* no. 53. Washington.

SMITH, A. LEDYARD

1961   Types of Ball Courts in the Highlands of Guatemala. *In* Essays in Pre-Columbian Art and Archaeology (Samuel K. Lothrop and others), pp. 100-125. Harvard University Press, Cambridge.

SMITH, MARY ELIZABETH

1973   Picture Writing from Ancient Southern Mexico: Mixtec Place Signs and Maps. University of Oklahoma Press, Norman.

SMITH, TILLIE

1963   The Main Themes of the "Olmec" Art Tradition. *The Kroeber Anthropological Society Papers,* no. 28, pp. 121-213. Department of Anthropology, University of California, Berkeley.

SNARSKIS, MICHAEL J.

1976   La Vertiente Atlántica de Costa Rica. *Vínculos,* vol. 2, núm. 1, pp. 101-114. Museo Nacional de Costa Rica, San José.

SOTHEBY PARKE BERNET INC., NEW YORK

1975   Sale 3792. Important African, Oceanic and Pre-Columbian Art: The Property of Jay C. Leff, Uniontown, Pensylvania. Sotheby Parke Bernet Inc., New York.

SPINDEN, HERBERT J.

1913   A Study of Maya Art: Its Subject Matter and Historical Development. *Memoirs of the Peabody Museum of American Archaeology and Ethnology, Harvard University*, vol. VI. Cambridge.

1947   An Olmec Jewel. *Bulletin of the Brooklyn Museum*, vol. IX, no. 1, pp. 1-12. The Brooklyn Institute of Arts and Sciences, Brooklyn.

STARK, BARBARA L.

1977   Mesoamerica. *American Antiquity*, vol. 42, no. 2, pp. 272-280. Society for American Archaeology, Washington.

STIRLING, MATTHEW W.

1940a   Great Stone Faces of the Mexican Jungle. *The National Geographic Magazine*, vol. LXXVIII, no. 3, pp. 309-334. National Geographic Society, Washington.

1940b   An Initial Series from Tres Zapotes, Vera Cruz, Mexico. *Contributed Technical Papers, Mexican Archeology Series*, vol. 1, no. 1. National Geographic Society, Washington.

1941   Expedition Unearths Buried Masterpieces of Carved Jade. *The National Geographic Magazine*, vol. LXXX, no. 3, pp. 277-302. National Geographic Society, Washington.

1943a   La Venta's Green Stone Tigers. *The National Geographic Magazine*, vol. LXXXIV, no. 3, pp. 321-332. National Geographic Society, Washington.

1943b   Stone Monuments of Southern Mexico. *Smithsonian Institution, Bureau of American Ethnology, Bulletin 138*. U.S. Government Printing Office, Washington.

1947   On the Trail of La Venta Man. *The National Geographic Magazine*, vol. XCI, no. 2, pp. 137-172. National Geographic Society, Washington.

1955   Stone Monuments of the Río Chiquito, Veracruz, Mexico. *Smithsonian Institution, Bureau of American Ethnology, Bulletin 157, Anthropological Papers*, no. 43, pp. 1-23. U.S. Government Printing Office, Washington.

1957   An Archeological Reconnaissance in Southeastern Mexico. *Smithsonian Institution, Bureau of American Ethnology, Bulletin 164, Anthropological Papers*, no. 53, pp. 213-240. U.S. Government Printing Office, Washington.

1961   The Olmecs, Artists in Jade. *In* Essays in Pre-Columbian Art and Archaeology (Samuel K. Lothrop and others), pp. 43-59. Harvard University Press, Cambridge.

1965   Monumental Sculpture of Southern Veracruz and Tabasco. *In* Handbook of Middle American Indians (Robert Wauchope, ed.), vol. 3, pp. 716-738. University of Texas Press, Austin.

1968   Early History of the Olmec Problem. *In* Dumbarton Oaks Conference on the Olmec, October 28th and 29th, 1967 (Elizabeth P. Benson, ed.), pp. 1-8. Dumbarton Oaks Research Library and Collection, Washington.

1969   Archeological Investigations in Costa Rica. *National Geographic Society, Research Reports*, 1964, pp. 239-247. Washington.

STIRLING, MATTHEW W., and MARION STIRLING

1942   Finding Jewels of Jade in a Mexican Swamp. *The National Geographic Magazine*, vol. LXXXII, no. 5, pp. 635-661. National Geographic Society, Washington.

STONE, DORIS

1966   Introduction to the Archaeology of Costa Rica. Revised edition. Museo Nacional, San José.

1972   Pre-Columbian Man Finds Central America: The Archaeological Bridge. Peabody Museum Press, Harvard University, Cambridge.

STONE, DORIS, and CARLOS BALSER

1965   Incised Slate Disks from the Atlantic Watershed of Costa Rica. *American Antiquity*, vol. 30, no. 3, pp. 310-329. Society for American Archaeology, Salt Lake City.

STRAUSS, JOYCE R.

n.d.   A Mirror Tradition in Pre-Columbian Art. Master's thesis, University of Denver, Denver, 1977.

STUART, GEORGE E., and GENE S. STUART

1969   Discovering Man's Past in the Americas. National Geographic Society, Washington.

STUART, L. C.

1964   Fauna of Middle America. *In* Handbook of Middle American Indians (Robert Wauchope, ed.), vol. 1, pp. 316-362. University of Texas Press, Austin.

SULLIVAN, THELMA D.

n.d.   Tlazolteotl-Ixcuina: The Great Spinner and Weaver. *In* Art and Iconography of Late Post-Classic Central Mexico, A Conference at Dumbarton Oaks, October 22nd and 23rd, 1977. Dumbarton Oaks Research Library and Collections, Washington. (In press.)

SWALLOW, R. W.

1937   Ancient Chinese Bronze Mirrors. Henri Vetch, Peiping.

SWEENEY, JEANNE W.

1976   Ceramic Analysis from 3 Sites in Northwest Coastal Guanacaste. *Vínculos*, vol. 2, núm 1, pp. 37-44. Museo Nacional de Costa Rica, San José.

Bibliography

SWITSUR, V. R.

1973   The radiocarbon calendar recalibrated. *Antiquity*, vol. 47, no. 186, pp. 131-137. Antiquity Publications Ltd, Cambridge.

TAYLOR, WALTER W.

1941   The Ceremonial Bar and Associated Features of Maya Ornamental Art. *American Antiquity*, vol. VII, no. 1, pp. 48-63. Society for American Archaeology, Menasha.

TERMER, FRANZ

1942   Auf den Spuren rätselhafter Völker in Südguatemala. *Die Umschau*, Jahrgang 46, Heft 26, pp. 389-392. Breidenstein Verlagsgesellschaft, Frankfurt.

1973   Palo Gordo: Ein Beitrag zur Archäologie des pazifischen Guatemala. *Monographien zur Völkerkunde, herausgegeben vom Hamburgischen Museum für Völkerkunde*, VIII. Kommissionsverlag Klaus Renner, München.

THOMAS, NORMAN D.

1974   The Linguistic, Geographic, and Demographic Position of the Zoque of Southern Mexico. *Papers of the New World Archaeological Foundation*, no. 36. Brigham Young University, Provo.

THOMPSON, ALLYN J.

1973   Making Your Own Telescope. Revised edition. Sky Publishing Corporation, Cambridge.

THOMPSON, J. ERIC S.

1939   The Moon Goddess in Middle America: with Notes on Related Deities. *Carnegie Institution of Washington, Publication 509, Contributions to American Anthropology and History*, vol. V, no. 29, pp. 121-173. Washington.

1941   Dating of Certain Inscriptions of Non-Maya Origin. *Theoretical Approaches to Problems*, No. 1. Division of Historical Research, Carnegie Institution of Washington, Cambridge.

1943   Some Sculptures from Southeastern Quezaltenango, Guatemala. *Notes on Middle American Archaeology and Ethnology*, vol. I, no. 17, pp. 100-112. Carnegie Institution of Washington, Division of Historical Research, Cambridge.

1962   A Catalog of Maya Hieroglyphs. University of Oklahoma Press, Norman.

1972   A Commentary on the Dresden Codex: A Maya Hieroglyphic Book. *Memoirs of the American Philosophical Society*, vol. 93. Philadelphia.

1973   Maya Rulers of the Classic Period and the Divine Right of Kings. *In* The Iconography of Middle American Sculpture, pp. 52-71. The Metropolitan Museum of Art, New York.

TOLSTOY, PAUL, and LOUISE I. PARADIS

1970   Early and Middle Preclassic Culture in the Basin of Mexico. *Science*, vol. 167, no. 3917, pp. 344-351. American Association for the Advancement of Science, Washington.

TOOMER, G. J.

1976   Diocles: On Burning Mirrors. The Arabic Translation of the Lost Greek Original. *Sources in the History of Mathematics and Physical Sciences*, 1. Springer-Verlag, Berlin, Heidelberg, and New York.

TOZZER, ALFRED M. (ed.)

1941   Landa's Relación de las Cosas de Yucatan: A Translation. *Papers of the Peabody Museum of American Archaeology and Ethnology, Harvard University*, vol. XVIII. Cambridge.

TRIGGER, BRUCE

1974   The archaeology of government. *World Archaeology*, vol. 6, no. 1, pp. 95-106. Routledge & Kegan Paul Ltd, London.

VAILLANT, GEORGE C., and SUZANNAH B. VAILLANT

1934   Excavations at Gualupita. *Anthropological Papers of the American Museum of Natural History*, vol. XXXV, part 1. New York.

VELSON, JOSEPH S., and THOMAS C. CLARK

1975   Transport of Stone Monuments to the La Venta and San Lorenzo Sites. In Three Papers on Mesoamerican Archaeology, pp. 1-39. *Contributions of the University of California Archaeological Research Facility* no. 24. Department of Anthropology, Berkeley.

VILLACORTA C., J. ANTONIO, and CARLOS A. VILLACORTA

1927   Arqueología guatemalteca. Impreso en la Tipografía Nacional, Guatemala.

VOGT, EVON Z.

1969   Zinacantan: A Maya Community in the Highlands of Chiapas. The Belknap Press of Harvard University Press, Cambridge.

WATERS, FRANK

1963   Book of the Hopi. The Viking Press, New York.

WEBER, WALTER A.

1945   Wildlife of Tabasco and Veracruz. *The National Geographic Magazine*, vol. LXXXVII, no. 2, pp. 187-216. National Geographic Society, Washington.

WEDEL, WALDO R.

1955   Archeological Materials from the Vicinity of Mobridge, South Dakota. *Smithsonian Institution, Bureau of American Ethnology, Bulletin 157, Anthropological Papers*, no. 45, pp. 69-188. U.S. Government Printing Office, Washington.

WESTHEIM, PAUL

1957   Ideas fundamentales del arte prehispánico en México. Fondo de Cultura Económica, Mexico and Buenos Aires.

WEYERSTALL, ALBERT

1932 Some Observations on Indian Mounds, Idols and Pottery in the Lower Papaloapam Basin, State of Vera Cruz, Mexico. *In* Middle American Papers, pp. 23-69. *Middle American Research Series, Publication No. 4.* Department of Middle American Research, The Tulane University of Louisiana, New Orleans.

WHITTEN, NORMAN E., JR.

1976 Sacha Runa: Ethnicity and Adaptation of Ecuadorian Jungle Quichua. University of Illinois Press, Urbana, Chicago, and London.

WICKE, CHARLES R.

1971 Olmec: An Early Art Style of Precolumbian Mexico. The University of Arizona Press, Tucson.

WILBERT, JOHANNES

1972 Survivors of Eldorado: Four Indian Cultures of South America. Praeger Publishers, New York, Washington, and London.

WILKERSON, S. JEFFREY K.

1972 La Secuencia Arqueológica-Histórica de Santa Lucia [Luisa], Veracruz, México. *Anuario Antropológico,* núm. 3, pp. 354-377. Escuela de Antropología, Universidad Veracruzana, Jalapa.

1973 An Archaeological Sequence from Santa Luisa, Veracruz, Mexico. *In* Studies in Ancient Mesoamerica (John Graham, ed.), pp. 37-50. *Contributions of the University of California Archaeological Research Facility,* no. 18. Department of Anthropology, Berkeley.

1974 Cultural Subareas of Eastern Mesoamerica. *In* Primera Mesa Redonda de Palenque, Part II: A Conference on the Art, Iconography, and Dynastic History of Palenque; Palenque, Chiapas, Mexico. December 14-22, 1973 (Merle Greene Robertson, ed.), pp. 89-102. The Robert Louis Stevenson School, Pebble Beach.

1975a Pre-Agricultural Village Life: The Late Preceramic Period in Veracruz. *In* Studies in Ancient Mesoamerica, II (John A. Graham, ed.), pp. 111-122. *Contributions of the University of California Archaeological Research Facility,* no. 27. Department of Anthropology, Berkeley.

1975b Resultados preliminares del estudio de ecología cultural en el norte-central de Veracruz durante 1973. *In* Balance y perspectiva de la antropología de mesoamérica y del centro de México, Arqueología I, XIII mesa redonda, pp. 339-346. Sociedad Mexicana de Antropología, Mexico.

n.d.a Ethnogenesis of the Haustecs and Totonacs: Early Cultures of North-Central Veracruz at Santa Luisa, Mexico. Doctoral dissertation, Tulane University, New Orleans, 1972.

n.d.b Huastec Presence and Cultural Chronology in North-Central Veracruz, Mexico. Paper presented at the XLII Congrès International des Américanistes, Paris, 2-9 Septembre, 1976.

WILLEY, GORDON R.

1962 The Early Great Styles and the Rise of the Pre-Columbian Civilizations. *American Anthropologist,* vol. 64, no. 1, part 1, pp. 1-14. American Anthropological Association, Menasha. (Reprinted 1971 *in* Anthropology and Art: Readings in Cross-Cultural Aesthetics [Charlotte M. Otten, ed.], pp. 282-297. The Natural History Press, Garden City, New York.)

WILLIAMS, HOWEL, and ROBERT F. HEIZER

1965 Sources of Rocks Used in Olmec Monuments. *In* Sources of Stones Used in Prehistoric Mesoamerican Sites, pp. 1-39. *Contributions of the University of California Archaeological Research Facility,* no. 1. Department of Anthropology, Berkeley.

WILLIAMSON, GEORGE

1877 Antiquities in Guatemala. *Annual Report of the Board of Regents of the Smithsonian Institution . . . for the Year 1876,* pp. 418-421. Government Printing Office, Washington.

WING, ELIZABETH S.

1975 Vertebrate Faunal Remains. *In* Archaeological Investigations on the Yucatan Peninsula (E. Wyllys Andrews IV *et al.*), pp. 186-188. *Middle American Research Institute, Tulane University, Publication 31.* New Orleans.

1978 Use of Dogs for Food: An Adaptation to the Coastal Environment. *In* Prehistoric Coastal Adaptations: The Economy and Ecology of Maritime Middle America (Barbara L. Stark and Barbara Voorhies, eds.), pp. 29-41. Academic Press, New York, San Francisco, and London.

WITTFOGEL, KARL A.

1956 The Hydraulic Civilizations. *In* Man's Role in Changing the Face of the Earth (William L. Thomas, Jr., ed.), pp. 152-164. The University of Chicago Press, Chicago.

ZERRIES, OTTO, DONALD W. LATHRAP, and PRESLEY NORTON

n.d. Shamans' Stools and the Time Depth of Tropical Forest Culture. *In* Irving Rouse Festschrift (Edwin S. Hall and Robert C. Donnel, eds.). (In press.)

346